CCF Colonialism in Northern Saskatchewan

David M. Quiring

CCF Colonialism in Northern Saskatchewan: Battling Parish Priests, Bootleggers, and Fur Sharks

UBCPress · Vancouver · Toronto

14   13   12   11   10   09   08   07   06   05   04   5   4   3   2   1

Printed in Canada on acid-free paper

National Library of Canada Cataloguing in Publication

Quiring, David M. (David Menno), 1948-
    CCF colonialism in Northern Saskatchewan : battling parish priests, bootleggers, and fur sharks / David M. Quiring.

    Includes bibliographical references and index.
    ISBN 0-7748-0938-8 (bound); ISBN 0-7748-0939-6 (pbk.)

    1. Saskatchewan, Northern – History. 2. Co-operative Commonwealth Federation – History. 3. Saskatchewan – Politics and government – 1944-1964. 4. Socialism – Saskatchewan, Northern – History. 5. Saskatchewan, Northern – Economic conditions. I. Title.

FC3525.2.Q57 2004   971.24'103   C2004-900291-0

Canadä

UBC Press gratefully acknowledges the financial support for our publishing program of the Government of Canada through the Book Publishing Industry Development Program (BPIDP), and of the Canada Council for the Arts, and the British Columbia Arts Council.

This book has been published with the help of a grant from the Canadian Federation for the Humanities and Social Sciences, through the Aid to Scholarly Publications Programme, using funds provided by the Social Sciences and Humanities Research Council of Canada.

Printed and bound in Canada by Friesens
Set in Stone by Brenda and Neil West, BN Typographics West
Copy editor: Audrey McClellan
Proofreader: Kirsten Craven
Cartographer: Eric Leinberger

UBC Press
The University of British Columbia
2029 West Mall
Vancouver, BC V6T 1Z2
604-822-5959 / Fax: 604-822-6083
www.ubcpress.ca

Contents

Acknowledgments

Numerous people and organizations have helped make this book possible. Personal experiences and conversations in northern Saskatchewan during the past decades kindled the interest that led to undertaking the project. Over the years, many northern residents and former government employees freely shared their knowledge, both informally and in formal interviews.

The facilities of the University of Saskatchewan and the faculty of its Department of History provided much of the support for researching and writing this book. W.A. (Bill) Waiser, who generously shared his knowledge and expertise about Saskatchewan and Canadian history, research, and writng, deserves special mention. Various other persons at the university also helped guide the research. These include K.S. Coates, B.T. Fairbairn, V. Korinek, L. Kitzan, J. Handy, J.R. Miller, L. Barron, and R. Bone. W. Morrison of the University of Northern British Columbia provided further valuable advice. The staff of the University of Saskatchewan Library, the Saskatchewan Archives Board, and the Glenbow Archives also proved helpful in many ways, facilitating this study. Financial support came through a University of Saskatchewan scholarship, a doctoral fellowship from the Social Sciences and Humanities Research Council of Canada, and the Messer Fund for Research in Canadian History. I express my gratitude for the generosity shown by these organizations and their people.

My wife Suzanne encouraged and supported me in carrying out this project. She accompanied me on various research trips and patiently tolerated the long hours devoted to researching and writing this book. I offer sincere thanks to her, other family members, and all others who helped with this research.

Introduction

Life in the southern part of the nation of Canada shaped my early development, much as it did that of most Canadians. Growing up in Swift Current, a spot on the CPR main line in the dry southern Saskatchewan prairie, gave me an early introduction to an environment dominated by humans. From the orderly blocks and streets of that small city to the neatly surveyed fields that surrounded it, mankind had taken control. Even the residents, from the youngest child to the oldest pioneer, followed a pattern of life controlled by clocks, schedules, and calendars. Yet a wild space survived in the midst of that well-ordered environment. Swift Current Creek flowed through the small city. In the water and on its banks survived traces of an untamed world. Fish swam in the water that rushed through rock-filled rapids, and trees and a vast variety of green plants thrived in the fertile soil bordering the stream. There, in this wild space, children also found a reprieve from the ordered world at home and school.

While little of a once untamed world survived in the south, the opposite situation dominated hundreds of miles to the north. My awareness that this other world existed came first from neighbours and relatives who travelled past where the fields ended. They brought back many large fish, along with tales of an enchanted world of rivers, lakes, rocks, and forests. Eventually, when I was a teenager, I welcomed my first opportunity to see that world. Trading labour as a fish filleter for trips to the north permitted me to spend days on windswept, rocky lakeshores. Several years later, my willingness to work in the north brought a job as a social worker with the Department of Welfare during the final years of Ross Thatcher's Liberal government in Saskatchewan. Although I was stationed in La Ronge, the job involved administering the department's programs in a large area extending to the Northwest Territories (NWT).

The wild spaces I found there in the north still proved fascinating. Thousands of square miles of unsurveyed land, water bodies that numbered in the tens of thousands, and countless millions of trees that formed the vast forests provided a natural environment unsurpassed in its beauty and possibilities for adventure. Yet the north also included people. It soon became apparent that the human population included two distinct groups: those with white skins and the dark-skinned Aboriginals. As a white employee of the southern-based government, it fell to me to apply programs purportedly designed to help northern Aboriginals overcome their economic and social problems. The human population, particularly the dynamics between the two distinct groups in the north, soon proved as fascinating as the natural environment.

Although my introduction to the north included no history lessons, I soon discovered that any substantial governmental presence in the region dated back only several decades. The Liberals and their predecessors, the Co-operative Commonwealth Federation (CCF), were the first governments to bother with the northern half of the province of Saskatchewan. Some of the same persons who had worked under the CCF still applied the programs designed by the Liberals. Most notably, my supervisor, John Edgerton Hugh Parsons, once had single-handedly provided the Department of Social Welfare presence in the north during the CCF era.[1] A tireless spinner of yarns, Hugh whetted my curiosity about that earlier time in the north with stories of his experiences as a social worker in remote communities. Various Department of Natural Resources (DNR) officers who had survived the change of government and the intervening years also provided a connection to the earlier CCF time.

Working as a social worker in the north encouraged my desire to know more about the relationship between Aboriginal northerners and the provincial government. My job existed largely because economic and social problems plagued the region, and I could not help but wonder how government might creatively deal with the issues. For the first months after my arrival, the answers to northern problems seemed clear, but this confidence faded as I became aware of various dilemmas. Yet it clearly seemed that government could do things differently and, in many cases, much better. Shortcomings existed, not only in policies made by a remote government in Regina, but also at the local administrative level, where petty officials twisted northern programs to add to their personal wealth and power. Cynicism and resignation that the north and Aboriginals were inherently dysfunctional pervaded the northern civil service.

When the pull of southern attractions proved irresistible, I left the rugged beauty of the Precambrian Shield behind. My work as a social worker in the forest-fringe area near Prince Albert ensured that my contact with Aboriginal families continued for many more years. Later, a career in the private sector included work on Indian reserves, which gave me a somewhat different perspective on life in those Aboriginal communities. A preference for life away from city streets and fields led to my family's choosing to live in the southern fringe of Saskatchewan's northern forest.

This proximity to the north made it easy to spend countless days and weeks there, both for recreation and study, over the past three decades. Travel by air, water, and road has permitted visits to many areas of this vast and always breathtaking region.

The north that residents and visitors experience today still bears the mark of events that began to unfold in the spring of 1944. At that time, newspaper headlines proclaimed that Saskatchewan voters had elected North America's first socialist government, the Co-operative Commonwealth Federation government, led by T.C. (Tommy) Douglas. Those early news reports did not mention that, unlike previous governments, the CCF had plans for the northern area. But in the months that followed, observers became aware that the CCF's vision for Saskatchewan included the north. Although preoccupied with introducing changes in the south, including economic diversification, modernization, and new social and health care programs, the CCF concern also extended to the ten thousand or so persons who inhabited the forested northern half of the province. In fact, it made dealing with the previously ignored northern part of the province one of its priorities.

The CCF interest in the north came from a number of sources. In an effort to avoid a repeat of the economic disaster of the Great Depression of the 1930s, the CCF looked to the north for help in diversifying the provincial economy. Northern resources might, it thought, free the province from its overreliance on agriculture, in particular the production of wheat for the world market. Additionally, in order to implement its ambitious plans to create new health and social programs, the CCF needed to greatly increase government revenues. Although the extent of northern wealth remained largely unmeasured, the CCF felt certain that development of the north could make the entire province more prosperous.[2] Some in the new government optimistically believed that the northern forests, waters, and rocks contained great resource wealth that could contribute to long-term economic diversity and stability.

Various other motivations drove the new government to action. Confidently believing modern ways superior to the old, the CCF set out to modernize the entire province, including the north. In 1944 southern Saskatchewan lagged behind much of the rest of the North American continent. Initiatives in the south included rural electrification, urban water and sewer systems, improved telephone service, road improvements, and new schools and hospitals. Modernizing the north presented a much more formidable challenge, since the northern infrastructure had changed little since the nineteenth century. Although the increasing use of airplanes offered an important transportation option for some, most northerners still travelled on the traditional water routes that traversed the north. The region lacked roads, railways, electrical service, and up-to-date communications systems. The absence of modern infrastructure limited the northern economy. While some extraction of furs, fish, timber, and minerals took place, transportation limitations prevented the economy from expanding. Large expanses of the north received little in the way of education, medicine, policing, and other government services.

Northern power structures also appeared unmodern. To the CCF way of thinking, the Hudson's Bay Company (HBC) and other fur traders operated an outdated and exploitive economic system. The new government viewed the HBC as the worst villain, believing it controlled Aboriginals through a Canadian version of the Third World's debt peonage system. The Roman Catholic and Anglican churches also held considerable sway in the region. In the opinion of CCF leaders, these churches carried out many functions, especially in the areas of health care and education, that rightly belonged to the state. The CCF did not oppose personal religion, but it wanted to separate the functions of church and state, secularize northern systems, and remove the Anglican and Roman Catholic presence in education, health care, and community leadership. Joe Phelps, the new minister of Natural Resources, saw a "pretty grim" situation and described most parish priests as fighting the government.[3] The CCF judged northern and Aboriginal society as outdated and problematic, with little worth salvaging. Unlike many northern Aboriginals, who did not see the need for or want widespread modernization of their homeland, the CCF considered it essential to bring the region into the twentieth century.

In addition to its plans to modernize the north, the CCF adopted an agenda of assimilating northern Aboriginals into modern Canadian society. Consistent with the view held by much of Canadian society at the time, this government viewed the Aboriginals' semi-nomadic, hunter-gatherer way of life as a primitive form of economic, political, and social organization, much inferior to the Euro-Canadian culture and its constant "progress." Yet the CCF worked to bring about assimilation with greater devotion than did most governments of the time. During its two decades in power, the CCF sought to direct and alter the lives of northern Indians and Metis. It sincerely believed that Aboriginals needed to adopt white ways of thinking and acting in order to have a viable future.

The CCF set another major goal for the north: to establish a socialist society there. In contrast, the party accepted that it had no choice but to live with a large degree of capitalism in the south. To interfere with agricultural and other businesses among the wheat fields and small towns of southern Saskatchewan likely would have brought political disaster. After spending more than a decade in the political wilderness, Douglas and his party had learned that lesson well. But the north was another matter; there the CCF found an area free from much electoral control, a place where its idealism could take root in concrete programs.

In deciding to promote socialist solutions in the north, the CCF launched what may qualify as its most radical and unique project. While the controversy that accompanied the introduction of medicare in 1962 attracted international attention, the imposition of a much more comprehensive socialism in the north hardly caused a stir outside the northern region. Like socialists elsewhere, the party believed that socialist-based rational planning offered solutions to society's existing problems and would result in a new and better world. The CCF hoped to replace the haphazard northern society that had grown up over the centuries. In the CCF plan, northerners would not only receive benefits, but would also freely share northern resources with the struggling southern economy.

Many of the politicians and bureaucrats who designed and implemented the northern programs of the CCF did not concern themselves with ideological purity. Although numerous programs introduced in the north were not examples of "pure" socialism, they did possess many socialist characteristics and reflected the influence of socialist ideology modified by the experiences of life on the prairie.[4] The party primarily applied an economic socialism, which increased government control over northern land and resources. This did not require nationalizing the land, since the province had received nearly the entire area as Crown land from Ottawa in 1930. The new government added strict control over the use of various resources, imposing a level of state regulation much greater than existed previously and in the south. Prior to 1944, the Liberal government allowed some transfer of resources, including land, trees, minerals, furs, and fish, to private hands. Exercising its lawful authority, the CCF withdrew the rights of private parties to own, extract, and sell most resources, reclaiming them for the "people of Saskatchewan." Joe Phelps wrote about a coming gradual transition "to social ownership in the industrial development of our Natural Resources." He hoped for eventual "complete social ownership and management of key industries in the development of our resources."[5] However, the changes that occurred did not seem distant or gradual to northerners. Almost overnight, Phelps and the CCF introduced socialist policies that transformed reality for most northerners and set long-lasting directions for the region.

Phelps's statement that private trappers, fishers, loggers, and miners had "taken millions of dollars out of our province as a result of planless ravaging" typified the CCF's view of the existing northern economy. The party also blamed private capital for northern underdevelopment. To end perceived abuses and to increase development, the CCF introduced various pieces of legislation that successfully restricted unfettered capitalism in the north. In no uncertain terms, the province advised those who made their living extracting renewable and nonrenewable resources that those assets belonged to the people of the province. Early actions included expelling outsiders from participating in the northern economy and giving economic opportunities to local people. Since very few larger companies operated in the north, those ideologically motivated attacks often jeopardized small, struggling, fishing, trapping, forestry, and retailing businesses.

Realizing that it could not simply wipe out the old, the CCF set out to design and build a better northern world. The government created new structures to institutionalize socialist forms of organization within the region. Crown corporations and marketing boards soon played instrumental roles in implementing the new northern socialist economy, handling the vital commodities of fish, fur, and trees.[6]

Once it held a firm grip on the northern economy, the CCF shifted some responsibility from Crown corporations and marketing boards to its newly created cooperatives. The CCF liked cooperatives because they excluded private capital and encouraged community ownership of assets. As well, the party thought that cooperatives would reduce costs and increase incomes for northerners. Premier Douglas himself strongly favoured cooperatives, viewing them as "the most important form of social ownership."[7]

While various other provincial governments and the federal government also worked to modernize their northern jurisdictions and assimilate Aboriginal populations, only the government of Saskatchewan sought to combine those tasks with the goal of building a socialist society. The CCF worked towards introducing socialism with a missionary-like zeal. Application of its socialist agenda meant that the path of development in northern Saskatchewan would differ substantially from that taken in other northern regions, especially from the middle 1940s to the early 1950s. By the late 1950s, several programs introduced by the federal government in the Arctic and on Indian reserves in the northern areas of the provinces increasingly resembled some implemented earlier by the CCF in Saskatchewan. But Ottawa did not go nearly as far or enter into as many areas of the society and economy as Douglas and his associates did. During the postwar decades, some provincial governments also instituted programs that resembled those of the early CCF. Quebec became interested in its northern region of "Nouveau Québec" by the 1960s. Across Canada, other provincial governments increasingly focused attention on their northern regions. Yet no other government in Canada allowed socialist ideology to guide its northern actions to the extent that the Saskatchewan CCF did. No one else went as far in seeking to remove pre-existing private enterprise, discourage the entry of new business, and promote public enterprise.[8]

Lacking models to follow, the new CCF government largely invented the form its northern socialism would take. Although the CCF plan for the north called for the creation of a local economy based on socialist principles and a sharing of northern wealth with the south, subsequent programs did not require that northerners receive an equal share of the province's wealth. While on the surface this may appear to contradict the goal of instituting socialism, the CCF justified this anomaly. The government strongly feared that northern Aboriginals would take advantage of generous social programs and become lazy; in a sense, then, the CCF limited benefits to northerners for their own good (discussed further in Chapter

10). In addition, the CCF simply ignored northern needs, knowingly permitting the continuance of Third World-like conditions in the northern half of the province. As a result, southern residents received many more benefits from social and health programs.

The CCF simultaneously imposed modernization, assimilation, and socialism, expecting their joint application to solve northern problems. Douglas and his ministers placed great confidence in the power of knowledge and planning applied by those with the benefit of social democratic enlightenment. They held a roughly equal lack of faith in the ability of northern Aboriginals to plan for their future. Although northerners resisted CCF plans for the north both at the ballot box and through numerous actions, this had little effect on the southern-based party. Even when its efforts led to failure, the CCF did not question its basic hypothesis or goals, but blamed imperfect subjects and methods, as we shall see in the following chapters.

Possibly as important as what the CCF set out to do in the north was how it sought to bring about change. The CCF used paternalistic, colonial methods to impose its agenda. Northern Saskatchewan already had a centuries-old legacy of colonial control. First Britain, then Canada, and finally Saskatchewan exerted authority over the area. During each phase, political and economic control remained largely outside the region. This situation was not unique. Governments had long established colonial control, both economically and politically, over far-flung regions of the globe. The years after the Second World War brought a global decolonization movement, which saw colonial masters gradually relinquish control over their former possessions. However, decolonization did not apply to internal colonialism within Canada. Instead, where one area held power over another, this colonialism frequently strengthened as the century progressed.

Similarly, the Saskatchewan CCF increased the province's colonial control over its northern region. Although northern Aboriginals accepted and valued the existing northern system, which had evolved under the direction of the traders and churches, the CCF decreed its end. Driven by the dual engines of unquestioning ethnocentrism and socialist fervour, CCF ministers and bureaucrats overpowered the north. The early CCF government brimmed with confidence that it would do things much better than had former governments and institutions. The region known as "the north," although covering about half of Saskatchewan, lacked political power. Its residents formed only 1 to 2 percent of the provincial population while the CCF held power. Only two elected Members of the Legislative Assembly (MLAs) represented northerners in the provincial capital of Regina, making it easy for the relatively massive southern population to dictate what happened in the north. The physical distance between the northern region and the centre of power also meant that the north became a distant periphery of the southern centre. About three hundred miles separated Regina from the near north, and seven hundred miles or more lay between the southern city and some remote northern areas. Only in the north could government impose the society it visualized without fear of repercussions at the polls. Northerners lacked the numbers to remove the CCF from power, and southern voters, who would not have tolerated similar programs closer to home, would not interfere in the remote north.

Even though most CCF officials had virtually no experience in or with the north, they consulted only minimally with northerners, white or Aboriginal, considering them incapable of analyzing their society or participating in designing improvements to it. Typical of a colonial situation, the CCF did not rely on local input. Some northern residents participated in surveys and possibly helped determine minor details of changes to resource policies, but that limited opportunity excluded most isolated and non-English-speaking northerners. The consultation process did not extend to the other economic and social engineering policies that quickly and dramatically altered reality for all northerners.

The early CCF government chose the Department of Natural Resources and Industrial Development (DNR) to serve as its strong colonial arm, greatly expanding its presence and power in the north. Other departments also participated, and bureaucrats from many departments visited the north. With few modifications, that far-reaching northern colonial system continued throughout the CCF's time in office. Some see an increased promotion of community development in the CCF's later years as decolonization.[9] Yet that claim minimizes the ongoing role played by the CCF in creating and operating the northern colonial system. It also does not recognize the colonial nature of the so-called tools of decolonization, including the forced promotion of cooperatives and community development used by the CCF.

Contradictorily, while the CCF wanted to assimilate Aboriginals, the colonial system perpetuated and reinforced the presence of two economies and societies in the north. More than before, the Aboriginal economy and society functioned separately from those of non-Aboriginals. Phelps and others in the CCF visualized happy, sober, educated, healthy, hard-working, and cooperatively-minded Aboriginals living in orderly settlements while participating in what the CCF viewed as "traditional" economic pursuits. The CCF believed that Aboriginals had a natural aptitude for trapping and fishing, while lacking the ability to participate in nontraditional industrial activities such as mining and forestry.[10]

Although no other jurisdiction sought to impose socialism as the CCF did in Saskatchewan, the CCF was not alone in Canada in creating a colonial system. In some respects a colonial or neo-colonial situation existed throughout other provincial norths and in the NWT. Colonialism grew at various rates, increasing greatly in some areas during and after the Second World War when capital and workers moved north to extract resources. The fragmenting of the Canadian north by provincial and territorial borders made it easier to impose colonialism, in northern Saskatchewan and else-where, by breaking a natural region into pieces. This limited the potential strength of the north. Tying northern provincial areas to more populous and powerful southern areas further facilitated colonialism.[11]

The first few years after the 1944 election victory brought the most aggressive intervention by the CCF. Joe Phelps, the powerful minister of Natural Resources, led a handful of dedicated bureaucrats in their mission. Yet problems soon beset the well-meaning small army. Even as the CCF proudly boasted it could logically plan a new and better society, chaos characterized its northern initiatives. Goals remained poorly articulated, while ad hoc natural resource development projects disrupted northern lives. This stage brought the most dramatic change to the north, as Phelps and other southern socialists fought to excise capitalist abuses and intro-duce socialism and strict state control. Often flying by the seat of his pants, Phelps energetically made and modified policies. Hope remained strong that, once the CCF worked the bugs out of its new system, the north would reap the benefits of the interventions.

A second stage in CCF northern policy began in the late 1940s. After vot-ers threw Phelps out of office in 1948, no other CCF politician possessed a similar dedication to reshape the north. The party also came to realize that diversification of the provincial economy through developing north-ern resources would not come about easily or cheaply. Financial reali-ties severely limited the CCF's options as well. While early optimism and hopes of a quick return on northern investments had helped loosen the purse strings after 1944, a more cautious fiscal approach characterized the 1950s. CCF interest in the welfare of northern people also faded. Erosion of earlier reforms took place, disillusioned radical staff members quit, and CCF attacks on the churches and the HBC eased somewhat. The CCF still did not successfully apply its self-touted planning ability to the north. Phelps's replacement as minister of Natural Resources, John H. Brockelbank, favoured action over contemplation, placing little emphasis on developing goals and plans.[12] The lack of effective planning became apparent in the unexpected consequences of CCF actions: health care improvements led to a population explosion, new roads brought social problems, market inter-ventions increased poverty, and social aid undermined self-reliance. The problems created by the CCF often proved more formidable than the old ones. Perplexed by its numerous failures and ongoing resistance from the northern population, the CCF lost faith that it could quickly and easily build a new northern society. Yet instead of giving up, it adopted subtler methods to impose the same goals on northerners. The new plan combined extensive anthropological study of northern Aboriginals with community development methods to achieve its goals. The modernizing, assimilation-ist, and socialist agenda remained, with DNR still the primary colonial ad-ministrator. This final stage continued until the defeat of the CCF in 1964.[13]

In many respects the story that has emerged is not a celebration of the CCF era in northern Saskatchewan. Instead of being liberated by the CCF from forces that the government viewed as corrupt and capitalistic, many northerners, both Aboriginal and non-Aboriginal, experienced a new and destructive oppression. Certain that its goals justified its actions, the CCF imposed its ideology and programs in the north, ignoring and overruling the desires of northerners, while attempting to bring modernization, assimilation, and socialism to the region. Unfortunately, destroying the old proved much easier than building a new and viable north.

In retrospect, some of the negative effects of the CCF presence came from its failure to reconcile its actions with its ideology. As a result, the CCF left a legacy riddled with contradictions. Even though it prided itself on being an intelligent, thoughtful government, it often acted on impulse and emotion. While the party thought of itself as a kinder, gentler alternative to capitalism, it built and employed an insensitive, heavy-handed colonial apparatus. At the same time that it claimed to care for northern Aboriginals, the CCF judged their culture as worthless and worked to assimilate them. There was inconsistency in the CCF attempt to impose economic socialism on the north while it opposed expanded sharing through social programs. Similarly, the CCF viewed northern wealth as belonging to all Saskatchewan residents, but it refused to share the province's wealth equally with northerners. Another major contradiction existed between the CCF choice of pre-industrial vocations for northern Aboriginals and its stated goal of assimilating Indians and Metis. CCF policies that established isolated Aboriginal ghettos also limited assimilation. Further, while the CCF wanted to modernize the north, it failed to devote the needed resources to bring this about, leaving northerners living in semi-modern poverty.

In addition to describing the CCF and northern society, both Aboriginal and non-Aboriginal, this book portrays Canadian society from the 1940s to the 1960s. The momentum of society's attitudes and beliefs exercised a powerful influence on events in the north, sometimes proving more powerful than the overt ideology espoused by the CCF. As a result, the CCF often behaved as a product of its time. The CCF claimed socialism as its ideology, but the more powerful ethnocentric beliefs that it shared with the larger society dictated many of its actions and helped determine the outcome of its projects.

Although forty years have passed since the CCF defeat at the polls in 1964, the record of this government in northern Saskatchewan has remained largely unknown outside the region. There are various reasons for this situation. Only recently have historians begun to study many aspects of the Canadian north. Yet the northern areas of the provinces have been more neglected by the historical profession than have areas of the Canadian territorial north. The attitude, which exists in some circles, that the true north does not extend below the sixtieth parallel can take attention away from regions like northern Saskatchewan. At the same time, the northern areas of some provinces have received more notice than has the northern part of Saskatchewan. Beginning in the 1940s, the Alaska Highway drew the attention of North Americans to northern British Columbia and Alberta. More recently, the Nisga'a land settlement and the *Delgamuukw* court decision, both relating to British Columbia, have directed the national spotlight onto that northern area. Similarly, the James Bay and Northern Quebec Agreement and related Aboriginal claims have drawn the attention of historians to northern Quebec. No such major event has attracted historians and those working in related disciplines to northern Saskatchewan.

Another reason that the history of the CCF era in northern Saskatchewan remains largely untold is that Canadians believe they know the history of the CCF in Saskatchewan. While many provincial politicians from the first decades after the Second World War have sunk into obscurity, large numbers of Canadians still recognize the name of T.C. Douglas. In popular mythology, Canadians associate Douglas and the Saskatchewan CCF with positive advances in social policy and particularly with the introduction of medicare. It is likely that few people think of the north when they think of Douglas and his party. As a result of the lack of study of the CCF's northern record, the picture of this government remains incomplete and inaccurate. Therefore, the significance of this book extends beyond providing information about, and an analysis of, two decades in northern Saskatchewan. It adds necessary information about the nature of the CCF in the larger Saskatchewan and Canadian arenas.

I used a variety of sources and methods for this exploration of the history of northern Saskatchewan during this period. As the dominant Canadian historical tradition has done, I relied heavily on archival sources. Without the information contained in the records preserved by the Government of Saskatchewan and various individuals, the story of events during this era would be largely lost. On the other hand, to rely only on these records would omit the voices of many northern people, both Aboriginal and non-Aboriginal. Interviews with numerous northern residents who remember the CCF presence have provided an invaluable check on archival sources and additional information. Drawing on both written and oral sources combines the traditions of historical transmission of both cultures, the Euro-Canadian and the Aboriginal.

A third source has contributed to this work, particularly to its conclusions. Without the interpretation of the observer, the information gathered remains little more than disjointed descriptions of incidents. In this book, as must almost certainly happen in every historical work, the various pieces of information join together to form a picture. While the data gathered conceivably could tell many different and possibly conflicting stories, one story has emerged, standing above the other possibilities, as most convincing and true. Although this picture may appear subjective and constructed to some, to me it has taken on the status of being a true recreation of events.

The narrative that emerges by combining the information from various sources may not be what some expect or want to hear. Some CCF goals for the north, including socialism and modernization, found and still find many sincere and devoted supporters. Many also would agree with Joe Phelps in his desire to end the reign of parish priests, bootleggers, and fur sharks in the north.[14] Large numbers of Canadians have placed the CCF and its leaders on a pedestal, thinking them above the failings that afflict ordinary mankind. Many look on the CCF and its successor, the NDP, as the originators of many of the best aspects of Canadian society. They accept that Tommy Douglas and his party helped save Canadians from the excesses of capitalism by developing and implementing a kinder, more humane society. The CCF record in southern Saskatchewan serves as one basis for this belief. Yet little is known about the actions of the CCF in the northern half of the province, where the party had much more freedom and power to demonstrate its nature. Examining the CCF record in the north can shed light on the nature of CCF socialism in the larger context of Saskatchewan and Canada.

The reader should not interpret this work as an attempt to blame the CCF and its program of modernization, assimilation, socialism, and colonialism for all the ills that came to plague the north. Other governments across Canada, including those that did not adopt socialist policies or other aggressive programs of directed change, experienced similar failures in their northern regions. This book does not seek to release Aboriginal society or those who promoted nonsocialist solutions from accepting some responsibility for life as it was lived in northern Saskatchewan. As this book demonstrates, Aboriginals possessed free will and some power, even when confronted by a powerful state. Also, the pre-existing Euro-Canadian capitalist and church institutions, which sometimes made victims of Aboriginals, certainly did not vanish completely with the election of the CCF. Although greatly weakened, the old forces continued to affect events during the CCF era.

Part One
At the Crossroads

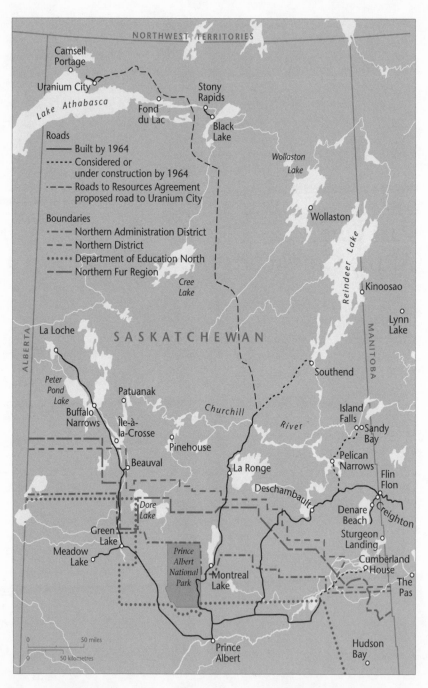

Map of northern Saskatchewan, showing major communities, administrative divisions, and road systems.

1
Another Country Altogether

Northern Saskatchewan found itself at a crossroads in 1944. Until that time the region, linked to the south primarily by the traditional waterways, had remained isolated from the twentieth-century society that had developed farther south. By the 1940s, technological advances in transportation and communications, combined with a growing southern hunger for northern resources, meant that the north's former isolation could not continue indefinitely. Further, the election of the Co-operative Commonwealth Federation (CCF), and its interest in the north, meant that the informal governance of the Hudson's Bay Company and the churches would have to make way for an expanded governmental presence. Developments in neighbouring provinces and the northern territories demonstrated that change would inevitably come to northern Saskatchewan, no matter who governed the province. Yet the nature of the impending transformation remained undetermined in 1944. The landslide election victory of T.C. Douglas and the CCF granted this party the authority to choose the direction at the crossroads. Although most northerners, and particularly the Aboriginal population of the region, paid little attention to the election of the CCF at the time, the new government held great power over the future of northerners.

On 15 June 1944, the CCF defeated W.J. Patterson's Liberals, winning 53.1 percent of the popular vote and forty-seven of fifty-two seats. Northern issues played little part in the outcome of the election, which was largely determined by southern voters. In the south, the Liberals had alienated supporters by their ineffective handling of the Great Depression of the 1930s and subsequent economic and social problems. In 1944 southern Saskatchewan appeared to be a beaten-down and obscure area that had not yet fully recovered from the devastation wrought by drought and collapsed grain markets. Poverty there had reached legendary proportions, dashing the hopes of the immigrants who had come to this place once thought to be a Garden of Eden. By provincial election day, although rains again fell and the war economy created a demand for prairie wheat, poverty still dominated. Patterson and his party lost further support by extending their term past the customary four years; voters simply tired of the long-serving Liberals. Even more importantly, the CCF and its energetic leader, Tommy Douglas, managed to convince voters that they offered a viable alternative to the old government. The party held out hope that its innovative solutions and benevolent planning would solve existing problems and prevent a recurrence of economic catastrophe. Additionally, the new government promised changes in education, health, and labour legislation.

Douglas and his colleagues in the CCF also owed much of their election victory to a seeming moderation of the party's earlier radical socialist policies. The CCF that northerners and other residents of Saskatchewan came to know formed in the early 1930s. The party sprang from various socialist and nonsocialist origins. Some of its strongest roots grew from the western Social Gospel movement of the early twentieth century. J.S. Woodsworth, the first leader of the national CCF organization, and others had long advocated the application of Christian principles to solve society's problems. Social Gospel influenced the Progressive Party in the 1920s, and when the Progressives faded, many idealists looked for a new political party that would apply Christian principles to everyday life.

Although the CCF did not turn against Christianity and continued to advocate various Christian ideals, it incorporated some secular influences. For decades, Saskatchewan's farmers had battled the power of large grain-handling companies and railroads. Those experiences formed part of the heritage of the CCF. Similarly, Saskatchewan people's reliance on cooperatives proved compatible with the ideals of the CCF. Support for the new party also came from radicalized workers who experienced defeat at the hands of big business after the First World War and who again suffered economic hardship during the Great Depression. These workers introduced views from a variety of European socialist movements. The CCF accepted ideas from the League for Social Reconstruction and its eastern Canadian intellectuals, who drew up the Regina Manifesto for the new party in 1933. At that time the CCF moved beyond advocating the limited social reforms of its predecessors in the Social Gospel, Progressive, and cooperative movements and identified itself as a socialist party.

Socialism has meant various things to different people at different times, and the version that existed in the 1930s in Saskatchewan did not necessarily mean the same thing that it meant in another place or time. The same observation can be made of capitalism, commonly considered the primary ideology competing with socialism. Early in the twentieth century, for example, capitalism incorporated a heavy dose of social Darwinism that, a hundred years later, even self-proclaimed capitalists likely view as primitive and harsh. Similarly, what various people mean by socialism has changed over time. For instance, the international image of socialism underwent dramatic change from the idealistic time before the Russian Revolution to the excesses of the Stalinist era. In order to understand the socialism of the CCF and its impact on northern Saskatchewan, one must view socialism and capitalism in the context of the CCF era.

Elements of the Regina Manifesto offer some of the clearest evidence about what the CCF meant by socialism. The manifesto, which for over twenty years formed the official ideological basis of the CCF, boldly stated that "No C.C.F. Government will rest content until it has eradicated capitalism and put into operation the full programme of socialized planning which will lead to the establishment in Canada of the Co-operative Commonwealth." Like socialists elsewhere at that time, the early CCF believed that the entire capitalist system suffered from "mortal sickness." It aimed to replace capitalism and the reliance on private profit as the "main stimulus to economic effort" with a "planned and socialized economy." The coming widespread "socialization" would include the "economic order," "all financial machinery," "transportation, communications, electric power and all other industries and services essential to social planning," and "health services." The party placed "the supplying of human needs" above "the making of profits."[1] Shortly before the party's first election victory in Saskatchewan, David Lewis, the national secretary of the CCF at the time, and Frank Scott, the national chairman of the CCF, indicated that the manifesto remained "the basic statement of C.C.F. philosophy."[2] The party did not develop a more moderate replacement for the Regina Manifesto for many years, even after winning office in 1944. For much of their time in office, when CCF politicians and bureaucrats spoke of socialism, they referred to the ideas and spirit of the Regina Manifesto.

CCF supporters and other socialists during the era from the 1930s to the 1960s probably would have agreed that the doctrine they espoused dealt largely with the economic order, although they believed that the effects of its implementation would resonate throughout all aspects of society. In their view, the state should exercise its authority to intervene in society in an effort to lessen economic and social inequalities. In addition, those socialists sought to institute a system that would prevent individuals from exploiting others and receiving large amounts of unearned income from property or investments. The welfare of the community took precedence over that of the individual. State intervention would result in a dramatic reduction of private ownership of resources and the means of production. Public ownership, Crown corporations, and cooperatives would play expanded economic roles. Strong elements of the socialism promoted by the CCF in the 1930s survived in the party into the 1940s and later.[3] Many in the CCF remained committed to battle against capitalism and promote socialism. Frank Scott, a long-time national chairman of the CCF who was present at the drafting of the Regina Manifesto, stated in 1950, "I disagree with those who say that the issue today is not between capitalism and socialism."[4]

Over time, the stark contrast between the two competing ideologies, socialism and capitalism, became blurred, and both appeared to lose their hard edges. In Saskatchewan the CCF itself contributed to that ongoing process by softening some of its earlier positions.[5] As the years passed, the CCF increasingly referred to itself as "social democratic."[6] The party continued to enjoy electoral success partly because southern voters, even those opposed to socialism, found some things to like in the usually nonthreatening social democratic program of the CCF.

For the most part, the debate among Saskatchewan politicians and voters about the extent of socialism in the CCF and its impact on the province remained fairly simple, with both sides believing that they knew the meaning of the term. Rarely did politicians explore the ideological complexities of socialism and capitalism or spell out what either ideology meant. A notable exception occurred in 1957 when Tommy Douglas and future Liberal leader Ross Thatcher squared off at Mossbank, Saskatchewan, over the issues of government intervention in the economy and Crown corporations. That debate became one of the more articulate skirmishes in Thatcher's "personal war on socialism."[7] In the years that followed, Thatcher did much to remind Saskatchewan voters of the CCF's socialist origins and doctrine. Without denying its heritage, the CCF sought to portray itself as a party that pragmatically dealt with the problems confronting the province.

Even though the CCF took pains to distance itself from radical socialism, a more moderate version of that ideology continued to identify and distinguish the CCF party and government in Saskatchewan. Especially during its early years in office, but also later on, CCF politicians, party members, and devoted bureaucrats continued to see the political world in terms of socialism versus capitalism. Opponents of the party viewed the political world in similar terms. Clearly, the CCF differed from other major political parties in Saskatchewan and Canada, none of which identified themselves largely by pointing to socialist ideology.

In 1944 Saskatchewan voters believed that the CCF had retreated from its former position of calling for a complete elimination of capitalism. Following unsuccessful elections in the 1930s, the party backed away from its more radical pronouncements and policies to attract a broader base of support. While the CCF originally wanted to nationalize farmland, it abandoned this policy in the 1930s. It then restricted its plans for social ownership to taking over financial institutions, public utilities, and some natural resources. The people of the province became familiar with the CCF while it served as the opposition in the legislature, during which time its moderate stance and advocacy for farmers assuaged the fears of some distrustful voters. CCF roots in the Christian Social Gospel and agricultural movements, and Douglas's position as a Baptist minister also helped allay the dread of communism. Consequently, the Liberals' characterization of CCF members as radical socialists or communists had little effect, and voters overlooked some of the more worrisome roots of the CCF. Farmers who did not support the earlier, more radical CCF policies, which threatened their survival as independent farmers, liked and came to trust the new CCF platform that offered to protect them and give them higher wheat prices. Many who feared Soviet-style socialism accepted the democratic Christian socialism advocated by the federation. By 1944 the CCF appeared to be a social reform party, and even some former opponents supported it.[8] By voting for the CCF, Saskatchewan electors did not necessarily vote for socialism.

Once in power, the CCF continued to moderate its socialism for southern Saskatchewan. Observers accurately see only a mild and very limited socialism in that region of the province during the twenty-year record of CCF government. Yet the party did not abandon all of its socialist inclinations, even in the south, and it adopted a cautious evolutionary approach that by 1964 had moved Saskatchewan towards becoming a "welfare state."[9] Some residents of the province became alarmed when, true to its philosophy, the CCF attempted a limited socialization of the southern economy after its election victory. The new government acted quickly, passing the Crown Corporations Act of 1945, which authorized government involvement in a variety of industrial and commercial enterprises. These new initiatives fell under the direction of Joe Phelps and his department, the former Department of Natural Resources, renamed the Department of Natural Resources and Industrial Development in keeping with its expanded mandate. Phelps, known as an idealistic dreamer, likely had the biggest job in the government, with responsibility for industry, natural resources, and remaking the electrical supply system.[10] While Douglas wanted to limit public ownership to monopolistic industries, Phelps managed to push his colleagues much further – into taking ownership of many non-monopolistic industries.[11] By establishing manufacturing industries for items that Saskatchewan previously bought from other provinces or countries, referred to as Import Substitution Industrialization (ISI), the party hoped to build a nonagricultural economy and use the profits to pay for social programs.[12] By 1948 the CCF had set up more than twelve Crown corporations. These operated buses, made bricks, tanned hides, cobbled shoes, processed wool, built boxes, refined salt, and slaughtered horses.

It soon became apparent that the CCF lacked business experience. As a result, all of the state ISI efforts folded, resulting in a loss of face and money. The CCF then retreated from attempting to establish extensive state ownership. This withdrawal, along with private enterprise's hesitancy to invest in a "socialist" province, meant the failure of the plan for economic diversification.[13] Douglas later acknowledged that government expansion into artificially created secondary industry did not work, blaming failure on the small market. He regretted some of the early experiments with Crown corporations. "We did too much in the first four years," he said, "and we unsettled a lot of people by trying to bring about a social revolution in almost every aspect of human life, instead of tackling two or three fields, and bringing people to this gradually."[14]

Soon the CCF moved even farther from radical socialism in southern Saskatchewan. Phelps's failure to win re-election in 1948 resistance from ordinary people and capital to socialism, and the Cold War all added to the "siege mentality" that developed in the CCF.[15] In 1948 Douglas and others "pledged fair play, assistance, and the assurance of no expropriation to private enterprise."[16] In spite of some embarrassing failures, the absence of a strong opposition helped the CCF win subsequent elections. Over the years, the party did implement many relatively noncontroversial aspects of its platform in the south. Largely thanks to the Canadian economic upturn of the 1950s, it went ahead with medicare, new labour legislation, rural electrification, telephone expansion, highway construction, and educational improvements.[17] Crown corporations, meanwhile, continued in safer enterprises, including in the monopolies of power, gas, and telephone. Provincially as well as nationally, the CCF distanced itself from a hard socialist line without completely relinquishing its image as a socialist party. Politicians and faithful supporters could point to small steps towards the goals established in the early days of the party's existence.

A very different situation existed in the north in 1944. The charm of Douglas and the CCF failed to sweep the northern region. Had the rest of the province voted as the north did, the CCF would not have won its landslide victory. The new government garnered only 7.4 percent of the vote in Athabasca constituency, compared to 80.7 percent for the Liberals, while Cumberland constituency voted 58.7 percent for the CCF, compared to 39.7 percent for the Liberals.[18] Since Status Indians could not vote, CCF support in the north came disproportionately from white residents. Had Indians voted, it is likely the Liberals also would have won in Cumberland. Many Indians belonged to the Roman Catholic church, which encouraged voters to support the Liberal party. Clearly the CCF lacked a mandate from northerners to impose its programs on the north in 1944, a situation that changed little over the next two decades.[19]

The north differed from the south in other ways, including in its history. In a sense, when the CCF turned its attention to the north in 1944, white residents of southern Saskatchewan revisited some largely forgotten roots. The Euro-Canadian presence in Saskatchewan and western Canada came from northern beginnings. Hardy white traders and explorers used natural water routes to visit the area that later formed northern Saskatchewan long before there was an interest in settling the southern prairie. Aboriginal people had lived in the hospitable bush for millennia, and the furs they trapped became the first major northern attraction for white people. The HBC founded Cumberland House as its first permanent trading post in the area in 1774. By 1800 various fur-trading companies strategically placed numerous trading posts on the maze of northern inland waterways. The Saskatchewan River provided access to the southeastern area of the north and to the Sturgeon Weir River, which led to the Churchill River. This water highway spanned the province from east to west. From near the western end of the Churchill system, Aboriginals and traders crossed the Methye Portage into the Clearwater River and the Mackenzie River watershed, which flowed to the Arctic Ocean. Aboriginals provided much of the labour for the trade, trapping furs and supplying traders with food from the land. Many white men took Aboriginal wives, which led to a substantial mixed-blood population in the area. Adding to the white presence, the Roman Catholic and Anglican churches had established missions in the north by the 1840s.

Although the southern area of what later became the province of Saskatchewan also once participated fully in the fur trade, by the 1880s the two regions followed divergent historical paths. Prime Minister Sir John A. Macdonald's vision for Canada led to the building of a southern transcontinental railroad by the 1880s and the influx of tens of thousands of white settlers who ploughed the prairie and parkland area. The growth of agriculture in the south diverted attention from the north, and the fur trade declined in relative importance to the economy of western Canada. After Confederation, the north was part of the North-West Territories until the creation of the province of Saskatchewan in 1905. The federal government placed the northern boundary of Saskatchewan at the sixtieth parallel, optimistically but unrealistically believing this to be the northern limit of agriculture. Partnering the north with the southern farming area appeared illogical from the northern point of view, since in reality the two areas had little in common. Yet creation of the province had little immediate effect on northerners, particularly because the federal government maintained control over Crown land and resources until 1930, when it transferred these to the province. Although most southerners seemed oblivious to the existence of the north, there were exceptions. Large lumber companies cut accessible trees, and some mining companies developed ore bodies in the region. In an effort to confirm the agricultural potential of the north, governments sponsored expeditions, including the federally supported travels of Frank Crean in 1908 and 1909, to explore the area. The city of Prince Albert, while outside the north, viewed its proximity to the region as a key to prosperity. Prince Albert National Park, established in 1927, became one of only a few successful major developments, creating a substantial tourism presence in the near north.[20] Many young white males also ventured north in the years before 1940, seeking the riches of fish and fur while escaping the ravages of the southern drought.

Prior to 1944, the Hudson's Bay Company and other traders had exerted considerable control in the north. The Roman Catholic and Anglican churches also played major roles in directing the lives of northerners. While northern Aboriginals may not always have welcomed the presence and actions of the traders and churches, a workable economic and social system resulted from the interaction between the newcomers and northerners. Aboriginals recognized and appreciated many of the services imported from outside by these forces. Among the most important benefits were the credit system created by the traders, which carried the needy through hard times, and the hospitals and schools established by the churches. Although sometimes government reimbursed the traders and churches for their efforts, neither the federal nor provincial government offered extensive welfare, health care, or education services in the north. Few bureaucrats ventured north, leaving the area unregulated and northerners doing much as they pleased. Even after Saskatchewan gained control over northern Crown lands in 1930, southern politicians, distracted by the Depression and the Second World War, largely ignored the north. It was not until the election of the CCF that government turned its attention northwards. When it did so, the CCF found an undeveloped, isolated north with no roads or railways entering it.

After Saskatchewan became a province in 1905, northern Saskatchewan formed a distinct geographic region within the province. Travellers immediately knew when they reached the north – the prairie grain fields disappeared and trees and lakes dominated the landscape. Farther north, rock outcrops became common. Not only in geographic terms but also in other respects it was, as Joe Phelps said, "another country altogether."[21] Northern Saskatchewan includes about half the province. Its definition has varied over time and for various purposes. All definitions use the sixtieth parallel – the line of latitude that divides Saskatchewan from the Northwest Territories – as the northern boundary, and the Manitoba and Alberta borders as the eastern and western boundaries. The southern boundary, however, is less certain, partly because governments have drawn and redrawn this line for a number of reasons. Different lines delineate the southern edge of Census Division 18 and federal constituency boundaries for Ottawa's purposes. The provincial definition of the north has a more complicated history. During most of the CCF era, a Northern Administration District (NAD) defined the north for purposes of natural resources administration. The NAD extended farther south in the east than in the west. On the east side it included Cumberland House, while on the west side it did not reach as far south as Meadow Lake. The NAD boundary ran roughly parallel to the northern limit of agricultural settlement in the province. Confusing things considerably, the CCF did not follow the NAD boundary when defining the north for provincial elections and the administration of education, health, and other government programs. As a result, numerous administrative lines criss-crossed on the map. However, the NAD line became the most widely recognized southern boundary of the north. For most purposes, this book also follows the NAD definition of the north.

The fixed borders that divided northern Saskatchewan from Manitoba, Alberta, and the NWT broke a formerly unified natural region into a number of powerless pieces. These areas shared a geographic, cultural, economic, and historic unity that political division disrupted. Splitting the north into many pieces helped create northern colonies of the south.[22] The act of division also took from the region much of its potential for future independent power and control. The location of the provincial boundaries lacked rationality from the point of view of the interests of northern Saskatchewan. The political boundaries also allowed the CCF to establish a unique direction for northern Saskatchewan, which diverged considerably from that of other northern jurisdictions. Only Saskatchewan attempted to reshape its northern region into a largely socialist society, and the province also led the way within Canada in its attempt to assimilate and modernize northern Aboriginals.

During the CCF era, the residents of various areas within northern Saskatchewan had little contact with each other. As modern communication and transportation links with the south increased in number, the traditional east-west water routes fell into disuse. In some cases this resulted in decreased contact and unity between widely separated areas of the north. The west-side area, extending from Beauval to La Loche, became distinct. On the opposite side of the province, Cumberland House and the Saskatchewan River delta formed a separate area. No longer did the fur brigades, once the lifeblood of the north, sweep along the waterways tying these communities together. The far north also formed a large, isolated region. Pockets of predominantly white settlement developed. La Ronge, located midway between Alberta and Manitoba, served as the CCF governmental centre within the north. Not far from the north shore of Lake Athabasca, Uranium City grew as a white mining community, and near the border with Manitoba, the white communities of Island Falls and Creighton formed separate enclaves. As time went on, links with the outside world grew, while those within the north atrophied. This situation facilitated the establishment of political and colonial control from outside and jeopardized the development of northern unity and power.

Inevitably, even though northerners appeared satisfied with many aspects of the existing regional economic and social system, change would have come to the north. Had it not been for the election of the CCF, that change likely would have come more gradually. But the new government brought abrupt change. Applying ideologically based planning and a firm, controlling hand, it turned northern development in directions it otherwise would not have taken. Taking control fit well with the party's belief that it possessed the duty and the ability to develop improved ways of doing things.

The CCF set out to apply rational planning not only to the north, but within its entire scope of influence. To do so, Douglas and his ministers relied on various sources for advice. Early advisors included the Economic Advisory Committee composed of "three ideologically sympathetic" University of Saskatchewan (U of S) faculty members, a Legislative Advisory Committee, and Carlyle King, the provincial CCF president and a U of S professor of English. In an effort to institutionalize planning within government, the CCF established the Economic Advisory and Planning Board (EAPB) on 1 January 1946 as its main economic planning mechanism. The EAPB also coordinated most government enterprises. In addition to its chairman, George Cadbury, the imported socialist scion of the Cadbury chocolate family, the EAPB included the maverick minister of Natural Resources, Joe Phelps, other members, and nine professional staff. The EAPB proved quite conservative, certainly more so than Phelps, and pulled back from promoting the institution of socialism in the south. Yet it did support Phelps's aggressive plans and actions in the north. In 1947 one section of the EAPB became a Crown corporation, the Government Finance Office (GFO), a holding company for Crown corporations. This move proved extremely significant for the north, since numerous Crown corporations would operate there. Chairman Cadbury held a lot of power in the north and the south, also managing the GFO and acting as the chief industrial officer. In another effort to rationalize government, the CCF established the Budget Bureau in 1946. It examined spending proposals before they reached the Treasury Board and had the task of connecting budget making and program evaluation with a view to the longer term.[23] The Budget Bureau exercised a profound influence over northern developments, controlling the purse strings and often deciding whether projects would proceed or not. Throughout its time in office, the CCF continued to value rational planning. Although centralized control remained, the government decentralized some research and planning by the early 1950s, delegating this to individual departments. In theory, this made the entire system of government a planning instrument. After its initial massive intervention in the north, the CCF passed much of the planning responsibility for the region to DNR. That department had a planning division by 1951, staffed largely by geographers.[24]

Self-assurance characterized the early CCF government. It confidently relied on its own planning expertise, proceeding without much public consultation. While Crown corporations played a large role in carrying out CCF plans for the north, the CCF did not hold public hearings into most of its new enterprises. Not even the legislature debated the corporations before their creation. Yet the highly touted group of planners in Regina included few with successful business experience, and some lacked the credentials to plan and run Crown corporations and the economy. As a result, numerous dreams and enterprises soon foundered when confronted with reality. With the most public of its failures behind it, the CCF deflected criticisms by having a Crown corporations committee deal with questions about the corporations after 1949.[25]

While southern voters and failed experiments limited the radicalism of the CCF in the south, government planners operated with far fewer restraints in the north. During its twenty years in office, the CCF implemented various aggressive projects to achieve its goals of modernization, assimilation, and socialism for the north. At the same time, Douglas and his colleagues sought to diversify the provincial economy, tap northern resource riches to help fund the coming prairie utopia, and bring justice to northern residents.

In 1944 the north stood at a crossroads, faced with inevitable modernization and change. The new government held the authority and power to decide the nature of much of this change and did not hesitate to quickly establish a firm direction for the north. Through a multifaceted initiative, it set out to build a northern socialist economy and society to replace the long-standing capitalist system. In doing so, the party demonstrated loyalty to socialist ideals as it defined them in its guiding Regina Manifesto. The CCF took advantage of the relative weakness of the north to apply its socialist beliefs much more than it could in the south. Although northerners had not asked for a socialist society, the CCF believed northerners would soon reap the benefits of socialism. The new north visualized by the dreamers in Regina would provide a modern environment for an assimilated, prosperous, healthy, and educated Aboriginal population. In addition, the north would play a major role in bringing prosperity to the entire province. The CCF confidently thought it could achieve these goals. While northerners did not share the vision, the CCF believed that it knew best.

In order to successfully introduce its plans to the north, the CCF needed to create an administrative structure and hire devoted people who agreed with its goals and methods. Failure to do so would jeopardize the CCF's northern plans and the economic future of the province. The challenge of building a new administrative system for the north soon provided a real test of Douglas and his colleagues' ability as planners.

Part Two
Building the Colonial Structure

2
From the Top

In order to introduce its ambitious plans to the north, the CCF created an administrative structure of a size unprecedented in the region. While its primary northern agency, the Department of Natural Resources and Industrial Development (DNR) also operated in the southern part of the province, the CCF gave DNR numerous special and greater powers to carry out its northern work. In the north, DNR and other government departments applied various programs, many of which the CCF designed specially for the region. The geographical isolation and the application of special programs made CCF efforts in the north resemble a large laboratory experiment. This analogy is apt insofar as the CCF broke new ground, since no government in Canada had ever tried to simultaneously introduce modernization, assimilation, and socialism to a large Aboriginal population. Yet unlike some who exercise great caution and skepticism when exploring uncharted territory, the CCF approached this project with immense confidence and did not admit the possibility of failure.

The CCF had no northerners in its caucus in 1944 from whom to obtain advice about northern matters. Joseph Lee (Joe) Phelps, a Wilkie-area farmer who represented the Saltcoats constituency in east-central Saskatchewan, became the key person to bring change to the north during the early CCF era. The mark of his efforts remained long after he left government. Phelps behaved like an ardent socialist, aggressively introducing socialism to the north. He was not a Marxist, unlike some who came to work for him, yet he described the result of the CCF coming to power as a "real revolution." Phelps's brand of socialism came from the southern Saskatchewan farm tradition, which viewed large private monopolies, including the Canadian Pacific Railway (CPR) and elevator companies, as the worst of capitalist villains. In the north the Hudson's Bay Company (HBC) became Phelps's primary capitalist target, although he extended his attack on northern capitalism to include some very small enterprises. Phelps's socialism justified his northern actions, actions that spoke of an immense self-assurance even within the unfamiliar northern environment. In a contradiction that

he, like some others in the CCF, seemed blind to, Phelps advocated socialism for the north and some other sectors of Saskatchewan's economy,
while continuing his own entrepreneurial farming enterprise.

Phelps had never visited northern Saskatchewan until after the June
1944 election. Nor did he possess a strong interest in the region. He only
reluctantly took the job of minister of Natural Resources and Industrial
Development, the CCF's most powerful northern position. He preferred
the other job he received, that of overseeing the Power Commission and
the electrification of southern Saskatchewan. However, characteristic of
Joe Phelps's style, he took on his new duties with great vigour. Not long
after the election, Phelps and his wife travelled to various parts of the
north in DNR's only plane. The visit seemed to kindle a passion in the
man to bring change to the region. Phelps described the north as a vast
new frontier, similar to space. While he seemed quite taken with the physical environment and economic potential of the region, Phelps saw much
that he did not like in the existing northern society. Trusting his first
impressions, he did not waste time on a prolonged study. Instead he
rapidly decided that white people, including unregulated fish and fur dealers, bootleggers, and priests, had caused many northern problems. Phelps
made three trips north by September 1944 to work on plans to introduce
changes to the trapping, fishing, and forestry industries.[1]

Believing that the north faced various crises, Phelps and his colleagues
hastily developed new policies and an administrative structure specifically
to introduce CCF solutions to the region. T.C. Douglas and his cabinet
generally supported Phelps's fur, fish, timber, and other northern initiatives. For several reasons, his party also gave Phelps an unusually large
degree of freedom to act independently in the north. Possibly most importantly, the CCF accepted the view that northern society was beset with
severe problems and not worth preserving. Wiping it out would leave a
clean slate on which to build a better society. Additionally, southern politicians knew or cared little about the north and let Phelps do as he pleased
there, as long as his actions did not create problems for them.

Phelps devoted great energy to the CCF's northern intervention. He
viewed the matter as a war of good against evil, easily substituting the
Hudson's Bay Company and other northern villains for the CPR and as-
sorted traditional adversaries of prairie farmers whom he already had
fought in the south. A missionary zeal characterized his northern campaign. Additional momentum came from Phelps's personality. Tommy
Douglas described him as a "steam engine in pants." Phelps typically tackled any project he deemed worthwhile with an all-out effort, trampling all
opposition. This fiercely determined man set out to remake the north and
the lives of its residents. Convinced that he acted in the best interests of
the province and northerners, he practically dismantled the existing economy and society over four years.

Phelps's unconventional style sometimes caused problems. He disliked even the loose controls imposed by cabinet, bureaucrats, and budgets, and often would not accept "no" as an answer. Phelps said cabinet thought he "did too many damn things" and did not see the same urgency that he did. Sometimes when Phelps acted without prior approval from cabinet, the CCF found itself with little choice but to support his actions. His successor as minister of DNR, J.H. Brockelbank, claimed that Phelps made people mad even when he did good things. In 1946 the *Saskatoon Star-Phoenix* perhaps expressed the concerns of many when it said "the blithe way in which the minister [Phelps] stacks one good intention on top of another to build his pretty dream castles would be amusing if it were not for the fact that he is a responsible minister and not merely an idle dreamer." The article described Phelps as having "undisputed nuisance value" while in the opposition, but thought he lacked "hard, shrewd common sense" once in power. Phelps became so animated at times, with his arms flying, that one reporter expected him to "'take off like a whip-lashed aeroplane.'" Phelps's style alienated political colleagues including T.C. Davis, the former Liberal attorney general, who suggested that Phelps's head should be put over the speaker's chair once he died. Davis also suggested slitting Phelps's throat. Some within the CCF may have wished they had taken Davis's advice, particularly when Phelps's actions dragged the CCF into controversies.[2]

Consistent with the establishment of a separate administration for the north, DNR took over the hiring of northern staff from the larger public service hiring organization. Phelps played an active role in the selection of staff, choosing those whom he thought would implement his ideas. He hired CCF supporters to fill both high and low northern positions, since only by having ideologically sympathetic persons administer policies could the CCF hope to successfully introduce its plans to northerners. The CCF even expected some whom it hired to work for the party when elections came along. CCF supporters, including some at La Ronge and Cumberland House, asked for employment, expecting special consideration because of their political affiliation.[3] Phelps refused to tolerate those who did not agree with him or work as he wanted, and he disposed of many staff. Although he wanted to weed "loafers" out of the larger civil service and even identified some employees for dismissal, others in the CCF safeguarded most jobs. Phelps did manage to fire fifteen of those under his command, including some senior employees.[4]

Phelps had trouble filling the critical position of deputy minister of DNR. After several quick changes, C.A.L. (Vern) Hogg, who agreed with Phelps's socialist ideas and in whom Phelps showed vast confidence, took over as deputy minister in 1946. Hogg played an important role in government for many years.[5] In 1953 J.W. Churchman became deputy minister.

Phelps apparently considered known Marxists to be ideologically suited to apply his plans to the north. He hired the Metis Albertans Jim Brady and Malcolm Norris, who openly espoused their more radical beliefs. Norris, one of the most influential Aboriginals to work for the CCF, came to Saskatchewan in 1946 from Alberta, where he and Brady had worked to organize fish cooperatives and the Metis Association of Alberta. Norris had also been president of the Metis Association and helped organize the Indian Association of Alberta. After moving to Saskatchewan he held various jobs with the CCF government, including DNR officer, researcher, advisor, promoter of mineral prospecting, and liaison between government and Aboriginals. Norris supported Phelps's interventions in the fur, fish, and timber industries and in developing marketing boards. Yet Norris also showed a loyalty to and understanding of Aboriginals. When people spoke of the "Indian problem," Norris told them that the white man, who did not understand, had the problem. He also worked as an organizer for the Saskatchewan Metis Society and the Union of Saskatchewan Indians. Although a CCF member, Norris took a position to the left of the CCF, joining the communist Labor Progressive Party (LPP) in 1957. He remained with the civil service until the end of the CCF time in office in 1964.[6]

Phelps welcomed Jim Brady to the ranks of the northern civil service as well. Likely more radical than Norris, Brady also had helped organize the Alberta Metis. Once in Saskatchewan, while maintaining his membership in the CCF, Brady also joined the communists in the LPP in 1947. He did not participate greatly in the LPP after 1953, possibly because of the party's lack of interest in helping with his northern activism. Brady also moved away from the CCF, not renewing his membership. This break with the party possibly occurred because the CCF overruled the nomination of Allan Quandt, a friend of Brady's, as the CCF candidate in 1952. Brady held several positions under the CCF government. He managed the Saskatchewan Government trading post at Deschambault Lake and worked as a DNR officer at Cumberland House. There his work went far beyond that of most DNR officers, since he helped establish a fishermen's cooperative, the first northern wood producers' cooperative, and a credit union. He also taught classes for adults, helped to create a village council, and put out a community newsletter.[7] Murray Dobbin, Brady and Norris's biographer, claims the CCF forced Brady to resign after Phelps's defeat as part of the CCF move away from radicalism. This allegation lacks credibility. Even after Phelps left, DNR thought highly of Brady, and in 1949 it rated him as "clearly superior in his position, very dependable." The Public Service Commission also approved his permanent appointment. By 1951 DNR attempted to put distance between Brady and Cumberland House by offering him a transfer to the far north. Apparently scandal had erupted in Cumberland House over rumours that Brady had fathered children by two local women. Rather than accept the transfer, Brady quit and moved to La Ronge. He spent most of his remaining years in the La Ronge area, where he earned the respect of many people. While there he organized area Metis, gained local renown for his large library, did some writing, and people turned to him for loans of money. He briefly returned to work for the CCF, joining his friend Malcolm Norris at the Department of Mineral Resources. His travels in 1960 to promote Aboriginal prospecting met with little success. By 1963 Brady possibly drank too much and appeared defeated. The disappearance of Brady and a male co-worker in 1967 while the two carried out mineral exploration in the Foster Lakes area has become one of the great mysteries of the north. Local people speculate that Brady met with foul play over an affair with a woman.[8]

Allan Quandt, another idealist, also went to work in the north for Phelps. By 1947 Quandt became the field supervisor and assistant superintendent for DNR's Northern District. A strong believer in socialism, Quandt approved of CCF plans for the north and expected to see "a really progressive programme" that would help humanity and produce great wealth. Quandt did not remain long with DNR, leaving soon after Phelps left. He took up permanent residence in La Ronge, where he and others in the local CCF Club acted as a perennial radical thorn in the CCF body.[9]

Other CCF adherents and sympathizers held high offices within DNR and other departments. These included Floyd Glass, Northern District superintendent and head of Saskatchewan Government Airways, and J.J. Wheaton and C.L. MacLean, northern administrators. Even long after Phelps left, the CCF hired ideologically sympathetic persons for top jobs in the north. A.H. MacDonald, a man with a strong commitment to socialism, became director of Northern Affairs in the late 1950s. Like Brady, some other employees proved only lukewarm supporters of the CCF. Glass, for example, left and set up Athabasca Airlines, in direct competition with the CCF airline. Employees who filled the lower ranks showed varying degrees of socialist fervour.

While Phelps wanted staff who agreed with his plans for the north, he resisted delegating authority even to senior employees. The minister frequently interfered in petty matters and demonstrated a lack of confidence in his staff's judgment. This undermined morale and at times created defiance. Not all district superintendents or other high-ranking employees complied readily with Phelps's order that they submit details of their daily activities. Those who defied Phelps or did not promptly carry out his orders received reprimands. He also closely monitored expenses. In one instance, Phelps wanted Northern Administrator J.J. Wheaton to watch his travel plans and expenses. He even criticized a DNR officer for charging fifty cents for lodging and thirty-five cents for meals when away on government business. Under Phelps, men held all the top jobs in DNR. Even within the realm of clerical work, he refused to give female office employees, whom he referred to as "the girls," much responsibility.[10] Working for Phelps was likely not always easy.

The Saltcoats voters rejected Phelps in 1948. It seems they felt neglected, since he spent little time in the constituency. His northern policies had also created controversy. After the loss, Phelps said that the Liberals had contributed to his defeat by hiring a northern fisherman to spread exaggerated stories about how Phelps ruined the north. Patronage and suspected corruption also likely added to Phelps's defeat. He hired acquaintances, including his brother Don Phelps, Allan Quandt, and K.E. Dickson, the manager of the Beaver Lake Fish Plant. The opposition discovered that Dickson came from Phelps's home area. It also did not help when the legislature heard that Phelps "stored" two nearly new one-and-a-half-ton trucks at his farm, letting his neighbours rent them from the CCF. While he claimed the government planned to dispose of the trucks anyway, the scandal hurt his reputation.[11] The CCF could have given Phelps another seat to run in but did not do so. When seven DNR bureaucrats asked Douglas to give Phelps a position in DNR, Douglas did not reply.[12]

With Phelps's departure, much of the energy went out of the northern program. His successors showed less interest in implementing innovative and radical policies in the north. Still, the CCF continued with a separate administrative structure and policies for the north and did little to undo Phelps's work. J.H. Brockelbank, the minister of Municipal Affairs from 1944 to 1948, became the new minister of Natural Resources. Brockelbank lacked Phelps's impatience and desire for quick change, but he did support the CCF commitment to bring modernization, assimilation, and socialism to the north and its inhabitants. As one example, he demonstrated his commitment to socialist solutions when he fought for the survival of the controversial compulsory fur marketing system in the 1950s. Brockelbank used a relaxed and orthodox "hands-off" style of running DNR, relying on his staff. He liked to keep in touch with the north, though, and travelled around the area most autumns in a CCF government plane.

In 1956 Brockelbank assumed ministerial duties for the new Department of Mineral Resources, also an important department for the north. Alec Kuziak then became the minister of Natural Resources. Kuziak distanced himself more from involvement with the north than had his two predecessors. During his time as minister, cabinet increasingly shared responsibility for decisions affecting the north.[13] Eiling Kramer succeeded Kuziak as minister, holding the position until the CCF defeat in 1964.

Throughout its time in office, the CCF maintained its commitment to introducing socialism and other interventionist programs in the north. Dobbin's claim that the CCF removed "radicals and native sympathizers" from positions of influence in the north after Phelps departed, leaving those who opposed Phelps's reforms in control, appears an exaggeration.[14] Norris remained, Quandt left voluntarily in 1949, and Brady also left willingly in 1951. The CCF did not undo its socialist economic reforms, and ideologically sympathetic persons continued to oversee programs.

In spite of a strong commitment to bringing change to the north, the CCF handicapped its northern program by not quickly passing legislation that would have facilitated its effort to establish a separate government structure and programs for the north. Finally recognizing this shortcoming, the legislature passed the Northern Administration Act, which it copied from the Local Improvement Districts Act of 1940. The new legislation took effect on 1 January 1949. The CCF hoped that this new authority would help coordinate northern activities and guide northern development. Yet the act proved to be poorly designed. It did not define northern problems or outline clear goals, and it failed to provide an adequate northern taxation system. The act and the administrative structure were unable to carry out CCF plans for the north, adding to the CCF's growing frustration over the intransigence of northern problems. Although the Budget Bureau questioned the suitability of the act as early as 1951, the CCF never did replace it. Instead, severe administrative structural design problems continued, contributing to program failures.[15]

In other respects the CCF did act decisively to bring change to the north. The new government chose Prince Albert, located on the banks of the North Saskatchewan River, as its main administrative centre for the north, even though the small city fell outside the north by all definitions. Prince Albert grew in stature, receiving the offices of the DNR's northern administrator, the headquarters of various DNR branches including Northern District, Forest Fire Control, Construction, and Communications, as well as the northern headquarters of Saskatchewan Government Airways. DNR also placed its assistant deputy minister there by 1949 to direct and coordinate northern programs. A grand new provincial office building opened there in 1948, in celebration of which the *Prince Albert Daily Herald* ran a "Northland Progress Edition." After describing La Ronge as "becoming the base for remote development," it said Prince Albert had "a new, greatly changed and infinitely more important position ... and plays a leading part in virtually everything happening in the entire north." Prince Albert retained its position as a secondary centre to Regina for northern activity throughout the CCF era, with high-level DNR, Agriculture, Cooperation, Education, and Social Welfare staff stationed there. Most of DNR's Planning and Research Group also worked in Prince Albert but Regina retained overall control of programs and policy design, a situation that sometimes caused conflict between the two offices.[16]

The CCF further demonstrated its commitment to northern change by establishing a new and distinct administrative structure within DNR to implement municipal, natural resource, and other policies in the region. For municipal administration purposes, the government had formerly designated the north as Local Improvement District (LID) "A." Government used LIDs in place of municipalities in areas it thought not ready for full municipal government. By 1946 the CCF did away with the LID designation and created the Northern District of DNR to handle municipal and other matters in the north. F. Glass held the position of Northern District superintendent.

Additionally, after creating and staffing the new Northern District, the CCF added the Northern Administration Branch (NAB) to DNR in 1947. J.J. Wheaton received the appointment of northern administrator. However, the new administrative system seemed hastily planned and illogical, creating confusion and inefficiency. The NAB had a separate staff from Northern District and operated within what became known as the Northern Administration District (NAD). The Northern District and NAD boundaries did not match, since the NAD covered all of the Northern District area plus an additional area to the south. As a result, DNR operated in the north with two distinct sets of staff, chains of command, programs, and geographic boundaries.

It is hard to imagine how the CCF, which prided itself on its abilities at skilful planning, could create this system and, worse, let it continue. Even those working under the system could not understand its logic or why the CCF did not design a workable system. Some of the greatest problems resulted from the decision to allow three pre-existing DNR districts – Meadow Lake, Prince Albert, and Hudson Bay – to each cover part of the northern area while also extending into the southern area. DNR staff in these three districts continued to handle some, but not all, matters far within the NAD boundary. The Prince Albert District extended nearly as far north as La Ronge, and the Meadow Lake District reached even farther north in the western area. The Northern District had eighteen subdistricts, Prince Albert had sixteen, and Meadow Lake had eight, each supervised by conservation officers.[17] For efficient administration, DNR needed only one structure in the north, operating within the larger NAD boundaries. Even employees found the system confusing.

After creating the NAD, the CCF seemed unsure what to do with the Northern District but refused to do away with it. It did not fill the Northern District superintendent position after Glass left, instead hiring Allan Quandt to work as Northern District assistant superintendent. He had relatively little authority, and his work overlapped with that of the NAB in many areas. DNR recognized the problems, and as a temporary fix, Wheaton supervised Quandt by 1949. Yet the two distinct administrative structures continued. Appearing frustrated, Quandt resigned from DNR in 1949. Further administrative confusion resulted from the CCF giving the northern executive assistant position, outside the normal chain of command, the power to supervise many of the DNR operations.[18] Boundary and jurisdiction problems never disappeared under the CCF, since only minor alterations of the southern boundaries took place.

Boundaries for other programs did not match with either the NAD or the Northern District boundary, adding to the problems. The Northern Fur

Region boundary jogged crookedly across the north, Public Health used its own boundaries, and provincial electoral boundaries frequently changed. Indian Affairs divided the north according to its priorities, and Census Division 18 included all of the north along with some southern areas. Although the multiple and overlapping divisions caused confusion and inefficient program delivery, the CCF never dealt with these problems.

The CCF gave the NAB's northern administrator most day-to-day power within the north. Wheaton and his successors held broad municipal responsibilities, including those normally carried out by a reeve and municipal council. The CCF also expected its northern administrator to coordinate the activities of all departments and administer Crown lands and the Northern Administration Act. The men who held this position helped determine details of CCF policy and how DNR staff introduced CCF projects to northerners. Wheaton left by about 1950, after which C.L. MacLean held the position for a number of years, followed by C.S. Brown.[19] Some reorganization took place in 1958, when the CCF appointed A.H. MacDonald as director of Northern Affairs, a new position that replaced that of northern administrator. This move accompanied new CCF northern initiatives, including expanded community development and social aid programs. The creation of the new organization continued the CCF policy of devoting a separate DNR structure to administer the north. MacDonald had charge of a revitalized Northern Affairs Branch (NAB), and sensibly the CCF did away with the Northern District. Yet confusion continued because the new NAB boundaries appeared the same as those of the former Northern District and did not extend as far south as the southern boundary of the ongoing Northern Administration District. The NAB had a west and east district, with a field supervisor in each. Cabinet also approved the creation of the Advisory Committee on Northern Affairs, which included high officials from various departments.[20] In a final reorganization just before leaving office, effective 1 April 1964, the CCF created separate resources and recreation branches, except in the north. There Northern Affairs continued to hold responsibility for resource, recreation, municipal, welfare, housing, and community development matters.[21]

In spite of the shortcomings of the Northern Administration Act and DNR's organizational structure, the act and DNR's role as a coordinating agency created a single departmental presence to a much greater extent in the north than in the south. This had potential advantages for introducing the aggressive CCF program of change to the north, since DNR held most of the responsibility for planning and implementation of plans. A major weakness resulted, though, because the CCF expected DNR officers to administer a wide range of programs, even though they lacked expertise in many of these areas. The departments of Health and Education had stronger separate northern programs than did most arms of government. Some departments increased their presence during the CCF years. By 1959 the Department of Co-operation had five cooperative management advisors, Public Health had about twelve professional positions, Education had an administrator and assistant, Agriculture had an agricultural representative, and Social Welfare had a supervisor and maybe one social worker.[22] The need for coordination of services increased as departments expanded their staff.

Throughout its era, for reasons of administrative efficiency and bringing directed change to the north, the CCF stressed coordinating northern programs to a far greater extent than those in the south. The term "coordination," while it may sound uncontroversial, carried a hidden meaning. It meant a coordinated implementation of the CCF program for the north. A lack of coordination within the colonial structure would compromise the CCF goals of imposing modernization, assimilation, and socialism. Some thought that the CCF could best coordinate services by creating a single northern agency, which would have powers even greater than those the CCF gave to DNR. The radicals of the La Ronge CCF Club and various CCF employees frequently discussed and promoted the idea of a single agency.[23]

Recognizing that its programs often did not work together towards its goal of bringing directed change to the north, the CCF perennially strove to improve coordination. In one effort it established the Advisory Committee on Northern Co-operative Education in 1952, which brought together people from various government organizations. A larger initiative began when cabinet created the Northern Advisory Committee (NAC) in 1953 to examine northern problems, recommend actions, and coordinate programs. Yet NAC lacked authority, and as the need for coordination increased, it proved unfit for the task.[24] Beginning at much the same time, the CCF expected DNR's newly hired anthropologist V.F. Valentine to improve coordination. He developed plans for unified action at the field level, creating an atmosphere of rising optimism in government that a coordinated intervention would finally take place. However, Valentine left in 1957, and most of his plans did not proceed.[25] The same year, J.A. Collier, the CCF's director of public relations, saw that the CCF was not meeting its goals for the north. Strongly denouncing the conflicting northern empires of various departments, he concluded that a single new department should handle all northern matters, with reviews at least twice a year to keep the "gentle sleep" from resuming.[26] Politicians also became impatient with the province's failure to bring change to the region. In 1958 five cabinet members, including Brockelbank and Kuziak, wanted action to improve coordination. Some then hoped that the revival of the Northern Affairs Branch and the appointment of MacDonald as its director would bring a coordinated government effort.[27] MacDonald soon pointed out that the new organization did not work because it lacked the authority to coordinate activities.[28]

After fifteen years of failed attempts to have the various branches of government work together, cabinet finally approved the idea of a single agency in 1959. The Budget Bureau worked to find a suitable structure. But the CCF again lost the will to create the mechanism that might have enabled it to more decisively work towards its goals for the north. Opposition to the idea of a single agency arose in some departments, and politicians turned against the idea, stopping its implementation. As the Center for Community Studies pointed out in 1963, departments continued to work at cross-purposes, hurting the application of CCF plans for the north. CCF inaction on improving coordination of services continued. Only much later, after the Liberals governed the province for two terms, did the NDP, the CCF's heir, create a single agency, the Department of Northern Saskatchewan.[29] While the CCF effectively attacked the northern status quo, a lack of coordination compounded the administrative inadequacies that handicapped its efforts to build a workable new system. Legislative and administrative shortcomings demonstrated that the CCF overestimated its ability to design and implement intelligent programs.

Immediately after the election in 1944, long before it recognized that it had failed to create an adequate administrative system, the CCF approached its interventions in the north with great optimism. A large increase in staff was required for the CCF to apply its aggressive new plans and extend control throughout the north. Prior to this, northern residents had enjoyed an unusual degree of freedom from governmental control. The CCF would not tolerate the continuation of this situation. The new government soon found large areas that natural resources officers had never visited. And some companies that should have paid royalties apparently had not done so for more than a decade. To create a presence in the region, DNR rapidly expanded northern field staff to about six by late 1945. It claimed to have most areas adequately staffed by 1948, with a total of eleven field officers, two junior field officers, and three Fish Board post managers helping fill gaps. Hiring continued, and by the early 1950s DNR had multiple staff at La Ronge, Cumberland House, and the border town of Flin Flon, while numerous other locations had one employee. DNR also changed the designation "field officer" to "conservation officer" (CO). Staff numbers grew further until the NAB had thirty-five employees in 1962, including seventeen COs. Prince Albert headquarters included a director, a supervisor of community development, two field supervisors, and specialists in municipal services, housing, and forestry.[30] Men held all top northern administrative posts during the CCF era, with the highest jobs occupied by women being those of nursing supervisor and welfare supervisor.

At the field level, COs ran the system. They provided law and order, interpreted conservation laws and various rules, administered municipal and social aid matters, acted as counsellors and patrons, carried news, made medical decisions, controlled tools and equipment, regulated access to many jobs, and, possibly most importantly, promoted government policies. They developed a reputation for operating with an appearance of great authority, an image reinforced by the use of police-like uniforms, airplanes, and powerful cars. A Center for Community Studies report compared the COs to British Colonial Service officers. According to the centre's Peter Worsley, the CO, with southern perspectives and an income much higher than that of most Aboriginals, appeared as a "local deity" with a "trinitarian nature." Within the northern environment, DNR dictated to the Metis much as Indian Affairs controlled Status Indians. While people could appeal over the head of the CO to his superiors or to a politician, these actions often proved futile, since the complaint usually came back to the CO for his opinion. In addition, local people lacked skill in making complaints.[31]

Cumberland House, the once-thriving hub of the fur trade, had fallen on hard times by 1944. Although the community's economic situation seemed no worse than that in most other northern areas, the CCF introduced an extraordinary number of projects there, including some socialist experiments. Along with the initiatives came a large number of DNR employees. Prior to Officer J. Johnson moving there in 1945, the community had only one permanent provincial employee, a nurse. By the end of 1945, DNR placed three staff there. It added four more by 1948.[32]

At least partly because it posted a large part of DNR's staff to Cumberland House, the CCF failed to establish a strong governmental presence as quickly and completely as it would have liked in some other areas. In particular, the far north remained under looser control. Wollaston Lake still did not have an officer in 1953, though senior DNR officials "agreed that practices in game, fur and fish in the Wollaston region are exceedingly bad." Accustomed to doing as they pleased, residents demonstrated hostility when DNR did visit. Yet DNR thought the population too small to justify placing a permanent officer there. DNR briefly had a headquarters at Cree Lake, largely to inspect Waite Fisheries' operations there. It ended this posting by 1953.[33]

Concerned about a continuing lack of supervision of northerners, DNR created the game management officer position in the early 1950s. This increased CCF control and supervision over trappers. DNR did away with most of these positions in 1956 when this work reverted to conservation officers.[34] Having responsibility for mineral resources work meant that DNR officers could devote less attention to other matters. The creation of the Department of Mineral Resources in the mid-1950s relieved DNR of most duties related to mining.[35]

A large part of DNR's work in the north involved enforcing law and order in the colony. Officers often acted reasonably when enforcing fur, fish, and game laws. At other times they officiously applied the letter of the law to Aboriginal people who did not understand English or the new laws. Morris Shumiatcher, T.C. Douglas's assistant, later wrote: "I never ceased to be shocked by the unyielding attitude of that department in its enforcement of laws that ostensibly had been passed as ameliorative measures to assist rather than to oppress those engaged in the fur industry."[36] The RCMP and voluntary deputy game guardians also aided with enforcement of the laws.

DNR engaged in relatively few prosecutions. This suggests northerners showed a high level of compliance with conservation laws. Fourteen northern DNR employees carried out only thirty-three game and fur prosecutions from 1951 to 1955, compared to 1,806 for the entire province. The RCMP prosecuted only six game and fur cases in the Northern Region during the same years. The pattern remained much the same for the next several years. Senior DNR officials repeatedly urged officers to increase prosecutions. In 1955 E.L. Paynter, game commissioner, denounced the attitude of DNR officer R. Lockhart, who had planned to overlook bush workers taking deer without licences. Paynter pointed out that even DNR Surveys Branch could not take caribou on the isolated boundary survey. The same year, A.T. Davidson, assistant deputy minister, made an issue of the scant prosecutions. In defence of his staff, Northern Administrator C.S. Brown pointed out that about one prosecution for every 1,430 persons occurred there per year, a level higher than that of one for 6,300 for the rest of the province. Yet in a memo to his officers, Brown then wrote: "An occasional prosecution, however mild the punishment, has an educational and beneficial influence."[37]

Even the few prosecutions that took place often involved trivial offences. Sometimes DNR prosecuted Aboriginals who failed to adapt to the new rules. In 1952 DNR found that a young Beauval area girl illegally sold moose meat for one dollar. Since her father had not properly tagged the moose hide, also an offence, DNR preferred to prosecute him for that instead.[38] In another case, DNR charged Ben Bradfield of Molanosa with unlawfully hunting and killing big game without a permit. DNR confiscated four pounds of moose meat, which it destroyed. The infraction cost Bradfield forty-nine dollars.[39]

Misunderstandings also could result in prosecutions. Many years after the event, an elderly Aboriginal woman related how DNR officers prevented her parents from trapping in their customary fashion. On an autumn day, the couple travelled by canoe through their trapping area, hanging traps in trees near where they planned to place them later, once the season opened. Although the pair broke no laws, DNR officers flying overhead landed. Likely not understanding the Cree-speaking couple's intentions, they confiscated the load of traps and laid charges.[40]

While DNR officers applied and enforced CCF policies at the field level, DNR also employed other staff. Consistent with the CCF emphasis on expert planning, DNR relied heavily on geographers to design and implement northern change. Over the years, many served in the planning office and as administrators. The department's staff included five geographers by 1954. Of these, three did administration, one mapping, and one geographic research.[41] DNR's Construction Branch also played a key role in CCF plans for the north. The CCF relied on this branch to provide much of the infrastructure in its colonial world. As head of the branch, R.N. Gooding exercised great authority, overseeing the building of roads and airstrips, organizing heavy trucking, providing heavy equipment for firefighting, and constructing buildings.[42]

The CCF considered it important to educate the northern public about its programs. For this purpose it created the Conservation Education Branch within DNR by 1953. This later became the Conservation Information Service. It distributed information, handled press releases, created the Northern News radio program, and worked with the public on conservation.[43]

Because of increased staff numbers and the CCF's ambitious plans for the north, it became important to train specialized staff. The government took a major step towards improving northern staffing when it opened DNR's Conservation Officers' Training School in Prince Albert in 1953. Eleven graduated from the first class after about nine months. DNR soon required trainees to spend time in the field before entering the training program to allow advance assessment of their suitability. The training program continued in the 1960s. In 1960-61, for example, DNR chose twenty-five candidates from 220 applicants before reducing the number further to fourteen after a two-month field proving period. All graduated from the six-and-a-half-month course, and DNR appointed four as conservation officers and ten as patrolman graduates. DNR also trained new candidates as well as existing officers in anthropological matters and community development techniques. DNR anthropologist V.F. Valentine began this specialized training in the mid-1950s. Later the Center for Community Studies provided much of this instruction.[44]

Once it had trained staff and they gained some northern experience, DNR wanted to keep them in the north. Low staff morale was one of the factors that worked against this. Complaints from staff in 1956 included problems with housing, transfers, and promotions. Assistant Deputy Minister Davidson blamed the grumbling partly on supervisors, who had asked the men if they had complaints. He considered this "a dangerous technique" and wanted a "firmer approach."[45] Morale seemed to worsen by the early 1960s. The repeated unsuccessful reorganizations and fruitless talk about a single northern agency contributed to staff losing faith in the CCF's planning expertise. In 1960, for example, Malcolm Norris, after obtaining a copy of a proposed NAB reorganization, called those who would fill higher positions "reactionary personnel" and field workers "dedicated fools." He compared it to "a Mexican Army arrayed with numerous Generals at the top with a meagre field force."[46] In 1962 Norris confided to Brady: "Dept filled with personnel jealousies and rivalries. A most unhappy state ... Hardly anybody can be trusted anymore."[47] Others also saw the problems. One observer compared a northern posting to "banishment to Siberia" in terms of career effects. Some employees felt alienated because they did not have the skills DNR came to value. Higher education and community development expertise increasingly mattered for career advancement.[48]

CCF northern staffing problems included a high rate of staff turnover and unsuitable attitudes towards Aboriginal people. In 1955 Brockelbank wanted civil servants to remain in the north for at least five years. He considered one or two years insufficient to develop a "proper perspective."[49] Yet in a typical situation, between 1950 and 1970, Public Health hired eighteen nurses to work at the one-nurse Sandy Bay hospital. One stayed for over five years, while nine stayed for only two to ten months.[50] Most teachers hired by the Department of Education also stayed only a short time. A majority of whites viewed their northern time as temporary. Not all liked the rugged outdoor activities the north offered, and many missed southern culture, including radio, television, movies, libraries, shopping, and countless other items. Alice Jenner of the Department of Public Health wrote: "It requires a missionary zeal, a strong conviction that something ought to be done about this, and an affection for the people to stay at this job."[51]

Like the hundreds of young, single government employees who fled the north after only a short time there, many married staff and their families also disliked living in the region. Mr. Stene resigned from DNR in 1951 because his wife did not want to move to Pelican Narrows.[52] Similarly, after DNR built an expensive new house at Buffalo Narrows for Mr. Halvorsen, his family stayed in the south where his children attended high school.[53] In 1954 Mrs. Laurier Poisson, the wife of the Île-à-la-Crosse conservation officer, wrote an irate letter to J.W. Churchman, DNR's deputy minister since 1953. She had already endured three years of isolation and inconvenience. Her outburst occurred when DNR built a new staff house there, not for the Poissons, but for another officer. Churchman reassured her that they did not intend the construction as a personal affront to her, and DNR transferred her husband out of the north later that year.[54]

The CCF made some efforts to retain northern staff by offering them extra compensation. Small isolation allowances and subsidized housing helped make up for higher prices and travel costs. Yet employees often found the incentives inadequate. "Being bushed" contributed to some frequently heading south at their own expense, and "social boredom" caused northern employees to eat and drink more. With complaints rising and DNR fearing increased resignations and transfer requests, it gathered information on the northern cost of living in 1957. The study found food costs were 32 percent higher in Uranium City than in Regina and were about 20 percent higher for the north overall than in Regina. DNR rent rates, however, stood at a lower level than in the south. Calculating various factors, the study found an increased cost of living for Uranium City of $1,250.17, compared to the allowance of $900. Some communities had larger discrepancies, while in others the allowance exceeded the difference in the cost of living, although calculations did not allow for additional travel costs. The situation improved somewhat by 1962, as employees of numerous departments could then charge some travel expenses when going on annual leave and to obtain medical treatment.[55]

One of the greatest obstacles to attracting and retaining staff was the dismal housing situation in most northern communities. Since few government employees would consider building or buying their own house in the north, and most areas offered virtually no modern rental accommodation, the onus fell on government to supply housing. The CCF did provide some staff housing, although it could have done much more. At first the new government bought existing housing, including some that proved inadequate. By 1949, for example, it owned a three-room shack at Stony Rapids, where Field Officer Oliver Shaw lived and worked. He conducted business in the presence of the two bachelors who lived there with him and various travellers who stopped in. DNR built a three-bedroom house for Shaw, who planned to marry. Beginning in 1949, DNR policy called for the department to charge rent to all staff using its housing. By 1952 a point system determined the rental rate, up to 12.5 percent of the employee's salary. DNR had about twenty-five residences by 1953, and the number continued to grow. Due to small budgets, the supply of adequate housing lagged behind the demand caused by rising staff numbers. La Ronge still had poor and overcrowded staff housing in 1956: two employees each occupied a "cottage," a radio operator lived in a renovated bunkhouse, one employee lived in the former government store, and several lived in an old house. All these staff members had wives and most had children.[56]

The CCF found itself in a double bind. If it did not provide housing, staff suffered, complained, and even quit. Yet where it built staff housing, government residences often stood out as the most lavish in the community. This helped create two distinct societies: the white middle class and the poverty-stricken Aboriginals. DNR built what it called "Type 1," "Type 2," and "Type 3" houses, but developed the superior "Type 5" design by 1952. It had six of the latter in 1953, each with water and sewer – luxury seldom seen in the north at that time. By 1957, DNR houses at Île-à-la-Crosse, Buffalo Narrows, and La Loche had basements; two to four bedrooms; bathrooms with tub, sink, and toilet; refrigerators in place or on order; propane or wood/coal stoves; furnaces; and other amenities. The CCF also frequently provided its houses with furnishings and electrical generators. Its dwellings often cost from $12,000 to $18,000, many times the cost of most northern homes.[57]

While many non-Aboriginal employees from the south found it difficult to adjust to or appreciate life in the north, the CCF continued to look in the south for nearly all its employees. It believed that northern Aboriginals lacked the ability or training to carry out most better government jobs. White people from outside the region held nearly all full-time jobs, while the CCF employed local Aboriginals primarily for temporary, low-paying work. Shortly after the election of the CCF, RCMP Corporal M. Chappuis at Cumberland House thought of Aboriginals as "hopeless" for the position of DNR officer, without "direct supervision."[58] In contrast to Chappuis's reservations, Oblate Father F.X. Gagnon lobbied the government to employ area men as wardens and fire guardians on the west side.[59] Still in 1950, DNR's Earl Dodds indicated the department would use some Aboriginal labour for roadwork, but needed experienced and reliable workers to run the equipment, which likely meant non-Aboriginals.[60] About half of the fire detection and prevention staff consisted of Aboriginals, with fire suppression crews usually all Aboriginal. But fires provided only short-term, low-paying work.[61]

The northern administrator held much responsibility for DNR's hiring decisions at the field level. Only in isolated cases did the department hire Aboriginals for more than short-term work, and difficulties only reinforced stereotypes. After hiring J. Favel as a Native patrolman at Patuanak, DNR considered firing him in 1954. Problems had arisen when CO L. Poisson set more rigid work expectations than Favel was accustomed to. C.S. Brown, northern administrator, wrote that Favel "has a number of the usual traits of the northern native and in some respects lacks a proper sense of responsibility." To deal with the situation, Earl Dodds of DNR spoke to Favel and "left him in some doubt of the permanency of his employment with us."[62] Public Health, which hired very few Aboriginals for work in its outpost hospitals, also encountered difficulties after hiring several local people. It let one person go for lack of ability and another for theft.[63] Additionally, northern Crown corporations seemed disillusioned in 1956 after Aboriginals quit their jobs, likely because of local pressure and jealousy.[64] The attitude that most Aboriginals lacked suitability for more than unskilled, occasional employment permeated the various branches of government that operated in the north.

In some exceptional cases, Aboriginals distinguished themselves and became trusted employees. Nap Johnson of Île-à-la-Crosse, for example, worked as a DNR Native patrolman and special constable for the RCMP.[65] A Metis, Norman MacAuley, also stood out. He held various positions, including manager of the government stores at Pinehouse and Deschambault Lake. In another positive case, DNR began a "pilot project of community development" in 1963-64, with Pelican Narrows area trappers electing a fur patrolman. DNR called the results "outstanding."[66] Yet the fact that only a handful of Aboriginals held permanent positions demonstrates the nature of CCF hiring policies as well as the lack of preparation of Aboriginals for wage labour.

Although racism appeared common in the northern environment, other factors also help explain the CCF record of employing Aboriginals. To have hired large numbers of Aboriginals for permanent positions would have required the committal of substantial resources for educating and training potential employees and the introduction of affirmative action programs. The CCF was not willing to take these steps. Instead, the CCF's dismal record in employing Aboriginals added to northern unemployment and underdevelopment.

Placing a large number of southern, white government employees in the north, instead of hiring the region's own people, widened a pre-existing rift within northern society and also worked against the CCF policy of assimilation. DNR officers, nurses, teachers, and other CCF employees formed a separate class within the small, primarily Aboriginal villages. Civil servants also became part of the white upper class in the larger communities. Government workers frequently considered themselves superior by virtue of their race. And the mandate given them by the CCF to bring forced change to northern Aboriginals gave them additional prestige and authority.

A large social distance existed between the racially based northern classes. Few whites doubted the superiority of their group – instances of white government employees lacking respect for Aboriginals abound. In 1954 a DNR employee at La Loche feared "turning Indian" if he stayed in La Loche longer than several years.[67] A teacher told how his opinion of Aboriginal males changed over twenty years, from thinking them "very nice and well-mannered" to seeing them as improvident, boastful, easily insulted, arrogant, and dishonest. He added, "The more they come in contact with the whites, drunkenness becomes their favorite pastime, as then they think they are real men."[68] A lack of knowledge of and interest in Aboriginal culture, ways, and languages contributed to the distance that existed between administrators and their subjects. In some cases Aboriginals established special relationships with DNR officers similar to the earlier "patron-client relationship" with the HBC, and officials had a special clientele who supported their programs as part of a system of reciprocal obligations. Here too a class system continued. Aboriginals also sometimes contributed to maintaining the distance between government employees and Aboriginals. Many felt "contempt and hostility" towards the CCF and its employees, largely because of conservation policies.[69]

The civil servants sent north to implement CCF programs usually felt safe living in their separate social enclaves within the Aboriginal communities. Exceptions occurred, though, as when a critical situation arose at Buffalo Narrows in 1957. Although Aboriginal males there had threatened the lives of Aboriginal females with knives while demanding "sexual submission," government employees and their families felt immune from the violence around them. C.S. Brown, northern administrator, claimed that "decent white women have been inviolable almost everywhere in the north." This changed when a repeat violent sexual offender raped the out-post hospital nurse, also causing brain damage and physical disability. Soon after, another repeat sexual offender broke into the house of J.B. McLellan, the CO, presumably to rape Mrs. McLellan, not realizing that her husband had returned from an extended trip. Although outraged, the CO persuaded local white people, including government workers, not to take vigilante action. He described the Aboriginals as eighteenth-century people, to whom laws designed for twentieth-century people should not apply. He also advocated the use of public whipping and stocks. The light sentence of three years received by the man who raped the nurse further outraged whites. She resigned from her job after the judge passed sentence. CCF employees approved of the two-year sentence meted out to the second offender for his less-serious offence. His sentencing "had a most worthy effect on the people in the region."[70] Many officials saw increased and more punitive law enforcement as the answer to these problems.

Sandy Bay government personnel charged with implementing CCF programs also experienced violence at the hands of local Aboriginals. In one case, the outpost hospital nurse, Miss Houston, and the hospital caretaker, J.H. Nichols, investigated a complaint of "neglected and starving" children. The children's drunken father lunged at the nurse with a knife. She ducked, and the knife stuck deep into the wall. One person commented, "It could have been a little worse the nurse could have been killed. Perhaps a human sacrifice is necessary ... for the last two years ... this loyal and devoted caretaker has protected the nurse ... If liquor is forced upon this little community I think we should employ male nurses only or shut-up shop."[71] Female government employees, especially provincial nurses who went into unknown situations in remote communities, found themselves vulnerable to mistreatment and violence. This danger added to the un-usually high turnover rate among nursing staff. Although incidents of Aboriginal violence directed against government employees did not occur frequently, those that took place spurred an increasing fear of Aboriginals among the southerners who came north.

Clearly, the CCF established a colonial structure in the north to implement its agenda of modernization, assimilation, and socialism. As in other colonial situations, control remained outside the region. Politicians and bureaucrats who lived far away chose goals, designed programs, and hired staff. While it used the pre-existing Department of Natural Resources as its primary colonial agency, the CCF created a separate administrative organization within DNR for the north. In effect, for many purposes the north had a separate governmental structure from the south. The CCF gave this organization great power, including that normally held by municipal governments. Unlike in the south, those living in northern Aboriginal communities could not elect their local governments and also had little say in electing the provincial government. About half of northern Aboriginals, the Status Indians, could not vote in provincial elections until 1960, and those northerners who could vote had little influence in determining CCF policies for the north, since the region had only two elected representatives in Regina. Outsiders made most decisions for northerners without consulting with the local people.

Imperfections plagued the northern colonial structure, belying the much-touted CCF planning expertise. Many working within the system saw the need for changes to the administrative structure, but the CCF failed to provide an efficient organization and appropriate legislation. This added to program failures and compromised the achievement of CCF goals for the north. From the point of view of northern Aboriginals, many of whom did not want the intrusive CCF presence, governmental inefficiency permitted their former society and ways to continue to some extent.

The CCF directed matters in the north "from the top." Various officials spoke about this. J.H. Brockelbank, Phelps's successor as the minister of Natural Resources, asked, "How would you get a change in the north except suggestions coming from the top?" He viewed Aboriginals as undemanding and as making only simple requests.[72] The department's deputy minister, J.W. Churchman, admitted that in the early CCF era "in many instances things were done in a dictatorial manner."[73] Morris Shumiatcher depicted the northern Aboriginals' "way of life" as "unacceptable" to CCF doctrines. "The lack of organization and the dearth of planning ran counter to the socialist ideal of what was best for the native," he said. "The C.C.F. assembled a vast clutch of administrators who undertook to change the habits of the native in the North to accord more perfectly with their own theories of social justice."[74]

The top-down colonial approach of the CCF brought many negative consequences to the north. It played an instrumental role in creating a deep rift in the northern society, with alienated Aboriginals on one side and a self-confident government and its employees on the other. With few exceptions, those who brought the CCF presence north did not come from the north. Many bureaucrats never even moved to the region, applying programs from southern offices. Most who did move north only did so temporarily, without making a long-term commitment to the region. The colonial presence also helped institutionalize and perpetuate unemployment, poverty, and social dysfunction within the Aboriginal community by ensuring that Aboriginals would not share equally in employment and economic opportunities. CCF colonialism effectively altered and remade practically every aspect of the northern economy and society, creating a reality very different from that which existed in 1944. Yet the result did not please northerners or the CCF. Most northerners had never approved of the CCF goals or the colonial presence, while the CCF could take little satisfaction in the many unforeseen and devastating side effects of its interventions.

With its newly created colonial apparatus in place, the CCF sought to introduce modernization, assimilation, and socialism to northerners. The new government actively worked to bring fundamental changes to how Aboriginals lived their everyday lives. Only an examination of CCF words and actions can demonstrate the party's intentions for the north and its population.

3
The Ultimate Solution

CCF politicians and bureaucrats felt certain of the superiority of Euro-Canadian culture over the traditional Aboriginal cultures of northern Saskatchewan. The new government did not hesitate to use its authority to impose white ways on Aboriginal people, aiming for their complete assimilation into the white world. In many respects the CCF efforts to assimilate Aboriginals broke new ground in Canada. During subsequent decades, other governments followed suit. An essential part of the CCF effort to assimilate Aboriginals included a large-scale forced movement to settlements where the government could teach Aboriginals to live as white men and women and better deliver its various programs to its subjects. CCF planners also thought that relocation to villages would help Aboriginals by providing them with the opportunity to benefit from modern ways. Yet, contradictorily, the establishment of separate Aboriginal settlements and pervasive racism worked against the goal of assimilation. For most Aboriginals the move from the bush came to mean a life lived in semi-urban squalor, and the better world visualized by the CCF remained far away. The expansion of mining and government also brought urbanization, as thousands of white people moved to the north. Two societies grew there: the relatively prosperous white and the destitute Aboriginal. The northern population increased dramatically, which particularly caused problems within Aboriginal communities. While the CCF could soon see the growing problems, it did not admit responsibility for these. Nor did it develop effective solutions.

Traditionally, northern Saskatchewan supported only a small population, possibly about five thousand at the beginning of the fur trade era. At that time, Cree and Dene (Chipewyan) people formed the population. The Dene lived a life centred on the barren land caribou, following seasonal caribou migrations between the tundra of the present-day Northwest Territories and the wooded area of northern Saskatchewan. The Cree inhabited the large woodland area to the south of the Dene territory. The fur trade brought various changes to where Aboriginals lived. One change occurred when Cree from farther east moved into northern Saskatchewan, joining with and sometimes displacing Cree already there. Dene people also moved farther south into former Cree territory. This occurred particularly on the west side of the province in the La Loche and Patuanak area. The Cree and Dene remained separate, with cultural differences and old animosities reinforcing their distinctness. Before the election of the CCF, northern Aboriginals continued to enjoy a great amount of freedom to follow their traditional lifestyle. They had little need for cash, since the northern environment provided them with most necessities of life. What they could not obtain from nature came from trading posts, where they traded furs and labour for the white man's goods.

Prior to CCF intervention, the two major outside influences on northern Aboriginals came from traders and missionaries. Both the fur trade and Christianity had left their mark. Certainly the fur trade had resulted in major changes. At one time, Aboriginals killed animals primarily to gain food and clothing, but they now systematically killed fur-bearers to supply the worldwide market for furs, and much about their lives revolved around trapping. The churches also had altered northern life. They concerned themselves with spiritual matters, medical care, and basic education, and introduced Aboriginals to some aspects of white society. The Aboriginal population included many devout Christians in 1944. Nearly all Aboriginals claimed to belong to a Christian denomination. The 1951 census counted 57 percent of Division 18 as Roman Catholic, 19 percent as Anglican, and 10 percent as United Church. Many Aboriginals combined aspects of their traditional beliefs with Christianity, finding the two compatible in many respects.[1] The change brought by the traders and churches had come slowly and over a long period of time. Aboriginals also enjoyed considerable choice in what aspects of the new ways and beliefs they would accept. As a result, Indians and Metis voluntarily accepted the churches and traders and the limited change and assimilation they brought.

Contact with other white people also increased before 1944. Thousands of southerners moved north during the 1920s and 1930s to trap, fish, mine, or farm in the forest fringe. Most newcomers left the north by the end of the Second World War. The southern economy strengthened, again providing jobs for the unemployed, and large numbers enlisted in the armed forces during the Second World War. Unlike the majority of white people, northern Aboriginals showed a strong attachment to their homeland and did not want to leave the area permanently. Most who left to fight in the war or work in wartime industry soon returned.

Government also influenced northern Aboriginals by 1944. Various treaties made between Indians and the federal government blanketed all of northern Saskatchewan, giving Ottawa legal title to ancestral lands. Treaty 5 covered the Saskatchewan River delta and the surrounding area.

Aboriginals in a large part of the southern area of the north had adhered to Treaty 6, originally designed primarily as an agricultural treaty for the prairie. Treaties 8 and 10 dealt with the rest of northern Saskatchewan and much of the larger Canadian north. In comparison to the earlier treaties signed for agricultural areas, government tailored these latter two treaties to the northern situation. Their signing took place largely to open the way for resource extraction.

Contact with white society split northern Aboriginals into three groups: Status Indians (also referred to as Registered or Treaty Indians), to whom the treaties applied; Non-Status Indians, who appeared Indian in all respects except by legal criteria; and Metis. The federal government held primary responsibility for Status Indians and had jurisdiction on reserves. At the time of the 1930 Natural Resources Transfer Agreement, which transferred Crown lands from Ottawa to Saskatchewan, various Dominion orders-in-council provided reserves for northern Indian bands. Clause 10 of the agreement allowed for the later transfer of land to Ottawa to meet treaty obligations. Many Status Indians had not moved onto reserves by 1944 and still enjoyed freedom to roam the bush. The establishment of reserves remained incomplete throughout the CCF era. Although nearly all Status Indians lived in settlements by the late 1950s, they did not necessarily live on reserves. La Loche, Fond du Lac, Black Lake, Stony Rapids, and Lac la Hache bands still had not settled on reserves. Some groups apparently had never asked for land.[2] And even when negotiations for reserve land took place, they commonly dragged on for decades. In the case of the La Loche Band (Clearwater River Dene Nation), for example, even though negotiations for a reserve began in about 1939, the matter still remained unresolved in 1964.[3] The province generally proceeded as if it had full ownership of northern land and resources, other than on established reserves.

Consistent with its desire to assimilate Aboriginals, the CCF discouraged expansion of the northern reserve system. In one instance in 1954, the CCF opposed a request by Indian Affairs for additional reserve land in the La Ronge area to accommodate the growing Status Indian population. DNR's deputy minister, J.W. Churchman, and director of Conservation, R.G. Young, viewed the reserve system as outdated and working against Indians' best interests. While it did not completely refuse to participate in expanding the number and size of reserves, the CCF wanted to control their expansion. Minister Brockelbank thought the Natural Resources Transfer Agreement allowed the minister of Natural Resources to choose land for reserve expansion. The CCF particularly wanted to stop extension of the reserve system in areas with recreational and mining potential, including in the area between La Ronge and the Churchill River.[4] In 1950 the province even tried to take back some land from Kitsakie Indian Reserve, which adjoined La Ronge, for townsite expansion. DNR claimed the residents made little use of the largely rock-and-muskeg-covered 139 acres, but the federal government found about sixty people and twenty homes there. The Indians also opposed surrendering the land, and Ottawa turned down the province's request.[5]

Some northern Metis, particularly those on the west side and in the Cumberland House area, appeared distinct from the Status and Non-Status Indians. Metis there had long-standing connections with the Metis of the prairie, and some had moved north after the Red River Resistance and the Northwest Rebellion. Yet in many communities, Non-Status Indian and Metis meant much the same thing. The government and others commonly used the term "Metis" to describe all Aboriginals who did not fall under the provisions of treaties. While cultural and racial differences between the groups often seemed nonexistent, the legal differences between Status Indians and the Non-Status Indians and Metis increasingly split communities, causing tension and conflict. Status Indians accepted the government definitions and also considered their Non-Status and Metis brethren as not real Indians, while the latter groups seemed critical of the Status Indians' dependence on Ottawa. Some Metis lived partially in both white and Indian cultures. The CCF's anthropologist, V.F. Valentine, agreed with a Metis fur trader's definition of a Metis as "'a man who, when he had money, lives like a white man, and when he has no money lives like an Indian.'"[6] The west-side Roman Catholic Metis carried French surnames, while mainly Scottish names identified the largely Anglican central and east-side Metis. More than in some areas to the south, cultural differences divided the Metis and the Status Indians of the Athabasca Region. Many of the Metis from Fort Chipewyan and Camsell Portage had Cree origins, while practically all Status Indians there were Dene. Disparities between federal and provincial services caused problems throughout the north, since Metis received fewer benefits and faced more restrictive hunting and trapping rules. On the other hand, Metis could legally drink liquor and vote, while Status Indians could not do so until 1960.[7]

Whether it considered them Metis or Indian, the CCF actively tried to assimilate all Aboriginals into white society. T.C. Douglas, other politicians, and bureaucrats confidently believed in the superiority of Euro-Canadian ways. They accepted a linear view of progress and thought the Aboriginals' hunter-gatherer, nomadic lifestyle represented a low form of economic, political, and social organization. Western society often held little respect for other cultures, as countless colonial situations throughout the world demonstrated. Ethnocentrism appeared even more strongly in the CCF than in some other sectors of society. The idealists of the party believed in the perfectability of society and that the group to which they belonged had progressed farther towards perfection than any other in the history of humankind. Additional justification for assimilation came from the socialists' use of class analysis. This theory minimized the importance of, and even discouraged, preserving racial and cultural distinctions. Within the northern CCF organization, for example, the Metis Marxists Norris and Brady viewed the class struggle as holding primary importance. The CCF appeared very sure about forcing assimilation on Aboriginals and did not give Indians or Metis a choice in the matter.

There is disagreement about whether the CCF aimed for integration or assimilation. Today, many view integration as acceptable, since it includes a higher level of respect for the other culture and allows aspects of it to survive. The term "integration" describes HBC and church policies prior to 1944, when Aboriginals enjoyed more choice about what they would accept from outsiders. The HBC preserved hunting and gathering, which fit with its own goals, and the churches maintained local cultures as much as religious changes the priests considered necessary would allow. In contrast, with successful assimilation, outside forces overwhelm the former culture, altering it until racial conflict and discrimination disappear. Strong links connect assimilation with colonialism.[8]

The controversy over whether the CCF worked for integration or assimilation exists largely because politicians and bureaucrats often did not differentiate between the two terms to describe their goals for northern Aboriginals. However, an examination of its words and actions reveals that assimilation and integration meant the same thing to the CCF government. Neither allowed for much survival of Aboriginal culture. Using today's terminology, the CCF generally followed a policy of assimilation. The government tried to assimilate all categories of Aboriginals, although the CCF attacked the Status Indians' culture less aggressively because it lacked full jurisdiction over this group. Yet the province worked with Ottawa to remove special treatment and status for Indians and move them from their traditional society into the Canadian mainstream. The CCF used DNR officers, teachers, health workers, and others to force assimilation.

The desire to assimilate Aboriginals extended to the top levels of the CCF administration. T.C. Douglas believed that "social and intellectual assimilation is absolutely vital." While he fostered the creation of Aboriginal organizations, this also fit with assimilation. He assisted the formation of the Union of Saskatchewan Indians in 1946, but the union did not operate independently and had a reputation as a captive organization that served CCF purposes. Douglas favoured ending reserves and wardship and wanted Saskatchewan to handle health, education, and welfare for Status Indians. In his view, "progress for Indians was measured in terms of integration," which meant assimilation.[9]

Many others within the CCF organization evinced a commitment to assimilating Aboriginals, which continued throughout the CCF era. Joe Phelps wanted Indian status ended and the province to administer Indian affairs. He did not favour "aborigine rights," which he interpreted as Natives wanting land and control. Phelps thought Indians should let "bygones be bygones."[10] Phelps's successor as DNR minister, J.H. Brockelbank, wrote: "We are convinced that the long-term solution to these social problems, is cultural assimilation."[11] In 1952, CCF politician W.J. (Bill) Berezowsky wanted to quickly put Aboriginals into the "melting pot." He blamed the lack of CCF support among trappers and fishermen on the HBC and the church helping Aboriginals remain distinct.[12] Four years later, Northern Administrator C.S. Brown described assimilation as an attainable goal, which they should "guide and speed" as much as possible.[13] Cabinet instructed minister J.H. Sturdy to head up a study into Indian problems and how to integrate them "as ordinary citizens in Saskatchewan." Dr. Lewis H. Thomas, Saskatchewan's provincial archivist, was to chair a subcommittee to help determine how to reach this goal.[14] Little changed as time went on. In 1962 DNR's C.L. MacLean, also a CCF candidate, described "economic and cultural assimilation" as "the only lasting answer to the so-called Metis problem."[15]

Some within the government spoke less about assimilation and more about integration by the 1960s. Official documents, including the 1960 Saskatchewan brief to the Joint Committee of the Senate and the House of Commons on Indian Affairs, referred to integration. Yet only the terminology changed. The CCF still wanted to see reserves disappear and viewed treaties and treaty rights as relatively minor rights that Status Indians would voluntarily give up. The new integration would tolerate only "vestigial ethnic traditions."[16]

From small beginnings in the mid-1940s, the CCF relied increasingly on community development methods to assimilate northern Aboriginals. Rather than attempting to bluntly force change, the more subtle community development efforts tried to convince Aboriginals that they should voluntarily accept the ways of white society. V.F. Valentine helped develop this program beginning in 1953. By the late 1950s the CCF relied heavily on the Center for Community Studies for policy direction in community development. Assimilation, although less forceful, remained central to the program. W.B. Baker, the centre's director, thought community development balanced assimilation with a respect for the integrity of Aboriginal culture. The centre also reflected the beginnings of a shift in societal attitudes from demanding assimilation to favouring integration. The centre took a neutral position in 1963: "Complete integration, i.e., the disappearance of the socially identifiable Indian, may not be accepted as a goal by everyone, but its achievement lies so far away in the future that there is no need for a consensus of opinion on this issue."[17]

Initiatives to give Indians the right to vote and drink liquor in the north and the south formed part of the CCF drive for assimilation. Douglas, possibly ahead of his time, already favoured full citizenship rights for Indians in 1943. The 1945 CCF convention also called for extending the vote to Indians. While other Indians appeared ambivalent, Chief Simon Linklater of Pelican Narrows supported the proposed changes. The matter gained urgency by 1958 when the province invited Status Indians to a conference, addressed by Douglas, at Fort Qu'Appelle. Chiefs and councillors did not support receiving the franchise then or in the following year. Thinking it knew best, the CCF gave Indians the provincial franchise anyway in 1960 and asked Ottawa to grant them liquor rights, which occurred in July 1960. Douglas reassured chiefs that the right to vote was a "new right" and would not affect Indians' "special rights."[18] Although many in the larger society considered it indefensible not to grant what they considered basic human rights, doing so served to increase assimilation by breaking down barriers between Indians and non-Indians. Where others saw discrimination, many Indians viewed not having the right to vote and drink as a defence for their culture.

Exerting control over Aboriginal organizations also helped the CCF with its agenda of assimilation, both in the north and the south. CCF involvement in Indian organizations co-opted their effectiveness at representing the issues of northern and other Indians. Douglas's assistant, Morris Shumiatcher, met with the northern chiefs in 1946 as one step in the formation of the Union of Saskatchewan Indians. The Federation of Saskatchewan Indians (FSI), which officially began in 1958-59, also felt strong CCF influence. CCF funding, which began in 1961-62, brought further provincial control over the organization. Malcolm Norris viewed the FSI as ineffective, describing it as existing in name only.[19]

The CCF seemed less concerned with controlling Metis organizations than those of the Indians, possibly because it considered the Metis to be already more assimilated. The Metis did not appear to speak effectively in defence of Aboriginal culture and represented little threat to the CCF program of assimilation. Disunity plagued Metis attempts to organize. Northern Metis formed the Saskatchewan Metis Association in 1943 as a rival to the Saskatchewan Metis Society (SMS). Douglas made some efforts in 1946 to organize the Metis, but failed due to rifts between northern and southern leaders. The CCF did little more to promote Metis organization. Malcolm Norris and Jim Brady struggled to organize the Metis over a long period of time but did not meet with much success. A La Ronge local of the SMS operated for a while, but the Metis appeared uninterested. Norris's and Brady's position as CCF supporters may have added to the failure.[20]

As one of its most forceful and prolonged efforts to bring assimilation, the CCF strove to take over the care of Status Indians from the federal government. This issue had great relevance to the north, since it was there that the CCF applied its most aggressive programs. The presence of a separate federal organization, which often followed different policies, threatened CCF plans to promote assimilation as well as its agenda of modernization and socialism. During the early part of the CCF era, Indian Affairs provided only minimal services in the north, which caused the province to repeatedly intervene with Indian Affairs on behalf of northern Status Indians in matters of housing, health, and welfare. The dearth of federal services in the north provided a logical reason for Saskatchewan to take responsibility. Various officials, including Phelps, wanted more cooperation with Indian Affairs on northern development, but in spite of seeming agreement for joint development and a partial transfer of services in 1947, nothing further came of this. Instead, Indian Affairs actually expanded its services and staff. Even after Indian Affairs started providing services superior to those offered by the province, the CCF continued to attempt to take over services to Indians. In 1956 the CCF appointed a committee under Sturdy to investigate Saskatchewan taking the services. Surprisingly, Sturdy recommended against a transfer of responsibility.[21] Yet the CCF continued to work for this. While still hoping to extend its jurisdiction onto reserves, the CCF first directed many of its efforts at Status Indians who did not live on reserves. In a move that affected many northern Indians, cabinet decided in 1957 to provide full social aid services to off-reserve Status Indians. Deputy Minister J.S. White of Social Welfare viewed extending provincial social aid on and off reserves as the "keystone" to solving "welfare problems."[22]

The province's efforts to take over federal services to Indians continued. In about 1960, Douglas asked for "joint provincial-federal conferences on Indian Affairs" to equalize services, including in the areas of infrastructure, education, medical care, and the extension of cooperatives.[23] The strength of the push to take over the services was demonstrated in 1961 when the legislature unanimously passed a resolution asking Ottawa to give complete Indian Affairs administration to any province that wanted this, providing that a majority of the Status Indians agreed. Concerned with the cost, Douglas suggested a twenty-five-year transition period to phase out federal financial support for Status Indians. Had Ottawa agreed, this change would have aided the CCF in applying its assimilation and other plans in the north and would have brought a nearly complete removal of the Indian Affairs presence from the north.

In 1963 Saskatchewan politicians and bureaucrats still strove to take over services to Status Indians. The director of Northern Affairs, A.H. MacDonald, expected Indians to resist attempts to make them "masters of their own destiny." J.S. White renewed his efforts to have the province take over the full range of social services on reserves, and the Department of Education proposed a complete transfer of Indian education to the province. A Community Development Branch submission wanted to see movement from reserves to urban areas. Premier Woodrow Lloyd led Saskatchewan's delegation to a Dominion-Provincial Conference on Indian Affairs called by Prime Minister Lester Pearson. Saskatchewan's brief spoke of reserves as an obstacle to Status Indians' off-reserve participation and portrayed assimilation and acculturation as desirable for Indian economic advancement.[24] This fit completely with the CCF's northern agenda of assimilation.

During the many years when Saskatchewan worked to take over services to Indians, it frequently appeared that the federal government would allow the transfer of responsibility to take place. Ottawa also wanted to see assimilation and an end to separate services, special status, wardship, and Indian reserves. Already in the 1940s the Joint Committee of the Senate and House of Commons wanted to see the shift of some services to the provinces. The transfer of responsibility for Indian health to National Health and Welfare in 1945, and the moving of Indian Affairs from the Department of Mines and Resources to the Department of Citizenship and Immigration in 1949, both fit with the plan of bringing full assimilation. In 1953 W.E. Harris, the minister of Citizenship and Immigration, opposed "treating Indians as a special class of citizens" and used this as a reason for not subsidizing northern Indian fishing with federal funds. In subsequent years, momentum to make the transfer grew. The Joint Committee of the Senate and the House of Commons on Indian Affairs' final report of 1961 encouraged shifting administration of Indian education and welfare to provinces and called for a Dominion-Provincial Conference to discuss the transfer of various matters. Yet the changes did not happen. Indian Affairs instead again expanded services. By 1963 it directed services from Prince Albert for Carlton Agency, which covered La Ronge and the northeast side, and from Meadow Lake for Meadow Lake Agency, which looked after the northwest side. Indian Affairs also had northern staff at Île-à-la-Crosse, Stony Rapids, La Ronge, and Pelican Narrows.[25] Ottawa remained ambivalent, though, refusing to give up assimilation as a goal. Great similarity existed between the CCF desire for assimilation and the position of the 1969 federal White Paper. Both governments emphasized treating all Canadians the same.

While Ottawa disappointed the province by not following through with the transfer of responsibility for Status Indians, at the end of its mandate, the CCF still hoped that northern and other Indians would voluntarily give up the treaties and move into white society. This wish also proved futile, since Indians increasingly emphasized group rights and the permanent relationship between themselves and the Canadian government based on the treaties. The CCF continued to oppose Aboriginal distinctness and the establishment of Indian self-government at the end of its time in office.[26] Any increase in Aboriginal independence jeopardized CCF assimilation and other plans for the north.

Although Saskatchewan failed to gain full jurisdiction over Status Indians, another attempt to assimilate northern Aboriginals succeeded to a greater extent. In one of its boldest initiatives, the CCF worked to move all Aboriginals who still lived in the bush into settlements. It would be inaccurate to suggest that no Aboriginals lived in villages prior to 1944 or that all wanted to continue living in the bush. Some movement to communities predated the CCF era, since the presence of fur-trading posts, missions, or boarding schools led to some Aboriginals living nearby. This occurred at numerous northern spots, including Île-à-la-Crosse, Cumberland House, and La Ronge. Treaties and the creation of reserves, although delayed in much of the north, also moved people into settlements. Montreal Lake offers an example. There the Cree adhered to Treaty 6 in 1889, wanting the protection of a treaty and a reserve. Fur-trading posts and the Anglican church also drew them to the settlement at the south end of the lake.[27] Yet C.H. Piercy, commissioned by the CCF to study the educational situation in the north in 1944, found nomadic Aboriginals who moved to trap and hunt for the winter and fish for the summer. Unable to carry many goods, they "squandered" their wealth and did not save for the future. Some already lived in or near settlements for six months of the year or permanently.[28] But no one prior to the intervention of the CCF had systematically attempted to eliminate the option that northern Aboriginals could live a nomadic life.

The CCF's politicians and bureaucrats had various reasons for wanting Aboriginals to end their unregulated wanderings. First of all, nucleation into settlements would make it easier to assimilate Aboriginals into white society. Village life would permit the CCF to efficiently apply education, health, housing, social, and other services to the formerly mobile population, which would gradually blend them into the larger society. Second, to its credit, the CCF believed that supplying these services would result in the improved health and welfare of northern Aboriginals. A third motivation came from the CCF desire to bring all aspects of the north under state control – to identify, count, and monitor the population. The new government refused to allow human life to continue in wild spaces beyond its control. Finally, placing people in communities would facilitate the introduction of modernization and socialism to the north.

Nucleation to the "micro-urban village" happened in northern Saskatchewan sooner than in most other areas of the Canadian north, largely because of CCF policies and actions. Provincial hospitals and schools pulled people into settlements. Ottawa's new family allowance system, which required children to attend school in order for mothers to receive the cheques, assisted the CCF with its plan. Additionally, the CCF's conservation area trapping system greatly limited mobility, and orderly fur marketing led trappers to spend more time in settlements, waiting for cheques from Regina. A complete shift to settlement life took time. Many continued to move between the village and their traditional hunting, trapping, and fishing areas, as dictated by the seasons. But over time, government programs inexorably solidified year-round residence in the communities.

Settlement life brought profound changes to northern Aboriginals. One of the greatest shocks came in the economic realm. While living on the land had sometimes been harsh, the natural northern environment had often abundantly provided the necessities of life. Village life made the formerly nomadic people instantly poverty-stricken. They lost much of their access to subsistence items and instead needed a constant supply of cash to live. Living in urban shacks, Aboriginals found themselves depending on welfare and other payments from government.[29]

Government nucleation policies also had devastating effects on family dynamics and gender roles. Men possibly experienced the greatest impact, losing much of their former status as providers for their families. Women received federal family allowance payments and often also the family's welfare payments. They frequently had a larger cash income than did their husbands, which increased women's status while decreasing that of men. Women also frequently received better educations than did men, and they took over much of the task of dealing with government bureaucracy. Male prestige declined further when CCF changes to the economic system resulted in trappers losing credit with traders. Although many trapped, fished, and hunted less than before, few other employment opportunities came their way. Consequently, they found themselves in the villages with time on their hands. When they did trap, fish, or hunt, they frequently did so with other men, rather than with their families. Men also found themselves under pressure to move away for job opportunities, while women could remain at home. The reduction of Aboriginal men's status and self-esteem, and their resulting dysfunctional actions, affected entire families and communities.

Certainly women and children also experienced stress as a result of moving to villages. Women helped less with trapping, lost traditional skills, underwent acculturation, and found themselves trapped in the village, caring for children. Yet in some respects, women experienced less cultural disruption than did men, since women's role as mothers continued and their traditional roles appeared more flexibile than those of men. Domestic problems grew as roles changed. Fewer people married, and many matrifocal families came about. Children assumed adult roles later in life, and the family held less social control than it once had. Parents' role as teachers of children also diminished. Schools often took over much of the education of children, teaching them white ways.[30]

The CCF prodding of Aboriginals into settlements included those Status Indians who had not chosen or moved to reserves. This process resembled the one followed by the federal government in the southern prairies beginning in the 1870s, when it signed treaties and drove Indians onto reserves. In the south this served the dual purpose of pushing Indians out of the way of white agricultural settlement and placing them in small areas where Ottawa could apply assimilative policies to make them behave like white men. Instead, contrary to the hopes of some, reserves often served as a barrier to assimilation. Similarly, although the sites chosen by the CCF for northern Aboriginals lacked reserve status, most villages became enclaves of the surviving Aboriginal culture. This jeopardized CCF goals.

Metis also found that the new government pressured them to live in designated and approved communities. One case from 1948 demonstrates the conflict that resulted from the different goals of the CCF and Metis. Rev. S. Cuthand, a Cree Anglican missionary and the secretary of the Saskatchewan Metis Society at La Ronge, sent a petition with about fifteen signatures asking for the survey of an area separate from the La Ronge townsite for the Metis. Numerous Metis lived, or in CCF terms "squatted," on land near the mouth of the river flowing into Lac la Ronge. Some had gardens and plots much larger than town lots. A.I. Bereskin, the provincial surveyor, responded by offering the Metis leases in two blocks in the townsite. He wanted to split the already small lots into two, making them about thirty-three feet in width. By moving the Metis to the townsite, Bereskin hoped to increase work opportunities, allow easier supervision of the liquor traffic, remove the risk of having a shantytown, and head off the demand for school and hospital services in the outlying area. The Metis had thirty days to accept the lots. While two applied for lots, others resisted, fearing friction with whites, a lack of peace, and the loss of space to garden and keep their dogs. The SMS intervened on behalf of the Metis. Its secretary, J.Z. LaRocque of Lebret, wrote: "Surely there is enough room in the Northern part of the Prov. to allow for permanent homes for our people." J.H. Sturdy, the minister of Social Welfare, opposed the separate Metis area since his "ultimate solution" for the "Metis problem" required "assimilation." Bereskin, J.J. Wheaton, the northern administrator, and J.W. Churchman, DNR's assistant deputy minister, all seemed to agree with Sturdy's position. Malcolm Norris, while not opposing nucleation, pointed out that whites had taken many available lots and that the Metis lacked "foresight and ability" to compete. He viewed the Metis as not yet ready to deal with whites and wanted government to protect them. Norris favoured the use of "miscellaneous use permits" to raise the status of Metis from squatter to permit holder.[31] Efforts to move Metis to the community continued.

With ongoing pressure from the CCF government and the attraction of expanding services, Aboriginals moved to dozens of communities across the north. On the west side, people moved to La Loche, Buffalo Narrows, Île-à-la-Crosse, Beauval, and various smaller settlements. Dene in the La Loche area formerly lived dispersed over a large area, including at Garson Lake, Descharme, and West La Loche. Some movement to the new community of La Loche took place prior to 1944. After the HBC store at West La Loche burned in 1937, the store manager and the priest encouraged the people to move to La Loche. There the construction of the school and store in 1940 and the hospital and convent in 1943 drew some from the outlying areas. The attraction of La Loche increased after the election of the CCF with the addition of a DNR headquarters and an RCMP detachment. Soon, in order to collect family allowances, parents needed to place their children in schools. As dependence on the services increased and new regulations removed former freedoms, Aboriginal people found it increasingly necessary to live in the community. Many would have preferred to stay where they formerly lived and felt tricked into moving by the white man. Unfortunately, at La Loche and elsewhere, the package did not include jobs. Instead people found unemployment and poverty.[32]

Near La Loche, Treaty 10 reserved four tracts of land on the Churchill River for Patuanak-area Dene. Long before the election of the CCF, the HBC traded from its store, which it built at Patuanak in 1921. Roman Catholic Father Moraud provided religious services for area people for almost fifty years until his death in 1965. After the Second World War, CCF fur programs and encouragement to attend schools drastically reduced seasonal nomadism. Aboriginals built log houses at Knee Lake, Primeau Lake, Dipper Lake, Cree Lake, and Patuanak. Later, the first four communities declined, while Patuanak increased in size.[33] There, as elsewhere in the north, in order to deliver services more efficiently, government wanted people to live in fewer and larger communities.

Farther south, the mainly Cree community of Buffalo Narrows became the primary supply centre for the west side. Again, the beginnings of the community predated the CCF era. A church and school operated by 1931, and a major economic opportunity appeared when Len Waite built a fish plant in 1943. The plant soon dominated the village physically and economically. With the election of the CCF came a new school and an outpost hospital. By 1953 Buffalo Narrows, with about eight hundred people, also boasted a DNR headquarters, an RCMP detachment, two hotels with cafés, four food stores, a poolroom, a sawmill, mink ranches, and an air base.[34]

Still farther south on the west side, Île-à-la-Crosse, Saskatchewan's second oldest community, also grew. The HBC trading post, which opened in 1779, became the first major attraction. Later, in 1846, Louis-François Laflèche and Alexandre-Antonin Taché founded the first mission in Saskatchewan there. Grey Nuns provided medical care and education from 1860 to 1996. Many Metis, including descendants of Red River French Canadians and Scots, chose to live in the area. By the mid-1950s services included a DNR headquarters, RCMP detachment, hospital, residential school, church, stores, hotel, café, and poolroom. As part of its taking control of northern communities, the CCF wanted a more compact settlement design to ease provision of services. DNR developed plans to relocate the community to the new highway, into a planned settlement. The province's plans for relocation fell through in 1957, largely because the federal government and the mission had other ideas. The mission built a new hospital and the RCMP a regional headquarters at the old site. It also seemed that Ottawa would build a public dock and that a new filleting plant would locate nearby. DNR then turned to organizing the old townsite.[35]

South of Île-à-la-Crosse, Beauval offered a school, an Indian residential school, a fish plant, a fruit plant, two stores, a café, and a poolroom by 1953.[36] DNR directed commercial development at nearby Beauval Forks at the junction of the highway to Buffalo Narrows. There the province wanted to lease, not sell, lots for service station and restaurant development.[37]

Not far away the CCF helped relocate Metis to a new community at Cole (Cold) Bay on Canoe Lake. The post office there received the name of Canoe Narrows. The move, with financial compensation to the Metis from Ottawa, took place to make way for the Primrose Lake bombing range. The province expected the Metis to use some of the money to help pay for the twenty-two new houses built there. However, residents allegedly spent the cheques on a drinking spree before the DNR officer arrived to collect the money. A one-room school opened in October 1962, adding to the permanence of the community. About twenty-eight pupils attended in the spring of 1963.[38]

West of La Ronge, at Snake Lake, the HBC established a post in 1786, and the first missionary visited the Dene population in 1899. After a small-pox epidemic in 1900-01 killed about half of the area people, survivors left for Patuanak or Stanley Mission. Cree Metis later moved into the area from the west side, forming a scattered village by 1939. Roman Catholics completed a church in 1944. Soon after its election, the CCF established a store there. School began in 1948, further increasing the draw to the set-tlement. DNR laid out a townsite and encouraged the Metis to settle in the surveyed area. But most Metis preferred to squat in the surrounding area. By 1950 only the government store manager, one other family, the store, and the church had located in the townsite. Eventually more complied with the CCF plan for them to move to the new site. In 1954 local initia-tive led to renaming the community Pinehouse Lake.[39]

Nucleation into settlements occurred later for some far northern Dene, including the Hatchet Lake, Black Lake, and Fond du Lac bands. A disor-ganized community grew at Wollaston Lake by 1954, with thirteen single whites, about twenty-five Status Indian families, and four Metis families in the area. Aboriginals still followed the caribou, and whites lived in their winter fishing camps. While the CCF delayed introducing trapping areas and other regulation to the locale, DNR officer Chas. Salt wanted to see the CCF intervene by establishing a village, airport, and compulsory school. Only three children had some education, about two years each. He noted: "We bring a little bit of the law to these people who have been doing pretty much as they please."[40] Over time, dependence on the caribou lessened and most moved to a settlement lifestyle. In 1956 DNR's R.N. Gooding chose a new site for the community prior to the government building a fish plant. A co-op store and a new mission helped gather people together in the settlement. The CCF's extension of the registered trapline program to the far north in 1958 represented another step in increasing control in the area.[41]

On the Fond du Lac River near the east end of Lake Athabasca, Stony Rapids began when the HBC established a store in 1927. The Roman Catholics also built a church. Many Dene, formerly from the Selwyn Lake area of the NWT, then spent more time at Stony Rapids. Others moved there from west-side Churchill River communities and the Brochet and Wollaston Lake area in the 1920s and 1930s. By the late 1940s so many Indians lived at nearby Stony Lake that they quickly depleted fish and firewood stocks. In 1951 the Catholic priest established a church some miles away at Black Lake, and the HBC and many Indians followed. Chief Louis Ditheda wanted to see the Indian school placed at Stony Rapids, but the priest won out and it went to Black Lake. A road, built by DNR for uranium development, linked the two communities. Black Lake's population soon surpassed that of Stony Rapids, and it also grew far beyond the ability of the area to support it, with ecological damage to the land, water, and forests. Although settlement life provided few jobs, the caribou-centred way of life largely disappeared. As happened elsewhere, many of those who still hunted and trapped did so largely for emotional reasons.[42]

In most areas the CCF encouraged Aboriginals to move to pre-existing communities. It embarked on a much more ambitious experiment at Reindeer Lake. There, on the lake's east shore, the CCF established the completely new community of Kinoosao (Co-Op Point) as a site for a filleting plant. Its proximity to the railhead at Lynn Lake, Manitoba, about fifty miles away, dictated the location of the new settlement, and Saskatchewan built a road to the Manitoba town. DNR surveyed the Kinoosao townsite in 1952 before leasing lots to fishermen and fish plant employees. The plant, which operated only in the summer, employed up to fifteen persons. By 1954 Kinoosao's population included two DNR officers, a schoolteacher, a storekeeper, six trapper-fishermen, and thirteen students. Attractions included the DNR headquarters, a school, a store, and a post office.[43] Yet most residents of the big lake lived far from the CCF's new settlement. About a dozen fishermen lived on islands in the central area of Reindeer Lake, while most area Aboriginals lived far away from Kinoosao in the Southend area. There, Status Indians of the Pelican Narrows band resided on an island reserve, and Metis occupied a village on the mainland.

Seeing that most Aboriginals had no intention of moving to Kinoosao, the CCF tried to move them there. The Roman Catholic church and some Southend people raised strong opposition to the CCF nucleation plans. The Indians wanted to move from the island since its location made transportation and firewood access difficult, but instead of complying with the CCF plan for them to move to Kinoosao, they and some Metis wanted to exchange land with the province and move to Sucker Point, northwest of Southend. They opposed moving to Kinoosao, citing its distance from their traplines, a shortage of fish there to feed their dogs, and a desire not to live so close to white people. Some who had helped build the Kinoosao filleting plant rued going there. They had drunk liquor and lost much money to white people in poker games. Roman Catholic Bishop Lajeunesse, wanting to protect the Aboriginals, raised concerns about the move to Kinoosao with T.C. Douglas. Yet the CCF did not retreat from its plans for nucleation at Kinoosao. It had already spent about $100,000 on Kinoosao's new DNR headquarters and fish plant and planned to build a school. Northern Administrator Brown thought the church and the HBC wanted to keep "the natives in isolation and comparative ignorance ... contrary to our policies and beliefs. We consider education and assimilation the only ultimate solution to the native problem." Minister Brockelbank dismissed the bishop's concerns about gambling, depicting gambling as part of Aboriginal culture. He wrote: "The only way the native will learn not to gamble is to experience losing his wealth permanently." He thought a "protectionist policy" prevented Aboriginal development. Although the CCF could not force Aboriginals to move to Kinoosao, its continuing encouragement and incentives resulted in many moving there.[44]

Much farther south, Cumberland House, the oldest settlement in Saskatchewan, lay on an island in the Saskatchewan River delta. It once had played an important role in river transport and the fur trade, and these activities had attracted Indian families to trade and work there. Treaty 5 of 1875 created a reserve near the post. After Father Charlebois asked the federal government in 1892 to allow Metis to remain, Ottawa traded 640 acres of land at Cumberland House for land elsewhere. This made room for a settlement for Metis and Non-Status Indians. By 1900 some Aboriginals lived there almost permanently.[45] After 1944, as elsewhere under the CCF, DNR acted as the local government. In 1946 DNR began a four-point development plan, which included muskrat habitat development, a sawmill, a farm, and improved education. About five hundred persons lived in the area in 1947, including about twenty-five whites. The presence of schools, a hospital, and government cheques accelerated nucleation.

The number of encampments and villages in the area dropped from ten to four by 1960. Cumberland House, with 453 persons, had three satellite communities: Pemmican Portage with 247 persons, Pine Bluff with 75, and Sturgeon Landing with 102. Metis comprised 76.4 percent, Status Indians 16.3 percent, and whites 7.3 percent of the area population. At Pemmican Portage, about three miles from Cumberland House, over half of the population lived on the reserve. That community included a school, a Northern Evangelical Mission, and Roman Catholic and Anglican churches. Pine Bluff, a reserve about twenty-five miles west of Cumberland House, offered a one-room Indian Affairs school and a winter HBC store. Most

Pine Bluff people moved to Cumberland House in the summer and back to Pine Bluff in September when school resumed. Attractions at Sturgeon Landing, thirty-four miles north, included a one-room school, a store, and a post office. Residents traded with The Pas and Flin Flon in Manitoba, some provincial administration came from Cumberland House, and treaty matters were handled from Pelican Narrows.[46]

The CCF preferred larger settlements to smaller ones, partly because it wanted to maximize the efficiency of its provision of services to northerners. Centralization of services at Kinoosao, Patuanak, La Ronge, and Cumberland House all demonstrate this preference. Refusal to provide services in smaller villages acted as an incentive for movement to the larger communities. An example comes from Dillon, about thirty water miles from Buffalo Narrows. Father A. Darche wanted to build a residential school at Dillon. The settlement already had a church, rectory, HBC post, school, about twenty houses, and a population of about 157 Status Indians and 122 Metis. To better meet the needs of the population, Darche wanted government to build a medical facility, but both the CCF and Ottawa opposed establishing an outpost hospital there.[47] CCF refusal to provide services in small villages pushed Aboriginals to the larger communities.

The foregoing description of nucleation of northern Aboriginals into predominantly Aboriginal communities does not mention all northern settlements. Similar congregation occurred elsewhere. Clearly factors other than the efforts of the CCF influenced the movement to centralized settlements, freeing the CCF from some of the credit or blame for the process. The traders, the churches, and the federal government all participated in moving the formerly nomadic people into an urban environment. Yet no other institution deliberately worked for nucleation to nearly the same extent as did the CCF. The strong efforts made by this government to establish new settlements where none existed before, such as at Wollaston and Kinoosao, clearly demonstrate the importance the CCF placed on nucleation. As the primary provider of services in the new north that it sought to build, the CCF wanted to establish an efficient service-delivery system. Additionally, and possibly more importantly, movement of Aboriginals to settlements would allow the government to apply its programs of assimilation, modernization, and socialism to the formerly dispersed population.

The new nucleation brought many problems. Previously, those moving to the small villages had often built houses where they wanted. Many preferred to build homes in clusters, determined partly by kinship ties. The CCF sought to impose order on the settlements and applied culturally inappropriate southern settlement designs to old and new northern communities. Urban planners wanted to place houses in neat rows along uniformly spaced streets, thereby reducing costs for surveys, services, and policing. Aboriginals resisted conforming to the new pattern. While not giving up on its efforts, the CCF lamented the problems of squatters, poor sanitation, and stray dogs. It also decried the lack of local organization at the same time as government officials displaced traditional leaders. The often unsatisfying lives in communities brought increased social problems, including violence and alcohol abuse. Yet for most Aboriginals the option of living in the bush no longer appeared practical or possible.[48]

Most northern villages housed only a few white residents but four communities had substantial white populations. At Uranium City, Creighton, and Island Falls non-Aboriginals formed the majority. The fairly even mix of Aboriginals and non-Aboriginals at La Ronge represented an unusual racial situation in northern Saskatchewan. And the CCF refused to spend much money on La Ronge, leaving it with inadequate services, while it designed and helped build the mining community of Uranium City almost overnight, providing it with an extensive infrastructure, hospital, and high school. Creighton, another mining community, also far surpassed most northern communities in development under the CCF. Private industry developed Island Falls. The disparity in development between white and Aboriginal communities existed because the Uranium City, Creighton, and Island Falls areas generated substantial revenues for the province and industry, while the other settlements drained provincial coffers, and industry had no reason to invest in infrastructure where it did not operate. CCF spending on northern communities was often directly related to the amount the government collected there.

Any examination of northern Saskatchewan would remain incomplete without discussing La Ronge. The community also serves as an interesting case study of urban development under the CCF. Although neglected, the stature of La Ronge rose considerably after 1944. The settlement had long served as a trading, mission, and educational centre. A survey of 316 acres in 1920 divided about two miles of lakeshore east of the Indian reserve. The HBC and Indian Affairs received much of the approximately 150 acres considered suitable for development. In turn, Indian Affairs allowed the Anglican residential school to locate on its land. By 1944 about twenty-four families lived in the community. The Anglican mission and school, two stores, a DNR officer, and an RCMP officer provided services. Much of the development in the surrounding area had followed an unregulated course, and many Aboriginals had squatted nearby.[49]

Seeing excellent potential for tourism and various forms of resource development, the CCF wanted to expand La Ronge. DNR consequently bought land from the HBC and Indian Affairs and laid out a townsite. A new survey of part of the settlement created residential lots measuring 65 by 130 feet, allowing residents room for a small garden and chickens. By 1946 the CCF built a filleting plant and sawmill and provided two-way radio and air service to the community. The new government aggressively assumed many of the roles formerly filled by the Anglican church and the

HBC, imposing its own plans. Although local people disapproved of much of what the CCF did there, it proceeded with minimal local consultation. CCF efforts to have the Anglican school removed proved controversial, but after the school burned, the issue seemed to disappear. Opposition also arose to the fish plant. The Anglicans' Reverend Fisher thought the plant brought negative changes, including increased drinking. There was also fear that a poolroom and dance hall would follow, adding further harmful influences. DNR's town and road layout plans raised controversy too. For a time, only a miserable road extended through the settlement, not following the survey plan.

While community people indicated interest in local government and participation in decision making as early as 1946, the CCF left control with DNR. White people felt left out of decision making, but Aboriginals held even less power. Within the townsite, a race-based class structure grew, with many of the dominant white people viewing Aboriginals as problematic. Whites expressed fear that Aboriginals would not properly care for a hypothetical community hall, and one person even wanted to see treatment of books at a future library to prevent transmission of disease.[50]

Even though the CCF used La Ronge as its base within the north, and DNR held responsibility for local government there, the province spent little on developing the community except for administration purposes. It provided a new administration building to house the Northern District office, Saskatchewan Government Airways, and the radio monitoring station, and two field officer residences. A new four-room school operated by 1948.[51]

La Ronge possessed great potential as a tourism, business, and governmental centre, and many private persons demonstrated interest in investing there. Yet the CCF put up obstacles to development, repeatedly turning away interested parties. This occurred partly because the CCF wished to protect some existing businesses, but primarily because of the CCF's failure to provide badly needed development land.[52] The federal government and the HBC still owned much of the land in the townsite, and the CCF's fish plant polluted an area of the lakeshore, preventing other development there. Further limits on development existed because the Indian reserve lay to the west, muskeg to the north, and the lake to the south. While some in government occasionally spoke about establishing a new townsite in a more suitable location, this never occurred. Instead, DNR's surveyor A.I. Bereskin and other officials made various efforts to squeeze development into the existing limited space. Several transfers of land from Ottawa to the province took place by the early 1950s, helping ease the congestion somewhat. Land obtained included the former Anglican school site.[53] Bereskin suggested the imaginative expansion plan of laying out two hundred lots on Kitsakie Island, about 1,200 feet from the townsite. He visualized a bridge, causeway, or ferry link to the mainland, but the development never happened.[54]

Even though the CCF insisted that it handle community planning at La Ronge, this proved inadequate and haphazard, further hurting development. While it offered the Metis only half-sized leased lots, the CCF allowed a few businesspeople to dominate much of the lakeshore. Outfitters leased prime lakefront land for low-density, poor-quality development, largely shutting out cottagers. Red Boardman, a tourism operator, leased prime lakefront land, formerly set aside by DNR as public reserve for a public park and camping site. A less fortunate entrepreneur, Vic Peterson, leased sodden swampland, where he located four modest cabins and an outhouse. Others waited for development land. By 1951 Allan Quandt, the former employee of DNR, had waited about three years for approval of a business lease.[55]

M.A. Welsh, district sanitary officer, kindly depicted La Ronge as having "a bad case of growing pains." A more candid description would have called it governmental neglect. The townsite lacked a safe water supply and an adequate sewage and garbage disposal system, so there was the risk of a typhoid or dysentery outbreak. As elsewhere in the north, Aboriginal sled dogs were a "scourge," fending for themselves in the summer when their masters did not use them. Welsh saw DNR as an obstacle to improvements, since he understood that DNR planned not to spend more on settlements than it collected in taxes. DNR already had spent much more on La Ronge than it raised there. Without development, La Ronge lacked the ability to generate tax revenue.[56]

DNR's tight control and inadequate administration of La Ronge continued for many years. Finally, by the mid-1950s, the CCF tired of its responsibilities there and decided that La Ronge should incorporate as a village. The province wanted this change to happen quickly. DNR's minister even supported a plan to threaten the local ratepayers association with an increase in the education mill rate to force its hand. A plebiscite approved incorporation, and the village began effective 1 August 1955. The change meant that villagers elected councillors, and the local government took over garbage collection, taxation, assets, and liabilities. The province retained control of public reserves until 1958.[57]

While La Ronge grew and offered a relatively large range of services, becoming the regional centre, the village lacked the tax base or resources to shake the legacy of underdevelopment. The CCF also failed to provide substantial aid. As a result, La Ronge continued without water, sewer, and other facilities. Possibly most surprisingly, this centre did not even have a hospital until 1960. By that time La Ronge had a population of about 568, while 884 lived nearby in a Metis area and on reserves. The residents of many outlying settlements also relied on La Ronge as a service centre.[58]

The situation seemed to brighten for La Ronge in the 1960s. By 1963 DNR offered lots for lease at a new development just south of La Ronge, known as Air Ronge. Also, following a multi-year project to drain a muskeg area, DNR approved village plans to expand to the north in 1964. The land provided space for a school and housing. The CCF undoubtedly made many contributions to the La Ronge area by 1964. Yet it could have done much more.[59] Inadequate development planning and a low level of spending handicapped the village. As a result, La Ronge remained badly underdeveloped with glaring shortcomings, particularly for its Aboriginal population.

The provincial neglect and miserly spending at La Ronge stands out even more sharply when contrasted with the situation at Uranium City. There, on the north shore of Lake Athabasca, the CCF created a new modern town. Not far away, Goldfields had grown into a bustling town in the 1930s, but it had unincorporated and become a ghost town after the Box Mine closed in 1942. The area received new life when the federal Crown corporation Eldorado began exploratory work for radioactive minerals in 1946. With the discovery of uranium, the area quickly developed. Goldfields briefly revived, but in 1952 the CCF began to build Uranium City at a central location. The provincial government managed development, aiming "to control or eliminate the establishment of company towns in the north." The Beaverlodge Local Development Area encompassed the mining area, although DNR also had a resident administrator there. The CCF quickly found the money to provide infrastructure, including electricity, a new four-room school, and a hospital.[60]

The Uranium City area boomed, employing about 1,500 persons in exploration and mining construction by early 1953. Pacific Western Airlines (PWA) flew in daily from Edmonton, and three Saskatchewan Government Airways (SGA) flights per week from Prince Albert also brought workers and supplies. The newcomers included many Europeans, making Uranium City an ethnic "melting pot." It soon had many businesses located on lots leased from the province. A 1955 report requested by the CCF cabinet projected a potential population of eight thousand and recommended the immediate construction of a twenty-five-bed hospital and a water and sewer system. Both projects quickly proceeded. Area mines, including Gunnar and Eldorado, also provided housing and other facilities. With the province's blessing, the Municipal Corporation of Uranium City and District began in 1956, looking after municipal, hospital, and education matters, operating independently.[61] Only four years after its founding, the infrastructure and facilities at Uranium City far surpassed those of La Ronge.

Although the CCF encouraged destitute Aboriginals to move to La Ronge and many other northern communities, the CCF tried to reserve Uranium City for tax-paying residents. Aboriginal squatters presented a problem, but by 1953 the government relocated them outside the hamlet limits. Concern resurfaced in 1956 about Aboriginals who lived in nearby tent camps and other bush dwellings. A provincial report called for a program to control Aboriginal settlement. Its authors thought Aboriginals lacked the preparation to integrate into the community and viewed them as an economic and social threat. The province feared Indians and Metis would raise the area's low welfare costs and that "unemployables and undesirables" would become a burden.[62] The CCF successfully helped exclude Aboriginals from the mining community, creating a white, prosperous microcosm of the south.

Another major area of white settlement grew on the Saskatchewan side of the border near Flin Flon, Manitoba. The main attraction for outsiders was the chance of employment with the Hudson Bay Mining and Smelting Company at Flin Flon. Since some workers preferred to live on the Saskatchewan side, several settlements sprang up. About 350 people lived in the unorganized "tin and shanty town" of Tobacco Road. The CCF spent little on this boundary area, instead relying on Manitoba and the mining company to provide much of the care for nearby Saskatchewan residents. The CCF leased the area to the Community Development Company of Flin Flon, which provided fire, police, health, road upkeep, and other services.[63] In 1953-54 the boundary area amalgamated with Flin Flon.[64]

Another settlement grew nearby at Creighton. DNR surveyed lots there, guided by "scientific community planning." The province leased, rather than sold, the lots to prevent speculation and land price inflation. Over the years the mining company paid many of the community's expenses, including those for education and a water and sewer system. Creighton incorporated as the first northern village in 1952, relieving DNR of local government responsibilities. It became a town by 1958. The population of Creighton and the boundary area continued to rise, reaching 2,287 in 1961.[65] Largely thanks to the services provided on the Manitoba side of the border, residents enjoyed many of the amenities available in southern communities. The nearby resort community of Denare Beach provided recreation for workers from Flin Flon and Creighton. Some Aboriginals also lived there. As in most communities, DNR kept strict control at Denare Beach, resisting efforts to develop local authority.[66]

Throughout the north, the CCF applied its socialist ideology when determining various details of life in both old and new settlements. The CCF vision saw Aboriginals living in state-owned communities, working at state-owned and cooperative industries. In socialist fashion the CCF retained state ownership of most of the land on which it placed northerners. The government often refused to sell land, insisting on leases instead. It also worked to take over some already titled land that had been transferred to private parties and the federal government before the province received control of Crown lands in 1930. This policy differed greatly from that used by the CCF in the south, where private persons commonly owned land. No clear rationale existed for the northern policy other than the CCF desire to impose state control and socialism on northerners. The policy had severe negative consequences since it limited northern development. Owners of homes and businesses generally preferred to own building sites because land ownership gave the developer greater security, and improvements on leased lots usually had a lower value than those on titled lots. Additionally, lessees needed government consent to obtain mortgages.[67]

Although the CCF seemed to relax its controls by 1949, in theory allowing the sale of lots in surveyed subdivisions, in reality, restrictive lease policies continued. These affected both Aboriginal and non-Aboriginal northerners. DNR persisted in signing leases in community after community. By 1961 the CCF adopted a policy not to sell land in new subdivisions in recreational areas. The policies led to an irate confrontation at the Denare Beach Ratepayers' Association meeting.[68] Inconsistent and excessively restrictive policies also deterred business investment, preventing northerners from improving communities and building an economic base. Those interested in beginning businesses had to lobby for development approval without knowing what arbitrary rules they might face. Not surprisingly, in view of the obstacles created by the CCF, DNR's supervisor of Northern Municipal Services, W.J. Bague, described the north in 1961 as economically sick.[69] In some cases DNR proved willing to make minor variations in its lease policies while maintaining strict general control.[70]

The new government was not satisfied with just moving Aboriginals from the bush into communities. It also decreed that the common practice of putting up a shack wherever seemed convenient had to end. Instead, northerners should live on surveyed and exactly delimited lots. Although the task of imposing order in the dozens of northern communities appeared formidable, DNR tackled this work almost immediately. Controller of Surveys A.I. Bereskin took over most survey work from DNR's Construction Branch. He held great independent power, deciding priorities and schedules for surveys and designing and planning communities. Development needs in the larger, predominantly white communities often took priority over the surveys of Aboriginal settlements, although the CCF never forgot to also survey the rapidly growing Aboriginal villages. Frequently, others in government prodded the surveyors to speed these surveys. In one case in 1947, for example, Northern Administrator Wheaton pressed for a survey at Snake Lake to avoid having "just that many more squatters on our hands."[71]

Aboriginals sometimes resisted CCF survey plans. In one case, resistance rose in 1950 when Bereskin set out to survey a townsite at the scattered Metis and Indian settlement of Sandy Bay. Unlike in many other areas, Aboriginals had settled in the community prior to the election of the CCF. Employment at the nearby Island Falls power plant had drawn them there. However, the people had built houses more or less where they wanted along more than half a mile of the scenic Churchill River shore. Bereskin

aimed to begin "a more orderly program of development." Most local people did not want the survey, preferring to live cheaply on unsurveyed land
to paying leases and taxes on small lots. It seemed many would move
to the bush before paying fees. Bereskin gave up in frustration, at least for
the time being. Instead he surveyed only a small townsite, including the
DNR, school, hospital, and Roman Catholic church areas and a ten-lot residential "test block."[72] Resistance to the surveys also arose elsewhere. At
Stony Rapids, people resented landscape changes designed by "city planners from the south."[73]

Some northern communities, including Île-à-la-Crosse, Buffalo Narrows,
and Cumberland House, had old surveys dating back to before the CCF
era. In these cases, former governments that did not oppose the idea of
private property in the north had issued titles, but neither government
nor residents had bothered to see that the legal paperwork remained up to
date. Many property owners had died or sold their lots, and most had
fallen many years into arrears in the payment of property taxes. The destruction of survey markers and random placement of buildings further
eroded the system. In these communities the CCF aggressively worked to
institute control, carrying out resurveys and restoring tax collection.

Cumberland House provides one of the more dramatic examples of the
CCF exerting authority in pre-existing communities. Residents there had
received titles to surveyed lots from the federal government in 1911, and
the HBC also owned and sold land. By the time the CCF came to power,
the survey, land registration, and taxation systems had broken down. DNR
took control, filing tax liens, taking over all properties, resurveying the
area, and then giving lots to the residents. By 1956 the CCF instituted
order there.[74]

The CCF also extended its governance to those who did not move to
communities or who still spent some time away from villages. By 1949
trappers and others could no longer build remote cabins wherever they
wanted without first securing occupation permits. DNR also sought to
regulate existing buildings in the northern bush. In a 1953 initiative it
turned its attention to about eighteen scattered sites, including cabins, a
store, and the Evangelical Mission, along the road south of La Ronge
and the east side of Montreal Lake. Control over property and residents
increased as the CCF era progressed.[75]

As part of the nucleation process, the CCF tried to force Aboriginals to
pay lease fees and taxes. However, one of the tactics it used to minimize
resistance to nucleation was to increase controls gradually, trying not to
create enough of an obstacle to prevent Aboriginals moving from the status of squatter to that of paying lease or permit holder. The government
kept lease rates low and varied these by ability to pay. DNR began a system
of basing lease charges on the classification of communities as developed,
semi-developed, or undeveloped. This method designated communities

that depended on fish and fur – in other words, Aboriginal settlements – as undeveloped. DNR kept lease rates low there, encouraging Aboriginal movement to the settlements. Protest arose within DNR, though. A.T. Davidson wrote: "It is a poor policy to continue to force the white residents to pay high taxes and lease rentals just to make up for the non-payment by Metis in the same community." By 1956 only about a quarter of residents in some settlements paid lease or permit fees. Those living the "white man's standards" paid fees and taxes, while those living the "native way" paid little.[76]

To facilitate property taxation, the Saskatchewan Assessment Commission assessed northern communities, starting by 1948. As with leases, the CCF tried to gradually ease Aboriginals into accepting this new responsibility, using an "introductory educational form of taxation." It raised taxes for "relatively advanced communities" to "more realistic levels" by 1954.[77] Further increasing the obligations of Aboriginals, the CCF introduced school taxes, and by 1955 most northern communities had educational levies based on property assessments and ability to pay. To the CCF, the principle of having Aboriginals pay seemed to matter more than the amount collected. The education tax paid only about 3 percent of the cost of northern education in 1956.[78]

Many Aboriginals continued to resist paying property taxes late in the CCF era, limiting the success of CCF efforts to exert control and order in the new settlements. Because of the pervasive poverty, government found it could do little to enforce the collection of taxes. Île-à-la-Crosse paid only $637.77 of the levy of $1,765.55 in 1960, Cumberland House only $580.29 of $1,127.30 in 1962, and Sandy Bay only $139.40 of $545.40 in 1962.[79]

The CCF pointed to the low level of revenue generated from local taxes and claimed that northerners did not pay for most services they received from the province. Yet only by omitting from their calculations the millions paid into provincial coffers through royalties and taxes on mining, forestry, fish, and fur could the CCF view the north as a welfare case. This creative accounting justified the province's low level of spending on northern Aboriginal communities. Although most northern Aboriginals complied with the CCF effort to move them to villages, once there, they encountered severe poverty and neglect by government.

In 1953, seemingly in response to a CCF cabinet inquiry, DNR's R.G. Young studied the issue of whether the north paid its way. He found that, with the inclusion of mining royalties, government income from the north stood much above expenditures. But he argued against counting mining income in the analysis. According to his estimate, the province would spend about $600,000 on various programs in one year. Not counting mining revenue, it would collect up to $200,000, including property taxes, sales tax, non-mining royalties, and licence fees. This left a shortfall of about $400,000. Young thought the main demand on funds came from Aboriginals, not from industrious and self-sufficient whites. He wrote that maybe cabinet should have asked whether "individual cultural groups were paying their way." He noted that even when assessed taxes, Aboriginals often did not pay. A lack of social stigma for not paying taxes, and even for imprisonment for ignoring tax liabilities, worked against CCF plans to have Aboriginals accept the responsibility of making payments to the government. In his view, Metis blew their money on liquor, lacked technical knowledge, and would experience "retrogression," resulting in a further financial drain.[80] Young's fear of increased expenditures came true when northern spending for six departments rose from $705,113 in 1951-52 to $1,270,105 in 1954-55. DNR spent over half of this amount, while Education, Health, and Welfare together expended less than DNR.[81]

Although efforts to nucleate Aboriginals proved successful, CCF plans for assimilation largely failed. CCF politicians and administrators became frustrated with Aboriginals and their seeming refusal to give up their distinct ways even once they were within the settlements. Doris Shackleton, Tommy Douglas's biographer, wrote: "The darkest problem facing Douglas, and the one he was least able to solve, was the degradation of the Indian people of Saskatchewan."[82] Other factors contributed to the degradation, but in the view of the CCF, Aboriginal lifestyles and culture played a major role. Aboriginals resisted accepting the Euro-Canadian ways and giving up their own culture.

Non-Aboriginals also contributed to the failure of CCF plans for assimilation. Two distinct societies solidified and grew, separating the region's Aboriginals from non-Aboriginals. The former remained separate from their social superiors, the white people, both government employees and others, who formed the rapidly growing white society. Many whites, both those already there and the newcomers, did not doubt their superiority and the corresponding inferiority of Aboriginals. The line between the two groups hardened as time went on. Women as well as men contributed to the two societies that grew up in the north. During the CCF era, the number of white women in the region increased greatly. Many accompanied their husbands, who went north to work for mining companies or government. Professional jobs with the government, most commonly nursing or teaching, also attracted large numbers of women to the north. In contrast to the poverty of Aboriginal women, most white women in the north lived a middle-class lifestyle.

Aboriginals suffered most from the racially based division that developed. Even while United States civil rights issues headlined Saskatchewan's newscasts, discrimination openly flourished in the north. The CCF knew of this situation. In 1952 outspoken CCF MLA W.J. Berezowsky recognized the presence of the two societies. He saw "class or racial distinction and prejudice" where whites deemed themselves a "superior people."

Aboriginals wanted acceptance by whites, who ignored them. Berezowsky wrote: "Only a few whites who have resided in a community for a lengthy period or who are idealists, treat these people as equals on occasion."[83] The CCF largely ignored the blatant racism in its own backyard and did not effectively deal with the situation.

Barriers between Aboriginals and whites increased in the 1950s when mining attracted thousands of white people to the area. Nongovernment employees often had even less contact with and understanding of Aboriginals than did government workers. Frequently, white people considered themselves morally superior and disapproved of much Aboriginal behaviour. In a blatant effort to keep Aboriginals away, Uranium City had a "one-mile exclusion zone" in which Aboriginals could not put up tents or build houses.[84] V.F. Valentine, DNR's anthropologist, likened the relationship between Indians and whites to a caste system, with the white man in the ruling caste. He described Metis as "outcasts," with little mobility possible out of their group. Some whites thought of Aboriginals as lazy and as having lower intelligence. Fearing lowered academic standards and contagious disease, they did not want their children to attend school with Aboriginals.[85] A 1958 government report said that many people, including numerous government employees, perpetuated the myth of Metis as a "shiftless lot" unable to care for themselves.[86]

Most who spent time in the north can describe the two societies in the communities they knew. One such person, DNR's anthropologist J.E.M. Kew, lived at Cumberland House in 1960. He reported that ethnic prejudice, power, and economic position separated people there. Within the upper social class, DNR officers and store managers stood at the top, while teachers, missionaries, RCMP officers, nurses, and other whites held less status and authority. Although they formed only a small minority, white people had all ten phones in the community. Using censure, whites pressured other whites to follow the rules of social segregation. A teacher who crossed the line was transferred. Intermarriage between whites and Aboriginals often brought increased status to the Aboriginal partner, while the white spouse risked losing status. Even though the churches and some in the CCF protested against the caste-like system, the upper class resisted and delayed change.[87]

Possibly the most startling tale of two societies came from the communities of Island Falls and Sandy Bay on the Churchill River. There, the oldest hydroelectric dam in the province's north generated power for the Hudson Bay Mining and Smelting mine and mill at Flin Flon. About forty white employees and their families, a total of about two hundred people, lived in the company town of Island Falls. They lived in luxurious company houses, including some about 1,800 square feet in size, with hardwood floors, french doors, and electric heat. Community facilities included a recreation centre, swimming pool, golf course, skating rink, and curling rink. Attracted by employment at the dam, Metis and Status Indians settled a short distance downstream at Sandy Bay. About eighty Aboriginal men laboured for the company at menial and unskilled jobs. In contrast to the luxury found in the nearby white community, many Sandy Bay residents lived in unmodern shacks, and even though the power plant stood about one mile away, they lived without electricity until 1958. The company did not permit its Aboriginal employees and their families to use the Island Falls recreation facilities. Nor did the company store allow these second-class customers past the counter, allegedly because white women did not want to shop with them. After Cree customers protested, the company set up a separate store for them.[88]

The discrimination and racism at Island Falls and Sandy Bay continued with the knowledge of the CCF. The government failed to intervene. In 1957 CCF Member of Parliament A.M. Nicholson saw little government interest in improving housing, providing electricity, or dealing with social problems.[89] The situation remained much the same when DNR anthropologist Walter Hlady studied Sandy Bay in the late 1950s. He thought the company set the tone of segregation except where necessary for work and to give the "impression that apartheid does not exist." Hlady blamed at least some of the social problems among the Aboriginals on the discrimination. In his view, alcohol helped the Aboriginals relieve the feeling of being second-class citizens. Residents drank large quantities of home-brewed "molly" on a daily basis. On weekends, men, women, and teenagers partied, spending much of their income on alcohol. Hlady described drinking and sex as the primary recreational activities.[90] Robin F. Badgley of the University of Saskatchewan found northern discrimination "most clearly crystallized" there, with residential, recreational, educational, medical, and even religious discrimination present. The power company educated white children and owned its own clinic. Island Falls also received religious services from Father Thibodeau separate from those at Sandy Bay.[91] These and other people pointed out northern racism. But the CCF simply ignored it. While the CCF wanted to move Aboriginals to settlements to make them into modern, assimilated socialists, its tolerance of, and collusion in, creating two societies worked against achieving this goal.

Nucleation to settlements brought some consequences not anticipated by the CCF. One of the most profound and unexpected changes, rapid growth in the Aboriginal population, soon overwhelmed politicians and bureaucrats and made already tenuous CCF plans even less likely to succeed. Population growth within the Aboriginal community occurred at least partly due to CCF interventions, including the CCF nucleation projects. The unpredicted expansion of the Aboriginal population added a new and overwhelming dimension to northern problems.

The dramatic rise in population occurred both among whites and Aboriginals. The number of persons in the north more than doubled under the CCF, from roughly 8,500 in 1944 to about 18,000 in 1964. During the same period, in contrast, the province's southern population changed little in size. The northern population increase came from two primary sources: a high rate of natural increase among Aboriginals and the influx of white people to the area. By 1958 the northern population of about 16,500 included 4,400 Status Indians, 4,600 Metis, and 7,500 whites, located in seven areas. Athabasca Region had the largest population, with about 4,500 residents, while only 50 persons lived in the Cree Lake area. The other areas fell somewhere in-between.[92] Most white people who came north worked in mining or related industries or for government, and since they paid taxes and did not depend on welfare, they did not worry the CCF. The largest number of non-Aboriginals concentrated in the Uranium City area, where the population rose from 250 in 1946 to about 4,500 by 1959. Similarly, the Creighton mining area grew from 129 in 1921 to 2,576 in 1961. Power generation at Island Falls added several hundred more white people to the north. In contrast to the gainful employment of white people, most Aboriginals did not hold steady jobs. The large increase in the numbers of Aboriginals who lacked adequate means of support distressed the CCF.

Infant mortality fell from an average of 109 per 1,000 in the 1952-56 period to 62 per 1,000 in the 1957-61 period. Since the Indian infant death rate still stood at about four times that for non-Indians, population growth could accelerate more as infant mortality fell further. The rate of natural increase in the north rose from 24.6 per 1,000 population in 1952 to 38.3 per 1,000 in 1961, more than double the rate in the south. Northern Saskatchewan's birth rate of 46 per 1,000 population in 1961 stood only a little behind that of Guatemala, which at 49 per 1,000 had the highest rate shown in a United Nations survey. West-side communities experienced a 52.5 percent increase in the Indian and Metis population from 1951 to 1961, or an average annual increase of 5.3 percent. This raised the Aboriginal population there from 2,433 to 3,694. Growth accelerated further, with the highest rates of natural increase occurring from 1959 to 1965.[93]

Although the CCF worried about the increase in the Aboriginal population, the government contributed to the population expansion with its nucleation and other policies. Population growth resulted from the decreased infant mortality and increased life expectancy made possible by the improved health services Aboriginals received in villages. Additionally, family allowance and welfare payments acted as incentives to have children, helping ensure that the pre-existing high birth rate would not fall, even when more infants survived childhood. Cheques increased with family size, and even small payments became important as the CCF shifted the society to a cash basis.[94] The Catholic church, the principal northern church, also likely added to the population increase by prohibiting birth control. Government and medical practitioners, although alarmed about the high birth rate, did not aggressively push birth control until long after the CCF left office. A relative lack of stigma among Aboriginals about illegitimacy also possibly added to population growth. Many unmarried women gave birth. The CCF saw a crisis in illegitimacy, and its Northern Advisory Committee spoke of "twisted domestic relationships," "drinking, loose-living and gambling," and of men fathering children by several women. In one year, eleven unmarried "girls," aged fourteen to twenty-five, expected children in one settlement. Indian births in 1958 included 27.4 percent classed as illegitimate, compared to 3.1 percent for the rest of the population.[95]

Population growth greatly contributed to the worsening economic situation in the communities to which the CCF moved Aboriginals. Pete Tompkins, a DNR employee, wrote: "The Neetows are breeding like mink and the population is mounting by leaps and bounds and as a result the fishing trapping etc are over crowded ... no one seems to know the remedy."[96] Along with the CCF failure to help Aboriginals move into new occupations, the population increase pushed northerners into welfare dependency. Some in government came to fear the growing population. G. Kinneard of Public Health, for example, saw the growing Aboriginal population as a "serious threat to peace."[97]

For two decades the CCF aggressively worked to shift Aboriginals from nomadic lives in the bush to residence in villages. Only in the confined space of settlements could government effectively modernize and assimilate Aboriginals and teach them the principles of socialism. Its pursuit of these goals did not allow the CCF to tolerate Aboriginals continuing to live unregulated lives on the land. The CCF added new settlements and expanded existing ones to house the formerly mobile population. A gradual but forceful introduction to the responsibilities of the Euro-Canadian lifestyle followed.

The CCF aimed for complete assimilation of northern Aboriginals. It wanted to eliminate distinctions within the Aboriginal group and between Aboriginals and whites. Yet even though Aboriginals moved to settlements, discrimination and racism grew, adding to the existence of a society deeply split by race and class. This rift worked against assimilation. An explosion of the northern Aboriginal population also contributed to the failure of CCF plans for assimilating Aboriginals. Instead of becoming fewer and less distinct, Aboriginals grew in number and increasingly became a separate force. Contrary to CCF hopes, northern Aboriginals would not become modern, assimilated socialists in one generation.

While vital to CCF plans, nucleation formed only one part of the new government's strategy to bring modernization, assimilation, and socialism to the north. In order to reach these goals, the north also needed a new and adequate infrastructure. Since it served as both the local and provincial government, the CCF held responsibility for providing much of this. Exploring the CCF record in the provision of northern infrastructure can help understand the CCF and its plans and actions.

4
A Deterrent to Development

CCF plans for the north made providing a modern infrastructure system urgent and imperative. Without this, the CCF could not adequately apply its policies; modernization, assimilation, and socialization would not take place; and northern wealth would remain beyond the reach of government and industry. The movement of Aboriginals to settlements and the growing northern population added further demands for services. Since it held responsibility for local, regional, and provincial governance in the north, most responsibility for providing northern infrastructure fell to the CCF. The party also discouraged private investment in industry and infrastructure, preferring to have government develop the north. Yet while wanting to remake the north, the CCF ironically refused to devote the necessary resources for this to succeed. As a result, the northern infrastructure remained extremely inadequate when the CCF left office after twenty years. Inevitably, then, a lack of government spending contributed to underdevelopment, poverty, and the failure to realize the potential of the north and its people. Shortcomings in infrastructure affected practically all aspects of northern existence, making the lives of most northern residents, with the exception of those in several white communities, unnecessarily difficult.

Its socialist orientation influenced the CCF's approach to building northern infrastructure. Because of ideological opposition to private industry, the CCF often refused to provide the support facilities needed for large-scale, high-quality development in tourism, forestry, and mining. Industry also did not trust the CCF, preferring to operate in more favourable political climates. Exceptions included the federally promoted uranium development in the Lake Athabasca area, where a number of private companies thrived along with the federal Crown corporation, Eldorado. In most areas of the north, though, private enterprise could not afford to operate because of the lack of infrastructure.

The CCF colonial system also affected northern infrastructure development. While politicians and bureaucrats claimed to have the interests of Aboriginals at heart, they refused to spend the money necessary to allow them to live in decent conditions. The decision to entrust DNR with most infrastructure development helped create a colonial situation and limited development. DNR received only meagre resources to work with – not nearly enough to provide necessary roads, water and sewer systems, electricity, communications methods, community buildings, and other facilities.

Northern Saskatchewan presented a picture of underdevelopment in 1944. Northern communication links traditionally followed the watercourses. Since no all-season roads penetrated the region, the water routes remained important. Four main water trade routes existed. One from Black Lake to Fort McMurray, Alberta, traversed Lake Athabasca and the rivers at each end. Another ran from Lac la Loche to Green Lake via Buffalo Narrows, Beauval, and the Beaver River. A third route allowed travel from Stanley Mission to Lac la Ronge and then to Montreal Lake. Finally, a fourth led from Reindeer Lake to the Churchill, then down the Sturgeon Weir to the Saskatchewan and on to The Pas, Manitoba. All four routes connected to road or rail systems, although two did so outside the province. As a result, many northerners dealt more with centres in Manitoba and Alberta than with those in southern Saskatchewan. People also used the water bodies as winter highways, when their frozen surfaces carried dog teams and sleds and much heavier Caterpillar tractor trains laden with goods.

Unlike neighbouring provinces, northern Saskatchewan had no railroads in 1944. Without rail transportation, economical extraction of ores and forest resources could not take place. While airplanes had already revolutionized some aspects of northern transport, air transportation suffered from serious limitations. Most residents and industry could not afford to use planes as a substitute for roads and railways. Air travel did help government administer the north and proved invaluable in cases of medical emergency. A limited telegraph system operated on the west side prior to 1944, but most areas had no access to telegraph, radio, or telephone communication. Many northerners had never seen an electric light. While southerners expected and received access to the provincial electrical grid, power lines did not reach the north. For drinking water, northerners still relied on water scooped from lakes and rivers. This water supply proved satisfactory prior to nucleation in settlements and accompanying pollution of shoreline areas. Also in the pre-settlement days, northerners did not need sewage or garbage disposal facilities. But by the 1940s these still did not exist in most areas, even where villages developed. The justice system remained rudimentary in 1944. Representatives of southern justice usually flew in from outside when situations became urgent. Further, northern communities had no form of representative or responsible local government. It is not surprising then that the CCF saw much room for improvement of the northern infrastructure when it took power. In order to modernize the north and create a viable economy there, the new government planned to devote large amounts of resources to building a new infrastructure to move people, goods, and information within and to and from the region.

In its first years in office it appeared that the CCF would rapidly open up the north to extract minerals and timber. J.T. Douglas, the first CCF minister of Highways, wanted to build roads to La Ronge, Île-à-la-Crosse, and Flin Flon. In 1947 the CCF claimed to be developing a "long-range plan" to provide access to all northern areas with development potential.[1] Yet confronted with high costs, CCF interest in northern resource development soon waned. Government then contented itself with easy royalty pickings from several profitable mining areas that relied on Manitoba and Alberta infrastructure. Soon building northern roads held little priority for the CCF. When J.T. Douglas retired in 1960, road construction remained largely stalled. Not a single road crossed the Churchill River, and many resource-rich northern areas had no road within hundreds of miles. Ironically, while the CCF refused to build the necessary northern road system, Saskatchewan constructed more miles of roads in the south than did any other province.

Northern Saskatchewan missed out on much development by not having a more extensive road system. Some, including DNR deputy minister J.W. Churchman, failed to recognize the importance of road access for mining exploration. Unambitiously, he seemed content to rely on water, rail, and air connections to Manitoba and Alberta.[2] Not all in government shared Churchman's attitude. Although he lacked the power to do much about the situation, Northern Administrator C.S. Brown in 1956 described inaccessibility as "a major and obvious deterrent to resource utilization and industrial development in northern Saskatchewan."[3] Economic development of ore bodies and of forestry resources required access, and most areas did not have the option of dealing with the road and rail systems found in adjoining provinces. Mining exploration and logging made little sense hundreds of miles from roads, since most companies could not afford to build the needed access.

Under the CCF, benefits from the two main northern mining developments flowed out of the province. The lack of a road to the Lake Athabasca area meant that supplies for Uranium City came primarily from Alberta, carried by barge from Waterways, Alberta. While Saskatchewan Government Airways provided scheduled air service from Prince Albert to Stony Rapids and Uranium City, Uranium City's main air link joined it to Edmonton. Pacific Western flights carried uranium, supplies, workers, and money. Stony Rapids, a regional government centre, and other communities in the Athabasca area also obtained most of their supplies from Alberta.

In a similar situation on the east side, the Creighton area, located just across the border from Flin Flon and its mine, relied on close ties to Manitoba. Benefits from the mine flowed to Manitoba, even though, for a time, nearly 90 percent of the ore processed came from Saskatchewan. Electricity to drive the mill also came from Saskatchewan, from Island Falls on the Churchill River.[4] Only Manitoba provided road and rail access to the area, ensuring that most supplies came from Manitoba.

People in other areas of Saskatchewan's north also relied on Alberta or Manitoba. Lacking access to southern Saskatchewan, residents of La Loche walked to the railhead at Waterways, Alberta. Manitoba's roads and railways carried Reindeer Lake, Beaver Lake, and Cumberland House fish to market. Residents from numerous communities travelled to Flin Flon or The Pas, Manitoba, for secondary education, shopping, medical care, and entertainment.

The CCF did build some northern roads. Its greatest early road-building achievement was the completion of the road to La Ronge, which formerly was accessible only by winter road. The Liberal government had began the road before the Second World War, and the army helped by building the first bridge over the Montreal River at La Ronge in 1944-45 as a training exercise. With the completion of the road in 1947, La Ronge became the first major northern community to have an all-weather road. Yet it still could take about eleven hours to cover the 185 rough miles to Prince Albert. Washouts frequently stopped travel in the spring. A winter road along the east side of Bittern Lake to Montreal Lake opened in 1947-48, shortening the distance from Prince Albert to La Ronge, but the CCF never developed this route into an all-weather road. The indirect route through Waskesiu remained the only reliable route to La Ronge during the CCF era.[5]

It soon became apparent that the CCF would only reluctantly and frugally spend money on northern roads. Saskatchewan tried repeatedly to secure federal funding for roads – or, preferably, have Ottawa assume complete responsibility for road-building projects. In 1952, for example, J.H. Brockelbank approached Ottawa for help with two roads. A proposed highway from Beauval to La Loche would serve over 2,600 people and open up fishing, lumber production, tourism, and mining exploration. Another suggested road north of La Ronge would initially reach Nemeiben Lake and eventually access the mineral and pulp potential of the Churchill Valley. Brockelbank also thought roads would help the government assimilate Aboriginals. After Ottawa denied the request because it considered the resources unproven, the CCF gave the projects little priority, working only slowly on the roads.[6]

While the CCF spoke of modernizing and developing the north, its actions contradicted its words. Frustration and failure usually resulted when northerners petitioned Regina to build roads. Buffalo Narrows residents approached the CCF in 1951 for the extension of Highway 4 from Île-à-la-Crosse to Buffalo Narrows. Winter travel over unsafe ice, which resulted in lost lives, gave urgency to the request. J.H. Brockelbank wrote in response: "We must remember that there are limits to the amount of money that can be spent for roads." Overlooking the large royalties government collected, he claimed they did not collect much tax revenue in the north and held out little hope for quick construction. Work finally began on the road in 1954-55, and with impatient ratepayers pushing, completion of the 167-mile-long road from Meadow Lake took place in 1956. Yet construction did not include bridges over the Beaver River or across Keizies Channel near Buffalo Narrows. A new bridge across the Beaver River ended ferry service there in 1962, but the CCF refused to spend the money to build a bridge across the dangerous Keizies Channel.[7]

The CCF also proved unresponsive to the needs of the rapidly growing Dene population at La Loche. While residents there petitioned for a road as early as 1950, J.W. Churchman considered this "entirely out of the question." He also questioned the validity of the petition, since all signatures appeared in the same handwriting. Someone likely signed for those who did not know how to sign their name, a common practice at the time. Faced with CCF inaction, local people took the initiative and began building a road to Buffalo Narrows. They quit after clearing several miles, overwhelmed by the size of the task of building a road by hand. C.S. Brown, DNR's northern administrator, repeatedly tried to obtain money to "grub stake" the local crew, but his superiors refused to help. The CCF eventually built a winter road by 1960, which helped reduce the cost of goods in the northern community. The all-weather road remained unfinished when the CCF left office in 1964.[8]

Faced with a lack of CCF interest in opening up the north, northern people tried to build a road to Lake Athabasca. The absence of a road forced the far north to deal mainly with Alberta and also handicapped development in a large area south of Lake Athabasca. J.F. Midgett, a fish trucker, built a trail to the Clearwater River by 1954.[9] A private company then used Dene workers to help blaze a route farther north. Their winter road to Uranium City first saw use in 1955, but it proved disappointing since it could operate only for a short time in the winter. In 1957 the Buffalo Narrows Ratepayers' Association asked the CCF to study building an all-weather road to Uranium City for community, tourism, and resource access.[10] But the CCF refused to build a west-side road to the far north.

Appeals from industry to open up the north also had little effect on the CCF. In 1957, at a conference on northern development sponsored by the Saskatchewan Chamber of Commerce, speaker after speaker lamented the lack of access to northern Saskatchewan. Alvin Hamilton, the new federal Conservative minister of Northern Affairs and Natural Resources, told the conference that he thought development of resources should come first. He disagreed with the emphasis of the CCF, which he thought preferred to spend money on welfare programs and other services.[11]

Refusing to support the local efforts to build a west-side road to Lake Athabasca, the CCF proposed a more expensive new route to Uranium City. The road would pass near Foster Lake and Cree Lake before crossing the Fond du Lac River near Stony Rapids. It would then follow the north shore of Lake Athabasca to Uranium City. Although this route encountered more difficult and costly road-building conditions, the CCF preferred it over the west-side route because it would not dead-end at the south shore of Lake Athabasca. It could also open access to minerals, pulp, fur, fish, and game in a large area.[12] Although the CCF recognized the importance of this road, it refused to pay for it. As a result, only about 25 of the 505 miles from La Ronge to Uranium City were constructed by 1959. Completion of the road looked doubtful by 1960 due to its high estimated cost of $21,850,000. The 140-mile section from Stony Rapids to Uranium City alone would cost an estimated $6,720,000.

However, Ottawa's Roads to Resources program brought new hope for construction of the road. The program, which also applied to other provinces, formed part of Ottawa's renewed interest in northern development under the Diefenbaker government. DNR minister Kuziak took credit for the program, claiming he suggested it to Ottawa. Saskatchewan's agreement with Ottawa had a maximum value of $15 million, with each party providing half of this.

Optimism that the middle and far north would finally have a road link to the south did not last long. Bickering ensued between the province and the federal government when Ottawa counted the value of the Diefenbaker Bridge over the North Saskatchewan River at Prince Albert as part of the Roads to Resources Agreement. This removed up to $2.5 million, and other road projects also used money from the agreement. It seemed that about four hundred miles of the Uranium City road would remain unbuilt. Demonstrating its lack of commitment to northern development, the CCF refused to complete the road unless Ottawa increased its contribution over that already agreed to. The CCF blamed Ottawa. Kuziak fumed: "The Federal Government talked much about their Vision in 1957 and 1958, but now this has faded out."[13] Yet the CCF also refused to commit more money.

With neither government willing to spend the required cash, the CCF wanted to move the route farther east because the agreement seemed to have enough money left to reach Southend, Reindeer Lake. The province thought a road to Southend was preferable to having the road end somewhere short of Cree Lake, going nowhere. While Ottawa at first agreed to the change of route, it then reversed its stand, fearing delay of the road to Uranium City.[14] Saskatchewan distrusted Ottawa's vague suggestion that the needed money would appear, and the Saskatchewan cabinet authorized changing the route. Construction began. By March 1962 the road to Uranium City cost $2,133,000, including the $313,000 bridge over the Churchill. It would cost another $3 million just to reach Southend, about eighty miles away.[15] In all the confusion, the CCF lost sight of its initial goal: to build a road to Lake Athabasca. The rocky and wet route followed north of La Ronge demanded higher road-building expenditures than did the gentler terrain north of La Loche. In the end, the CCF refused to build either road to the far north.

The decision to build the road to Southend also made the CCF's recent development of a community and filleting plant at Kinoosao on the other side of Reindeer Lake look short-sighted. The CCF located Kinoosao there because of its proximity to the railhead at Lynn Lake, Manitoba. Instead of spending money building roads at home, the CCF paid much of the cost of building and maintaining the sixty-mile road to Lynn Lake, fifty-eight miles of which fell within Manitoba.[16]

Delays in building the vital Hanson Lake Road to the Creighton area also demonstrated the province's lack of commitment to northern development. As part of its initial burst of enthusiasm for northern development, the CCF began to build this road soon after assuming office. The province also turned to the federal government for help. But since Ottawa refused to participate, work stalled by 1948, even though only 100 of the road's 230 miles remained unbuilt. Little happened until 1958, when Ottawa included the road in the Roads to Resources Agreement. Finally the Hanson Lake Road opened in 1962, providing access to Creighton, Flin Flon, Deschambault, and Pelican Narrows and facilitating tourism, forestry, and mining. Yet the long construction delay had limited development in a large area for most of the CCF era.[17]

Residents of a number of east-side communities desperately wanted road access to the outside. The CCF seemed not to care. Lacking a road to a larger community in Saskatchewan, Cumberland House residents dealt with The Pas, Manitoba, ninety miles away by water or forty-five miles by winter road. Various initiatives over the years teased residents with promises of a road. In 1952-53, H.R. Knutson wanted $600 to build a Caterpillar road that would connect with a Manitoba road twenty-five miles away. DNR minister Brockelbank seemed to like the idea, but thought Knutson might cut his price. Nothing happened. The federal Prairie Farm Rehabilitation Administration (PFRA), which explored agricultural potential in the area, bulldozed a winter road east towards The Pas in 1953-54 and also worked on a road to the west to the Sipanok Channel. A winter road resulted, making limited travel possible between Nipawin, Cumberland House, and The Pas. Pressure for a proper road increased in the winter of 1954 when the Carrot River-The Pas Agricultural Development Route Association organized a cavalcade and travelled the winter road.

The winter road already helped shift trade patterns from The Pas to Nipawin and Prince Albert. Faced with rising pressure from local residents, by 1962 the CCF finally selected a tentative route for an all-weather road, estimated to cost from $675,000 to $1,120,000. Yet this did not include a bridge over the dangerous Saskatchewan River at Cumberland House. Crossing the river in winter became increasingly hazardous after the CCF built the Squaw Rapids dam, since water releases created unsafe ice conditions. One woman drowned when a vehicle broke through the ice; an RCMP Bombardier and a DNR bulldozer fell through; and large trucks could not cross the river. At the time of the CCF defeat in 1964, the CCF had not even finished building the dirt road. A bridge remained an impossible dream given the lack of CCF spending in the north.[18]

The Cree, Metis, and white residents of Sandy Bay and Island Falls also yearned for a road link to the outside. The most practical route led south to Pelican Narrows and then on to the Hanson Lake Road. Although work began on a location survey by 1961, the road held a low priority for the CCF. In 1964 the Island Falls-Sandy Bay Road Association, whose letterhead read "Open the North with Roads," pushed the CCF and Ottawa to build the road. They feared the Roads to Resources fund would not have enough for their road. On the other hand, the Saskatchewan Chamber of Mines exerted pressure not to divert attention or money from completing the road to Reindeer Lake. These communities did not receive a road under the CCF.[19]

Initially only three road projects – Hanson Lake (Smeaton to Flin Flon), La Ronge to Uranium City, and Otosquean (Hudson Bay to The Pas) – fell under the Roads to Resources Agreement. Additions to the agreement, without adding any new money, included the Diefenbaker Bridge, the road from Squaw Rapids to Cumberland House, and the Island Falls access from the Hanson Lake Road. To the end of 1963, expenditures under the program reached about $10,672,700.[20] The program never did include enough money to build all these roads, and neither the CCF nor Ottawa provided the needed money.

The CCF proved miserly in building access roads from main roads as well, looking to others for help. In 1961 it appeared Ausland's Mink Ranch would pay half the cost of a road to Deep River from the Buffalo Narrows Road.[21] The same year, Indian Affairs agreed to share the cost of a road and bridge across the Beaver River to improve access to the Beauval Indian Residential School.[22] The CCF sometimes produced impressive statistics about the miles of roads it built. For example, DNR built about 2,500 miles of access and fire roads in a ten-year period to 1957.[23] Unfortunately, many of these were nothing more than rough trails.

While the CCF built few roads to the outside, it also refused to devote much money for local mine access roads, even in the economically active Lake Athabasca area. Saskatchewan generally only offered to pay up to one-third of the cost of these roads. The province, Ottawa, and Nisto Mines shared the cost of building the first mining road in 1950. Ottawa, Saskatchewan, and the mines also split the approximately $150,000 cost of building a fifteen-mile access from Black Bay to Eldorado and other mines. Yet Gunnar Mine remained isolated in 1960 for lack of a nine-mile road. Ottawa insisted the mine pay a third of the cost. The mine refused, and Saskatchewan would not pay the entire cost.[24]

DNR received the responsibility for building most northern roads. Motivation for using government crews came from a desire to save money and also from the CCF preference for public over private enterprise. An ongoing dispute with Ottawa resulted, with the federal government pushing Saskatchewan to tender northern road construction to private companies.[25] Saskatchewan sometimes relented. Cabinet also decided in February 1964 that the Department of Highways should take over responsibility for all northern roads, which meant a diminished responsibility for DNR.[26]

Although northerners often asked for roads, their construction also met opposition since roads proved a mixed blessing. Some traders thought roads would bring competition and loss of business, and churches feared roads would carry in more whites, drinking, and trouble.[27] The CCF did not share this desire to protect traders and Aboriginals from outside forces. In fact, the CCF wanted to put private traders out of business and assimilate Aboriginals. The greatest reason for the continuing lack of road access to most areas of the north was the CCF refusal to spend the required money.

At the end of the CCF era in 1964, no road extended to the far north. Most communities lacked ground access, and resource development often faltered for want of roads. The CCF's road policy contradicted its stated commitment to developing and diversifying the northern economy. Instead, governmental penny-pinching ensured that northern underdevelopment would continue.

Most Aboriginal northerners, even those who lived in communities with road access, did not own a motor vehicle. They relied heavily on public transportation. The new CCF government acted quickly to meet the transportation needs of some northerners by providing bus transportation and freight service through its Crown corporation Saskatchewan Transportation Company (STC). Government vehicles carried freight to and from La Ronge by 1947, and bus passenger service began by 1948. Service increased from once a week to four times weekly by 1953.[28] But STC services remained limited in the north, mainly due to the lack of roads and a loss of interest by the CCF. Lacking alternatives, many northerners depended on taxis for trips within communities and to travel longer distances. Some even took taxis to their traplines. Seeing unregulated business, the CCF introduced regulations to govern taxis at Uranium City in 1952.[29]

Along with its failure to build badly needed roads, the CCF built no rail-roads in the north. This deficiency greatly limited mining and forestry development since these industries often needed railways for economical operation. Industry repeatedly asked for railways. While the CPR and CNR showed some interest in building rail lines, the CCF did not offer help. T.C. Douglas, unlike John A. Macdonald, did not give railways money to open new frontiers. A proposed pulp mill in 1957 called for extension of the CNR line north from Paddockwood. The project did not proceed. In 1958 the CCF cabinet, not willing to spend the money itself, considered asking the federal government to build a railway to Uranium City and on to Great Slave Lake.[30] But railway construction never went beyond the talking stage. Lines in northern Manitoba and Alberta continued to take business from Saskatchewan, as transportation patterns still ran east and west out of Saskatchewan's north.

With few alternatives present, the traditional water routes continued to carry people and goods in vessels of various types, from canoes to barges. In an early burst of enthusiasm, DNR bought a used barge from the War Assets Corporation and began to move supplies and equipment between Cumberland House and The Pas in 1947. The service did not last long. The barge again saw use in 1951, but by 1954 it sat unused, stuck in a mud bank.[31] As in other things, CCF interest in improving water transportation had waned as the years passed. Booth Fisheries of The Pas proved more reliable. It provided service to Cumberland House, hauling freight, mail, and passengers to and from The Pas, by water in summer and by Bom-bardier in winter.[32] On the west side, DNR provided scheduled barge ser-vice between Beauval, Fort Black, Île-à-la-Crosse, and Buffalo Narrows, and nonscheduled service to Dillon, Patuanak, and Clear Lake by 1949.[33]

On a much larger scale, Northern Transportation Services, a federal Crown corporation, used barges to carry goods from the railhead at Water-ways, Alberta, along the Athabasca River and across Lake Athabasca to Uranium City, Camsell Portage, Fond du Lac, and Stony Rapids. Freight volume grew as uranium mining increased. In 1955, for example, the corporation transported 470,000 gallons of gasoline to Imperial Oil in Uranium City. The federal Department of Transport placed markers, buoys, and lights as navigation aids, and the federal Department of Public Works dredged the river channel to maintain sufficient water depth for the barges. The large lake often proved hazardous, as when eight men died in a tugboat sinking in 1956, and barges could not compensate for the lack of road or rail access, since the long winter severely limited the shipping season. In one demonstration of the difficulties involved, a boat towing eight barges loaded with material for Gunnar and Eldorado froze into the ice in 1956.[34] Lac la Ronge also saw much water transportation, although on a smaller scale. In 1957, for example, about 150 commercial boats and two barges operated there, dodging the lake's many hidden reefs. Because of a lack of roads, vessels carried materials and supplies to mineral exploration sites on the Churchill.[35]

Water transportation cost the CCF virtually nothing, other than the expense of some docks and a few barges. Not wanting to spend money on improving water transportation, the CCF pressed Ottawa to assume many of the costs involved. To ask the federal government to help with this made some sense since Ottawa had a limited responsibility for inland waterways. But in many cases it remained unclear whether the federal government or the province had responsibility for northern docks and wharfs. Bickering and delays resulted. In one case, only after Ottawa refused to help did the CCF resign itself to building a new dock at the Snake Lake filleting plant.[36] The province also delayed building wharves at Île-à-la-Crosse and La Ronge, hoping that the federal government would provide the facilities. In the meantime, safety was compromised and local impatience grew.[37] Experience taught Saskatchewan that Ottawa would more likely refuse to build a wharf if the province chose the site. In order to avoid refusal at Kinoosao, the CCF let Ottawa pick the exact spot for the filleting plant. The strategy worked, and the federal Department of Public Works built a wharf.[38] Ottawa also built wharves at Buffalo Narrows, Stony Rapids, and Dore Lake, while Saskatchewan built those at La Ronge, Snake Lake, Wollaston Lake, and Beaver Lake by 1955.[39] Both governments continued to pass responsibility back and forth, with neither wanting to spend money. Although water transportation provided a cheap alternative to building roads and railways, CCF spending on this remained paltry.

Transportation by aircraft also provided a cheaper alternative for the CCF. Establishing and operating an air service cost far less than constructing and maintaining an adequate road or rail network. The CCF's total investment in planes and airstrips would not have built one major northern road. Unfortunately, air travel had many limitations. Airplanes did not meet many of the everyday transportation needs of northern residents, who could not afford to hire a plane every time they needed or wanted to go somewhere. For its part, industry could not feasibly pay high air transport rates to move most mineral and forest products. Consequently, the growing use of aircraft did not end northern underdevelopment.

Aircraft quickly became indispensable for the CCF, which lacked other means of transportation. The government immediately recognized that it could not monitor, control, and administer its northern colony without planes. Shortly after the 1944 election victory, Joe Phelps toured the north by airplane, something he could not have done otherwise. At first the CCF relied on DNR to meet its air transportation needs. Quickly expanding its fleet, DNR had ten planes by 1947, mainly Second World War craft bought from the Dominion War Assets Corporation. Floyd Glass, the northern superintendent, also piloted planes and headed the Aircraft Division, which had its offices, hangar, and repair facilities at Prince Albert. DNR planes carried civil servants from various departments, provided medical transportation, flew Fish Board fish, and helped with fire protection. Pilots also worked as DNR field officers. A new Crown corporation, Saskatchewan Government Airways (SGA), took over responsibility for air service from DNR in 1947. This company provided an expanded commercial air service in the northern air space. The CCF eliminated much competition by buying M & C Aviation Co. of Prince Albert and its subsidiary, Aircraft Skiis Ltd.[40]

By 1954 SGA had eleven pilots and about twenty aircraft, which flew charters and provided scheduled service on five routes. SGA operated from bases at Prince Albert, La Ronge, Uranium City, Beaver Lake, and Stony Rapids. A modest expansion and updating of the SGA fleet and services continued, and by the end of 1958 the investment in SGA totalled $675,000. The company had earned a surplus of $175,000. The province changed SGA's name to Saskair in 1962. By 1964 it flew on four routes, which terminated at Uranium City, Buffalo Narrows, Beaver Lake, and Wollaston Lake.[41]

Claiming it could provide better service if it operated a monopoly, the CCF opposed private aircraft companies flying in northern Saskatchewan. Initially the federal Air Transport Board and Ottawa seemed to support the monopoly. However, over SGA's objections, the board approved an application by Waite Fisheries to operate a commercial air service on the west side in 1949. SGA also opposed a charter licence for Athabasca Airways, which Floyd Glass and Russell Karels applied for. The pair claimed SGA did not provide adequate service. Glass, SGA's former head, considered it "time that people realized that the monopolistic government enterprises were not healthy for the development of the province." Athabasca Airways began operating in 1955, and La Ronge Aviation Services started in 1960. SGA also lost its battle to eliminate competition when PWA received the route from Prince Albert to Saskatoon and Regina. With Ottawa's refusal to support the SGA monopoly, options for northern flying expanded. By the late 1950s PWA operated scheduled flights to Uranium City, five or six companies provided charter services, and some mining companies operated their own airplanes. Ottawa had frustrated CCF plans for a state-owned air monopoly in the north.[42]

Most northern planes landed on water or ice, using floats or skis, but larger planes and some small planes landed on wheels using airstrips. Unless a community had a landing strip, planes could not land during the spring or fall due to thin ice on the rivers and lakes. DNR built many northern strips. An inexpensive gravel surface runway opened at La Ronge in 1947. The province also provided landing facilities at Stony Rapids, Snake Lake, Cumberland House, Île-à-la-Crosse, Buffalo Narrows, La Loche, and Cree Lake. Private interests built other airstrips, and Ottawa built one at Beaverlodge. Not all isolated communities received landing strips under the CCF. These found themselves cut off from the outside during freeze-up and breakup.[43]

The new government recognized the importance of providing a system of rapid voice communication in the north. This seemed essential for various reasons, including the CCF's need to efficiently administer its colony. Given the state of technology in the 1940s, two-way radio seemed the most practical choice for improving northern communication. The CCF took the initiative by giving DNR responsibility for expanding the pre-existing system of about sixty radios. After briefly operating its first base station at Emma Lake, DNR moved the station to Prince Albert. The system grew considerably, with airplanes, Bombardiers, and government vehicles receiving radios. DNR operated a monopoly, allowing the public to send radiograms, for a fee, and renting radios to private interests. In 1955 DNR experimented with new lightweight walkie-talkies, which weighed only a little more than twelve pounds. By 1958 DNR used permanent operators at eight key stations: La Ronge, Foster Lake, Stony Rapids, Uranium City, Buffalo Narrows, Meadow Lake, Prince Albert, and Hudson Bay. DNR officers' wives often operated the radios in remote settlements. These women normally received five dollars per month for this work in 1955, which was seen by many as a ridiculously small amount. The radio service proved controversial and inadequate. Shortcomings included frequent breakdowns, a lack of privacy for personal and medical matters, and a lack of full-time emergency service. In addition, white people controlled communications, since a shortage of radios and high rental rates prevented most Aboriginals from having a radio.[44] The service became indispensable, but the CCF devoted only small resources to it and did not keep up with technological advances. As a result of this neglect, the north lacked a modern communication system in 1964, which added to the syndrome of underdevelopment.

Most Saskatchewan residents took telephones for granted during the CCF era. Saskatchewan Government Telephones (SGT), a Crown corporation, received a monopoly over telephone service in the south beginning in 1947 and quickly upgraded the telephone system there. In contrast, telephones continued to be absent in most northern communities. In a typical response, the CCF ignored La Ronge residents who demanded telephone service in the early 1950s. Even Manitoba showed more interest in providing telephone service in northern Saskatchewan than did the CCF. Manitoba Telephone Company offered to link Flin Flon and Denare Beach in 1955. Although a modern connection to the outside world remained a dream, La Ronge, Uranium City, and Buffalo Narrows eventually received local telephone service by the early 1960s. DNR also set up limited local service in some other communities using obsolete telephones from southern rural systems.[45] Most northern communities, including fairly large communities like Cumberland House and La Loche, still did not have even local telephone service in 1964. Although it held a provincial monopoly on telephone service, the CCF failed to spend the money needed to build a northern telephone system.

The CCF also refused to provide electrical service to most northerners, even though it created and enforced a monopoly over power distribution in the province. Saskatchewan Power Corporation (SPC) began operating in 1929, but remained small until the election of the CCF. Joe Phelps oversaw the early modernization of the power system in the south and the building of a power grid there, and by the mid-1950s southern Saskatchewan enjoyed a modern power system.[46] Yet Phelps, with responsibility for both SPC and the north, did not bring the two together. Power lines still did not reach most northern communities in 1964, and most Aboriginals did not have access to electricity. The lack of an adequate northern electrical generation and distribution system greatly hampered development within communities and for industry.

Although few northerners used electricity in 1944, government, mining, business, and non-Aboriginals soon considered it essential. The hum of gas- or diesel-powered generators producing electricity for government operations and white residents formed part of the colonial scene in northern communities. Bright light shone from the windows of government houses, while Aboriginal homes gave off the flicker of candles, gas lanterns, or wood-burning stoves. The CCF considered it necessary that its employees have electricity. DNR sent a generating plant to Buffalo Narrows in 1954, hoping to calm the wife of the DNR officer, who had become "extremely nervous and neurotic" after a neighbour who supplied electricity moved away.[47] Each government department, including DNR, Education, and Health, often had its own plant. The four outpost hospitals received "full-time electric power" by 1958.[48]

Several communities received more advanced electrical supplies, although only after long delays. Denare Beach residents petitioned government for electricity in 1953, but did not obtain this until about 1958, when they received a link to the Island Falls dam.[49] SPC procrastinated in supplying power to La Ronge, even though cabinet in 1951 recommended SPC investigate providing electricity to the rapidly growing centre. SPC and DNR eventually helped set up a diesel generating plant at the local fish-processing plant and a small distribution network for limited community use. Yet the province refused to operate the generators. Instead a local man, Carl Louis, leased and operated the system. In 1956, when La Ronge became a village, DNR turned over the distribution system to the village. SPC finally took increased responsibility in 1958, when it bought the assets.[50] At Buffalo Narrows in 1955, the annual ratepayers' association meeting passed a resolution asking for a generation unit. In an uncharacteristically quick response, SPC installed power lines and street lights in 1956. Waite Fisheries generated and sold the electricity for the system.[51]

Buffalo Narrows finally received a power line from the outside in the early 1960s.

Rather than take responsibility for providing electricity in most northern communities, the CCF encouraged the formation of power cooperatives. Yet the province endangered the cooperatives' success by offering inadequate support. After SPC built the diesel-powered generating and distribution system at Stony Rapids, government expected the twelve-member co-op to survive with minimal help. In 1957 the membership could not pay for about eight thousand gallons of fuel that it needed to order and have delivered by barge before freeze-up. Still struggling, the cooperative had a deficit of $2,455.93 for 1960, which almost doubled by the end of September 1961.[52] Cumberland House also experienced problems with its cooperative generation system. The DNR officer in 1964 described the three generators as "a pile of junk." Only one would operate, while the co-op lacked the funds to rent a new generator from SPC.[53] In 1961 the cooperative at Sandy Bay obtained its power from the Island Falls generating dam, but the agreement gave it only up to 50 kVA of power. Most residents used little power.[54] Power co-ops also supplied energy to some homes at Île-à-la-Crosse, Denare Beach, and Pelican Narrows in the late 1950s. Many of the poorer people still lacked access to electricity, even where the co-ops operated.

Exceptions to the lack or shortage of electrical power in northern settlements existed in the predominantly white communities. Industry and residents there found ways to obtain electricity, which they considered an essential service. Uranium City received electricity from hydroelectric dam projects at nearby Wellington Lake and Waterloo Power Stations and from diesel generation.[55] Creighton received modern power lines from the Northern Power Company in 1948.[56] Island Falls obtained abundant power from the company dam. Although the CCF also often failed to take responsibility for providing electricity for industry, this government seemed to place industry's needs ahead of those of remote communities. In 1957 David Cass-Beggs, SPC's general manager, viewed providing power for mining and other industry as SPC's main mandate in the north.[57] SPC also held responsibility for natural gas distribution in the province. Not surprisingly, the province did not extend the southern natural gas distribution system to the north, not even to the larger, easily accessible communities near the south.

Ironically, northern hydroelectric dams generated electricity for export from the region. Outside interests imposed the dams for the benefit of distant companies and people, adding another facet to northern colonialism. The dams caused serious damage to the northern environment, local economy, and lifestyles without bringing benefits to most small communities. Aboriginal people affected by the projects today claim that government and industry did not consult with them prior to constructing the dams, and some question whether government had the right to proceed without the consent of northerners.[58] While some insist that the treaties surrendered the land alone, not water rights, the federal and provincial governments acted as if they had the right to do as they wished with the water as well as with the land.

Churchill River Power Company, a subsidiary of Hudson Bay Mining and Smelting Company, built the first major northern dam at Island Falls on the Churchill River to supply power to the mine and mill at Flin Flon. While the CCF had nothing to do with the original construction of the dam, the structure profoundly influenced the economy and society in that part of the north throughout the CCF era. Two very different and conflicting stories describe the process of establishing the dam. The official version of events says public hearings took place in 1928. The company then built the dam, which began operating in 1930. Saskatchewan issued a fifty-year licence. Virtually no Status Indians had settled in the Island Falls area prior to construction of the dam. Chief Cornelius Ballantyne tried to establish a reserve there prior to construction of the dam, but he was unsuccessful and interest in his project faded after he died. With construction of the dam, Indians came seeking jobs, moving from the Pelican Narrows area to the new village of Sandy Bay near the dam site.[59] The other version of the story, based on Aboriginal oral history, denies the fairness of the public hearings. It claims establishment of the reserve went ahead before the mining firm wanted to build the dam. Once the company spotted the prime Island Falls hydro site, Ottawa, which controlled Crown lands until 1930, took the reserve from the Indians. Government then claimed that the reserve never existed there but that it instead was located at Sturgeon Weir Indian Reserve, over a hundred miles to the southeast.[60]

In either case, the dam disrupted life on the no longer free-flowing Churchill. It flooded Aboriginal houses upstream, lowered the downstream water level, reduced water quality, hurt animal and bird populations, and eliminated the prized black sturgeon, leaving only the regular lake sturgeon. Flooded trees caught fishing nets and lines, and people may have died as a result of water releases from the dam, which made winter ice unsafe for travel. The dam also brought liquor and social problems from outside. A pimp and two female prostitutes operated on a nearby island for a time until an RCMP investigation caused them to flee.[61]

In 1942-43, the Churchill River Power Company built a storage dam at Whitesands Rapids on the Reindeer River to help stabilize the water supply for Island Falls. This second dam raised the level of Reindeer Lake by up to ten feet and caused the near disappearance of muskrat, beaver, and mink; destruction of spawning grounds; reduced fish harvests; and other difficulties. Local people received no compensation.[62]

These two dams continued operating throughout the CCF era, disrupting the lives of Aboriginals and removing wealth from the area. While nearby communities lacked electrical power, the operation produced over $270 million in electricity by 1971. Saskatchewan received more than $3 million in water and land rental. From 1930 to 1971, revenues to the province gradually increased, roughly equal to the rate of inflation. The CCF seemed content to pocket the money instead of using it to provide northern Aboriginals with electricity.[63] Provincial revenues from the dam probably could have paid for modern generating and distribution systems in all northern communities.

The CCF built a dam of its own at Squaw Rapids, upstream from Cumberland House, damming the mighty Saskatchewan. SPC completed the project in 1962. The province had not involved Cumberland House people in planning for the dam and seemed unconcerned about possible negative downstream effects. While government forecast benefits for the Cumberland area, including flood control and agricultural development, the dam soon proved a major disaster for the local people. Varying water levels hurt fish, waterfowl, fur-bearers, and big game animals. The dam also made the river ice – the main winter highway – unsafe for travel.[64]

Dams comprised another aspect of northern colonial underdevelopment during the time of the CCF. Outside forces imposed the large, permanent structures with virtually no local consultation. While they provided some employment to residents, their development and operation largely ignored northern needs. The most substantial benefits from dams went outside the region, leaving northerners a legacy of social problems and underdevelopment. Governments also gave minimal consideration to environmental effects, destroying priceless river environments.

Even more than electricity, which most people could live without, northern settlements needed safe drinking water and sanitation facilities. Without these services, risks to life and health mounted. Yet, predictably, the pattern of underdevelopment and governmental neglect also applied to these areas of infrastructure. While the CCF encouraged Aboriginals to move to settlements, it added to the dismal conditions there by refusing to fund or take responsibility for providing water, sewage, and garbage disposal services. The poverty-stricken Aboriginals lacked the resources to build the systems themselves.

In contrast to its neglect of Aboriginal communities, the CCF in the mid-1950s gave Uranium City a proper water and sewer system, estimated to cost about half a million dollars.[65] Government and industry ensured that the white settlements of Island Falls and Creighton also enjoyed sewer and water services, and the CCF saw to it that many of its employees in remote settlements received these benefits. Setting a double standard, it considered water and sewer systems essential for non-Aboriginals, while lamenting that Aboriginals did not know the sanitary ways of the white man.

Instead of providing Aboriginal communities with safe water and sanitation options, the CCF blamed Aboriginals and their lifestyle for sanitation problems. Numerous government reports decried the filthy conditions under which Aboriginals in settlements lived. The few white people in the communities often had the only outhouses. Part of the problem arose because the former nomads, not appreciating the hazards involved, transferred sanitation standards from the bush to the village. Methods that worked on the land did not work in permanent settlements, and excrement from people and hundreds of sled dogs lay around communities. Rain rinsed the ground surface, and runoff washed into the lakes or rivers next to which communities invariably sat. Fish-processing plants contributed to the pollution by dumping offal into the water. Residents then took their drinking water from the polluted water bodies. In a typical situation, a "horrible mess" existed at Wollaston Lake in 1950. Tourist fishing parties left "thoroughly disgusted." Little changed by 1953 when the Wollaston post manager of Saskatchewan Government Trading (SGT) described the Aboriginal camp as a "disease ridden, filthy place." Although government knew of the situation, it did not provide a remedy. Another report in 1960 said the Indian people "merely wander back into the bush."[66] Surface runoff and the fish plant continued to pollute the water supply. Similar stories came from other communities.

CCF officials placed hope for improved sanitation on educating the Aboriginal people in constructing toilets and obtaining safe water. One sanitary officer viewed educating Aboriginals as a "difficult and long term project."[67] Yet the CCF spent little on education programs. Further, as demonstrated by the situation at Cumberland House, education had its limitations. There, although war veterans with experience in the outside world exerted a positive influence and many residents had outhouses, the water remained unsafe to drink. Allan Quandt described the Cumberland House water supply as "very bad" in 1946. It seemed responsible for health problems.[68] The CCF ignored the warning and did not provide safe water. The village continued to lack a good water supply in 1951, when RCMP Constable Crawford organized the boy scouts to help dig a public well. However, heavy rain caved in the unfinished well and the project ended.[69] While education helped, only money could provide proper wells and sewage disposal systems. Blaming Aboriginals and their lack of knowledge relieved the CCF of the need to spend this money. Government gave neither DNR nor Public Health the authority or resources to provide the needed facilities.

Even the larger settlement at La Ronge lacked a safe water and sewage system, seemingly because it did not provide large resource revenues to the province. Human waste concentrated in dirt pits under outhouses, and people dumped household water on the ground. Much litter and garbage lay around because La Ronge had no lanes in which to hide garbage and garbage cans, and had no garbage collection system. In 1951 Public Health judged that only two of the seven wells there were safe. Many residents used lake water, polluted by the fish plant and runoff. Fear of typhoid and other water-borne diseases caused concern in the Department of Public Health. Deaths from typhoid, blamed on polluted lake water, had occurred some years earlier at Goldfields, and this memory lent credence to the fears. As a positive aside, Public Health found few flies at the dilapidated fish plant, "sprayed inside and out with DDT." Even though it held responsibility as the municipal government of La Ronge, the CCF refused to spend the money required to improve sanitation. In 1952 G. Kinneard of Public Health thought it unlikely much would change until La Ronge incorporated.[70]

However, its incorporation in 1956 did not end the sanitation problems. The struggling village lacked the money to build the necessary infrastructure systems, and the province did little to help. Some continued to blame the Aboriginals. In 1960 Robin F. Badgley of the University of Saskatchewan concluded that "it is impossible to change the ways of the Indians." Aboriginals had reacted with animosity when Dr. Cook of La Ronge tried to clean up the local reserve. After Cook threatened to withdraw medical care, garbage burned for four days and "38 trucks of garbage were removed from the reserve." Some claimed the doctor discriminated against the Indians, as he had not dealt with open sewers at the hotel and poolroom.[71] Sanitation problems also persisted elsewhere. Reports from Wollaston and Snake Lake said that Indians still did not use privies. Fish plants continued to endanger water quality at Wollaston, Deschambault, and Snake Lake.[72]

The CCF, aware of the atrocious sanitation situation, did not want to spend even the relatively small amount of money required to monitor the situation. Instead it made several efforts to have Ottawa contribute money for inspections. A National Health grant, which paid for a sanitary officer's salary and travel costs, finally provided hope for modest improvement by 1962. The officer's duties included extending sanitary inspections to as many settlements as possible.[73] While health inspections of northern communities increased, the CCF failed to provide the needed infrastructure systems in any Aboriginal communities. It demonstrated little commitment to improving water, sewer, and sanitation services there throughout its mandate.

In addition to needing physical infrastructure, northern communities required other systems, including those for local government and law and order. With few exceptions, the CCF retained control over local government, giving local people little say over what happened to their communities. DNR, the CCF's colonial arm, handled municipal matters, including property taxation and public works. Most local government remained rudimentary and very limited in power under the CCF. Exceptions developed at Uranium City, where a municipal corporation cared for the local needs of its largely white population. La Ronge and Creighton, with many white residents, also incorporated.

The CCF possessed little interest in establishing truly responsible local government outside white areas for several reasons. First, the province viewed the northern resource base as inadequate to support local government. This reason only made sense when the government ignored the large tax and royalty revenues paid by the mining and other industries to Regina. But the CCF looked at the Aboriginal communities separately and saw that they produced little tax revenue. Second, the CCF did not consider Aboriginals ready to handle even limited self-government and did not trust them to make decisions.

At times, while maintaining strict colonial control, the province tried to give the impression of involving northerners in local government. In 1949 Assistant Deputy Minister J.W. Churchman wanted DNR to present ideas to the rudimentary local councils and ratepayers associations "in such a way as to let the people think it came from them." Similarly, DNR's Jim Brady, while wishing to maintain a nondictatorial appearance, did not want DNR to recognize local councils elected without DNR supervision.[74]

DNR helped develop some local councils and ratepayers associations, although it held onto all real authority. Cumberland House had no elected local government until 1948, when residents chose a council of three members. The council could not act alone but needed to wait for DNR to approve its recommendations. Yet DNR refused to act on resolutions because it disapproved of the political leanings of members. DNR's Quandt reported to Churchman: "We deemed it a necessary lesson to show these people that if they want to follow reactionary leadership and not help the small progressive nucleus of their own kind in the Cumberland community, that we follow a very niggardly policy as far as special works is concerned for some time. Already it is giving results." The reference to "reactionary leadership" likely referred to the Liberal affiliation of council members, and the "lesson" DNR wanted to teach was that the local people should not elect representatives who did not support CCF "development plans" for the area. Teaching the lesson did not meet with complete success, though, as at least one of the initial council members, Pierre Carriere, remained a thorn in the side of the CCF for the rest of its era.[75]

To help administer northern communities, DNR appointed W.J. Bague to the position of supervisor of Northern Municipal Services in 1951. He worked to develop ratepayers' associations, authorized by the Northern Administration Act. Contradicting its efforts to maintain control, DNR spoke of "autonomous municipal administration" as the goal for all northern communities. Though it had difficulty generating local interest, DNR established a ratepayers' group at La Ronge in 1951. DNR also helped create ratepayers' associations at Denare Beach, Île-à-la-Crosse, and a few other communities. The associations generally had three-person councils with no authority and which could only make recommendations to DNR.[76] Their level of activity depended largely on how much stimulation DNR applied.

Even though the CCF did not trust Aboriginals to govern northern communities, local people sometimes demonstrated interest and ability in handling local affairs. An example of this comes from Cumberland House. The DNR-sponsored ratepayers' association there had become dormant by 1961, seemingly due to the lack of interest of the former conservation officer. And his replacement had not revived the organization. Yet the community found other avenues for limited self-government, including the Legion, the women's organization, the recreational club, and the school committee. A community council, unfunded by the CCF, also formed, its creation seemingly stimulated by the Center for Community Studies, located at the University of Saskatchewan. Unlike many of the white-dominated ratepayers' associations, the nine-member elected council included only four whites. Although the CCF did not allow the relatively vibrant council to advise DNR on spending – only a ratepayers' association could do that – the council did take over various local government functions, including a community cleanup, dog control, and recreation projects. Local Aboriginal people demonstrated their genuine interest in local government by continuing the council even after the white members left.[77]

Under the CCF only a few northern communities moved to a system of municipal government. Three settlements – Uranium City, La Ronge, and Creighton – did so by 1964. DNR's half-hearted efforts to organize local governments elsewhere brought poor results, and by 1962 only six ratepayers' associations existed: at Denare Beach, Île-à-la-Crosse, Buffalo Narrows, Beauval, Cumberland House, and Sandy Bay. Most communities lacked even this type of advisory body. The government's concentration on ratepayers' associations, which only included those who paid property taxes, disenfranchised those who did not pay property taxes. The associations excluded large numbers of non-taxpaying Aboriginals, often leaving white people holding the most influence.

In the twilight years of the CCF government, the Center for Community Studies called for a more responsible system of local government than the ineffective, powerless ratepayers' associations. The centre recommended the creation of councils with greater responsibility, elected by all residents and not just by ratepayers. It suggested that government should advise the councils, not the other way around. Shortly before it lost office, but too late to act, the CCF appeared willing to amend the Northern Administration Act, end ratepayers' associations, and allow the establishment of Northern Community Areas administered by Local Community Authorities.[78]

Throughout the CCF era, Saskatchewan's justice system also proved inadequate to meet northern needs. Courts and treatment facilities remained based in the south. Additionally, since the southern government retained control, northerners had little influence over the administration of justice in the region. Northern justice issues seemed to raise little concern in Regina. Even outrage from the northern white community on those occasions when Aboriginal crime affected non-Aboriginals had little effect on spurring the CCF to design a system appropriate to the region.

The north received only spotty policing in 1944, with RCMP occasionally patrolling by dogsled and canoe. Joe Phelps saw little need for change, blaming northern crime on southerners, the "bootlegger and white man chiseler." During the early CCF years, DNR and the RCMP cooperated to keep law and order. Although DNR initially had only one airplane, Phelps claimed it quieted down the north, since people never knew when the government would arrive.[79]

Appointed justices of the peace (JPs) handled most northern cases, which commonly involved summary convictions. Usually a white person, possibly the schoolteacher, minister, or a local businessman, acted as JP. Positions often stood vacant due to resignations and the attorney general's delay in appointing replacements. In 1957, for example, Île-à-la-Crosse, Buffalo Narrows, Beauval, and Stony Rapids all awaited the appointment of new JPs. In the meantime, the vacancies made work difficult for DNR and the RCMP.[80]

Visiting magistrates from the south judged the next level of cases. This system suffered from various shortcomings. The accused and witnesses from outlying areas needed to travel long distances to attend the hearings or trials, while proceedings were delayed as they awaited the magistrate's next visit. No magistrate was based in the north during the CCF era. Possibly even worse, magistrates appeared to have a closer relationship with local white authority figures than with Aboriginals, a situation that may have compromised the administration of justice. Northern Aboriginals sometimes questioned the fairness of the system. Cumberland House residents suspected the RCMP constable influenced the magistrate in advance, but they seemed to accept this with a "general ignorance of civil rights and judicial process."[81]

White people proved much more vocal than Aboriginals in expressing their dissatisfaction with the justice system. But while Aboriginals felt the system treated them too harshly, white people called for expanded law-and-order services and more severe treatment of Aboriginal offenders. The white community's concerns frequently involved drunk Aboriginals, delinquent children, and wild sled dogs. White northerners blamed "soft" justice for many Aboriginal social problems.

The practice of contracting northern policing to the RCMP helped the CCF distance itself from responsibility for reforming glaring inadequacies in the police and justice systems. The provincial attorney general's department, responsible for justice and the official liaison between the province and the RCMP, also proved unresponsive, even to appeals from within government. Buffalo Narrows provides an example of ongoing problems. After receiving a "permanent" RCMP constable by 1952, the village became "much more orderly."[82] But the officer left by 1954, and RCMP policed

Buffalo Narrows from Île-à-la-Crosse. The Buffalo Narrows ratepayers' association and C.S. Brown of DNR complained, and the RCMP agreed to
again station an officer there.[83] In 1957, again without an RCMP officer,
terror reigned among whites at Buffalo Narrows following the rape of the
public health nurse and the possible attempted rape of a DNR officer's
wife. Since some did not believe that the courts would handle the matter
properly, vigilante action, including lynching, appeared possible. Reports
said that drunks roamed unmolested by the RCMP, visitors found themselves bothered by the local people, and break-ins and thefts occurred
almost nightly. When the RCMP officer did fly in, he had to borrow a car
or truck to travel within the local area. Brown described Buffalo Narrows
as "the most lawless and immoral community in the Northern Administration District." He, many citizens, and the ratepayers' association all
called for improvements to the justice system. Brown opposed having the
magistrate from Meadow Lake, whose work he described as "rather dis-
turbing," preside over court cases in the Buffalo Narrows region. People
were also concerned by various alleged instances of miscarriages of justice
as well as by the attorney general's reversal of some harsher sentences.
White residents suggested reforms for the system, saying that at least two
Mounties should live in Buffalo Narrows, and the community should receive a local jail. The critics thought this would end the custom of well-
travelled prisoners flying back from luxurious holidays in southern cells
and receiving a hero's welcome from other Aboriginals. Whites also wanted
exemplary local humiliation of offenders, and "sexual monstrosities" put
away in a mental institution. DNR's minister, A.G. Kuziak, added to the
uproar by calling on the attorney general to reform northern justice.
Although Buffalo Narrows again received a "permanent" RCMP officer in
1958, the province did not make the major changes demanded by northerners. Problems with law and order continued in the community.[84]

White people claimed that the northern justice system did not work at
Sandy Bay either. There, "The Council of Good Order," which included the
priest, the Island Falls nurse, the Sandy Bay nurse, three Sandy Bay teachers, the DNR officer, and the MLA, signed a petition in 1955, complaining
about the policing situation. The RCMP officer lived a short distance away,
in the comfortable community of Island Falls, rather than at Sandy Bay
with its problems of public drunkenness, contraband liquor, homebrew,
child abuse, accidents, and misery. Complainants said that Aboriginals
lacked respect for "anybody and anything" and were "worse than animals." The deputy attorney general, J.L. Salterio, refused to intervene with
the RCMP beyond making the Mounties in Regina aware of the concerns.[85]

People at Denare Beach repeatedly begged for improved policing, while
the CCF continued to deny responsibility for this. By 1953 seasonal use of
the resort area had grown greatly, and numerous people lived there year-
round. Yet the RCMP from Flin Flon patrolled the community only about

once a week during the busy summer season and refused to create a summer detachment. Policing shortcomings continued in 1957. Even though there were up to five thousand people in the vacation area, the RCMP had only one car and two constables available for work outside Flin Flon. The Manitoba detachment considered the work in Saskatchewan "complimentary, and not obligatory." Saskatchewan's attorney general appeared unable or unwilling to improve the situation.[86]

While the white community complained loudly when the justice system failed to protect them from Aboriginals, CCF neglect of justice issues possibly affected the Aboriginal community even more. An uproar resulted when Aboriginal men threatened the safety of white women at Buffalo Narrows, yet female Aboriginals had long suffered sexual assaults from both Aboriginals and whites. At La Ronge, sexual contact between visitors and local girls or women, sometimes with consent and sometimes without, caused concern. On one occasion, some locals, including Quandt and Brady, reportedly forced the RCMP to tell some men to leave La Ronge "over the issue of pregnant native girls." A group of girls also formed a "bubble-gum gang" for protection against rape by white visitors.[87] In 1957 teenage girls in Buffalo Narrows felt unsafe "to even go to a show, a jiving class, or Church," for fear of attack from "sexual maniacs."[88] Many members of the white community did not make an issue of crime until it affected them.

Disproportionate numbers of northern Aboriginals spent time in jail. By about 1957, 60 percent of northern males aged sixteen to thirty had been in prison an average of 1.75 times. Aboriginals comprised about one-quarter of men and one-fifth of women in provincial correctional facilities in 1963. Since the north had only short-term holding facilities, convicted persons served longer sentences in the south. Non-Aboriginal northerners, thinking that jail time outside had no stigma for Aboriginals, frequently disapproved of sending prisoners south. They called for the establishment of northern jails and for prisoners to perform local work. The RCMP rejected the idea since it could fly prisoners out more cheaply.[89]

Concerns about northern juvenile delinquency, raised mainly by white people, also went largely unaddressed. Inadequate numbers of police and social workers, and the complete absence of northern treatment facilities, contributed to problems in the area. Uncharacteristically, the Department of Social Welfare sent group workers, Professor and Mrs. Hill, to Buffalo Narrows in 1957. The Hills saw youths' problems as "boredom and lack of stimulation."[90] Whites in many communities wanted curfews to curb Aboriginal youths, but controls rarely resulted. Buffalo Narrows did institute a 9:00 p.m. curfew in the late 1950s, complete with an enforcer. The system ended when the judge would not support it.[91]

Under the CCF colonial system, white people from the south enforced most laws in the north. In a positive development, by 1960 the RCMP involved some Aboriginal northerners in policing through a special constable program. In one situation a local Metis man at Cumberland House worked as a special constable. He acted as an interpreter, guide, and assistant to the regular constable, managing to hold the confidence of both the people and the constable.[92] While the special constable program seemed a step in the right direction, the CCF still refused to devote major resources to issues of law and order in the north.

Since the CCF gave DNR the responsibility of governing most northern settlements, this department also held responsibility for protecting northern communities from fires. The Northern Administration Act allowed for the appointment of DNR field officers as deputy fire commissioners, allowing them to act in emergencies, though not compelling them to do so.[93] The communities with larger white populations, including Creighton, Uranium City, and La Ronge, established some firefighting services. La Ronge received more fire protection than did most communities, relying on a rudimentary voluntary brigade by 1952. But the CCF refused to spend much money, even after the fire commissioner's office recommended buying equipment to fight fires at La Ronge. By the 1960s, fire protection there remained inadequate for the scattered village, reserve, and surrounding area's population.[94] The smaller, predominantly Aboriginal settlements received virtually no equipment specifically to fight local fires. Overall, the province did not take its duty to protect northerners from fires very seriously.

Underdevelopment also characterized the area of banking and credit services. Although the CCF introduced a cash economy to the north, most communities had no bank or credit union, forcing residents to deal with local merchants to cash cheques and obtain limited credit. Even La Ronge only received its first bank, the Bank of Montreal, in about 1956. A few CCF-directed credit unions operated briefly. One was established at Cumberland House by the early 1950s, and Buffalo Narrows received a credit union by the late 1950s, although it dissolved in the 1960s.[95]

Northern postal service fell largely outside CCF control. The formerly sporadic mail delivery improved from 1944 to 1964, likely partly because northerners sent many petitions to the Postmaster General asking for improvements. SGA, which regularly flew to most communities, held the contract to carry the mail on its airplanes. Although larger communities received post offices, stores still handled the mail in smaller villages. Complaints arose when residents thought that storekeepers tampered with the mail. People suspected that stores returned parcels from outside mail-order companies, such as Eaton's, to reduce competition, and that they intercepted cheques to apply them to accounts owing.[96] In spite of upgrades, much of the northern postal service remained far below southern standards.

Northern mass media remained underdeveloped from 1944 to 1964. Minimal access to newspaper and radio service, and the absence of television long after its arrival in southern Canada in 1952, added to the feeling of isolation many southerners felt when they moved to or visited the north. Most local newspaper enterprises did not last long, and none brought together the concerns of northerners. No radio or television station broadcast from within the area. Radio signals from the south varied greatly in strength, with US signals among the strongest late at night. One Cumberland House Metis woman remembers listening to Wolfman Jack from a faraway US station.[97]

The CCF did transmit one radio program from the south to the north. Beginning in the 1940s, Prince Albert's CKBI broadcast "Northern News," a program produced by DNR and paid for by DNR and Crown corporations. Northerners eagerly awaited the program, largely because it included personal messages. Government used the opportunity to provide information and propaganda about the Fur Marketing Service and other CCF programs.[98] This broadcast gave the CCF control over much of the dissemination of information in the north. Opposing points of view lacked a forum of equal power.

Northern recreation facilities also remained underdeveloped during the CCF's time in power. Although DNR acted as the municipal government for most northern communities, its political masters devoted only paltry resources to recreation. Aboriginal communities consequently received virtually no facilities unless local white people organized to provide some. Father Lavasseur took the initiative at Buffalo Narrows by 1958 and organized the Buffalo Narrows Advancement Club. The group dismantled and moved two buildings from the obsolete Fort Black Mid-Canada Line radar base and rebuilt these into an indoor skating and curling rink.[99] The CCF made a minimal effort to address the lack of recreation facilities by the early 1960s. It gave DNR a $5,000 budget to give matching grants to help communities build facilities, including rinks and community halls. Since the north had dozens of communities, the money did not go far. DNR then reallocated part of this meagre budget and could not give the Denare Beach Community Club $500 without overspending.[100] In an unusually generous act, the CCF passed an order-in-council in 1961 approving $500 to help the Pemmican Portage Sports Club build a hockey rink.[101] Glaring contrasts continued to exist between Aboriginal and white settlements. Many Aboriginal communities did not even have a large room or gymnasium, attached to the local school or elsewhere, to accommodate local functions.

The northern infrastructure system established and maintained by the CCF bore many colonial characteristics. Most white people received a much higher standard of services than did the thousands of Aboriginal people, who lived in poverty. No longer able to live in the bush, they lived in dismal, unmodern settlements. Frequently, much as in matters of personal poverty, the CCF blamed northern Aboriginals for deficiencies in northern community infrastructure systems. At the same time, government removed millions of dollars from the north through various royalties and taxes. In most instances, the CCF did not apply policies with a socialist bent when it came to spending money on the welfare of northerners, including infrastructure. Yet, the socialist principles of the CCF strongly influenced its plans and projects to restructure the northern economy.

Part Three
The Segregated Economy

5
Never Before Have We Been So Poor

One of the CCF's major goals was to diversify the provincial economy. The devastating failure of the once-dominant agricultural sector during the Great Depression, and the realization that Saskatchewan had almost totally missed out on industrial development, motivated efforts to expand the range of economic activity. Diversification offered hope for long-term economic stability and prosperity. The redesigned Department of Natural Resources and Industrial Development, led by Joe Phelps, provided the organizational structure for working towards this goal. Taking control of and modifying the northern economy formed a key part of the CCF diversification plan. The new government accepted the stereotypical view of the north as a storehouse of great riches. But while the north did hold treasures, it did not freely give them up. Only a great investment of effort and money could wrest these from the rugged environment. The CCF divided northern resources into two groups: those it thought Aboriginals should participate in harvesting and those it considered beyond the scope of Aboriginals' abilities to extract. It largely reserved trapping, fishing, and subsistence farming for Aboriginals, while thinking non-Aboriginals should handle mining, forestry, and tourism.

The CCF applied socialist ideals to all major areas of the northern economy. It firmly believed that resources belonged to the people of Saskatchewan and not just to entrepreneurs who removed the wealth. True to this belief, the government imposed state control over the extraction of northern resources. Crown corporations, marketing boards, and cooperatives structured Aboriginal trapping and fishing, and a socialist model shaped northern farming. In the non-Aboriginal economy, the CCF took over most of the forest resource, to which it applied socialist principles. Lacking expertise in mining, it contented itself with raising royalties and taxes for this industry, while reserving the right to take it over later on.

Policies established by the CCF suffered from glaring contradictions that it did not address and that remain difficult to explain. An obvious contradiction appeared between the party's often-stated desire to assimilate Aboriginals into white society and the CCF segregation of Aboriginals into the more traditional sectors of the northern economy. On one hand, the assimilation policy implemented by the CCF required and encouraged Aboriginals to give up a nomadic lifestyle, live in a cash economy, learn English, and become literate. Yet on the other hand, economic segregation and the CCF failure to help Aboriginal northerners move into industrial occupations, including mining and forestry, guaranteed that complete assimilation would not happen. Occupational segregation ensured that Aboriginals would not leave their communities in large numbers since they had no way of receiving the job training needed to survive outside the region.

Promotion of Aboriginal trapping by the CCF contradicted its plan to move people from the bush into settlements. Traditionally, Aboriginal families spent prolonged periods, several months at a time, living on remote traplines. This obviously could not continue if the CCF wanted to assimilate Aboriginals in settlements. The CCF partially resolved this dilemma by changing how people trapped. It looked on trapping as a male activity and condoned men's absences from the settlement as long as women and children remained there. Instead of allowing trappers to trap wherever they wanted, which would have resulted in severe overcrowding on traplines near the villages, the CCF assigned trapping areas to groups of men. Some trappers received areas near the village, allowing them to frequently return to their homes and families. But many traplines lay farther away, forcing those who wanted to trap to spend prolonged periods of time away from their homes. Often the pull of families and village life meant that little trapping took place. It also meant that families trapped much less frequently together.

Economic policies established by the CCF for the north also contradicted those it followed in the south. Socialist ideology guided the CCF's northern economic plans much more than it did elsewhere. The party imposed state ownership and control over furs, fish, timber, and retail sales and applied socialist forms of organization to vital parts of the northern economy. At the same time it used its power to limit the role of private capital in the region. In contrast, the CCF quickly abandoned most of its state interventions in the southern economy, continuing state ownership there mainly in utility monopolies. The CCF's northern actions demonstrate that the party did not abandon its socialist ideology and that, given the opportunity, it preferred and did not hesitate to apply socialist solutions.

CCF politicians and planners visualized northern Aboriginals efficiently and contentedly harvesting renewable fur, fish, and game resources. Using compulsion, the CCF largely reserved these resources for Aboriginals, expelling many non-Aboriginals from participating in their extraction. The CCF imposed a structure of Crown corporations, marketing boards, and cooperatives to provide organizational and marketing services for furs and fish. Southern planners, however, grossly misjudged the capacity of these resources to support the northern Indian and Metis population. The forced reliance on fur and fish consequently soon formed a structural part of northern poverty and underdevelopment. The CCF watched this situation worsen, without finding solutions.

The CCF saw two types of problems in fur, fish, and forestry: those caused by resource mismanagement and those created by capitalist abuses. It developed an integrated program, using "sustained yield management" and socialist ideology, to address both issues. The new government successfully applied conservation principles to ensure a sustainable supply of furs, fish, and game, but its desire to replace capitalism with socialism proved more difficult to satisfy. Yet the CCF's socialist ideology influenced resource policies more than did conservation considerations.

Of all CCF actions, its intervention in the fur industry raised the most opposition among northerners. The new fur programs quickly and permanently altered how and where trappers worked and dramatically changed their relationship with fur traders and the government. Trappers, both Aboriginal and white, had not asked for or wanted most of the changes brought by the CCF.

Phelps and his colleagues justified their actions partly by pointing to depletion of fur-bearing animals. Allan Quandt of DNR, in an accurate description, blamed resource depletion on "mankind bent on personal power and material wealth being gained."[1] Prior to 1944, non-Aboriginals, many of whom only spent winters in the north and lacked a long-term commitment to the region, increasingly dominated trapping. These trappers often responded to the strong demand for furs by taking as many fur-bearing animals as possible. Depletion of fur stocks resulted. Beaver particularly declined in number, becoming rare in many areas of the north by 1944. The CCF was interested in restoring fur stocks and held no ideological opposition to harvesting fur resources. It sought a balance between overuse and underuse, considering underutilization as wasteful as overutilization.[2] DNR proved skilled at managing fur resources, with its actions ensuring adequate stocks in most cases. The game commissioner, a position held by E.L. Paynter for much of the CCF era, and the Game Branch controlled many aspects of the fur industry.[3] While the fur situation in 1944 clearly justified the introduction of conservation controls, the CCF could have addressed the conservation issues without imposing socialist solutions.

Until 1944 the Hudson's Bay Company (HBC) and other private fur traders bought and marketed the furs brought to them by trappers. Traders only stayed in business by making a profit from their operations. Long experience taught them how much they could pay for furs and how to successfully operate the crucial credit system on which trappers depended.

Most northerners did not deal much with cash, but relied on traders to provide them with needed goods throughout the year. Trappers then repaid their debts with furs. Traders held great influence in northern society, acting as economic advisors, bankers, and welfare agencies.

Influenced by its socialist beliefs and desire to modernize the north, the CCF found the northern system of control by capitalist traders unacceptable. It decreed that the old ways could not continue. The party believed that traders imposed their will on dependent Aboriginals and did not see the fur trade as a mutually beneficial agreement between Aboriginals and traders.

Various people in the CCF organization characterized the HBC as the greatest northern villain. T.C. Douglas justified creating the CCF's compulsory Fur Marketing Service, which became the dominant force in fur handling, by saying: "There was only one thing to do to save them from the exploitation by the Hudson's Bay Company." George Cadbury, the top CCF planner, thought the HBC kept trappers in near permanent debt.[4]

Joe Phelps was likely one of the HBC's greatest foes. Myth and misinformation provided the basis for much of his crusade. He had already judged the HBC before he set out to gather evidence against the company for an address to the legislature, a speech that would "expose" HBC exploitation of the Aboriginals. Phelps asked RCMP corporal C.E. Wenzel for details about unfair HBC dealings. The best Wenzel offered was rumours that both the HBC and a private trader charged five squirrel pelts for one box of matches and that the HBC gave special beaver licences only to those who sold their furs to the HBC. He referred Phelps to six other possible informants. Phelps wrote to these six, saying, "The people have been exploited very much in their trading, both by free traders and the Hudson's Bay Company." One of the six, himself a free trader at Stanley Mission, claimed that unfair trading practices did not exist when more than one trader operated in an area, as at Stanley Mission. Another respondent, Albert VanderKracht of Lac la Ronge, observed to no one's surprise that northern prices exceeded southern prices. He also complained about the large supply of vanilla extract stocked by a free trader for people who "do not go in for cakes much," implying that the trader sold the vanilla as a substitute for alcohol. Thus armed, Phelps raised the issue in the legislature in 1945. Following his characteristic style, he relied largely on rhetoric, even wanting to "challenge the validity of the Hudson's Bay Company charter issued by King Charles II in 1670." Phelps also claimed that the HBC and the CPR did not "rightfully own" land granted them.[5]

Phelps lacked legal grounds for a challenge to the old firm's presence in the north. The CCF did manage to use the Mineral Taxation Act to successfully coerce the HBC into surrendering most of its mineral rights, but HBC stores remained open. The company skilfully handled Phelps, by cooperating in some instances and promoting conservation. The new government tried various ways to replace the old capitalist paternalistic model with its new socialist paternalistic model. Phelps led the effort to assume HBC functions, including in the areas of fur buying, retailing, social services, and leadership.

Those who criticized the HBC, including Phelps, did not seem to realize that the company had long ago lost its overwhelming, dominant position in the fur trade and that many other traders competed with it. The company handled about 45 percent of the wild fur exports of $2.3 million from Saskatchewan in 1943-44, while within the larger Canadian scene it handled only 23 percent of furs.[6] The CCF did not approve of small traders either, but it did not oppose them with the same vehemence. Driven by its ideological opposition to free enterprise, the party wanted to put all capitalist traders out of business. This attack caused uncertainty and losses for merchants, who could not buy furs while the CCF revamped policies.[7]

Once Phelps and some other radicals left government and the CCF socialist fervour eased, the CCF and HBC relationship improved. The province reduced its efforts to open government-owned northern stores and asked the HBC if it would sell its stores, but the HBC refused.[8] Some radical CCF members continued to complain about the HBC. In 1960 the La Ronge CCF Club claimed the HBC charged an Aboriginal customer 280 muskrat pelts, which sold for $1,120, for a used ten-horsepower motor. The motor soon broke down.[9] Rumours also persisted that the HBC illegally took Aboriginals' cheques from its post offices to repay debts.

Northern opposition to CCF actions arose partly because many trappers did not share the party's critical view of the HBC. Instead, they appreciated the valuable services the HBC had long provided. In many cases, while government projects came and went, the HBC provided a stable and reliable economic and welfare institution. Aboriginals especially depended on the credit system offered by the HBC and other traders, which let them obtain goods and pay for them later with their fur harvest. Conversely, CCFers viewed the credit system as one of the primary northern evils because they thought it allowed traders to pay low prices for furs, sell goods at high prices, and paternalistically treat Aboriginals as children. The CCF also wanted northerners to use a cash system to pay for their licence and lease fees, royalties, and taxes. Phelps considered it "absolutely necessary" to end northerners' reliance on credit, and swift action followed. The CCF succeeded in breaking the old system by making the marketing of some types of furs compulsory through the Saskatchewan Fur Marketing Service.[10] This move caused trappers to lose most of their credit, since traders could no longer buy the furs to repay debts. While the shift to cash appeared inevitable, the CCF prematurely forced this transition in an extremely disruptive and destructive fashion.

Although the credit system allowed traders to exercise paternalistic control over Aboriginal trappers, it operated harmoniously, and customers wanted to see it continue. At Île-à-la-Crosse, families were either a "Hudson's Bay family" or a "Marion family." Because the free trader, Marion, protected and cared for them, the Metis called him "boss." Most did not complain about his prices for fear of hurting the paternalistic relationship.[11] Because traders knew the trapping ability and probable income of each family, they ensured that trappers bought essentials. A trader who extended too much credit for luxury items or vanilla would not stay in business, since the trapper's income likely would not pay for it. The old system also spread buying power throughout the year. Some trappers with large families received as much as $200 per month in credit, while those with few dependents received less. Men gained prestige from their credit limit, which reflected their ability as trappers and hunters. The HBC cared for its customers, even giving out free food at Christmas. One person recalls that the HBC "promised to look after us, just like a pension ... they treated all the old people the same way."[12] The sometimes inflated prices helped pay bad debts and carry customers through hard times, with trappers, and not taxpayers, ultimately paying the cost. The credit system effectively encouraged work and helped moderate drunkenness and crime. Hugh Mackay Ross, a long-time HBC employee, said his company "understood how they felt about tomorrow. It might never come." Ross also described Phelps as "a rabid socialist" who thought the HBC wanted to keep Aboriginals "enthralled in debt."[13]

Less controversially, the CCF sought to facilitate conservation and equalize opportunity for Aboriginals and whites in trapping. The federal government helped Saskatchewan with this by entering into the Northern Fur Conservation Area Agreement. The first ten-year agreement took effect on 18 July 1946 and applied to the area north of the fifty-third parallel. The pact created a Fur Advisory Committee to advise government. More dramatically, it allowed the CCF to establish a Fur Conservation Block that would blanket the north, where the province would apply conservation and other policies. Ottawa and Saskatchewan were to spend up to $50,000 annually to develop and administer northern fur resources, with the province contributing 40 percent. Because the north had a large number of Status Indians, the federal government would pay 60 percent. The funding soon proved inadequate, and even though Ottawa gave extra, Saskatchewan wanted more. The province contributed $352,000 from 1946 to 1957, while the federal government provided $412,400. On expiry of the first agreement, the two governments signed another ten-year agreement to run until 31 March 1966.[14]

On the surface the CCF appeared to allow affected parties some opportunity for input into the design of fur policies. After distributing about fifteen thousand questionnaires to trappers, fur ranchers, and fur dealers in 1944, the CCF claimed to have the support of 96 percent of trappers, 88 percent of fur ranchers, and 81 percent of fur dealers for its plans. Phelps also met with trappers on a trip north in 1944, holding meetings in "all northern communities" to introduce policies. In another effort, the Saskatchewan Fur Marketing Association, the corporation that controlled the newly created Saskatchewan Fur Marketing Service (SFMS), established an advisory committee. It met only once. Field officers' conferences gave DNR staff an opportunity to make recommendations.[15]

The process used by the CCF to gather public opinion suffered from serious flaws. First, the CCF already seemed to have decided that it would intervene aggressively to structurally alter the fur business. Second, many who completed questionnaires and attended meetings did not understand the true nature of CCF plans. Finally, the process excluded many, particularly Aboriginals who could not read or write and did not complete the questionnaires. The widespread opposition that soon arose contradicted CCF claims of general support for its actions.

Some of the unhappiness with the CCF intervention in trapping resulted because the new government prevented many trappers, particularly non-Aboriginals, from continuing to trap. Southerners who had formerly come north to trap seasonally found themselves shut out. The CCF required a one-year residence period, the recommendation of the area trappers' association, and the approval of DNR before allowing an outsider to trap. In effect, this policy reserved northern trapping for the area's residents.[16] The CCF further restricted trapping in the region by limiting it to those who did not have a major source of income outside trapping or fishing – in other words, Aboriginals. This rule eliminated trapping by many white northerners, including priests, bureaucrats, teachers, and businesspeople.[17] The CCF enforced this policy less strictly with Aboriginals than with whites, likely revealing its true intent. The policy of not permitting people to earn income from more than one occupation had no precedent in the province. Even Joe Phelps, responsible for the edict, received income from various sources, including farming and politics. In one case the policy ended the long-standing conservation and trapping efforts of the North of 55 Mink Ranch, made up of Churchill River Power employees. The CCF rejected their plans to continue operating because the group did "not make their living from this source," even though they proposed forming a cooperative and using Aboriginal labour to improve the trapping area.[18] In another case, in 1950-51 the CCF stopped long-time trapper Alvin L. Akre from trapping after he became the principal at the Candle Lake School. Feeling unfairly treated, Akre complained that a fellow trapper, Nemo Sackett, worked at many activities. On the advice of W.J. Berezowsky of DNR, the Fur Advisory Committee then disqualified Sackett from trapping. Minister Brockelbank supported the decision, and the action appeased Akre. Although not many women trapped in the north, the new policy also applied to those who did. DNR refused a trapping licence to Mrs. Hanson because her husband worked for DNR, even though she had long trapped in the area.[19]

Yet in the case of the Aboriginal trapper Matthew Natwejus, who had other employment in the Island Falls area, the CCF overlooked its rule.[20] It enforced the regulations more strictly against white than Aboriginal trappers because of the CCF belief that Aboriginals had a natural aptitude for trapping and fishing and that they would not succeed in other industries. Not all who worked for the CCF agreed that Aboriginals had an aptitude for "traditional occupations," including trapping. In the 1950s, V.F. Valentine and R.G. Young described as "perhaps the greatest paradox" the fact that the average Metis did not do well at trapping or fur preparation.[21] The banning of southern trappers and those with other sources of income removed some of the best and most efficient trappers from the industry. These policies became part of the CCF tolerance of inefficiency in the trapping industry.

Shutting out numerous good trappers did more than just raise opposition to the CCF. Unexpectedly, the policy was a factor in some remote areas becoming undertrapped by the mid-1950s. The attraction of village life, increased access to welfare, and falling fur prices contributed to a loss of interest among many Aboriginals in trapping outlying areas. Even then the CCF continued to protect Aboriginal trapping. Some in the government questioned the policies. A.T. Davidson, assistant deputy minister of DNR, and other officials agreed that "too much security was being given these men."[22] DNR tried to reverse the situation by encouraging trappers to get out and take furs. It operated an "access trails" program in the northwest area in 1958-59 to allow ground access to remote areas, and also provided two "camp trade" outpost stores, which allowed for longer stays on traplines.[23] In another effort, DNR flew two trappers from the Buffalo Narrows area into an undertrapped area in 1961, also offering fur pickup and a trip out at Christmas.[24] Yet Aboriginal interest in trapping in difficult-to-reach areas waned further, even though fur stocks increased. Wild fur production dropped to a seventeen-year low in 1964.[25] The CCF stuck to its belief that Aboriginals should trap and did not open the industry to those it excluded. It continued to hope that Aboriginals would trap the remote areas more intensively.

In another controversial move, the CCF broke the north into group trapping areas. It intended to administer the areas as "large wild fur farms." The move to group trapping, consistent with the new government's socialist preference for group action over individual enterprise, reversed the previous Liberal administration's plans for an individual trapline registration system. Group trapping forced cooperation between trappers. It also brought heavy regimentation, as government involved itself in an unprecedented manner in many aspects of trapping. DNR officers closely oversaw the operation of the groups and their activities. Government was even involved in determining group membership. In order for individual trappers to sell their right to trap, DNR and the group needed to approve of the buyer. Regulations also required that the group notify Indian Affairs of vacancies. The establishment of the trapping areas proceeded quickly. On 3 April 1945, at Phelps's request, an order-in-council created the Cumberland House-Pine Bluff Conservation Area. It became the first of ninety-nine areas eventually established. Conservation areas included 3,584 trappers by 1950. Part of the far north remained outside the program until its extension to the northern boundary of Saskatchewan in 1958.[26]

Even though the structure of the new trapping areas appeared to favour Aboriginal trappers, they also opposed the program. Resistance arose partly because the new divisions often violated traditional trapping arrangements. A CCF supporter at La Ronge wrote in 1945: "We have had a lot of agitation here about the trapping leases and got only 29 votes for Bowerman [federal CCF candidate]."[27] Cumberland House trappers repeatedly agitated for changes to trapping areas, wanting expansion of trapping area A28 to include excluded parts of their traditional trapping territory. Their wishes sometimes conflicted with the desires of Sturgeon Landing trappers. CCF rules also barred some Cumberland House trappers who trapped on the nearby HBC lease, including vocal Pierre Carriere, from trapping in A28. This led to protests, which the CCF did not appreciate. Game Commissioner Paynter described Liberal supporter Pierre Carriere as the "chief agitator."[28] Even though the full trapping area system did not reach the far north until later, DNR did not wait to impose some new boundaries there. This led to Stony Rapids residents in 1949 repudiating their chief. DNR had drawn a new dividing line between the traditional hunting and trapping areas used by the Stony Rapids and Fond du Lac groups in an effort to increase trapping of beaver by Fond du Lac trappers faced with "extreme poverty." The chief wrongly received the blame for this division, and DNR reevaluated its decision.[29]

Along with its creation of trapping areas, the CCF imposed trappers councils in each area. Members of trapping areas elected five persons to each local council. Indians, Metis, and whites, where present, enjoyed equal rights on the councils. Paynter claimed: "This is the first time in the history of the province that Indians have been treated equally with all others." Ironically, government itself became the primary obstacle to effective operation of the councils. DNR kept strict control, dominating council meetings, setting agendas, and making final decisions. Since trappers could not set quotas, determine selling prices, or relieve overcrowding of trapping areas, the councils held little real power. Consequently, trappers often showed minimal enthusiasm for meetings. Only twenty-four of eighty-six members attended one meeting at Cumberland House in 1954-55.

DNR continued to call the meetings in 1960, although by then it allowed trappers to chair some of the gatherings.[30]

Even in the remote far north, where it delayed introducing trapping areas, the CCF quickly imposed a system of trapping licences and fur royalties. In 1945 Phelps seemed alarmed when he heard that trappers at Fond du Lac trapped in an unregulated fashion, without licences. Even though Status Indians would receive licenses free of charge, the CCF wanted to regulate *all* trapping. The province also wanted Ottawa to establish fur rehabilitation areas on Indian Reserves, which could serve as the federal equivalent of the provincial trapping areas.[31] Some northern Saskatchewan residents, including a number with a traditional claim to do so, hunted and trapped in the NWT. Increased regulation also soon reached that area. Beginning in 1949, those who trapped in the NWT had to have federal licences.[32] This supported CCF efforts to regulate trapping in the province's most remote reaches.

In addition to resenting the increasing regimentation and fees imposed by the province, trappers also opposed the CCF's new conservation measures. In the interests of restoring endangered fur populations, the CCF wasted no time in placing strict controls on the harvest of beaver and muskrat. Many areas had virtually no beaver left in 1944. Muskrat numbers also had declined due to overtrapping and the 1930s drought, which dried up marsh habitat. Phelps closed muskrat and beaver seasons, although he knew this action would hurt Aboriginal trappers. Many trappers found the trapping bans reduced their incomes. Phelps optimistically thought that construction work on the road to La Ronge and work programs could help fill the income gap.

The CCF's fur conservation program applied to the entire province. In the Precambrian area north of the Churchill River, beaver management held priority, while in the northern Saskatchewan River watershed, muskrat management took precedence.[33] Habitat modification formed a major part of the CCF plan to restore beaver and muskrat populations. Largely funded by the Northern Fur Conservation Area Agreement, the CCF built dams and flood control structures in various areas. On the west side, F.X. Gagnon, the Oblate priest from the Beauval Indian Residential School, knew his area well and advised government on the placement of dams. There and elsewhere, DNR built many dams over the years. In 1949-50 alone it built thirty-nine dams.[34]

Southern beaver stocks stood at a much higher level than those in the north in 1944. Consequently, DNR live-trapped beaver in the south and relocated them to the north. The province worried that Aboriginals would hurt the program by killing the beaver before they had a chance to reproduce. To help prevent this from happening, DNR wanted Father Gagnon to "instruct the natives that these beaver were planted for their benefit and that they should not be molested."[35] During 1946 and 1947 DNR transplanted

1,127 beaver, raising their number in most areas to a level considered sufficient for propagation. Relocation carried on, though, including to the far northern area of Stony Rapids in 1952. While it was costly to fly beaver that far, Brockelbank hoped the effort would have a "psychological effect" on the Dene and result in an improved attitude to conservation. The program continued, with about 3,500 moved north by 1955.[36]

Under the CCF, Cumberland House's low-lying, wet delta area received a disproportionate amount of governmental and private attention directed at restoring and increasing fur stocks. The new government inherited numerous lease arrangements, for much of the area, entered into by the former Liberal government. One HBC lease extended to 1964, while another expired sooner. In response to drought drying up the marshes and damaging muskrat habitat, the HBC had begun the largest fur conservation program in northern Saskatchewan on leased land at Cumberland House in 1938. The HBC seemed to have somewhat altruistic motives for leasing the marshes. It wanted to restore fur populations, help Aboriginals become independent, demonstrate that "large-scale conservation schemes" could work, and encourage governments to take action. The company built a headquarters and manager's residence, along with dams, dykes, and canals to control water levels and improve muskrat habitat and production. It spent about $200,000 by the early 1960s on structures.[37]

Even though the HBC project increased local employment and income, Phelps and the CCF did not like the company's involvement. Viewing the leases as capitalist oppression of the northern people, the CCF tried to cancel them. These efforts met with partial success when the HBC gave up the area north of the river. It kept the lease south of the river, probably the more profitable of the two areas. Governmental pressure continued for this lease to end as well.[38] The CCF seemed overly suspicious about HBC intentions and did not fully appreciate the dramatic increase HBC efforts brought in fur production and income. The HBC lease, for example, produced 110,708 muskrat in the 1953-54 season compared to only 16,000 taken from the nearby A28 fur conservation area. Careful management, contracts with trappers, regular fur pickups, and the provision of traps and grubstakes helped bring the HBC success. Although some local people resented the HBC presence, many better trappers wanted to trap for the company. At least one person in government did not agree with his political masters' opposition to the lease. Game Commissioner Paynter recognized the HBC's administration was superior to that of DNR. He opposed cancelling the lease until DNR could improve its management.[39]

Eventually opposition from the CCF and some local trappers appeared to wear down the HBC. Even though the lease did not expire until 1964, in 1960 the company asked DNR to end the lease. With justification, the HBC viewed the project as successful. While the company had lost about $175,526, its efforts had restored fur stocks and benefited the local community. During twenty-two years of company control, production had approximately quadrupled, muskrat and beaver trappers received $830,000, and the HBC paid wages of $150,000 to local staff. The province had also benefited, collecting more than $185,000 in lease fees, royalties, and SFMS commissions from the HBC over the years. Seemingly anxious to leave, the company offered the province a house, ten other buildings, and various assets for $30,000 and did not ask any compensation for the approximately $200,000 spent on dams, dykes, and canals. DNR, shrewdly sensing that the HBC might take less, offered $20,000, which the HBC accepted.[40]

Once in control of the former HBC lease, the CCF set out to use the area as part of its community development program. While DNR's H. Read wanted to eliminate all appearance of paternalism, contradictorily, he paternalistically spoke of government paying for deficits. Government recognized that Aboriginal payments on the project's purchase cost might not amount to more than token payments. Also paternalistically, the CCF decided the plan would proceed in spite of lukewarm local support. Only about 25 percent of those eligible voted on the government's plan, with fifty voting for and forty against proceeding. Aided by the province, in 1961 local trappers organized a cooperative and the Cumberland Fur Project began. But the pattern of paternalism continued. The CCF repeatedly bailed out the money-losing organization, while the Federal-Provincial Fur Agreement paid off the debt to Saskatchewan.[41] The new operation proved costly to taxpayers and likely lowered fur production and local income. Yet the CCF clearly preferred an expensive and dependent cooperative over the former productive and independent HBC operation. The cooperative structure only thinly disguised the CCF preference for socialist organization; in effect the fur project became a government enterprise.

Various other fur leases in the Cumberland House area dated back to the Liberal era. Again demonstrating its socialist preference and opposition to private enterprise, the CCF strove to end leases held by private parties and partially succeeded in doing so. In contrast, it did not oppose the Indian Affairs lease of the Sipanok area west of Cumberland House. Indian Affairs operated a successful conservation program there, aiding trappers from Red Earth and Shoal Lake reserves.[42] A large nonprofit conservation project begun by Ducks Unlimited in the mid-1940s received a warm welcome from the CCF. The organization also carried out water control work for the CCF in the former HBC lease area in the 1960s. By 1963 Ducks Unlimited had spent about $240,000 on area water control.[43]

DNR also ran its own conservation projects in the Cumberland House area. Of the various organizations and persons who worked on projects there, DNR likely ran the least productive operation. Early water control projects, including those directed by Jim Brady in the late 1940s, seemed promising. Local people participated, using wheelbarrows to build earthen dams. Some structures extended to one and a half miles or more in length. As DNR interest rose and ebbed over the years, however, its dams often fell into disrepair.[44] Yet the CCF seemed less concerned about the inefficiency and ineffectiveness of its own operations than with eliminating more efficient and effective private operations. The CCF also undid some of the positive effects of conservation efforts when it built the Squaw Rapids hydroelectric dam upstream on the Saskatchewan River. Beginning in the early 1960s, fluctuating water releases repeatedly damaged fur habitat. Although angry residents blamed the dam for damaged fur stocks and many other problems, the province paid little attention to the outcries.[45]

Overall, though, efforts to restore beaver and muskrat populations succeeded at Cumberland House and elsewhere. The CCF had overreacted by imposing overly severe restrictions on beaver and muskrat trapping in some areas in 1944-45. Seeming to recognize this, the province again allowed trappers to take muskrat in most parts of the province and some beaver under special permits in 1945-46. The new conservation efforts soon bore fruit. The beaver harvest averaged about 1,200 per year in the eight years before the federal-provincial program began, while during the first ten years of the program trappers took an average of about 12,000 per year. By 1949 DNR saw "splendid progress." It described the trapper as "a fur farmer in the wild." The beaver harvest reached over 34,000 in 1954-55. In spite of a large price decline, down from an average of $40 in 1945 to $9.69 in 1954, Minister Brockelbank claimed government actions helped increase income by over $225,000. Production remained high, while prices did not recover. In 1958-59 trappers in the conservation block took 31,164 beaver, which sold for an average of $9.04, compared to 1,260 taken in 1946-47 that brought an average price of $31.80.[46]

Muskrat production also increased dramatically from its low point in 1941-42. In the years from the beginning of the conservation program until 1952, muskrat production averaged 477,541 per year compared to 230,084 for the same number of years before the program began. Production reached 951,065 in 1952-53. Although conservation played a part in this recovery, muskrat numbers naturally rose and fell in a cycle. The most productive muskrat area, the Cumberland delta, provides an example of how water conditions and disease caused large fluctuations. Flooding and refreezing of the water in 1947 led to DNR closing the muskrat season there. The area muskrat harvest dropped from 126,407 in 1946 to nil in 1948, causing destitution and the consequent distribution of relief.[47] This demonstrates that, even with conservation controls in place, uncertainty remained.

As part of its conservation efforts, as well as to exert control over the formerly uncontrolled north, DNR closely regulated trappers and their activities. In one new initiative, DNR required northern trappers to carry out beaver censuses. Yet officials sometimes distrusted the trappers' counts. In one case at Stanley Mission, DNR suspected that trappers inflated numbers, thinking this would give them a higher beaver quota. The suspicions seemed well-founded since the beaver house count fell from 1,860 to 986 after DNR threatened to take away trapping rights. The department also found trapping violations there, including beaver houses chopped open.[48] Another new regulation required trappers to submit annual reports within thirty days of the end of the trapping season. DNR refused future trapping permits for noncompliance. New controls also closely regulated the taking of fur-bearers other than beaver and muskrat, as in the early 1950s when DNR issued no fisher or marten permits. Additionally, the province set trapping seasons. These varied by species, with some beginning as early as October.[49]

The CCF's strict controls on trapping caused dissatisfaction across the north. Some thought the regulations contributed to poverty and hardship. Residents at Pelican Narrows, a poor community, called for a beaver quota.[50] At Island Falls, Horace Morin complained when DNR closed an area to trapping, since people did not have the canoes or dogs to allow them to trap farther away. He also objected to the policy that allowed only married men to receive beaver licences. Phelps's office consulted with Churchill River Power, whose superintendent expressed surprise that Morin complained, since Morin had a reputation as a docile, lazy person.[51] At Cumberland House in 1948, Pierre Carriere sent a fifty-six-name petition to DNR asking for an open beaver season. Trappers there also wanted changes to trapping areas.[52] As well, the quota system for muskrats raised complaints. One protester at Cumberland House in 1950 claimed that after the government stopped muskrat trapping the previous year, the remaining ten thousand muskrats died anyway.[53] On the other side of the province, at Buffalo Narrows, a trapper found that the CCF's new rules devastated his formerly profitable occupation.[54]

Many northerners resented paying the fees related to trapping. While they effectively resisted property taxes by refusing to pay them, the CCF system for collecting fur royalties foiled resistance by requiring payment at the point of sale. Royalties varied over time and by species. At one point in the late 1950s royalties ranged from a low of two cents for squirrel and jack rabbit to seven cents for muskrat, one dollar for beaver, fisher, and mink, and $1.25 for otter. Fur royalties and licence fees totalled about $3.8 million from 1944 to 1963, much more than the CCF spent on fur programs.[55]

The fiercest and most damaging northern resistance to the CCF arose because the new government decided to force the marketing of beaver and muskrat, other than muskrat from the HBC lease near Cumberland House, through a newly created Crown corporation, the Saskatchewan Fur Marketing Service. Idealistically, the CCF sought to provide a "safe, sound market for trappers and fur farmers." It also wanted to give trappers the highest possible prices and improve the quality and prestige of Saskatchewan furs. Although Phelps justified creating SFMS by claiming overwhelming support from trappers, fur farmers, and dealers, that unity of purpose soon seemed elusive.[56]

In addition to whatever altruistic motives it may have had for creating SFMS, other goals motivated the CCF's creation of the new Crown corporation. Likely most importantly, placing fur marketing under a Crown corporation structure fit with the government's socialist agenda, which preferred public over private enterprise. Granting power to SFMS also took much of the power away from private traders, thought responsible for keeping Aboriginals in debt peonage and poverty. Further, the CCF did not trust trappers or traders. Handling the furs itself helped the CCF enforce its trapping controls and collect royalties.[57] Additionally, the CCF looked to SFMS for revenue. Phelps wanted to use initial profits to expand DNR and expected SFMS to return a dividend to government.[58] SFMS did generate considerable revenue. It charged a commission of 5 percent plus other fees. In turn it paid various fur collection agents, including DNR, the Fish Board, priests, and others, a fee of about 1 percent of the selling price. By 1962 the Crown corporation earned a surplus of $412,319 and possessed a contingency reserve of $25,000.[59]

With characteristic interest, Phelps oversaw details of establishing SFMS. After the first manager, W.H. Lefurgey, did not satisfy the minister, A.J. Cooke took over as manager in November 1945. SFMS wasted no time in scheduling fur auctions at its building in Regina. At four auctions from January to June 1945, sales totalled about $520,000. Phelps soon claimed that SFMS succeeded in raising prices for trappers. Seeing the early success, he planned to expand government activity into tanning and processing furs and making fur coats. In his excitement he ordered a muskrat coat from Winnipeg, made with Saskatchewan skins.[60]

Many in the northern part of the province did not share Phelps's enthusiasm for SFMS. The compulsory fur marketing system quickly raised widespread opposition, much more than the conservation measures did. Many unhappy SFMS customers complained, with some saying they received only a small percentage of what they should have from the sale of their furs.[61] In one case SFMS paid $22.28 for thirty-six wolf pelts, which it sold for $106.05.[62] In 1948 Rev. G.J. Waite of Montreal Lake railed against charges much higher than the 10 percent fee he thought the CCF had promised. Charges reached 25 percent for fisher pelts, including royalties. Waite spoke of the CCF and its "Soviet system" robbing "my Indians."[63] L.E. Blanchard, MLA for Cumberland, wrote to Brockelbank in 1949: "The Indians tell me never before have we been so poor ... they are getting desperate." Brockelbank dogmatically replied: "I think you will agree with me that it would be very undesirable in the interests of your constituents to leave them completely at the mercy of the fur dealer as they were in the past."[64] A letter from Deschambault Lake, originally written in Cree, read: "For me I feed my dogs, when I have finished using them, all summer I feed them even when they are not working for me since I expect that they will be working for me again, but now, as far as we can see it is as if they are trying to starve us to death and children."[65] Chief Robert McKay of Red Earth Reserve complained to Brockelbank after SFMS destroyed rejected muskrat pelts. He reminded Brockelbank that he recently told trappers that nothing would please him more than to have the trappers call him "brother."[66] On the west side a Metis trapper still bitterly recalls how compulsory marketing destroyed the profitability of muskrat trapping.[67] The opposition to SFMS came from across the north.

The reaction to SFMS became so strong that the usually reserved Aboriginals left no doubt that they did not approve of the new policies. DNR's anthropologist, V. Valentine, experienced the opposition first-hand when he moved to the north. The Metis he knew particularly disliked compulsory fur marketing, which destroyed the credit system and did not replace it with a reliable substitute. "For most people, all present wrongs are believed to have been caused by the present Government," Valentine wrote. Aboriginals "had only contempt and hostility for the Department of Natural Resources, and for the Provincial Government generally." He reported: "I couldn't walk two steps without being accused of being some kind of a CCF spy or some other damn thing ... it was all focused on the way in which the resources were being administered, and specifically, the compulsory aspects of beaver and muskrat."[68]

Resistance to compulsory fur marketing became part of a generalized opposition to the CCF presence and policies. Laurie Barron describes Aboriginal opposition as "an indictment of the very notion that the CCF was walking in Indian moccasins." The older generation particularly resisted, and Aboriginals fought back by continuing to use the HBC when they could.[69] Valentine thought the Metis felt "robbed of their natural heritage and that the new programmes are rapidly bringing about the disintegration of their society. The resentment is such that to be called a 'C.C.F.'er' is an anathema."[70] Some of the strongest open resistance to CCF policies came at Cumberland House. In 1947 a recording secretary at a community hall meeting admonished Pierre Carriere "for his anarchistic expressions and conduct at past meetings."[71] And in 1948 R.T. Francis, a forestry student, wrote: "I have heard from some great rumors that these people are very hard to get along with, i.e. what we have done for them in the past two or three years was more or less ignored by these people."[72]

Although trappers and other northerners disagreed strongly with CCF fur policies, they often chose mild methods, including petitions, to register their opposition. In 1949, for example, a petition from 147 Lac la Ronge area trappers and fishermen requested "the removal of compulsory marketing of fish and furs through socialist boards." Formal opposition from Aboriginals often depended on white advisors, as most Metis and Indians lacked education or experience with the white man and his policy and decision-making process. A language barrier also existed, as Aboriginals spoke primarily Cree or Chipewyan. Often a literate white person organized a petition, which arrived in Regina with numerous Xs made by those who could not sign their names.[73] Many trappers and others used passive resistance, not cooperating with CCF fur and other projects. In the north, the powerless aimed more to minimize the negative impact of CCF programs than to bring structural changes. They delayed, faked compliance, and affected ignorance and incompetence. Most resistance remained unorganized, although silent understandings and informal networks effectively worked against CCF plans. A Saskatchewan Metis Society study found that Aboriginals used "accommodating language" when speaking to officials. They gave the answers they thought would please the officials, and they did not reveal their true "deep feelings and decisions." The report said: "Accommodating answers make things run more smoothly in the colonized world."[74] Resistance of various types to CCF fur policies continued to rise.

The CCF did create one mechanism through which trappers could register their concerns over fur policies with government. Beginning in 1950 the CCF used annual trappers conferences at Prince Albert as one of its main ways to communicate with trappers. DNR provided most of the initiative, financing, and organization. Northerners participated increasingly by 1953, when ninety-one delegates from fifty-two conservation areas attended meetings conducted in Cree, Chipewyan, and English. Yet DNR and white trappers from fringe areas often dominated. DNR anthropologist J.E.M. Kew depicted the organization as "dictatorial" and "paternalistic." The meetings acted as a "safety valve" for hostilities and as an "educational tool" for government, and with few exceptions did little to alter government policies. DNR continued its close supervision of the organization in the 1960s and still gave grants to delegates.[75]

Northern trappers had company in their opposition to compulsory fur marketing through SFMS. Fur traders and dealers throughout the province resisted the new measures. Complaints from dealers flooded in to Regina. Schneider and Einarson, traders at Deschambault Lake, complained of forged signatures in support of SFMS and said Indians had been told that shipping their furs to SFMS would help the Red Cross. They wondered too if SFMS would collect debts owed them for advances to trappers. The pair soon sold their post to the CCF, which opened a government store there. Similarly, the HBC worried about collecting debts from trappers who shipped furs to SFMS. In 1944 the Raw Fur, Hide, Horsehair and Wool Dealers' Association opposed the creation of SFMS. When Phelps considered forcing the marketing of all ranch and wild fur through SFMS, the Lestock Silver Fox and Fur Association unanimously opposed the plan.

Fearing the worst, Jewish fur dealers in Saskatoon asked for one year to close out their affairs. Fur dealer Mick Fyck wrote to Phelps: "Do you think Mr Phelps that fur dealers were making so much profit on buying furs that you wanted to take this away from us?" Even after trying the new system, the Raw Fur Dealers' Association remained opposed to SFMS in 1948. It offered to handle furs, keep records, oversee quotas, collect fees, and "become keen guardians."[76] But the CCF largely ignored the concerns of these capitalist merchants, whom it viewed as part of the problem in the fur industry. Instead of listening to opponents, the province worked to reduce and even eliminate their involvement in the business.

The HBC also resisted dealing with the SFMS. Regulations allowed the old company to handle muskrat furs from its Cumberland House lease. Phelps wanted to end this practice and to have the HBC market these furs through the Crown corporation. But after selling a trial shipment of muskrats through SFMS, the HBC decided to market the furs in London. The HBC justified this by claiming it wanted to help the British government reestablish the London fur market, which had ended during the war.[77] In effect, the decision weakened the marketing force of SFMS.

Although opposition to SFMS remained fierce in various quarters, a recovery in fur prices to "exceptional" levels helped the corporation succeed. From 1944 to 1946 it marketed nearly $2 million in furs. One large auction in August 1947 offered buyers the skins of 83,848 muskrat and 1,712 beaver and produced sales of $254,400.30. About thirty brokers and agents from outside the province attended, including representatives from twelve New York firms. After the sale, A.J. Cooke personally travelled north to distribute returns, which would allow trappers to buy trapping equipment and avoid debt. Many trappers seemed less concerned about the future and quickly spent the cash. SFMS added two storeys to its building in Regina, and Cooke declared that he had seen no equal to the new second-floor display area. He also claimed SFMS sales brought prices that equalled or exceeded those at any sale on the continent. SFMS sold about $8 million in pelts by January 1951 and earned a total surplus of $277,611 by the end of 1953.[78] In financial terms the Crown corporation appeared successful.

In some cases SFMS raised the prices of furs received by trappers. In 1947, for example, it paid eighty-six cents for muskrat, while the HBC paid seventy-five cents for those from its lease at Cumberland House. DNR's Malcolm Norris surveyed fur prices at La Ronge and concluded that the HBC and other private interests paid far less for furs than did SFMS. In one example offered, large mink sold at La Ronge for thirty-five dollars, while they had a market value of about sixty dollars. A report commissioned by Phelps for November and December 1947 concluded that trappers who sold to private interests lost about $128,000 compared to SFMS prices.[79] The government's claims seemed exaggerated. In reality the differences were often small, not large enough to support accusations of unfair treatment by private dealers. Traders could justify paying lower prices for furs since they did not know in advance what prices they would receive for them. Unlike SFMS, dealers paid for furs when they received them. Dealers also incurred costs by operating in isolated settlements and offering credit. Further, they did not receive the operating subsidies received by SFMS. The Crown corporation received government financing, market protection, and free labour from DNR officers who collected furs.

Even though the CCF boasted that SFMS provided protection and financial benefits to trappers, many of these captive customers did not believe the government's claims. Rejecting government statistics that they benefited from the compulsory program, trappers correctly pointed out that they received lower prices for many furs than they had years before on the open market. While weakening world fur markets caused much of this decline, the CCF received the blame. Delayed payments from SFMS and lost credit at local traders also continued to irk many northerners. Consequently, opposition to compulsory fur marketing intensified. As early as 1949, faced with complaints from Liberals, dealers, and trappers, Minister Brockelbank considered abandoning the policy, even though SFMS earned a profit. As protests increased, DNR's deputy minister, C.A.L. Hogg, and game commissioner, E.L. Paynter, also questioned continuing the compulsory program. Even DNR officers became apathetic about SFMS. With the opposition reaching overwhelming proportions, Brockelbank again reluctantly spoke of ending compulsory marketing in 1954. The final blow to the system came when the usually docile annual trappers convention, which had previously supported compulsory marketing, voted to end the system in 1955. The Fur Advisory Committee blamed Aboriginal delegates for the result, since most white trappers at the convention favoured compulsory marketing. In a weak effort to salvage the crumbling system, Brockelbank suggested increasing the initial payment for furs. Finally the CCF government, worn down by persistent and growing opposition to SFMS, allowed open marketing of beaver and muskrat pelts during the 1955-56 fiscal year. The primary reason compulsory marketing ended was persistent pressure from trappers. Government wanted to continue the system, even though the main initial justification for creating the system, the need to protect fur stocks, was no longer a concern.[80]

From the point of view of many northerners, SFMS had failed. During its time as a compulsory service the Crown corporation helped destroy the former northern economy while it did little to raise incomes. It possibly left Aboriginal northerners "poorer than ever."[81] The CCF also broke a promise to use the $412,319 surplus to promote the industry and increase social services. Instead the money went into general revenue.[82] However, from the CCF point of view, compulsory marketing succeeded. It largely accomplished at least one of the original purposes, playing a key role in the party's ideological attack on northern capitalism, including the HBC, private traders, and the credit system. Compulsory fur marketing helped weaken these institutions.

SFMS continued operating as a noncompulsory service after 1955. Once northern trappers received the freedom to choose a buyer, many of them avoided the hated marketing system. Largely because of support from southern trappers, SFMS handled 60.6 percent of the total wild fur catch in 1961-62. Yet this represented a considerable decline in market share. Under the compulsory system, SFMS had handled 74.5 percent of furs in 1949-50. During nineteen seasons of operation SFMS marketed more than $25 million in furs, more than half of Saskatchewan's wild fur production.[83]

Although the CCF used a heavy hand in various matters – banning trapping by southerners and those who had jobs, imposing group trapping areas, and forcing marketing through the SFMS – it chose not to use its power to reduce the number of Aboriginal trappers to a rational number. Instead, government institutionalized overcrowding. The number of northern trappers increased from 1,747 in 1947-48 to 2,055 in 1959-60. Practically all Aboriginals who wanted to trap received permission to do so. The Fur Advisory Committee and later the Program Co-ordinating Committee held responsibility for approving new trapping licences. While recognizing the poor economic outlook for trapping, the Program Co-ordinating Committee claimed vocational alternatives did not exist and turned down few applicants. It allowed thirty to forty new trappers per year. By 1959-60, Cumberland House area trappers, operating in one of the north's most productive areas, had a mean gross income of only $328, down from $464 in 1953-54. There and elsewhere many trappers failed to cover expenses. Since few could earn a living on the trapline, trapping increasingly became an activity rather than an occupation. Allowing many to trap, rather than limiting trapping to fewer participants, added to the failure of the CCF plan to have trapping form one of the primary bases of the northern Aboriginal economy.[84]

In an initiative closely related to trapping, the CCF encouraged northern fur farming. Politicians, bureaucrats, and many others viewed farming captive animals on fur farms as the future of fur production. Due to changing markets, during the 1940s mink ranches replaced the once-popular fox ranches. Northern mink ranching interested the CCF because it would use coarse fish and offal from fish plants as feed and offered hope for economic diversification. Many mink ranches started up, particularly in the Buffalo Narrows and Île-à-la-Crosse area. That region produced more than a quarter of the provincial mink production by 1955-56.[85] About ninety-four fur farms operated in the province by 1959, with 49,534 mink consuming approximately 5,685,372 pounds of coarse fish.[86] White people raised most furs, but the CCF saw potential for Aboriginal participation and wanted them to enter the business. However, since it had no program to help Aboriginals become fur farmers, CCF encouragement existed more in spirit than in fact. Various DNR officials spoke about creating programs to move Aboriginals into fur farming, and the Center for Community Studies visualized a great expansion in northern mink ranching, with up to another sixty ranches on the west side and more elsewhere. The CCF, the centre, and experts all guessed wrong in seeing a bright future for fur farming. Prices crashed by the mid-1960s. Only twenty-one licensed mink ranches remained in the province by 1970.[87]

Success greeted CCF efforts to restore and control fur stocks. Beaver once again felled trees and built dams, and muskrat played in thriving marshes. Yet the CCF hope that its multifaceted fur intervention would bring prosperity to Aboriginals remained unrealized. In many cases the poverty of trappers worsened. The provincial government could not control some of the causes for this. It could not reverse the long decline in world fur prices, which reduced the profitability of trapping. In 1960-61 Canadian wild fur production totalled only $12,360,000 compared to $16,092,000 in 1923. Beaver prices fell from an average of $27.36 in 1947-48 to $11.17 in 1959-60, and muskrat from $2.29 to $0.82. For 1959-60, Status Indian trappers averaged returns of $476, Metis of $313, and whites of $606. Trapping incomes fluctuated wildly, as seen in the northern block's drop to $684,932.24 in 1963-64 from $984,702.25 the previous year. Artificial fur, ranch fur, and foreign competition all hurt the industry, though pressure against using fur-bearing animals had not yet risen and was not a factor.[88]

CCF policies contributed to trapping's failure to form a base for the northern Aboriginal economy. Although fur stocks rose, trappers failed to increase the amount of fur taken. By 1960 wild fur production exceeded that of the first year of the conservation program only once. Some remote areas saw little trapping, since many trappers preferred to trap near settlements. Some Aboriginals also lacked interest in trapping, even close to home. By protecting inefficient and unmotivated producers and not opening trapping to outsiders, the CCF failed to bring much-needed efficiency and rationalization to trapping. Consistent with socialist principles, the CCF wanted to spread trapping income among virtually all northern Aboriginals rather than have fewer and better trappers receive substantial incomes. Skilled and ambitious trappers consequently could not earn a good living at trapping. The CCF forced socialist principles on a reluctant trapping industry. It did so by expelling entrepreneurs from trapping, imposing a group trapping model, opposing profit-oriented traders, and compelling marketing through the state-owned SFMS. Northerners resisted CCF ideology and actions, hurting the success of CCF plans.

Another aspect of the CCF trapping interventions, that which strove to end the credit system and replace it with a cash system, also proved a dismal failure. Barred from buying beaver and muskrat, traders cut the amount of credit they gave. This forced trappers to return from the trapline frequently for supplies, a change from the earlier arrangement when they obtained enough goods for extended, efficient stays in the bush. As well as refusing to give credit, SFMS did not pay for furs at the time of delivery. Instead it used a system of initial and final payments, but even the initial payment would not arrive for weeks or months. Trappers reportedly camped near the post office, drinking and gambling, waiting for cheques that often proved much smaller than expected. The new cash system brought feast and famine, since many quickly spent their fur cheques. Examples abound. Few bought traps for the next winter from cheques that arrived in the spring and summer. When fur income peaked at Cumberland House in 1946, trappers received cheques of $1,200 to $4,000. Many quickly spent the money and then went on relief. Montreal Lake became a "bootleg paradise" when fur cheques arrived, with up to seven taxis bringing liquor in one night. Reverend Waite blamed the increased drinking on what he referred to as the "Soviet system" introduced by the CCF.[89] Under the CCF system, trappers commonly ended up broke and without credit, which increased dependence on social aid. The government seemed surprised when its tampering with the centuries-old credit system caused serious new problems.

The CCF made weak efforts to fix its replacement for the credit system, mainly by talking about issuing payments in numerous installments. Indian Affairs and DNR unfruitfully discussed a multiple-payment system for Montreal Lake in 1948. The HBC agreed to help DNR implement a three-payment system for the Cumberland House area, but the system broke down in 1950 when two fur payments came too close together. RCMP Constable Crawford noted this resulted in "considerable excess drinking." In 1950, C.A.L. Hogg, DNR's deputy minister, favoured implementing a larger system to hold back fur income for "bad times." Action did not follow, and since the CCF seemed less concerned about the increased drinking and poverty than about ideology, the problem continued.[90]

Credit did not disappear completely. Since private traders could still buy some types of fur, they continued to extend some credit to trappers. But the amount was possibly only one-tenth the former credit limit. Additionally, traders allowed limited charge accounts for mothers, who would use the next family allowance cheque as collateral. Other government cheques also served as collateral, particularly if the trader handled the mail and could intercept the cheque. While the CCF opposed credit, even its stores reluctantly issued credit at times.[91] Forced fur marketing ended by 1956, but CCF opposition to credit continued. One observer in 1964 saw it as a "medieval approach," which regarded credit as "bad" because it allowed people to live beyond their means.[92] The mighty credit system of the old fur trade was never rebuilt, and instead of reducing northern problems, the CCF's ideological attack on northern credit proved disastrous, contributing to economic inactivity, welfare dependency, poverty, alcohol abuse, and social problems. Morris Shumiatcher, Douglas's former assistant, also saw many negative effects from the CCF intervention.[93] The CCF supplanted the former paternalism of the HBC with the paternalism of government control and the welfare state. Also, ironically, the CCF chose to destroy the northern credit system at the same time that southern householders and farmers increasingly relied on credit.

As an adjunct to its attack on the private fur trade and credit system, and as a central part of the new society it sought to create in the north, the CCF established a chain of retail stores. True to the party's socialist vision, the stores operated under a Crown corporation structure. The province simultaneously tried to build its share of the retail market and put private retailers out of business. One effect of the CCF giving itself a monopoly over buying beaver and muskrat was to discourage private traders from remaining in business. With the profitability of their businesses in jeopardy, some traders quit. In one case, Schneider and Einarson, disgruntled with the SFMS, sold their store at Deschambault to the government. The HBC proved more resilient. Although the CCF also tried to buy the thirteen northern HBC posts in 1944, the company did not sell. This refusal did not stop the CCF, which opened new stores. Most of the pressure for government to enter retailing came from ideologically sympathetic southern socialist politicians and bureaucrats, not from northerners. George Cadbury of EAPB and Allan Quandt wanted to see government stores. And Malcolm Norris and J.J. Wheaton viewed the government stores as the "main spring" for the new northern economy.[94]

In its first retail effort the CCF established Saskatchewan Government Trading Services (SGT) as a division of the Fish Board. In order to have administration of the stores close to the north, the CCF placed SGT's head office in Prince Albert. An SGT store began at La Ronge in 1945.[95] Posts also opened at Snake Lake, Wollaston, Beaver Lake, and Birch Rapids by 1948.

The new government stores received heavy subsidies from the province. One of the more unprofitable stores operated at Deschambault. Many Aboriginals there preferred to trade with a private store at Pelican Narrows, about twenty-eight miles away. An inconvenient location and a poor stock of goods also hurt the operation. The CCF considered closing the post, partly because it thought the area had "a poor class of native," not interested in hard work. Yet it remained open, operating much as a social service, with the Fish Board assuming losses. Malcolm Norris and then Jim Brady managed the post, trying to influence Aboriginals to change trading patterns and deal with the SGT store.[96]

The Fish Board and DNR subsidized various stores by providing staff and facilities and by flying store goods free of charge on flights to pick up fish. Additionally, DNR gave SGT cash subsidies in exchange for SGT doing DNR work at Deschambault, Wollaston, and Snake Lake. SFMS also helped SGT by deciding in early 1949 that SGT should collect its furs in most locations where SGT stores operated. This would give SGT a commission for handling the furs as well as possibly increase sales of goods to trappers. In another form of subsidy, the CCF sold goods below cost at times, causing dissatisfaction with higher prices at private posts. In one case, cheap flour at Wollaston brought buyers more than 100 miles.[97]

Patience with the ongoing financial losses began to wear thin when it became apparent that the CCF knew little about retailing or about the northern retail situation. By 1947, contradicting the CCF claim of HBC price gouging, Norris found SGT stores could not compete with the HBC, which sold goods for about the same price SGT paid wholesale. Poor buying jeopardized the La Ronge store, which had a stock of three or four tons of foul sausage, enough fishing lead to last for an estimated fifty years, and moth- and mouse-eaten socks and coats. In an effort to save money, the CCF operated stores in ramshackle rented or second-hand buildings. As part of an effort to stop the financial bleeding, government closed its Beaver Lake store by 1949. The Wollaston operation, on which people had come to depend, hung in the balance. Happily, the situation at La Ronge improved and it received a large modern store in 1952. By 1953, in keeping with its loss of enthusiasm for northern programs, the CCF did not want to expand its system of stores and became more interested in turning the stores into cooperatives.[98]

Part of the responsibility for the difficulties experienced by SGT belongs to the CCF's ideological opposition to the credit system. Because many northerners found it nearly impossibly to live without credit, the SGT stores' usual insistence on dealing in cash presented an ongoing obstacle to attracting customers. The stores sometimes gave in to pressure from customers and allowed some buying on credit. Although store managers could see the need for credit, those above them sometimes did not agree. In 1947, for example, James F. Gray, resident director of the Saskatchewan Lake and Forest Products Corporation, which controlled the Fish Board and its SGT stores, stopped the use of credit. As a result, since people could not wait for slow CCF fur payments, some stores lost much trade and their future appeared to be in jeopardy. After various DNR staff applied pressure, Gray agreed to allow the Snake Lake store to extend credit, but only in cases where another government department or a regular government or salary cheque would guarantee payment.[99]

Even though the Fish Board, under which the stores operated, went out of business by 1949, CCF stores continued. Saskatchewan Marketing Services took over Saskatchewan Government Trading Services and two other divisions – the Fur Marketing Service and the Fish Marketing Service. In time the CCF became more adept at running its stores, which then operated fairly successfully for much of the 1950s. SGT operated stores at Stanley Mission, Cumberland House, Lac la Ronge, Snake Lake, Wollaston, and Deschambault. By 1956-57 SGT had nineteen employees, fixed assets of

$124,351, sales of $610,053, and a net surplus of $15,335. The benefit of SGT stores remained uncertain, though, since many northerners did not want to deal with the unpopular CCF and its stores. The HBC and other private traders continued to dominate sales in most villages.[100]

The limited success of the CCF stores did not end the government's efforts to remake the northern retailing environment. As early as 1950 the CCF viewed SGT as a temporary measure until cooperatives could take over. The province began an aggressive program of creating cooperative retail outlets by the mid-1950s. In one of the earliest initiatives, DNR's anthropologist V.F. Valentine helped organize the Fort Black Co-op Store at Île-à-la-Crosse in 1955. The province gave funding and the credit society provided a loan. Things looked good for a time, with the co-op underselling local stores, paying a dividend, and buying many furs. Some problems arose when free traders opposed Valentine's efforts, and older people feared losing their security at the HBC or Marion's store. But the store survived. In 1957 and 1958, CCF officials pointed to it and other cooperative efforts in the Île-à-la-Crosse area as proof that Metis could successfully operate complex businesses. Yet even this model store repeatedly needed extensive aid. It failed about five times by 1970, with the province helping it reopen each time. One observer said the store ran much like a welfare agency, with credit carelessly given. Patrons reportedly also blackmailed the manager into giving them more credit by threatening to complain to the Co-op Management Advisor about the operation.[101] Other areas tried to emulate the early success at Île-à-la-Crosse. Co-op stores opened at Buffalo Narrows and Beauval by 1957.[102]

Possibly spurred by high prices at the HBC store, local interest in a co-op store grew at La Loche by 1958. A comparison of prices at the HBC store in La Loche and the co-op store in Buffalo Narrows revealed that a group of items cost about 15 percent more at La Loche after allowing for extra transportation costs to the area. Local promoters of a co-op found willing allies in Paul Godt of the Department of Co-operation and Miss M. Crawley of Social Welfare, who did not like HBC ways. The CCF took over the project, expecting it would need to maintain control. P. Spaulding of Co-operation wrote: "The meaning of co-operation, the value of loyalty to the organization, the value of money, thrift, and industriousness in the sense that they are meaningful to Canadians have little or no meaning to the residents of La Loche." The Department of Co-operation planned the store, and the CCF supplied most of the funds, expecting residents to provide only wall logs and $1,000 towards the estimated $31,000 cost. The store officially opened in 1959, with T.C. Douglas in attendance. It failed in the 1960s, apparently because the manager gave credit too leniently.[103]

The CCF further increased its imposition of co-op stores and the number of these retail outlets by turning SGT posts into cooperatives. Pressure for making the change came from various quarters. The Northern

Advisory Committee (NAC) pushed for the changeover of SGT stores to cooperatives. It wanted the province to provide a 100 percent guarantee, carry losses, and place less emphasis on making a profit. Amendments to the Guarantee Act, allowing a 100 percent guarantee for some co-ops, followed. The Officials' Committee on Northern Affairs, a newly appointed group, began meeting in 1958 to study changing SGT and the Fish Marketing Service to cooperatives. SGT then transferred its stores to Northern Co-operative Trading Services (NCTS) on 31 March 1959. The CCF extended credit for the full sale price of $275,000. NCTS, along with the new Co-operative Fisheries Limited (CFL), was a "second tier co-operative." This meant that local co-ops held memberships in the central cooperatives. An appointed southern board of directors oversaw the operation, while the CCF spoke of a five-year transition period to northern control. Some local participation existed, including at Cumberland House where an elected local board advised the central board. The co-ops also began using Aboriginal managers. In its first full year of operation, NCTS, together with CFL, did business of $1,862,432.03. Although it earned a surplus of $80,000, government paid much more than this in subsidies. Driven by ideology, the CCF continued to insist that northerners would have cooperatives whether they wanted them or not. Many of the new cooperatives became not much more than another form of CCF socialist enterprise. Little local initiative and interest existed, but the CCF thought support would come in time.[104]

At one point, NCTS stores operated at Cumberland House, Deschambault, La Ronge, Pinehouse, Stanley Mission, and Wollaston, in addition to co-op stores at Beauval, Buffalo Narrows, Île-à-la-Crosse, La Loche, Patuanak, Pelican Narrows, and Kinoosao. A floating co-op store also conducted business from a barge on Churchill Lake, following fishermen.[105] The stores likely lowered prices for goods and reduced the cost of living, especially where no competition had existed.[106]

Ongoing strong involvement by the CCF ensured that the co-ops continued while that government remained in power. But a lack of true local support and the CCF failure to solve the "production credit problem" – or failure to advance credit appropriately – became fatal flaws once the co-ops had to stand on their own. Faced with continuing losses, the new Liberal government, which defeated the CCF in 1964, discontinued the operation of NCTS. It first allocated part of the purchase debt to local cooperatives and then wrote off the remainder owing.[107] With the artificial props reduced, the number of co-ops dropped dramatically.

The CCF had a dream for northern prosperity. Politicians and bureaucrats made and implemented ambitious plans to fundamentally alter the northern economy, particularly the Aboriginal economy. They visualized Aboriginals successfully pursuing "traditional occupations," including trapping. At the same time the CCF sought to protect northerners from the ravages of the capitalist system. This brought an ongoing attack on capitalist fur traders and the long-standing credit system. To replace capitalist relationships in the fur trade, the CCF introduced Aboriginals to various forms of socialist and cooperative organization, including SFMS, SGT stores, and cooperatives. Working from its base in the south, the socialist government imposed its ideologically inspired plans on northerners, using paternalistic and colonial methods. Subsequent events disappointed the CCF. Aboriginals opposed the Crown corporation form of ownership, detested compulsory marketing, and lacked interest in cooperatives. Further, trapping, even when reserved for northern Aboriginals, failed to provide the hoped for prosperity. But the CCF did not place all of its hope for northern economic reform on its fur and retail projects. It simultaneously intervened in other aspects of the economy. In another major initiative, the CCF reorganized the fishing industry. This endeavour also proved challenging, with many unforeseen pitfalls.

6
At the Point of a Gun

Commercial fishing formed the second major sector of the northern Aboriginal economy visualized by the CCF. In many respects policies for the fishery resembled those for the fur industry; they formed part of the same CCF economic master plan. As with trapping, this government reserved commercial fishing primarily for northerners. In its view, greedy capitalists from outside the region had long dominated the industry, hurting local participation and removing wealth from the northern economy. In another parallel to its trapping policies, the CCF wanted to increase Aboriginal participation in the fishery and spread the income from fishing to a large number of Aboriginals. Those in government believed that Aboriginals possessed a natural aptitude to fish and that fishing could form one of the main activities in a new, prosperous Aboriginal economy. Promotion of Aboriginal fishing contradicted the CCF plan to modernize and assimilate Aboriginals just as the CCF policy on trapping did. Instead of moving Aboriginals into the modern world, fishing reinforced a pre-industrial, segregated lifestyle.

The CCF applied its socialist philosophy to the intervention in the fishery much to the same degree it applied it to the fur industry. James F. Gray, who soon would head the new Crown corporation in charge of fish, expressed the belief of many in the government when he said that fishermen did not own the fish. They believed that benefits from fish belonged to all the people of Saskatchewan.[1] Socialist ideology also influenced the CCF's choice of Crown corporations to buy, process, and market fish. To improve the enterprises' chances of success, the CCF created and enforced a monopoly over fish processing and marketing in a large part of the north. At the same time it discouraged and limited private investment in the fishery and created a hostile climate for capital. Further, as with furs, the CCF preference for socialist solutions led to the eventual creation of a largely artificial cooperative structure to handle fish.

Commercial fishing had long operated successfully with minimal government involvement. At least it seemed successful from the point of view of many involved in the business. Fishing formed the third largest industry in Saskatchewan in the mid-1940s. Hundreds of people fished, with little depletion of fish stocks. In the 1944-45 fiscal year the fish haul totalled about 13,397,427 pounds. Since many isolated lakes, including Wollaston and Reindeer, had no licensed fishermen, there was potential for considerable expansion.[2] Prior to CCF involvement, white fishermen, processors, and dealers dominated northern fishing. They provided the necessary capital and organization for a profitable fishing industry. While Aboriginal people relied partly on fish to feed themselves and their dogs, most seemed uninterested in commercial fishing. Some commonly worked for non-Aboriginal fishermen. For several reasons, most fishing took place in the winter. Because the north had virtually no roads, Caterpillars and other tractors economically pulled sleighs loaded with frozen fish along ice-covered waterways and winter roads. The natural refrigeration of the cold northern winter also allowed caught fish to keep well. In contrast, fish netted in summer quickly spoiled unless kept on ice or under refrigeration.

The new government seemed to want advice about the fishery and appointed a royal commission to study the subject. Commission members included University of British Columbia professor A. Clemens, A.A. McAllister from Flin Flon, Supervisor of Fisheries A.H. MacDonald, A. Mansfield of Prince Albert, and Dr. D.S. Rawson of the University of Saskatchewan. The group began its work in 1946 and reported in February 1947. It made seventy-five recommendations. Among other things, it suggested ways to improve markets and adjust freight rates and advised giving "Indians and Metis a proper place in the commercial fishing industry." The report also stressed the importance of the fishery to the north.[3]

However, the CCF had already formed its own opinions about the fishery. In spite of this industry's past success, government disapproved of the structure and operation of the northern fishery. It thought the middlemen, who bought, marketed, and exported the fish, took too much while fishermen received too little. Its socialist convictions told the CCF that an unregulated capitalist system inevitably resulted in abuses and excessive profits going to business owners. Natural Resources minister Joe Phelps claimed that unscrupulous fish buyers had bled the north and, along with fur buyers and bootleggers, "skinned" the people. J.H. Brockelbank thought dealers had "ways and means" of controlling Aboriginals, keeping them in near-perennial debt. Subsequent events proved the CCF analysis of price-gouging wrong. The fishermen's share of the selling price of fish dropped from the 1939-43 period, when they received an average of 48 percent of the market price, to the 1955-59 period, when, under CCF regulation, they received an average of only 47 percent.[4] It remains unclear why the CCF appointed the royal commission, since it did not wait for the commission's report to act.

Politicians and bureaucrats rapidly designed and implemented a three-pronged program to remake the fishing industry, targeting the production, marketing, and quality of fish. As in trapping, the CCF, with a few exceptions, gave priority to northerners in fishing.[5] In colonial fashion it only applied this principle to the menial fishing positions, while outsiders managed the fishery. Residents on lakes received first priority for licences in various areas of the north. With the ejection of many outsiders, northerners comprised about 94 percent of area fishermen by the late 1950s.[6]

Phelps and the CCF claimed a groundswell of support for intervening in the fishing industry. Some fishermen, particularly those who fished in the southern part of the province, did agree with the CCF plans. For example, a fishermen's meeting at Meota, addressed by Phelps, voted unanimously for marketing through the Fish Board. Also, about 85 percent of fishermen who answered a questionnaire supported the creation of a marketing board.[7] But the CCF survey failed to accurately reflect the opinion of northern Aboriginals, most of whom could not read or complete a questionnaire. It also did not give much weight to the opinions of those fishermen and dealers whom the CCF wanted to expel from the fishery.

Acting quickly, the CCF set up a complex organization to manage fish processing and marketing. It created Saskatchewan Fish Products (SFP) in 1945 to operate filleting plants, and later that year added the Saskatchewan Fish Marketing Board to buy and sell fish. George Cadbury, the top hired CCF planner, agreed with replacing "competitive interests" with a marketing board. In a May 1946 reorganization, the CCF formed Saskatchewan Lake and Forest Products Corporation (SLFPC), which had three divisions: the Fish Board, the Timber Board, and the Box Factory. Phelps held the position of chairman of the corporation. James F. Gray, resident director of SLFPC, also took over responsibility for the Fish Board, and D.F. Corney became its general manager in December 1946. The Fish Board also had three parts, with A. Mansfield in charge of sales, K.E. Dickson heading up production, and Gray looking after trading posts. The Fish Board, with its head office in Prince Albert, operated in six areas by 1948: Lac la Ronge, Beaver Lake, Meadow Lake, Wollaston Lake, Reindeer Lake, and Pelican Narrows. The CCF felt optimistic about its fishing intervention, and zeal for the program extended into the ranks of Fish Board employees. In 1947 Art Lucas, the new sales manager, wrote: "I am satisfied more every day that the stand we have taken in the fishing industry is basically right ... to drive the thin edge of the wedge into an industry dominated by exploitation + racket."[8]

Men dominated all levels of the CCF fishery. Only one woman, Mrs. E. Welsh, served on the first board of directors. Welsh, who qualified for the board because she had organized and served as president and manager of the defunct Reindeer Lake Fisheries Ltd., did not last long. The Flin Flon area Trades and Labor Council complained to Phelps that the Fish Board had hired a woman whose husband had a job with the mine. The council wanted a "just distribution of employment." Phelps considered Welsh's appointment as temporary and terminated her services effective 31 March 1946. He offered the approaching end of the fish delivery season as the reason for her dismissal. Yet men remained on in their positions.[9]

Unlike the fur industry, in which the CCF justified its intervention by citing conservation needs, the fishery was not depleted. Instead, justification for Phelps's fish policies came from a timely crisis; *Triaenophorus crassus* cysts infested whitefish, endangering the industry. The minister credited these parasites, not CCF ideology, with making the construction of CCF fish-processing plants necessary. While harmless to humans, the cysts, which infested the flesh of the fish, made the product unappetizing. The United States had already stopped many large shipments of infested Saskatchewan whitefish, endangering the industry. Filleting the fish, candling the fillets, and then cutting out the cysts could make even heavily infested fish acceptable to the US market. While the province administered fishing, fishery regulation, including establishing export standards, fell under the authority of Ottawa. To deal with the infestation, Ottawa and Saskatchewan co-operated in introducing a system of grading lakes as A, B, and C lakes by 1943-44. The "A" designation allowed the sale of unfilleted fish even if they were lightly cyst-infested, a "B" grade required filleting and candling, and "C" lakes awaited inspection. By January 1946 the process designated fifty "A" and twenty-eight "B" lakes in Saskatchewan.[10]

New regulations that allowed no more than fifty cysts per hundred pounds of fish took effect 14 November 1944. One official minimized the potential impact of the new regulations. He thought that even if the crisis stopped northern fishing, this would affect only 944 part-time fishermen, including 589 "half-breeds and Indians who, no doubt, trap in season." Faced with opposition from fishermen, who thought it impossible to operate under the new regulations, Phelps wanted the standard eased to allow the marketing of substandard fish within Saskatchewan. The chief inspector for the federal Department of Fisheries admitted that the only reason for the regulations was to increase exports to the US. Ottawa then allowed a more lenient standard of ninety cysts per hundred pounds of fish for local sales. Political opponents took advantage of this relaxing of regulations to accuse the CCF of selling second-rate fish, fish not good enough for Americans, to Saskatchewan residents. The new quality-control measures and a shift of fishing to lakes with low infestations proved effective in improving the quality of fish exported to the US, and there was a 73.5 percent reduction in rejections at the US border.[11]

Since private interests already owned fish plants, the CCF did not really need to go into the fish-processing business. The existing industry, even

though it lacked the facilities to fillet all the fish required by the new regulations, seemed willing to expand its capacity. But instead of allowing the
industry to respond to the crisis, the CCF imposed a government monopoly on fish processing in large areas of the north. It built its first two fish
plants at La Ronge and Beaver Lake.

Construction of the La Ronge plant, which began in 1944, proved a
fiasco. Long delays occurred due to winter weather and disputes between
project managers. Some wanted construction to stop. DNR's acting deputy
minister, L.C. Paterson, favoured abandoning the plant and instead building it in Prince Albert as "a monument to this Government in the establishment of industry." La Ronge residents wished the plant relocated to
English Bay, farther north on Lac la Ronge, a location they considered
more suitable. A. VanderKracht, one of only three paid-up CCF members
in La Ronge, complained that local people did not receive construction
employment. His complaint possibly lost credibility when another CCF
supporter described him to Phelps as "half out of his mind anyway." VanderKracht unhappily quit the party. Although the CCF stuck to its plan
and the building was eventually completed, its foundations soon settled,
causing floors and machinery to tilt precariously. Complaints arose about
staff drunkenness, a lack of supervision of female employees, and venereal
disease among the staff. One report said few of the thirty-two employees
could "state what his or her duties are." Axel Olsen, the manager and an
SFP director, lost his managerial position due to alleged incompetence
but remained on staff. Neither Olsen nor his replacement, Mr. Bodner, the
Fish Board chairman, spent much time at the plant, leaving it "virtually
unmanaged." Pollution from the plant also brought grievances. In 1947
the latest plant manager, M.A. McCabe, blamed complaints on the Liberal
"propaganda machine." Yet Dr. A.O. Blackwell, who checked the plant,
found dirty and inadequate conditions.[12] The plant's sorry saga continued
in the years to come.

Construction of the Beaver Lake plant, located not far from Flin Flon,
went much better. It opened in 1945, managed by K.E. Dickson. SFP also
built two large two-storey staff houses there. Indian fishermen, whose light
dog teams allowed them to travel on the thin early ice, began bringing fish
in December. As at La Ronge, the plant hired many surplus staff. Fishermen, who paid for poor management through lower receipts for the fish
caught, criticized the inefficiencies.[13]

The province established bonded warehouses at Flin Flon, Big River, and
Meadow Lake where inspections took place. Most exported fish passed
through Flin Flon or Prince Albert, which had rail lines. The Fish Board
hired Don Phelps, a Wilkie area farmer and Joe Phelps's brother, to manage the Flin Flon warehouse, paying him $200 per month. Don advised Joe
on various aspects of fish handling, and the brothers agreed that "much of
our field staff don't seem to know what it is all about." Although Don later

left the job for his farm, he returned to temporarily manage the Beaver Lake Fish Plant in the winter of 1947-48. He took no pay, "on account of family relations," although he billed the Fish Board for expenses, including the cost of wages for his hired man on the farm.[14]

While the CCF claimed its fish intervention was for the benefit of northern Aboriginals, this philosophy did not apply to the construction and operation of the plants. Although some Aboriginals worked there, white people dominated. Dickson, who helped with the construction at La Ronge, said, "The native help here is not very dependable ... another 6 or 8 good men would be more economical than those we are using at present." The dozens of employees at both plants in early 1946 included few, if any, Aboriginal persons.[15]

The Fish Board built numerous other fish plants throughout the north. It viewed Pelican Narrows, located at the head of three lakes, as an ideal location for a fish-processing plant and established one there by 1946. The Crown corporation also located smaller facilities at Sturgeon, Suggi, Windy, Deschambault, Snake, and Wollaston lakes and at Birch Rapids and Stanley Mission. Meadow Lake received the board's main plant for the Meadow Lake area. Elsewhere on the west side, the government operated ice houses and packing plants at Île-à-la-Crosse, Lac la Plonge, and Canoe, Arsenault, Keely, and Green lakes.[16]

Winter roads, which passed over frozen water surfaces and muskeg, allowed for the economical transport of fish from outlying lakes to the processing plants. Caterpillar tractors, often operating on unsafe ice, opened roads and pulled sleighs loaded with fish. While the province had some tractors, private persons owned most of those used. From January to March 1946, Reindeer Lake and its treacherous ice alone claimed seven Caterpillars and a number of lives. After one incident, when two privately owned tractors fell through the ice and one man had a close call, Don Phelps told his brother Joe, "I would not feel too sorry for the freighters as they are mostly owned by fish companies."[17] The board also used snowmobiles and airplanes to pick up fish in some areas.

The Fish Board soon experienced mounting problems. Miscalculations in stock management led to a situation where the board bought a lot more fish than it sold. For practical reasons it dealt mainly in frozen fish, while the market wanted and paid higher prices for fresh fish. In the fall of 1947 government already had large quantities of fish stored in Prince Albert, Regina, Winnipeg, Montreal, Toronto, and Minneapolis and sold only about one-third of the fish it bought the next winter. While it had a huge stock of some types of frozen fish, the board could not meet the demand for fresh fish. Had government not paid for the mounting financial losses, the Crown corporation would have quickly fallen into insolvency.[18]

Desperate to sell the stockpiles of fish, the province worked to increase exports. Learning the fish business by trial and error, the Fish Board located agents in New York City, Montreal, and Toronto. Board sales managers travelled extensively, developing markets. They met with some success but fish quality problems continued to endanger the hard-won marketing achievements. The new CCF plants continued to operate under lax controls and often failed to produce an acceptable product. Even after filleting, candling, and excising, many cysts remained in the flesh. The chief inspector for the Department of Fisheries thought that the processing methods used could not produce acceptable fillets from highly infested lakes. While some infested fish slipped past the inspection system to the US, many did not. After a rejection of fish in 1947 caused the loss of the fish and the shipping costs, the board's sales manager, A. Mansfield, threatened to quit unless he received "a definite guarantee that this kind of negligence will not go on." The introduction of voluntary pre-inspection of export whitefish in 1947 helped somewhat. Rejections at the border fell by over 60 percent, but the US still blocked the import of ten thousand pounds of pre-inspected fish. The classification of lakes also continued. By 1948, 168 lakes were classified, with 93 in the "A" category and 75 in the "B" category. Fish from "A" lakes, which did not need processing, became the preferred fish. The federal government also continued its efforts to improve the fish product, introducing even stricter inspection regulations in 1950.[19]

Needing to dispose of the stocks of frozen fish, the CCF tried to sell fish to Saskatchewan residents. Since the province's people ate less fish than the average Canadian, potential for market expansion seemed good. A winter mail-order program and commercial locker plants helped dispose of heavily infested fish that could not meet export standards. Len Waite, a private fish dealer who also sold fish by mail order, opposed the CCF dumping of inferior fish on residents, fearing destruction of the local market for fish. Yet the province continued selling infested fish, operating on the premise that the cysts presented no health risk to consumers. The mail-order program proved reasonably successful. In 1951-52 the CCF sold about a million pounds of fish with a total of 2,785,607 pounds sold in the province. With patronage dropping off, it ended its mail-order business in 1955. Overall fish sales within Saskatchewan also fell, dropping to about 1,360,000 pounds in 1959. In the end, the policy of selling substandard fish likely played a part in consumers losing interest in fish.[20]

The CCF tried other ways to dispose of surplus fish. Willing to try innovative solutions, it built canning and smoking operations at Meadow Lake and Prince Albert. Optimism remained, even after the experiment lost $9,854.03 from 1 April to 30 September 1947. Expansion of the program saw DNR buy a portable quick-freeze unit and smoke house and refrigerated transportation. But the board failed to find the needed market or produce a product with sufficient consumer appeal. With the fish market at its lowest point since 1939, the desperate board marketed smoked fish from a truck in Montana in 1948. Government eventually let the canning and smoking operations die, with the last operation at Prince Albert ending in about 1949.[21]

For various reasons, the CCF also promoted a shift from winter to summer fishing. The strong demand for fresh fish provided a major incentive for this change, and improved technology, including the increased use of refrigeration and rapid transportation of fish by airplanes, made this possible. Fishing in summer also fit well with the CCF plan for the Aboriginal economy, since trapping took place primarily in winter. Staggering trapping and fishing would spread economic activity and income throughout the year. While many fishermen resisted the pressure to fish in summer, the gradual shift did take place over the next decades. By 1962 fishers netted 67 percent of the annual catch during the summer. The following year, of about 900 fishers, more than 500 fished only in the summer, about 200 only in winter, and about 200 in both seasons.[22]

Financial losses mounted in spite of the government's ability to legislate rules that operated in its favour and against potential competitors. In an extremely controversial move, the CCF gave its plants a large advantage over private buyers and processors by prohibiting the latter from operating within seventy-five miles of Fish Board plants. This created a compulsory marketing situation in about one-third of the northern area, where fish had to pass through government plants. The CCF monopoly forced dealers and processors to move to other areas, leave the province, or close down. In one case, a private plant at Deschambault Lake closed in 1945. Convinced of the ideological and moral correctness of its actions, the CCF seemed unconcerned about the damage its policy caused. Although the record soon showed that the government plants often produced inferior fillets, Phelps justified the monopoly by expecting them to produce a superior product. He wrote of "the absolute necessity of having all fish go through our own Plant in order to insure a quality product." The CCF rigorously enforced the seventy-five-mile rule, with the notable exception of allowing Len Waite to operate at Dore, Smoothstone, Cowan, and Snake lakes.[23] The board also extended its operations outside the compulsory marketing zones. It entered into various arrangements, including for filleting at the Canada Packers Plant in Prince Albert and for DNR to buy fish at Cumberland House.[24]

By 1947, faced with criticism from fish dealers, Phelps and some in the Fish Board wanted to expand government's monopoly and take over all handling of Saskatchewan fish. Phelps believed that putting dealers out of business in the forest industry squelched criticism, and he thought a complete monopoly might do the same in fishing. Blaming opposition on vocal dealers, who feared the CCF threat to their livelihood, diverted attention from the severe problems that plagued the CCF production, quality control, and marketing methods.[25]

While still considering the creation of a complete monopoly, Phelps allowed some private fish buying and processing to continue in the north, mainly on the west side. Len Waite and his Big River-based Waite Fisheries dominated there, efficiently buying, processing, and marketing "Arctic Brand" fish. Waite built a large filleting plant at Buffalo Narrows and placed smaller plants elsewhere. F.M. Clark also handled fish on the west side. In 1945-46, Clark handled 976,293 pounds of fish, while Waite handled 1,065,986 pounds.[26]

The relationship between Phelps and Waite appears puzzling given the minister's vehement condemnation of fish dealers. Phelps treated Waite with great respect. Although not a CCF member, Waite managed to preserve his business while helping the CCF take over much of the rest of the industry. He advised Phelps on the fishery, even allowing the Fish Board to use his filleting plant blueprints to build almost exact copies. Phelps actively protected Waite from the Fish Board, other dealers, and fishermen. When Waite complained to Phelps that others wanted to process fish near Waite's Dore Lake plant, Phelps promised to do "everything in our power" to keep competitors away. The board also let Waite operate within the seventy-five-mile exclusion zone of its La Ronge plant. When Phelps wanted to take over all fish processing, he did not abandon Waite, but tried to buy out his plants and put Waite in charge of the board's production division. Waite did not seem to oppose selling his plants, possibly seeing a favourable outcome for himself either way. He cooperated when in 1945 the Crown corporation took his plant at Dore Lake, before transferring it back to Waite in 1946. For a time the board also held options to purchase Waite's plants at Buffalo Narrows and Big River. Aided by Phelps, Waite soon enjoyed a near monopoly in some west side areas, in spite of strong opposition from other processors and fishermen.[27]

By siding with Waite, the CCF ignored one of its main reasons for involvement in the fishery – to protect fishermen from buyers' control. Some complained about Phelps's preferential treatment of Waite. K.E. Dickson of the Fish Board boldly told Phelps: "You are being openly accused of being in with Len Waite and his operations and there must be some reason for this and we cannot ignore public opinion altogether." DNR acted as a conciliator when Dore Lake fishermen went on strike against Waite's monopoly in 1946. In 1948 the province sided with Waite against Dore Lake fishermen on the issue of splitting winter and summer quotas. Fishermen there wanted to be able to divide the take between the winter and summer as they wished. The CCF decreed 75 percent of the 600,000 pound quota as the summer catch, and reaffirmed Waite's monopoly.[28] Surprisingly, the capitalist Waite successfully coexisted with the socialist Phelps. While Phelps clearly appreciated Waite's advice and help, the relationship remained puzzling. Waite lost his protector with Phelps's defeat in 1948. Under DNR's new minister, J.H. Brockelbank, the dealer met with harsher treatment.

Although Waite prospered, the Fish Board's problems mounted. Phelps's alleged overwhelming support from fishermen for his interventions seemed elusive, with the compulsory aspect of the program particularly raising controversy. A report about the La Ronge plant said: "Some fishermen stated that 'they were selling their fish to the Government at the point of a gun.'" Many opposed the CCF plan. R.F. Bradfield of Montreal Lake "refused to work under a dictatorship"; fishermen in the Primrose and Cold lakes area defied regulations by taking fish to Alberta, which offered higher prices. Opposition to the Fish Board increased as its errors and losses grew.[29]

The Fish Board proved a financial disaster, largely because the CCF knew little about the fishery. Dreams of processing low-value, parasite-infested fish from remote lakes and selling them at a profit proved unrealistic. Board accountant W.J. Bague admitted that "optimistic reports ... have been more or less guesswork." At times, because of low prices and the reluctance of fishermen to deal with the Crown corporation, the board could not find enough fish for efficient operation of its newly built plants. Flying fish from Wollaston and other remote lakes in small planes also brought losses. Board manager K.E. Dickson became very dissatisfied, tendering his resignation in 1947. Although he remained, Dickson thought they had squeezed all they could out of fishermen.[30]

Failure of the Crown corporation also became inevitable because the CCF wrongly thought northern fishing profitable enough for the board to act as a social agency and still make a profit. In one instance the board gave medicine and food to sick Dene at Wollaston Lake. In spite of these efforts, three of the Dene died. In another case a board plane flew a five-hundred-mile round trip to bring a patient to Flin Flon. The corporation also lost money on its stores, which it operated partly to provide a service. The CCF expected the board to provide supplies to Aboriginal fishermen, operate on unprofitable lakes, inefficiently prolong fishing to increase employment, and involve as many fishermen as possible. The province issued 1,700 licences, thinly spreading the potential benefit from fishing and reducing fishermen's incomes to a paltry $100 to $500. Even former supporters of the CCF fishery policy came to question its wisdom. Some blamed inefficient Aboriginal fishermen for the troubles. Dickson and other board managers called for limiting operations to the less remote, heavy-producing lakes and using competent fishermen. The managers also wanted the board to ignore social issues. Yet a dilemma existed. Without controls, efficient white operators would again sideline Aboriginals.[31]

After Phelps left, a long-overdue review of CCF fishing policies took place. Faced with mounting losses and controversy, the CCF decided to kill the board, bury its failures, and try again. The Fish Board passed from existence on 31 October 1949, with an accumulated deficit of $364,264.37. In its place rose the Saskatchewan Fish Marketing Service (SFMS). DNR took over responsibility for much of the new operation, including guaranteeing prices and absorbing losses. The government still ran the La Ronge plant, tendered out operation of the plant at Beaver Lake, and closed the Meadow Lake plant.[32]

The CCF seemed chastised and more wary after its costly education in the Fish Board fiasco. The disaster also damaged the credibility of CCF planners. SFMS acted less aggressively than had the Fish Board, forcing its compulsory service only where at least 51 percent of the fishermen on a lake voted to deal with it. Those at Beaver Lake, La Ronge, Deschambeault, and Pelican Narrows decided to use the service. Fishermen at Snake Lake rejected using SFMS by a margin of twenty-one to one. Some who did not want to deal with SFMS, as in the Canoe Lake area, later changed their minds. Remaining firm in his ideological opposition to private enterprise, Brockelbank said, "The fish dealers got hold of them and taught them a lesson the hard way."[33]

In reality, SFMS proved popular largely because fishermen wanted to participate in a floor price system established by the CCF. Support payments proved costly at first, but less so by the 1960s due to better markets and marketing. By 1959 government spent a total of about $265,000 supporting prices. However, government only offered this program in some areas of the north. A correlation exists between the areas where fishermen supported SFMS and where government offered the floor price plan. Both programs operated much more on the east side than on the west side.

At best SFMS produced a mixed record of success. With its organizers still in shock from the Fish Board failure, the new organization particularly lacked clear goals and consistent methods. After several years of confusion, the CCF again acted more assertively and increased SFMS operations. Government had already transferred most former Fish Board assets to DNR, and it continued the clever system where DNR and its relatively large budgets would absorb much of the financial risk for fish interventions. This approach helped the SFMS ledgers appear healthy, while large expenses hid in the DNR books. To its advantage, SFMS leased the plants at La Ronge, Beaver Lake, Pelican Narrows, and Deschambault, warehouses at Flin Flon, Prince Albert, and Dilke, and other assets from DNR beginning 1 December 1952. The system allowed SFMS to avoid heavy capital expenditures; it only built small processing plants at Pinehouse and Pelican Narrows. Under the new system, SFMS also reduced its risk by acting as a marketing board and not actually buying the fish, unlike the Fish Board.[34] In 1951-52, SFMS operated on forty-eight lakes, handling 5,317,834 pounds of fish. The amount of fish it dealt with fluctuated, dropping to 4,385,404 pounds in 1954-55. In 1957 SFMS marketed about 47 percent of the provincial catch.[35] In comparison to the Fish Board, it appeared successful.

With the larger resources of DNR backing the SFMS operation, the CCF used the fish enterprise to aid with various noneconomic goals. The province called upon the Crown corporation to help with the task of modernizing, assimilating, and socializing northern Aboriginals. Reindeer Lake provides a notable example. Commercial fishing there had ended when fish stocks declined, likely due to a control dam built in 1942 on the outflowing Reindeer River for the Island Falls hydroelectric project. Once fish stocks recovered, SFMS began a temporary operation on the lake in 1951. Committing large amounts of money, DNR then built a permanent filleting plant and settlement at Kinoosao, also known as Co-Op Point, just inside the Saskatchewan border. The CCF, with Manitoba's cooperation, built a road from the formerly remote location to the railhead at Lynn Lake. In 1953, forty-one white and Aboriginal fishermen, operating as a cooperative, held fishing licences. The province then actively encouraged Aboriginals to move to the new community, where they could live in a modern, assimilated, cooperative environment.[36]

Similar events took place at Wollaston Lake. Icelanders from the Lake Winnipeg area first commercially fished there in 1944-45. Although the Fish Board took over the marketing in 1945-46, the CCF allowed the Icelanders to remain, since they had established permanent residence on the lake. In 1951 fishermen unanimously approved marketing the fish from the lake through the SFMS for the next five years. But before this time passed, the lake closed to fishing due to heavy parasite infestation of fish. The closing jeopardized the livelihood of about fifteen white or Metis fishermen and ten Status Indians, who worked mainly as assistants. Spurred by a strong demand for fish in New York, cabinet in 1956 decided to build a filleting plant at Wollaston, reversing an earlier decision. Cabinet also wanted to save money on social aid costs and asked how much the plant might reduce social aid expenditures. It seemed the plant could provide a substantial increase in local income of up to $80,000 per year and reduce future subsidies. The province visualized creating a new community with a joint Indian Affairs and provincial school and a federal hospital. Movement to the community could also help the scattered people "properly carry out their responsibility as citizens." DNR's R.N. Gooding flew over the area to choose a plant and townsite location. DNR then built the plant, the cost of which rose dramatically from an initial estimate of $40,000 to about $75,000, and leased it to SFMS. An estimated 152 people lived at Wollaston Lake, including 16 whites, 19 Metis, and 117 Indians.[37]

Both economic and noneconomic motivations drove the CCF fishery interventions in the 1950s. Over time, marketing problems eased and the market for whitefish fillets grew greatly. This should have increased the potential benefit of the fishery for northerners, but government usually responded only slowly to business considerations and market demands, thereby limiting the output of the fishery and its impact on the northern economy. As the situations at Reindeer and Wollaston lakes demonstrate, in several cases the province did react to supply the market. On those occasions, while noneconomic considerations likely remained of utmost importance, government also became caught up in trying to meet the demands of the market.

In order to maintain its position in the fishery business, the CCF also needed to spend money on existing operations. After years of problems, by the mid-1950s the La Ronge plant deteriorated from bad to unacceptable. About eight inches of lake water stood in the engine room, and the filleting and fish receiving rooms had water between the floor joists. Floors sloped, and the roof appeared in danger of collapse. DNR budgeted $45,000 to replace the plant, which took place by 1956.[38] Construction also began on a new plant at Pelican Narrows, where mostly Status Indians fished and processed fish. DNR wanted Indian Affairs to contribute $20,000, while Saskatchewan would guarantee a $10,000 loan and give about $18,000 in assets and a grant. A cooperative would operate the plant and own it on repayment of the loan. After lengthy delays waiting for Indian Affairs funding, construction resumed in 1959.[39]

The fishery required ongoing subsidies, although fish royalties collected since the mid-1940s helped pay for plants and floor price payments. Levies stood at one cent per pound on trout and half a cent per pound for pickerel and whitefish. From 1949 to 1959 the CCF collected about $117,000 through SFMS and likely a similar amount from private dealers, paying more than half of the estimated $400,000 cost of filleting plants.[40]

In spite of considerable spending by the CCF, the politicians and top bureaucrats failed to effectively manage the fish plants. Inadequate management also plagued the day-to-day operations. Sanitation problems seemed especially inexcusable. While the CCF used DNR to enforce cleanliness at private plants, it continued to tolerate a lower standard at its own plants. In one case in 1950, government allowed the Pelican Narrows plant, condemned because it did not have a concrete floor, to continue operating. Yet DNR soon closed both of Waite's Cree Lake plants for a lack of concrete floors. Waite promptly remedied the deficiency. In 1951 Fishery Officer F.M. Mitchell, on inspection of the Beaver Lake plant, found a "terribly rotten, stale fish smell" pervading the plant, as well as confusion and inefficiency. He threatened to close the plant, but gave it one year to improve. In 1956 Fishery Officer G.R. Bowerman found poor sanitation at Beaver Lake and Kinoosao. The new La Ronge plant seemed even worse, with extremely poor sanitation and cleanliness. There Bowerman found a huge quantity of rotten fish, with some green from deterioration. In contrast, when he inspected the Waite Fisheries plant at Buffalo Narrows he found it well-planned, modern, and clean.[41] Waite also produced a superior product, without government funding, and he provided more consistent opportunities to fishermen, steadier employment in his plants, and better working conditions than did government.

Thanks to his close working relationship with Phelps and willingness to cooperate with the CCF, Waite successfully survived the initial CCF on-slaught on the northern fishery. But after Phelps left in 1948, the CCF be-came noticeably less friendly towards the entrepreneur and his business plans. Government repeatedly limited Waite's plans to expand his fish-processing and sales operations during the 1950s. It also refused to give him a mon-opoly over buying fish in the areas where he operated, even though the CCF ensured that its own SFMS enjoyed a monopoly. Waite soon described himself as feeling "provoked and frustrated at the seeming lack of interest by the Government of Saskatchewan, as well as the Federal authorities, in the development of an industry which could so easily bring stability and ultimate satisfaction to all concerned."[42]

Yet Waite persisted in his efforts. After his plant at Buffalo Narrows burned, Waite wanted to rebuild. To help ensure his success, he asked the CCF to grant him an assured fish supply and a virtual three-year monop-oly on whitefish from "B" lakes in that area. He also offered to guarantee fair prices to area fishermen, and 166 signatures supported his plan. But Assistant Deputy Minister J.W. Churchman opposed Waite and recom-mended the CCF consider building a plant there instead. Churchman sup-ported his position by referring to T.C. Douglas's policy of wanting to turn fish marketing over to cooperatives. Waite built the plant anyway in 1951, without receiving the assurances he sought. His investment of about $130,000 in the new, modern plant represented a far greater amount than the SFMS ever spent on any one plant. Instead of appreciating Waite's efforts, in 1954 DNR again threatened his Buffalo Narrows operation by supporting a new competitor. Even though the competitor's operation appeared makeshift, Waite seemed concerned.[43]

While the CCF permitted Waite to rebuild his plant at Buffalo Narrows, it repeatedly blocked efforts by the entrepreneur to build a new filleting plant at Île-à-la-Crosse. Frustrated Île-à-la-Crosse residents, many of whom supported Waite's plans, petitioned Douglas for a fish plant in 1957. Waite offered to have a plant operating by midsummer. Instead, DNR's V.F. Valen-tine and other officials wanted to invest government money in building a cooperative plant. In 1958 cabinet finally approved building the co-op plant, blocking Waite's plans. Waite also wanted to build a plant not far away at Patuanak, but met resistance from Father Moraud. The Roman Catholic priest feared the project would bring demoralization and "hotels, beer parlors, theatres." As a result of government and church opposition to Waite's plans, development of the west-side fish industry suffered. In spite of its dismal record in fish processing, government preferred to spend public money and oversee the new plant rather than allow the expansion of Waite's proven and efficient private operation.[44]

Farther north, although the CCF had not taken the initiative to provide processing facilities at Cree Lake, for a time it appeared this government would prevent Waite from expanding his operations there. Waite was one of the first to fish on the big lake, beginning operations in 1945. In 1957 he started moving his Dore Lake plant to Cree Lake after DNR verbally approved his establishing a new plant there. Dissension then arose within DNR. One official wanted to see a cooperative plant instead, although he thought it might fail due to a lack of road access. In the end, DNR approved Waite's plan.[45]

Continuing uncertainty about whether government would expand its operations and displace or expel Waite and other private operators hurt the industry. Although the CCF decided not to take over Waite's operation in the 1940s, cabinet in 1955 authorized SFMS to talk to Waite about buying him out. After lengthy delays the minister and other officials met with Waite in 1957. Waite reaffirmed his willingness to sell his entire operation, with insured assets of $890,000.[46] Although the province did not proceed with the purchase, the threat continued that the CCF might take over the fishery in northern areas where it did not yet operate. Understandably, private operators preferred safer places to invest.

While successfully preventing the private fishing and processing industry from reaching its potential, the CCF operated SFMS in an uninspired manner. Mediocre management often led the half-hearted effort, further hurt by poor equipment and inefficient fishermen. SFMS, DNR, and the Department of Co-operation all held responsibility for the program, but little coordination of efforts took place. The CCF seemed reconciled to losses, although questions sometimes arose in the legislature. Higher fish prices, an increased focus on meeting market demand, and subsidies helped SFMS survive. Saskatchewan fillet output rose from 998,338 pounds in 1950-51 to 2,634,210 pounds in 1957.[47] Yet it could have risen much higher with better management and more private investment.

Even though the succession of Crown corporations proved unable to adequately manage and expand the fishery, CCF politicians and bureaucrats did not admit defeat. Many in the party had long held a vision, consistent with their socialist ideology, to move the fishery to a cooperative structure. Already in 1945 Phelps spoke of turning the plants over to the fishermen "as soon as they have learned the art of co-operating." The 1946 royal commission suggested creating fishermen's groups, and the board of directors of Saskatchewan Fish Products wanted a cooperative structure. The Fish Board promoted local bodies, and weak groups existed by 1947 at La Ronge, Beaver Lake, and Meadow Lake, though they lacked a constitution or a central organization. Later, T.C. Douglas often spoke of wanting to move SFMS to cooperative control. Criticisms of losses and the SFMS's creating dependence added pressure to make this change.[48]

While the Crown corporations continued operating, some early cooperative development took place in the fishery. A fishermen's cooperative began at Cumberland House in 1950. Co-ops also began at Beaver Lake and Reindeer Lake in 1950, although the Beaver Lake co-op soon collapsed.

The co-op at Reindeer Lake fared better. Although they relied heavily on provincial funding and direction, fishermen there participated in operating the first cooperative filleting plant in Canada. The number of co-ops continued to grow. By 1957, 45 percent of fishermen had joined co-ops, and the organizations handled 36 percent of the fish. But these statistics hid much of the reality. In the case of the cooperative at Cumberland House, for example, although ninety-seven members from the four area communities joined by 1959-60, prosperity did not follow. The area included 10.6 percent of the province's fishermen but yielded only 2.4 percent of the provincial fish production. Fishermen there received a meagre median gross income of $145. Further, the cooperatives often began and continued only in response to considerable governmental prodding. Even some in government proved willing to point out the shortcomings of this approach. One provincial official, J.A. Collier, claimed the CCF set up the co-ops "PDQ" without doing the "basic work" to make them true co-ops.[49]

After years of deliberation, the CCF finally took the step of replacing SFMS with a new cooperative processing and marketing structure. A cabinet meeting led to the organization of the Fisheries Policy Committee, which in 1957 recommended the province build a federated cooperative structure. A report said: "The growth of fishermen's co-operatives has been slow and in any case more nominal than real ... these co-operatives are largely devoid of function and in main exist in name only." Government visualized that the new co-op would assume existing assets, build new facilities, and take over Waite's operation. The organization would have a total fixed asset value of about $762,000. The CCF would grant $350,000, leaving the balance to be repaid over ten years. The province would also give annual grants and operational subsidies, and provide working capital of up to $1 million. A.G. Kuziak, DNR minister, liked the idea, hoping cooperatives would make northerners "self-reliant and self-respecting."[50]

Kuziak and Douglas altered some details of the plan, and cabinet endorsed replacing SFMS with cooperatives. The Co-operative Fisheries Limited Act passed in April 1959, creating Co-operative Fisheries Limited (CFL). Control stayed in the south; the appointed board of directors had only one northern member. The board included two fishermen as associate directors by 1960, but it seemed that the CCF would not allow an elected board until CFL repaid one-half of the principal. Local co-ops did little accounting or managing, and the CCF thought fishermen lacked readiness to run the operation.[51] Brockelbank said, "This co-op will be a co-op in name and in principle – but not in ownership for the time being." He added, "What we are trying to do is to make a century of progress for the people of the North in a generation."[52] Some opposed the move to CFL, including D.F. Corney of the Fisheries Policy Committee and the strongly socialist La Ronge CCF Club. The club thought CFL promoted "a new class of entrepreneurs within the protective orbit of the co-operative movement and their possible re-emergence as a revivified exploiting stratum operating within the restricted range of the co-operative field."[53]

The province implemented the cooperative structure at the field level in spite of little local initiative among fishermen. Politicians and bureaucrats continued to dominate and retain strict control of CFL. A strong central organization directed matters, partly because the CCF thought local groups lacked the necessary education, experience, and "communication infrastructure." With more than a decade of experience in the fishery, in some respects the CCF ran the co-op quite skilfully. It established a processing and storage operation at Prince Albert. CFL charged a marketing fee of 12.5 percent, which brought a surplus of $50,000 to distribute in its first full year of operation. By 1962 fishers owned equity of $341,240 in CFL, and the eighteen member co-ops held $139,901.85 of share capital. CFL handled fish for about two-thirds of Saskatchewan's fishermen by 1963, 47.1 percent of the catch.[54] In contrast to its policy for private operators, the CCF allowed CFL a monopoly if 70 percent of area fishermen wanted to deal with CFL. This support sometimes proved difficult to obtain. At La Ronge from 1962 to 1964, fishermen repeatedly did not go along with efforts to have them deal with CFL.[55]

Some old problems persisted under the CFL structure. It still used a system of initial and final payments, as had the Fish Board and SFMS. As a result, fishermen at Patuanak in 1961 waited for fish cheques, much as they did for government fur cheques. Fish prices also still varied from lake to lake, depending largely on transportation costs. In 1960, for example, "A" whitefish from Montreal Lake brought twenty cents per pound compared to only six cents for those from Wollaston. Similarly, La Ronge trout brought thirteen cents compared to 6.5 cents at Wollaston.[56] The unfair system in which some areas participated in the floor price plan, while others did not, continued. Inequities in prices and subsidies contributed to low and inadequate earnings.

Throughout its time in office the CCF encouraged large numbers of Aboriginals to engage in commercial fishing. In 1959-60, 934 Northern Affairs region residents held fishing licences, a peak in participation. Buffalo Narrows had one of the highest rates of adult male participation at 60.8 percent, as did Cumberland House at 45 percent. Only 17.5 percent of men fished in the La Ronge-Stanley Mission area, and nearly none did so in the Fond du Lac area. The government encouraged Aboriginals at Fond du Lac to increase their participation in the fishery.

Yet a high rate of participation in the fishery did not bring economic prosperity. Instead, contrary to CCF hopes and in spite of its massive interventions through the Fish Board, SFMS, and CFL, destitution increased. For many Aboriginals, fishing became part of a lifestyle of poverty. A correlation existed between the number of people fishing and the severity of their poverty. Île-à-la-Crosse had about twice as many fishermen as needed.

Lac la Ronge typically had about seventy-five licence holders instead of the thirty the lake could support. The average fisherman at La Ronge in the summer of 1947 received an income of $189.90, which was $8.85 less than estimated expenses. In the Cumberland House area in 1947, although many fished, fishing only comprised 4.24 percent of the economy. In 1952-53, 122 fishermen at Big Peter Pond near Buffalo Narrows earned an average of about $261.20, while they spent about $256.70, without counting motor or canoe repairs. The twenty or thirty people who worked at Waite's plant earned much more. Still in 1962, most northern fishermen earned only about $500 per year, not enough to provide a motor, a boat, and ten nets, plus money to live. DNR in 1958 claimed that about 1,500 people depended on fishing for most of their livelihood. This statement seemed false, since relatively few could live on their earnings from fishing, and most needed to rely on other income.

While CCF dreams of adequate incomes for the vast majority of Aboriginal fishermen did not come true, some white fishermen and a small number of Aboriginals did manage to make a living fishing. Of sixteen operators at Beaver Lake in 1946, two white men received 44 percent of the revenue. By 1960, four fishermen earned from $5,000 to $10,000 at Wollaston and Reindeer Lakes, where fishermen of Scandinavian origin played an important role.

Poor transportation, inefficiency, lack of skill, underutilization, undercapitalization, low prices, small lakes, and too many fishermen all contributed to worsening poverty in most Aboriginal communities. In most cases, income from fishing merely served as a small supplement to similarly meagre trapping income. It soon became clear that commercial fishing offered Aboriginals nothing more than a life of poverty.[57]

Ironically, while overcrowding characterized the situation on many lakes, some remote lakes saw much of the quota unused. As in trapping, many Aboriginals wanted to work near their village homes and ignored opportunities farther afield. In one year, 1959-60, over one million pounds of the Reindeer Lake whitefish limit stayed in the lake. Lake Athabasca fishers took less than one-third of the two-million-pound whitefish and pickerel quota, and much of the trout limit often remained untaken.[58] If properly managed, the resource in these areas could have supported a number of additional fishermen.

Several CCF fisheries policies ensured that underuse of fish stocks in remote areas and the resulting loss of income would continue. It blocked southern fishermen, who had traditionally proven themselves willing to travel long distances to catch fish, from participating. It also failed to extend funding to developing the fishery in large areas of the north. Instead of operating on more of the large lakes with unused quotas, SFMS operated almost completely east of the third meridian. The guaranteed price plan also applied only north of the fifty-fourth parallel, which again excluded some potentially productive areas. Additionally, although the province did not hold responsibility for Status Indians, it often provided more help for them than for Metis and whites. As an example, the expensive Wollaston Lake plant served thirty-five Status Indians and only twenty-six Metis and ten whites. The province also invested heavily at Pelican Narrows, primarily a Status Indian area. Oddly, while neglecting many Non-Status fishermen, the CCF continued to spend much on Status Indian fishing, including paying for fishery losses, floor price supports, and deficits at its stores. Clearly, provincial policies contributed to the low level of income from the fishery.[59]

Unwilling to itself devote the financial resources needed to provide adequate support to the entire northern fishery, the CCF begged for federal aid. As in other areas where the province asked for help, Ottawa chose to give very little. A Federal Price Support Act, designed to help fishermen in abnormal market lows, paid out only once in 1952-53. It seems only Wollaston and Reindeer Lake fishermen benefited, since other fishermen delayed asking for help. In 1950 Ottawa indicated it would not subsidize Indian fishing, and Indian Affairs refused repeated requests from Saskatchewan for help. It claimed Status Indians paid taxes to Saskatchewan and opposed "treating Indians as a special class of citizens." Indian Affairs did give some help to Status Indian fishermen by providing supplies and a one-time contribution of $25,000 for the construction of the Pelican Narrows plant. Hope for federal help increased in 1964 with the first Federal-Provincial Conference on Fisheries Development, which called for a national fishery development program. Formation of the Federal-Provincial Prairie Fisheries Committee in 1964, and the subsequent creation of the Commission of Inquiry into Freshwater Fish Marketing, also provided hope for increased federal spending. But the effects of these initiatives did not appear until after the CCF era ended.[60]

The benefit derived from CCF interventions appears dubious. The quantity of fish taken in 1944 remained unsurpassed by 1956, and the 1944 landed value of $1,032,000 was not reached again by 1956, when it stood at $784,000. Using inflation-adjusted dollars, the landed value of production fell by about 55 percent from 1944 to 1956.[61] Some improvement occurred by the 1960s, when the long-term trends in production, demand, and prices all rose. Annual production from 1945 to 1951 remained below ten million pounds per year, while from 1960 to 1964 production surpassed fourteen million pounds. From 1961 to 1963 Saskatchewan was the top Canadian producer of whitefish and lake trout. In 1962-63 gross market value reached $3,114,797.90, of which fishermen received $1,477,448.38. Much of the production came from the Northern District.[62] The increase occurred largely due to improved markets and prices and not because of extraordinary CCF actions. Production levels remained far below the potential of the fishery. Also, the fishermen's share of the market value of fish did not increase, even though the CCF eliminated many of the private dealers it accused of enriching themselves at the fishermen's expense.

Many fishermen could not see that they benefited from the CCF fishery interventions. This contributed to the situation where, as in trapping, compulsion by government and resistance from fishermen characterized the CCF interventions in the northern fishery. The province refused to tolerate violations of its fish-processing monopolies. In one high-profile case in 1951, the national media focused critical attention on the CCF policies after DNR seized fisherman John Ivanchuk's fish and equipment at Reindeer Lake. The alleged crime involved Ivanchuk and a pilot who illegally delivered Ivanchuk's fish to a dealer at Flin Flon rather than to the Beaver Lake SFMS. Ivanchuk clearly preferred to sell his fish privately, and the pilot considered compulsory marketing "unconstitutional." The *Ottawa Citizen* called the law "vicious legislation." Likely because of the publicity, DNR returned Ivanchuk's goods and did not proceed with charges.[63]

Aboriginal fishermen resisted CCF fishery controls in many small ways. In order to force compliance, DNR sometimes acted severely. In one case in 1951, when DNR and RCMP officers used the authority of the Liquor Act to search the tent of Moise Laliberte, a Status Indian from Pine Bluff, they found some sturgeon hooks attached to wet line. Laliberte claimed Indian Affairs gave him the hooks years earlier, but charges resulted. In court, speaking through an interpreter, Laliberte agreed with the Mountie's testimony and said he did not care what the court did to him. DNR asked the Justice of the Peace for more than the minimum penalty, and Laliberte received a fine of $150 and costs or sixty days in jail. A.H. MacDonald, director of Fisheries, thought the severe penalty should have an exemplary effect on other fishermen.[64]

Unlike Laliberte, fishermen at Cumberland House in 1953 became defiant and fought back. DNR began actions against two men after an officer found nets placed without identifying tags. The local fishermen's co-op promised to pay fines, and someone contacted T.C. Douglas, charging DNR with interference. DNR stopped one prosecution after the suspect sent for counsel and it appeared that a new Justice of the Peace would hear the case. Fishery Officer F. Mitchell wrote: "I would suggest that this gang have been pampered too much, and instead of trying to initiate some program of their own they are sitting waiting for handouts ... There were 25 men in a new poolroom in midafternoon ... They have no thought of conservation and only a rudimentary idea of what co-operation means." Mitchell told the DNR officer to continue enforcement and not to be stopped by a threat of being beaten up, even though an RCMP officer had been beaten. Northern Administrator C.S. Brown offered contradictory comments, thinking "young Conservation Officers were too strict and over-enthusiastic," while also seeing habitual violation of fisheries regulations by Aboriginals.[65]

Fishermen also resisted the CCF-promoted change from winter to summer fishing. At Big River in 1944, all fishermen opposed the change, citing high wastage, low-quality summer fish, and damage to fish stocks done by fishing prior to the fall spawning season. Agreeing with the CCF, Waite wanted to see about two-thirds of the fishery as a summer fishery.[66]

Even though northern Aboriginals' income from commercial fishing remained small, fish from Saskatchewan's countless northern lakes brought various other benefits to northerners and outsiders. Fishers outside the commercial industry took large numbers of northern fish. Sport anglers hooked a rising number, and they and commercial fishermen both pressured the CCF for preferential treatment. Four other categories of fishing took place. Non-Indians purchased domestic licences to net fish for personal use; tourists bought franchise licences to net whitefish; Status Indians obtained free permits to net fish for their own use; and fur farmers used fish. DNR issued 456 domestic licences and 1,341 licences to Status Indians in 1944-45. In 1958-59 the domestic fishery took about 1,166,900 pounds and the Status Indian fishery about 1,786,000 pounds, while franchise fishing accounted for about 17,108 pounds in 1961. Fur farmers paid fees based on the type and number of animals fed with fish. The industry used rough fish, including tullibee, suckers, and burbot, and low-priced pike and offal from fish plants, peaking at about 6.5 million pounds of fish used in 1956-57. The province closely regulated these various types of fishing. Here, in contrast to the situation in the commercial fishery, the CCF did not introduce controversial policies.[67]

In addition to the disappointing impact of its commercial fishery policy on the northern economy, difficulties arose with CCF efforts to conserve fish stocks. Unlike in the fur industry, where strict controls restored stocks, the province failed to introduce adequate measures to compensate for the increased demand placed on fish stocks. Biological surveys of lakes began in the 1940s, supervised by Dr. D.S. Rawson of the University of Saskatchewan Biology Department. Yet in spite of ongoing studies and control efforts, unwanted changes in fish populations took place, including at Big Peter Pond Lake, where desirable whitefish, pickerel, and jackfish declined greatly in proportion to other species. Across the province at Cumberland House, sturgeon, valued at nearly one dollar per pound, swam in the Torch and Saskatchewan rivers. But sturgeon numbers declined, and from 1950 to 1962, fishermen took only about seven thousand pounds of sturgeon per year. Government blamed fishermen for the depletion of sturgeon and tried to strictly enforce quotas, but, unexpectedly, it was not overfishing but pollution from outside the region that brought a virtual halt to that potentially lucrative fishery. "Gross pollution" from Edmonton, Saskatoon, and other cities increasingly damaged the Saskatchewan River system and its sturgeon and other fish stocks. Dams also hurt fish. Early water-control structures included the Island Falls Dam on the Churchill, which generated power for the Hudson Bay Mining and Smelting Company at Flin Flon, and the

Whitesand Dam on the Reindeer River, which provided water control for Island Falls. By 1963 the Saskatchewan Power Corporation dam at Squaw Rapids on the Saskatchewan, upstream from Cumberland House, also blocked fish movement, possibly further hurting fishing in the polluted delta.[68]

Confident in its ability to plan a better north, the CCF once confidently visualized fishing and trapping becoming the two primary bases for the Aboriginal economy. Fisheries policies formed part of the CCF effort to impose a northern socialist economy in which Aboriginals would happily cooperate, pursuing "traditional" occupations. Socialism in action imposed Crown corporations, marketing boards, and cooperatives, while eliminating some private enterprise. At the same time the CCF colonial structure paternalistically controlled the fishery. While it imposed strong control and limited private investment, this government refused to devote adequate resources to develop the potential of the fishery. Additionally, substandard management promoted mediocrity. After twenty years of interventions, at best the CCF-controlled fishery brought only moderate benefits to northerners. While the plan included many northern Aboriginals in the fishery, the vast majority earned only meagre incomes, often not enough to cover operating costs. CCF policies contributed to the fishery becoming part of the northern lifestyle of poverty. The CCF plan for the northern economy also included other elements. While the southern socialists did not encourage substantial participation by Aboriginals in some sectors of the economy, they did think northern Aboriginals could engage in subsistence farming.

7
Just One Jump Out of the Stone Age

Along with trapping and fishing, the CCF reserved northern agriculture largely for Aboriginals, expecting them to engage in subsistence farming based on a socialist model. The new government used its colonial structure to apply socialist ideology to northern agriculture in a manner that southern farmers would not have tolerated. It retained ownership of and control over farmland and directed the most minute aspects of farming operations. The policies prevented interested northerners and southerners from expanding northern farming. At the same time, the CCF proved inept at farming and frequently demonstrated how not to farm. New agricultural programs brought few benefits to the north.

Northern agriculture was not only an important part of the northern Aboriginal economy visualized by the CCF, but also constituted an integral part of the province's community development plans. While community development in Saskatchewan was in its infancy in the 1940s, even then the CCF introduced some community development projects to the north. As the years went by, the CCF placed increasing emphasis on these programs. This accompanied a realization that the interventions in trapping and fishing were not working. Community development programs then played a crucial role in CCF plans to develop the Aboriginal economy. These projects included not only agricultural initiatives but also fur, fish, and cooperative development programs. Research-based, experimental community development plans brought new life to the CCF vision for the north. By the late 1950s, community development programs carried the primary responsibility for bringing economic and other change to northern Aboriginals. The CCF spoke of involving northerners in community development and used cooperatives, ratepayers' associations, and fur councils to include token northern input, but DNR officers continued their role as the primary development catalysts.

Much of northern Saskatchewan saw no economic activity other than trapping and fishing before 1944. While some optimists believed successful agriculture could extend far into the forest, the north presented severe challenges to would-be farmers. The underlying rock of the Canadian Shield emerged in many areas, and even where there was a layer of soil, it usually lacked fertility. Frosts shortened the growing season to the point where few crops could mature. There were pockets of fertile soil and a more hospitable climate near some water bodies, where rivers dropped fertile sediments, and the proximity of rivers and lakes moderated temperatures. The largest areas of fertile soil and favourable climate were found in the Saskatchewan River delta and the lower west-side area near Beauval. There, farmers had long grown crops and raised livestock. Fur traders and missionaries initiated agriculture, and some Aboriginal people became interested in growing food as well.[1]

DNR, the CCF's colonial arm, administered northern Crown land, including agricultural land. Consequently, the Department of Agriculture, with its greater agricultural expertise, had little involvement in northern agriculture.[2] Yet a lack of knowledge about farming matters cannot completely explain the fiascos that followed.

During its two decades in power, the CCF government expended most of its northern agricultural effort at Cumberland House. Over the course of many centuries, the mighty Saskatchewan River had deposited rich, fertile soil in its delta there. Cumberland House sat in the delta on Pine Island, a low-lying piece of land of about fifteen thousand acres. The Bigstone River divided Pine Island from Spruce Island, also known as Farm Island. It consisted of about 3,500 acres. A white man, Thomas Harvey, leased Farm Island from about 1929. The farmer employed up to nine people, raised up to four hundred cattle, and sold butter and eggs to area residents. However, Harvey left in about 1940, and by 1944, when the CCF came to power, local agriculture consisted mainly of raising gardens, cattle, and feed for horses and cattle.[3]

The CCF attempted to apply a socialist model to Aboriginal farming. Under this plan, the state, not private persons, owned the land. Also, instead of farming alone, Aboriginals would farm cooperatively. Some likened the CCF plan for northern farming to peasant farming. Peasant farming is usually associated with pre-industrial societies, where large landowners dominate tenant farmers. Images of poverty-stricken farmers, who have no viable alternatives but to continue working for their oppressors, come to mind when speaking of peasants. In the case of northern Saskatchewan, the CCF was the landlord. Aboriginals, much like peasants, would farm small plots of land using horses and antiquated equipment. They would give lease payments to the government, and the agricultural products would help provide them with a subsistence level of living.

Governmental interest in developing northern farming initially came largely from Joe Phelps. On a visit to Cumberland House shortly after the CCF took power, the minister noted the potential of the local grass to feed cattle. DNR viewed nearly all of Spruce Island and over one-half of Pine Island as arable. Drainage and flood control presented the main challenges. DNR sent J. Johnson to the area in 1945 to launch a four-point community development project, which included muskrat habitat development, a sawmill, education, and a farm.[4] DNR's Allan Quandt also played an important role when he went to Cumberland House in 1946 to assess agricultural possibilities. Like others, he saw the area's potential to provide much-needed local food. Quandt, a socialist, opposed private farms and favoured CCF-subsidized farming on Spruce Island using surplus Aboriginal labour managed by the CCF. Quandt saw obstacles, though, including Aboriginal distrust of white people, created by past "lying and cheating" of white men to Aboriginals and the area being "just one jump out of the Stone Age." He concluded: "If over a period of a hundred years we succeed in bringing about a reasonable change I feel the effort is well worth it." Quandt found support among local white people for the idea of a CCF farm. He even won the qualified support of Reverend Parker, the Anglican minister, who feared outside influences, contrary to the "progress" wanted by Quandt. Local people then met and unanimously voted for the project.[5]

The CCF quickly put its farming plan into action at Cumberland House. DNR's R.N. Gooding bought the mostly used machinery, and Tom Leia managed the farm, which had about three hundred acres broken by 1947. The farm grew produce, some of which DNR sold and some of which local people received for working in the garden. A work-and-wages program employed locals to make hay. With Phelps pushing, DNR bought chickens and low-grade cattle by 1948, but after flooding hurt crops, Quandt ordered most livestock sold. He wanted to see the project obtain a better grade of cattle. DNR also spoke of using a five-year plan to improve the farm. Politicians and bureaucrats from outside dominated the operation. Although government claimed the farm was for the benefit of the local Aboriginal population, none from this group worked at the farm for a salary in 1948.[6]

After Phelps's defeat in 1948, the new minister, J.H. Brockelbank, also enthusiastically involved himself in the farm. He found and considered buying a French coach stallion from Quebec, but another DNR official questioned the need to raise horses. Brockelbank offered advice on the choice of a bull, preferring an Aberdeen Angus to a Shorthorn. He also "supplied" a John Deere Model B tractor. Under his leadership, the operation grew. An ambitious building program included a manager's house and office, a barn, a hay shed, a two-storey henhouse, a cattle shed, a workshop, and a granary.[7]

By 1950 problems at the farm increasingly jeopardized its successful operation. Although various officials commanded the enterprise, it became difficult to tell who was in control. Additionally, the agricultural representative J.D. Neilson and others spoke of a lack of definition of the farm's purpose. Neilson wanted to turn the project into a demonstration farm, using two full-time staff instead of local part-time labour. In his view, the farm should run like a business, generate a profit, and show the Metis how to farm rather than try to "rehabilitate" them by hiring them. To achieve this end, Neilson wanted to increase the cultivated area to six hundred acres, move authority from Prince Albert bureaucrats to the farm manager, and improve accounting methods. For his part, E. Dodds, field supervisor, wanted more mechanized equipment. He noted that most locals did not want to work there. Poorly chosen machinery and wet conditions added to the problems. R.N. Gooding noted other deficiencies, which included a delay in beginning a school milk program, poor cattle quality, and chickens that did not produce well. He also criticized Leia's care of the machinery and questioned whether Leia should work there. Understandably, Leia's morale seemed low. He thought his superiors were "down on him."[8]

DNR soon accepted Neilson's idea of expanding the project to serve as a demonstration farm. By 1951, Brockelbank chose one of five options presented by Neilson. He elected to concentrate on cattle, hogs, and chickens, while growing a cash crop on one hundred acres to reduce the risk. The new plan required more farm buildings and living quarters for possibly three employees and their families. The farm would operate much like a Crown corporation. But a major letdown soon occurred when DNR found it only had 150 acres broken, instead of the 340 acres claimed by Leia. This discrepancy was surprising since many officials with farm backgrounds had visited the farm, and someone should have noticed the error. As a result, DNR needed to clear and break much more land than expected. In spite of an excellent harvest, with wheat producing over forty bushels an acre, the farm lost $1,701.80 from April to December 1951.[9]

The new plan did not last long. In 1952 DNR's E. Dodds considered the demonstration farm a failure and recommended leasing the land to a new farmer, whose demonstration of successful farming methods would inspire Aboriginals. Brockelbank agreed, and cabinet decided to rent the farm and dispose of the stock and equipment. After advertisements ran in major newspapers, DNR selected W.M. Miner and his two associates, University of Saskatchewan (U of S) graduates. But the trio lost interest when government refused to give them financial assistance to farm. Lack of road access to markets likely formed the main obstacle to farming without help.[10] Failure to rent the land likely pleased local people, who opposed bringing in outside farmers.

Local opposition to the government farm also rose. J. Brady questioned the CCF right to take over or to privatize the land, describing it as communal land. He claimed that government had failed to establish even one local Aboriginal in agriculture, that the project used Aboriginals as temporary, unskilled labour, and that it aimed for profit, not education. Locals saw the farm as "an imposed evil." They thought the CCF lacked confidence in them. Yet Brady also doubted the local Aboriginals, whom he depicted as "barely emerged from a semi-nomadic background ...

emotionally at variance with the concepts and usages of a strictly seden-
tary mode of life."[11]

Following the failure of several of their plans, the CCF and DNR wal-
lowed in indecision about the farm. In 1953 the DNR deputy minister,
J.W. Churchman, tried to interest the Prairie Farm Rehabilitation Administration (PFRA) in taking it for an experimental farm. DNR disposed of its
swine and shipped twenty-one head of cattle to Winnipeg, fearing they
would soon die of advanced age. DNR had butchered some beef the previous winter, but local people did not want to eat the meat, and DNR sold it
for five dollars per quarter as dog food. Likely for lack of another plan,
Brockelbank then approved renting the farm to local people in forty-acre
plots. This new plan meant a return to rehabilitation as a goal. The heavily subsidized program would involve eight "fairly high calibre Metis"
supervised by DNR. The Metis seeded up to twenty acres each, but a "fine
start" abruptly ended in June when floods hit.[12]

Cabinet reversed the latest rehabilitation plan in January 1954, deciding
that the farm should either support itself that year or stop operating.
Northern Administrator C.S. Brown found the decision rather confusing,
and Brockelbank appealed to T.C. Douglas for the rehabilitation program
to continue. Brockelbank thought he had attended the cabinet meeting
that made the new plan, but seemed unable to remember participating in
making the decision. He described the cabinet minute as "confusing and
rather meaningless."[13] Flooding again hurt farming in 1954, with no crop
put in on Farm Island. A feed shortage resulted, and winter "ice conditions" led to the loss of some cattle in the river.[14]

Chaos grew, while the farm earned $300 and cost $6,000 in 1955-56.
Dodds considered "DNR activities in Cumberland to be approaching an all
time low." Neilson told a meeting that the people did not really need farm
income, since they did quite well from natural resources. Senior officials,
however, wanted to buy two more bulls. Brown lamented the long-term
policy confusion, writing: "In no instance was any policy decision completely followed through in field administration." Fearing that stopping
farming would cause deterioration of assets and risk DNR's investment,
Brown wanted to rent the farm to a private party. Operating on his own
plan, Turnbull, the latest farm manager, wanted money to make the farm
self-sufficient with cattle and chickens. He wrote: "I think much has been
gained as far as the native is concerned. I actually think he has gained
more than we can estimate or actually value in terms of money." In 1957
Brown wanted to buy one or two more bulls, while Churchman hoped the
Department of Agriculture would take over the farm.[15]

Confusion continued, and the farm operated without a plan "on a
maintenance basis." Broken land reverted to willow growth, while DNR
waited to see what part the farm could play in a community development
plan, on which the CCF increasingly relied to solve northern problems.

The Social Credit candidate in 1960 "saw lots of buildings; but little farm-ing." By 1961, J.E.M. Kew, in Cumberland House to work on community development, described the farm as "at a stand-still" and saw a low level of Metis enthusiasm for the imposed farming. Under the CCF, Metis agri-culture had declined. Local people held less land, and fewer people owned cattle than prior to CCF involvement. The Metis owned sixty-eight cattle in 1947, while in 1960 they had only about twenty-four. DNR owned ninety-five cattle in 1960, up from twenty-one in 1948. The CCF seemed largely responsible for the decline of farming because local people had to compete with the DNR farm for the use of farm machinery and with the cheap subsidized food grown by the farm. Further, the program taught farm labour, not farm management, and the low wages it paid did not act as an incentive to farm. The CCF also failed to provide capital and land to local people. Kew spread some of the blame onto the local people, who censured those who appeared too ambitious.[16]

Turmoil continued in 1961. By that time the CCF had spent about $110,000 on the farm, not counting the tens of thousands spent by poli-ticians and bureaucrats on air flights to Cumberland House and for their expenses and salaries. Farm revenues over the years brought in about $18,985, and capital assets totalled about $17,135. Numerous people made suggestions to bring success to the operation. Neilson wanted a coopera-tive farm, but Kew saw this as potentially "disastrous," with too many organizational problems. Outside parties seemed interested in buying the assets. The local community council wanted to rent the farm, but Minister A.G. Kuziak and a Department of Agriculture specialist wanted Agriculture to operate a training farm. DNR's R. McKay thought the farm could solve various problems including those of population increase, a high cost of living, unemployment, resource depletion, malnutrition, and low education. He wrote: "I am positive that the farm will work, that is if it is tried."[17]

By 1962 the latest farm manager had quit, and DNR used a "native boy" to care for the farm. DNR and an interdepartmental committee created by the Treasury Board seemed to agree on some things. The Canadian Voca-tional Training Centre (CVTC) at the U of S should train young Aborigi-nals, who would alternate between the Centre and farm placements. Some graduates might take over the DNR farm, some would work for farmers outside the area, and some would farm on a proposed land development project. Looking for local input, officials met with thirteen residents to dis-cuss the farm. The meeting lacked direction and adjourned after one par-ticipant, described as "apparently in high spirits," passed out. By 1963 the CVTC plan seemed in jeopardy, partly because local people demonstrated little interest. The following year, the Treasury Board still delayed and had not made a decision on the future of the farm. Government refused to lease the farm to an interested outsider because a study of the delta area would take at least two years. Another committee also studied the farm.[18]

With the CCF election loss in 1964, eighteen years of CCF farming ended on Farm Island. Not one Aboriginal farmed the island's fertile soil. Government had blocked local farming, demonstrated how not to farm, and failed to bring any discernible "rehabilitation." At the same time, the province's actions had discouraged and alienated those who once had possessed enthusiasm for farming on the island.

The CCF also applied its control, planning, and agricultural expertise to Pine Island, the larger island on which Cumberland House sat. The province owned most of the land there, ownership that the CCF carefully guarded. DNR rented eight or nine parcels of land to Aboriginals, with about thirty acres cultivated in 1950. Local people wanted to expand mixed farming, and to facilitate this they asked to have land surveyed into eighty-acre plots. But DNR made other plans. Brady recommended DNR survey a large area into forty-acre leases, a scheme in which at least sixteen persons then seemed interested. The tenant farmers would have three years to make improvements and break twenty acres, with the DNR farm serving as a "Mother Farm." In theory, this would help develop "a new economy and way of life." Without warning, DNR then turned to a cooperative model. By 1951 it had surveyed eight plots of forty acres that people would lease and operate as a cooperative. DNR would break the land, supply machinery, and supervise, while the people would farm in a pre-industrial manner, using mainly horses. Brady, who had supported the earlier plan, did not like the new idea to use what he called "small peasant methods" of farming. While the local people waited, government delayed. DNR failed to carry out its commitment to prepare the land and had only seventy acres broken by 1952. Deputy Minister Churchman then questioned the plan and thought they should increase the farm size and not use horses. DNR dallied, citing the need for more study, while local interest waned.[19]

While the two islands in the Saskatchewan River offered potential for farming, much greater agricultural possibilities awaited in the larger Saskatchewan River delta area. Various studies in the 1940s and 1950s, including by the U of S, the federal Department of Agriculture, and PFRA, all found arable soil suitable for agriculture. Soil surveys identified several hundred thousand acres of arable land by 1954. Influenced by socialist ideology, the provincial Royal Commission on Agriculture and Rural Life in 1954 visualized leasing, not selling, primarily grain-growing farms of at least 250 acres to experienced farmers. The PFRA and Manitoba proceeded with a pilot project in the delta, the Pasquia Land Settlement Project, which overlapped into Saskatchewan. While Saskatchewan agreed to an easement, it would not sell the portion of reclaimed land in Saskatchewan. That would have conflicted with the CCF policy of only leasing land. Manitoba did sell its land to farmers and by 1953 had spent about a quarter million dollars on the project. PFRA investigated the Cumberland House area again in 1957, and a Department of Agriculture official visualized projects possibly five times the size of Manitoba's 100,000-acre project. An interdepartmental committee in 1962 pointed to about one million acres of suitable land. At much the same time, the Center for Community Studies visualized farmland for "several hundred farmers," including some Aboriginals. An order-in-council in 1963 established the Saskatchewan River Delta Development Committee to again investigate. At that time, reclamation costs varied from about sixteen to sixty-two dollars per acre.[20] Clearly, a lack of study or of farming potential were not the reasons farming did not begin.

Some approved of CCF inaction in the expansion of farming in the larger delta area. Local Aboriginals repeatedly opposed the idea of outsiders coming to farm nearby. In 1950 residents expressed "grave concern" about opening up farming, and DNR's Gooding feared they might not get enough of the good land.[21] Developing the delta into farmland also might reduce Aboriginals' trapping incomes. Further, some feared drainage would flood Cumberland House. The HBC also opposed widespread agriculture. It worried about the future of its fur lease and the trappers' incomes if land drainage and agriculture went ahead. Concern increased when PFRA used bulldozers in the HBC lease, destroying many muskrat houses. As an alternative to the larger plan, the HBC suggested farming could take place on a narrow strip of higher land, one-quarter to one-half mile wide, along the Saskatchewan. This option would affect the HBC operation much less.[22] A mixed development of trapping and agriculture could have partially addressed the concerns of Aboriginals and the company. Yet opposition to farming from Aboriginals and the HBC does not explain why the CCF did not proceed with putting delta land into agricultural production.

In spite of the delta's well-established agricultural potential, the CCF lacked the political will to spend the hundreds of thousands of dollars required to develop farming there. The government also prevented private capital from participating by refusing to sell land on the islands and in the larger delta area to outsiders. At the same time, CCF actions and policies kept local people from farming. Had the CCF applied these policies to southern Saskatchewan, farmers would have revolted or stopped farming since they could not have operated under the type of restrictions imposed by the CCF in the north. The Saskatchewan delta, despite great agricultural potential, remained undeveloped. After twenty years of intervention and study, the CCF could not point to one farmer it started farming.

Extensive farming did not make sense for most of the rest of the north, but agricultural potential did exist in some other small areas. In 1943 J. Mitchell of the U of S Soils Department studied the Meadow Lake to Buffalo Narrows area and reported his findings to the Department of Agriculture. He found some farming, including at the Beauval mission, which also had a flour mill and sawmill powered by turbines in the La Plonge River. The soil at Île-à-la-Crosse grew "very good gardens," and Dr. Lavoie raised fruit trees there. A few cattle and horses grazed at Buffalo Narrows. At Buffalo River, nearly all the Dene had good gardens, and the nearby Dillon River flats provided hay and grazing for many cattle and horses. While scattered areas could support farming and gardening, and some expansion of these activities could take place, Mitchell saw no great agricultural potential.[23]

Additional surveys of northern agricultural potential took place by 1950, including those by A.R. Brown of the Department of Agriculture's Co-operative Extension Program, T.R. Coupland, assistant professor of Plant Ecology, and H.C. Moss of the U of S Soils Department. Other than in the Cumberland House region and in some west-side areas, good agricultural land lay mainly in pockets near streams and lakes. Interest in substantial agricultural developments still appeared from time to time, as in 1957 when Agricultural Representative J.D. Neilson thought the Clearwater River valley north of La Loche might grow food to supply Uranium City. A 1964 estimate suggested the provincial forest had about three million arable acres, although much of this needed drainage or clearing.[24]

Even in areas with little arable land, the CCF tried to increase Aboriginal farming and gardening. Government hoped to increase food self-sufficiency and to shift eating habits from heavy dependence on meat to include more vegetables. Although Aboriginals already ate potatoes, they consumed relatively few other vegetables. J.D. Neilson promoted northern agriculture, beginning work as the northern agricultural representative in 1950. While he worked for the Department of Agriculture, DNR paid some of the costs and seemed to direct many of his activities. Neilson helped develop large community gardens at Snake Lake and La Loche, and numerous settlements received gardening equipment. The CCF sometimes tried to motivate Aboriginal gardening by using prizes. In 1961, for example, it provided $500 for prizes.[25] The University of Saskatchewan also continued to help develop agriculture. Along with the agricultural representative, its Horticultural Department in 1952-53 studied the suitability of various grains, legumes, vegetables, and fruit. Additionally, the university's extension department and the Canadian Vocational Training program helped with canning and/or cooking courses at Beauval, Île-à-la-Crosse, and Montreal Lake.[26] The CCF focused much of its agricultural effort on children by promoting 4-H clubs. Establishing the clubs was Neilson's main long-term aim. Government seemed to hope that the children would continue to grow food when they reached adulthood. But the 4-H program also had other functions, including providing citizenship and leadership training and teaching Aboriginal children about the outside world by sending them south on excursions. By 1963, clubs included 522 members in about nine communities. White people often dominated leadership roles at the community level, although Neilson worked to have Aboriginal people take over as leaders.[27]

In an additional effort to encourage northern self-sufficiency in food, the CCF promoted northern ranching. Although remote and deep in the forest, Pinehouse already had a few cattle in 1950. These included those of J. Cockburn, the SGT store manager, who ran afoul of DNR when he failed to obtain a permit for wild hay. The CCF introduced its own project there in 1953, hauling in a cow behind a Bombardier. Three local people received five heifers and a bull the following year. While the plan called for repayment with heifers, a later report said: "Those chosen were not promising individuals ... One man lost all his animals by drowning ... dogs, kids and cattle did not mix ... so the individual living in the settlement in 1957 transferred his cattle to the remaining one living on an island." By 1958 the herd numbered thirteen, and it seemed the project might succeed. Government also encouraged raising cattle elsewhere, including at Buffalo Narrows. Overall, the livestock projects remained small. Seemingly motivated by a desire to preserve opportunities for northerners, the CCF blocked farmers from the south from establishing cattle operations on the west side.[28]

The CCF also involved itself in some other northern agricultural efforts. True to its preference for cooperatives, it encouraged the Vegetable and Fruit Growers Co-operative, which formed at Île-à-la-Crosse in 1954. Government provided machinery, with the co-op to repay half the cost over ten years.[29] The province also saw potential for wild berry production in the north. Assisted by the agricultural representative, a small frozen-blueberry marketing project operated at Beauval by 1953. Additionally, the Department of Co-operation studied marketing berries.[30] Wild rice became of interest by 1963 with the experimental planting of four hundred pounds of wild rice. The province viewed the growing of wild rice as an economic opportunity for Aboriginal northerners. Relying on government subsidies, La Ronge Industries Ltd. of La Ronge carried out much of the initial development and marketing work. In 1964 the company harvested about fourteen thousand pounds of wild rice, valued at $7,000.[31]

Besides the money it misspent at Cumberland House, the CCF spent little on northern agriculture. Officials, including Assistant Deputy Minister A.T. Davidson and Northern Administrator C.S. Brown, did not expect or favour a rapid "wholesale development of agriculture." In spite of some promotion of farming, they and other officials seemed to care little whether agriculture would form a significant part of the northern economy. The Department of Agriculture established the Special Demonstrational Livestock and Crop Production Assistance Policy in 1957, but it had an annual budget of only $5,000. Cutbacks for 1961-62 eliminated the full-time assistant agricultural representative position, while Agricultural Representative Neilson found himself overworked and with inadequate financing for larger projects. Inconsistent planning and a lack of money plagued northern agricultural programs. No substantial agricultural growth took place there under the CCF.[32]

The failure to develop northern agriculture, combined with disappointing results in the fur and fishing industries, meant that CCF plans for a
new Aboriginal economy did not materialize. Believing that it needed to
deal with the increasing northern dysfunction and poverty, the CCF came
to rely on community development programs and techniques to bring
social and economic health to the region's Aboriginals. Even before losing
faith in its initial direct and forceful policies, the CCF had spoken of community development. The new government initiated its primary early
community development project at Cumberland House in 1945. Three of
the four aspects of that project – the DNR farm, a muskrat habitat project,
and a sawmill – all directly strove to improve the Aboriginal economy. But
the development plans at Cumberland House foundered with the ongoing
fiasco at the farm, declining fur incomes, and the failure of local people to
show interest in forestry. Aboriginals had correctly expected "another of
the white man's failures." Yet instead of giving up on community development, the CCF increasingly relied on this method.[33]

The province chose a refined version of community development. More
subtle than earlier policies, the new community development offered the
hope that northerners would internalize and apply CCF ideals to their
lives. Aboriginals would then voluntarily follow the CCF plans for them
and become productive members of Saskatchewan society. The CCF continued to use its colonial apparatus to apply the new programs, using DNR
and other government departments to introduce expanded community
development projects to the north.

In order to increase the effectiveness of community development, the
CCF incorporated quite sophisticated community studies into the development programs. The government hoped that study would provide a
grasp of Aboriginal societal dynamics and guidance on how to reach its
economic and social goals for Aboriginals. The studies began by the late
1940s. Malcolm Norris undertook an economic and social survey of some
villages in 1947.[34] In 1948 the CCF asked Richard I. Ruggles of McMaster
University to survey northern "social conditions" and "physical characteristics" to help clarify social and economic development issues. The same
year, in an early effort to combine research and community development,
DNR asked the Fish Board, Social Welfare, Agriculture, Education, Public
Health, and the Saskatchewan Recreational Movement to study the Cumberland House area and to make plans for about five years.[35]

The growth of community development in northern Saskatchewan par-
alleled its increasing use by other western governments to solve problems
of underdevelopment at home and abroad. Community development called
for facilitators to stimulate and direct communities toward goals that, ideally, the communities should set or at least participate in setting. The CCF,
however, did not include northern communities in most goal setting or in
determining and implementing strategies to meet goals. Instead, the CCF's

colonial approach extended to its community development projects, with decisions made outside the region. In 1948, for example, A.O. Aschim, a forester, suggested a DNR-directed forestry-based program to supplement other programs in developing a diversified economy at Cumberland House. Yet he saw an obstacle in the local attitude to "material progress." He thought many had "the intelligence of a school child, but the obstinance of a Missouri mule," and he saw community leaders as a "hindrance to progress." Aschim wanted to exclude community leaders from the decision-making process.[36] Similarly, the following year Assistant Deputy Minister J.W. Churchman, Malcolm Norris, and Jim Brady all wanted to see strong government direction in community development. Norris said, "If the initiative comes from the people themselves it sometimes takes years."[37] To achieve success, community development required spontaneous and enthusiastic local initiative. Subsequent failures proved the need for local support.

When the CCF's various efforts at Cumberland House encountered failure and a loss of direction, the province turned its attention to developing communities in the west-side Buffalo Region, from Beauval to La Loche. Anthropologist V.F. Valentine, first hired for the summer of 1952, returned in 1953 and joined DNR's permanent northern staff. His job became to advise the CCF on how to "provide a more secure, happier life for the residents of our more remote areas." Dr. Harry B. Hawthorne of UBC evaluated Valentine and his work for DNR. Hawthorne was "favourably impressed" and deemed Valentine well qualified to work as an anthropologist. He added: "The essential problem of the Metis today is that they are unable to help themselves ... It would be presumptuous to try to account for the failures of intelligent, patient men who have tried to aid the Metis." Hawthorne proposed a three-year program to bring change among the Metis. DNR's Planning Office, staffed by several geographers, also studied the Buffalo Region and provided data for CCF interventions there.[38]

CCF politicians and bureaucrats alike recognized the paternal and colonial nature of their northern programs, which seemed the antithesis of ideal community development models. They also claimed to understand that they needed to change their methods of dealing with the region's Aboriginals. Churchman, while acknowledging the failure of CCF plans for assimilation, placed faith in Valentine's study. Churchman thought that, once the CCF had more information, it could alter its programs so the Metis would accept them better. For his part, J.H. Brockelbank told Premier Douglas and other cabinet members, "We have helped to foster a 'beggarly' attitude on the part of these people in which they have come to expect that the Provincial Government will carry the whole burden of solving their dilemma, while they do nothing." J.A. Collier, a CCF employee from Regina who studied the region, critically described the colonial situation, where the "great white father" tried to remake the north, with "almost all *done for* and damn little *done with*" the northern people.

In 1958 A.G. Kuziak, the minister of Natural Resources, thought Valentine's work helped government understand that the initiative had to come from local individuals to work together to deal with problems. Clearly, these and other officials claimed to understand the need for Aboriginal self-determination. Yet they and those who designed and applied the new community development programs at the field level wanted Aboriginals to change rapidly and in particular ways. Two men who influenced the shape the programs would take were R.G. Young, a DNR geographer, and Valentine; both wanted Metis to move from what they saw as irrelevant lives. This goal contradicted their desire to let Aboriginals spontaneously choose, reject, and change aspects of the invading culture. Left to their own choices, Aboriginals well might choose not to change. Officials became accustomed to saying that any solution to the "problem" had to involve northerners. Yet since the plan to change Aboriginals remained nonnegotiable, the approach remained highly directed.[39]

Although its basic goals for northern Aboriginals remained unchanged, the CCF soon placed most of its hope for achieving these on Valentine and his community development program. After carrying out a general study of the north, Valentine began a pilot project exploring techniques of change at Île-à-la-Crosse. He lived there for about two years beginning in 1955. The anthropologist agreed with the CCF's desire to introduce cooperatives into the north. He thought the development of cooperatives and community development should go hand in hand, with cooperatives acting as the key to community development. Valentine successfully encouraged formation of a co-op store, a co-op fish marketing association, and a power co-op at Île-à-la-Crosse. Although Indian Affairs nearly lured him away in 1956, the CCF induced him to stay, giving him a hefty raise. Valentine's primary responsibility became expanding the northern community development and rehabilitation program approved by Douglas and cabinet.[40]

While Valentine worked on developing new plans, community development and "Northern Native Rehabilitation" projects remained small. In addition to DNR's efforts, other departments, including Co-operation, Social Welfare, and Health, increasingly engaged in community development projects. Co-operation employed an anthropologist at Prince Albert and representatives for Buffalo Narrows and the east side. But a lack of coordination plagued the various attempts to work for community development. M. Miller, DNR director of research and planning, placed some of the blame for the program's shortcomings on Northern Administrator Brown. Critically, Miller commented: "Brown, humbly and quite properly, makes no more claims for the present 'program' than that it is a series of remotely related measures which directly and indirectly help provide the natives with seasonal work. There is no policy involvement on their part." With dismay Miller added: "Brown has no proposals to offer to alter the situation, nor does he seem unduly perturbed by it." Yet responsibility for the program shortcomings could have attached to many others besides Brown.[41]

Thanks to Valentine, the community development program soon did show promising signs of life. Phase One of DNR's new plan, the Île-à-la-Crosse stage, had ended in 1956. Valentine claimed success; the Île-à-la-Crosse study demonstrated that "encouraging the greater participation of local people in community affairs" could solve some Metis problems. The anthropologist then moved to Regina to plan the expansion of the program. Phase Two of the project would employ "action-research" to apply research and community development at Cumberland House. The CCF chose this community because it was the largest Metis settlement and had natural resources, high literacy, local initiative, a reputation as a "major problem area," and a long history of failed government projects. Direction for the project would come from Valentine and his assistant, who would live in modern conditions at The Pas, Manitoba. Valentine would have the help of a deputy minister's committee of seven, a five-member research team, seven special consultants, and four technical consultants, working with a multilevel community structure. Various departments approved the interdepartmental effort. Thinking even further ahead, Valentine visualized a third phase, in which they would apply the lessons learned at Cumberland House to other communities. But before Phase Two could begin, Valentine quit and moved to the federal civil service. This brought a "temporary halt" to the project. His leaving possibly saved Cumberland House from the worst insult yet from the CCF. The full-blown plan did not proceed under Valentine's replacement.[42]

After Valentine left, the community development and related cooperative programs also faltered at Île-à-la-Crosse. It seemed the local people had not internalized the cooperative values. DNR sent E.N. Shannon, who conceded he had no training in the matter, there to continue the work. His goals were to integrate the Metis and end their special treatment in the areas of resources and hospital tax collection.[43] Needless to say, his tough approach to community development and attempts to force integration and impose new responsibilities encountered resistance.

Basic principles of community development had fallen by the wayside, as Valentine and the other community development workers acted without community support. Several experts warned about proceeding alone. In 1957 Carl C. Taylor of Arlington, Virginia, an expert on community development, questioned the dynamic role played by Valentine and cautioned that action should await "development of the consciousness of the people."[44] A 1957 government document also quoted a warning from J.R. Rees, director of the World Federation for Mental Health. Rees said that trying to shape new developments in other cultures can produce unfortunate consequences and do great harm.[45] The CCF did not heed the warnings.

The province remained committed to the strategy of community development and Valentine's "action oriented" and "applied research" approach, even after he left. Tom Wylie, the new director of anthropological research, lived and researched at Cumberland House in 1959. DNR also spoke of possibly hiring three more anthropologists to work in the north. It even saw some success and claimed that local people took initiative in building the Buffalo Narrows recreation centre, the Île-à-la-Crosse curling rink, and the La Loche co-op store, while DNR remained in the background.[46]

Another major effort at community development had begun in 1957, when the CCF and the University of Saskatchewan sponsored the independent Center for Community Studies, located at the U of S. The centre's director, W.B. Baker, oversaw a consulting division guided by Dr. Harold R. Baker, a training division headed by Dr. Darwin D. Solomon, and a research division led by Dr. Arthur K. Davis. By 1960 the centre had developed an interdisciplinary team with fourteen professional positions. After researching some southern communities, it turned to the north in 1959, guided by anthropologist Charles Brant of Portland State College.[47]

DNR and the centre entered into a three-year contract from 1 April 1960 to 31 March 1963. A budget of about $220,000 would pay for research, training, and seminars aimed at improving the situation of northern Metis. The centre delivered community development training for many DNR and other government staff and offered community leadership courses in numerous northern communities. For the study, the centre relied on professionals, including the English anthropologist Dr. P.M. Worsley, the economist Helen L. Buckley, the anthropologist J.E.M. Kew, and many others.[48]

A preliminary report from the centre by 1961 described the northern situation as colonial and as a microcosm of two-thirds of the world. Yet the centre also praised the CCF for the steps it took against northern colonialism. It blamed the colonial situation in the north on "200 years of white control" and not on the CCF. The study failed to recognize the primary role the CCF had played in strengthening and perpetuating the northern colonial situation. Colonialism also continued in the community development program, although the CCF claimed "a decisive break with past tradition." Compulsion remained a dominant feature of community development, which W.B. Baker described as "planned change" and as "rational manipulation of impinging forces."[49]

DNR kept the primary responsibility for community development, which ranked as one of its main tasks. Nineteen conservation officers (COs) at ten northern headquarters worked as the primary development workers, overseen by a supervisor of community development. Yet the program lacked viability. The few weeks' training given to the officers did not adequately prepare them for the tasks expected of them. Further, even if they mastered the necessary skills, DNR expected them to carry out conflicting authoritarian and facilitating roles. The CCF also continued to

rely on anthropologists, but in spite of their relatively high level of training, they also failed to produce quick results. One anthropologist, J.E.M.
Kew, who spent time at Cumberland House, lost faith in the government's
plan. "I have seen the odd blurb in the COMMONWEALTH [CCF/NDP
newspaper] about the great Northern development projects," he wrote.
"But I suspect there is a great difference as always between what the seers
in Regina hand out to their lackeys and what the Indians on the Bigstone
[reserve] receive as they walk that long main street of La Ronge." In reality, most areas saw little community development. Some in DNR attributed the ongoing failures and northern problems to Aboriginals. As one
example, in 1963 W.R. Parks, DNR's director of forests, blamed DNR failures at Cumberland House on "the general apathy and unreliability of the
natives ... They need to develop a sense of responsibility."[50]

Not many successes came about, but when one did occur, DNR did not
hide its pleasure. In the Pelican Narrows area in 1963-64, DNR instituted a
community development pilot project that saw trappers elect an Aboriginal
fur patrolman. The band chief and fur councillors guided his activities.
A.H. MacDonald, director of Northern Affairs, described it as "a remarkable
achievement with respect to the involvement of the people in managing
their own affairs."[51] But the CCF could point to few other successful projects.

The CCF made an additional community development effort in 1962,
establishing the Community Development Branch within the Department
of Municipal Affairs. Ray Woollam received the task of creating local government structures and moving responsibility to local people. He left in
1963, after doing some community development work at Green Lake and
Canoe Lake.[52]

Although the CCF preferred to retain control over community development work, Roman Catholic priests also saw community needs. As a
result, they designed and operated several development projects. Father
Chamberland of the Beauval Indian Residential School and Father Darche
of Buffalo Narrows each offered some vocational education in the late
1950s. Father Darche also developed the Young Men's Centre and Unity
Training Centre at Buffalo Narrows. In the latter project, helped by a $500
grant from the province, Darche arranged for two female community
workers to come to the training centre in early 1964. He also asked the
CCF for lumber to build an alcohol education centre at Buffalo Narrows.
Overall, the CCF preferred to run projects itself and gave the church projects little support.[53]

The province's northern community development efforts often consisted largely of creating cooperatives. These came about primarily
through CCF initiative, with many of the same staff working to develop
communities and create cooperatives. Co-ops became part of the CCF
effort to solve northern problems through the introduction of socialist
ideals. In colonial fashion, the CCF kept paternalistic control, not trusting

northerners to run businesslike operations, and preventing movement of full responsibility to the local level. There were cooperatives in retail, trapping, the fishery, forestry, housing, and handicrafts. Even with heavy subsidies, retail cooperatives did not usually lower prices dramatically, and cooperative marketing could not make the inefficient resource industries profitable.[54] In some cases, co-ops lowered prices and improved incomes, but not enough to overcome poverty, since the larger structure of the northern economy played the dominant role.

During its first five years in government, while it introduced the bluntest and most aggressive programs aimed at transforming the north, the CCF's efforts to encourage northern cooperatives remained minimal. Largely due to Jim Brady's work, Cumberland House saw the most extensive cooperative development in the late 1940s. Local enthusiasm for cooperatives remained strong there for a time. In 1950 H.E. Chapman, director of Extension Services for the Department of Co-operation, helped conduct a cooperative school for about thirty-five men. Attendance rose to about 250 in the evenings, when women and children came to view cooperative films. By 1952 fur, wood products, sturgeon fishing, and retail co-ops and a credit union operated there. But these all soon failed. In the case of the fur co-op, which disbanded by 1953, local support seemed to evaporate when trappers found that the co-op did not give them the freedom to control trapping regulations and sell furs to whom they wished. It seems they thought the co-op would let them circumvent the CCF regulations. A Cumberland House fur cooperative again operated by 1963, apparently successfully run by trappers.[55]

Although the Department of Co-operation hired its first field man for the north in 1949, it was not until the 1950s that the CCF devoted large resources to cooperatives. The department developed its Extension Services branch and helped found the Co-operative Institute in 1955. By this time the CCF had chosen Île-à-la-Crosse for its first major effort to found co-ops. There, V.F. Valentine, the DNR anthropologist, promoted cooperatives as part of the CCF pilot project in community development. The CCF also approved a co-op advisor by 1956 for Île-à-la-Crosse. Promotion of co-ops proceeded largely by trial and error, with efforts made in some areas of the north and not in others. After two years as a field worker, Terry Phalen succeeded Harold Chapman as the department director of Extension Services, a position he held for fifteen years. By 1959 the department had five northern cooperative management advisor positions.[56] In another significant development, the Northern Handicrafts Co-operative Association Ltd. began as an all-woman organization at La Ronge in 1960. Substantial advisory and monetary help from the province and a strong demand for the handicrafts helped the co-op succeed for a time. About eighty producers participated by 1962.[57]

Ideally, cooperatives spring from local enthusiasm, motivated by a desire to join in meeting a community need. Government involvement, while supportive, should remain nondirective. But under the CCF, government dominated, while northern enthusiasm remained weak at best. As a result, the CCF relied on long-term compulsion to create and maintain co-ops. This compromised the independence and effectiveness of the cooperative movement. DNR, responsible for most northern development, particularly pushed cooperatives. The Department of Co-operation sometimes demonstrated a greater awareness of proper cooperative principles and seemed more concerned with the economic viability of co-ops, but the aggressive approach prevailed. At times the CCF justified its promotion of co-ops by asserting that Aboriginal culture had a tradition of cooperation that would make cooperatives work well, a view Terry Phalen shared in 1956. However, in later reflections he changed his mind about the predilection of Aboriginals to cooperate. Phalen also acknowledged that the program grew primarily due to CCF actions and not from local initiative. He described cooperatives as the "corner-stone" of the CCF development plan for the north. Clearly the northern co-op program remained a CCF enterprise. It lacked meaningful links to the larger cooperative movement, including Federated Co-operatives Limited or other southern cooperatives.[58]

Trapping, fishing, and agriculture comprised the three primary parts of the economy visualized by the CCF for northern Aboriginals. All three failed to meet CCF expectations, and it became increasingly clear that the poorly conceived and implemented programs would not build a successful new northern economy and society. Once it realized this, the CCF increasingly turned to community studies and community development methods to design and implement changes. Yet these new efforts also failed to solve northern problems. Instead, the Aboriginal economy weakened further and social problems grew. There was, however, another economy that existed in the north at that time, which could have brought stability, if not prosperity, to northern Aboriginals.

8
A Pre-Industrial Way of Life

The CCF government accepted and perpetuated the notion that Aboriginals were not ready or suited for industrial occupations. It thought trapping, fishing, and subsistence agriculture, all restructured following socialist principles, should form the basis for the Aboriginal economy. While the northern economy also included the industries of forestry, mining, and tourism, the CCF helped reserve these mainly for non-Aboriginals and did little to encourage Aboriginal participation in these areas. However, Tommy Douglas and his cohorts' socialist philosophy affected not only the Aboriginal sector of the economy. They also applied a socialist model to forestry, taking ownership of the resource and control of the industry. The province chose not to take over mining, preferring instead to increase government revenues by raising taxes and royalties. In spite of these disincentives, federal interest and a strong US uranium market continued to drive mining development for most of the CCF era. In the area of tourism, government imposed strict regulations and controls while permitting private persons to operate businesses. The socialist reputation and policies of the CCF alarmed potential investors, limiting development in the most promising sectors of the northern economy. Further limits on economic growth came from the underdeveloped state of northern infrastructure. With the exception of some mining companies, major firms stayed away. As a result, the northern economy satisfied few. Non-Aboriginals saw little future for themselves there, while Aboriginal people found themselves excluded from most opportunities that did arise. Even the CCF failed to meet its goals, failing to diversify the provincial economy and bring prosperity to the north.

Although trees covered northern Saskatchewan, a lack of road or rail access meant that most areas had seen virtually no logging by 1944. The forest industry had heavily logged accessible areas, leaving a false impression of forest depletion. No major wood processors operated in the province. Relatively little mining development – certainly much less than in some other provinces – had taken place in Saskatchewan. A scarcity of major discoveries and the remoteness of known ore bodies accounted for the relatively small role mining played in the economy. For a time, miners dug for gold on the north shore of Lake Athabasca, but their community of Goldfields became a ghost town with the onset of the Second World War. Various small mines brought little benefit to the province. One large mine operated in 1944 at Flin Flon, Manitoba, where Hudson Bay Mining and Smelting mined much of its ore from the Saskatchewan side of the border. Tourism played only a minute role in the northern economy before the CCF assumed office. No roads entered the north; only water or air transportation could bring visitors to appreciate the remote northern attractions. Virtually no tourism facilities awaited the few who ventured north. Given the lack of previous development, northern Saskatchewan offered the CCF great opportunities for expansion of economic activity in 1944.

In keeping with its socialist principles, the CCF claimed most of Saskatchewan's forest resources for the people of the province, ejected private companies, and created a state apparatus to run much of the industry. For the most part, government did not use the forests for Aboriginal economic development or promote Aboriginal involvement in forestry. CCF actions demonstrated that it considered forestry primarily a non-Aboriginal activity. Additionally, even had government wanted to involve Aboriginals in forestry, most Aboriginal communities continued to lack road access. Without adequate transportation, no large-scale forest industry could operate.

Saskatchewan's tree cover stretched to its northern boundary, but the southern part of the forested area, south of the Canadian Shield and often covering less than one hundred miles from north to south, formed the province's prime commercial forest zone. By the early 1900s the largely US-based forest industry had heavily logged the prime white spruce stands in the accessible areas. Mills in Prince Albert and elsewhere sawed the trees into lumber, much of which left for markets outside the province. With the easiest pickings taken, some lumber barons left the province. Largely uncontrolled cutting continued, though, including during the Great Depression and the Second World War. The postwar years saw the release of pent-up housing demands, and Canadians clamoured for lumber.[1] When the CCF assumed power, most logging and processing of trees took place near the southern edge of the northern forest. Some forest areas looked depleted, particularly those near roads or waterways. While heavy timber covered the area farther north, a lack of road access and the smaller size of the trees meant most of the commercial potential went untapped. Additionally, secondary forest industries were few, and Saskatchewan failed to capitalize on the full potential of the trees cut there. No pulp or paper mill operated in the province, but trees were exported to mills in Manitoba and Ontario.

Much as it did in trapping, the CCF justified intervening in forestry partly by claiming gross depletion of the resource. And as with furs and fish, the CCF's socialist beliefs determined its actions. In the party's view, private entrepreneurs had enriched themselves by taking what did not belong to them while mismanaging the forest resource. Consequently, the CCF believed that it should claim the northern trees for all residents of the province. Saskatchewan's people would not actually receive the trees, but the CCF would handle them for their benefit.

Once again, Joe Phelps led the charge against an existing industry. Acting quickly, he and his colleagues established the Forest Products Marketing Board. Creation of the Saskatchewan Timber Board (STB) followed in September 1945. This Crown corporation received a mandate to cut, log, saw, purchase, and manufacture timber products. New policies allowed private interests to cut and process state-owned trees only as agents of the Timber Board, which let tenders for logging, sawing, planing, and delivering green lumber. The Timber Board then processed and sold the lumber. It also extended its control to pulp, ties, posts, and poles from Crown lands. T.C. Douglas cleverly compared the new set-up to hiring someone to cut an agricultural crop, with the province the landowner. The CCF also used the analogy of partners. Where the CCF saw a partnership between government and industry, however, loggers and sawmill owners experienced coercion. Optimistically, the CCF foresaw higher returns to producers, lower prices for consumers, and profits that would pay for social services for grateful citizens. The futures of those who depended on the forest industry seemed to cause the party little concern.[2]

Before introducing the most controversial policy changes, similar to its interventions in fishing and trapping, the CCF made a show of gathering input from a variety of people. Phelps consulted twelve MLAs about the changes. He also surveyed industry people, asking if they favoured "contract logging by tender of Crown timber." Sixty-six percent of respondents supported the scheme. Contradictorily, in the same year many operators opposed the forced selling of lumber to the board. The CCF ignored the opposition, claiming to have over 90 percent support from operators and sawmill owners.[3]

Much of Phelps's alleged support from the industry soon evaporated when the reality of the new system became clear. Operators had not understood the extent to which the CCF meant to take over the industry. Some Norquay-area companies, which had met with Phelps, apparently thought the board would help market their lumber. Opposition increased when operators found the new system created financial hardship by paying much less for lumber than the open market did. Citing a desire to eliminate inefficient operators, the Timber Board refused to grant a rate increase. It frequently found itself accused of not paying enough. Further resistance arose when, as with trapping, the marketing board system endangered credit. Small loggers and sawmills could not obtain credit from buyers to whom they could no longer sell. Larger companies did not like the new policy either. The Pas Lumber Company, the largest holder of licensed timber berths, agreed to try the plan only after a three-day meeting in Regina with the CCF. A 50 percent royalty increase on berth timber raised additional opposition from the Manitoba Saskatchewan Forest Products Association in 1945.

But the CCF demonstrated confidence in its actions. It characterized adversaries as persons unhappy about losing their profitable situation. James F. Gray, the resident manager of Saskatchewan Lake and Forest Products Corporation, compared those waiting for the Liberals to return to power to someone waiting for the sheriff or police to leave in order to get back into business. Ignoring the opponents, the CCF even dropped operator representation on the board, which had included two operators and one ex-operator. Its experience introducing the new forestry policies taught the new government a valuable lesson: taking over the entire forest industry seemed to reduce opposition, presumably by weakening opponents.[4]

Again, as in its fishing and trapping interventions, most of the "capitalists" targeted by the CCF consisted of small family operations. Hundreds of loggers and small sawmill operators worked in the forest-fringe area, providing mainly meagre incomes. Although CCF policies greatly affected their livelihoods, most could do little to fight back. While, in terms of business size, most forestry operations resembled the small southern farms, the CCF did not interfere with farmers' operations. The CCF found it much easier to take control of forestry operations since this industry relied heavily on trees from provincially owned Crown lands. Also, those who worked in forestry represented a much less potent political force than did the much larger number of farmers.

Internal opposition did arise to the CCF plan. C. Philip Reed, a DNR officer at Love, testified before the Saskatchewan Royal Commission on Forestry, alleging political interference by an MLA in forestry. Phelps did not tolerate this dissension and took Reed to task over his testimony. Defiantly, Reed then attacked Phelps, accusing him of failing as an "Industrial Tycoon," of employing teachers and farmers to run the forest program, and of hiring employees before advertising the jobs. As a result, he said, Phelps had "left instead of right hand men."[5] In another incident, someone in 1948 filled a road washout in the Paddockwood area with manure and put up a sign designating it as a "CCF culvert." The local DNR officer, fed up with the heat he took for unpopular CCF policies, wrote a nasty letter to the Timber Board manager, complaining of board operations.[6] These incidents did not make a noticeable impression on the CCF.

In addition to taking over the industry, the CCF worked to conserve the forest resource. The primary controversy from conservation programs resulted when the CCF overestimated forest depletion in the 1940s. The

Saskatchewan Royal Commission on Forestry, appointed by the CCF in 1945, played a role in the design of forest conservation measures. The commission's mandate did not extend to looking at the controversial issue of the CCF takeover of the industry. Phelps and his colleagues had already made that decision. The commission's 1947 report suggested practical actions, including using aircraft and parachutists to protect the forest from fires. It also recommended a forest inventory and expanding markets for unused forest growth. Many of the nonsocialist aspects of the CCF forest policy were based on the commission's findings. In subsequent years, the CCF stressed research, protection, and management of the forest. To help manage the resource, DNR began a forestry school at Prince Albert in 1946 to train forest managers, enrolling primarily southern students. The province also developed a plan to space the cutting of white spruce over twenty years and began a forest inventory. Drastic cuts in quotas resulted. But cutting again increased somewhat with the implementation of the Dore-Smoothstone management plan in 1950-51, which brought most remaining large blocks of white spruce under management. The CCF rejected clear-cutting, which was common before, and set minimum size limits for trees cut. Government operated four tree nurseries in 1946, and some reforestation took place through replanting. DNR decided to curtail its northern forest nursery program by 1948, thinking the forest regenerated "more quickly and efficiently" on its own. Apparently changing its mind, DNR built a new forest nursery north of Prince Albert by 1961.[7]

Protecting the forest from fire formed a major part of the plan for forest conservation. The province formed the first smoke jumper group in Canada in 1947. By 1955 the forest protection network included eighty-five fire towers and staff at nearly fifty locations. DNR taught Aboriginals to fight fires in the late 1950s and depended heavily on them for manual labour on fire lines. DNR divided the north into two zones by 1961, with the area south of the fifty-seventh parallel and the Beaverlodge area receiving "top priority." Elsewhere, DNR often let fires burn themselves out.[8]

During the years of CCF management, the northern forest industry remained small, limited by CCF policies. Consistent with its socialist ideology, the province encouraged two types of forestry operations: government-owned and cooperative. Government mills included Timber Board and DNR mills. The board operated eleven yards and had forty-nine employees by 1947. After reorganization in the 1950s, the Timber Board fell under the direction of Saskatchewan Forest Products (SFP), which also included Saskatchewan Wood Enterprises, formerly the Prince Albert Box Factory. The STB opened a new mill at Big River in 1950 and also owned a sawmill at La Ronge and later at Air Ronge, which stopped operating by about 1954. In 1950 the STB set up a pole department to supply power poles, with Northern Wood Preservers at Prince Albert preserving the poles. SFP handled a volume of more than $5 million of products by 1954. It ran eight yards and eight planing mills located in the forested area in 1964. By then it paid the provincial treasury about $5.9 million in surpluses.[9]

Under CCF management, logging did increase a little in the area north of the prime commercial belt, particularly in the La Ronge, Buffalo Narrows, Cumberland House, and Flin Flon areas. Those sawing lumber in the latter two areas could rely on Manitoba's roads and railways to carry the product to markets. Before 1959 the annual value of Northern Region forest products averaged from $750,000 to $1 million, a paltry amount given the size of the resource.[10]

While some lumber left for outside markets, local northern people also needed wood products. To help meet this demand, the Timber Board made lumber available to northerners. In cases where residents would use the product themselves, the board sometimes sold them this lumber at reduced prices. Lumber sold by the Timber Board also helped build northern schools, hospitals, and community buildings. DNR helped meet the northern need for lumber as well. Larger DNR mills worked at Pemmican Portage, Buffalo Narrows, Île-à-la-Crosse, Beauval, and Lac la Ronge, while smaller portable operations sawed and planed lumber for Fish Board buildings, schools, teacherages, and homes in many other villages. One or two lightweight units could fit in airplanes, although it seems these saw little use. When communities used DNR mills, local people supplied labour, paid timber dues, and later also paid the sawyers' wages and gas and oil costs. With the expansion in the 1960s of the northern housing program, DNR bought more mills and another planer. Some small private mills also helped meet the local need for lumber. Veterans, trappers, fishermen, and prospectors could receive free timber-cutting permits.[11]

Joe Phelps's northern vision did not include forestry as a major option for Aboriginal people.[12] Even after he left government, the CCF continued to consider forestry primarily as a non-Aboriginal activity. Various experiments involving Aboriginals in the industry reinforced this point of view. The largest CCF project to involve Aboriginals in commercial logging and sawing lumber operated at Cumberland House. In this case, the CCF remained true to its ideology by using a cooperative structure. DNR helped establish Cumberland House Wood Products Co-operative in 1950. Using a DNR-owned steam-powered sawmill, the co-op should have thrived. It received great advantages over other operations, including concentrated high-grade cutting areas and extensive aid. Instead, due to poor management and maintenance, the government lost at least $4,000 from 1949 to 1951. In 1951-52, again operating with DNR money and supplies and with a potentially profitable contract for 500,000 board feet, local people lacked interest in working. They took out only about 200,000 board feet and failed to saw the trees into lumber. The government employees who oversaw the operation were frustrated. DNR's Shaw wrote, "You cannot trust these people with valuable machinery as in the course of a very short time you will have nothing left but scrap." Director of Forests W.R. Parks later described the co-op's first two years of operation as a "complete failure" except for providing some local work. The co-op ended operations after three winters when it did not have $500 needed for repairs.[13]

After some years passed, in 1962 the CCF again tried Aboriginal forestry work at Cumberland House. Government revived the wood co-op, and prospects looked rosy with a ten-year supply of spruce-budworm-damaged wood, at a cutting rate of about one million board feet per year. Fearing failure, local people resisted the project, but with prodding they reluctantly agreed to the plan. Outsiders managed the operation, but this did not prevent problems from arising – indeed, a lack of community control may have increased the difficulties. Local people attempted sabotage, the new beer parlour took workers away on drinking bouts, and some developed "itchy feet." Determined to remove the wood, the CCF imported Metis workers from Green Lake, but the newcomers soon allied with opponents of the project. At a high cost, DNR then hired an outside crew, which employed mechanical logging in place of the horses used until then. DNR estimated the first season's loss at $6,003.33, although local people received about $16,500 from the operation and it lowered welfare costs. Social aid had risen dramatically from $10,199 in 1960 to $53,747 in 1962-63, and the CCF decided to continue the project. Even with a provincial grant and loan backing for 1963-64, optimism again proved unfounded. This time the manager left, and crawler tractors and heavy trucks broke through the river ice, allegedly weakened by water releases from the Squaw Rapids dam. The operation cut only 575,000 board feet, and there was a net loss of $6,733. Yet the Department of Co-operation saw success and gave another grant. Loan guarantees stood at $22,000 by 1964. The CCF stubbornly stuck with its artificial cooperative, even though private operators would not have needed subsidies and may have provided more jobs and income. As much as anything, these experiences at Cumberland House likely reinforced the CCF belief that Aboriginals could not participate in forestry in a substantial way.[14]

A somewhat different CCF-supported forestry cooperative operated at Buffalo Narrows. There, in 1960, twelve residents, including DNR's L. Reznechenko and G. Parsons of the Department of Co-operation, each invested $100 in a sawmill. The sawmill incorporated as the Buffalo Narrows Sawmill Co-operative in 1961 and obtained a CCF-backed loan of $10,000. But financial difficulties followed. The co-op made no payments in the first two years and by 1964 accumulated other debts of $6,500. Although the co-op resisted, DNR then took over the mill, adding it to the department's operations.[15] In this case, the province tired of the ongoing problems, even though local initiative existed and the co-op operated more like a true cooperative. Contradictorily, the artificial co-op at Cumberland House continued with CCF support. One likely reason for this was that the CCF viewed the social and economic needs as being greater at Cumberland House and used the cooperative to try to meet them. Additionally, the CCF considered it pressing to remove the spruce-budworm-damaged wood at Cumberland House.

In addition to the Crown corporations, DNR operations, and cooperatives, some private concerns continued to log and saw lumber. But they could only do so by accepting the strict new CCF controls. Various operators held timber berths in 1944, granted in 1930 or earlier by Ottawa. Phelps and the CCF bought back many berths, spending about $150,000 on these purchases by 1948 and leaving only seven operators holding berths. The Pas Lumber Company remained the largest, with rights to 123.18 square miles, down from 224.19 square miles in 1945. It agreed to build a high utilization sawmill, on which the CCF held a purchase option. Hundreds of small sawmills also still operated. Located mostly in the forest-fringe area, they sawed for the Timber Board and individuals who owned land outside the provincial forest. The forest industry employed about 3,523 people in the province in 1947.[16]

It often seemed that the CCF intentionally created obstacles to timber access, thereby discouraging use of forest products. In one case in 1948 and 1949, Nisto Mines wanted to cut timber in the Stony Rapids-Black Lake area for its mining operation. Although suitable timber grew in the area, DNR refused to grant cutting permission, citing a possible future local demand. Unrealistically, DNR suggested the mine might cut timber in an inaccessible area hundreds of miles to the southwest and then bring it by water through Alberta and along Lake Athabasca.[17] In another instance, in 1953 DNR sabotaged a private contractor in the Beaver Lake area by giving him small amounts of timber in about seventeen scattered areas, making economical operation impossible. Private operations at Green Lake and Meadow Lake also experienced difficulty obtaining trees. DNR's district superintendent, A. Hansen, wrote that the Meadow Lake sawmill owner constantly expanded and tried to put the onus on DNR to supply timber. Yet the operator had no choice but to look to DNR, which controlled all timber on Crown land. This type of attitude on the part of the province prevented development of the great potential of the timber industry.[18]

Development of the forest industry suffered further from the CCF's great exaggeration of forest depletion. Although the detailed forest inventory soon contradicted the early alarm over depletion, in 1949 the CCF still justified its intervention by citing unscrupulous cutting, conservation, and management practices. One official said it would have taken "only a few years until we had no marketable timber left."[19] The CCF eventually did revise its idea of what it considered "commercially productive." Then, in a complete about-face, in 1952 DNR claimed that Saskatchewan possessed "one of the largest remaining untapped rich forest areas of North America." By 1956 the CCF estimated about fourteen billion board feet of saw timber and six billion cubic feet of pulpwood remained unharvested in the commercial forest zone. Yet the CCF continued its strict control over access to the forest resource. The annual depletion in 1955 totalled only about 30 million cubic feet, while available volume grew by about 220 million cubic feet. Simultaneously, Saskatchewan imported large amounts of wood products. Mr. Atkinson, the superintendent of the Nisbet Plywood Company, called it "gross under-utilization."[20]

Northern District lumber production eventually increased with improved road access. In keeping with the CCF belief that Aboriginals lacked suitability as forestry workers, most forestry labour came from the south. In one example, only about fifty northerners worked in bush operations in the winter of 1958-59. Director of Forests W.R. Parks blamed this on Aboriginals' lack of dependability, claiming they often did not return to work after receiving their pay and going home.[21] In 1962-63, while the Northern Administration Branch (NAB) area produced 8,356,623 board feet of lumber, the industry remained tiny compared to the size of the resource. The north had only sixteen of the province's five hundred sawmills. Only 255 of 2,700 men working in forestry and sawmills in 1961 laboured in the tree-covered north.[22]

Even with the realization that forest depletion was a myth, provincial production increased little, from $3.9 million in 1948 to $4.2 million in 1958. Its value varied from $2.4 to $4.5 million in the intervening years. Forestry as a percentage of the net value of commodity production dropped from 0.7 percent to 0.5 percent. While little harvesting of trees took place, some still tried to blame the situation on the pre-CCF era. In 1959 the Stanford Research Institute, in a CCF-commissioned report, echoed CCF sentiments. The institute blamed low output on past overcutting, while contradictorily seeing underutilization of most wood species.[23]

As its time in office lengthened, the CCF found itself blamed for the continuing stagnation of the industry. The inability to bring a pulp and paper industry to Saskatchewan became one of the government's greatest failures in management of the forest resource. Producing pulp and paper could have employed thousands in the bush and mills, using otherwise nonsalable trees. It also would have brought badly needed revenue and economic diversification. Beginning in the 1940s, some in government, including cabinet and DNR's Industrial Development Branch, recognized the potential of pulp and paper. Several false announcements of mills took place in the mid-1950s. Skepticism greeted the CCF promise before the 1956 election of three thousand jobs and a $60-million mill for Prince Albert. The mill idea soon vanished. Another plan in 1962 also fell through.[24] In spite of the CCF's uncharacteristic willingness to use private investment for this development, capital, frightened by the government's socialist reputation, stayed away. After the defeat of the CCF in 1964, the new Thatcher Liberal government quickly and successfully negotiated a pulp mill for Prince Albert. It also obtained an agreement for a second pulp mill at Dore Lake, a deal that the NDP cancelled by paying compensation when it came to office in 1971.

Although trees covered the northern half of the province, at the end of the CCF era, Saskatchewan ranked last among the provinces in per capita forest production, at about eight dollars per capita. The province produced less than half of the lumber it consumed, forest-related industries employed only about three thousand people, and a lone large nonportable sawmill operated, owned by the CCF. While dismal production figures and missed opportunities stood out, the CCF praised its sustained yield policy and the work of its Crown corporation, the Saskatchewan Timber Board.[25] The CCF refused to acknowledge its inability to properly manage the forest industry. In spite of possessing little knowledge about the industry, government stubbornly continued its destructive control.

In contrast, the CCF recognized its limitations regarding mining. Consequently, unlike its approach to all other major northern resources, the province did not involve itself directly in extracting, processing, or selling minerals. Yet CCF policies and actions greatly affected mining. Socialist ideology, high royalties, and the lack of infrastructure prevented northern mining from realizing its potential. Saskatchewan's relatively small northern mining industry existed in spite of CCF policies, not because of them.

DNR retained responsibility for administering mining policies until the CCF created the Department of Mineral Resources in 1953. Joe Phelps knew little about mining. He later described himself as "almost flabbergasted" with the mineral development job. Realizing his limits, Phelps relied heavily on others, using his deputy minister, Vern Hogg, a geologist, as the "main sparkplug" while exercising caution that things would not "backfire." The minister viewed mining development as less urgent than fur, fish, and timber, which he thought needed crisis intervention. Minerals would keep in "nature's storehouse." While it deliberated, the CCF decided to allow private capital to participate in mining. The province reserved the right to take over mining later on. But the CCF did not give the mining companies free rein. Consistent with its ideology, the CCF thought mining companies had added to their wealth by exploiting the people. Much as in forestry, Phelps visualized a partnership between government and industry, although with the mining companies running the mines.[26]

The CCF soon proved an unfriendly partner by passing the Mineral Taxation Act in 1944. Since the owners of much of Saskatchewan's titled land owned the mineral rights, the CCF wanted the landowners either to give up the mineral rights or pay an ongoing tax. The CPR, which owned large amounts of land, lost its effort to have the Supreme Court disallow the legislation. Introducing an additional disincentive to mining, for the first time in Canada the CCF charged royalties for mineral depletion on private lands.[27]

Raising royalties for ore extracted from public lands also proved irresistible for the CCF. Phelps viewed increasing royalties as a satisfactory alternative to socialization of mines. The new government then raised royalty rates for larger mines, affecting the only large mine operating in the north, Hudson Bay Mining and Smelting at Flin Flon. Phelps pledged not to socialize the mine. Taking it over would have proven difficult anyway, since the mill and part of the ore body sat in Manitoba. Royalties collected there rose from $178,808 in 1944 to an estimated $1.23 million in 1946, about a sevenfold rise. In a sense, the increase turned the operation into a gold mine for the CCF. The mine continued operating in spite of the dramatic increase in royalty payments. Over $36 million of ore passed through the Manitoba mill in 1949, with about 74 percent of the rock coming from the Saskatchewan side. The operation employed about 2,600 people.[28] Yet, CCF taxation and royalty increases discouraged mineral exploration, and distrust existed that the CCF government would take over discoveries.

Although CCF taxation and royalty increases discouraged mineral exploration, and mining companies distrusted the CCF government, fearing it would take over discoveries, the province took some action to counteract depressed mining activity. In an apparent attempt to offset the negative effects of its policies, the province applied a sliding royalty scale, based on profits, beginning in 1947. The CCF also soon promised "full protection to exploration interests." In another liberalizing move, cabinet changed government policy to allow uranium prospecting, which had until then been banned. Ottawa still controlled the sale of all uranium.[29] Recognizing the mining industry's need for information, the province began the Saskatchewan Geological Survey in 1948. Using airplanes, government carried out magnetic and electromagnetic surveys, and field teams worked on mapping.[30]

In an additional move designed to change the low level of mineral exploration, in 1945 the CCF developed a five-year plan to train prospectors. Dr. J.B. Mawdsley of the University of Saskatchewan helped design the program, which initially trained about twenty men at the university. DNR then taught and aided prospectors through the Prospectors' Assistance Plan. The department helped by providing free air transportation, equipment, and assaying, and by waiving fees. Malcolm Norris looked after many of the administrative details. New discoveries included radioactive minerals at Lake Athabasca and near Lac la Ronge. Thinking the area north and east of Lake Athabasca had received enough stimulus, in 1950 the CCF confined the program to the area south of latitude 58 degrees, 30 minutes. It provided further encouragement to the mining industry by beginning an annual prospecting school at La Ronge in about 1953. The program still operated for three weeks a year in 1964. A Prospectors' Assistance Plan also continued.[31]

The CCF recognized the potential for Aboriginals to participate in prospecting. It viewed Aboriginal bush skills as an asset in the search for minerals. Under the Native Prospectors' Assistance Plan, DNR taught prospecting to Aboriginals in their own language at La Ronge and elsewhere. The modest program sent two pairs of Aboriginals into the field in 1949. Each person received $100 a month and supplies. A blow to the project occurred in 1950 when Indian Affairs withdrew funding, apparently because J.P.B. Ostrander, the regional supervisor of Indian agencies, opposed Norris's involvement. Ostrander said Norris stirred up criticism of Indian Affairs educational policies. But the program and Norris's involvement with it continued in the 1960s, although Mineral Resources had taken it over from DNR.[32] In addition to the CCF-sponsored teams, many Aboriginals worked for private firms, making up as much as 85 percent of some crews. They did mostly unskilled jobs, including cutting lines.[33]

Even though it saw a place for northern Aboriginals in prospecting, the CCF did not visualize them as miners. Politicians and bureaucrats accepted the view that Metis and Indians lacked the preparation, skill, and ability for highly structured industrial work. Mining companies shared this view and hired few Aboriginals. Typically, in 1959 nearly all of the 2,700 mine workers came from outside the area. Blaming Aboriginals' "pre-industrial" way of life, DNR claimed: "Native workers generally have been unable to adapt to a way of life that requires work underground and regular hours as hardrock miners."[34]

Although the CCF claimed success for its efforts to increase mining activity, most areas of the north did not experience dramatic results. Saskatchewan produced metallic minerals valued at $20,342,885 in 1943-44, compared to $25,455,751 in 1950-51.[35] Metallic minerals, including uranium, declined in relative importance under the CCF. They comprised 84.5 percent of the provincial mineral production in 1945. This plummeted to 16 percent by 1964, mainly due to the development of southern petroleum and potash resources.[36] In addition to the negative effect of the CCF socialist ideology, the province's failure to provide adequate infrastructure systems contributed to the slow rate of northern mineral development. While prospectors could fly or paddle into remote areas, efficient removal of most minerals required road or rail access.

Extraordinary international demand and encouragement from Ottawa made the uranium industry the exception to the pattern of little mining development in the north. Washington's desire to buy as much uranium as possible drove the development of uranium mines at Lake Athabasca. Canada entered into large contracts with the US Atomic Energy Commission by 1948. Lucrative agreements set prices and quantities for five-year periods. Eldorado Mining and Refining Ltd., a federal Crown corporation, mined and subcontracted to fill the commitments. Dramatic price increases, government payments for infrastructure, favourable depletion allowances, and a three-year tax exemption for new mines made profitable operation possible, even in remote northern Saskatchewan. Eldorado staked more than 150 claims in the Lake Athabasca area by 1947. Both the federal and provincial governments also lifted restrictions against private prospecting for uranium. A staking boom began in 1952 when Saskatchewan opened some new areas, with 252 claims recorded the first day. Eldorado, as the only legal purchaser of uranium ore and concentrates, built a processing mill on the north shore of Lake Athabasca in 1952. Other area mines, including Gunnar, Ace, and Lorado, produced uranium for Eldorado at a guaranteed price. By 1953 the CCF's Economic Advisory and Planning Board claimed the province's production had "almost doubled the free world's reserves of uranium." Saskatchewan led Canadian uranium-producing districts in output from 1953 to 1957. Disastrously for the industry, US and British demand for uranium fell in 1958. The US did not exercise options on Canadian uranium after contracts expired in 1962-63. Some mines closed, and Saskatchewan's uranium production fell to $19,902,485 by 1964 from $44,561,832 in 1957.[37]

Even at its peak, uranium mining proved uncontroversial, and there were no public hearings or strict environmental controls. Although it knew that the US nuclear weapons program formed the main market for uranium in the 1950s, the CCF still supported uranium mining. Contradictorily, many CCF supporters wanted disarmament and participated in the Ban the Bomb movement. Brady and Norris, for example, marched against the bomb at the Regina legislature in 1961. At the same time, the two promoted northern prospecting. Canadian sales contracts did not limit uranium to nonmilitary uses until 1965.[38]

While friendly to federally directed uranium mining, in other respects CCF policies hurt the mining industry. In 1957 E.F. Partridge, president of the Saskatchewan Chamber of Mines, described the CCF as doing little for the industry but wanting high taxes and royalties. By 1956 the CCF reinvested less than 5 percent of the annual revenues it collected from mining back into the industry, compared to almost 15 percent in 1944.[39] CCF policies in the areas of royalties, taxes, and infrastructure also discouraged mining development and added to overall northern underdevelopment.

Tourism formed the third primary sector of the non-Aboriginal northern economy under the CCF. Lush forests, fast-flowing rivers, profound lakes, and lichen-covered rock provided a natural environment for a large variety of recreational activities. Some in the new government seemed to possess a vision for northern tourism. Phelps described northern Saskatchewan as "another country altogether," while DNR depicted the north as "a potential summer playground for literally millions of people."[40]

Few tourists went north before the mid-1940s, although the occasional party flew in to fish a remote lake, and some adventurers canoed through parts of the north. The completion of the highway to La Ronge in 1947 opened up that part of the north to tourists. La Ronge quickly became the primary northern tourism destination. In 1951 about six thousand tourists arrived in the until-recently isolated village. The number included about 4,100 Americans from thirty-six states. Since they stayed longer and spent more than did Canadians, Americans were encouraged to come. The province sponsored US sportswriters to visit La Ronge to fish. But largely due to a lack of spending on infrastructure, the settlement was "strictly a man's camp," and few families came along. Facilities remained rudimentary, with no campground, no place to buy a legal drink, no filleting table for people to clean their own fish, hazardous water and sanitation facilities, and inadequate emergency services. The growth that did occur lacked regulation, and inexperienced people with small financial resources provided services in low-budget facilities. At the same time, CCF policies limited development. By 1951 DNR turned away parties interested in building further tourist camps at La Ronge, claiming it had enough accommodation for the time being. In fact, La Ronge had run out of suitable surveyed land, and the CCF failed to provide space for further development there. Some outfitters built operations at Hunter Bay, a remote spot without road access on the other side of Lac la Ronge. DNR worked to formalize arrangements there through leases for commercial and residential buildings.[41]

In spite of the limits on development, angling soon surpassed commercial fishing in economic value at La Ronge. To avoid damaging public relations with sport fishermen, and to save game fish for them, by the late 1940s DNR closed Lac la Ronge to summer commercial fishing. Indian Affairs supported the decision, since it saw little interest among Indians in commercial fishing anyway. Soon the government fish plant, built for the commercial fishery, handled primarily tourists' fish in the summer. La Ronge grew as a tourist centre built on angling, with trout making up about half of the sport fish taken. Winter commercial fishing took place largely to reduce whitefish numbers to protect game fish stocks. Elsewhere, a multiple-use policy applied to most lakes, allowing both commercial and sport fishing.[42]

Angling interest at La Ronge fell as depletion of game fish stocks soon occurred. As early as 1948, DNR tried to shift angling pressure to the Churchill River by establishing a canoe route for tourists. After rejecting a 174-mile-long route with twenty-three steep portages as "too tough for popular use," the department chose a route from La Ronge to Stanley Mission, which required only two days each way. DNR also spoke of dispersing tourists by extending the road north to other lakes and broadening the area's appeal by improving facilities. By 1950, with pressure continuing on the fish stocks at Lac la Ronge, DNR limited the number of pike anglers could catch.[43]

Although modest expansion of facilities at La Ronge took place by the 1950s, much of the development remained of low quality. Tourists frequently complained to DNR about dirty and inadequate tourist camps, poor equipment, and guide rates fluctuating with demand. Visitors who booked a cabin, ended up in a tent; a boat shortage kept some on shore; and a guide wanted to sleep and not fish. The fish plant's filleting and shipping service also proved unreliable.[44] Some gradual improvement took place. By 1953 ten outfitters had invested about $600,000, and the village boasted four "good" cafés, a nine-room hotel, and four stores. DNR also finally provided badly needed camping facilities. To promote the area to Americans, the CCF advertised and made movies. Yet even with improvements, the tourism development remained overly rustic, and by 1964 many tourists again complained about unsanitary conditions in most restaurants.[45]

An additional disincentive to tourism came from severe restrictions imposed by the CCF on private cottage development in the La Ronge area. With few exceptions, government prohibited cabins on the shoreline. It also allowed only minimal cottage development on the big lake's hundreds of islands, in spite of a strong demand. Those who did manage to build on islands had to content themselves with leasing and not owning the building sites. After turning down the request of a California man in 1962 for a thirty-year exclusive right to develop and sell or lease islands on Lac la Ronge, the CCF decided to sell islands itself, but soon reverted to leases.[46]

Second only to La Ronge, the Denare Beach area, on Beaver Lake near Flin Flon, received a considerable amount of tourism development. There, as at La Ronge, DNR controlled policies, planning, and surveys, while private persons carried out small developments within the parameters set by the CCF. Much more development of cottage potential took place there than at La Ronge, and by 1958 Denare Beach had about 250 cottage lots.[47] Also on the east side, employees at the Island Falls power plant on the Churchill built dozens of cabins on the dam reservoir, apparently with the company's consent but without the province's permission. The company had no lease for the land, but only a development licence. It appears the cabin owners paid neither lease fees nor taxes.[48] Surprisingly, the CCF allowed this unregulated situation to continue, while regulating even remote trappers' cabins.

Other than at Beaver Lake and Lac la Ronge, the north continued to offer little tourism or cottage development accessible by road. The west side missed out almost completely on opportunities for tourism. Poverty-stricken, slum-like communities and a lack of facilities scared tourists away. Even had people wanted to visit the area, a lack of roads limited access. While the CCF built a road to Buffalo Narrows in 1956, most other areas remained isolated. Some in DNR dreamt of developing tourism on the west side, but without substantial spending on infrastructure the dreams could not come true.[49]

Many tourists who could afford to do so flew to one of the numerous fly-in fishing camps. There, visitors could enjoy the pristine environment away from the squalor of Aboriginal villages. Forty-one of ninety-three Public Health-approved tourist camps in the north in 1961 operated only as fly-in camps, but they brought little benefit to the north. Typically, owners lived outside the region and carried profits back with them to the south at the end of the season.[50]

Tourism contributed relatively little to the larger northern economy, and Aboriginals benefited even less than did non-Aboriginals. Indians and Metis played only a small role in tourism, mainly working for white employers as fishing guides. An exception existed at Cumberland House, where local people guided hunters in the 1940s and owned outfitting camps by the 1950s. But even there a Regina-based non-Aboriginal business built possibly the largest operation. While doing little to encourage Aboriginal involvement in owning tourism-related businesses, the CCF supported their working as guides. The province considered imposing standards for guides, but no regulations were established and in 1951 a DNR report described some of the guides as "completely useless." More successful tourist operators preferred to use white guides, which worked against maximizing Aboriginal employment. In the areas to which tourists travelled, guiding continued to provide seasonal income for some northern Aboriginals. One-third of the La Ronge Aboriginal workforce guided in 1956, earning about $62,000. Commercial fishing had never returned more than $27,000 to local fishermen.[51]

Hunting brought fewer tourists to the north than did fishing, partly because the CCF severely restricted caribou, moose, and elk hunting. Barren land caribou still appeared abundant in 1944, but their numbers soon declined precipitously. Sport hunting of barren land caribou closed by the early 1950s, although Aboriginals continued to take large numbers for their own use. Due to overhunting, virtually no moose or elk remained in many areas in 1944. Later on, as moose populations increased and the province eased restrictions, more southern hunters came north to hunt these large animals. The Cumberland House area in particular saw moose stocks rise dramatically. Hunters of waterfowl also came to the delta area. Yet a lack of road access limited hunting there, and fewer than two hundred hunters flew in each year.[52]

CCF officials sometimes assumed the role of tourists, taking advantage of business trips to hunt. While they spoke of the need for conservation of game resources, their actions sometimes proved inconsistent with their words. Joe Phelps and other officials flying with him shot four caribou in 1946. Their plane could not carry all of the meat, so they left some behind. Phelps later wrote: "The boys all thought they had a real outing."[53] In another case in 1951, five officials, concerned by reduced caribou herd sizes and hunting violations, did an aerial check of the animals on the west side. They found numerous planes in the area for the caribou hunt. They then killed four caribou themselves.[54]

Efforts to attract tourists to northern Saskatchewan remained modest. In the 1940s the province made some attempt to attract American anglers, but it was not until 1957 that it created the Department of Travel and Information to promote use of recreational facilities. Private concerns united by forming two new tourism associations by 1957: the Northern Saskatchewan Tourist Association based in Prince Albert, and the North-West Tourist Association for the west side. Investors also took advantage of the opportunities presented by the completion of new roads. Various small-scale developments grew, including at Jan Lake and Missinipe.[55] But in spite of great potential, northern Saskatchewan likely received less than 1 percent of Canadian tourism. Even many Saskatchewan residents shunned the area, preferring to holiday in neighbouring provinces and states. Although the CCF said it recognized the northern potential for tourism, in 1959 the Stanford Research Institute saw little effort to develop this.[56]

Dreams of a booming northern tourism industry failed to become reality. Instead, the north missed a golden opportunity for economic development. Various factors accounted for this. A lack of governmental spending on infrastructure certainly played a part in keeping tourists out. Additionally, the government's socialist ideology discouraged large-scale private tourism development. Although the CCF rejected the idea of applying its Crown corporation model to tourism, an unfriendly atmosphere to private investment and unnecessarily strict control over development ensured that the area received none of the large investment in tourist facilities seen in various other Canadian wilderness areas. Further, northern poverty and lifestyles hurt tourism. Southerners turned away in disgust and fear from the sight of poverty-stricken Aboriginals living in unpainted shacks in treeless, garbage-littered communities. Many refused to vacation in a wilderness dotted with slums. Cheaply built facilities, uncommunicative Aboriginals, incidents of violence, and rude tourism operators also hurt repeat business.[57]

Although the policy was not always clearly articulated, the CCF separated the northern economy into Aboriginal and non-Aboriginal sectors. Through numerous actions, the province reserved the benefits from forestry, mining, and tourism largely for white people. The newly constructed colonial structure retained control of forestry, with Crown corporation head offices, forestry administration, and the CCF's main sawmill all located in the south. A combination of CCF hostility to private industry, a preference for state and cooperative development, underfunding, misjudging forest resources, and a lack of infrastructure removed forestry as a major element of the northern economy. Clearly, CCF forestry policies added to northern unemployment and underdevelopment.

The province also did little to help Aboriginals enter the mining industry. Instead, discriminatory attitudes and a lack of affirmative action programs ensured that Indians and Metis would not receive major economic benefits. Beyond working sporadically on prospecting crews, few Aboriginals had much involvement with mining. The CCF did allow private capital to explore for minerals and develop mines, but the severe lack of infrastructure and a reluctance by the mining industry to trust a socialist government contributed to mining activity remaining at a low level in the north. Uranium mining, driven by exceptional US demand and steered by Ottawa, proved the primary exception.

Tourism formed the final major aspect of the northern economy. Neither the government nor private parties made major investments in tourism. Obstacles to tourism development included the lack of good highways, rail connections, and major airports. The north's glaring social and economic problems also proved incompatible with attracting visitors. CCF ideology and policies possibly hurt tourism most of all. While it invested little, the CCF did not try to attract major private capital, and fear of socialism kept investors away. Additionally, the government's policy of allowing little private land ownership hurt development both of facilities and cottages. The CCF's strict controls proved effective at keeping growth out. Failure to develop the potential of tourism deprived northern people and the province of a major potential source of economic development.

Under the CCF, the northern economy consisted of six main industries: trapping, fishing, farming, forestry, mining, and tourism. Through numerous policies and actions, the CCF reserved the first three mainly for Aboriginals, while doing little to encourage their participation in the other three. This situation existed partly because Aboriginal people already possessed experience at trapping and fishing, and farming promised to increase northern self-sufficiency. The CCF viewed these three occupations as within Aboriginal capabilities, given close supervision. To increase Aboriginal participation in these industries also required relatively small investments of time and money, and it seemed realistic to expect quick, positive results in these areas. Further, many Aboriginal people lacked readiness to pursue nontraditional occupations. To move them into forestry, mining, and tourism would have required a large investment of time and money, particularly for education and vocational training initiatives. In addition to not wanting to devote the resources necessary to accomplish this vocational shift, the CCF had doubts about the ability of Aboriginals to work at new occupations, which limited its actions. Largely excluded from trapping, fishing, and farming, non-Aboriginals dominated forestry, mining, and tourism. While various politicians and other CCF officials outlined occupational policies, the government's actions spoke most loudly.

The influence of socialist ideology appears much more strongly in CCF policies for the north than for the south. In southern Saskatchewan, most people experienced a mild CCF socialism primarily through health programs and utility monopolies. In contrast, a very different CCF socialism shaped the northern economy, actively determining the character of trapping, fishing, farming, and forestry, while more passively influencing mining and tourism. Crown corporations, marketing boards, and cooperatives became instrumental parts of the CCF's northern presence. The CCF especially wanted Aboriginals to accept and use socialist forms of ownership and organization. It also expected Aboriginals, in socialist fashion, to share northern wealth with the entire province. Had the CCF applied its socialist ideology to northern welfare, health, and education services, it might have alleviated the worsening plight of northerners to a considerable degree. Instead, the CCF followed very different principles when it came to establishing social policy.

Part Four
Poverty-Stricken and Disease-Ridden

9
Scarcely More Than Palliative

Once in power, Tommy Douglas said, "In terms of technological progress we will measure our success by what society does for the underprivileged, for the subnormal, for the widow, for the aged and the unwanted child."[1] The severe suffering of many Saskatchewan residents during the Great Depression had confirmed and strengthened the CCF's commitment to establish socialistic economic and social programs to create a more humane and caring society. Convinced of the enlightened nature of its ideology, the CCF also wanted northerners to accept its socialist values. Residents of the region should share with each other and give northern resource wealth to all residents of Saskatchewan. Yet the CCF proved hesitant to apply its socialist ideals to northern welfare, social service, health, and education programs. This contradiction existed partly because the CCF feared that Aboriginals would take advantage of generous programs. Receiving something for nothing might spoil them and further weaken their reputedly weak work ethic. CCF planners suspected that Aboriginals had not yet internalized the socialist ideal of working for the good of the larger society and might not work if they could live without doing so. Some in government also thought that since Aboriginals paid little in taxes, they should not expect to receive much back. Additionally, neglect of northern needs took place simply because residents of the north did not have a voice and political influence in Regina, the distant political centre.

CCF policies resulted in a situation where southerners received enhanced welfare, health, and education services, while their capitalist economy remained intact. Meanwhile, the new government applied the reverse to the north. It imposed a largely socialist economy and expected northerners to fend for themselves in the area of social benefits. Only in the north, where the relatively small number of residents lacked a strong voice, could the CCF neglect various pressing social needs while removing much personal economic freedom.

Few residents of northern Saskatchewan depended on welfare payments in 1944, even though many lived in poverty by southern standards. As the CCF era progressed, Aboriginal lifestyles changed and as a result the capacity of trapping, fishing, and hunting to support the growing Aboriginal population greatly diminished. Work-for-welfare programs became the favoured method to keep northerners from starving. Those who could not work received lower welfare benefit rates than those paid to recipients in the south. In the closing years of its mandate, when worsening poverty overwhelmed Aboriginal communities, the CCF loosened its welfare purse strings and increased payments to northerners. But job creation efforts, other than those providing short-term make-work projects, remained minimal. The dominant Aboriginal poverty of the CCF years manifested itself in increasing social problems, crime, delinquency, child neglect, disease, and semi-urban slums.

Prior to 1944 governments accepted little responsibility for the welfare of northern residents. Over the previous decades, both the federal and provincial government had introduced modest programs directed at alleviating the direst poverty of some "deserving poor," including the aged, physically disabled, and widows. Some northerners received government aid. Those residing in settlements more often received this help than those living in the bush. Many illiterate northern Aboriginals who might have qualified for assistance did not know of the programs and did not apply. A lack of knowledge of how to deal with bureaucracy and a shortage of staff to dispense governmental charity added to the low level of payments. Saskatchewan had no welfare worker or social worker stationed in the north, and Indian Affairs, which was responsible for the Status Indian population, provided virtually no social services there.

Aboriginal people traditionally helped each other through hard times, sharing the bounty of the land within a relatively small group. Credit from the Hudson's Bay Company (HBC) and other trading companies provided needed goods throughout the year, and the traders carried trappers and their families through lean times. In some cases the HBC even looked after people when they grew old, remembering their service to the company when young. Aid for the needy also came from the Roman Catholic and Anglican churches. While paternalistic, this old system provided security to northerners and alleviated suffering.

The federal family allowance plan became the first major social program to affect the north. Ottawa passed enabling legislation in 1944, and payments began in 1945.[2] Dramatic change followed, instigated by the requirement that children had to attend school in order for mothers to receive the cheques. Families moved to villages to enable school attendance, while men spent time away from their families, fishing and trapping. The payments of five dollars per month per child provided a large part of the cash many required. People still lived largely from the land, eating surprisingly large quantities of wild meat, making garments from animal skins, and using logs to construct shelters.

Provincial welfare payments to northerners remained low until the early 1960s. Although rates rose somewhat, the CCF persisted in paying lower rates in the north than in the south. Many northerners also lacked access to full welfare services, since DNR officers handled most welfare administration. The CCF did not design special welfare programs for the northern or Aboriginal population but instead applied frugal versions of its southern programs. A belief that Aboriginals were responsible for their poverty justified the provision of inferior services in the north. Yet, not willing to allow northerners to starve, the CCF alleviated some of the direst poverty. For the most part, the CCF did not use welfare payments to buy political peace in the north since relatively little organized unrest existed.

A brief examination of CCF social policies in the south shows more clearly the contrast with its northern program. Of the three areas of social spending – welfare, health, and education – the CCF spent the most money on improving health and education services. It devoted relatively little money to enhancing welfare programs, in spite of saying in 1948 that welfare recipients no longer received payments as charity but out of society's responsibility. The Economic Advisory and Planning Board's 1947 statement, that the province could not afford to ensure a "decent standard of living for all," more accurately described CCF policies. Provincial spending on education and health rose much more quickly than spending on social aid under the CCF. During the war, welfare spending took 52 percent of the education, health, and welfare budget, but welfare's share declined to about 18.1 percent by 1953. Although its own Budget Bureau was already severely criticizing the social aid program by 1952, the CCF did not implement the bureau's recommendations until 1959.[3] Much of the "progress" in welfare policies by 1964 occurred because of the growing economy, improved finances, higher taxation, and changes in societal attitudes towards social aid. CCF idealism played a lesser role in bringing change.

While the CCF did not shower the southern poor with great generosity, it applied a much more frugal policy to the north. Politicians, advised by their bureaucrats, decided northern welfare policies. CCF ministers of Social Welfare were O.W. Valleau from 1944 to 1948, J.H. Sturdy from 1948 to 1956, T.J. Bentley from 1956 to 1960, and A.M. Nicholson from 1960. Continuity existed in the higher echelons of department staff, with J.S. White serving as deputy minister from the 1940s to 1964.[4]

After its election, the CCF introduced some structural changes to the welfare program, partly based on the reform plan of the former Liberals. The new government passed the Social Aid Act in 1944, repealed the Direct Relief Act, and created the Department of Social Welfare. This department brought Child Welfare, Old Age Pensions, Social Aid, Welfare Services, and Corrections together. Its name changed to Department of

Social Welfare and Rehabilitation in 1949 when it took over veterans' rehabilitation activities. While social services grew much more slowly than did education and health services, the CCF greatly increased Social Welfare's staff numbers. They rose from 157 to 646 by 1949 and to about 800 by 1957.[5] Douglas likely approved of the sense of urgency and zeal that existed among the staff. Many shared his vision to have society take responsibility for its weakest members.

For many years after 1944 the Department of Social Welfare relied on various categorical programs to meet specific needs, using means tests to determine eligibility. It applied these more in the south than in the north. Needy mothers, the aged, the blind, and the disabled in the south received help from separate programs, but in the north the CCF preferred to use a basic welfare program for all. This policy, which primarily reduced benefits paid to the unemployable, grew from the CCF desire to prevent Aboriginal dependency on welfare.[6]

Although the CCF recognized the northern social and economic problems, the minimal social services it provided did not begin to adequately address the needs. Rather simplistically, the CCF thought Aboriginals needed rehabilitation. Departmental reports repeatedly spoke of the need for Aboriginal "rehabilitation." Use of this term placed the fault for indigency and other shortcomings on the individual or group, while absolving the larger society of responsibility. In 1952 the Budget Bureau acted as the government's conscience by pointing out the inadequacy of Saskatchewan's rehabilitative services for "depressed minorities," including for Aboriginals. It called them "scarcely more than palliative."[7] Yet in the years that followed, rehabilitation programs continued to lack clear goals or consistency. Various organizations, including the departments of Social Welfare, Natural Resources, and Municipal Affairs, all worked on their own projects.

During the early CCF years, the Local Improvement District (LID) Branch of the Department of Municipal Affairs held responsibility for social aid in the north. The LID inspector and the RCMP administered much of the social welfare program. With the establishment in 1947 of the Northern Administration District, responsibility for social welfare administration moved to DNR.

The CCF chose not to post even one of the hundreds of staff in the newly expanded Department of Social Welfare to the north. Instead, workers from the south ventured north on quick trips. Nor did the CCF create a separate social welfare administrative region for the north. Rather, the department administered the north as part of southern regions. Prince Albert served as the primary centre to provide northern welfare services. Recognizing that it lacked much of a presence in the north, the department delegated many northern services to DNR. Natural resources officers, trained to manage natural resources, also governed the human population. In the south the Department of Social Welfare, perennially lacking in funding, public esteem, and popular support, nonetheless had staff with a moderate to high level of skill and training. In contrast, DNR officers received little preparation for administering welfare programs. Both DNR management and field staff lacked expertise in welfare administration.

For many years George Burgess, a Welfare Services Division officer from Prince Albert, helped DNR administer welfare programs. Conservation officers often issued short-term assistance by giving out "requisitions," a paper that "clients" exchanged for goods at the store. Longer term assistance required the approval of Burgess or another welfare officer. Central office in Regina then mailed "payroll" cheques to the clients. For a time the system seemed to work well from the point of view of DNR; in 1950 its officers kept "a close check on indigent and ailing people." But some in the department soon came to dislike handling social services and fought to rid themselves of the responsibility. This reluctance did not add to the quality of service provided.[8]

Asking DNR to provide welfare services fit with the CCF desire to have one department handle and coordinate northern services. Yet since the province failed to hire or train the skilled staff needed to administer social welfare programs, assigning this work to DNR confirmed the low priority northern social services held for the CCF. Using DNR to apply these programs saved government large amounts of money on administration and programs. In the opinion of the CCF, northern social services did not warrant a regional office, a local office, or any resident staff. As a result, the north received a much lower level of social aid, child welfare, and other social services than did the south. In contrast, the CCF created Mineral Resources as a separate department from DNR to oversee the important work of mining.

An additional justification for DNR's involvement in northern welfare administration came from its acting as the municipal government for the north. Elsewhere in Saskatchewan, municipalities administered most social aid, with the province and municipalities sharing the relief costs. Many southern jurisdictions employed specialists for this work. The province also provided them with advice and suggested payment schedules. Since the north lacked a true municipal system and DNR collected little in taxes there, Social Welfare paid 100 percent of the relief costs. Ottawa, in turn, helped pay social aid costs, following various formulas. Effective 1 January 1958, the federal government paid 50 percent of most social aid costs.[9]

Until its demise in 1949, the Fish Board helped fill the need for northern social aid. It provided supplies to fishermen, operated on uneconomic lakes, prolonged fishing to allow local fishermen longer employment, and provided food, medicine, and transportation to the ill. This generosity contributed to its failure.[10] The Fish Board's losses taught the CCF to operate the Saskatchewan Fish Marketing Service and Co-operative Fisheries Limited, the Fish Board's successors, in a more businesslike manner and not use them to provide social aid.

Indian Affairs held primary responsibility for Status Indians, who, at least as long as they remained on their reserves, did not qualify for most provincial programs. Yet for several reasons the province frequently provided social aid to Status Indians. Many of them had not permanently located on reserves. In addition, for many years Indian Affairs offered minimal social aid programs in the north. Since it employed only seventeen social workers in all of Canada, it had virtually no specialized staff to handle social services in northern Saskatchewan. As time went on, Ottawa increased social services to northern Indians.

Federal and provincial services appeared similar in many respects. Both levels of government shared the suspicion that Aboriginal people would easily become dependent on welfare, a risk that rose as programs increased in generosity. A 1947 federal-provincial meeting about northern social aid saw agreement "that 'giving' too freely of any commodity was not a sound policy to these people, who seem to become more careless with added help." Officials agreed that subsidies to the fishery formed a more acceptable method of helping Indians, who "were in a sorry state." Indian Affairs did give some "rations" to widows, orphans, and indigents on its "Rations List." Need in the Status Indian community often surpassed that in the Non-Status group, and the federal government had a reputation for providing services inferior even to those offered by the province. Status Indians could not yet receive old-age pension payments, and only 35 percent of the elderly who would have received old-age pensions, had they not been Indian, received rations. It seems that the rations program used a less generous eligibility criteria than did the old-age pension program. Payments under the rations system often did not amount to much. In 1956-57, Indian Affairs' Carlton Agency, responsible for much of Saskatchewan's north, issued welfare payments totalling only $600. Yet Indian Affairs thought the Indian agent doled out money too freely. It disallowed an expenditure of six dollars for curtains, a window shade, and a tablecloth for an elderly widow, describing this as a "dangerous precedent." Status Indians received family allowances, but often, to prevent misuse, the Indian agent handled the cheques and saw that children received "certain necessities." Indian Affairs sometimes set up a family allowance credit with a local trader, against which the family could draw from an approved list of goods. The list did not include basics like flour or lard required to make bannock, since the families should spend the allowance on "extra foods needed by growing children." These controls did not apply to non-Aboriginals. Beginning in the late 1950s, Indian Affairs loosened its purse strings, but liberalization remained slow. It did not issue cash or cheques to Indians until 1959. Inadequacies in the federal welfare system for Status Indians continued to place extra pressure on the provincial system.[11]

In its first years in office, the CCF also spent little on northern welfare, but its politicians and bureaucrats perpetuated a false myth of high northern welfare costs. After almost a full year of CCF government, provincial northern social aid spending totalled only $73,224.94 annually, apparently including old-age pensions, mothers' allowances, and social aid. The CCF viewed even this small expenditure as excessive. Joe Phelps, who opposed direct relief, thought he saw welfare dependence. He said that northerners, anxious to buy liquor, asked, "When am I going to get my relief cheque?" According to Phelps, the chief Indian spokesman at Cumberland House wanted to know what the government would do to bring in social aid. Phelps replied that he wanted to move people off social aid and use it only as a last resort. He hoped that fur, fish, and forestry industries would eliminate much of the need for social aid. Northern Administrator J.J. Wheaton expressed a similar attitude in 1947 when he wrote that many recipients viewed social aid as a "life pension." The Île-à-la-Crosse area, where thirty-eight applicants accounted for almost half of the northern recipients, particularly concerned him. Using income information from the Saskatchewan Fur Marketing Service, he launched an investigation of payments. Cuts then took place at Île-à-la-Crosse, where the number of recipients dropped to twelve by the spring of 1948. L.M. Marion, the area's Liberal MLA, complained about the disqualifications, claiming that those cut off received even less from trapping a few rats (muskrat) than they formerly had from social aid. Social Welfare staff also worked to minimize northern welfare expenditures. For example, the department did not want to use mothers' allowances in the north, preferring to use social aid instead. Burgess feared mothers "will be content to sit back and not work." Apparently white mothers in the south would not lose their work ethic if the government increased aid payments, but northern Aboriginal women would. Possibly showing some reservations about the harsh northern policies, DNR's assistant deputy minister J.W. Churchman asked Deputy Minister Hogg in 1948 whether he thought they acted too severely in handling social aid cases.[12]

Concern over austere policies seemed fleeting. CCF politicians and bureaucrats continued their tight control over the purse strings, limiting payments during 1947-48 to 229 northerners. Social aid payments, not including categorical allowances, totalled $8,838.34, or less than one dollar per capita. Of this amount, food allowances comprised $8,717.53, with fuel and miscellaneous costs accounting for only $120.81. In comparison, overall spending for the province reached $1,123,092.24, or well over one dollar per capita. Northern recipients also received much lower payments for nonfood items. During 1948 and 1949, family payments ranged from five to thirty dollars per month, often appearing unrelated to the size of the family unit. One family of five received thirty dollars per month, while another family of seven received only twelve dollars. Most payroll recipients received social aid for a lengthy period of time, often because of chronic unemployability. Even these people received virtually nothing other than payments to buy food. During the 1948-49 fiscal year, from eighty to ninety-one families received payroll cheques at a cost of $13,081. Emergencies added further costs. This increased spending apparently triggered another administrative crackdown. With "closer supervision," spending again fell in the following year. To control spending, George Burgess instructed DNR officers on proper procedures. The northern administrator took central control over issuing emergency relief requisitions, taking this responsibility from DNR officers. In an emergency, the officer had to arrange a temporary credit at a store and request a requisition to cover this.[13]

By the 1950s the poverty in northern Aboriginal communities deepened. As a result, Northern Administration District (NAD) social aid spending rose during 1951-52 to $22,263. Food allowances accounted for most of the expenditure, while northern fuel, clothing, shelter, and miscellaneous payments remained behind those in the south. Reflecting increasing Aboriginal poverty, in 1954-55, 484 northern recipients received $40,193.27 of a total of $1,539,620.08 paid in the province. By this time, northern per capita welfare costs surpassed those in the south. Yet spending per northern recipient remained below the southern level.[14]

Northern poverty and the demand for social aid grew for various reasons. While the Aboriginal population grew rapidly, their sector of the economy did not keep pace. More people fished and trapped, but per capita income decreased from these sources. Additionally, the CCF destruction of the credit system, which formerly carried people through lean times, added to destitution. Under the new system, many found they had the money to drink, gamble, and spend lavishly for short periods of time before applying for social aid. DNR's anthropologist, V.F. Valentine, pointed out another reason for the increased dependency. "The Government is felt to have taken away all of the natural resources that really belonged to the people," he observed, "and by taking them without the consent of the people it must pay." He also thought Aboriginals began to accept the government view that they could not manage their own affairs. They could no longer live in the old ways and did not fit into the new ways either.[15]

The formal arrangement that saw DNR handle northern social aid at the field level ended in about 1951, although DNR still reluctantly issued food orders in urgent cases until a social welfare officer could arrive. DNR minister J.H. Brockelbank preferred that Social Welfare take over full responsibility for this work. Yet politicians did not move to institute this change. Even though need continued to increase, in 1955 Social Welfare still had only one travelling social worker to handle both social aid and child welfare. "Accumulated demands" meant the social worker could not meet many of the needs when he visited settlements. Possibly more seriously, prevention received little attention. With the obvious failure of the system to provide services, several senior DNR officials again wanted to take over social aid administration. This change would allow the social welfare worker to concentrate on child welfare. A minor increase in services came in 1956 after the lone worker, Hugh Parsons, requested a transfer. Social Welfare then appointed Miss M. Crawley, a "highly trained welfare supervisor," and Mr. Paul Fritz, social worker, to cover the entire north. Crawley undertook a study of welfare needs. She recommended giving DNR full responsibility for social aid and increasing social aid payments as part of a "balanced, developmental program." In line with her recommendations, DNR took over both Public Assistance and the Hospital Services Plan in 1958-59, except in the incorporated municipalities of La Ronge, Creighton, and Uranium City. This freed "professional welfare workers" to devote more attention to less routine matters. A new Social Welfare Act also treated the Northern Administration Branch (NAB) as a municipal government, which gave legislative force to the arrangement.[16]

In spite of variations in service delivery, DNR officers served as the primary distributors of social aid during the CCF era. The officers used considerable discretion in administering aid. In one case, charges of unfair social aid administration arose at Cumberland House in 1950. The complainant said that the Metis DNR officer, likely J. Brady, helped fewer than half of the people, those who were "drunk every week." At the same time, many children went to bed hungry. A study of Île-à-la-Crosse in the 1960s said DNR officers used "ideosyncratic solutions [sic]," often not following welfare regulations and giving aid to those who did not qualify. New officers would first cut ineligible people from social aid and then reinstate them when the officers developed close relationships with the local Metis.[17]

Various factors brought another large increase in northern social aid payments in the late 1950s and early 1960s. As before, population continued to rise and the northern economy lost further viability. The CCF also became more concerned about guaranteeing the rights of recipients, one of the main goals of the Social Aid Act of 1959. Barriers to employables receiving assistance decreased. Prior to this, only unemployables could usually receive long-term aid. Further, Aboriginal northerners became more demanding as they discovered they had a right to receive welfare. Peter C. Tompkins, a Metis DNR officer, contributed to this awareness by broadcasting a radio information program telling Aboriginals about new social aid programs. Many became increasingly accustomed to life on welfare and saw few ways to earn a living.[18]

Provincial social aid for the NAD rose more than tenfold from 1950-51 to 1960-61, climbing from $17,020 to $174,181. Even so, rates remained below those in the south. Services also varied between communities. Of six areas in 1960-61, Sandy Bay depended on social aid the least, with only 20 percent of residents on welfare, while 59.6 percent of Cumberland House people depended on aid. Within the entire NAD, 33.8 percent of the population received help. The payments per recipient also varied, from an average of $65 at Sandy Bay to $92 at Île-à-la-Crosse, and $83 for the entire NAD. Outside the more prosperous areas of Uranium City, La Ronge, and Creighton, 864 of 1,069 NAD families received some social aid. Federal and provincial payments, including family allowances, pensions, and social aid, totalled about $1,041,000, an amount almost equal to the combined income from fur and fish. Other forms of government payments provided more income than did social aid. Social aid spending rose further in 1961-62, when it reached $238,307.07, including $156,921.19 in permanent aid and $81,385.88 in emergency payments. Increased spending did not bring prosperity. At Sandy Bay, one family lived in a tent on a lakeshore in minus thirty-five degree weather. Also, in spite of the rising demand for help, the CCF still did not provide adequate staffing. Social Welfare employed only two workers to visit the entire north, neither of whom had professional degrees.[19]

A tug-of-war took place over social aid rates. Various voices within government had the ear of the politicians, encouraging them to maintain rates at a low level. DNR staff and some officials frequently pushed for reduced payments. At one point it negotiated with Social Welfare to pay lower food allowances in the north than in the south. Even then, DNR officers, clergy, and others still viewed the lower rates as too high. The CCF-sponsored Center for Community Studies opposed liberalizing welfare and wanted to see alternatives to social aid. On the other side, champions of welfare rights and higher rates included some civil servants, some MLAs, and the Federation of Saskatchewan Indians. Faced with rising complaints, the CCF promised in the 1960 election campaign to bring northern rates in line with those in the south. Director of Northern Affairs MacDonald also reluctantly buckled to pressure in 1961. He recommended adopting the higher southern rates, which paid 95.5 percent more for two adults and five children than the northern schedule: $133.00 compared to $68.00. At the same time, MacDonald feared higher rates would have a disastrous, debilitating effect on trapping and fishing unless the DNR could use work programs to dispense the aid. A cabinet committee agreed that the province should pay the same rates in the north and south, with some adjustments for rent and fuel payments and deductions made because northern people ate more fish and game. The CCF raised the rates in 1962-63, when 4,071 northerners received aid of about $325,589. Expenditures rose further in 1963-64 to $390,737.46. But even with the new rates, a large differential remained between northern and southern payments. During 1963-64 the NAD had an average monthly cost of $16.79 per recipient compared to the provincial average of $25.92.[20]

A major change in social aid came with a slow shift from the various categorical programs, which determined eligibility through a means test, to one program using a needs test. With means-tested programs like old-age pensions, the amount paid did not vary with individual need. Different programs also had different eligibility requirements. The Budget Bureau, as early as 1951, pointed out the administrative confusion caused by the categorical programs and suggested moving to only one program. The Social Aid Act of 1959 brought needs tests and the budget deficit method of calculating benefits for social aid payments. This method calculated applicants' eligible expenses and income. Over the following years the department phased out various categorical programs and means tests. Since northerners had never received full access to categorical programs, this change affected the north less than the south. But in spite of claims that the new system would meet needs more fairly, northerners still experienced differential treatment.[21]

The CCF government never fully accepted the principle that northerners should receive payments equal to those in the south. For a number of reasons the province consistently paid lower social aid rates in the north than in the south. Obviously the alleviation of northern poverty held little priority in Regina. Southerners also accepted the false stereotypical view that northern Aboriginals could always live off the land and did not need much money. Possibly most importantly, though, politicians and bureaucrats feared that generous payments would hurt the morale of northerners and take away their incentive to work. Diminishing returns from trapping and fishing added to the danger of welfare dependency because even low welfare payments amounted to more than most received from trapping and fishing. This removed the incentive to work and made the once honourable occupations of trapping and fishing little more than hobbies for many. Even if northerners wanted to support their families by setting traps or nets, they likely could not do so. Pressure to maintain welfare rates at a low level also came from the common belief that Aboriginals felt little shame when they received welfare. According to this line of reasoning, because nearly all in a community received aid, no stigma existed, adding to the movement to social aid. One observer, the Oblate priest L. Lavasseur, said that Indian people valued sharing and honoured those who gave to others. To accept the help of the government agent, the new provider, "is to honour him as once the chief was honoured when he distributed the spoils of the hunt." Anthropologist J.E.M. Kew thought Cumberland House residents viewed social aid as their right as citizens of Saskatchewan after they heard of this right at a public meeting in 1959.

Perhaps some Aboriginals did lose interest in working as government aid became more readily available. If so, this would fit with the observation of early fur traders who noticed that Aboriginal trappers failed to respond to higher fur prices by producing more furs. Instead, since they needed to trap less to obtain the necessities of life, they took fewer furs. On the other hand, many Aboriginals opposed and lamented the shift to welfare that took place under the CCF. Aboriginals recognized that along with government cheques came increasing poverty, a lack of meaningful employment, loss of self-esteem, and worsening social problems. By almost any standard,

Aboriginals were the biggest losers as their society shifted to welfare dependency. To suggest that only white people could see the growing problems, while Aboriginals did not understand or care what happened to them, lacks credibility.[22]

Many northerners and others, both Aboriginals and non-Aboriginals, viewed the introduction of welfare to northern Saskatchewan as the greatest error made there by government. In one case in 1963, Elizabeth Montgrand of La Loche spoke up at a local meeting attended by the minister of Social Welfare, A.M. Nicholson. Although her neighbours ridiculed her, she also wrote to Nicholson. Montgrand opposed giving social aid to single girls with babies because this encouraged illicit relationships and having babies. She favoured giving social aid to sick and deserving widows instead. In his reply to Montgrand, Nicholson refused to address these issues. Father Mathieu of La Loche, who observed the effects of social aid first-hand, blamed the program for ruining northern people, since they stopped working and lost self-respect. Morris Shumiatcher, former assistant to T.C. Douglas, viewed the welfare program for Aboriginals as a major mistake. He claimed Douglas had "political nymphomania," since he never learned to say no. Shumiatcher blamed many Aboriginal problems on welfare dependence. He also attributed the high Aboriginal crime rate and social problems to welfare. The CCF received blame both for introducing welfare and for not paying enough. Both criticisms missed the mark, since the more serious and underlying issue remained the absence of viable alternatives to welfare.[23]

Although the flow of welfare payments to northerners increased from a mere trickle to a steady stream under the CCF, Douglas's government consistently preferred to pay northerners to work rather than give them welfare. The CCF expected able-bodied men to labour in "work-and-wages" programs. This policy had various precedents. Indian Commissioner Edgar Dewdney required Cree to work for rations in 1879 as part of the federal government's effort to exert control over the plains Indians.[24] More recently, governments had provided relief in exchange for work on public works projects during the Great Depression. Promotion of these programs by the CCF seems surprising, since in recent decades left-wing parties have opposed similar policies. Yet the socialist CCF government wholeheartedly wanted the northern poor to work for their food in varied programs.

Several motivations explain the CCF affection for work-and-wages projects. Importantly, the work performed sometimes benefited the community by providing useful services or building small infrastructure projects. Both government and northern residents could see the value of the benefits provided. But the main source of the CCF preference for make-work projects was a fear of Aboriginals losing their work ethic. Convinced that Aboriginals would easily become dependent on welfare and idle, the government instituted work programs that combined assistance with activity.

DNR operated a work-and-wages program to reduce relief at Cumberland House by 1947. Although the community found itself in desperate straits, DNR refused to give employable recipients social aid. Instead it paid out what it called "advances," requiring residents to sign agreements for repayment. Workers repaid most of the $4,018 advanced by gravelling the road to Pemmican Portage and making hay at the government farm. Phelps objected to paying in advance, calling it "a very dangerous practice" that perpetuated "the credit and debt system." "Special Works" programs in the community included labour at the government farm and sawing lumber. Following flooding and failure of the fur harvest in 1948, DNR's Wheaton thought they "might need to administer a complete community under Government control." DNR continued to use the Special Works program to lower welfare payments at Cumberland House, spreading the work among residents with families. Payment varied with family size. A worker with six or more dependents could receive up to fifty dollars per month. Special Works programs also operated at Île-à-la-Crosse and Beauval by 1948, and in 1949-50 program workers cut trees for the Timber Board at Cumberland House and La Ronge. The CCF continued to use make-work projects in many parts of the north in the years that followed.[25]

Make-work schemes proved an inadequate substitute for true employment. At times government recognized this and cut back payments. When doing so, it seemed to forget that withdrawing the artificially created employment would cause welfare payments to rise. Northerners also became dependent on the projects and resisted government efforts to reduce them. When DNR cut back the program at Cumberland House in 1954, B. McKenzie, a CCF supporter and self-proclaimed "Key Man of Mr. Bill Berezowsky, M.L.A.," lost his job at the DNR farm. The unemployed man and the CCF MLA quickly objected. McKenzie complained that the CCF did not provide jobs, in contrast to the HBC manager who found work for ten men in Manitoba. McKenzie also pointed to poverty in the community, saying, "Lots of kids go to bed with out supper." In reaction, C.S. Brown, northern administrator, wrote: "The workings of governmental financing is far beyond the scope of his imagination. He seems to be strongly of the opinion that all governments take care of their supporters by providing employment. This situation has been created and aggravated by past policies of pouring money into this quagmire settlement." Berezowsky believed the story about hungry children and wanted to see a works program. Even Brown conceded that Cumberland House had "no employment, no credit, and no money other than pensions and family allowance." The protests brought little in immediate results, although DNR did give the paltry amount of $400 for "small work projects."[26]

Even though it sometimes questioned the wisdom of work-and-wages programs, the CCF continued to use them to reduce direct relief. In 1955 some DNR officers thought "even women with children should be encouraged to do something." The progressive Miss Crawley of Social Welfare also supported the use of work-for-wages programs in 1958. She pushed for a project under which Cumberland House workers would have cut and sold firewood to residents, with social aid paying for the wood. Her department refused to advance $1,000 for the project. She also wanted to see a larger program that would train people and use local labour, in place of heavy equipment, to build roads. Work programs continued to operate sporadically in many villages. During the winter of 1961-62, with about half of the people at La Loche already on relief, residents avoided starvation by eating squirrels and rabbits. Anxious to minimize welfare payments, DNR asked the Treasury Board for money to establish a sawmill program.[27]

Revival of the Cumberland House Wood Products Co-operative in 1962 helped the CCF provide employment as an alternative to welfare in that area. Because of the worsening economic situation and liberalized welfare policies, social aid costs had risen by about 500 percent since 1960. Even though local people responded to the debt-ridden forestry project with apathy and resistance, the CCF saw success, since it provided work and training and reduced social aid costs. Government continued to operate the cooperative, without much local support. DNR portrayed Cumberland House as a self-destructive community where people would not work together or take advantage of government efforts. A.H. MacDonald, the director of Northern Affairs, thought places like Cumberland House needed a year-round work program to provide an alternative to idleness and welfare dependency. After the majority of people there received relief in 1962-63, DNR launched a project of roadwork, fireguard construction, and garbage pickup, using community development funds.[28]

Ottawa and Saskatchewan shared the costs of various work programs in the late 1950s and early 1960s. The Municipal Winter Works Program included $10,000 to hand-clear a winter road from Buffalo Narrows to La Loche in 1959-60. The program also helped DNR with a muskeg drainage project at La Ronge, keeping some unemployed off social aid for a while. Money for workers to clear rights-of-way for roads came from the National Employment Service of 1960. The Community Employment Program, which began in 1962, paid out wages of $31,838 over three years to La Ronge and Pelican Narrows men. Three projects in 1961-62 and six in 1962-63 received funding from the Winter Works Incentive Program. For 1963-64, due to poor trapping and fishing, the program expanded to about $200,000. The various projects effectively reduced social aid rolls. In 1960-61, out of a labour force of about 2,800, northern social aid recipients included only eighty-six able-bodied persons. Prosperity did not result from the work though. Daily average project wages of $7.42 in 1962-63 were less than half the average provincial wage. Additionally, the programs, primarily designed for the south, did not fit northern employment patterns. In the south unemployment was often highest in the winter, but in the north summer often brought the highest need for aid because most trapping took place in the winter. As a result, northern projects would have been more effective had they extended to summer.[29]

Late in the CCF era, unemployment continued to worsen. To ease suffering, the province proposed many Municipal Winter Works Programs for 1963-64. One project that proceeded hired Stanley Mission workers to build an airstrip. In appreciation of the work, Malachi McLeod, representing the "Metis and Non-Treaty People," thanked Eiling Kramer, minister of Natural Resources. "If not for this, a lot of people would be hungry ... We would not like to go on Relief, because then, a lot of people would not want to work," he wrote. Ottawa also contributed $50,000 as its share of a forest improvement project for the Meadow Lake and Beauval/Île-à-la-Crosse area. Kramer wanted Ottawa to fund future forestry work and wrote to the federal minister of Forestry, Maurice Sauvé: "These people are anxious to work and earn a living for their families. The overall cost in dollars is little more than Social Aid costs while the results in human dignity are manifold." Even with the artificially created work, social aid in some areas rose by about 40 percent that winter.[30]

CCF work-for-wages projects would likely have expanded had Ottawa not withdrawn support for some programs. Kramer, who preferred these projects to demoralizing and degrading social aid, failed to obtain funding. In 1964 Judy LaMarsh, minister of National Health and Welfare, claimed the Unemployment Assistance Act did not allow them to "share in assistance to persons who perform work for the assistance they are granted." Recognizing the need for a solution to "one of the oldest and most intractable problems in the history of social welfare," she held out hope this policy might change.[31] A discordant note also came from Saskatchewan's Department of Social Welfare, which joined Ottawa in opposing the programs. The department claimed that the projects encouraged poor work habits, interfered with others' employment, had higher administration costs than social aid, stigmatized individuals, and violated people's rights. Ottawa's willingness to cost-share welfare but not work programs fortified the department's position.[32]

Pressure for continuation of work-and-wages programs came from CCF politicians, DNR staff, and community members. The projects recommended by officials and community leaders included sawing lumber, building houses for indigents, erecting thirteen fire halls, constructing portages, working on roads, providing recreational facilities, and many other initiatives. The estimated cost stood at $153,522 for 1963-64. Even the Center for Community Studies liked work-and-wages programs, contending the government and people of the province did not know of the "urgent need in the North for make-work projects and developmental programs of every kind." In its final budget the CCF provided for a large work-and-wages program. This government's commitment to using artificially created work as an alternative to social aid remained strong.[33]

In spite of the proliferation of welfare and work programs, poverty characterized the CCF era in the north to a far greater extent than in any other region of Saskatchewan. Visitors from the south, unaccustomed to seeing widespread destitution and suffering, reacted with shock. Mrs. John A. Bell of Moose Jaw wrote Premier Douglas in 1948. She told him of conditions at Montreal Lake, where up to ten people lived in one room and many lacked adequate medical care, food, and clothing. "Mr. Douglas, you are a Minister of the Gospel, as well as the head of our government. Please in the name of our Lord Jesus Christ won't you see that something is done for these poor people, now before winter sets in," she appealed. Many who spent more time in the north viewed poverty as a normal part of the colonial situation, where a small group of white people lived a middle-class lifestyle while the Aboriginal population lived in privation. As time went on, the level of destitution likely increased, even though government payments rose dramatically. Various forces, including CCF policies, eroded the traditional sources of sustenance and income.[34]

The CCF justified its draconian northern welfare measures partly by continuing to believe that northerners could rely on the bush for food and other necessities. Yet many Aboriginals discovered that the land would no longer feed or support them. Few moose remained when the CCF came to power, although subsequent conservation measures helped restore their population in some areas. Overall, though, northern Aboriginals could no longer depend on the large animals as much as before. In the far north, Dene sometimes waited in vain for the declining herds of barren land caribou to migrate south. By 1951 Canada's caribou population had fallen to about 670,000 from possibly 1.75 million in 1900. A further drop to approximately 300,000 took place by 1955. Wastage by Aboriginals – including killing animals for their hides, killing more than needed, using caribou for dog food, and not using the entire carcass – all added to the decline. According to Mr. Terry of DNR, one Dene killed 125 caribou in the fall and was almost out of meat by January. The recorded kill in Saskatchewan dropped to about four thousand in 1961. DNR attempted to preserve the caribou supply for Aboriginals by teaching them to conserve. After finding a group of Stony Rapids area Indians with many slaughtered caribou, a DNR officer lectured them on proper use of the animals. They told him "they were very glad to have [him] drop in and tell them these things." Yet he felt certain that they and two priests who were with them would again feed their dogs caribou that night.[35]

Lifestyle changes, brought at least partly by CCF policies, also contributed to the decreased reliance on traditional foods and increased northern poverty. Aboriginals traditionally ate the flesh of animals they shot, fur-bearers caught in their traps, netted fish, and a variety of birds. A constant supply of meat kept those living on the land alive. Favoured foods included many species not thought of as edible by others. As game became scarcer, and with the decline of trapping and the shift from bush to settlement life, there was less access to wild meat, and eating habits changed. Many became dependent on store-bought food. This shift added to poverty since Aboriginals now required cash to feed their families. Decreased reliance on other natural products from their environment also made poverty more acute. Aboriginals increasingly needed and wanted many of the trappings of a Euro-Canadian lifestyle. Nations that appeared wealthy when they lived from the bounty of the land now lived in poverty.

Although Aboriginals complied with the government's wish that they move to settlements, most lacked the income necessary to live comfortably in that environment. Unemployment, low incomes, and poverty went hand in hand. Early in its time in office, the CCF optimistically set out to increase fish and fur incomes, largely reserving these occupations for Aboriginals and relying on socialist forms of organization and marketing. Yet during a twelve-month period in 1945-46, the trapper who received the most from the Saskatchewan Fur Marketing Service in the La Loche district took in only $160.83. The highest earner in the La Ronge district obtained only $299.06. At Cumberland House, Thomas Cook topped the list of thirty-seven trappers, receiving $383.32. Many trappers earned less than $100. Fishermen did not fare much better. During a twelve-month period in 1946 and 1947, the Fish Board's Beaver Lake plant paid out $14,819.37 to fifty fishermen, with about half of the fishermen earning less than $100. Lac la Ronge area fishermen did somewhat better, with 118 fishermen receiving $45,372.67. Average fishing incomes stood at about $300 per year. In comparison, Saskatchewan males in 1946 had average earnings of $1,245 and women earned an average of $767.[36]

While politicians and bureaucrats knew that northern Aboriginals lived in poverty, they often ignored the larger picture and instead focused on instances of financial mismanagement. In 1947, for example, Malcolm Norris surveyed northern incomes. He found average annual incomes of $91.15 at Île-à-la-Crosse, $102.73 at Patuanak, and $124.48 at Beauval. Fishing and Len Waite's fish plant raised incomes at Buffalo Narrows to a still unacceptable level of $345.49. But in spite of these dismal numbers, the situation he found at Cumberland House provided support for the stereotyped view that Aboriginals could not handle money. Thanks to an unusually good muskrat harvest, the Cumberland House area's 525 residents received $51,428.85 from trapping. Their income totalled $92,331, an amount that probably gave the average family more than $1,000 in income. Norris described how residents quickly spent the windfall on liquor, horses, and household equipment. Before long the community fell into dire straits and required large-scale welfare and work programs. A.O. Aschim, a forester who visited Cumberland House in 1948, wrote: "I have never visited any settlement that subsisted on so meagre and insufficient diet for properly keeping body and soul together." He blamed welfare dependence on "the absolute inability of these people to intelligently budget and purpose proper values."[37]

In the mid-1950s, DNR employees V.F. Valentine and R.G. Young demonstrated a similar attitude. They attributed poverty to Metis culture and a philosophy of life that condoned blowing money on nonessential items. At one store, Metis spending included 8.1 percent on tobacco and 26 percent on dry goods. The pair thought this was too high. Southerners also frequently lamented the amount northern Aboriginals spent on liquor. Within the CCF government, the contention that Aboriginal northerners could not manage money reached the status of undisputed belief. Whether or not this was true, focusing on this issue detracted attention from the fact that, even had Aboriginals managed every cent they received with the utmost frugality, the northern economy still doomed them to live in dire poverty.[38]

Little changed in the years that followed. Poverty remained pervasive in 1958, when Miss Crawley of Social Welfare described the situation. La Loche experienced a food shortage, with government money as the only source of income. Beauval fishermen, who had taken the year's limit of fish the summer before, did not have their usual winter fishing income. DNR also expected a "crucial" situation in about two weeks at Pinehouse, one of the poorest settlements. Poor prospects for fishing and trapping at Montreal Lake and Cumberland House and unemployment at La Ronge and Uranium City added to the grim outlook.[39] Crawley's political masters rarely reacted with adequate short-term or long-term answers. Too often the blame for northern poverty continued to fall on the victims of inadequate government policies.

As time went on, the failure of CCF attempts to increase northern incomes by intervening in the trapping and fishing industries became increasingly obvious. Over thirteen years, La Loche trappers averaged annual trapping incomes of $280. In 1959-60, of 238 Aboriginal fishermen and trappers at La Ronge, only 56 earned over $1,000 from these activities, while 126 earned under $500. More than half of northern fishermen in 1960 likely earned under $500 from fishing, while some lost money. La Loche residents received per capita incomes of about $175 that year, while incomes at Cumberland House stood at about $325. At relatively prosperous La Ronge in 1962, per capita incomes, including family allowance and various other payments from government, averaged about $320. In comparison, the average per capita Saskatchewan income in 1958 already stood at $1,245. In further contrast to the pitifully small northern Aboriginal incomes, Saskatchewan males received an average of $3,290 in 1961, while females earned $1,974. Those working for northern mines did even better, with mine foremen receiving an average of $6,597 and miners $5,496. Income discrepancies between Aboriginal and non-Aboriginal workers made Aboriginal poverty stand out all the more. Chronic poverty meant that trappers and fishermen sometimes lacked even sled dogs and the other equipment needed to trap and fish.[40]

Degrees of poverty existed. La Loche stood out as one of the most destitute among the dozens of communities stricken by chronic poverty. Hugh Mackay Ross, who travelled the north for the HBC, described La Loche as "poverty stricken and disease ridden" and "the hell-hole of the fur trade." For a number of years the people ate largely fish for part of the year, and some did not have even that. Rampant tuberculosis worsened the suffering.[41] Several Aboriginal communities in the north received higher incomes than others, although poverty still dominated even there. Of trappers and fishermen, those in the northeast area did better than most, earning an average combined trapping and fishing income of $1,742 for 1959-60. On the west side, Buffalo Narrows benefited from the presence of Waite's fish plant and other fish buyers. But even there, white people held many of the better jobs, and unemployment and underemployment combined with social problems to doom many Aboriginals to poverty. Earnings from the Island Falls generating dam gave Sandy Bay residents the highest income of any northern Aboriginal settlement, yet incomes remained far behind those of white employees at nearby Island Falls. Alcohol abuse, not low incomes, received much of the blame for the severe poverty at Sandy Bay. Typical of comments by government personnel, one of the many nurses who briefly served in the community saw alcohol as the main "stumbling block" to improvement.[42]

Aboriginals, who experienced first-hand the failure of the CCF plan for trapping and fishing to support them, frequently looked for wage labour to help them survive. Fighting forest fires provided one of the few opportunities to earn wages within the north, but it usually offered only sporadic employment and low incomes. In a dry year with many fires, Aboriginals might find a few weeks' or even a few months' work on fire lines. In other years they might obtain only a few days' work. In one case, of sixty-seven men from Pelican Narrows who fought fires in 1961, only four earned more than $100. Guiding also provided little income. In 1957, for example, 122 guides averaged a little more than $300 per year. By 1963 only twenty-five to thirty guides worked regularly from June to September, earning about $600. Of thirty-eight Aboriginal workers who participated in a study at La Ronge in 1961, only six worked for wages on more than a casual basis, and twenty-six earned a total of less than $1,000. Since La Ronge possessed a relatively brisk economy, it can be assumed that much worse situations existed elsewhere.[43]

Indians and Metis could have benefited to a much greater degree from wage labour. A primary obstacle to their moving into waged and salaried positions came from the belief, shared by government and industry, that Aboriginals lacked readiness or suitability for industrial activities. During most of the CCF era, the Uranium City area offered the best-paying employment in northern Saskatchewan. Although thousands of white workers moved from outside to work there, already by 1951 Eldorado and other mines no longer wanted to hire Aboriginals. Companies claimed they had tried hiring people from the local area but found them unreliable. The CCF government passively accepted the view that mining work did not suit Aboriginals, although it did see manual labour on prospecting crews as suitable work for them. It made several minor attempts to increase Aboriginal employment. In one effort the province considered relocating Non-Status Indian workers to the Uranium City area from high-unemployment areas like La Loche and Beauval. Business opposed the plan, and the belief in Aboriginal unsuitability for wage employment solidified. One contractor claimed it was cheaper to fly white men from Edmonton than to hire Aboriginals. He described Aboriginals as untrainable, unreliable, and dirty. As an example of unacceptable behaviour, he mentioned that an Aboriginal man had taken company food to feed his family. DNR's R.G. Young saw a "foundation" for the companies' hiring policies, saying, "We know what the Metis is likely to do once he has acquired a small amount of cash – the urge for Bacchanalian revels is too great." Closing mining to Aboriginals meant the loss of the primary opportunity for employment. Mining generated income of $89.7 million in 1958, compared to $1.2 million from fishing and trapping combined. The booming industry employed over two thousand workers in 1958, and in 1962 Eldorado alone employed 564 persons. This number included only eight northern Aboriginals. Mining employment could have virtually eliminated northern unemployment.[44]

An additional source of jobs for northern Aboriginals could have come from the provincial government. But the CCF employed few Indians or Metis for more than part-time work. Non-Aboriginals dominated the skilled, better-paying jobs and even the less skilled jobs, including those of caretaker and housekeeper at outpost hospitals. In 1960 DNR's A.H. MacDonald blamed Aboriginal unemployment on a desire to stay on reserves, lack of skills, and "irregular work habits and lack of job responsibility." He added, "The Indians believe Queen Victoria promised to look after them 'as long as the sun shines and the rivers run.'" Demonstrating a typical attitude of resignation, in 1962 DNR thought the province could not solve the "employment crisis," since this required the help of all levels of government.[45] Woodrow Lloyd, Douglas's successor as premier, made a weak effort in 1963 to change this situation. He told his cabinet colleagues to employ Aboriginals wherever possible in the north. Yet at the same time he said the province already employed Aboriginals "in every case possible except in those jobs where special skills were required and not available among native people." The deputy minister of Social Welfare, J.S. White, made a similar claim. He said his department had hired several Aboriginals and that they had the same opportunity if they had the "necessary qualifications and are personally suitable."[46] While the CCF said it gave Aboriginals equal employment opportunities, it did not use affirmative action programs, and resignation typified its response to Aboriginal unemployment. Aside from its interventions in trapping and fishing, the provincial government made few efforts to provide Aboriginals with permanent employment.

Within Aboriginal communities, government, missions, stores, mink ranches, and fish plants offered some wage labour. Twenty-four local persons held jobs at Île-à-la-Crosse, one of the larger communities, in 1956. Fourteen worked at the mission, one for the RCMP as a special constable, and one patrolled for DNR. At La Loche in 1958 the hospital provided two jobs and DNR employed a local patrolman. That left hundreds of potential employees without work. Mink ranches and Waite's fish plant gave Buffalo Narrows one of the highest rates of employment, but there were still not enough jobs. Only five Metis men held full-time jobs at Cumberland House in 1960. Of these, one worked for the RCMP as a special constable and DNR employed two. In some communities, white people held all jobs, leaving Aboriginals to rely on welfare and the failing traditional economy. As the end of the CCF era approached, likely fewer than 10 percent of Aboriginal male workers held full-time jobs. Society offered northern women even fewer employment opportunities. The best most could hope for was to work cooking or cleaning for white people or clerking in a store.[47]

Given the absence of local jobs and adequate welfare programs, many Aboriginals left their northern home to work as migrant workers. At times the CCF pushed them to do so. After flooding and failure of the fur crop in 1948, DNR encouraged all "movable labour" to leave Cumberland House. In another instance, in 1951 west-side workers toiled in the Big River area under a DNR-sponsored project. During many years there was a large movement of workers to jobs outside Saskatchewan, including to the port of Churchill, Manitoba, and to the Alberta sugar beet fields. In 1964 alone, the agricultural representative, J.D. Neilson, placed 250 northerners in the beet fields. Most northerners did not like to spend prolonged periods of time away from the north. The prejudice and cultural barriers that commonly greeted them made spending time away from their own communities difficult. Additionally, migrant workers felt the pull of home and returned for family and social reasons. This form of work became part of the economic and social pathology of the north. Financial rewards to the labourers remained small and failed to lift them out of poverty. Further, migrant labour contributed to personal and familial instability. V.F. Valentine, the anthropologist, considered migrant labour to be a cause of the disintegration of marriages. The workers often could not support their families, and their wives preferred men with better incomes.[48]

In spite of Aboriginals' strong preference to remain in the north and the poor record of successfully placing them in southern jobs, some in government came to view permanent relocation to the south as a positive option. DNR's Valentine and Young had already spoken of relocation by the mid-1950s, when they visualized a voluntary program to help some move to the south to work at new trades. Overall, though, the CCF government did not promote or support any large-scale relocation, preferring to deal with unemployment and poverty with a series of short-term measures. Even after 1960, when confronted with the continuing decline of trapping and fishing and the rising cost of welfare, the CCF remained ambivalent about relocating Aboriginals to the south. The Center for Community Studies, which studied the north for the CCF, called for training and relocation programs. But the centre did not take a strong stand in favour of relocation. Obstacles it identified included southern unemployment, northerners' lack of preparation for work and life in the south, and southern attitudes. The centre favoured giving Aboriginals a choice in the matter. It also called for training northerners to fill existing jobs in the north, creating new jobs, and revamping the fishing and trapping industries. To keep Aboriginals in the north also fit with the CCF belief in their unsuitability for wage employment, which relocation of the worker would not change.[49] Lacking any program to train or relocate northerners, the CCF adopted a policy of paying increasing amounts of welfare.

Many of the academics who worked on the Center for Community Studies's northern study strongly disagreed with the centre and CCF position. *A Northern Dilemma*, edited by Arthur K. Davis, contained the research results and opinions of these scholars. Seeing the inability of fish, fur, and game to support northerners, the authors called for large-scale relocation to the south. They favoured a two-pronged approach, which would see government lessen northern suffering while promoting movement out of the area. The report referred to northern communities as "Outdoor Custodial Institutions," which could only support a fraction of their populations. Increased education and employment programs, combined with reductions in social aid, make-work, and other programs that helped non-viable communities survive, would encourage relocation. The centre's Vernon C. Serl called for "ruthless rationality." The authors disagreed with the CCF belief in the unsuitability of Aboriginals for wage employment and blamed unemployment and poverty on a lack of opportunity. The report recognized that life in the south would not be easy for relocated Aboriginals. A centre study had found that while few northern Aboriginals relocated to the south, those who did frequently lived on welfare or worked at jobs with low skill levels. The "chasm" Aboriginals had to cross in moving to the city was much greater than that faced by rural whites moving to the city. Yet the study found that those Aboriginals who moved to cities were much better off than those who remained in the north.[50]

While disagreement continued about whether northern Aboriginals should leave their northern homes to seek opportunities in the south, no one seriously pursued the most obvious solution to the pervasive unemployment. Neither the CCF, the centre, nor the dissenting researchers advocated a massive transfer of existing northern jobs from the white community to the Aboriginal community. Certainly most Indians' and Metis' lack of training and other preparation to assume jobs in mining, forestry, and government made a rapid change of this nature impractical. Yet without aggressive affirmative action and training programs there was virtually no chance of alleviating northern poverty. Few even spoke of moving Aboriginals into the non-Aboriginal-sector jobs as a long-term goal.

While Davis and his colleagues strongly disagreed with some aspects of CCF northern policies, neither group wanted government to make the "Outdoor Custodial Institution" too comfortable, though their reasons differed. The researchers feared that providing amenities in northern villages would prevent Aboriginals from leaving for the south. For its part, the CCF, which did not care if northerners left the north or not, did not want to spoil Aboriginals by giving them too much too easily. Housing policy was perhaps the most dramatic embodiment of this philosophy. From its early time in office this government knew of and lamented the conditions under which Aboriginals lived, but it deliberately devoted only paltry resources to improving Aboriginal housing. The beginnings of more generous housing programs did not appear until the 1960s, and even then these developed little under the CCF.

Prior to moving to settlements, many northern Aboriginals lived in tents in the summer and trapping cabins in the winter. When they moved to villages, they did not have the resources to build adequate, modern houses, so they threw up small, inexpensive shacks. These tiny homes frequently lacked modern conveniences, were often unpainted inside and outside, and sometimes had only a dirt floor. In contrast, the residents of several communities enjoyed much better housing. The quantity of adequate accommodation in a community strongly correlated to the size of the white population, with Uranium City, Island Falls, Creighton, and La Ronge having the most adequate housing. Some white people initially lived in small, unmodern houses, but most ensured that this situation quickly changed. For example, although Uranium City's dwellings in 1955 still included fifteen tents and tent shacks and 129 houses with less than three rooms, the community's housing and services improved rapidly in the following years. Similarly, housing on the Saskatchewan side of the border at Flin Flon underwent rapid improvement. Before long, most northern non-Aboriginal workers lived in relatively large and modern houses.[51]

The primary CCF housing program for "better homes" for Aboriginals consisted of providing a portable sawmill if enough demand existed in a community. To ensure that northerners did not receive something for nothing, government expected local people to pay for the mill's operating and maintenance costs. This program did not provide nearly the amount of lumber required, other building materials, or the training necessary for building good houses.

An odd situation developed in 1948 and 1949 when the CCF attempted to coerce the Roman Catholic church into providing lumber for northern housing. The province seemed equally or more interested in attacking the church. For many years, some missions had owned sawmills and sawn lumber for their own and the community's use. Much of this lumber had helped build Aboriginal houses. The CCF suddenly introduced a new policy that ended the practice of allowing schools and missions to obtain the trees needed to make lumber. Yet the Île-à-la-Crosse, Canoe Lake, and Beauval missions all wanted lumber. Various officials, including Allan Quandt of DNR, decided that the missions could only obtain lumber if they cut an equal amount for local people. Quandt doubted that the missions had provided much lumber to local people in the past. He also chastised the Catholics, saying that alongside their "magnificent structures" stood "the hovels that people call homes ... Certainly this would indicate a lack of faith with their own parishioners." Since local people did not want an amount of lumber equal to that which the missions wanted that year, DNR did not allow the missions to saw any lumber in 1948. DNR stuck to the same policy the following year. After Father Remy of the Île-à-la-Crosse mission complained to J.H. Brockelbank about the restrictions, cabinet approved new regulations that allowed permits for churches and community buildings. Brockelbank then again altered the rules, prohibiting Father Remy from taking more than ten thousand board feet unless the mission sawed a matching amount for other local users. In another instance, DNR wanted the church to improve housing at Pelican Narrows. This time, government acted more diplomatically. It offered Father Guilloux use of a DNR mill to build a rectory, hoping that "he could help us induce the people to take out material for both his Rectory and for homes for the community."[52]

Admittedly, the churches did not provide the resources required to improve northern housing to an acceptable level. But neither did the CCF, which strove to take over northern leadership from the priests. By the early 1960s the province devoted little money or energy to deal with the horrendous northern housing conditions. A 1960-61 study of housing in five settlements found that the average dwelling of eighteen by twenty feet had two rooms and six occupants, while about one-third of the buildings had only one room. No Aboriginal houses included running water or flush toilets, and cheap, light, "airtight" wood heaters heated many homes. At Cumberland House, where the quality of housing surpassed that of many communities, an average of 8.9 people lived in the average 2.6-room house. In contrast, the mean Canadian house size was 1,041 square feet in 1960.[53]

A modest expansion of northern housing programs accompanied the introduction of expanded welfare programs in the closing years of the CCF era. Consistent with its ideology, beginning in 1959 the CCF involved cooperatives in providing housing. Cabinet allowed DNR to guarantee a limited number of housing improvement loans made by the Saskatchewan Credit Society. The department backed loans totalling a paltry $17,000 in 1960-61. The CCF preference for cooperatives fit well with the Credit Society's requirement that it could only lend to cooperative societies. Newly created local housing cooperatives and existing co-ops, including Northern Co-operative Trading at Pinehouse and La Ronge, handled loans and collected payments. After repeated delays by cabinet, the system of having the Credit Society provide CCF guaranteed loans did expand.[54]

Another sign of the province's growing interest in assisting northerners obtain adequate housing came when DNR hired a housing supervisor. Among other things, he gathered housing designs suitable for the north. The department estimated a need for about a thousand new houses to eliminate overcrowding in "one-room hovels." Pinehouse received the first CCF-built public houses in the north in 1960. But government efforts lacked unity, with the Timber Board working at cross purposes to the new housing project. The Crown corporation preferred to have no involvement with the program, insisted on receiving its full cost for lumber, and suggested using cooperatives to supply lumber.[55]

Some government staff reacted with compassion to northern Aboriginals' housing plight. Seeing the unmet need for improved housing, individual DNR staff members tried several innovative solutions. Their efforts, while laudable, appeared pathetically inadequate. A few times, DNR obtained "several hundred dollars" from Social Welfare to buy "some old shack," which DNR then renovated and rented to welfare recipients. The system did not work well, since people still ended up with "only a mean shack." In 1961 A.H. MacDonald, director of Northern Affairs, suggested taking the Goldfields Trust Fund of $4,504.47 to allow DNR crews to build three or four "emergency houses." Materials would cost from $1,000 to $2,000 per house. DNR would then rent out the houses, using the revenue to build more units. In his submission to the Treasury Board asking for permission to use the fund, Minister Kuziak wrote: "At best the housing situation is deplorable and at its worst it is desperate. Hundreds of people are living in sub-standard shacks in slum conditions ... Probably the most urgent need is for housing for the aged."[56]

The housing program grew in 1961-62. Three categories of northerners could use the plan: those who could afford to make house loan payments but lacked a down payment, those who lacked income to buy better housing, and the old and infirm. Building Supervisor A.J. Feusi helped Pinehouse residents build ten houses, financed by the Credit Society. Projects also operated at La Ronge, Beauval, Île-à-la-Crosse, La Loche, and Buffalo

Narrows in 1962. The Pinehouse program catered to purchasers with earned incomes, allowing them ten years to repay the loans, while the other projects provided housing mainly for welfare recipients, with Social Welfare paying the rent. Provincial efforts to improve housing included operating three portable sawmills and training some northerners to install electrical wiring.[57]

The extent of provincial housing initiatives remained small given the size of the need for better living conditions. Most communities received virtually no assistance to improve housing stocks, while a fortunate few settlements received attention. Metis at Cole (Cold) Bay on Canoe Lake, who had undergone relocation from the RCAF Primrose Lake bombing range, benefited from a unique housing project in 1962 and 1963. With government giving direction and financing, local workers provided much of the labour to complete twenty-two houses. The province expected the Metis to help pay for the houses with money they would receive as compensation for the loss of land on the bombing range, but the repayment plan went awry in 1963 when the people failed to pay the required $8,000 towards the cost of the houses. Four days passed before the conservation officer learned that residents had received the compensation money. He then "found everyone drunk and the money all spent."[58]

False hope of a major expansion in the northern housing program arose in 1964. The CCF bought sawmills for La Loche and La Ronge, raising the number of its mills to six. It also prepared legislation to expand the northern housing program, approved a provisional housing board, and approved making loans to finance housing and "industrial or business enterprises." DNR received responsibility for the housing program. A.H. MacDonald spoke of a $100,000 program for 1964, and the provincial budget of February 1964 mentioned "broadened opportunities" for northerners. The CCF decided to go ahead and build seventy-five houses, using maximum loans of $3,000 and $500 grants. Yet, surprisingly, the province made the program conditional on receiving help from Ottawa's Canada Mortgage and Housing Corporation (CMHC). Saskatchewan knew that most CMHC programs did not apply to the north and should have realized that Ottawa would not change its policies overnight. Predictably, CMHC refused immediate aid for the larger housing plan, agreeing only to give technical help and housing grants of $400 to $500. As a result, the CCF drastically cut back its housing program and refused to contribute the money it had budgeted.[59]

Even with the expanded CCF housing program of the 1960s, there was a huge difference between the housing the CCF built for the public and that built for its employees. Public housing cost about a third of civil servant housing. The average public house cost $4,900 in 1964. Yet by the 1950s, DNR was already spending about $13,000 to $16,000 per staff house at Buffalo Narrows, Pelican Narrows, and Cumberland House.[60] DNR also insisted that its employees receive the benefit of modern conveniences, while public housing lacked water, sewer, or central heat. This double standard reinforced the colonial image established by the CCF and its departments in the north.

When the CCF's era ended, the province's modest efforts had dealt with only a minuscule portion of the need for better northern housing. Overcrowding continued. Teachers complained about students not having adequate study conditions, missionaries feared a lack of privacy discouraged "certain Christian moral values," and medical personnel thought overcrowding and poor sanitation caused health problems. Inadequate housing stood out as one of the most visible symptoms of the larger problems of low incomes and poverty. Even as some housing improved, many northerners lacked the money to pay for utilities and furnish and maintain houses. Deplorable situations went unchecked. In one case a senior citizen, Celestine McKay, asked for help for house repairs, but because he and his wife received old-age assistance, Social Welfare would not help. DNR also refused aid. Eiling Kramer, the minister of DNR, heard about the situation. Instead of intervening on behalf of the old couple, he blamed a priest, Father Darche, for raising false hope that the McKays and others would qualify for repair and other housing programs.[61]

Shortly after the CCF left office, people still lived in a settlement near Creighton called Mile 86. Aboriginal squatters there included senior citizens. They lived in "dwellings" built "largely from material salvaged from the adjacent waste disposal ground ... on small islands in a swamp" that was used as a tailings disposal site by the mining company. The tailings had killed all vegetation, and an odour, which a sanitary officer thought emanated from cyanide used in the milling process, pervaded the "dismal place." The officer pointed out that "equally poor housing can be found in almost every northern community."[62] To suggest that the CCF failed to meet the housing needs of northerners does not adequately describe the situation. A more accurate statement would be that the CCF ignored the housing plight of northerners, devoting only a token effort to deal with this aspect of poverty.

A high and increasing level of social problems provided another symptom of worsening northern poverty. Children and families experienced some of the most negative consequences of the rapid economic and societal changes that took place during the CCF era. The Department of Social Welfare held responsibility for northern child welfare and family services, even though it had no staff resident in the north. Only one visiting staff person, who also had responsibility for administering social aid and other departmental programs, commonly handled this entire half of the province. This lack of staff often allowed the suffering of children and families to run its natural course, free from government intervention.

Soon after coming to power, the CCF acted to increase provincial involvement in providing services to children in need. A new Child Welfare

Act, introduced in 1946, replaced the former act, which expected local children's aid societies to provide child welfare services. The new act gave the minister of Social Welfare wardship of children in care and brought a shift from local to provincial responsibility. Eventually, by 1960, all local societies turned their caseloads over to the province. Social Welfare took the expanded responsibilities seriously. It placed much of its trained staff in child welfare and viewed protection services as their "basic service" to prevent community problems. Child protection caseloads peaked in 1948, when over 2,100 families received services. Caseload numbers declined to approximately 550 by about 1960.[63] But unfortunately, the CCF's emphasis on prevention and child welfare did not extend to the north.

For the south, the new government rapidly increased child welfare staff, although a perennial shortage of trained personnel continued. Since Saskatchewan offered no social work training, those pursuing a professional degree studied outside the province. From 1944 to 1960, 126 staff trained under departmental sponsorship. These people comprised much of the department's professional staff. Less-trained social welfare workers worked at more menial tasks, including in financial aid programs.[64]

Although the Social Welfare structure included a specialized Child Welfare Branch, this branch did not usually provide any staff for the north. Instead, the department let the Welfare Services Division look after northern child welfare. It had increased services by then, and yet in 1961 Social Welfare still had only two workers to administer all northern programs. As a result, it applied a much looser standard of neglect in the north than in the south. The department admitted that many northerners received only "token service." Urgent cases sometimes brought emergency visits by social workers. Because they did not have the resources to support the families through times of crisis, the workers frequently apprehended large groups of children (they could apprehend children up to age sixteen). In a typical situation, drinking parents left their children with a relative or a babysitter. Days later the caregiver tired of looking after the children and notified the RCMP or DNR, which called Social Welfare. Indian Affairs, which had even fewer social work staff than Social Welfare, also called on the province in cases of life and death on reserves.[65]

Governmental neglect of northern children worsened when no department wanted to accept financial responsibility for the region's wards and child welfare services. Although legislation gave DNR, the local government, responsibility for paying, it resisted. In 1950, DNR's deputy minister, C.A.L. Hogg, wanted Social Welfare to pay, or at least keep charges to a minimum. At the time, twelve wards had come from the north. Their care cost the province about $1,920 in total annual maintenance costs. Hogg particularly objected to charges for flying magistrate Lussier and social worker Burgess to northern child welfare hearings. The deputy minister wanted hearings only when charges were laid for "gross neglect." Although the provincial auditor told DNR it should pay, and DNR budgeted $3,600 in 1951 to support up to fifteen wards, the department still resisted, citing the north's lack of a large tax base and economic maturity.[66]

Northern children apprehended by social workers frequently found themselves quickly transported to southern foster homes, where they waited for the court system to determine their fate. Hearings took place within three weeks, presided over in the north by a travelling circuit judge. Judges relied heavily on the recommendations of the apprehending social worker, who usually presented the department's case in order to save money. Parents rarely hired a lawyer or called witnesses, and the judge, after listening to the social worker and his witnesses, passed judgment. Not until 1963 did an amendment to the act allow the department to pay parents' legal fees, although many likely did not know of this right. Beginning in 1946, some parents voluntarily gave their children into non-ward care for up to twelve months, particularly when children needed medical care away from home. But the department placed most children in foster homes against the parents' wishes.

Beginning in 1945, as an alternative to permanently committing children to the minister, judges could make temporary committal orders for up to twelve months or return the children to their parents with supervision. Often one temporary order followed another, and children experienced ongoing uncertainty while waiting in foster homes. Sometimes the children returned to their northern homes, but social workers frequently considered the parents incorrigible and recommended that judges make the children permanent wards of the minister. The resulting permanent wardship orders usually lasted until age twenty-one, although Social Welfare could discharge its responsibility earlier.[67]

Because the north had few approved foster homes, most wards went to southern homes. The experiences of northern children in these foster homes varied greatly. In some happy cases, children and foster families formed long-term, meaningful relationships that continued once the child reached adulthood. Some less fortunate children moved from family to family, failing to find a comfortable and secure home. Society stigmatized foster care, including the wards and the foster families who cared for them. Wards found that playmates ostracized them because of their race and history of family problems. For their part, foster homes received few rewards beyond the satisfaction of knowing that they performed a useful service. Although the common belief was that foster parents took in children for the money involved, in reality, in order to provide an acceptable level of care, foster families frequently had to subsidize the meagre rates paid by government. In 1946 Saskatchewan gave foster homes only sixty-five cents per day for children under age twelve and up to one dollar per day for those twelve and older. Rates remained low in the following years. The province often paid for clothing by requisition, which made foster parents and children stand out in the stores. In time the CCF loosened its purse strings slightly and included an allowance for Christmas presents in the December cheques. This replaced the former procedure under which the department provided presents.[68]

Removing children from northern Aboriginal communities and placing them in modern southern white foster homes brought intense cultural shock to the children. The loss of contact with their families and the northern environment brought further stress. Living in the south for a prolonged period of time made the children's eventual return to their families and communities difficult and fraught with problems. Many were unable to function in either society. As an alternative to foster care, neglected children sometimes found themselves placed at boarding schools, including those at Beauval and Montreal Lake. Sometimes this kept them out of ward care and closer to their families. Early in its mandate the CCF government recognized the advantages to children of keeping them in the north. Although the Metis community of Green Lake fell outside the Northern Administration District (NAD), its milieu resembled that of various northern areas, and Social Welfare opened a children's shelter there in 1947, with a capacity of about twenty-five children. After expansion, an average of forty-two children lived there by 1951. The facility closed that year, however, for a variety of reasons that included difficulty in attracting staff, isolation, a lack of local services, and a shift in preference to foster homes. Mildred Battel, the director of child welfare, said the institutional standards made it difficult for children to return home. Yet the only alternative for most children was placement in southern foster homes, hardly an adequate solution. Metis, including many from the north, comprised about 80 percent of children in care in the Prince Albert Region in 1962.[69]

Many children placed in southern foster homes became candidates for adoption. Because adoption brought a commitment to the children from the new parents, the department preferred this as the plan for permanent wards. Few people came forward to adopt older children or family groups, and placement of Indian and Metis children proved particularly difficult. By the 1960s the department used churches, newspapers, radio, and television to try to find homes for the children. Although few in number, most families who adopted Aboriginal children from the north were white. (Status Indians adopted by non-Indians did not lose their treaty rights, and Non-Status persons adopted by Status Indians did not gain treaty status.) Given the difficulty of finding adoptive homes for Aboriginal children, many permanent wards from the north lived and grew up in southern foster homes.[70]

Reflecting the dominant values of its time, the CCF government placed far less emphasis on preserving Aboriginal culture than on teaching children religious values. Religion remained important in society, and Social Welfare preferred to place children in homes where they would receive "a sound code of life and a Christian philosophy of living." Government also wanted to see continuity in a child's religious affiliation. As a result, committal orders included a designation of religion as Protestant or Roman Catholic. This added to the difficulty of finding foster and adoption homes for northern children. About 90 percent of northern wards came from Roman Catholic families, while more southern families belonged to Protestant denominations. Faced with a shortage of suitable homes, the department at times overrode the court's designation of religion. Priests sometimes compensated for this by providing religious instruction to Catholic children placed in non-Catholic homes.[71]

The systemic neglect of northern children extended to the region's delinquent and handicapped children. Since the CCF failed to establish any treatment centres in the north, children whose behaviour the foster care system could not handle were placed in southern institutions. Facilities in Regina included the Boys Industrial School, Embury House, Dales House, and the Girls' Hostel, while Saskatoon had Kilburn Hall. Government also moved handicapped northern children to southern institutions, where many lived out their lives far from home and family. Moose Jaw's Valley View Centre opened in 1946, the first provincial training school for mentally handicapped children and adults. Private institutions also opened their doors to northern children.[72]

Under the CCF, government involvement in providing a variety of social programs reached a level without precedent in Saskatchewan. Most of this growth took place in the south. While the province also increased welfare and social services in the north, the level of service offered there remained inadequate and far below that in the south. Incongruously, though, on a per capita basis the northern need for services soon far surpassed that of the south. Rapid population growth, changing Aboriginal lifestyles, and the many CCF interventions in the economy and society combined to create an untenable situation where northerners could no longer survive without state aid. Dependency on social aid grew to the point that many feared losing this, much as others fear losing their source of income. But the CCF, which helped destroy the former northern economy, failed to devote the resources needed to provide an alternative to welfare.

Welfare under the CCF kept northerners alive and pacified them, preventing open revolt. The CCF tried to keep welfare payments to needy northerners at a low level, preferring to supplement these with work-for-wages programs. It believed working for aid would help preserve Aboriginals' self-esteem and work ethic. Frustration, for all concerned, accompanied the work projects because they did not provide a long-term solution to northern unemployment. The reliance on work-for-wages programs, though they may have seemed preferable to welfare, failed to address the economic and social problems created by the lack of meaningful employment and by CCF interventions in the north.

As the CCF era closed, poverty blanketed the northern half of the province. Large Aboriginal families struggled to survive on about $1,000 per year. But in a change from the early days of Joe Phelps's fervour for reform, the CCF lacked ideas and commitment to deal with northern problems. The dream once held by the CCF of Aboriginals earning their living from restructured trapping and fishing industries had died. Instead of creating northern prosperity, CCF policies had contributed to the collapse of the traditional northern economy. While the north had enough jobs to employ the entire local work force, government and industry brought in thousands of white employees. The CCF accepted and perpetuated the myth that Aboriginals could not work at steady wage labour. In place of meaningful jobs, work-for-wages programs supplemented meagre welfare payments to keep northerners alive. The government justified continuing its inferior northern welfare services by saying it did not want to take away Aboriginals' work ethic and increase dependency. An additional reason for limiting social aid payments came from the common view that northern Aboriginals fell into the category of the undeserving poor, squandering their money and refusing to help themselves.

While it made child welfare a priority in the south, the CCF neglected the welfare of northern children. It committed only the most minimal resources to child protection and prevention services in the north. Inadequate staff numbers, a total absence of local treatment facilities, and a miserly attitude towards paying for services added governmental neglect to parental neglect. Children often suffered the most, as northern social problems grew and family dysfunction went unchecked.

In addition to welfare services, the larger category of social programs included health and education services. Increasing contact with Euro-Canadian society meant that some Aboriginal health problems increased. With rapidly improving health care a reality in the south, it became unconscionable that northern Aboriginals would live without medical services. The changes that swept the north under the CCF also made it imperative for northerners to receive formal education. Without schooling they had little chance of escaping from their lives of deepening poverty. As they lacked financial resources, most northerners depended on the CCF for the provision of both these vital services.

10
Dollars Are Worth More Than Lives

One of the primary rationales offered by the CCF for providing a lower level of welfare services in the north than in the south was that government did not want to spoil northern Aboriginals and weaken their work ethic. In other words, the CCF applied a form of "tough love," paternalistically acting in northerners' best interests. Based on this, logic then suggests that a truly caring government would institute more generous policies in other areas of social spending that did not offer the potential for abuse by Aboriginals. Yet underdevelopment also characterized the provision of both medical care and education in the north during the CCF era. This government proved as tight-fisted in these areas of social policy as in welfare spending. Southern socialists designed and controlled northern health and education systems, imposing, in colonial fashion, policies they thought adequate for northerners. Their socialism did not include a generous sharing with some of the province's poorest, and outright neglect of northerners' needs resulted. This situation also raises questions about the CCF's motivation for offering substandard welfare services in the north. It appears the primary reason for low levels of spending on welfare, medical care, and education was simply that government did not want to spend much on the north and its people. Since northern Aboriginals lacked a strong voice, and neglecting them had few repercussions at the polls, the situation continued.

In spite of their inadequacy, humanitarian caring certainly motivated some of the CCF initiatives in the area of social programs. Additional motivation for involving government in the provision of welfare, health, and education services came from the CCF desire to displace the traditional forces of the north – the fur traders and churches – from their positions of power. This party and government refused to tolerate continuation of the traders' paternalistic credit system, which also served as a major part of the northern social safety net. As well, this government sought to take over the secular functions of the churches in the areas of medical care and education.

Without doubt, Tommy Douglas felt a genuine desire to provide residents of Saskatchewan with socialized hospital and medical care. He and others in the CCF believed that a lack of financial resources should not deprive anyone of the benefit of medical care to preserve life and restore health. During the first years after the party's election victory, it appeared that the north and its residents would share in the benefits brought by this idealistic approach. The CCF set out to provide a basic humanitarian level of northern health care through a network of remote outpost hospitals. But after an energetic beginning, CCF enthusiasm for improving northern health services waned. Outright neglect of northerners' medical needs continued unchecked. During the twenty years of the CCF era, the quality of northern health care remained far behind that available in the south. Northerners either did without many services or travelled to the south to obtain care.

Woodrow Lloyd, the long-time CCF minister of Education and Douglas's successor as premier, brought devotion and understanding to the area of educational reform. A former teacher and past-president of the Teachers' Federation, he knew education from the inside. Lloyd and the CCF strove to reorganize and improve education throughout the province, including in the north. If the CCF hoped to modernize and assimilate northern Aboriginals, it needed to teach English, reduce illiteracy, and prepare northerners academically and vocationally for their new lives. Rapid educational expansion extended elementary education to most communities with the aim of enrolling nearly all northern children in school. However, CCF efforts soon stalled. By 1964 illiteracy and low educational achievement remained common. The province spent little on northern education. Most northerners still did not have access to secondary school education, and government offered no vocational or professional education. Without education, the region's Aboriginal people had little hope of rising from their lives of poverty.

Prior to 1944 the Anglican and Roman Catholic churches provided most northern medical care and education. On the west side, Roman Catholics operated an infirmary at the La Loche mission and a hospital at Île-à-la-Crosse, and a nurse lived at Beauval. A nurse at La Ronge's Anglican residential school provided medical services. Some other health care initiatives also predated the CCF era. Local people had spearheaded the building of an outpost hospital at Cumberland House. The Red Cross also became interested in providing health care from northern outpost hospitals, although this plan had not advanced far prior to the election of 1944. C.H. Piercy, sent north by the CCF to study education, saw an "urgent need for medical services" at Stony Rapids, Fond du Lac, Camsell Portage, Buffalo Narrows, Snake Lake, Sandy Beach, and Clear Lake.[1] The churches also provided most northern education before 1944. Anglicans operated schools in the central and eastern area of the north, including at La Ronge and Montreal Lake. Roman Catholics provided education on the west side at Île-à-la-Crosse, La Loche, and Beauval. Catholics and Anglicans shared the education of Aboriginals at Cumberland House. Since most areas had neither church hospitals nor schools, this meant many persons rarely, if ever, saw a doctor or nurse and never attended school.

Clearly, if they were to share in the coming provincial utopia visualized by the CCF, northern Aboriginals needed improved medical care and educational opportunities. They suffered more from some medical conditions than most residents of the province. Although most of the epidemics that once decimated Aboriginal peoples had passed, tuberculosis continued to ravage the population. Many women died in childbirth, a high percentage of children did not survive infancy, and northern Aboriginals died at an earlier age than did most Canadians. In the area of education, modernization made it urgent for the CCF to expand learning opportunities for northern Aboriginals. Without this they could not cope with change or participate in new opportunities.

In comparison to the north, southern Saskatchewan enjoyed superior health and education services prior to 1944. A partially socialized medical system operated under the former Liberal government, with a municipal doctor system and free medical service in about one-third of municipalities. Yet the province suffered from severe shortages of trained personnel, equipment, and hospital facilities. Seeing the need, the CCF promised to expand health services. Southern residents also enjoyed education opportunities superior to those available in the north. An extensive system of elementary and secondary schools served the agricultural and urban areas of Saskatchewan. While the province had only one university, in Saskatoon, this offered a broad range of education. It did not yet include a medical school. As in health care, the CCF saw room for educational improvements.[2]

Premier Douglas personally took the job of minister of Public Health from 1944 to 1949, a move that confirmed the importance he placed on reforming and expanding the health care system. Also importantly, the CCF created the Health Services Planning Commission in 1944, giving it responsibility for planning facilities and introducing and managing hospital insurance. The same year, the CCF appointed the Health Services Survey Commission, which gave outside experts a prominent role in formulating recommendations for health care reform. Members of the commission included the chairman, Dr. Henry Sigerist of Johns Hopkins University; Dr. Fred Mott, the US deputy surgeon general; and Dr. Mindel Sheps of Winnipeg. The authors of the resulting Sigerist Report also addressed the northern situation. As a sign of things to come, they wrote: "The far northern part of the Province is so sparsely populated that it will not be possible to supply it with complete medical services now."[3]

Reform of the medical care system became one of the new government's main initiatives. CCF enthusiasm for improved health care did not flag and resulted in the introduction of various innovative programs during the next twenty years. Health care spending rapidly increased from 6 percent of the budget ($1,852,079) in 1943-44 to 20 percent ($10,246,194) in 1947-48. By 1951-52, health spending took 51.8 percent of welfare, education, and health expenditures. While the CCF delayed introducing full medicare until 1962, it implemented the Saskatchewan Hospital Services Plan (SHSP) in 1947 as a compulsory program to provide hospital care. In another major initiative the CCF provided an air ambulance service. It quickly implemented the free cancer treatment legislation already passed by the Liberals and introduced free treatment for mental illness. Those receiving old-age and blind pensions, mothers' allowances, and social aid also no longer paid for medical care. The CCF rapidly built new hospitals, and many new doctors practised in them. It built a medical school in 1953 and the University Hospital in 1956, both in Saskatoon. As a direct result of their electing the CCF, the residents of southern Saskatchewan received greatly improved medical care.[4]

The new health care programs in southern Saskatchewan embodied the CCF's socialist conviction that the state should care for its citizens. While most residents of the south did not support the new government's socialistic economic plans for their region, the province's involvement in medical care won the support of many. Accessible medical care became the main identifying feature of benign prairie socialism. In its 1933 Regina Manifesto and repeatedly thereafter, the CCF called for a full medicare program. The Saskatchewan Hospital Services Plan, which began 1 January 1947, partially met the goals of the manifesto. It required residents to pay an annual fee of five dollars per person or thirty dollars per family. In return, residents received unlimited hospital care. Although it was based on socialist principles, the medical profession liked much about the plan, which added to doctors' incomes and improved the health care system. Fearing a loss of autonomy, doctors successfully opposed the aspect of the CCF plan that would have put them on salaries. By the end of 1947, SHSP covered 93 percent of the provincial population. SHSP did not help most northerners, since its compulsory aspect did not extend to the north. The CCF wanted to go farther and introduce full medicare, which would include payment for out-of-hospital medical services. Because of financial limitations and a desire to see Ottawa contribute financially, however, the CCF delayed its introduction. The government, by then led by Woodrow Lloyd, finally implemented the Medical Care Insurance Act on 1 July 1962. Bitter controversy and the withdrawal of services by most doctors greeted the introduction of medicare. To settle the dispute, the CCF compromised, allowing doctors to continue with a fee-for-service system.[5]

Prior to the CCF era, the Department of Public Health provided few services in the north. Under the CCF, this department received responsibility for most northern health care, aided by DNR. Public Health's Medical Services Branch provided medical and dental care for northern indigents beginning in 1945, and the Health Services Act of 1946 allowed the Department of Social Welfare to designate indigents.[6] The federal Indian Health Services (IHS) provided care in several areas with large Status Indian populations.

Douglas and his party's health care vision did not include full participation of the north in the new initiatives. Since the government seemed content to allow a much lower standard of care in that half of the province, northerners benefited comparatively little from the health care reforms and innovations in medical care. Although northern communities lacked road access, only the south had planes and personnel specifically dedicated to the air ambulance program. Instead of building modern northern hospitals, the CCF provided a modest expansion of the pre-existing "outpost hospital" system. It placed lone nurses in charge of these. For a time, only one doctor served the entire northern area. All major facilities, including sanatoria to treat tuberculosis, remained in the south.

Even the compulsory aspect of SHSP did not extend to the north for most of the CCF era. The CCF began a noncompulsory scheme there in 1948. As a result, many non-Aboriginal northerners received coverage while most Aboriginal northerners did not. The CCF claimed that most northerners did not want the program and could not afford it. Certainly some did oppose a compulsory SHSP plan. In one incident, Reverend G.J. Waite of Montreal Lake, wrongly believing the plan was compulsory, sent in twenty dollars for his 1951 premium. He addressed his payment to "The Little Kremlin" in Prince Albert. J.H. Brockelbank, DNR's minister, took offence, pointing out that various government staff had shed blood defending Waite's freedom of speech. He asked Waite to stop "hurting the feelings of my staff by calling names." Still thinking the plan compulsory, the next year Waite again sent twenty dollars to "The Kremlin" in Prince Albert. Waite wrote: "We don't yet have to have a permit to breathe or think or speak."

The CCF assertion that it was respecting the wishes of northerners in this matter lacked credibility, since its other northern actions demonstrated that it did not mind using compulsion. Nor did it mind compelling southerners to participate in the plan. Limiting the northern program to those who would voluntarily pay removed the poorest segment of the population and violated the spirit of the plan. Some of the neediest qualified for care as indigents, but large numbers of northerners had no medical coverage. No statistics exist to document how many persons went without medical treatment. The CCF aggravated the situation in 1952 when, in an apparent cost-saving measure, the Health Services Planning Commission decided that Public Health should not pay SHSP premiums for indigents but should pay their hospital bills instead. This added additional stigma to indigency. SHSP covered only 1,355 persons in the NAD in 1953, about 17 percent of the population, not counting Status Indians. Leaving the majority of northerners without SHSP coverage violated the CCF's principles and the spirit of its reforms. The primary reason for having separate policies for the north and the south appeared to be that government, knowing that most northerners could not afford the plan, did not want the administrative and policy difficulties of creating a workable plan for the north.[7]

Cabinet finally decided that compulsory SHSP coverage should extend to the NAD effective 1 January 1959. This decision had little to do with compassion but instead was spurred by financial considerations. In order to receive full cost-sharing for SHSP costs from Ottawa, Saskatchewan needed to extend coverage to all northerners. With money on the line, the CCF quickly found a way to include northerners in the program. DNR bought health coverage for all northerners outside Uranium City, La Ronge, and Creighton – about eight thousand people. The department dutifully tried to collect the fees (twenty dollars per adult, five dollars per child, or forty-five dollars per family by that time), although it quickly became an onerous task. DNR gathered only $14,900 of $47,300 owing in 1959. Since most northerners did not have jobs, DNR could not garnishee their wages, and collecting through property taxes did not work, since many residents held no property. Collections in 1962 in the La Loche area reached only 10.3 percent, although nearly 80 percent of residents at Sandy Bay, Molanosa, and Dore Lake paid. DNR collected only 36.3 percent of total levies in 1964. The department did not need to collect for Status Indians, since IHS paid for SHSP coverage for this group.[8]

Discrimination against northern residents also appeared in the CCF policy regarding health regions. The use of health regions allowed a measure of local control over the provision of health care. While the government considered it essential for southern people to receive the benefits of this system, it failed to extend this method of organizing health delivery to the north. Existing regulations did not allow for health regions in unorganized areas, and the CCF did not introduce legislation that would have allowed the creation of a northern health region. The absence of local control over health care reinforced colonialism.[9]

Instead of trusting northern people to make health care decisions, the CCF expected its top colonial administrator, DNR's northern administrator based in Prince Albert, to manage much of the northern medical system. He looked after SHSP, medical and hospital expenditures, medical flights, ground transportation, and nonhospital care.[10] Public Health also had responsibilities in the north, though it directed matters there from an even greater distance. Dr. Totton, the north's part-time medical health officer, worked from his Regina office. He visited the north quarterly, doing some clinical work and supervising outpost hospitals. A director of nursing services oversaw northern nurses, and sanitation officers occasionally visited. Public Health recognized the need to move administration north, at least to Prince Albert, but waited for Totton to retire, placing his convenience ahead of northern health needs. He finally retired in 1954, midway through the CCF time in office. The Northern Health District then began. Dr. A.C. Irwin, the new medical health officer, supervised northern staff, including the nursing supervisor and part-time public health inspector. Irwin and the other top personnel operated from their base in Prince Albert. The colonial methods of health care delivery continued. Even the designation of the north as a "health district" remained unofficial, without any legislative basis.[11]

As its primary northern health initiative, the CCF created a network of four outpost hospitals. A Red Cross outpost hospital had opened at Buffalo Narrows in 1947, and the CCF took this over in 1948. The new system also included the log Cumberland House hospital, which residents had helped build around 1940. To complete the system the CCF built new outpost hospitals at Stony Rapids and Sandy Bay. Although largely completed by 1948, the hospital at Sandy Bay did not open until 1950. The establishments were referred to as hospitals but had more in common with infirmaries or clinics. The outmoded facilities had little staff and no laboratory or x-ray equipment for many years. Their medical staff usually consisted of one resident nurse, referred to as a "supervisor," who provided a wide range of medical services. One of the CCF's early efforts involved encouraging northern mothers to give birth in the hospitals. Although the College of Physicians and Surgeons did not approve and viewed the use of midwives as "regressive," the province sent two nurses to the School of Nurse Midwifery in New York in 1945. Public Health then placed its first two midwives at Cumberland House and Buffalo Narrows.[12]

With its four small outpost hospitals operating by 1950, the CCF rested on its laurels. The following years saw little spending on the outpost hospitals and no expansion of the system for medical care in predominantly Aboriginal settlements. Yet the need for medical care increased as the population grew rapidly and new communities sprang up. None of the new villages, some created by the CCF, received the services of a resident nurse. Even the existing outpost hospital system suffered. The province repeatedly refused to replace Cumberland House's small log hospital. After the Treasury Board refused Public Health's latest request for funds to build a new hospital in the mid-1950s, G. Kinneard of Public Health wrote "things are tough all over." Doctors rarely visited most outpost hospitals, with the exception of the Buffalo Narrows facility. Due to its nearness to Île-à-la-Crosse, the doctor from there did attend to the Buffalo Narrows hospital. This facility provided the largest volume of service of all outpost hospitals for much of the CCF era, a situation that led to the nurse receiving the help of a nurse's aide in 1957. After years of delay, the Treasury Board approved $36,900 for a Buffalo Narrows hospital extension in 1963.[13]

Unlike their response to many other CCF initiatives, northern Aboriginals welcomed government health care initiatives. Aboriginals quickly developed faith in and became dependent on government-provided medical care. Outpatient visits at outpost hospitals increased greatly by the 1960s. In contrast, after years of heavy use, the number of inpatient days declined. Patients who required hospitalization increasingly travelled to better-equipped hospitals outside the region. Outpatient visits at Buffalo Narrows, for example, increased from 1,550 in 1952 to 4,552 in 1963. Inpatient care days, not including maternity, fell from 600 in 1953 to 251 in 1961. Similar patterns developed elsewhere.[14]

While nearly all northern Aboriginals needed to travel long distances to access reasonably modern medical care, west-side residents in the Île-à-la-Crosse area enjoyed superior services. St. Joseph's Hospital in that community delivered the most extensive medical care in the north during most of the CCF era. While the Roman Catholic church built and managed the facility, Saskatchewan and Ottawa participated by providing some funding. The only doctor in the north for many years, Dr. P.E. Lavoie, practised there for nineteen years until he retired in 1953. Dr. K. Hoehne briefly filled in until Dr. M.W. Hoffman arrived. Hoffman remained until 1973. In response to the need for improved services, the church built a large, new, forty-five-bed facility in 1958, administered by Oblates and operated by Grey Nuns.[15]

Dr. Hoffman, a devout Roman Catholic, performed Herculean tasks in a large area, partially compensating for the inadequate provincial and federal systems. His workload included caring for thirty to forty hospital patients and visiting patients in surrounding communities. Recognizing his contributions, Public Health and Indian Affairs paid his salary. Public Health even tried to build a house and office for him in 1955, but the Treasury Board turned down the request. The department also wanted to hire another doctor to help and relieve Hoffman, who did not take a holiday from 1954 to 1960. Approval for a second doctor finally came, effective 1 April 1959, but a series of fiascos followed. Long delays resulted while Public Health looked for a doctor. Then, over the next few years, three doctors each in turn proved unsuitable and stayed only a short time. One remained long enough for Dr. Hoffman to take a six-week leave in 1963.[16]

Roman Catholics also continued to provide medical care at their much smaller St. Martin's Roman Catholic Hospital in La Loche. In some respects, even this modest facility offered services superior to the province's outpost hospitals. Two nurses worked there, and the doctor from Île-à-la-Crosse sometimes visited. Saskatchewan participated by paying some ongoing operating costs and a per diem rate for patients. At the same time, government kept a close eye on expenditures. It became concerned about the "extraordinary" volume of service in 1954, when 3,110 inpatients and 4,914 outpatients visited the hospital. Instead of viewing these figures as a sign that the facility required expansion, Public Health suspected that patients abused the service. Dr. Irwin speculated that the population of about seven hundred had "nothing else to do, so for entertainment, 13 or 14 of them 'drop in' at the hospital, daily. Now that we are paying for the service, this figure will probably rise." Although Dr. Irwin described the hospital as "of the worst possible design," the CCF provided no alternative to the modest church facility.[17]

After the CCF's initial creation of the outpost hospital network, it only built new hospitals in the largely non-Aboriginal communities of Uranium City and La Ronge. This situation left dozens of Aboriginal settlements without any medical care and required residents to travel long distances for even simple medical procedures. In 1948 northern hospitals handled about 75 percent of the region's medical work, with outside hospitals caring for the rest. Radio communication and medical flights helped make the system work.[18] By the early 1950s Buffalo Narrows, Sandy Bay, Stony Rapids, and Cumberland House each had a rating of four beds, while the church hospitals had a rating of ten beds at La Loche and twenty-two at Île-à-la-Crosse. By 1954 the north had three doctors. The one at Île-à-la-Crosse mainly cared for Aboriginal people, while the two at Uranium City primarily served the local white populace. Twelve nurses in the region included four at Île-à-la-Crosse and two at La Loche.[19]

Outpost hospital nurses performed heroic feats in caring for the large populations that flocked to them for care. In addition to the challenge of providing medical services far beyond those normally required of nurses, these women dealt with ongoing trials, including stoking wood furnaces, poor water and sewage systems, and erratic electrical supplies. Slow modernization of the facilities took place, and by 1963 all four outpost hospitals had full-time electrical service and oil heat.[20] Nurses often received some help from ancillary staff, which consisted of a female housekeeper and a male caretaker. The housekeeper commonly lived in the hospital, providing companionship for the nurse. Usually the caretaker lived elsewhere, although he sometimes also lived in the hospital. In those cases he served as a guard for the nurse and premises. Nurses frequently felt threatened by drunken and violent community members and welcomed protection. Most housekeepers and caretakers worked under "labour service classification," since Public Health said they did not meet union agreement standards. This also proved convenient for government, since the labour service classification deprived employees of sick leave and controls on hours of work. It might appear that the housekeeper and caretaker positions could have provided some local employment for Aboriginals, but Public Health preferred to hire white employees even for nonprofessional positions. Several failed attempts to hire local people reinforced this practice. In one case the Aboriginal caretaker at Cumberland House lost his job because of "a lack of mechanical ability." In another instance the department fired an Aboriginal housekeeper at Sandy Bay for theft. As a result, Public Health had no full-time Aboriginal employees in the north in 1963, although it hired some local people for special projects and as relief help for caretakers or domestics.[21]

The Lake Athabasca area presented a picture of two standards of health care – one for the mining community of Uranium City and another for the numerous outlying Aboriginal communities. The Stony Rapids outpost hospital nurse and a Public Health nurse from Uranium City cared for area Metis. The nurses also often cared for Status Indians, since Indian Health Services had no nurse in the area. Further, Uranium City doctors did not want Status Indians to visit their offices because of the low fees paid by Ottawa. IHS finally hired a nurse for Uranium City in 1957, but she left by 1959. G. Kinneard, director of the province's Regional Health Services Branch, then agreed to have Public Health take over the IHS work, with reimbursement. Dr. Irwin opposed this agreement, since it condoned a reduction in services and placed additional strain on the busy provincial nurses.[22]

In contrast to the low level of services provided for Aboriginals in the far north, the white population of Uranium City received far superior medical service. Beginning in 1952, Eldorado operated a six-bed hospital for a time. Uranium City also obtained a seven-bed hospital, moved there from Goldfields. A new twenty-five-bed hospital opened there in 1956, with its contruction funded by the federal and provincial governments, and was administered by the municipal corporation. Robin F. Badgley of the University of Saskatchewan (U of S) described it as "magnificent," with "the most modern equipment available." The Gunnar mine also built a seven-bed facility nearby. Three physicians practised at Uranium City in 1959, more than in the rest of the north combined. Meanwhile, the far north's Aboriginal communities continued to rely primarily on the services provided by overworked Public Health nurses.[23]

While the experience at Uranium City demonstrated that the province could provide adequate medical care in remote areas, the province chose to leave La Ronge in the category of medical have-not communities. On the surface it seems surprising that the provincial government neglected the health needs of this area's residents. After all, this rapidly growing community served as the primary northern government and tourist centre. One feasible explanation for the ongoing neglect of medical needs there is that the CCF looked at revenue generated in an area and the racial composition of the population when deciding what services to provide. Revenues the province received from tourism at La Ronge remained small compared to those generated by the mines at Uranium City. Also, the La Ronge area population included a large number of Aboriginal people and many fewer white people than at Uranium City. No other explanation seems likely for the CCF refusal to provide health care at La Ronge. The province did not build an outpost hospital there and only began part-time Public Health nursing services in 1950. Even the federal government made a better response to the desperate need, posting an Indian Health Services nurse there. Unfortunately, the busy nurse often refused to see non-Indian patients. The provincial Public Health nursing position became full-time in 1953, but the province expected Nurse Broome to cover a huge area, including Montreal Lake, Deschambault, Stanley Mission, Foster Lake, Wollaston Lake, and Reindeer Lake. Lacking even an office, Broome first worked from her home, then out of a trailer she bought, then from the Fire Control building, and by 1957 from a rented cabin. Emergency calls interrupted planned clinics, and she carried a large workload, with residents, tourists, transients, and miners depending on her at all hours. Although a part-time nurse and IHS provided some help, Broome viewed her patients as neglected. When the badly overworked Broome asked for a ten-month leave in 1958, the lack of medical care became even more desperate. Shortly before, in 1957, Dr. Irwin described La Ronge as "our busiest centre." Yet the village still had no hospital or doctor. The two doctors who had some responsibility there, Irwin of Public Health and Stoker of IHS, both lived in Prince Albert and worked largely as administrators. A physician finally established a private practice at La Ronge in 1958, and after sixteen years of minimal medical care under the CCF, the La Ronge hospital opened in 1960, built by the federal and provincial governments at a cost of $500,000. The facility greatly increased services, with twenty staff and a capacity of twenty-five patients. Yet La Ronge continued with only one doctor, which limited use of the hospital, including for surgeries that could not be performed by one doctor alone.[24]

Although non-Aboriginals formed a large percentage of the population in the Creighton and Denare Beach area, Saskatchewan provided virtually no medical services there. The CCF relied on Manitoba to care for Saskatchewan residents of the area. This arrangement seemed sensible, since nearby Flin Flon, Manitoba, offered relatively advanced medical and hospital facilities. If Saskatchewan had provided these services it would have meant an expensive duplication of efforts. Manitoba also provided public health services to Creighton and the boundary area, receiving reimbursement from Saskatchewan and Creighton. Saskatchewan Public Health retained responsibility for Denare Beach, about fourteen miles from Creighton, although it provided little service there. While there were discussions with Manitoba about taking over this work, the matter lost urgency by 1964. Denare Beach's school closed, and area children received public health services at school in Creighton.[25]

Most areas of the north continued to lack adequate medical services by the 1960s. Statistics paint a misleading picture. In 1960 the north had five physicians, one sanitary officer, about thirty-five nurses and nurses' aides, five midwives, and approximately 124 hospital beds, which provided 6.9 beds per 1,000 persons, compared to 7.6 per 1,000 for the province. These statistics falsely suggest a reasonably high level of medical care.[26] But doctors lived only at Île-à-la-Crosse, Uranium City, and La Ronge. Nurses also lived in relatively few settlements. This left dozens of settlements in the vast area without any medical services. The large Wollaston Lake-Reindeer Lake area, with its growing settlements of Southend, Kinoosao, and Wollaston, received no provincial hospital or nurse from the CCF. Since outpost hospitals resembled clinics more than hospitals, the figures on hospital beds also mislead. Outpost hospitals remained a cheap alternative to more adequate care. By 1963 building costs for the outpost hospitals since 1944 totalled $76,261.04, an amount less than the cost of one fish plant built in the mid-1950s. Yet these small, understaffed facilities provided medical care for much of the north. Even late in the CCF era, the entire west side had no public health nurse; Regina had repeatedly ignored Dr. Irwin's request for a budget to hire one. This nursing shortage particularly affected remote areas like Canoe Lake, where in 1961 about 145 Non-Status Indians and whites lived among the Status Indian population. Dore Lake also still lacked regular public health services in 1964. A school had opened there in 1961, attracting about 140 people formerly scattered at Dore, Smoothstone, and other lakes. While well aware that this settlement existed, the CCF did not offer its residents even the regular care of a visiting public health nurse.[27]

Scanty medical care combined with dismal living conditions and sometimes inadequate parenting skills to cause a high number of infant deaths. Hundreds of newly born children died, including many whose deaths appeared preventable. During six months in 1958, for example, of twenty-one infant deaths, nine died "unattended" by medical personnel. Five of eight who died from respiratory infections had not received treatment in hospital or at an IHS station. Respiratory infections and gastroenteritis, both often treatable conditions, claimed many lives. The government knew that improved health care could make a difference and save lives. In 1958 Dr. Irwin blamed some "needless infant deaths" on inadequate medical care in "really isolated areas." With an air of resignation, G. Kinneard, director of the Regional Health Services Branch, thought needless deaths would continue to occur. And the problem did continue. From June to August 1963, twenty-two infants died. Dr. Irwin wrote: "For the most part, northern Saskatchewan is an 'underdeveloped' country and all the methods and skills being employed elsewhere in the world, should be tried closer to home." Yet these circumstances did not stir the Regina-based government to action.[28]

Certainly, the infant mortality rate could have been much higher. The shift to births in hospitals, where nurses/midwives delivered most babies, did save lives. Public Health required its nursing supervisor and outpost hospital supervisors to have midwifery certificates. Aboriginal women welcomed the opportunity to give birth in one of the outpost hospitals. By 1963 the percentage of northern births in hospitals stood near the provincial average, with few mothers dying in childbirth. While the province encouraged expectant mothers to use the hospitals, problems occurred. Not knowing when their child would come into the world, women often arrived at the hospital much too early. This overloaded the outpost hospital facilities. Additionally, some midwives complained that pregnant women had "very high expectations of service" when they went to hospitals for their "annual vacation." There was a decline in births at the outpost hospitals by 1964, to 77 from 104 in 1952, largely due to the referral of more difficult cases to larger hospitals. Although women did not like to go to the more distant hospitals, they often arrived there long before the birth, causing accommodation problems. The establishment of hostels at La Ronge and Île-à-la-Crosse by 1960 helped alleviate the situation.[29]

Dual jurisdiction, where the federal government cared for Status Indians and Saskatchewan for other northern residents, caused endless problems in the provision of medical care. Since 1945 Indian Health Services had fallen under National Health and Welfare, yet the department only slowly expanded its services in the north. As a result, when there was much sickness among Indians in 1947, the Fish Board arranged for treatment. Even after IHS increased its services, the province still often provided health services to Status Indians at outpost hospitals. Although Ottawa paid for some of this, Public Health felt burdened and considered the reimbursement inadequate. At Stony Rapids, expectant Indian women often arrived days or weeks before the birth of their baby, sometimes bringing along another child. Mothers also escorted sick children and stayed at the hospital. IHS refused to pay the full rate for the extra care. Eventually IHS operated its own nursing stations at La Ronge and Sturgeon Landing and a hospital at Pelican Narrows. By 1960 an IHS doctor "periodically" toured the north, and IHS nurses visited some reserves.[30]

Since neither the provincial or federal governments devoted adequate budgets to northern health care, Public Health and IHS often traded services. Problems resulted, though, because IHS split northern Saskatchewan into two areas, with the Athabasca area administered from Edmonton and the rest from an IHS office in southern Saskatchewan. Public Health found the Edmonton office particularly difficult to deal with. As an example of the difficulties, a federal "Treaty party," which provided travelling medical care while distributing annual treaty payments, refused to x-ray some Metis in the Athabasca area in 1954 in spite of a high rate of active TB. Treaty parties elsewhere did x-ray non-Indians. When responsibility for the Athabasca area shifted to IHS in Regina by 1955, cooperation between the two levels of government likely improved.[31]

The thinly stretched health care services would not have adequately met the needs of even a relatively healthy population. Yet Aboriginals suffered more from some diseases than did non-Indians, much as they had during an earlier time when affected by epidemics brought by the white man. During the CCF era, poor sanitation, housing, and diet aggravated a possible lack of immunity to some diseases. In 1964 Indians still died of measles at a rate about twenty times greater than the general population. Influenza and the often related pneumonia or upper respiratory infections also killed Indians at five to twenty times the national rate.[32]

Medical officials focused considerable attention on two diseases: venereal disease and tuberculosis. They often spoke of the two in the same breath. But while government could force treatment for VD, it could not do so for TB. In the 1940s, Northern Administrator J.J. Wheaton described these diseases as "in a very disastrous state." Public Health's Dr. Totton thought the greatest need existed among Status Indians, although IHS offered few services to them. Diagnosis and treatment of VD improved under the CCF, and cases of advanced syphilis declined in number. By 1960 Dr. Irwin, while admitting the north had a higher rate of VD than elsewhere in Saskatchewan, complained about the stereotype that said "every resident of northern Saskatchewan is suffering from venereal disease." The incidence of VD appeared to rise with increased contact with white people, particularly lower-class white people as opposed to richer tourists and government workers. The north had 163 cases of gonorrhea and five of syphilis reported in 1963. Increased staffing might have brought a more rapid improvement. At the end of the CCF era in 1964, not even one follow-up visit took place per case.[33]

Tuberculosis proved even more devastating, continuing rampant among Aboriginal northerners long after it subsided among whites. TB remained the leading killer of Indians until 1952. Although treatment became commonplace, it disrupted lives, since the average length of stay in southern sanatoria stood at almost thirteen months. The Saskatchewan Anti-Tuberculosis League, not the province, provided most TB services, paid for with fundraising, municipal levies, provincial and federal payments, and user fees. League sanatoria operated at Fort San, Saskatoon, and Prince Albert. Additionally, some Indians received treatment at IHS hospitals. Metis also suffered from TB, comprising 20 percent of new cases in 1950 while making up less than 2 percent of the population. There were great breakthroughs in the treatment of TB by the early 1950s. Diagnosis efforts increased, BCG vaccinations began, and streptomycin came into general use, all helping greatly. The death rate from TB among Canadian Aboriginals fell to 60.1 per 100,000 by 1954 from 579.1 per 100,000 in 1946.[34]

Isolation and the low level of medical care meant that northern Aboriginals felt the devastating effects of tuberculosis more than did those in the southern part of the province. Even though diagnosis and treatment programs had expanded by 1950, tuberculosis still killed forty NAD residents that year. This number included twenty-three Status Indians, although they formed only about 34 percent of the region's population. The northern TB death rate stood at 400 per 100,000, compared to a provincial rate of 18.5. The league stepped up its efforts to diagnose the disease among northerners. In 1952 Miss J. Walz, a former outpost hospital nurse, began to work for the League in an aggressive program using portable x-ray equipment. At La Loche alone the project discovered twenty-three active cases in 1953. The general infection rate stood at 62 percent, reaching 89 percent in the twenty to twenty-four age range. In eighteen months Walz visited most northern settlements, tested 7,021 people, and gave BCG to 2,383 people. Outpost hospitals also administered the vaccine, but only sporadically. At Buffalo Narrows in 1957, for example, only one of forty-nine newborns received the vaccine. The BCG program for infants still looked shaky in 1964, partly because of varying attitudes among nurses to the vaccine.[35]

The League continued its campaign against the epidemic. It provided x-ray equipment, paid for with federal grants, to the outpost hospitals at Cumberland House, Sandy Bay, and Buffalo Narrows. Ottawa also helped by sending a doctor and x-ray equipment along with most of its annual Treaty parties. Additionally, the expansion of the road system allowed the use of heavier and more reliable x-ray machines transported by vans. The province seemed less interested in participating in the battle. Although his department received the x-ray machines at outpost hospitals free of charge, Dr. Irwin protested the League charging Public Health $82.55 for chemicals and film at Sandy Bay. He wrote: "This is only the beginning of what may be an expensive proposition." DNR, as the municipal government for much of the NAD, did pay substantial sanatoria levies to the League. In a typical situation it paid $25,000 for 1957. The concerted efforts led by the League brought positive results, reducing the northern TB death rate to forty per 100,000 by 1960. As the disease declined, northern patient days in sanatoria fell from 25,169 in 1956, to 7,083 in 1963.[36]

Statistics do not adequately convey the difficulties tuberculosis brought to northerners. In addition to the suffering caused by illness and early death, extended stays in southern sanatoria disrupted the lives of survivors and their families. Patients from the north needed to adjust not only to institutional life, but also to life in the south, where all sanatoria were located. Many feared treatment, partly because many early patients who went south died. Although fears eased as the treatment success rate improved, northerners still resisted moving to the institutions. This resistance resulted in higher expenses and reduced efficacy of treatment. Patients frequently "eloped," fleeing for home. One young girl, afflicted with advanced TB, broke her hip jumping from a second-storey window. Many others escaped successfully. In July 1959, for example, four patients "eloped." The same month, three received disciplinary discharges, including a man who refused to keep a cast on his tubercular ankle, an insolent young woman, and an elderly drunk. Robin F. Badgley of the University of Saskatchewan wrote that, at the first admission, sanatoria gave Indians a "warm welcome," but on readmission patients received "severe treatment."

One sanatorium director reportedly said to a returning Indian, "Well, you black bastard, you're back are you." While the law did not provide for forced detention, compulsion took place. Efforts to force treatment included using the RCMP to return runaways and treating some in locked mental wards. In 1961, with the Prince Albert Sanatorium scheduled to close, it seemed the elopement problem might worsen, since northern patients needed to go even farther from home for treatment.[37]

Much of the credit for the rapid reduction of the incidence of tuberculosis during the 1950s and 1960s belongs to advances in treatment. Thanks to the efforts of the Saskatchewan Anti-Tuberculosis League, northerners quickly benefited from the new methods of diagnosis and treatment. For its part, the CCF failed to lead the attack. Neither it nor the league provided a northern treatment facility in spite of the epidemic proportions of the disease there.

Northerners also suffered from various chronic medical conditions, including those brought on by aging. Yet government did not build or fund even one northern nursing or special care home. In contrast, the south had sixty-four government-supported or -licensed special care homes or housing projects in 1962. Northern Aboriginals could apply for admission to southern geriatric centres and nursing homes, but few did so. The Department of Social Welfare admitted that selection methods gave Status Indians little chance of admission to seniors' homes and housing. As well, many feared going to southern chronic care homes, partly because they viewed southern care facilities as "graveyards." In one case an outpost hospital cared for a seventy-five-year-old diabetic and arthritic widower for ten days, but could not give him long-term care. In another instance in 1951, DNR saw the plight of seventy-six-year-old Andrew Raun, a blind Cumberland House area trapper who lived "in a deplorable, filthy state in his cabin on the Mossy River." Officials seemed convinced that he could not continue to live alone in the bush, but the north had no facility to care for him. Although Raun badly needed income from trapping, and area trappers approved of him trapping near his cabin, DNR refused him a beaver permit. After he set his traps anyway, DNR charged him with illegally trapping six beaver. Reverend Parker, the Justice of the Peace, fined Raun $250 and $4.50 costs, which represented more than one year's blind pension for the man, or sixty days in jail. Raun went to jail. DNR and the Justice of the Peace seemed less concerned about the trapping violation than about protecting the blind man from himself. While in jail he had an operation on his toe nails, which possibly had not been cut for years. E.L. Paynter, game commissioner, wrote: "It is quite a problem to know just what to do with people like this. Many of them think they should have the right to live and die as they wish ... I am inclined to recommend that the proceeds of the fur involved should be given to him." While politicians and officials could see that many old and ill people required care, government provided no facility to care for them. Many preferred to manage as best they could in the north, rather than move to the culturally distinct south, far from their family and community.[38]

Given the small number of clinics and hospitals in the north, many residents lived far from the nearest facility. Since most communities lacked road access, air transportation provided the only method of quickly moving patients to obtain treatment. The prohibitively high cost of air travel made government assistance essential for Aboriginal and other patients. Appropriately then, as a major aspect of its plan to improve health care, the CCF established the Air Ambulance Service in February 1946. It charged patients a fee of twenty-five dollars plus ten dollars per passenger for in-province flights, a rate that continued unchanged in 1958. But this program again demonstrated how the CCF provided a lower level of service in the north than in the southern part of the province. In the south the service had its own planes and staff. By the late 1940s it expanded rapidly from having only one plane based in Regina to also operating from a Saskatoon base. It used four planes and its own pilots and nurses. In contrast, charter flights carried most northern patients, often without escorts.[39]

The CCF's top official in Prince Albert, the northern administrator, oversaw the transport of northern patients, authorizing chartered medical flights. Patients frequently needed to travel to Prince Albert. In those cases he also arranged ground transportation and patient care in and outside hospital. Because of the distance from home, patients who needed to remain near medical care often stayed in Prince Albert for long periods of time. DNR expected them to pay for transportation and accommodation if they could afford to do so. Otherwise government paid for them as indigents.[40]

With provision made for air evacuation of patients, Public Health's Dr. Totton thought patients should come to the doctor, rather than the other way around. Other officials agreed. In 1948, when Mrs. Baptiste Misponas refused to get on the plane that came to take her to the hospital, the province rigidly followed this policy. Although her husband asked for a doctor to visit her, DNR's Allan Quandt said, "It is to be assumed that the lady will die unless her condition changes for the better."[41]

Sometimes the air ambulance system worked as planned in the north, and planes arrived to transport patients. But at times the lack of a specialized northern service jeopardized lives. While the CCF claimed that Saskatchewan Government Airways (SGA) planes would carry northern patients, the system failed on the day in 1948 when Clements Bradfield gave birth at the north end of Montreal Lake. She became very ill, and local women attending to her could not help. Early in the morning, Harold Udey drove Clements' husband, Ben, to the DNR Bittern Creek Radio Station, about fifty miles to the south, to radio for an airplane and doctor from Prince Albert. Udey later claimed that the DNR radio operator in Prince Albert said no doctor was available and gave the impression that no plane would come without advance payment. It seemed a Bradfield from Montreal Lake had not paid previous bills. Unexpectedly, a plane soon left Prince Albert bound for Île-à-la-Crosse, with Dr. Lavoie and Nurse Walz on board. Having heard of Mrs. Bradfield's plight, the pilot made a detour to Montreal Lake. While people on the ground heard the plane's engine at about 10:30 in the morning, low cloud prevented the pilot from landing and he flew on to Île-à-la-Crosse. Even though the cloud soon lifted, no other plane came. Clements died at about 3:00 p.m. Officials refused responsibility, in spite of complaints from Udey and Reverend G.J. Waite, who buried the woman. Northern Administrator Wheaton thought it odd that no one had driven the sick woman to Prince Albert. Seemingly implying that the Bradfields were not among the deserving poor, Deputy Minister Hogg told Premier Douglas that the Bradfields had not taken advantage of work opportunities earlier that year. Udey wrote to Douglas reminding him of a recent speech he gave at La Ronge in which he said "the plane was available for all and that payment for same was not a factor." Waite, who said he had voted for the CCF, wrote: "Under the Communism of the Provincial Govt. it looks as if dollars are worth more than lives." Wheaton refuted the charges of communism, blaming Liberal propaganda. Waite's second letter to Wheaton referred to Phelps as "Dictator J. (Stalin) Phelps" and to the CCF "Soviet system."[42]

The lack of a dedicated northern air ambulance system also adversely affected other patients. In another incident, for example, official business took priority over a medical emergency in 1948. A government official and a pilot were flying north in a radio-equipped Stinson when they received a call regarding a sick Indian girl at Burnt Lake, southwest of Reindeer Lake. Not wanting to stop, they flew on to Wollaston Lake. The two finally landed at Burnt Lake the next day. Since the girl seemed too ill to sit up in the plane, they left without her. Had the girl lived in southern Saskatchewan and required air evacuation, a suitable plane, complete with medical staff and equipment, would have arrived promptly.[43]

Even though the northern air ambulance service remained inferior to that in the south, it continued to operate. Northern patients, rich and poor alike, came to depend on the flights. During 1949, for example, planes transported a hundred patients, including seventy-five carried by SGA. Hospitals admitted fifty. Fourteen died. The province allowed carefully chosen persons to authorize flights. By 1954 DNR officers, Dr. Hoffman, outpost hospital nurses, and some local designates performed this function. The posting of Dr. Irwin to Prince Albert after 1954 also helped improve the service. Compassionately, he "stressed that it was better to call nine planes for ambulance cases if in doubt, than to let one patient die." Service improved by the early 1960s, at least for the southern area of the north. Then the specialized planes and staff from Saskatoon sometimes flew to Île-à-la-Crosse, La Ronge, and Cumberland House. But the system still depended heavily on commercial aircraft to carry patients. This continued to prove unreliable at times, including when DNR commandeered aircraft to fight forest fires. In those cases, pilots refused to fly medical flights without DNR's permission. Since most northern communities did not receive hospitals or road access by 1964, the area's residents continued to rely on aircraft to carry them to medical facilities. The service made 199 emergency flights in the north in 1962-63.[44]

Without doubt the air ambulance program provided a much-needed service to northerners. But the province discriminated against northerners by providing an inferior service compared to that in the south. This situation extended to practically all other areas of northern health services. Most northerners received little beyond the most basic health services from the government, which considered things like optical and dental care as luxuries. As a result, white residents often obtained these services outside the region, while Aboriginals usually did without.

Although northerners suffered from vision problems much to the same extent as people in the south, the north had no resident optometrist by 1964. Some visited occasionally. In a rare initiative, Public Health arranged for an optometrist to travel to six communities in 1949. He supplied sixty sets of glasses. Another went north in 1955, and one again in 1957, visiting twenty schools with 1,429 students. A lack of funding jeopardized the project. Yet Uranium City received a much higher level of optical care. About 90 percent of its residents received service in Edmonton, and Prince Albert optometrists also visited there. By the 1960s, after IHS hired an ophthalmologist, Status Indians often received better care than did the Metis.[45]

A similar situation applied to dental care. No dentists lived in the north, other than at Uranium City, and white northerners obtained most dental services outside the region. With the movement to settlements and the accompanying change to a southern diet, Aboriginal dental health likely deteriorated after 1944. Their dental care remained deplorable, causing great suffering. The medical doctor from Île-à-la-Crosse, Dr. Hoffman, did many extractions, and emergency flights carried some dental patients south. Some in government recognized the dire need to improve dental health. In 1954 several officials, including C.S. Brown, northern administrator, and Dr. A.E. Chegwin, the director of Public Health's Division of Dental Health, wanted the province to institute a northern dental service. Ottawa had recently begun a program for Status Indian children, and Chegwin felt pressure to match this. But the CCF refused to institute the program. Instead, Public Health helped pay for the odd clinic, including one described as "an orgy of extractions."[46]

Public Health officials who saw the need did not give up; they continued to pressure their political masters for funding. Unfortunately, the department again failed to obtain funding in 1955. This time, the Budget Bureau refused to grant $8,500 to pay for two dentists to each provide five weeks' annual service. After the CCF refusal, the Junior Red Cross began a five-year pilot project at Cumberland House and Île-à-la-Crosse in 1957, with a budget of $15,000. At seven Cumberland House clinics, dentists performed 851 extractions and 1,577 fillings. Eight Île-à-la-Crosse clinics provided 927 extractions and 2,061 fillings. The program brought a great improvement in child dental health in the two communities. Dr. Irwin also arranged for a Prince Albert dentist, Dr. E.J. Gaudet, to visit Sandy Bay in 1962, where in five days he saw 158 patients and did 303 fillings and 727 extractions. Gaudet's rapid work led to controversy within government, but Dr. Irwin defended the quality of the dentist's care.

The five-year Red Cross project clearly demonstrated the advantages of providing dental care to children, but when it ended, the CCF refused to continue, let alone expand, the program. The Red Cross and a National Health grant then funded the program for an extra year at Cumberland House and Île-à-la-Crosse. Children in most other communities still received virtually no dental care.

A.E. Chegwin prepared to leave Public Health in 1963, but before leaving he vehemently condemned the CCF record, including its failure to implement recommendations from the Sigerist report from the 1940s. He called the lack of northern dental service "discrimination with a vengeance" and made a last effort to expand the northern children's dental program, asking for a $20,000 cost-shared program. The CCF refused the request, even though Ottawa approved $10,000.[47] IHS continued to provide superior dental care to Status Indians, holding twice-annual clinics using private dentists. In contrast to the province, IHS also located modern dental fixtures at the Beauval Indian Residential School and La Ronge Hospital.[48] At the time of the CCF defeat in 1964, northern dental care for most northern residents remained minimal. Several officials, including Irwin and Chegwin, had tried to improve the situation, but the CCF refused to devote money for even a modest service. The existence of two standards, under which those who moved to the region from outside received care while many of the region's original inhabitants did not, formed part of the CCF's northern colonial world.

Malnutrition, caused in part by poverty and an inadequate diet, also affected the health of many northerners. The province involved itself in combatting dietary deficiencies by encouraging gardening and combining nutrition programs with education. Teachers gave out cod-liver oil, powdered milk, and hard biscuits, although the programs remained sporadic and inadequate to meet the need. For several years in the 1940s the CCF provided $100 per classroom for noon lunches. But, claiming abuse by those who ran the programs, government took over central control of purchasing. Cuts also took place. In 1948, after the CCF ended school lunches at the north end of Montreal Lake, a teacher there appealed to the Red Cross to provide them. He described the people as "badly undernourished," with many bringing dry bannock and lard for lunch. By the early 1950s the federal government, concerned about the nutrition of Status Indian children, helped redesign the aircrew survival rations biscuit to meet the needs of a ten-year-old boy. Finding them "reasonably acceptable to Indian School Children," the government annually gave out thousands of pounds of the hard biscuits, which had a shelf life of about five years.[49]

Dr. Hoffman found "critical" malnutrition among children at La Loche, possibly the north's poorest community. He repeatedly tried, and failed, to have DNR fund a nutrition program. At the time, the Department of Education provided only twenty-five cents per year per child for this purpose. In 1962 a CCF official from Regina, Ray Woollam, visited La Loche and told Premier Lloyd about the situation. Yet an inspection by Doctor Irwin and other officials did not confirm the complaints and found the Catholic sisters at the school providing hot chocolate and vitaminized biscuits to the children. A report described the children's nourishment and clothing as no worse than elsewhere in the north. This statement possibly served more as an indictment of the sorry state of nutrition in other communities than as an absolution of the situation at La Loche.[50]

Several more thorough studies pointed to severe nutritional deficiencies. A 1956 National Health and Welfare study found health defects, many of which proper nutrition could improve, in about three-quarters of subjects.[51] A project at Pinehouse and Pelican Narrows from 1958 to 1961 demonstrated that close supervision by a nurse or teacher could improve nutrition and hygiene. Once the study ended, problems returned, aggravated by desperate living conditions in the settlements.[52] As in other areas of northern health and welfare, the province devoted very little money and effort to improving nutrition. Parents and the community also sometimes failed to carry out their responsibilities in this area, leaving the children to suffer.

Further problems, health as well as social, resulted from alcohol abuse. For too many Aboriginals, the government-encouraged movement of people to settlements brought a shift from occasional sprees to chronic drinking. A relatively idle and unsatisfying existence in settlements, which often supplanted active lives on traplines and in fishing camps, fostered drinking. Replacing credit with a cash system also increased alcohol use, since traders no longer managed customers' incomes to make them last. Both provincial and federal bureaucrats soon recognized the relationship between the arrival of fur cheques and heavy drinking. A movement grew among provincial and federal bureaucrats to pay for furs in monthly installments. Since the effort remained half-hearted and trappers resisted, the plan failed.[53]

Society increasingly stereotyped Aboriginals as alcohol abusers. With some justification, officials and other whites blamed increasing northern crime and social problems on Aboriginal alcohol use. Nearly all manslaughters occurred after the killer drank. V.F. Valentine, the anthropologist, wrote that "aggression and hostility characterizes Metis behavior while drunk." Speculation suggested that Aboriginals drank because liquor made them into an "Ogimow," or big man. The Center for Community Studies thought a high level of anxiety led to excessive drinking, and that Aboriginals had not internalized the controls of white society. Less academic analyses suggested Aboriginals could not handle liquor or just liked to drink.[54]

The health and social problems created by drinking were aggravated by the CCF setting a double standard for the sale of liquor in the north. In colonial fashion it allowed outlets in communities with large white populations, while denying them for Aboriginal villages. Restricting access to alcohol in effect criminalized drinking for many northerners and drove determined drinkers to imbibe unsafe substitutes for alcohol. Status Indians could not legally drink in Saskatchewan until 1960. To combat bootlegging, Joe Phelps tried to open beer parlours to Indians, but cabinet rejected this idea. Later, Douglas and the CCF did support giving Indians the right to drink, and beginning in 1960 they could do so off reserves. But Indians still could not drink on reserves after 1960, which added to the public drunkenness seen in northern towns. Although the law did not prohibit Metis from drinking, the government used its regulatory power over the sale of liquor to attempt to prevent them from drinking. As a result, even most larger northern communities had no place to legally buy liquor. Lacking legal access to alcohol, Aboriginals who wanted to imbibe relied on bootleggers, homebrew, and alcohol substitutes.[55]

The province particularly opposed easy access for northern Aboriginals to the relatively cheap liquor sold in liquor stores. Likely partly because of its fear that Aboriginals would obtain large quantities of spirits, the government also did not want to see liquor stores even in predominantly white communities. As a result, northerners who wanted to drink commonly did so in beer parlours or "licenced premises." Alcohol served by the drink cost much more than that from a liquor store. This raised the cost of drinking, leaving less money for essentials. The province issued licences for beer parlours at Denare Beach and Goldfields, communities with many white residents, before 1950. With white people, both residents and visitors, demanding access to liquor, Northern Administrator C.L. MacLean wanted additional licensed premises for the "more progressive areas." He thought it time to give northerners a voice. But while residents preferred a liquor store to licensed premises, he did not want them to have that choice. The CCF considered La Ronge, with its large white and tourist population, a suitable place for a beer parlour. Even though it suspected a majority opposed the outlet, the CCF allowed a new hotel to open a beer parlour and bar in 1952. In the coldest weather, a group of concerned La Ronge men made sure that drunks ejected from the premises arrived home without freezing to death. The village received its first liquor store only in 1958.[56] In contrast to the situation at La Ronge, the CCF opposed a beer parlour for the largely Aboriginal community of Buffalo Narrows in the early 1950s, even though a petition signed by 161 people favoured an outlet. DNR minister Brockelbank unrealistically wanted the local people to cooperatively control bootlegging instead. About four years later, even with church and widespread community support for the legalized sale of liquor, the hotel still could not sell beer. Eventually some easing of restrictions to liquor access took place, and in a few cases officials allowed local votes to determine if communities should have beverage rooms. Buffalo Narrows and Cumberland House held votes by 1962.[57]

The province's policy of limiting northern access to legal alcohol increased reliance on questionable alternatives. Instead of reducing bootlegging, CCF policies likely increased this activity and did little to slow the bootleggers' business. Carried by planes into remote settlements, bootleggers sold the liquor for about ten times its normal value. For those communities with road access, taxis served as the primary liquor haulers. Stories circulated about liquor-laden taxis arriving in Aboriginal communities at the same time as welfare and fur cheques. Even though the CCF introduced a licensing system for cabs, these problems continued. Enforcement efforts also had little effect. In 1957, for example, the Village of La Ronge and the DNR both worked to put one notorious taxi operator out of business. Northern Administrator C.S. Brown described him as "a thorn in everyone's side," who "contributed more to the general demoralization of the younger native people in La Ronge than any other person." Yet in spite of crackdowns, taxis continued to carry liquor to Aboriginal communities.

Many people found cheaper alternatives to bootleg liquor. Some developed skill at fermenting potatoes and other things. A Sandy Bay resident later derided Walter Hlady, the CCF anthropologist, for writing that the community's homebrewed "molly" lacked potency. He claimed Hlady himself passed out from drinking the brew. Traders also sold large quantities of vanilla extract to people who baked few cakes. Many of those desperate for a drink risked their health imbibing household cleaners and cosmetic products. Late in the CCF era, Aboriginal communities still depended largely on costly illegal liquor and dangerous substitutes. Even though they used various cheaper alternatives to bottled liquor, Hlady estimated that Sandy Bay residents spent 20 to 30 percent of their total income on alcohol. Similar situations existed in numerous other settlements.[58]

The government preferred to limit Aboriginals' access to alcohol instead of introducing educational and treatment programs. Although everyone knew that the control efforts failed dismally, the CCF provided virtually no alcoholism treatment in the north. In the Uranium City area, with its predominantly white population, the Alcoholism Foundation of Alberta provided a limited program. Even those in southern Saskatchewan who suffered from alcohol problems received little help. The Bureau on Alcoholism opened its first counselling and referral centre in Regina only in 1959.[59]

Neglect and discrimination characterized provincial policies and actions in numerous areas of health care from 1944 to 1964. While it helped alleviate some blatant problems, the CCF devoted insufficient resources to meet northern medical needs. Northerners received an overall level of service far below that in the south.

In addition to health and welfare programs, CCF northern social policy included a crucial third area, that of education. Believing that education could bring the changes it desired to the north, the new government quickly implemented an aggressive program of universal, secular schooling. From long experience, governments knew that taking Aboriginal children into schools offered the opportunity to more effectively mould their young minds. CCF educational expansion, along with family allowances and the restructured economy, pushed Aboriginals into settlements. Although he objected to describing CCF educational efforts as "disruptive," J.H. Brockelbank admitted that education forced people into settlements and "changed their way of life, which was one of the intentions of the whole program." Clearly education played a major part in the CCF effort to assimilate northern Aboriginals. Colonial methods served the CCF when educating northerners. Administrators and teachers from outside the region designed and implemented education programs with virtually no local consultation.[60]

The CCF had no detailed information about the state of education in the north, so soon after its election victory it sent C.H. Piercy north to survey the educational system. Piercy made a whirlwind trip through the region, gathering statistics and impressions. His subsequent report strongly criticized the existing situation, which saw the churches provide most education and left many communities without a local school. Piercy found nineteen schools in six categories: Indian day, Indian residential, private day, private boarding, community day, and public schools under the School Act. Of 1,164 children aged six to fifteen, about 568 received no formal education, and no schools operated in eighteen settlements or areas. Since the School Act required attendance only if people lived within two-and-a-half miles of a school, many who attended school did so voluntarily. White children in remote areas often took correspondence courses, with 117 doing so in 1944. Only seven of seventeen teachers held first-class certificates, while some had no qualifications. The situation uncovered by Piercy appalled observers and confirmed CCF fears of an inadequate, priest-dominated education system.

Piercy made various recommendations calling for aggressive government intervention. He visualized one large northern school unit that would encompass all areas. The new system would include many new day schools and two boarding schools, one for the east and one for the west. As in residential schools, education would include practical training, with those in the upper grades devoting half of their time to learning work skills. Piercy preferred to hire female teachers, especially where they and a nurse could share accommodation to combat "solitude and loneliness." Teachers would receive improved housing and an increase in pay. They would also move at least once every three years to ensure they did not adopt Aboriginal standards and lose their inspirational value. Additionally, Piercy wanted northerners to help pay for the new system. He called on the CCF to survey and assess property and collect school taxes.[61]

During subsequent years, the CCF based numerous educational policies on Piercy's recommendations. In his position as education minister from 1944 to 1960, Woodrow Lloyd supported and oversaw the plan for educational reform. The CCF implemented Piercy's plan for one large northern administrative area, even though the vast size of the north created ongoing problems. Since some areas of the school unit were five hundred miles or more from others, and control over northern education remained in the south, communication proved challenging. The province also created the Northern Areas Branch of the Department of Education to oversee northern schooling. Piercy himself spearheaded the effort to reduce the churches' role and introduce a universal, secular, northern education system. As the administrator of education, he worked from his headquarters in Prince Albert and wielded great power, simultaneously carrying out the functions of "principal, supervisor, superintendent, chief executive officer and school board." Yet Piercy thought the north did not need his full attention, and at his request he also became the school superintendent for the city of Prince Albert. T.H. Waugh, who took over in 1949 when Piercy retired, also held much power. In the mid-1950s he was principal for twenty-one centres and superintendent for Creighton and Uranium City. K.C. Hendsbee replaced Waugh by 1958.[62]

The new educational system included some minimal provisions for local input and control. Cumberland House's organized school district, which dated back to the 1930s, continued in operation. In communities that had not organized as school districts, the School Act required the election of three-person local school committees. They looked after school property and made recommendations to the province, though they held little real power. The province also tried to involve local people by having them pay for education. Beginning in 1949 a ten-mill education tax on assessed property helped buy fuel and pay a caretaker, but this taxation remained a largely token effort. In 1949 operating costs for schools totalled $82,230.65, while the tax levy stood at $4,450 with only $1,973.78 collected. In 1964 taxes and grants in lieu of taxes provided only $22,397 of expenditures of $1,029,525.[63]

Piercy and the CCF wanted to remove the churches from their role in educating northern children. The province thought the state could "more efficiently" educate children than the church could. However, recognizing the necessary role residential schools played in educating the children of the still-migrant population, Piercy wanted to see two new residential schools established and operated by government. This plan did not proceed, it would seem largely because the federal government did not help implement it. Ottawa favoured a continuing role for the churches in educating Status Indians in residential schools and did not join the CCF in its attack on the northern church-run schools. The federal government wanted to increase the number of residential schools, but it accepted church involvement. Roman Catholic schools taught many Status Indians, and Ottawa's ongoing support for these institutions explains their survival in northern Saskatchewan.[64]

The CCF plan to push the Catholics out of education did cause alarm on the west side. The church feared that Piercy's desire to build a government boarding school at Île-à-la-Crosse would lead to closure of its day and boarding school. In addition to Ottawa's lack of support for the CCF plan, L.M. Marion, the Liberal MLA, came to the church's aid. The province then agreed to rent classroom space from the mission, pay teachers' salaries, and help pay the students' board. Piercy also failed in his effort to pay mission teachers less than the full salary scale of $1,200 per year. Contrary to his wishes, Roman Catholic education continued to dominate and even thrive on the west side. The Roman Catholics built several new schools at Île-à-la-Crosse by 1964, where nuns and lay teachers taught 331 pupils from kindergarten to grade eight. About one hundred children, many of whom stayed in the mission's boarding facilities, came from outside the community. Roman Catholic residential education also continued in a series of schools at Beauval. Additionally, Catholics offered education at La Loche. With CCF fervour against church-run education easing, the Northern Advisory Committee went so far in 1954 as to encourage the Catholics to open a new residential school at La Loche. But while the church seemed willing, the Department of Education refused to pay a rate per child of one dollar per day, and the plan did not go ahead. Buffalo Narrows, a newer community on the west side without the tradition of church education, received a succession of secular schools.[65]

Roman Catholic involvement with education also continued at Cumberland House. In the 1960s the school's staff of five still included two nuns. Voluntary religious instruction took place after school hours, taught to Catholics by a nun and to Protestants by a Protestant teacher.[66] The CCF also allowed religious instruction to take place in other schools where desired by the local people.

In contrast to the survival of Roman Catholic schools, the Anglican presence in education practically disappeared. For a time the Anglicans shared the education of children with the Roman Catholics and the province at Cumberland House. Anglicans also had long operated the All Saints Residential School at La Ronge. Piercy targeted this school for replacement by a government residential school. While this plan did not proceed, the Anglicans did not rebuild All Saints after it burned in 1947. With church-led education gone at La Ronge, secular education took place at Old Gateway School. Pre-Cambrian School opened in 1958 as an integrated school, with Ottawa paying $158,130.03 of the cost. This was the first provincial school in the north to teach home economics and shop work. New Gateway School was constructed by 1961.[67]

The CCF government also wanted to take over educating Status Indian children from Indian Affairs. Both governments often worked together to educate Status Indians, and Indian Affairs schools on reserves followed the provincial curriculum. Strong support for integrating all Status Indian students into the provincial system came from T.C. Douglas. For a time it appeared that the federal government would transfer educational responsibilities for Status Indians to the province, and in 1948 the Special Joint Committee of the Senate and House of Commons recommended educating Status Indian children alongside other children. The new Indian Act of 1951 helped increase integration, although Roman Catholic opposition likely contributed to the new act not following the JCSHC recommendation to abolish church schools for Status Indians. By 1953 a federal-provincial agreement provided for integrated education at Pelican Narrows, and numerous similar agreements followed. Even Aboriginal senator James Gladstone opposed building schools on reserves. There was a consensus that Status Indians needed to attend integrated schools to prepare them for the larger world. Teaching Status Indians also provided money to the province, since Indian Affairs paid tuition fees and a portion of capital costs. It covered about 28 percent of northern school construction costs from 1945 to 1962. Yet in spite of the shift to provincial education, most of the north's 1,311 Status Indian students in 1965 still attended Indian schools or the Beauval Indian Residential School. The once-powerful tide that had strongly pushed for integration also lost force. As an early sign of things to come, in 1955 Chief Simon Linklater of Pelican Narrows wanted Status Indian control of their education. He also wanted to see more emphasis on teaching "Indian ways of life" and opposed educating Indian children in residential schools.[68]

In spite of disappointing efforts to take over education from the Roman Catholics and Indian Affairs, the CCF expanded the province's educational presence in the north. By 1948 it had built twelve new schools and five new teacherages and almost doubled the number of teachers. About thirty teachers taught 1,261 students in eighteen schools. A small number of students attended high school outside the region. In 1950-51, for example, ten students received government assistance to do so. School attendance in provincial schools continued to rise because of the Aboriginal population explosion, pressure on parents for children to attend school, the arrival of white families attracted by mining, and Status Indian children attending Saskatchewan schools. Expansion continued. During its first ten years in office, the CCF provided twenty-one new schools, ranging from one-room portables to nine-room schools, and eleven new teacherages. Sixty-four teachers, including eighteen Roman Catholic sisters, twenty-seven other women, and nineteen men, taught in the north in 1954-55. Enrollment totalled 2,213. By 1957-58 there were 104 teachers and 3,137 students, and only five one-room schools remained. The province also gave some encouragement to adult education and offered some night classes and basic English instruction, though these efforts remained extremely limited.[69]

In order for the CCF to meet its goal of providing a modern Canadian education to the scattered northern population, it needed to spend large amounts of money. Teaching the isolated, largely illiterate, and non-English-speaking population should have required a much higher level of per capita spending than in the south. Yet the CCF funded northern education at a lower level. Capital and operating costs combined, from 1946 to 1962, stood at 86 percent of that for Saskatchewan schools overall. Northern capital expenditures from 1945 to 1962 totalled $1,188,246, an inadequate amount in view of the dozens of communities that needed schools.[70] Few northern schools received the amenities enjoyed by southern schools. To cut costs, the Department of Education rejected DNR deputy minister Hogg's suggestion in 1948 that it build a large hall at the Cumberland House school that could be used to show motion pictures for adult education. Hogg wanted northern schools to double as community centres, but government did not provide the money for this.[71] Some areas remained without a teacher or school. At Cree Lake in 1952, local people expected Junior Field Officer Berezowsky, who was once a schoolteacher, to teach the ten school-age children.[72] While Kinoosao did receive a school and teacher in about 1952, the teacher, Frank Remarchuk, lived in the school since the community still had no teacherage.[73] Schools in Aboriginal areas also had a higher ratio of students to teachers than those in southern school units. In 1950-51 teachers in "Metis Schools" taught an average of 39.3 students compared to 20.3 in other school units. This situation improved gradually, and by 1964-65 "Metis Schools" enrolled 22.1 students per teacher, a similar ratio to that in southern schools. By the time Douglas left provincial politics in 1961, northern education remained basic and without frills. Most northerners who wanted to attend high school still needed to move to the south. Relatively few did so.[74]

The CCF's strong early interest in northern education faded by the 1950s and 1960s. Various factors justified the government's reluctance to spend much on northern education. A continuing low level of northern tax funding and weak demand from northern parents for education contributed to this. Possibly more importantly, the belief that Aboriginals should pursue traditional, nonindustrial vocations reinforced the view that they did not need much education. Government also concluded that Aboriginals would not, and possibly could not, benefit fully from educational opportunities. Expanded education opportunities had only slowly increased northern Aboriginal literacy and educational achievement. Many northerners still could not sign their names, and large numbers remained outside school. Exceptions existed. Some communities, including Cumberland House, seemed to have a higher acceptance of and level of education, possibly due to a longer history of education there.

Without doubt the CCF efforts to educate Aboriginals proved disappointing. Most Aboriginal students did not progress as the system expected, with some needing four years to complete grade one. In a typical situation, of ninety-three students at Sandy Bay in 1959, twenty-three attended grade one while grades eight and nine had only two students each. Northern Aboriginal students often dropped out by grades four to six, rather than at grade eight or higher as occurred in urban schools. In the early 1960s only 3 percent of students in northern provincial schools, outside the organized areas, were in grade nine or higher, compared to 25 percent for the province overall.

But reasons other than limited student ability appeared responsible for the low level of achievement. Many children remained outside schools. At Buffalo Narrows in 1951-52, for example, only 57 percent of the eligible children aged six to fifteen attended school. Erratic attendance, not speaking English well, and a lack of kindergartens contributed to underachievement. Since they could help prepare the non-English-speaking and culturally distinct students for the coming years in school, kindergartens appeared particularly important. But the first kindergarten opened only in 1957. The scarcity of northern high schools also contributed to the small number in higher grades.[75]

Clearly the province failed to introduce an educational system tailored to the needs of northern Aboriginal students. In some cases, poorly trained teachers and an inappropriate curriculum hampered the success of CCF educational plans. On average, northern teachers possessed lower qualifications than those in the south. While teacher training improved, by 1962 only 32 percent of teachers outside the mining areas held Professional Standard Certificates, compared to 52 percent in the province overall. Most teachers also lacked preparation and training for the unique challenges they would face in the north. Some special training for northern teachers took place in the early 1960s, when Father André Renaud offered a summer course at the University of Saskatchewan. Overall, though, little specialized training existed. A high rate of teacher turnover aggravated teaching problems. Inexperienced teachers often fled the north after only a short time there. And in spite of some efforts to create a northern curriculum, teachers continued to inculcate southern knowledge and values. Only late in the CCF era did government make a substantial effort to reexamine the inappropriate curriculum. A Curriculum and Text Book Committee was set up after the Center for Community Studies released a report in 1963.[76]

In contrast to the situation in Aboriginal villages, white communities benefited from culturally appropriate curriculum and enjoyed educational facilities comparable to those in the south. Uranium City received a $50,000 four-room school in 1953, shortly after its founding. Much expansion followed. The community obtained the first high school in the north in 1958. Private industry also helped educate white students in the Uranium City area; Gunnar and Eldorado mines opened their own schools. In the Creighton area, in exchange for exemption from land, property, and business taxes, the Hudson Bay Mining and Smelting Company paid many education costs. The company first helped pay for students to attend school in Flin Flon and then gave a new four-room school to Saskatchewan in 1950. At Island Falls, Churchill River Power Company paid the teachers who taught white students in the company school.[77]

Improving working conditions for northern teachers held importance for the CCF. The construction of modern teacherages, even in isolated poverty-stricken communities, allowed teachers to live in relative comfort. A welcome break from the isolation of northern communities came when teachers attended the annual teachers' convention in Prince Albert. Government also paid other transportation costs for teachers placed in some remote communities. The province standardized teacher benefits, and their pay, which came from central office, included isolation bonuses of up to $300 per year. However, reflecting society's values of the time, married men's salaries included an additional $250.[78]

The province recognized and repeatedly spoke of the need for vocational training to improve use of traditional resources and provide new skills to northerners as the viability of traditional occupations declined. However, the CCF offered no vocational education programs within the region. The Roman Catholics made more concrete efforts to provide vocational training than did government. In 1958 Father Chamberland of the Beauval Indian Residential School offered carpentry and motor mechanics training to five people, three of whom found jobs in the south. He also taught "domestic science, children's care, and home making" to about ten women. When the priest wanted the Department of Labour to certify the school for apprenticeship training in 1959, A.H. MacDonald, director of Northern Affairs, preferred that the CCF start its own program. Yet the departments of Labour and Social Welfare seemed unwilling to take the lead. Father Darche of Buffalo Narrows also set out to teach vocational skills to Aboriginals. In 1959 he wanted the Young Men's Centre at Buffalo Narrows to offer trade and cooperation training. He hoped to combat the spread of social aid and help unemployed young men find work. This time

MacDonald recommended the Treasury Board approve a matching grant of up to $10,000.[79]

Instead of training Aboriginals in the north, the CCF brought a small number of people to southern schools. The lack of high school and vocational training in the north and the resulting movement of some students to take education in the south fit with the belief some held that the north could not provide a viable future for Aboriginals. But the CCF did not wish to move northerners to the south. The primary reason for poor educational opportunities in the north simply was the CCF's refusal to spend much on northern education. Likely the largest vocational education program for northerners operated in the early 1960s, when the province brought young men and women to attend the Canadian Vocational Training Centre in Saskatoon. Yet the CVTC program proved disappointing, since only 55 percent of students completed a three-month course and the market did not need the semi-skilled graduates. Saskatchewan also tried using the CVTC program to train northern farm workers, including some from Cumberland House, but this did not work out either.[80]

By the time the CCF left office in 1964, its attempt to educate northerners had brought largely disappointing results. Many who had spent years attending school remained illiterate, and most northerners continued life with a very low level of education. At the same time, government policies and actions had helped destroy the viability of the traditional economy, increasing the need for a formal education. The new education system established by the province in the north, particularly that in Aboriginal communities, remained inferior to that in the south. Government also failed to move responsibility for education in most communities to northerners, retaining colonial control over education from Prince Albert and Regina.

The CCF consistently devoted inadequate resources to meet northern needs in the crucially important areas of welfare, health, and education. In spite of greater needs and higher service delivery costs in the north, in many instances the CCF spent less per capita on northerners than on southerners. This government encouraged and frequently coerced northerners to accept its socialist vision for the north. Aboriginals were to share with each other by using socialist forms of organization while pursuing traditional economic activities. Through its resource taxation and royalty policies, the CCF also required northerners to share their region's wealth with the south. Yet the CCF version of socialism did not share Saskatchewan's social programs equally with the disadvantaged of the north. In addition, the CCF dreams for the northern Aboriginal economy and society did not come true. As a result, after twenty years of CCF interventions, northerners found themselves mired in hopelessness and poverty.

Epilogue
We Will Measure Our Success

As the second decade of its time in office neared its end in the early 1960s, the CCF knew that its economic and social programs had not created a northern utopia. Instead, the region's economic malaise and social dysfunction clearly had worsened. The government also could see that it had not achieved its goals of modernizing and assimilating northern Aboriginals. Neither had it convinced most northerners to embrace socialism. Lacking other answers, the CCF maintained its hope that community studies and community development would lead the way to a brighter future.

By August 1963 the northern research of the Center for Community Studies, overseen by Arthur K. Davis, had produced sixteen papers. Of these, the centre's director, W.B. Baker, chose *The Indians and Metis of Northern Saskatchewan: A Report on Economic and Social Development* as the official summary report. Premier Woodrow Lloyd and the CCF approved of the document, which gave them a clear direction to follow for northern programs. The report called on the CCF to take the primary role in developing the north. It suggested a twenty-three-point development program that included mining, forestry, mink ranching, agriculture, and government service – at a projected cost for the first year of more than $1.8 million. Under the plan, community development would continue to play a crucial role in implementing northern change. The centre referred to the fur area councils, the ratepayers' associations, and cooperatives as institutional parts of the community development process. However it said the CCF needed to improve its development methods. Few projects qualified as true development projects since the CCF spent most of the program budget on roads and minor infrastructure projects.

While it criticized some aspects of the CCF programs, the centre told the CCF what it wanted to hear. The report absolved the CCF of most blame for northern problems, ignoring much of the negative role the CCF had played in the northern colonial world. Instead the report's authors blamed the HBC and the churches for colonialism, even though the CCF had long ago dethroned these old rulers. The centre flattered the CCF by depicting it as a liberating force that strove to give control to northerners. Government accepted the report and hoped it would guide "policy and procedures for many years to come."[1] Optimism grew as it seemed that the CCF northern saga might still have a happy ending. The centre's analysis of problems and its detailed list of solutions offered hope that, with the commitment of large monetary and manpower resources, the CCF might yet reach its goals for the north.

Yet the official report and the new northern plan soon lost credibility. The primary attack on these came from within the centre, from Davis and numerous other respected senior staff researchers. After years of extensively studying the north, they had developed very different ideas about what the CCF should do there. These researchers, many of whom possessed careers independent from their work for the centre, seemingly were not afraid to depict the situation with detachment and impartiality. In contrast, the centre's dependence on CCF goodwill for its survival may have influenced its report. The dissenters thought the CCF and the centre had a strong bias that called for "cultural pluralism" and "local self-development" and would not allow for radical new approaches to dealing with the north. The newly defined CCF goals seemed meaningless to their opponents. Cultural pluralism contradicted active assimilationist policies, and "developing" Aboriginal communities without addressing the lack of an economic base made little sense. Davis and his cohorts claimed cultural pluralism would not work in northern Saskatchewan, condemned the CCF's community development work, and called for a large-scale movement of people from the north to southern urban centres. The CCF continued to support the centre's official report and the plan for tinkering with the existing northern economy and society. It also rejected the dissenters' ideas, including their call for moving northern Aboriginals into the more active economy of the south.

W.B. Baker suppressed the findings Davis and the others wanted released, and they left the centre. Davis described the dissenting reports as "not very radical or 'hot'," but they criticized CCF policies and "did not fit the 'bleeding heart' approach" of the official report. He predicted that "Baker's censorship will probably wreck the Centre." While Baker tried to block those who left from publishing their findings, the CCF government, just before leaving office in 1964, agreed to publication. Although greatly delayed, *A Northern Dilemma: Reference Papers* incorporated the work of numerous scholars, primarily distinguished sociologists and anthropologists, including P.M. Worsley, Herbert C. Taylor, Henry Zentner, Philip T. Spaulding, Vernon C. Serl, Arthur K. Davis, William D. Knill, Harry B. Hawthorne, and Cecil L. French. The suppression of their work had largely succeeded, though, since their report remained obscure, while the centre's official report received promotion and saw large circulation.[2]

The Center for Community Studies did not recover from the controversy. An employee wrote: "The Centre is still operating and will continue to do so *until and if* the time that Thatch – the Snatch – gets into office and decides to throw us out! However, I have even heard comments from some Liberals who claim that we are necessary, and that we will continue in existence after they get in." The optimism proved unfounded, and after their 1964 election victory the Liberals reduced funding to the centre. Premier Ross Thatcher thought the program wasteful and nonproductive. The centre's record of telling the CCF what it wanted to hear also did not help it survive, and it soon closed.

The CCF never had a chance to try the recommendations made in the centre's report. Whether Lloyd and his colleagues actually would have spent the millions of dollars on northern programs called for by the centre remains a matter for speculation.[3]

In the spring of 1964, Thatcher and his Liberals defeated the tired twenty-year-old CCF government. The north that the CCF handed over to the Liberals bore little resemblance to the region in 1944. Changing times had brought some of this alteration, but much of it came because of CCF intervention. The party could point to some of its achievements with pride. Health care initiatives had helped reduce infant mortality and increase life expectancy, new schools ensured that most children could learn to read and write, roads reached some villages, and most Aboriginals lived in houses arranged in rows on surveyed lots in settlements. On the other hand, CCF failures stood out clearly for all to see. The new north included a social malaise and a dysfunctional economy incapable of supporting the exploding Aboriginal population. Northerners and onlookers from outside alike saw little hope for a bright future. Many of the region's more than twenty thousand people subsisted in village slums. Families rarely trapped or fished together anymore, since these had become activities for men. Women cared for children in the settlements. Although cash had largely replaced credit as the northern currency, an increasing amount of the money came from welfare programs.

While it had succeeded in bringing major change to the north, the CCF failed to meet practically all of its objectives for the area and its people. In many respects the region remained stuck in the past, even more so than northern areas in neighbouring provinces. Modernization of the infrastructure system had stalled primarily due to the CCF losing enthusiasm and refusing to spend the money required to build modern transportation and communication systems. A lack of infrastructure profoundly diminished economic development and prosperity. Some roads penetrated the north, but most areas remained isolated. Since not even large companies could operate profitably in an area without infrastructure, development and various related benefits remained limited. Uranium City, Saskatchewan's uranium capital and northern showpiece, relied more on links to

Alberta than to Saskatchewan. Creighton, adjacent to the large mine at Flin Flon, dealt more with Manitoba than with Saskatchewan. Fish caught on Reindeer Lake and other east-side lakes moved to markets through Manitoba. Most communities also lacked links to the provincial electrical and telephone systems, and no radio or television stations broadcast within the north.

Efforts to modernize other aspects of the northern world also failed. The CCF had sought to build a new and up-to-date economy there. Its dream for the north envisioned non-Aboriginals labouring in the governmental and industrial sectors of the economy while Aboriginals happily and prosperously earned their livelihood from updated trapping and fishing industries, supplemented by income from farming. But while career opportunities for non-Aboriginals did expand, trapping and fishing declined in importance. Fur and fish prices and production could not keep pace with the rapidly expanding population, and poverty engulfed Aboriginal workers. Additionally, CCF control and ineptness in the area of agriculture ensured that farming's potential to support northern Aboriginals was not realized. Further, a lack of facilitation for Aboriginals to work in government administration, mining, forestry, and tourism helped rule out those promising sources of livelihood. While the number of jobs held by non-Aboriginals from outside the region could have eliminated Aboriginal unemployment had they held those positions, neither the CCF nor industry seriously tried to move Aboriginals into that work. As a result, extreme poverty afflicted nearly all northern communities during the CCF era. Northerners increasingly relied on welfare instead of on the north's abundant resources. For the Aboriginal population in 1964, economic problems seemed much worse than they had twenty years earlier. Hope largely had disappeared.

The government's plans to modernize and expand social programs also did not meet expectations. While the province arranged for its natural resources officers to pay out increasing amounts of social aid, payments per recipient remained at a level far below that in the south. Also, much as before, only one or two southern-based social work staff served the area. The burgeoning need for child welfare, counselling, and preventative services went largely unmet. Medical care remained rudimentary in most areas of the north. Widely spaced outpost hospitals, usually staffed by a lone nurse, could not meet more than basic medical needs. Most communities had no medical personnel or facilities. The larger hospitals available in several northern centres could not adequately treat many patients, and northerners frequently travelled to the south or an adjacent province to obtain medical, optical, and dental care. In the field of education, the CCF greatly expanded elementary school education opportunities, but the new system did not meet Aboriginals' learning needs. Achievement levels remained low. Few aspired to obtain a high-school education, and most who did so had to leave their home communities for the south. Further, the CCF provided no post-secondary education in the north.

As part of its effort to modernize the north, the CCF had effectively toppled the Roman Catholic and Anglican churches from their traditional positions. The provincial government's actions also reduced Aboriginals' reliance on the HBC and other traders. Unfortunately for the people of the region, government failed to replace the old church- and trader-dominated society with a workable alternative.

In its second major initiative, the CCF sought to assimilate northern Aboriginals into Canadian society. The party did not understand or respect the value of Aboriginal culture, considering it not worth preserving. To aid with assimilation, the CCF speeded nucleation of the formerly migrant population into villages. By the end of the CCF era, few northerners still lived in the bush. Another part of the province's plan for assimilation involved taking over responsibility for Status Indians from the federal government. The CCF hoped this transfer would lead to using only one set of rules and programs for all citizens. After a partial transfer of jurisdiction from Ottawa to Saskatchewan, the process stalled. Overall, though, the CCF partially met its goal of assimilating Aboriginals, since Indians and Metis adopted many Euro-Canadian ways. Yet twenty years of applying assimilative pressures helped create a people who could not function as whites or Aboriginals, and dependency on the state increased.

The CCF achieved even less success in reaching its third goal of creating a northern socialist economy and society. Northerners consistently resisted the government's efforts to implant socialist ideals and structures. Imposed economic programs that relied on socialist forms of organization lasted only as long as the colonial masters administered them. During the CCF era, numerous Crown corporations operated in the north in addition to those that typically provided services in the south and in other Canadian jurisdictions. The CCF used Crown corporations to impose public ownership within a number of the region's main economic sectors; these included trapping, fishing, forestry, retail sales, and air transportation. In time the CCF increasingly turned to a modified form of cooperatives to implement its programs, although it did so with the heavy hand of compulsion and control. Northerners would "cooperate," whether they wanted to or not. Simultaneously, while building structures inspired by socialism, the CCF strove to reduce the power and role of a wide range of private enterprises. In a related effort, the CCF kept strict control of almost all land. Through its frequent insistence on leasing rather than selling commercial, agricultural, and even residential property, the province limited and blocked private development.

Perhaps more northerners might have welcomed the CCF's brand of socialism had it included sharing the province's wealth equally with northern residents. But the party primarily limited its socialist plans for the region to redesigning the economy. Politicians and bureaucrats feared that an equal sharing of the province's wealth would spoil the Aboriginal people, who then would inappropriately take advantage of the generosity. The CCF used that line of thinking to justify providing only miserly social welfare, health, and education benefits to the not-yet-deserving poverty-stricken northern masses. The southern-based party showed great callousness in ignoring the worsening plight of northern Aboriginals. While Tommy Douglas said, "We will measure our success by what society does for the underprivileged, for the subnormal, for the widow, for the aged and the unwanted child," apparently CCF concern did not extend equally to northern Aboriginals.[4]

The pre-eminent place the CCF gave to socialist economic policies in its northern program contradicts its record in the south. Numerous previous studies have concluded that this was not a strongly socialist government.[5] Yet an examination of the CCF's northern record reveals that many in the party felt a passionate devotion to socialist philosophy and policies. In numerous ways the CCF made clear its preference for replacing traditional capitalist institutions with those that bore a socialist mark. Replacing Hudson's Bay Company and other privately owned stores with government-owned retail outlets, taking over the pre-existing airline industry, forcibly substituting government enterprises for private logging and wood-processing companies, legislating private fish processors out of business and building government-owned processing plants in their place, creating and enforcing a government monopoly on the purchase and resale of furs, introducing various government marketing boards, restricting private land ownership, reserving the right to take over mineral extraction from the private sector, and numerous other policies and actions all represented a dramatic change from the way things were done in northern Saskatchewan before and after the CCF era. Socialist ideology, whether "pure" or not, drove much of the CCF effort in northern Saskatchewan. No other compelling explanation exists for many of the CCF policies and actions.

Those who have suggested that the CCF abandoned many of its socialist ideals in exchange for power have based that observation on the party's record in southern Saskatchewan. The power of southern voters helped ensure that CCF socialism in the south fit within the region's predominant free enterprise agricultural and small business tradition. In contrast, northerners lacked the voice and electoral clout to determine CCF policies for their half of the province. Most southerners cared little what the CCF did in the northern bush. That indifference granted the CCF free rein to dictate socialist-inspired solutions for the north.

A newly constructed colonial apparatus allowed the CCF to impose its ideas and plans in the north. The government relied on its planning mechanisms in Regina and Prince Albert to design the futures of northerners. Paternalistically, little consultation took place with residents of the region, who lacked genuine and meaningful input into CCF plans. Colonial bureaucrats applied projects within the north. Although the colonialism became somewhat more subtle as the CCF era evolved, compulsion and direction from outside continued to characterize the administration of provincial programs in the north.

Strong and directive government characterized the CCF era. The party possessed confidence that it could forcibly introduce change, thinking that in time the objects of its wise planning would recognize the greatness of the gifts given them. Northerners found themselves powerless to repel the CCF's well-meaning onslaught. After all, southerners outnumbered northerners by nearly a hundred to one in 1944, and northerners lacked effective representation in the legislature, with only two representatives. Many northern Aboriginals also did not possess the necessary language and other skills to influence the CCF.

Yet the CCF northern experiment failed to modernize, assimilate, or socialize northerners. Failure occurred for three primary reasons. First, after a quick and energetic start under Joe Phelps, the CCF did not devote the quantities of energy, money, and personnel needed to implant and sustain change. While the party had ambitious plans for the north and the region's people, in reality it neglected this half of the province and its population. Second, in spite of its image as an intelligent government, the CCF's research and planning mechanisms failed. Douglas and his colleagues never gained an adequate understanding of the north or its people. Without a plan based on realistic analysis, even well-intentioned efforts to deal with problems were little more than stabs in the dark. And finally, the colonial government's efforts failed because it refused to involve northerners in planning and implementing changes. Although northern votes mattered little, northerners largely determined the fate of CCF plans. Resistance in various forms characterized the Aboriginal response to the CCF plans. In both active and passive forms, local resistance helped block government from meeting its goals. Resistance gave northerners some power, if not in designing CCF plans, at least in determining the outcome of CCF projects.

Contradictory influences determined the shape of CCF interventions in northern Saskatchewan. Without doubt, socialist ideology accounted for much of what this government did in the region. Additionally, though, CCF politicians and bureaucrats acted as products of their time, influenced by various nonsocialist and nonpolitical beliefs and attitudes. As a result, to examine the CCF record in northern Saskatchewan also illuminates Canadian society in the first two decades after the Second World War. Saskatchewan's idealists often behaved in ways similar to nonsocialist governments elsewhere in Canada. The mixing of a preference for socialist solutions with various other influences explains many of the contradictions that plagued Douglas's government. Often the party appeared simultaneously enlightened and unthinking, compassionate yet unfeeling, and tolerant but bigoted.

The presence of ideological contradictions and impurities raises the intriguing possibility that those inconsistencies may explain many of the CCF's failures in the north. Perhaps more socialism, not less, would have brought a happier ending to the story. Unfortunately, the historical record cannot offer firm answers about what might have happened had the planners and bureaucrats applied untainted socialist principles to the design of their northern programs. But evidence does suggest that northern Aboriginals would have resisted any imposed foreign programs, no matter how pure or well-intentioned. Possibly even more than they opposed the socialism of the CCF, many northern Aboriginals resented the CCF desire to remake their lives. It seems unlikely that Aboriginal northerners would have embraced any outside efforts to bring rapid, directed change to their society.

Similarities exist between northern Saskatchewan and other areas in the vast Canadian north. Yet the CCF era in northern Saskatchewan was unique in many respects. While governments in other parts of Canada also expanded their northern presence in the postwar years, none relied heavily on socialist ideas for guidance in designing policies for the region. Other governments established Crown corporations and operated some businesses, but none did so to the extent seen in northern Saskatchewan. Neither did any other jurisdiction attack free enterprise or the capitalist system with the fervour of the Saskatchewan CCF. In its north, that party sought to stamp out pre-existing capitalistic participation in numerous areas of the economy.[6] No other region of Canada allowed socialist philosophy to determine government policies to the extent that occurred in northern Saskatchewan.

The CCF presence left a lasting mark on northern Saskatchewan. Conservation efforts helped bring about a long-term restoration of fur and game stocks. Cooperatives, whose origins dated back to the CCF cooperative development programs, struggled on in some communities, helping meet residents' needs. CCF programs increased Aboriginal participation in fishing and trapping, a legacy that still lives on in those industries. Northerners continue to live in the villages selected by CCF planners and laid out by government surveyors. And some of the old roads built by the CCF still carry people and goods. While some of these things proved to be mixed blessings, they became part of northern Saskatchewan.

Clearly negative signs of the CCF presence also remained after 1964. In the opinion of many, then and now, an unfriendly business climate and fear of socialism did depress economic development under the CCF, and a legacy of severely limited infrastructure remained throughout the northern region, restricting possibilities for communities, individuals, and industry. During subsequent years, northerners, industry, and governments worked to overcome the severe underdevelopment in the tourism, forestry, and mining sectors that characterized the CCF era. Less tangible effects also endured. Bitterness towards powerful and interventionist governments remained. Some northerners who remember the CCF still vigorously condemn that government and its actions. The effects of the CCF and its policies on the residents of the north should not be overlooked or taken lightly.

As the chapters of this book demonstrate, CCF programs shaped northern Saskatchewan and made a difference. But often those differences, both positive and negative, seemed dwarfed by larger forces that swept across northern Canada. Over several decades the influence of traders and churches declined, traditional Aboriginal ways came under attack, and interventionist governments extended their presence. A malaise increasingly overwhelmed the region during the CCF era and following years. Observers who looked at northern Canada often saw little but problems, both economic and social. Dismal statistics gathered in northern Saskatchewan closely resembled those from other areas of northern Canada. Canadians across the northern reaches of the nation lived with high rates of illiteracy, unemployment, poverty, welfare dependency, and social problems. Few northern areas enjoyed a viable economy.

The CCF clearly underestimated the seriousness of the growing economic and social dysfunction that came to plague the north, but it is possible that northern Saskatchewan would have followed other northern areas of Canada in a similar downward spiral even if the CCF had not intervened. And if Douglas and his party had not worked to dismantle the old system in the north and speed its demise, in time other factors likely would have brought an end to the old ways. In some cases CCF efforts did little more than speed or slow that process.

No matter how inevitable the increase in northern problems may seem, however, the evidence demonstrates that the CCF intervened aggressively in northern Saskatchewan. The CCF tried to do things differently. Its members firmly believed that their socialist philosophy would make a positive difference in the lives of northerners.

The primary reason for emphasizing the socialist and other northern policies of the CCF is not to blame the CCF for failures in the region. Instead, knowing the history of the CCF era in the north allows observers to see the CCF legacy, even today. It helps those who wish to know about northern Saskatchewan understand why the region developed as it did. Similarly, the purpose of providing evidence of CCF socialism in the north is not to condemn socialism as an ideology. But this information does add to the ongoing discussion of the nature of the CCF and socialism in Saskatchewan. Based on the information presented here, my contention is that the CCF was a socialist party to a greater degree than observers often recognized. Admittedly, this book sometimes does not portray CCF socialism in a sympathetic light. Neither does it support the CCF's interventionist modernization, assimilation, and colonial policies. The various policies applied by the CCF worked together to overwhelm the north in an unprecedented intervention.

From their point of view, northerners endured twenty years of CCF intervention in their lives. Those two decades brought the destruction of much of the traditional northern power structure, economy, and society. The CCF ensured that parish priests, bootleggers, and fur sharks no longer dominated the north. In time, the day of the CCF also passed.

Appendix A
Comments on Collection of Oral History

The collection of information for this study included interviewing numerous people who lived in the north during the CCF era as well as some who worked there for the CCF government. Meeting the people who lived in the north and hearing the details of their stories added a dimension of reality to the research experience. Various older audiotapes of interviews with CCF politicians also provided information. Both types of interviews proved extremely valuable in some respects. They particularly provided a sense of the deep emotions that surrounded the CCF northern interventions. Dedicated politicians and bureaucrats believed they acted in the best interests of the province's residents, including northerners. On the other side, many northerners disliked and resisted the new and intrusive government presence. Although Tommy Douglas enjoyed nearly universal respect among those interviewed, few northerners had positive things to say about the party he led. Almost forty years after the defeat of the CCF, passions still flare at the mention of its name. Written sources do not convey the depth of this feeling. Oral accounts help provide a sense of what really happened in the north during the twenty years of CCF government and allow the researcher increased intimacy as an observer of this history.

Differences of opinion exist about the value of oral history in helping provide an accurate image of the past. Supporters of the use of oral history sometimes privilege these memories about the past, claiming them to be equally or more valid than original written records. Others question the reliability and value of orally transmitted historical accounts, thinking them affected by faulty memory, wishful thinking, or outright dishonesty. This debate appears particularly relevant for northern Saskatchewan. A large number of the region's Aboriginals possessed only limited literacy and wrote little about themselves or government. On the other hand, government bureaucrats filled thousands of files with their written observations about northerners. To look at only written sources means viewing the relationship between the government and northerners through white, male, bureaucratic eyes. Yet the researcher should not ignore government files. These have proven a surprisingly rich source of information, divulging many candid comments and observations and revealing much about the CCF politicians and bureaucrats who worked with and within the North.

While valuable in other respects, interviews proved unreliable for providing accurate details about various events in the north. Many of those interviewed, both on tape and informally, had poor recollection of when things occurred. Some interviewees claimed they had a poor memory and likely could not remember much of value. Even those who thought they could remember events frequently confused decades and governments. Some trappers who trapped during the CCF era did not recall that government's compulsory fur-marketing policies. Various interviewees moved seamlessly from one time period to another, as if events in the 1940s and 1980s happened at much the same time. While this perception of events may have merits, it does not supply accurate information about a specific time. Political preferences also influenced some stories, with CCF/NDP supporters viewing events differently from Liberal supporters.

Several examples can demonstrate the shortcomings of oral history. In these cases the oral account does not agree with written sources, and in some cases the spoken word appears clearly wrong. In one instance, Joe Phelps, in an interview carried out by an interviewer years ago, indicated he and his wife toured the north not long after the CCF victory of 1944. He spoke about visiting Uranium City and going down the Eldorado uranium mine shaft. Since neither Uranium City nor the mine existed until about eight years later, what does this say about the other information contained in the interview tape? In another situation, an Aboriginal interviewee in La Ronge described the prosecution of her father for an alleged trapping violation. She spoke about the large number of Aboriginal people lined up for court at La Ronge, leaving the clear impression that they were there because of violations of natural resources policies. Yet original prosecution records and statistics for the north reveal extremely low numbers of prosecutions for fish, fur, and game offences. In another recent interview, a former government employee spoke about going to Cumberland House shortly after the election of the CCF to investigate farming potential there, only to find the people already farming. Yet his written report from over fifty years ago, including a diary of his time there, contradicts this. In writing the report he did not mention much Aboriginal farming. He left the impression that the establishment of farming would take much time and patience because the people did not know the value of farming. Another example of disagreement between oral and written sources comes from Sandy Bay. Walter Hlady, the CCF anthropologist, lamented the heavy Aboriginal drinking of bought liquor and homebrewed "molly." One former resident took offence at Hlady's suggestion that molly lacked alcohol content. The interviewee recalled that Hlady had quite a different experience with molly while at Sandy Bay, including passing out from drinking the brew. In some cases it becomes difficult to know which version to believe.

While oral and written sources do not always agree, and some information obtained from oral sources may lack accuracy and comprehensiveness, oral history has value. The memories of persons who lived through events can confirm or contradict other sources. They also balance archival records, which primarily contain accounts of the actions and thoughts of white, male politicians and bureaucrats.

The literature about oral history in northern Saskatchewan is small. Since few precedents exist, I learned about the pitfalls and benefits of oral history in this situation partly by trial and error. In one of the few relevant studies, Keith Goulet compares oral and written history about Sandy Bay. He concentrates largely on the history of the dam built by the Churchill River Power Company. In "Oral History as an Authentic and Credible Research Base for Curriculum: The Cree of Sandy Bay and Hydroelectric Power Development 1927-67, an Example," Goulet concludes that oral history, as given by the Cree elders of the area, provides true and credible information. He finds that other evidence confirms about 45 percent of the oral evidence.

Other writers provide information about oral history in the context of the larger Canadian north. Julie Cruikshank, who has collected oral history in the Yukon, cautions against using positivistic methods to attempt to extract "facts" from oral history and against viewing it out of its social context. Although she points out that both oral and written histories qualify as social constructions, which change over time, she seems to move away from the relativism of postmodernism in her recent work. A positivistic view does allow for one interpretation of history representing the truth more accurately than another. This increases the importance of oral history, since oral history can confirm, add to, or contradict other information. Cruikshank claims that written histories represent the point of view of colonial institutions and that they incorporate, alter, and swallow stories. Robin Ridington, in *Trail to Heaven: Knowledge and Narrative in a Northern Native Community*, provides another model for collecting northern Aboriginal history. He spent time with the Beaver, or Dunne-za, people of northwestern Canada. His research relies on sources not usually used by historians, including myths, visions, and dreams. The role that oral transmission of events can play in a historical study remains controversial. Historians and those in related disciplines need to continue to experiment with and discuss the part oral history can play in enhancing our perception of the past.

As demonstrated by the endnotes, archival and other written sources provided the bulk of detailed information for this study of northern

Saskatchewan, yet oral sources played an important role, influencing much of the tone of this work. Although interviews provided relatively few details about northern events, they exposed the feelings of northerners and CCF politicians, helping bring this research to life. Both types of sources meshed, working together to form an image of Saskatchewan's north from 1944 to 1964.

Appendix B
Electoral Record

Two provincial constituencies, Athabasca and Cumberland, usually covered the entire area of northern Saskatchewan since 1908. Details of northern electoral boundaries frequently changed, but Athabasca generally encompassed the northwestern and far northern areas, while Cumberland contained the southeastern area. At times, Meadow Lake constituency also included part of the southwestern area of the north.

In 1944 northern voters elected the Liberals' Louis Marcien Marion of Île-à-la-Crosse to represent Athabasca and the CCF's Leslie Walter Lee of Choiceland for Cumberland. In that election the Liberals won the Athabasca constituency with 80.7 percent of the vote, compared to 7.4 percent for the CCF. Cumberland voters, who voted nine days later than the rest of the province, voted 58.7 percent for the CCF, compared to 39.7 percent for the Liberals.

Northern voters did not overwhelmingly reject the CCF at the polls. For the elections held from 1944 to 1960, the CCF won six of thirteen constituency contests, while the Liberals won five, the Social Credit one, and an Independent one. Liberals dominated in the southwest sector of the north. The CCF won Athabasca only in 1956 and Meadow Lake in 1960. On the other hand, the CCF commanded more support in Cumberland, where Liberals won only in 1948.

The presence of non-Aboriginal voters likely contributed to CCF northern electoral success. Although most Status Indians belonged to the Roman Catholic church, which often opposed the CCF, they did not receive the provincial vote until 1960. The Metis, also mostly Roman Catholic, quite possibly supported the Liberals more than the CCF. Although Aboriginals outnumbered non-Aboriginals by a margin of about two to one, it is probable that non-Aboriginals comprised the majority of active voters.

Liberal Deakin Alexander Hall represented Cumberland from 1913 until the CCF's Leslie Walter Lee defeated him in 1944. In 1948 Liberal Lorne Earl Blanchard beat the CCF's Joseph Johnson, a DNR officer. CCF candidate William John Berezowsky then won each election from 1952 to 1964. More left-wing than many in his party, he looked for a rise of northern militancy to bring a reformed socialist society to the north.

Liberals had represented Athabasca since 1908. Liberal Louis Marcien Marion won there in 1944, receiving 626 votes to 57 for the CCF. In 1948, Marion, then running as an Independent, defeated the CCF's Axel Olsen. In 1952 Liberal James Ripley triumphed over the CCF's C.L. MacLean. John James Harrop of the CCF took over in 1956. Allan Guy, Liberal, defeated the CCF's Allan Quandt in 1960. Guy won again in 1964.

Liberal Hugh Clifford Dunfield captured the Meadow Lake seat in 1952. In 1956 Social Credit's Alphonse Peter Weber took over as MLA. Martin Semchuk of the CCF won in 1960, while Liberal Henry Ethelbert Coupland proved victorious in 1964.

A number of current and past DNR employees ran for the CCF. Joseph Johnson ran in 1948, Axel Olsen in 1948, C.L. MacLean in 1952, and Allan Quandt in 1960. None won election.

A weak opposition and strong partisan support for the CCF characterized the situation in the legislature during much of the long CCF era. After winning forty-seven seats to the Liberals' five in the 1944 election, in 1948 the CCF dropped to thirty-one seats, while the Liberals rose to nineteen. The CCF recovered somewhat in 1952. Even though it lost much popular support in 1956 and even more in 1960, the party remained in power. The opposition remained weak, since Liberals, Social Credit, and Conservatives often split the vote. The rise of the Social Credit party likely helped the CCF stay in power. In 1956 Social Credit candidates won 21 percent of the vote.

The provincial Tories remained weak during the CCF era. No Conservative won a seat in 1944. The party won one seat in 1948, with 8 percent of the provincial vote. Rupert Ramsay became leader in 1944. Alvin Hamilton led from 1949 to 1957, followed by Martin Pederson.

Walter Tucker replaced William Patterson as Liberal leader in 1946, a position Tucker held until 1953. Asmunder (Mindy) Lopston then acted as house leader until the election of Hamilton "Hammy" McDonald in 1954. Ross Thatcher replaced McDonald in 1959. Thatcher led his party to victory in 1964.

The northern area also elected federal representatives. Mackenzie Constituency included much of northern Saskatchewan, including the far northern area. The CCF's A.M. Nicholson became the MP in 1940 and held the seat until 1949, when he lost to Liberal Gladstone Mansfield Ferrie. Nicholson won re-election in 1953, but again lost in 1958, this time to Conservative Stanley James Korchinski. Nicholson then switched to provincial politics, winning in Saskatoon for the CCF in 1960. He became the provincial minister of Social Welfare and Rehabilitation. While MP for Mackenzie and later as minister of Social Welfare, Nicholson played an active role in northern Saskatchewan.

Prince Albert Constituency covered much of the less remote north, including the La Ronge district. William Lyon Mackenzie King represented the constituency until Edward LeRoy Bowerman, CCF, defeated him in 1945. A Liberal, Francis Heselton Helme, defeated Bowerman in 1949. John Diefenbaker won there as a Progressive Conservative in 1953. He represented the area until 1968, when the area became part of Mackenzie Constituency.

Notes

Introduction

1 The Department of Social Welfare became the Department of Welfare under the Ross Thatcher Liberal government.

2 John Richards and Larry Pratt, *Prairie Capitalism: Power and Influence in the New West* (Toronto: McClelland and Stewart, 1979), 99-106, 126-128, 177.

3 *Saskatchewan Archives Board* [*SAB*], R-38, J.L. Phelps, interview by Craig Oliver, audio tape, April 1965; R-A1113, J.L. Phelps, interview by Murray Dobbin, audio tape, 1976.

4 See Chapter 1 of this book for a more detailed discussion of what socialism meant to the CCF and to other socialists.

5 Department of Natural Resources and Industrial Development, *The Natural Resources of Saskatchewan* (Regina: DNR, 1945), Foreword by J.L. Phelps.

6 *SAB*, S-M15, Box 2, "Canning Equipment, 1945-1946," Correspondence with Fisheries Research Board of Canada; S-M15, Box 2, "Crown Corp. General File," Murray D. Bryce to J.L. Phelps, 18 February 1946; S-M15, Box 5, "Dominion-Provincial Conference, 1945-1946, (1)," "Provincial Natural Resources Policy in Their Relation to the Dominion Proposals"; S-M15, Box 5, "Economic Advisory Board Recommendations, 1945-1946," H.F. Berry to G.W. Cadbury, 15 April 1946; S-M15, Box 8, "McCabe, M.A., Lac La Ronge Plant, 1946-1947," "Radio Address By The Honourable J.L. Phelps," January 1947; S-M15, Box 17, "General Correspondence, 1944-1946. (3)," Sec. of Phelps, to A.F. Barker, 5 April 1946; S-M15, Box 18, "Glycol"; S-M15, Box 18, "Sask. Industrial Development Branch, 1944-1946," H.G. Rondlesome to H. Lewis, 1 November 1945, H.W. Monahan to Phelps, 26 February 1946; Thomas Hector Macdonald McLeod, "Public Enterprise in Saskatchewan: The Development of Public Policy and Administrative Controls" (PhD diss., Harvard University, 1959), 86.

7 Thomas Hector Macdonald McLeod and Ian McLeod, *Tommy Douglas: The Road to Jerusalem* (Edmonton: Hurtig Publishers, 1987), 175.

8 Frank J. Tester and Peter Kulchyski, *Tammarniit (Mistakes): Inuit Relocation in the Eastern Arctic, 1939-63* (Vancouver: UBC Press, 1994); Edith Iglauer, *Inuit Journey: The Co-Operative Adventure in Canada's North* (Madeira Park, BC: Harbour Publishing, 2000). Possibly the clearest examples of similar programs instituted at a later date elsewhere in northern Canada come from the Northwest Territories. The events documented by Tester and Kulchyski and Iglauer for the NWT bear striking similarity to some CCF programs. Part of that can be explained by the hiring of former Saskatchewan CCF bureaucrats to institute programs in the Arctic. Vic Valentine and Paul Godt were two such employees who moved to the federal civil service, working in community development and cooperative development programs in the NWT. While in Saskatchewan, Valentine in particular supported various CCF-led challenges to the old capitalist forces of the north.

9 *Glenbow Archives*, M125, James Brady Collection, s. VI, f. 41, "Metis, 1952-63," P.M. Worsley, "Confidential," "A Provisional and Exploratory General Outline of the Research

Aspect of Contract Program TR-1: The Study of Northern Saskatchewan," 25 October 1960; P.M. Worsley, "Bureaucracy and Decolonization: Democracy from the Top," in *The New Sociology: Essays in Social Science and Social Theory in Honor of C. Wright Mills*, ed. Irving Louis Horowitz (New York: Oxford University Press, 1971), 378. P.M. Worsley of the Center for Community Studies described the CCF as "a government which is favourably disposed to *assisting* the process of decolonization." In 1964 he claimed that the provincial government, "with a markedly co-operative ethos, and a strong belief in popular participation in 'devolved' government, is engaged in decolonizing the province's undeveloped north."

10 F. Laurie Barron, *Walking in Indian Moccasins: The Native Policies of Tommy Douglas and the CCF* (Vancouver: UBC Press, 1997), 202; Philip Ballantyne, *The Land Alone/Aski-puko* (Saskatchewan: n.p., 1976), 136.

11 Geoffrey R. Weller, "Managing Canada's North: The Case of the Provincial North," *Canadian Public Administration* 27, 2 (Summer 1984): 197-209; Geoffrey R. Weller, "Political Disaffection in the Canadian Provincial North," *Bulletin of Canadian Studies* 9, 1 (Spring 1985): 71-78; Kenneth Coates and William Morrison, *The Forgotten North: A History of Canada's Provincial Norths* (Toronto: Lorimer, 1992), chapters 2, 3, and 4; Robert M. Bone, "Summary and Recommendations," in *Regional Socio-Economic Development*, ed. Robert M. Bone et al. (Saskatoon: Institute for Northern Studies, University of Saskatchewan, 1973), 13; W.A. Arrowsmith, "Northern Saskatchewan and the Fur Trade" (master's thesis, University of Saskatchewan, 1964), 79. Various efforts made over the years to unify the different jurisdictions included those by Lew Parres, a Flin Flon mining engineer, and Richard Rohmer, who developed the idea of a Mid-Canada Corridor. These attempts failed and the colonial situation continued.

12 *SAB*, A 1109, J.H. Brockelbank, interview by Murray Dobbin, audio tape, Regina, 19 August 1976; S-M16, A.M. Nicholson Papers, v. VII, f. 3, "Parks and Lands Branch, 1961-63," Brockelbank to Premier Douglas and All Cabinet Members, 10 October 1955.

13 Murray Dobbin, "Prairie Colonialism: The CCF in Northern Saskatchewan, 1944-1964," *Studies in Political Economy: A Socialist Review* 16 (1985): 28. Dobbin sees a third stage, from 1960 to 1964, with the CCF opening the way for neo-colonialism and the future penetration of capital. This appears doubtful as instead, after 1960, the CCF greatly increased the welfare state in the north, and growth of infrastructure and the penetration of outside capital remained small.

14 *SAB*, R-A1113, Phelps, interview by Dobbin, 1976.

Chapter 1: Another Country Altogether

1 Co-operative Commonwealth Federation, "Regina Manifesto," 1933.

2 David Lewis and Frank R. Scott, *Make this Your Canada* (Toronto: Central Canada Publishing Co., 1943), 121.

3 Seymour Martin Lipset, *Agrarian Socialism* (Berkeley, CA: University of California Press, 1971); Walter D. Young, "Socialism," in *The Canadian Encyclopedia*, vol. 3, ed. James H. Marsh, 2nd edition (Edmonton: Hurtig Publishers, 1988), 2035.

4 Frank R. Scott, *A New Endeavour: Selected Political Essays, Letters, and Addresses*, edited and introduced by Michiel Horn (Toronto: University of Toronto Press, 1986), 93.

5 Norman Penner, *From Protest to Power: Social Democracy in Canada, 1900-Present* (Toronto: Lorimer, 1992), 87-103; Alan Whitehorn, *Canadian Socialism* (Don Mills, ON: Oxford University Press, 1992), 35-66.

6 Alan Whitehorn, "Social Democracy," in *The Canadian Encyclopedia*, vol. 3, ed. James H. Marsh, 2nd edition (Edmonton: Hurtig Publishers, 1988), 2025. In this item, Whitehorn offers a definition of social democracy. He points out that social democracy is one form of socialism. Having rejected revolutionary socialism and communist socialism, the CCF chose a version of socialism known as democratic socialism. In the case of Saskatchewan, that meant that before the CCF could institute socialist policies, the citizens of the province needed to democratically elect the CCF. Although often synonymous with democratic socialism, the term "social democracy" may downplay its origins in socialist ideology and seem less threatening to some who oppose more radical socialism.

7 David E. Smith, *Prairie Liberalism: The Liberal Party in Saskatchewan 1905-1971* (Toronto: University of Toronto Press, 1975), 279.

8 Ivan Avakumovic, *Socialism in Canada: A Study of the CCF-NDP in Federal and Provincial*

Politics (Toronto: McClelland and Stewart, 1978), 168-170; Raymond Merle Sherdahl, "The Saskatchewan General Election of 1944" (master's thesis, University of Saskatchewan, 1966), 165-175; Smith, *Prairie Liberalism,* 245.

9 Evelyn L. Eager, "The Conservatism of the Saskatchewan Electorate," in *Politics in Saskatchewan,* ed. Norman Ward and Duff Spafford (Don Mills, ON: Longmans Canada, 1968), 14; Bill Harding, "The Two Faces of Public Ownership: From the Regina Manifesto to Uranium Mining," in *Social Policy and Social Justice: The NDP Government in Saskatchewan during the Blakeney Years,* ed. Jim Harding (Waterloo, ON: Wilfrid Laurier University Press, 1995), 305; Peter R. Sinclair, "The Saskatchewan CCF: Ascent to Power and the Decline of Socialism," *Canadian Historical Review* 54, 4 (December 1973): 419-433.

10 Terms such as "likely" or "probably" represent this writer's best guess. In the absence of firm evidence to support a stronger statement, it is preferable to use a term such as this.

11 A.E. Blakeney, "Saskatchewan's Crown Corporations: A Case Study," in *Proceedings of the Fifth Annual Conference of the Institute of Public Administration of Canada, Saskatoon, September 9-12, 1953,* ed. Philip T. Clark; Harding, "The Two Faces of Public Ownership," 283; Crown Investments Corporation of Saskatchewan and Gordon W. MacLean, *Public Enterprise in Saskatchewan* (Regina: Crown Investments Corporation of Saskatchewan, 1981), 11; Jean Larmour, "The Douglas Government's Changing Emphasis on Public, Private, and Co-Operative Development in Saskatchewan, 1944-1961," in *"Building the Co-Operative Commonwealth": Essays on the Democratic Tradition in Canada,* Canadian Plains Proceedings 13, ed. J. William Brennan (Regina: Canadian Plains Research Center, University of Regina, 1984), 176-177, 290.

12 C.H. Higginbotham, *Off the Record: The CCF in Saskatchewan* (Toronto: McClelland and Stewart, 1968), 66; John Richards and Larry Pratt, *Prairie Capitalism: Power and Influence in the New West* (Toronto: McClelland and Stewart, 1979), 103-105.

13 DNR, *Annual Report,* 1952, Intro. letter from C.A.L. Hogg to J.H. Brockelbank.

14 Lewis H. Thomas, ed., *The Making of a Socialist: The Recollections of T.C. Douglas* (Edmonton: University of Alberta Press, 1982), 293, 349.

15 Richards and Pratt, *Prairie Capitalism,* 139-143.

16 Larmour, "The Douglas Government's Changing Emphasis," 161-167; Thomas, *The Making of a Socialist,* 170.

17 John H. Archer, *Saskatchewan: A History* (Saskatoon: Western Producer Prairie Books, 1980), 281; Avakumovic, *Socialism in Canada,* 174-179; Thomas Hector Macdonald McLeod and Ian McLeod, *Tommy Douglas: The Road to Jerusalem* (Edmonton: Hurtig Publishers, 1987), 181; Penner, *From Protest to Power,* 114-118.

18 Sherdahl, "The Saskatchewan General Election," 158-159, 202-204. Northerners elected the Liberal L.M. Marion of Île-à-la-Crosse to represent Athabasca constituency and the CCF's Leslie W. Lee of Choiceland to represent Cumberland constituency.

19 V.F. Valentine, "Some Problems of the Metis of Northern Saskatchewan," *Canadian Journal of Economics and Political Science* 20, 1 (1954): 90-91. At La Loche, Buffalo Narrows, Île-à-la-Crosse, and Beauval, the CCF received only 65 votes in 1952 compared to 569 for the Liberals. Not only in 1944, but throughout the CCF era, northern voters demonstrated their resistance to key CCF policies for the north through opposition on election day. The lack of the franchise for Status Indians until 1960 and the possibility that a high white voter turnout could outweigh Metis opposition suggest that the relatively neutral electoral record, which saw the CCF win about half of northern electoral contests from 1944 to 1964, may not accurately show the opposition to the CCF. Even taken at face value, the northern electoral record shows a lower level of support for the CCF than in the province overall. Had the entire province voted as the north did, the CCF would not have formed the government for much of the twenty-year time period.

20 G. Abrams, *Prince Albert: The First Century, 1866-1966* (Saskatoon: Modern Press, 1966); W.A. Waiser, *Saskatchewan's Playground: A History of Prince Albert National Park* (Saskatoon: Fifth House Publishers, 1989); W.A. Waiser, *The New Northwest: The Photographs of the Frank Crean Expeditions, 1908-1909* (Saskatoon: Fifth House Publishers, 1993).

21 *Saskatchewan Archives Board [SAB],* R-A1113, J.L. Phelps, interview by Murray Dobbin, audio tape, 1976; R-8452, J.L. Phelps, interview by J. Larmour audio tape, 1 June 1982.

22 Kenneth Coates and William Morrison, *The Forgotten North: A History of Canada's Provincial Norths* (Toronto: Lorimer, 1992), chapters 2 and 3.

23 Dennis Gruending, *Promises to Keep: A Political Biography of Allan Blakeney* (Saskatoon: Western Producer Prairie Books, 1990), 21; G.W. Cadbury, "Planning in Saskatchewan," in *Essays on the Left: Essays in Honour of T.C. Douglas*, ed. Laurier LaPierre et al. (Toronto: McClelland and Stewart, 1971), 54-56; Avakumovic, *Socialism in Canada*, 178-179; Richards and Pratt, *Prairie Capitalism*, 108, 129-133.

24 M. Brownstone, "The Douglas-Lloyd Governments: Innovation and Bureaucratic Adaptation," in *Essays on the Left: Essays in Honour of T.C. Douglas*, ed. Laurier LaPierre et al. (Toronto: McClelland and Stewart, 1971), 66, 68; *SAB*, S-NR 1/4, DNR, 167 B3, "Northern Region, April 1st, 1956," N. Dist. Field Officers' Conf., 9-13 January 1951.

25 Robert Tyre, *Douglas in Saskatchewan: The Story of a Socialist Experiment* (Vancouver: Mitchell Press, 1962), 25; Thomas Hector Macdonald McLeod, "Public Enterprise in Saskatchewan: The Development of Public Policy and Administrative Controls" (PhD diss., Harvard University, 1959), 160-227.

Chapter 2: From the Top

1 Murray Dobbin, *The One-And-A-Half Men: The Story of Jim Brady and Malcolm Norris, Metis Patriots of the Twentieth Century* (Vancouver: New Star Books, 1981), 169-170; John Richards and Larry Pratt, *Prairie Capitalism: Power and Influence in the New West* (Toronto: McClelland and Stewart, 1979), 118; *Saskatchewan Archives Board [SAB]*, R-A1113, J.L. Phelps, interview by Murray Dobbin, audio tape, 1976; R-8452, J.L. Phelps, interview by J. Larmour audio tape, 1 June 1982; S-M15, Box 17, Joseph Lee Phelps Ministerial Papers, "General Correspondence, 1944-1946 (2)," J.L. Phelps to T.C. Douglas, 5 September 1944.

2 F. Laurie Barron, *Walking in Indian Moccasins: The Native Policies of Tommy Douglas and the CCF* (Vancouver: UBC Press, 1997), 140; John H. Archer, *Saskatchewan: A History* (Saskatoon: Western Producer Prairie Books, 1980), 272; Richards and Pratt, *Prairie Capitalism*, 98 and 110; *SAB*, R-A 1008, J.H. Brockelbank, interview by B. Richards, audio tape, 1976; R-A 1109, J.H. Brockelbank, interview by Murray Dobbin, audio tape, Regina, 19 August 1976; R-A1113, J.L. Phelps, interview by Dobbin, 1976; R-971, J.L. Phelps, interview by B. Richards, audio tape, 1976; R-8453, J.L. Phelps, interview by J. Larmour, audio tape, 1 June 1982; "Beaver Farming," *Saskatoon Star-Phoenix*, 24 January 1946.

3 *SAB*, S-M15, Box 17, "Game Branch, 1944-1946 (5)," B.L. Keighley to J.L. Phelps, 10 August 1944 and 14 August 1944, L.C. Paterson to Phelps, 18 August 1944.

4 Thomas Hector Macdonald McLeod and Ian McLeod, *Tommy Douglas: The Road to Jerusalem* (Edmonton: Hurtig Publishers, 1987), 129-130; *SAB*, R-971, J.L. Phelps, interview by Richards, 1976; "Another Importation," *Prince Albert Daily Herald*, 15 February 1946. The CCF wanted proven sympathizers and socialists as deputy ministers and in senior positions, and many CCF supporters held high positions. Socialist orientation often acted as a primary criteria in hiring. Controversy over nepotism and patronage raised opposition in the press and elsewhere.

5 *SAB*, R-8452, Phelps, interview by Larmour, 1982. Mr. Doakes, deputy minister when the CCF took over, did not support Phelps's ideas and asked for reassignment. L.C. Paterson became acting deputy minister, followed by H. Lewis as deputy minister, who did not satisfy Phelps.

6 Murray Dobbin, "Prairie Colonialism: The CCF in Northern Saskatchewan, 1944-1964," *Studies in Political Economy: A Socialist Review* 16 (1985): 13; Dobbin, *The One-And-A-Half Men*, 188, 219; *SAB*, R-A1113, Phelps, interview by Dobbin, 1976; *Glenbow Archives*, M125, James Brady Collection, s. VI, f. 53, "Sask. Metis Notes, 1947-1952," M.F. Norris to W. Bryce, 3 May 1948; M125, s. III, "Correspondence, 1933-67," f. 22, "Norris, 1945-1967 (Mining and Native Rights)," M.F. Norris to J. Brady, November 1964; W.O. Kupsch and S.D. Hanson, eds., *Gold and Other Stories As Told to Berry Richards* (Regina: Saskatchewan Mining Association, 1986), 161. Liberal MLA John Cuelenaere and Premier Ross Thatcher ordered Norris dismissed in 1965, after which he worked for the Friendship Centre in Prince Albert. Norris died in 1967 following a stroke.

7 Dobbin, "Prairie Colonialism," 14; Dobbin, *The One-And-A-Half Men*, 195; *Glenbow Archives*, M125, s. VII, f. 68, "Sask. Govt., 1946-1949," J.F. Gray to J.P. Brady, 21 July 1947; *SAB*, S-NR2, DNR-ADM, (A) Subject Files – August 1944-April 1949, f. 2, "Administration Branch (W.H. Roney)," W.H. Roney to A.K. Quandt, 20 August 1948.

8 Dobbin, *The One-And-A-Half Men*, 180-181, 213; *Glenbow Archives*, M125, s. III, "Correspondence, 1933-67," f. 22, "Norris, 1945-1967 (Mining and Native Rights)," M.F. Norris to Dr.

R.L. Cheesman, 26 July 1960; M125, s. II, f. 8, "Personal," 1952-62, various items. Local people in La Ronge speculate about who killed Brady and his companion and offer suggestions about the motivation for the alleged killings. The stories remain unsubstantiated.

9 *SAB*, S-NR 1/4, 137 C, "Northern Region" (3 files), A.K. Quandt to J.W. Churchman, 26 November 1947.

10 *SAB*, R-907.2, J.H. Brockelbank Papers, v. II, f.12, "J.J. Wheaton, Northern Administrator," J.L. Phelps to J.J. Wheaton, 5 March 1948; S-M15, Box 5, "District Superintendents' Progress Reports, 1945-1946," Progress reports and related correspondence; S-M15, Box 16, "Fur Marketing, 1944-1946 (2)," Minister of Natural Resources to A.J. Cooke, 21 September 1945; S-M15, Box 18, "L.S. Horne, 1945," Phelps to A.G. MacAskill, 4 October 1945.

11 *SAB*, A 1008, Brockelbank, interview by Richards, 1976; R-971, Phelps, interview by Richards, 1976; S-M15, Box 29, "Saltcoats Constituency, 1945-1946 (2)," J.L. Phelps, to A.K. Quandt, 27 November 1944; S-M15, Box 29, "Questions, 1945-1946 (2)," Questions in the Sask. Legislature 1946 and question by Mr. Proctor, 7 March 1946.

12 Dobbin, *The One-And-A-Half Men*, 174; Evelyn L. Eager, *Saskatchewan Government: Politics and Pragmatism* (Saskatoon: Western Producer Prairie Books, 1980), 57; *Glenbow Archives*, M125, s. VI, f 58, "1933 – 1964, reprint from *The News Optimist* (North Battleford, SK), "A Fighter reenters politics: Joe Phelps will seek nomination, January 27," 10 January 1962.

13 *SAB*, A 1008, Brockelbank interview by Richards, 1976.

14 Dobbin, "Prairie Colonialism," 38.

15 DNR, *Annual Report*, 1953, 149; *SAB*, S-M16, A.M. Nicholson Papers, v. VII, f. 3, "Parks and Lands Branch, 1961-63," J.A. Collier to R. Brown, 27 November 1957; "Welfare and Development Policy for Northern Saskatchewan," December 1957; Appendix A, "On Welfare and Development Policy for Northern Saskatchewan"; Vernon C. Serl, "Action and Reaction: An Overview of Provincial Policies and Programs in Northern Saskatchewan," in *A Northern Dilemma: Reference Papers*, vol. 1, ed. Arthur K. Davis (Bellingham, WA: Western Washington State College, 1967).

16 Gary William David Abrams, *Prince Albert: The First Century 1866-1966* (Saskatoon: Modern Press, 1966), 353; DNR, *Annual Report*, 1949, 135; Department of Natural Resources, *The New North: Saskatchewan's Northern Development Program, 1945-1948* (Regina: DNR, 1948), 18; *Progress Report from Your Government: A Survey of Saskatchewan Government Activity* (Regina: Bureau of Publications, 1948), 35; *SAB*, R-517, Northern Health District, v. XIII, f. 10, "Various Services," 1950-73, Dr. S.L. Skoll to Dr. A.C. Irwin, 29 September 1965, and attached draft of "Proposed Reorganization of the Northern Health District," 12; "Civilization's Northern Drive Shatters Furthest Isolation: La Ronge Story Seen Revealing North's Future," *Prince Albert Daily Herald*, 1 May 1948; Serl, "Action and Reaction."

17 DNR, *Annual Report*, 1955, 60-63; DNR, *Annual Report*, 1957, 62; *SAB*, R-517 Dept. of Health, Comm. Health Services Br. (GR-278), (Records of Central Office, the 13 Health Regions and the Northern Health District), v. XIII – N. Health Dist., f. 9, "Organization," 1951-71, Dr. A.C. Irwin to Dr. G. Kinneard, 26 June 1956.

18 DNR, *Annual Report*, 1951, 149; *Glenbow Archives*, M125, s. II, f. 7, "Personal," 1922-51, A.K. Quandt to "Dear Fellow Workers," 11 April 1949; *SAB*, S-NR2, (A) Subject Files – August 1944-April 1949, f. 38, "Northern District (A.K. Quandt)," N. Dist. Field Officers' Conf., Prince Albert, beginning 31 January 1949, Speech by J.W. Churchman; R-907.2, f. II 4a, "J.W. Churchman, Deputy Minister, March 1948-March 1949," Churchman to C.A.L. Hogg, 17 September 1948; R-907.2, f. II-12, "J.J. Wheaton, Northern Administrator," Budgets, N. Dist. and N. Admin., 1948-49; 1949-50; 1950-51; 1951-52, 29 November 1947; R-907.2, f. II-12, "J.J. Wheaton, Northern Administrator," Wheaton to Hogg, "Re: Progress Report – Northern Administration District – Spring and Summer 1948"; J.L. Phelps to Wheaton, 5 April 1948; S-NR 1/4, Deputy Minister and Assistant Deputy Minister Files, 167 B3, "Northern Region, April 1st, 1956," 1949 N. Dist. Field Officers Conf., Prince Albert, SK, 31 January-1 February 1949, Churchman, "Administration of the North"; S-NR 1/4, 230, "Northern Region – General," v. 1, 1948-31 December 1954, J.H. Brockelbank to all N. Admin. Staff, 1 August 1949; Wheaton to R.T. Cook, 19 March 1948; S-NR2, (A) Subject Files – August 1944-April 1949, f. 2, "Administration Branch (W.H. Roney)," Roney to C.A.L. Hogg, 14 September 1948; S-NR2, (A) Subject Files – August 1944-April 1949, f. 9, "The Chains of Control"; S-NR2, (A) Subject Files – August 1944-April 1949, f. 38, "Northern District (A.K. Quandt)," N. Dist. Field Officers' Conf., Prince

Albert beginning 31 January 1949, Speech by Churchman; S-NR 2, C, "Personnel Files, 77," "A.K. Quandt."

19   The record does not indicate the exact year when Wheaton left.

20   DNR, *Annual Report*, 1959, NA 3, xvi; *Glenbow Archives*, M125, s. VII, f. 65, "Fisheries, 1957-1965," M.M., "Fisheries Policy – as of October 1958," 26 September 1958; *SAB*, S-NR 1/5, v. I. f. 20, (162R), "Consultative Committee on Northern Affairs, 1958," "Additional Information re Names proposed as possible Directors." The committee included T.K. Shoyama, Dr. B.N. Arnason, C.S. Edy, J.W. Churchman, and A.H. MacDonald.

21   DNR, *Annual Report*, 1965, 3.

22   *SAB*, A 1109, Brockelbank interview by Dobbin, 1976; S-NR 1/5, I, 39, (230) "Northern Region, 1957-1959," D.D. Tansley to A.W. Johnson, "Alternative forms of organization for administration of provincial programmes in Northern Saskatchewan," 10 February 1959; S-NR2, (A) Subject Files – August 1944-April 1949, f. 38, "Northern District (A.K. Quandt)," N. Dist. Field Officers' Conf., Prince Albert, beginning 31 January 1949, Speech by J.W. Churchman.

23   F. Laurie Barron, *Walking in Indian Moccasins: The Native Policies of Tommy Douglas and the CCF* (Vancouver: UBC Press, 1997); Dobbin, "Prairie Colonialism," 31.

24   *SAB*, S-M16, v. VII, f. 3, "Parks and Lands Branch, 1961-63," Brief by N. Adv. Comm. on Metis of N. Sask., 1955; J.A. Collier to R. Brown, 27 November 1957; "Minutes of the First Meeting of the Northern Advisory Committee," 9 December 1953; "Welfare and Development Policy for Northern Saskatchewan," December 1957; App. A, "On Welfare and Development Policy for Northern Saskatchewan."

25   *SAB*, S-NR 1/5, v. I, f. 45, (236), "Rehabilitation and Welfare, 1956-1958," M. Miller, "Welfare and Development Policy for Northern Saskatchewan," December 1957.

26   *SAB*, S-M16, v. VII, f. 3, "Parks and Lands Branch, 1961-63," J.A. Collier to P. Spaulding, F. Warwick, J. Elliott, T. Phalen, R. Lavoy, P. Godt, R. Brown, 29 October 1957; R. Brown to A.G. Kuziak, 7 January 1958; S-M16, v. VII, f. 3, "Parks and Lands Branch, 1961-63," Collier to Brown, 27 November 1957.

27   *SAB*, S-M16, v. VII, f. 3, "Parks and Lands Branch, 1961-63," A.G. Kuziak to Cabinet, 22 April 1958; T.J. Bentley, J.W. Erb, W.S. Lloyd, J.H. Brockelbank, and Kuziak to Cabinet, 3 February 1958; S-M16, v. VII, f. 4, "Tour of Northern Saskatchewan, 1959," M. Miller, "Some Problems and Premises of Policy for the Development of Northern Saskatchewan," Center for Community Studies Seminar, Saskatoon, 6 October 1958; S-NR 1/5, v. I, f. 20, (162R), "Consultative Committee on Northern Affairs, 1958," Cabinet Memo., Cabinet Min. 8494, 20 May 1958; A.G. Kuziak to Cabinet, 18 April 1958; J.W. Churchman to Kuziak, 31 January 1958; Churchman to Kuziak, 31 March 1958.

28   *SAB*, S-NR 1/5, v. I, f. 20, (162R) "Consultative Committee on Northern Affairs, 1958," A.H. MacDonald to A.G. Kuziak, 17 July 1958.

29   Barron, *Walking in Indian Moccasins*, 173-175; Helen L. Buckley, J.E.M. Kew, and John B. Hawley, *The Indians and Metis of Northern Saskatchewan: A Report on Economic and Social Development* (Saskatoon: Center for Community Studies, University of Saskatchewan, 1963), 39-41, 51-52; Dobbin, "Prairie Colonialism," 31; Dobbin, *The One-And-A-Half Men*, 209; Queen's University, "Municipal Government for Northern Saskatchewan" (Kingston, ON: The Institute of Local Government, Queen's University, May 1975), 6, 8; *SAB*, S-NR 1/5, v. I, f. 39, (230), "Northern Region, 1957-1959," A.H. MacDonald to J.W. Churchman, 26 February 1959; D.D. Tansley to A.W. Johnson, "Alternative forms of organization for administration of provincial programmes in Northern Saskatchewan," 10 February 1959; Churchman to MacDonald, 16 February 1959; Serl, "Action and Reaction," 64.

30   DNR, *Annual Report*, 1950, 146; DNR, *The New North*, 18; L.D. Lovick, ed., *Tommy Douglas Speaks* (Lantzville, BC: Oolichan Books, 1979), 102; *SAB*, R-907.2, v. II, f. 12, "J.J. Wheaton, Northern Administrator," Wheaton to J.L. Phelps (2 items), 21 February 1948; S-M15, Box 2, "Accounts Branch, 1945-1946"; S-NR 1/4, 167 B3, "Northern Region, April 1st, 1956," N. Dist. Conf., 5-10 October 1953; S-NR 1/4, 167 B3, "Northern Region," N. Dist. and Admin. Org. Chart, 26 September 1951; S-NR 1/4, f. 430, "Game and Fur Branch, E.L. Paynter, Game Commissioner," 1951 Game Br. Report to Field Officers' Conf.; S-NR 1/4, 137 C, "Northern Region" (3 files), A.K. Quandt to J.W. Churchman, 26 November 1947; S-NR2, (A) Subject Files – August 1944-April 1949, f. 38, "Northern District (A.K. Quandt)," Quandt to J.F. Gray, 20 July 1948; Quandt to Churchman, 15 April

1948; Serl, "Action and Reaction." DNR had 344 permanent employees, including 63 in Fisheries, Forestry, and Wildlife research and planning, and staff had risen about 22 percent since 1952.

31 J.E.M. Kew, *Cumberland House in 1960* (Saskatoon: Center for Community Studies, University of Saskatchewan, 1962); Dobbin, *The One-And-A-Half Men*, 212; P.M. Worsley, "Bureaucracy and Decolonization: Democracy from the Top," in *The New Sociology: Essays in Social Science and Social Theory in Honor of C. Wright Mills*, ed. Irving Louis Horowitz (New York: Oxford University Press, 1971), 383; W.A. Arrowsmith, "Northern Saskatchewan and the Fur Trade" (master's thesis, University of Saskatchewan, 1964), 126-127.

32 Kew, *Cumberland House*, 8; *SAB*, R-907.2, v. I, f. 2, "Cumberland House Settlement," M.F. Norris to J.J. Wheaton, 22 October 1947, Report attached "Office of the Northern Administrator Report of an Economic and Social Survey of the Cumberland House District," October 1947; S-M15, Box 2, "Accounts Branch, 1945-1946"; S-NR 1/4, 235, "Cumberland House – General," v. 1, June 1948 to 31 August 1950, G. Burgess to J.S. White, 7 October 1948.

33 *SAB*, S-NR 1/4, 230, "Northern Region," A.T. Davidson to J.W. Churchman, 14 May 1953; S-NR 1/4, f. 230, "Northern Region – General," v. 1, 1948-31 December 1954, Churchman to A. Davidson, C.S. Brown, A.H. MacDonald, and E.L. Paynter, 24 April 1953; S-NR 1/4, f. 230, "Northern District – General," v. 2, 1954-56, C. Salt to Brown, 18 March 1955; Brown to Salt, 31 March 1955; S-NR 1/4, 235, "Cree Lake" (2 files), J.J. Wheaton to Churchman, 15 July 1949; Churchman to C.L. MacLean, 8 July 1952; R.T. Francis to Brown, 28 July 1953; Brown to A.T. Davidson, 4 August 1953. DNR's Chas. Salt paddled to Wollaston in 1954, remaining for about eight months. It took him time to gain the trust of the area's wary people, but he claimed he did so. Salt turned against DNR, criticizing it for collecting as much money as possible. He placed most of the blame for prosecutions on DNR and attributed infractions primarily to ignorance of the law. Although he wanted to remain, DNR sent him to Cumberland House, saying Wollaston's low population did not justify a permanent officer.

34 *SAB*, R-907.3, f. 4, "Dominion Government Departments: Citizenship and Immigration (J.H. Brockelbank: Natural Resources)," "Report on the Interim Meeting Saskatchewan Fur Advisory Committee, Prince Albert – July 11th and 12th/52"; S-NR 1/4, 167 B3, "Northern Region," Minutes of N. Region Cons. Officers' Conf., 15-19 October 1956; S-NR 1/4, f. 430, "Game and Fur Branch, General, 1951-1955," A.T. Davidson to J.W. Churchman, 4 October 1956.

35 *SAB*, S-NR 1/4, 230, "Northern Region," N. Admin. Office to J.W. Churchman, 25 March 1953.

36 Morris C. Shumiatcher, *Welfare: Hidden Backlash* (Toronto: McClelland and Stewart, 1971), 99.

37 DNR, *Annual Report*, 1958, 75; *SAB*, R-907.2, v. II, f. 10b, "E.L. Paynter, Game Commissioner, September 1953-April 1955," "Recapitulation of Prosecutions Under Game and Fur by Districts 1951-52 to 1954-55"; S-NR 1/4, f. 213, "Game and Fur, General, 1949-1957," Paynter to J.W. Churchman, 7 January 1955; S-NR 1/4, f. 433, "Prosecution – Poaching, Illegal," August 1956-31 December 1957, "Recapitulation of Prosecutions under Game and Fur by RCMP in Departmental Regions 1951-52 to 1955-56"; "Recapitulation of Prosecutions Under Game and Fur by Regions 1951-52 to 1956-57"; S-NR 1/4, f. 433, "Prosecutions," April 1954, v. 2, C.S. Brown to A.T. Davidson, 21 July 1955; Brown to N. Dist. COs, 21 July 1955; "Recapitulation of Prosecutions under Game and Fur by Districts, 1951-52 to 1954-55."

38 *SAB*, S-NR 1/4, f. 230, "Northern Region – General," v. 1, 1948-31 December 1954, E. Dodds to C.L. MacLean, 17 January 1952.

39 *SAB*, S-NR 1/4, f. 433, "Prosecutions," B.A. Matheson to A.T. Davidson, 16 February 1955; Matheson to Davidson, 21 July 1954.

40 Janet Fietz, interview by author, La Ronge, SK, July 1999.

41 A.T. Davidson, "Role of Geographers in Northern Saskatchewan," *Canadian Geographer* 4 (1954): 33-38; *SAB*, S-NR 1/4, 112D, "Geographers" (2 files), J.W. Churchman to D. Cass-Beggs, 19 February 1949; W.H. Roney to Office of the N. Exec. Asst., 7 March 1949; Churchman to E.E. Chorneyko, 16 August 1954; R.G. Young to Prof. W.J. Talbot, 16 October 1954.

42 *SAB*, S-NR 1/4, 167 B3, "Northern Region, April 1st, 1956," N. Dist. Field Officers' Conf., 9-13 January 1951; S-NR2, (A) Subject Files – August 1944-April 1949, f. 39, "Northern Executive Assistant (R.T. Cook)," DNR Circular No. DM-1, 27 December 1948.

43 DNR, *Annual Report*, 1953, Intro. letter from J.W. Churchman to J.H. Brockelbank, and 99; *Progress: A Survey of Saskatchewan Government Activity* (Regina: Bureau of Publications, 1955), 15.

44 DNR, *Annual Report*, 1953, 163; DNR, *Annual Report*, 1954, 75-76; DNR, *Annual Report*, 1955, 86; DNR, *Annual Report*, 1956, 101; DNR, *Annual Report*, 1961, 159-160.

45 *SAB*, S-NR 1/4, 230, "Northern Region – General," v. III, 1957-, A.T. Davidson to D.G. Wesley, 21 November 1956; S-NR2, (A) Subject Files – August 1944-April 1949, f. 2, "Administration Branch (W.H. Roney)," J.W. Churchman to Roney, 27 September 1948; S-NR2, (A) Subject Files – August 1944-April 1949, f. 37, "Northern Administration (J.J. Wheaton)," A.K. Quandt to Churchman, 15 December 1948.

46 *Glenbow Archives*, M125, s. III, "Correspondence, 1933-67," f. 22, "Norris, 1945-1967 (Mining and Native Rights)," M.F. Norris to J.P. Brady, September 1960.

47 *Glenbow Archives*, M125, s. III, "Correspondence, 1933-67," f. 22, "Norris, 1945-1967. (Mining and Native Rights)," M.F.N. to Jimmie, 1962.

48 *SAB*, S-NR 1/5, v. III, f. 8, "Buffalo Narrows, 1963-66," E.L. Paynter to J.W. Churchman, 29 December 1961; Serl, "Action and Reaction."

49 *SAB*, S-M16, v. VII, f. 3, "Parks and Lands Branch, 1961-63," J.H. Brockelbank to Premier Douglas and All Cabinet Members, 10 October 1955.

50 *SAB*, R-517, v. XIII, f. 64, "Sandy Bay – Outpost Hospital, 1961-1973," E.L. Miner to Dr. A.J. Walker, 14 September 1971.

51 *SAB*, S-NR 1/5, v. III, f. 11, "La Ronge, 1962-67," Mrs. A. Jenner, "Nutrition Education – Northern Saskatchewan," 12 December 1965.

52 *SAB*, S-NR 1/4, f. 113 C, "Northern Region" (3 files), C.F. Oatway to Northern Administrator, 31 October 1951.

53 *SAB*, S-NR 1/4, f. 137 C, "Northern Region" (3 files), A.T. Davidson to J.W. Churchman, 24 July 1953.

54 *SAB*, S-NR 1/4, f. 137 C, "Northern Region" (3 files), Mrs. L. Poisson to J.W. Churchman, 20 October 1954; Churchman to Poisson, 26 October 1954; C.S. Brown to A.T. Davidson, 15 November 1954.

55 *SAB*, R-658, Dept. of Health, Reg. Health Serv. Br., v. I, f. 8, "Northern Health District: Northern Co-Ordinating Committee – Subcommittee – Incentives, 1962-1970," T.M. Spencer to Co-Operation, Mineral Resources, Natural Resources, Public Health, 1 October 1962; S-NR 1/4, f. 230, "Northern Region – General," v. III, 1957-, C.S. Brown to T.H. Preston, Att: D.G. Wesley, 17 May 1957; "Report on Northern Cost of Living," DNR, 1 June 1957.

56 *SAB*, S-NR 1/4, f. 137 C8, "La Ronge" (3 files), A.T. Davidson to J.W. Churchman, 5 October 1956; C.S. Brown to Davidson, 19 December 1956; S-NR 1/4, f. 137 C, "Northern Region" (3 files), Brown to Davidson, 22 June 1956; Churchman to W.H. Roney, 19 April 1949; NAD, DNR Residences, 1953 Assessed Values, Mill Rates and Levies; S-NR 1/4, f. 137 C8, "La Ronge" (3 files), DNR, "Determination of Departmental House Rentals as Per Formula Submitted 28 November 1952," S-NR 1/4, f. 137 C10, "Stony Rapids," R.N. Gooding to Churchman, 21 June 1949.

57 *SAB*, S-NR 1/4, f. 167 B3, "Northern Region," E. Dodds, "Northern District Housing Policy," N. Dist. Conf., 9 October 1953; S-NR 1/4, f. 230, "Northern Region – General," Volume III, 1957-, 1957 Housing Survey.

58 *SAB*, S-M15, Box 2, "Cumberland House, 1944-1945," J.L. Phelps to Corporal M. Chappuis, 2 August 1944; Chappuis to Phelps, 20 August 1944.

59 *SAB*, S-M15, Box 18, "General Correspondence, 1944-1946," F.X. Gagnon to J.L. Phelps, 9 August 1945.

60 *Glenbow Archives*, M125, s. VII, f. 60, "Co-Ops 1950-1962," Report of Co-Op. School Prince Albert, 13-21 June 1950.

61 *SAB*, S-NR 1/4, f. 236, "Rehabilitation and Welfare – General," v. 2, M. Miller to J.W. Churchman, 29 May 1957.

62 *SAB*, S-NR 1/4, f. 113 C, "Northern Region" (3 files), C.S. Brown to A.T. Davidson, 16 June 1954; S-NR 1/4, f. 236, "Rehabilitation and Welfare – General," v. 2, M. Miller to J.W. Churchman, 29 May 1957.

63 *SAB*, R-517, v. XIII, f. 10, "Various Services," 1950-73, Dr. M.S. Acker to A.K. Davis, 12 February 1963.
64 *SAB*, S-M16, v. VII, f. 3, "Parks and Lands Branch, 1961-63," "Minutes of Northern Advisory Committee Meeting," 9 February 1956.
65 Robert Longpré, *Ile-a-la-Crosse 1776-1976: Sakitawak Bi-Centennial* (Île-à-la-Crosse, SK: Ile-a-la-Crosse Bi-Centennial Committee and Ile-a-la-Crosse Local Community Authority, 1977), 54.
66 DNR, *Annual Report,* 1964, 43.
67 *SAB*, S-NR 1/4, f. 167 B3, "Northern Region," Minutes of N. District Cons. Officers' Conf., Prince Albert, SK, 4-8 October 1954.
68 June Cutt Thompson, "Cree Indians in North-Eastern Saskatchewan," *Saskatchewan History* 11, 2 (Spring 1958): 45.
69 Serl, "Action and Reaction," 15-24.
70 *SAB*, S-M16, v. VII, f. 3, "Parks and Lands Branch, 1961-63," C.S. Brown to A.T. Davidson, 29 October 1957; J.B. McLellan to Brown, 16 October 1957; S-NR 1/5, v. I, f. 76, (411), "Buffalo Narrows. 1957-1961," L.M. Reznechenko to Attorney General of Canada, 29 January 1958; Brown to Davidson, Assistant Deputy Minister, 30 January 1958; Brown to Davidson, 22 April 1958.
71 *SAB*, R-517, v. XIII, f. 65, "Sandy Bay, 1960-1972," Dr. A.C. Irwin to Dr. G. Kinneard, 8 January 1959; Attached note from (M.P.) Edwards.
72 *SAB*, A 1109, Brockelbank, interview by Dobbin, 1976.
73 *SAB*, S-NR 1/4, DNR, 167 B3 "Northern Region," Minutes, 1954.
74 Shumiatcher, *Welfare*, 98.

Chapter 3: The Ultimate Solution

1 *Saskatchewan Archives Board [SAB]*, Dept. of Health, Comm. Health Serv. Br., v. XIII, f. 9, "Organization," 1951-71, R.F. Badgley to Dr. M.S. Acker, 3 May 1960; "The Rat Race: What Have We Done for the Indians in Stony Rapids?" *Weekend Magazine*, 13 June 1970, 10-14. Many missionaries and priests showed great commitment to northerners. The Evangelical Church also increasingly became part of the northern scene.
2 *SAB*, DNS-1, DNS, (GS-201), III, A, 123, "Stony Rapids/Black Lake Band, 1961-1974" (2 folders), Dr. G.F. Davidson to J.W. Churchman, 22 December 1961; N.J. McLeod to A.H. MacDonald, 11 January 1960; S-NR 1/4, DNR, 235, "Dillon"; S-NR 1/4, DNR, 235, "Pelican Narrows."
3 Evangeline Lemaigre, "La Loche: Its History and Development," unpublished essay (April 1978), 15-18.
4 *SAB*, R-907.2, II 4b, "J.W. Churchman, Deputy Minister May 1951-July 1954," J.H. Brockelbank, to Churchman, 30 July 1954; Churchman to Brockelbank, 22 July 1954; R.G. Young to Churchman, 15 July 1954.
5 *SAB*, S-NR 1/3, DNR, G-1-7, "Community Planning, General 1948-50," C.A.L. Hogg to L. Fortier, 30 March 1950; Fortier to Hogg, 5 July 1950; A.I. Bereskin to Hogg, 7 February 1950.
6 V.F. Valentine, *The Metis of Northern Saskatchewan* (Regina: DNR, 1955), 2, 18.
7 Henry S. Sharp, "The Kinship System of the Black Lake Chipewyan" (PhD diss., Duke University, 1973), 18-19; Helen L. Buckley, J.E.M. Kew, and John B. Hawley, *The Indians and Metis of Northern Saskatchewan: A Report on Economic and Social Development* (Saskatoon: Center for Community Studies, University of Saskatchewan, 1963), 5; James B. Waldram, "The 'Other Side': Ethnostatus Distinctions in Western Subarctic Native Communities," in *1885 and After: Native Society in Transition*, ed. F. Laurie Barron and James B. Waldram (Regina: Canadian Plains Research Center, University of Regina, 1986), 279-295; Robert Jarvenpa, *The Trappers of Patuanak: Toward a Spatial Ecology of Modern Hunters*, National Museum of Man Mercury Series, Canadian Ethnology Service Paper No. 67 (Ottawa: National Museums of Canada, 1980), 5 and 61-62.
8 June Helm, Edward S. Rogers, and James G.E. Smith, "Intercultural Relations and Cultural Change in the Shield and Mackenzie Borderlands," in *Subarctic*, ed. June Helm, vol. 6 of *Handbook of North American Indians*, ed. William C. Sturtevant (Washington: Smithsonian Institution, 1981), 150, 157; M.L. Lautt, " Sociology and the Canadian Plains," in *A Region of the Mind: Interpreting the Western Canadian Plains*, ed. Richard Allen (Regina: Canadian

Plains Studies Centre, University of Saskatchewan, 1973), 137; Robert Davis and Mark Zannis, *The Genocide Machine: The Pacification of the North* (Montreal: Black Rose Books, 1973), 9, 176; Vernon C. Serl, "Action and Reaction: An Overview of Provincial Policies and Programs in Northern Saskatchewan," in *A Northern Dilemma: Reference Papers*, vol. 1, ed. Arthur K. Davis (Bellingham, WA: Western Washington State College, 1967), 15. Cultural genocide also may occur in the assimilation process. Cultural genocide can mean political, social, and economic disintegration. Education, language policy, resource exploitation, nucleation, and welfare programs can all contribute to cultural genocide.

9   Doris French Shackleton, *Tommy Douglas* (Toronto: McClelland and Stewart, 1975), 204; James M. Pitsula, "The CCF Government and the Formation of the Union of Saskatchewan Indians," *Prairie Forum* 19, 2 (Fall 1994): 131-151; L.H. Thomas, ed., *The Making of a Socialist: The Recollections of T.C. Douglas* (Edmonton: University of Alberta Press, 1982), 243-244.

10 James M. Pitsula, "The CCF Government in Saskatchewan and Social Aid, 1944-1964," in *"Building the Co-Operative Commonwealth": Essays on the Democratic Tradition in Canada*, Canadian Plains Proceedings 13, ed. J. William Brennan (Regina: Canadian Plains Research Center, University of Regina, 1984), 205-225; *SAB*, R-A1113, Joe Phelps, interview by Murray Dobbin, audio tape, 1976.

11 *SAB*, R-907.3, Brockelbank Papers, 7b, "Dominion Government Departments: Resources and Development," Brockelbank to R.H. Winters, 8 November 1952.

12 *Glenbow Archives*, M125, James Brady Collection, v. VI, f. 55, "CCF 1949-1964," B. Berezowsky to Brady, 2 July 1952.

13 *SAB*, S-NR 1/4, 230, N. Region, C.S. Brown, "Northern Saskatchewan – A Special Problem," 8/3/56.

14 *SAB*, S-M16, v. XV, n. 14, "Indians, 1955-64," T.J. Bentley to J.S. White, 7 February 1957. This archival record does not mention Thomas's reaction or subsequent role in carrying out the plan.

15 DNR, *Annual Report*, 1952, 168.

16 James M. Pitsula, "'Educational Paternalism' Versus Autonomy: Contradictions in the Relationship Between the Saskatchewan Government and the Federation of Saskatchewan Indians, 1958-1964," *Prairie Forum* 22, 1 (Spring 1997): 47-71; James M. Pitsula, "The Saskatchewan CCF Government and Treaty Indians, 1944-64," *Canadian Historical Review* 75, 1 (March 1994): 24. By 1960 Ray Woollam worked as executive director of the Committee on Minority Groups, which replaced the Committee on Indian Affairs, and he helped coordinate CCF Indian and Metis policies. J.H. Sturdy chaired the committee until T.C. Douglas took over, a position he held until leaving for federal politics in 1961. Woollam favoured giving Indians the vote and liquor rights. The Committee on Minority Groups was replaced by the Community Development Branch of the Department of Municipal Affairs on 1 September 1962. Woollam left in 1963.

17 Buckley, Kew, and Hawley, *The Indians and Metis of Northern Saskatchewan*, 51; W.B. Baker, "Some Observations on the Application of Community Development to the Settlements of Northern Saskatchewan," 8.

18 *Glenbow Archives*, M125, v. VI, f. 56, "CCF 1954-1961," T.C. Douglas to my Indian Friends, 30 May 1960; Pitsula, "The CCF Government and the Formation of the Union," 131; *SAB*, S-M16, v. XX, f. 7, "Indians, 1958-63," Address by T.C. Douglas to Conf. of Sask. Indians, Fort Qu'Appelle, 30 October 1958; Prov. Conf. of Sask. Indian Chiefs and Councillors, Fort Qu'Appelle, 30-31 October 1958; "Tribal Chief Criticizes North School System," *Hudson Bay Post-Review*, 14 December 1955.

19 *Glenbow Archives*, M125, III, "Correspondence, 1933-67," f. 22, "Norris, 1945-1967 (Mining and Native Rights)," M.F. Norris to J. Brady, 15 February 1962; James M. Pitsula, "The Thatcher Government in Saskatchewan and Treaty Indians, 1964-1971: The Quiet Revolution," *Saskatchewan History* 48, 1 (Spring 1996): 3-16; F. Laurie Barron, *Walking in Indian Moccasins: The Native Policies of Tommy Douglas and the CCF* (Vancouver: UBC Press, 1997); Thomas Hector Macdonald McLeod and Ian McLeod, *Tommy Douglas: The Road to Jerusalem* (Edmonton: Hurtig Publishers, 1987), 139-140. Shumiatcher advised Douglas for a time, while J.H. Sturdy, an "expert" on Indians, later became Douglas's special assistant.

20 Shackleton, *Tommy Douglas*, 200-204; *Glenbow Archives*, M125, VI, 53, "Sask. Metis Notes, 1947-1952," Joseph Ross, Pres. and Norman J. Pansien (sp?) to Dear Friends, 23 June 1949;

John H. Archer, *Saskatchewan: A History* (Saskatoon: Western Producer Prairie Books, 1980), 287-288; Barron, *Walking in Indian Moccasins*, 34-45; Murray Dobbin, *The One-And-A-Half Men: The Story of Jim Brady and Malcolm Norris, Metis Patriots of the Twentieth Century* (Vancouver: New Star Books, 1981), 171-173; Proceedings of the Conference of the Metis of Saskatchewan (July 1946); Document 116, in David E. Smith, ed., *Building a Province: A History of Saskatchewan in Documents*, (Saskatoon: Fifth House Publishers, 1992), 379.

21 *SAB*, Brockelbank Papers, II-12, J.J. Wheaton to A.G. Hamilton, 1 October 1947; Wheaton to Phelps, 30 April 1948; Wheaton to J.P.B. Ostrander, 19 September 1947; Meeting report, Prov. and fed. reps. of Dept. of Indian Affairs, 7 October 1947; Resolution, Meeting, Dept. of Indian Affairs, DNR, and Fish Board, 7 October 1947; Minutes of Meeting of N. Co-ord. Committee, 23 April 1948; S-NR2, DNR, 19 (A), August 1944-April 1949, Fisheries Branch (A.H. MacDonald), J.W. Churchman, Summary of Meeting in Minister's Office, 16 September likely 1948; 34 (A), August 1944-April 1949, Min. of Natural Resources (Brockelbank)," Churchman to Phelps, 14 May 1948; McLeod and McLeod, *Tommy Douglas*, 140.

22 *SAB*, S-M16, v. XIII, f. 264, "Public Assistance, Indians and Metis, 1952-64," J.S. White to Col. Laval Fortier, 18 February 1958; White to Dr. G.F. Davidson, 26 July 1960; White to J.W. Erb, 19 February 1958.

23 *Glenbow Archives*, M125, series VI, File 56, CCF 1954-61, Douglas, To my Indian Friends, 30 May 1960.

24 Pitsula, "The Saskatchewan CCF Government," 51; *SAB*, S-M16, v. VIII, f. 1, "Planning Board, 1953-63" (1 of 2), J.S. White to A.M. Nicholson, 16 May 1963; S-M16, v. XIII, f. 264, "Public Assistance, Indians and Metis, 1952-64," A.M. Nicholson to J.S. White, 11 June 1963; "Treaty Indians and Northern Administration," 18 November 1963; S-M16, v. XV, f. 14, "Indians, 1955-64," M.H. Greenwood to G.J. Darychuk, 8 August 1963; "Proposals by the Department of Education for the Extension of Provincial Educational Services to Treaty Indian People," 1963; "Proposals by the Department of Social Welfare and Rehabilitation for Extending Provincial Welfare Services to Registered Indians," November 1963; "Saskatchewan Brief to the Dominion-Provincial Conference Indian Affairs," Draft, November 1963.

25 H.B. Hawthorne, *A Survey of the Contemporary Indians of Canada: A Report on Economic, Political, Educational Needs and Policies*, vol. 1 (Ottawa: Indian Affairs Branch, vol. 1 – 1966), 386-403; Morris Zaslow, *The Northward Expansion of Canada 1914-1917* (Toronto: McClelland and Stewart, 1988), 297-300, 302; P.E. Moore, "Medical Care of Canada's Indians and Eskimos," *Canadian Journal of Public Health* 47, 6 (June 1956): 229; Richard C. Daniel, *A History of Native Claims Processes in Canada 1867-1979* (Ottawa: Department of Indian Affairs and Northern Development, 1980), 132-133; *SAB*, R-907.3, 4, "Dominion Government Departments: Citizenship and Immigration," W.E. Harris to J.H. Brockelbank, 5 October 1953; S-M16, v. XV, f. 14, "Indians, 1955-64," "Summary of Findings and Recommendations (From the Second and Final Report to Parliament by the Joint Committee of the Senate and the House of Commons on Indian Affairs)," 8 July 1961.

26 Pitsula, "The Saskatchewan CCF Government," 23, 51.

27 Peter Goode, Joan Champ, and Leslie Amundson, *The Montreal Lake Region: Its History and Geography* (Saskatoon: Sentar Consultants Ltd., 1996), 40.

28 C.H. Piercy, "Survey of Educational Facilities in Northern Saskatchewan, Part 1: The Areas in the Remote Northern Part of the Province of Saskatchewan," unpublished paper (18 December 1944).

29 James G.E. Smith, "The Ecological Basis of Chipewyan Socio-Territorial Organization," in *Proceedings: Northern Athapaskan Conference, 1971*, vol. 2, ed. A. McFayden Clark, National Museum of Man Mercury Series, Canadian Ethnology Service Paper No. 27 (Ottawa: National Museums of Canada, 1975), 389-461; Robert Jarvenpa, "The Ubiquitous Bushman: Chipewyan-White Trapper Relations of the 1930s," in *Problems in the Prehistory of the North American Subarctic: The Athapaskan Question*, ed. J.W. Helmer, S. Van Dyke, and K.U. Kense (Calgary: Archaeological Association, Department of Archaeology, University of Calgary, 1977), 165-183; Murray Dobbin, "Prairie Colonialism: The CCF in Northern Saskatchewan, 1944-1964," *Studies in Political Economy: A Socialist Review* 16 (1985): 16; Robert M. Bone and Milford B. Green, "Jobs and Access: A Northern Dilemma," *Journal of Canadian Studies* 18, 3 (Fall 1983): 95; V.F. Valentine, "Some Problems of the Metis of

Northern Saskatchewan," *The Canadian Journal of Economics and Political Science* 20, 1 (1954): 93; Valentine, *The Metis of Northern Saskatchewan*, 10-13; V.F. Valentine and R.G. Young, "The Situation of the Metis of Northern Saskatchewan in Relation to His Physical and Social Environment," *The Canadian Geographer* 4 (1954): 55.

30 Churchill River Basin Task Force, *Churchill River Basin Task Force Report* (September 1972), 30; Buckley, Kew, and Hawley, *The Indians and Metis of Northern Saskatchewan*, Chapter 2; Jane A. Abramson, "Women and Work in Northern Saskatchewan," Draft, June 1975; Miriam McNab, "From the Bush to the Village to the City: Pinehouse Lake Aboriginal Women Adapt to Change," in *"Other Voices": Historical Essays on Saskatchewan Women*, ed. David DeBrou and Aileen Moffat (Regina: Canadian Plains Research Centre, University of Regina, 1995); Dobbin, "Prairie Colonialism," 22; Robert M. Bone, *Canadian Western Northland: Some Observations and Examples from Northern Communities* (Saskatoon: Institute for Northern Studies, University of Saskatchewan, 1974), 66.

31 *SAB*, S-NR2, DNR-ADM, (A), "August 1944-April 1949," f. 37, Northern Administration (J.J. Wheaton), J.H. Sturdy to J.Z. LaRocque, 22 September 1948; LaRocque to Rev. S. Cuthand, 28 August 1948; LaRocque to Sturdy, no date given; Cuthand to LaRocque, 6 August 1948; A.I. Bereskin to C.A.L. Hogg, 1 November 1948; Bereskin to Hogg, J.J. Wheaton, and A.K. Quandt, 15 July 1948; Wheaton to J.W. Churchman, 23 December 1948; Churchman to Wheaton, 14 December 1948; Malcolm F. Norris to Hogg, 25 November 1948; "Civilization's Northern Drive Shatters Furthest Isolation: La Ronge Story Seen Revealing North's Future," *Prince Albert Daily Herald*, 1 May 1948.

32 LeMaigre, "La Loche," 10; John H. Hylton, *The La Loche Report*, prepared for Saskatchewan Municipal Government, 15 October 1993, 6-7; *SAB*, R-517, Dept. of Health, Comm. Health Services Br., v. XIII, f.22, "Policy – Sanitation," 1951-65, District Sanitary Officer to Mr. Schaeffer, 14 April 1953.

33 Jarvenpa, *The Trappers of Patuanak*.

34 Amisk Planning Consultants, *A Community Planning Study for Buffalo Narrows*, 1978; *SAB*, R-517, Dept. of Health, Comm. Health Serv. Br., v. XIII, f. 22, "Policy – Sanitation," 1951-65, District Sanitary Officer to Mr. Schaeffer, 14 April 1953.

35 Northern Village of Ile a la Crosse, "Ile a la Crosse ... Northern Saskatchewan's Best Kept Secret"; Robert Longpré, *Ile-a-la-Crosse 1776-1976: Sakitawak Bi-Centennial* (Île-à-la-Crosse, SK: Ile-a-la-Crosse Bi-Centennial Committee and Ile-a-la-Crosse Local Community Authority, 1977); *SAB*, R-517, Dept. of Health, Comm. Health Serv. Br. v. XIII, f.22, "Policy – Sanitation," 1951-65, District Sanitary Officer to Mr. Schaeffer, 14 April 1953; S-NR 1/4, DNR, 137 C, "Northern Region" (3 files), C.S. Brown to A.T. Davidson, 22 April 1957; S-NR 1/4, DNR, 231 B, "Buffalo Narrows, 1949-1957," N. Admin. to J.W. Churchman, 3 November 1950; S-NR 1/4, DNR, 235, "Buffalo Narrows," Davidson to Churchman, 1 March 1957; S-NR 1/4, 235, "Ile a la Crosse," Brown to H.M. Ross, 22 April 1957; S-NR 1/4, DNR, 551 C, "Northern Region," v. 1, 1950-57, Brown to Davidson, Att.: A.I. Bereskin, 23 April 1957; Brown to Davidson, 22 June 1956; Brown to Davidson, 7 May 1957; R.G. Young to Davidson, 30 October 1956.

36 *SAB*, R-517, Dept. of Health, Comm. Health Serv. Br., v. XIII, f. 22, "Policy – Sanitation," 1951-65, District Sanitary Officer to Mr. Schaeffer, 14 April 1953.

37 *SAB*, S-NR 1/4, DNR, 231 B, "Buffalo Narrows, 1949-1957," C.S. Brown to A.T. Davidson, 14 November 1956; A.I. Bereskin to Davidson, 7 January 1957; Brown to Davidson, Att.: Bereskin, 23 January 1957.

38 *SAB*, R-517, Dept. of Health, Comm. Health Serv. Br., v. XIII, f. 25, "Construction and Housing, 1961-1965," M.A. Welsh to Regional Health Services Branch, Att.: Dr. M.S. Acker, 3 January 1963; R-517 Dept. of Health, Comm. Health Serv. Br., v. XIII, f. 21, "Policy – Medical Care," 1955-73, Dr. A.C. Irwin to Acker, 8 April 1963.

39 *SAB*, S-NR 1/4, DNR, 235, "Snake Lake" (2 files), A.I. Bereskin to G. Couldwell, 17 August 1954; C.L. MacLean to J.W. Churchman, 5 April 1950; Couldwell to A.I. Bereskin, 4 August 1954; W.K. Riese to MacLean, 19 July 1950; Underwood McLellan Ltd., *Pinehouse Planning Study* (Saskatoon: The UMA Group, 1981), 86.

40 *SAB*, S-NR 1/4, DNR, 167 B3, "Northern Region," Minutes of N. District Cons. Officers' Conf., Prince Albert, SK, 4-8 October 1954.

41 James G.E. Smith, "The Chipewyan Hunting Group in a Village Context," *Western Canadian Journal of Anthropology* 2, 1 (1970): 60-66; Smith, "The Ecological Basis," 389-461.

42 Sharp, "The Kinship System"; Robert M. Bone, ed., *The Chipewyan of the Stony Rapids Region,* Mawdsley Memoir No. 1 (Saskatoon: Institute for Northern Studies, University of Saskatchewan, 1973), 1-80; Robert M. Bone, *The Geography of the Canadian North: Issues and Challenges* (Toronto: Oxford University Press, 1992), 67.

43 *SAB,* DNS-1, DNS, (GS-201), v. VIII, f. 7, Laverne Olson, "History and Culture Report – Kinoosao (Co-Op Point), no date; S-NR 1/4, DNR, 235, "Reindeer Lake – South End," A.I. Bereskin, "Topographical Report on Subdivision E. Side of Reindeer Lake Locally known as Co-Op Point," 5 March 1952; Bereskin to J.H. Brockelbank, 11 March 1952; L.S. Cumming to J.W. Churchman, 4 June 1954; Bereskin to Churchman, 17 June 1954; S-NR 1/4, DNR, 235, "South End – Reindeer Lake," A.T. Davidson to L.S. Cumming, 9 February 1954; Churchman to Cumming, 11 March 1954; Cumming to Davidson, 2 February 1954.

44 *SAB,* S-NR 1/4, DNR, 235, "Reindeer Lake – South End," J.W. Churchman to Bishop Lajeunnesse, 24 December 1952; T.C. Douglas to J.H. Brockelbank, 24 October 1952; C.S. Brown to Churchman, 12 November 1952; Brockelbank to Douglas, 31 October 1953; Petition from South End of Reindeer Lake, Sask., to Premier Douglas, 20 July 1952; S-NR 1/4, DNR, 235, "South End – Reindeer Lake," C.L. MacLean to Churchman, 21 November 1950.

45 J. Howard Richards, *Recreation Potential of the Saskatchewan River Delta Area* (Ottawa, ON: Canada, Department of Forestry and Rural Development, ARDA, 1966), App: Cumberland House: Historical Summary, 12-13.

46 J.E.M. Kew, *Cumberland House in 1960* (Saskatoon: Center for Community Studies, University of Saskatchewan, 1962), 16, 22-27; *SAB,* R-907.2, Brockelbank Papers, I-2, "Cumberland House Settlement," M.F. Norris to J.J. Wheaton, 22 October 1947, Report attached "Office of the Northern Administrator Report of an Economic and Social Survey of the Cumberland House District," October 1947; S-NR2, DNR-ADM, (A), August 1944-April 1949, 2, Admin. Br. (W.H. Roney), "Essay Contest Air Trip Itinerary," DNR, about 1948.

47 *SAB,* R-517, Dept. of Health, Comm. Health Serv. Br., v. XIII, f. 9, "Organization," 1951-71, Dr. A.C. Irwin to Dr. F.B. Roth, 29 September 1954.

48 James W. Vanstone, "Changing Patterns of Indian Trapping in the Canadian Subarctic," *Arctic* 16, 3 (September 1963): 158-174; James B. Waldram, "Relocation, Consolidation, and Settlement Pattern in the Canadian Subarctic," *Human Ecology* 15, 2 (1987): 117-131; *SAB,* S-NR 1/4, DNR, 167 B3 "Northern Region," Minutes of N. District Cons. Officers' Conf., Prince Albert, SK, 4-8 October 1954.

49 Buckley, Kew, and Hawley, *The Indians and Metis of Northern Saskatchewan,* 9; *SAB,* S-NR 1/4, DNR, 235, "La Ronge," "An Investigation of Problems Related to the Development of Recreational Resources of Lac la Ronge," C.S. Brown to C.A.L. Hogg, 1951 or 1952.

50 *SAB,* S-M15, Box 7, Joseph Lee Phelps Ministerial Papers, "Fish Products, 1944-1946 (3)," Dr. G.C. Darby to J.L. Phelps, 16 April 1946; C.M. Bedford to Darby and Dr. J.B. Kirkpatrick, 26 March 1946; S-M15, Box 10, SLFPC, "W. Bague, 1947-1948," W.J. Bague to J.F. Gray, 28 November 1946; S-NR 1/3, DNR, G-1-7, "Community Planning, General 1948-50," A.I. Bereskin to C.A.L. Hogg, J.W. Churchman, 23 September 1948; S-NR 1/3, DNR, G-1-7, "Community Planning, Northern and Parks," 1945-48, A.I. Bereskin to Phelps, C.A.L. Hogg, 30 September 1946; A.I. Bereskin to Phelps, 3 December 1946; "Lac la Ronge Townsite," no date or author; Bereskin to Hogg, 24 July 1946; Bereskin to D.A. Cunningham, 1 May 1947; S-NR 1/4, 235, "La Ronge," Bereskin to Churchman, Hogg, 26 June 1950.

51 *SAB,* S-NR2, DNR, (A), August 1944-April 1949, 2, "Admin. Br. (W.H. Roney)," "Essay Contest Air Trip Itinerary," DNR, about 1948; S-NR2, DNR, (A), August 1944-April 1949, 38, "Northern District (A.K. Quandt)," Quandt, Ass. N. Dist. Supt., Ann. Rpt. N. Dist., 1 April 1947-31 March 1948; "Civilization's Northern Drive Shatters Furthest Isolation: La Ronge Story Seen Revealing North's Future," *Prince Albert Daily Herald,* 1 May 1948.

52 *SAB,* S-NR 1/4, DNR, 230, "Northern Region," A.T. Davidson to C.A.L. Hogg, 18 June 1951; S-NR 1/4, DNR, 231 B, "La Ronge – General" (5 files), J.H. Brockelbank to J.W. Churchman, 30 August 1950; N. Admin. to Churchman, 11 September 1950; S-NR 1/4, DNR, 235, "La Ronge (1)", Churchman to A.G. Stangel, Annaheim, SK, 16 January 1953.

53 *SAB,* S-NR 1/4, DNR, 230, "Northern Region," A.I. Bereskin to C.A.L. Hogg, 13 April 1951; Bereskin to Hogg, 2 August 1951; S-NR 1/4, DNR, 231 B, "La Ronge – General" (5 files), Director, Dept. of Citizenship and Immigration, Indian Affairs Branch, to J.W. Churchman,

10 November 1952; Churchman to J.P.B. Ostrander, 15 January 1952; C.S. Brown to Churchman, 24 October 1952; E. Dodds to Churchman, 2 January 1953; Churchman to C.L. MacLean, 5 November 1951; S-NR 1/4, 235, "La Ronge (1)," Bereskin to Hogg, 7 February 1950; Bereskin to Hogg, 2 March 1950; S-NR2, DNR, (A), August 1944-April 1949, 37, "Northern Administration (J.J. Wheaton)," Bereskin to Wheaton, 7 January 1949.

54 *SAB*, S-NR 1/4, DNR, 230, "Northern Region," A.I. Bereskin to C.A.L. Hogg, 15 October 1951; Bereskin to Hogg, 24 October 1951; Bereskin to Hogg, 15 October 1951; S-NR 1/4, DNR, 235, "La Ronge," "An Investigation of Problems Related to the Development of Recreational Resources of Lac la Ronge," C.S. Brown to Hogg, 1951 or 1952.

55 *SAB*, S-NR 1/4, DNR, 230, "Northern Region," C.L. MacLean to J.W. Churchman, 20 April 1951; Churchman to C.A.L. Hogg, 26 July 1951; S-NR 1/4, DNR, 231 B, "La Ronge – General" (5 files), Hogg to Churchman, 31 July 1950; MacLean to Churchman, 15 August 1950; N. Admin. to W.K. Riese, 6 June 1950; S-NR2, DNR, (A), August 1944-April 1949, 37, "Northern Administration (J.J. Wheaton)," A.I. Bereskin to Churchman, W.T. Ritchie, 14 December 1948; J.J. Wheaton to Churchman, 4 December 1948.

56 *SAB*, S-NR 1/4, DNR, 235, "La Ronge," M.A. Welsh, "Lac La Ronge," 17-20 July 1951; A.H. MacDonald to J.W. Churchman, 18 October 1951; Churchman to C.L. MacLean, 22 October 1951; Churchman to MacLean, 7 December 1951.

57 DNR, *Annual Report*, 1956, 77; *SAB*, S-NR 1/4, DNR, 231 B, "La Ronge – General" (5 files), C.S. Brown to A.J. Gossen and Co., 28 January 1958; Brown to A.T. Davidson, 30 August 1957; A.T. Davidson to J.W. Churchman, 31 October 1957; S-NR 1/5, DNR, I, 80, (415), "La Ronge, 1955-1961," Davidson to Churchman, 22 February 1955; Davidson to Churchman, 17 August 1955; C.S. Brown to Davidson, Att. Churchman, 12 July 1955; Brown to Davidson, 12 August 1955; John McIntosh to Churchman, 28 July 1955.

58 Helen L. Buckley, *Trapping and Fishing in the Economy of Northern Saskatchewan*, Report No. 3, Economic and Social Survey of Northern Saskatchewan (Saskatoon: Research Division, Center for Community Studies, University of Saskatchewan, 1962), 119-121; *SAB*, DNS-1, DNS, (GS-201), v. VIII, f. 10, "History and Culture Report – La Ronge," Vicky Roberts, "History and Culture – La Ronge," no date.

59 *SAB*, S-NR 1/5, DNR, v. I, f. 80, (415), A.G. Kuziak to Treasury Board, 28 December 1959; Office of the Dir. of N. Affairs to J.W. Churchman, 24 November 1959; Office of the Dir. of N. Affairs to Churchman, 2 October 1961; Office of the Dir. of N. Affairs to Churchman, 14 June 1961; S-NR 1/5, DNR, v. III, f. 11, "La Ronge, 1962-67," A.I. Bereskin to Mrs. L.E. Gibson, 6 February 1964; Office of the Dir. of Northern Affairs to Churchman, 23 August 1963; "The Government's Contribution to Lac la Ronge," 26 August 1964, no author.

60 DNR, *Annual Report*, 1951, 150; DNR, *Annual Report*, 1953, 153; DNR, *Annual Report*, 1954, 64; *SAB*, S-NR 1/4, DNR, 167 B3, "Northern Region," E.N. Shannon, "Uranium City Development," N. Dist. Conf., 9 October 1953; S-NR 1/4, DNR, 230, "Northern Region," C.L. MacLean to J.W. Churchman, 22 January 1951; S-NR2, DNR, (A), August 1944-April 1949, 35, "Municipal Affairs, Department of," L. Jacobs to J.W. Churchman, 13 May 1948; Economic and Planning Board, *Saskatchewan Economic Review* (January 1953), 15.

61 DNR, *Annual Report*, 1955, 63; DNR, *Annual Report*, 1957, 71; Dept. of Mineral Resources, *Saskatchewan's Metallic and Industrial Minerals* (Regina: DMR, 1961), 42-43; K. Izumi and G.R. Arnott, *A Guide for Development: Uranium City and District* (Regina: Community Planning Branch, Dept. of Municipal Affairs, 1956), 22-23; M.K. McCutcheon and R.G. Young, "The Development of Uranium City," *The Canadian Geographer* 4 (1954): 60; *SAB*, DNS-1, DNS, (GS-201), v. VIII, f. 12, "History and Culture Report – Uranium City," D. Belanger, F. Halkett, C. Dusseault, "History and Culture – Uranium City," no date; S-M16, v. VII, f. 3, "Parks and Lands Branch, 1961-63," "Report on a Study of the Beaverlodge Area," 15 June 1955; DNR, *Annual Report*, 1956, 76.

62 Izumi and Arnott, *A Guide for Development*, 22-23, 63; *SAB*, S-NR 1/4, DNR, 167 B3, "Northern Region," E.N. Shannon, "Uranium City Development," N. Dist. Conf., 9 October 1953.

63 *SAB*, R-907.2, f. I-3a, "Flin Flon-Creighton Area 1942-1944"; S-M15, Box 18, "C.A.L. Hogg," Hogg to J.L. Phelps, 27 September 1944; R-907.2, f. I-3b, "Flin Flon-Creighton Area 1944-1948," J. McIntosh and S. Young for J.H. Brockelbank, 3 February 1945; S-NR 1/3, DNR Dep. Min., G-1-7, "Community Planning, Northern and Parks, 1945-48," A.I. Bereskin, "Report on Community Development Company Area," 25 May 1946; "Flin Flon-Creighton

Area 1944-1948," "Flin Flon Brigade Ignored Fire; Was in Saskatchewan," *Star Phoenix* (Saskatoon), 21 January 1946.

64 DNR, *Annual Report,* 1954, 63.

65 DNR, *Annual Report,* 1953, 152; DNR, *Annual Report,* 1957, 70; DNR, *Annual Report,* 1958, 78; DNR, *Annual Report,* 1959, N.A. 25; *SAB*, R-907.2, f. I-3d, "Flin Flon-Creighton Area 1950-1952," C. Steventon to J. McIntosh, 12 November 1951; J.W. Churchman to C.F. Oatway, 17 October 1951; W.J. Bague to Churchman, 21 November 1951; S-M15, Box 7, "Fish Products (3)," K.E. Dickson to J.L. Phelps, 11 April 1946; S-M15, Box 36, "Doidge, J. (Publicity), James Hayes (Research Sec., DNR)," 4 June 1946; William D. Knill and Arthur K. Davis, "Provincial Education in Northern Saskatchewan: Progress and Bog Down, 1944-1962," in *A Northern Dilemma: Reference Papers*, vol. 1, ed. Arthur K. Davis et al. (Bellingham, WA: Western Washington State College, 1967), 205.

66 *SAB*, S-NR 1/4, DNR, 235, "Denare Beach" (2 files), clipping from Flin Flon newspaper (probably the *Daily Reminder*), "C.C. Sparling Heads Denare Beach Ratepayers Assoc.," 30 July 1953; E.R. Thompson to Mr. Brockelbank, 11 August 1953; C.S. Brown to A.T. Davidson, Att: A.I. Bereskin, 25 September 1953; C.S. Brown to Davidson, 25 September 1953.

67 *SAB*, S-NR 1/4, DNR, 231 B, "La Ronge – General" (5 files), W.T. Ritchie to J.W. Churchman, 20 April 1949; S-NR 1/4, DNR, 235, "La Ronge, Publicity," Churchman to Parker E. Dragoo, 21 May 1952. Leases also proved easier for DNR, as it could more easily lease unsurveyed land than sell it.

68 DNR, *Annual Report,* 1961, 107; *SAB*, S-NR 1/4, DNR, 167 B3, "Northern Region, April 1st, 1956," 1949 N. Dist. Field Officers' Conf., Prince Albert, SK, 31 January-1 February 1949, J.W. Churchman, "Administration of the North"; S-NR 1/4, DNR, 235, "Denare Beach" (2 files), Harry Fenster to Jack Herbert, 11 January 1955; R.G. Young to C.S. Brown, 1 February 1955; S-NR 1/4, DNR, 231 B, "Buffalo Narrows, 1949-1957," C.L. MacLean to Churchman, 10 July 1951; MacLean to Churchman, 7 August 1951; MacLean to Churchman, 13 July 1951; MacLean to Churchman, 21 August 1952; S-NR 1/5, DNR, I, 88, (426), "Cumberland House – General, 1961," Young to Mr. Armstrong, 15 March 1961; A.H. MacDonald to Young, 16 March 1961.

69 *SAB*, S-NR 1/5, DNR, 76, (411), "Buffalo Narrows, 1957-1961," C.S. Brown to A.H. MacDonald, 18 April 1961; MacDonald to J.W. Churchman, 24 April 1961.

70 *SAB*, S-NR 1/4, DNR, 231 B, "Buffalo Narrows, 1949-1957," C.L. MacLean to Soldier Settlement and Veterans' Land Act, 12 September 1950; C.S. Brown to A.T. Davidson, 2 December 1955; R.E. Brooker to MacLean, 7 June 1950; S-NR 1/5, DNR, v. I, f. 76, (411), "Buffalo Narrows. 1957-1961," A.H. MacDonald to C.S. Brown, 8 January 1960; J.W. Churchman to MacDonald, 19 February 1960; S-NR 1/5, DNR, v. I, f. 88, (426), "Cumberland House – General, 1961," R.G. Young to Mr. Armstrong, 15 March 1961; A.H. MacDonald to R.G. Young, 16 March 1961. At Buffalo Narrows the CCF allowed a veteran, J.A.C. Good, to use leased land as collateral in order to obtain a loan through the Soldiers Settlement and Veterans Land Act. In another case at Buffalo Narrows the CCF lease policy endangered the future of the family of elderly Tom Pederson. It appeared that Pederson, in poor health, would soon die. This would end his lease and put his wife and family, who relied on social aid, in jeopardy. After intervention by the ratepayers' association, the CCF made a show of having Minister Brockelbank and Deputy Minister Churchman personally present the title to Pederson. Controversially, R.G. Young, DNR's assistant deputy minister, approved the sale of four lots at Cumberland House to an outfitter from Regina in 1961. A.H. MacDonald, the director of Northern Affairs, questioned the decision, which broke the policy not to sell land.

71 *SAB*, R-907.2, f. II-12, "J.J. Wheaton, N. Admin.," Wheaton to J.L. Phelps, 5 December 1947.

72 *SAB*, S-NR 1/4, DNR, 235, "Island Falls," A.I. Bereskin to C.A.L. Hogg, 1 August 1950.

73 D. Poelzer and I. Poelzer, *Resident Metis Women's Perceptions of their Local Social Reality in Seven Northern Saskatchewan Communities,* a preliminary descriptive report for submission to the Saskatchewan Native Women's Association and to the women interviewed in the original field research (1982), 115.

74 *SAB*, S-NR 1/4, DNR, 235, "Cumberland House – General," v. 1, June 1948-31 August 1950, J.J. Wheaton to J.W. Churchman, 21 September 1948; S-NR 1/4, 235, "Cumberland House – General," v. 2, September 1950 to 1957, C.S. Brown to Churchman, 23 January

1953; Brown to Churchman, 6 January 1953; S-NR 1/4, DNR, 235, "Cumberland House – 1953-1956," A.I. Bereskin to Brown, 10 May 1954; Brown to A.T. Davidson, 10 December 1953; S-NR 1/4, DNR, 551 C, "Northern Region," v. 1, 1950-57, R.G. Young to Churchman, 12 September 1955.

75 *SAB*, S-NR 1/4, DNR, 137 C8, "La Ronge" (3 files), Map of Montreal Lake-La Ronge Highway area showing cabins and camps, 21 August 1953; B.A. Matheson to A.T. Davidson, 16 August 1953; S-NR 1/4, DNR, 230, "N. Dist. – Gen.," v. 2, 1954-56, C.S. Brown to Davidson, Att: J.W. Churchman, 15 December 1954; S-NR 1/4, DNR, f. 430, "Game and Fur Branch, Gen. 1948-1951," C.L. MacLean to Matheson, 16 July 1949.

76 *SAB*, S-NR 1/4, DNR, 167 B3, "N. Region," Discussion Report of N. Dist. Field Officers' Conf., 9-14 October 1951; Minutes N. Reg. Cons. Officers' Conf., 15-19 October 1956; S-NR 1/4, DNR, 230, "Northern Region," A.T. Davidson to C.A.L. Hogg, 13 March 1952; S-NR 1/4, DNR, 231 B, "Buffalo Narrows, 1949-1957," C.L. MacLean to J.W. Churchman, 10 July 1951.

77 DNR, *Annual Report*, 1951, 150; DNR, *Annual Report*, 1954, 63; *SAB*, R-907.2, II-12, "J.J. Wheaton, N. Admin.," Wheaton to C.A.L. Hogg, Re: Progress Report – NAD – Spring and Summer 1948; S-NR 1/4, DNR, 137 C6, "Goldfields," J.H. Jansen to J.H. Brockelbank, 8 June 1950; S-NR 1/5, DNR, I, 80, (415), "La Ronge, 1955-1961," W.J. Bague to A.H. MacDonald, 27 September 1961; S-NR2, DNR, (A), August 1944-April 1949, 38, "N. Dist. (A.K. Quandt)," N. Dist. Field Officers' Conf., Prince Albert, SK, 31 January 1949, Speech by J.W. Churchman.

78 *Progress: A Survey of Saskatchewan Government Activity* (Regina: Bureau of Publications, 1955), 66; *SAB*, S-NR 1/4, DNR, 167 B3, "N. Region," Minutes of N. Region Cons. Officers' Conf., 15-19 October 1956.

79 *SAB*, S-NR 1/5, DNR, III, 4, "NAD, 1962-67," "Local Development 1962 Tax Levy and Comparisons," no date or author.

80 *SAB*, S-NR 1/4, DNR, 230, "Northern Region," R.G. (Roy) Young to J.W. Churchman, 26 June 1953.

81 *SAB*, S-NR 1/5, DNR, I, 39, 230, "N. Region, 1957-1959," "Northern Population," no author or date.

82 Shackleton, *Tommy Douglas*, 203.

83 *Glenbow Archives*, M125, s. VI, f. 39, "Historical Notes, 1932-1959," W.J. Berezowsky to Members of Advisory Comm. on N. Dev., 30 September 1952.

84 Dobbin, "Prairie Colonialism," 24-25.

85 Valentine, *The Metis of Northern Saskatchewan*, 29-30.

86 *SAB*, S-NR 1/5, v. 1, f. 16, (137K), "Filleting Plants, 1955-59," "Proposal to Organize a Co-Operative Fish Processing Organization at Ile a la Crosse," 1958.

87 Kew, *Cumberland House*, 112-127. Information about the class system also comes from a variety of other sources. A record of service in the armed forces helped Metis move up the social ladder there and elsewhere. The prestige that came from military service helped elevate some to positions like that of special constable or game management officer.

88 *SAB*, S-M16, v. XV, f. 14, "Indians, 1955-64," A.M. Nicholson to Col. H.M. Jones, 12 July 1957; Philip Ballantyne, *The Land Alone/Aski-puko* (Saskatchewan: n.p., 1976), 135; Richard H. Bartlett, "Indian and Native Rights in Uranium Development in Northern Saskatchewan," in "Uranium Development in Saskatchewan," special issue of *Saskatchewan Law Review* 45, 1 (1980-81): 39-40; Keith Goulet, "Oral History as an Authentic and Credible Research Base for Curriculum: The Cree of Sandy Bay and Hydroelectric Power Development 1927-67, an Example" (master's thesis, University of Regina, 1986), 135-138.

89 *SAB*, S-M16, v. XV, f. 14, "Indians, 1955-64," A.M. Nicholson to Col. H.M. Jones, 12 July 1957.

90 *SAB*, S-NR 1/5, v. I, f. 69, "General – Northern Affairs, 1958-1961," W. Hlady, "Island Falls White Attitudes," 24 June 1959; Hlady, "Summary, A Social and Economic Study of Sandy Bay," Survey, June-September 1959 (Regina, SK: Department of Natural Resources and/or Department of the Environment, 1959).

91 *SAB*, R-517, v. XIII, f. 9, "Organization," 1951-71, R.F. Badgley to Dr. M.S. Acker, 3 May 1960.

92 Adrian A. Seaborne, "A Population Geography of Northern Saskatchewan," *The Musk-Ox* 12 (1973): 49-57; DNR, *Annual Report*, 1961, 102; Jim Wright, "Saskatchewan's North,"

Canadian Geographical Journal 45, 1 (July 1952): 32-33; *SAB*, S-M 16, A.M. Nicholson Papers, v. VII, f. 4, "Tour of North Saskatchewan, 1959," "The Present, the Potential, and the Planned for Northern Saskatchewan," background data for the National Northern Development Conference, Edmonton, 1958, no author given; W.A. Arrowsmith, "Northern Saskatchewan and the Fur Trade" (master's thesis, University of Saskatchewan, 1964), 61-64. The Census Division 18 population, without the Local Improvement Districts in its southern area, totalled 4,221 in 1921, 8,540 in 1946, and 17,687 in 1961. The population of Indian reserves totalled 2,365 in 1921, 3,087 in 1946, and 3,727 in 1961, while the off-reserve population rose from 1,856 in 1921 to 5,453 in 1946 and to 13,960 in 1961. In the late 1950s the Cumberland area had about 900 people, with 200 Status Indians, 600 Metis, and 100 whites. The La Ronge area was home to about 3,500 people, including 2,000 Status Indians, 900 Metis, and 600 whites. The Buffalo area's 3,800 persons consisted of about 900 Status Indians, 2,140 Metis, and 760 whites. Churchill Region included about 3,230 persons, with 630 Status Indians, 500 Metis, and 2,100 whites, counting 1,700 in Creighton. Athabasca had 4,500 residents, consisting of 350 Status Indians, 300 Metis, and 3,850 whites, with most of these in Uranium City. The Reindeer-Wollaston area held about 520 residents, with 300 Status Indians, 150 Metis, and seventy whites. Only about fifty persons lived in the Cree Lake area. This number includes about twenty Status Indians, ten Metis, and twenty whites. Numerous factors make it difficult to determine northern population with accuracy. Varying definitions of the north, a migratory Aboriginal population, a transitory white population, and mixed federal and provincial jurisdictions add confusion. While all of the NAD fell within Census Division 18, the division included an area south of the NAD. Population estimates varied widely, as in 1951, when DNR counted a NAD population of 9,657 while figures based on the census included 11,580 persons. Saskatchewan Hospital Service Plan records possibly offered the most accurate figures, although they also sometimes included an area outside the NAD.

93 Arrowsmith, "Northern Saskatchewan and the Fur Trade," 61-72; Buckley, Kew, and Hawley, *The Indians and Metis of Northern Saskatchewan*, 11-15, 107; *SAB*, R-517, Dept. of Health, Comm. Health Serv. Br., N. Health Dist., v. XIII, f. 7, "Budget Estimates," 1956-73 (3 folders); E.L. Miner to Dr. M.S. Acker, Re: N. Health Dist. B Budget 1965-66 – Request for Add. P.H.N. I Pos., 28 May 1964; Seaborne, "A Population Geography," 49-57.

94 Marcel L'Heureux, interview by author, La Ronge, SK, July 1999. Marcel L'Heureux, social worker, supervisor, regional director, and deputy minister, thinks government should have set a ceiling on the number of children for which it would pay welfare.

95 *SAB*, R-517, Badgley to Acker, 3 May 1960; S-M16, v. VII, f. 3, "Parks and Lands Branch, 1961-63," Brief by the N. Adv. Comm. on the Metis of N. Sask., 1955; Appendix A, "On Welfare and Development Policy for Northern Saskatchewan," no date or author; "Welfare and Development Policy for Northern Saskatchewan," no author, December 1957.

96 *Glenbow Archives*, M125, Series III, f. 24, "Correspondence, 1933-67, Tompkins, Peter C., 1951-66," From Pete to Jimmy, 12 March 1952.

97 *SAB*, R-517, v. XIII, f. 10, "Various Services," 1950-73, Dr. G. Kinneard to Secretary, Northern Advisory Committee, Re: Medical and Health Services, NSAD, 8 June 1955.

Chapter 4: A Deterrent to Development

1 DNR, *Annual Report*, 1947, Intro. letter from C.A.L. Hogg to J.L. Phelps; Jean Larmour, "Jack Douglas and Saskatchewan's Highways," *Saskatchewan History*, 38, 3 (Autumn 1985): 106.

2 *Saskatchewan Archives Board [SAB]*, S-NR 1/4, DNR, Dep. Min. and ADM Files, f. 230, "Northern Region," J.W. Churchman to R.G. Robertson, 23 November 1954.

3 *SAB*, S-NR 1/4, 230, "Northern Region," C.S. Brown, "Northern Saskatchewan – A Special Problem," 8/3/56.

4 *SAB*, S-M15, Box 18, Joseph Lee Phelps Ministerial Papers, "Hudson Bay Mining and Smelting Company, 1944-1946," J.L. Phelps to A.M. Nicholson; J.S. Bevan to Phelps, 5 March 1945. During 1943 HBM&S mined 242,682 dry tons of ore in Manitoba and 2,015,956 dry tons in Saskatchewan.

5 David W. Friesen, *The Cree Indians of Northern Saskatchewan: An Overview of the Past and Present* (Saskatoon: Department of Anthropology/Archaeology, University of Saskatchewan, 1973), 15; DNR, *Annual Report*, 1948, 121; La Ronge Heritage Committee, *Our Roots:*

A History of La Ronge (La Ronge, SK: Lakeland Press Ltd., 1981), 52; *SAB*, S-M15, Box 17, "General Correspondence, 1944-1946" (3), Asst. Sec. to F.R. Smith, 2 April 1946; S-NR 1/5, v. I, f. 131, "Roads – General – 1956-61," J.W. Churchman to K.M. Stevenson, 19 January 1960; W.O. Kupsch and S.D. Hanson, eds., *Gold and Other Stories As Told to Berry Richards* (Regina: Saskatchewan Mining Association, 1986), 146.

6 *SAB*, R-907.3, J.H. Brockelbank Papers, f. 7b, "Dominion Government Departments: Resources and Development (J.H. Brockelbank: Natural Resources)," J.H. Brockelbank to R.H. Winters, 8 November 1952; Winters to Brockelbank, 8 December 1952; S-M15, Box 5, "Dominion-Provincial Conference, 1945-1946 (1)," Untitled, 8.

7 DNR, *Annual Report*, 1955, 64, 72; DNR, *Annual Report*, 31 March 1957, 42; "Historic Motorcade up to Buffalo Narrows," *Saskatoon Star-Phoenix*, 17 November 1956; Institute for Northern Studies, *Beauval Community Planning Study* (Saskatoon: University of Saskatchewan, 1979), 12-13; *SAB*, R-517, Dept. of Health, Comm. Health Services Br. (GR-278), (Records of Central Office, the 13 Health Regions and the Northern Health District), Northern Health District, v. XIII, f. 61, "Buffalo Narrows – Outpost Hospital, 1957-1972," Memo for file, 16 March 1965; S-NR 1/4, f. 235, "Buffalo Narrows," J.W. Churchman to A.T. Davidson, 24 October 1955; S-NR 1/4, f. 235, "Buffalo Narrows," J.H. Brockelbank to Mr. and Mrs. D. Le Chasseur, 16 August 1951; S-NR 1/5, v. I, f. 76, (411) "Buffalo Narrows, 1957-1961," Churchman to A.H. MacDonald, 23 January 1961; Churchman to M.A. Laird, 25 January 1961; H. McPhail to A.G. Kuziak, 20 June 1961; Kuziak to McPhail, 6 November 1961.

8 DNR, *Annual Report*, 1961, 102; *SAB*, R782, DNR (GR-24-3), v. I, f. 4, "Branch Heads Meetings, 1963-1968," "Minutes of the Branch Heads' Planning and Policy Committee," Meeting No. 53, Meadow Lake, SK, 16 September 1964; S-M16, A.M. Nicholson Papers, v. XIII, f. 293, "Rehabilitation, Metis, La Loche, 1958-62," P. Spaulding to J.T. Phalen, 20 January 1958; P. Godt, "Co-Operative Store Project for La Loche"; S-NR 1/4, f. 235, "La Loche," Petition from "People of La Loche" for summer road; C.L. MacLean to J.W. Churchman, 26 January 1950; Churchman to MacLean, 10 February 1950; S-NR 1/5, v. I, "General," f. 131, "Roads – General – 1956-61," A.G. Kuziak to A.R. Guy, 16 November 1961; R.N. Gooding, "Construction Division Road Program for 1959-60," 22 May 1959.

9 *SAB*, S-NR 1/4, f. 167 B3, "Northern Region," Minutes of N. District Cons. Officers' Conf., Prince Albert, SK, 4-8 October 1954; S-NR 1/4, f. 230, "Northern Region," C.A.L. Hogg to J.W. Churchman, 10 August 1951; Churchman to J.F. Midgett, 5 September 1951.

10 "Historic Motorcade up to Buffalo Narrows," *Saskatoon Star-Phoenix*, 17 November 1956; *SAB*, S-NR 1/4, f. 235, "Buffalo Narrows," Resolution by Buffalo Narrows Ratepayers' Assoc., 30 January 1957; J.H. Brockelbank, "Address" to Northern Saskatchewan Development Conference, Saskatoon, SK, 20-21 November 1957, 2; S-M 16, A.M. Nicholson Papers, v. VII, f. 4, "Tour of North Saskatchewan, 1959," "The Present, the Potential, and the Planned for Northern Saskatchewan," background data for the National Northern Development Conference, Edmonton, August 1958, no author given.

11 F. Alvin G. Hamilton, "Address," Northern Saskatchewan Development Conference, Saskatoon, SK, 20-21 November 1957, 2, 8.

12 *Glenbow Archives*, M125, James Brady Collection, s. VI, f. 47, "Miscellaneous (Native Rights and Northern Development), 1947-1965," M.M., "The Present, the Potential, and the Planned for Northern Saskatchewan," background data for the National Northern Development Conference, Edmonton, 1958; *SAB*, S-NR 1/5, v. I, "General," f. 134, "Roads to Resources, 1960-61," "Roads to Resources," booklet for federal officials visit, September 1960.

13 DNR, *Annual Report*, 1959, N.A. 25; *SAB*, S-NR 1/5, v. I, "General," f. 134, "Roads to Resources, 1960-61," R.J. Genereux to S. Wiltshire, 29 June 1960; A.G. Kuziak to A. Hamilton, 31 March 1960; Kuziak to W.D. Ross, 4 November 1960; Hamilton to J.H. Brockelbank, 6 September 1960; Brockelbank to Hamilton, 26 August 1960; Brockelbank to Hamilton, 19 September 1960.

14 *SAB*, S-NR 1/5, v. I, "General," f. 134, "Roads to Resources, 1960-61," L.T. Holmes to C.G. Willis, 14 November 1960; A.G. Kuziak to W. Dinsdale, 21 March 1961; Dinsdale to Kuziak, 13 April 1961; Dinsdale to Kuziak, 14 June 1961.

15 *SAB*, S-NR 1/5, v. I, "General," f. 134, "Roads to Resources, 1960-61," A. Hamilton to J.H. Brockelbank, 22 September 1960; L.T. Holmes to C.G. Willis, 14 November 1960; A.G.

Kuziak to W. Dinsdale, 21 March 1961; Dinsdale to Kuziak, 13 April 1961; Dinsdale to Kuziak, 14 June 1961; Kuziak to Dinsdale, 19 July 1961; J.W. Churchman to Brockelbank, 7 December 1961; Cabinet Secretary to Premier Douglas, Kuziak, W.S. Lloyd, Brockelbank, C.G. Willis; Cabinet Minute No. 936, 16 August 1961; Kuziak to Dinsdale, 5 September 1961; Dinsdale to Kuziak, 20 September 1961; E.J. Goos to J.G. Diefenbaker and W.S. Lloyd, 17 November 1961; To J.H. Brockelbank, "Re: Northern Roads," 1960 or 1961; S-NR 1/5, v. III, f. 34, "Road to Resources, 1957-64," "Roads to Resources."

16 DNR, *Annual Report,* 1957, 42; *SAB,* DNS-1, Dept. of N. Sask, (GS-201), v. VIII, f. 7, L. Olson, "History and Culture Report – Kinoosao (Co-Op Point)"; S-M 16, A.M. Nicholson Papers, v. VII, f. 4, "Tour of North Saskatchewan, 1959," "The Present, the Potential, and the Planned for Northern Saskatchewan," background data for the National Northern Development Conference, Edmonton, September 1958; S-NR 1/5, v. I, "General," f. 131, "Roads – General – 1956-61," S.W. Schortinghuis, to J.W. Churchman, 26 August 1959; Schortinghuis to Churchman, 5 July 1960; Churchman to J.G. Cowan, 9 August 1961; R.G. Young to Churchman, Att: M.K. McCutcheon, 17 October 1961; J.G. Cowan to Churchman, 20 November 1961.

17 DNR, *Annual Report,* 1959, Co 6; DNR, *Annual Report,* 1963, 118; *SAB,* S-M15, Box 2, "Construction of Roads," J.L. Phelps to H.J. Miles; J.W. Nejedly to H.R. Mackenzie, 2 February 1940; S-M15, Box 5, "Economic Advisory Board Recommendations, 1945-1946," DNR Activities Summary for 1945 and 1946 Plans, 2; S-M15, Box 7, "Fish Products" (3), Phelps to K. Dickson, 28 March 1946; S-M 16, A.M. Nicholson Papers, v. VII, f. 4, "Tour of North Saskatchewan, 1959," "The Present, the Potential, and the Planned for Northern Saskatchewan," background data for the National Northern Development Conference, Edmonton, September 1958, no author given; S-NR 1/5, v. I, "General," f. 131, "Roads – General – 1956-61," R.N. Gooding, "Construction Division Road Program for 1959-60," 22 May 1959; S-NR2, (A) Subject Files – August 1944-April 1949, f. 19, "Fisheries Branch (A.H. MacDonald)," J.W. Churchman, Summary of a Meeting Held in the Minister's Office, 16 September likely 1948; R. Gooding, interview by author, Prince Albert, SK, August 1999.

18 J.E.M. Kew, *Cumberland House in 1960* (Saskatoon: Center for Community Studies, University of Saskatchewan, 1962), 30-31; *SAB,* S-M16, v. VI, f. 1, "General, 1962-63," J.W. Churchman to A.M. Nicholson, 8 June 1962; S-M16, v. VIII, f. 1, "Planning Branch, 1953-63" (1 of 2), "Cabinet Conference on Program Planning, May 21-22, 1963"; S-NR 1/4, f. 230, "Northern Region," C.S. Brown to A.T. Davidson, 13 January 1954; Carrot River-The Pas Agric. Dev. Route Assoc. to J.H. Brockelbank, 21 January 1954; S-NR 1/4, f. 235, "Cumberland House – General," v. 2, September 1950-57, Brown to Davidson, 13 January 1954; Brockelbank to J.W. Churchman, 8 December 1952; S-NR 1/5, v. I, f. 74, (408), "Cumberland House Farm, 1957-1961," "Historical Chronology on the Cumberland House Farm," S-NR 1/5, v. III, f. 20, "Cumberland House – General, 1962-67," E. Kramer to Tr. Board, 26 September 1963; J.S. Sinclair to A.H. MacDonald, 21 October 1963; E. Fiddler to R. Thatcher, 3 March 1965; J.M. Cuelenaere to Miss E. Fiddler, 26 March 1965; S-NR 1/5, v. III, f. 34, "Road to Resources, 1957-64," "Roads to Resources."

19 *SAB,* S-M16, v. VII, f. 2, "Parks and Lands Branch, 1961-64," A.G. Kuziak to A.M. Nicholson, 5 March 1962; S-NR 1/5, v. I, "General," f. 131, "Roads – General – 1956-61," A.R. Guy to A.H. McDonald, 17 July 1961; Kuziak to Guy, 16 November 1961; S-NR 1/5, v. III, f. 34, "Road to Resources, 1957-64," "Roads to Resources"; S-NR 1/5, v. III, f. 34, "Road to Resources," E.J. Goos to E. Kramer, 23 December 1963; Island Falls-Sandy Bay Road Assoc. to A. Laing, 18 April 1964; Island Falls-Sandy Bay Road Assoc. to E. Kramer, 20 April 1964.

20 *SAB,* S-NR 1/5, v. III, f. 34, "Road to Resources, 1957-64," E. Kramer to A. Laing, 18 December 1963; J.M. Cuelenaere to A. Laing, 29 May 1964. Expenditures included: Otosquean road – $1,650,000, Hanson Lake road – $5,700,000, Uranium City road – $1,710,000, Prince Albert bridge – $1,560,000, Cumberland House road – $50,000, and Island Falls road – $2,700.

21 *SAB,* S-NR 1/5, v. I., "General," f. 131, "Roads – General – 1956-61," R.N. Gooding to R.G. Young, 24 November 1961; J.W. Churchman to Gooding, 7 December 1961.

22 *SAB,* S-NR 1/5, v. I, "General," f. 131, "Roads – General – 1956-61," A.G. Kuziak to M. Semchuk, 14 April 1961; N.J. McLeod to J.W. Churchman, 21 August 1961; Paul Hurly, "Beauval, Saskatchewan: An Historical Sketch," *Saskatchewan History* 33, 3 (Autumn 1980): 102-110.

23 Department of Natural Resources, *The New North: Saskatchewan's Northern Development Program, 1945-1948* (Regina: DNR, 1948), 10; Martin Semchuk, "Transportation Panel," Northern Saskatchewan Development Conference, Saskatoon, SK, 20-21 November 1957; *SAB*, S-M15, Box 2, "Construction of Roads," Dep. Min., Dept. of Highways to J.L. Phelps, 27 July 1945; S-NR2, DNR-ADM, (A) Subject Files – August 1944-April 1949, f. 10, "Construction Branch (R.N. Gooding)," R.N. Gooding to C.A.L. Hogg, 18 February 1949.

24 Economic and Planning Board, *Saskatchewan Economic Review* (November 1951), 7-8; *SAB*, R-907.3, f. 7a, "Dominion Government Departments: Resources and Development (J.H. Brockelbank: Natural Resources)," R.H. Winters to Brockelbank, 27 February 1951; S-NR 1/4, f. 230, "Northern Region," J.W. Churchman to R.G. Robertson, 23 November 1954; S-NR 1/5, v. I, "General," f. 134, "Roads to Resources, 1960-61," J.R. Woodward, to A.G. Kuziak, 28 March 1960; W.D. Ross to T.C. Douglas, 3 June 1960; Submission to Brockelbank, "Re: Northern Roads," likely 1960 or 1961; Kuziak to W. Dinsdale, 19 July 1961.

25 *SAB*, S-NR 1/5, v. I, "General," f. 134, "Roads to Resources, 1960-61," A. Hamilton to A.G. Kuziak, 14 April 1960; Kuziak to Hamilton, 5 April 1960; S-NR 1/5, v. III, f. 34, "Road to Resources," A. Laing to E. Kramer, 2 March 1964; C.C. Willis to L.T. Holmes, 13 March 1964.

26 *Proceedings "Resources for People" Saskatchewan Resources Conference*, Saskatoon, SK, 20-21 January 1964, 256; *SAB*, R646, "Saskatchewan Department of Social Services," Info. Services, "Saskatchewan: The Province and its People," 1965, 14; S-NR 1/5, v. III, f. 34, "Road to Resources, 1957-64," L.T. Holmes to J.W. Churchman, 1 September 1964.

27 *SAB*, R-517, v. XIII, f. 9, "Organization," 1951-71, R.F. Badgley to Dr. M.S. Acker, 3 May 1960.

28 La Ronge Heritage Comm., *Our Roots*, 53.

29 *SAB*, S-NR 1/4, f. 230, "Northern Region," Various documents.

30 Gary William David Abrams, *Prince Albert: The First Century 1866-1966* (Saskatoon: Modern Press, 1966), 272; J.C. Parres, "Transportation Panel," Northern Saskatchewan Development Conference, Saskatoon, SK, 20-21 November 1957; *SAB*, S-M 16, A.M. Nicholson Papers, v. VII, f. 4, "Tour of North Saskatchewan, 1959," "The Present, the Potential, and the Planned for Northern Saskatchewan," background data for the National Northern Development Conference, Edmonton, September 1958, no author given; S-M16, v. VIII, f. 1, "Planning Board, 1953-63" (2 of 2), D.H.F. Black to Pres. and Members of Exec. Council, 19 November 1957; "Minutes of the Cabinet Committee on Planning and Budgeting," 18-22 November 1957; S-NR 1/5, v. I, f. 39, (230), "Northern Region, 1957-1959," Cabinet Sec. to Premier and six Ministers, Cabinet Minute No. 8762, 26 September 1958.

31 *SAB*, R-907.2, J.H. Brockelbank Papers, v. I, f. 2, "Cumberland House Settlement," M.F. Norris to J.J. Wheaton, 22 October 1947; R-907.2, v. II, f. 4b, "J.W. Churchman, Deputy Minister, May 1951-July 1954," J.H. Brockelbank to J.W. Churchman, Att: E.E. Chorneyko, 12 July 1954; R-907.2, v. II, f. 6, "R.N. Gooding, Supervisor of Equipment and Construction," "Minutes Road Committee," Meeting, 18 April 1952; S-NR 1/4, f. 235, "Cumberland House – General," v. 2, September 1950-57, E. Dodds to C.L. MacLean, 25 October 1951.

32 J. Howard Richards, *Recreation Potential of the Saskatchewan River Delta Area* (Ottawa, ON: Canada, Department of Forestry and Rural Development, ARDA, 1966), App.: Cumberland House: Hist. Summary, 10.

33 DNR, *Annual Report*, 1950, 149.

34 *SAB*, S-NR 1/4, f. 230, "Northern Region – General," v. 2, 1954-56, J.W. Churchman to J.R. Baldwin, 10 October 1956; S-NR 1/4, f. 230, "Northern District – General," v. 2, 1954-56, C.S. Brown to J.H. Brockelbank, 8 November 1956.

35 *SAB*, S-NR 1/4, f. 551 C, "Northern Region," v. 1, 1950-57, C.S. Brown to A.T. Davidson, 12 November 1957.

36 *SAB*, S-NR 1/4, f. 235, "Snake Lake" (2 files), C.L. MacLean to J.W. Churchman, 29 July 1952: R-907.3, f. 6, "Dominion Government (General)," Office of the Minister of Pub. Wks. to J.H. Brockelbank, 3 October 1952; R.N. Gooding to J. Barnett, 27 July 1953.

37 *SAB*, S-NR 1/4, f. 235, "La Ronge (1)," C.S. Brown to A.T. Davidson, Att.: J.W. Churchman, 17 October 1953; H.A. Young to Churchman, 24 August 1955; S-NR 1/4, f. 235, "Ile a la Crosse," A.T. Davidson to J.W. Churchman, 4 May 1955; Laurier Poisson to E. Dodds, 22 June 1954.

38 *SAB*, R-907.3, f. 6, "Dominion Government (General)," J.H. Brockelbank to A. Fournier, 27 April 1953; Office of the Minister of Pub. Wks. to Brockelbank, 11 May 1953; S-NR 1/4, f. 235, "Reindeer Lake – South End."

39 *SAB*, S-NR 1/4, f. 230, "Northern District – General," v. 2, 1954-56, C.S. Brown to A.T. Davidson, Att. E.E. Chorneyko, 18 March 1955.

40 DNR, *The New North*, 16; DNR, *Annual Report*, 1947, Intro. letter from C.A.L. Hogg to J.L. Phelps, 1 September 1947; *SAB*, S-M15, Box 5, "Economic Advisory Board Recommendations, 1945-1946," DNR, Summary of 1945 activities and plans for 1946, 1; S-M15, Box 36, "Doidge, J. (Publicity)," News Release, DNR, January 1947; Thomas Hector Macdonald McLeod, "Public Enterprise in Saskatchewan: The Development of Public Policy and Administrative Controls" (PhD diss., Harvard University, 1959), 103-105.

41 J. Howard Richards and K.L. Fung, *Atlas of Saskatchewan* (Saskatoon: University of Saskatchewan and Modern Press, 1969), 174; *Public Enterprise in Saskatchewan* (Saskatchewan: Government Finance Office, 1964); *Progress Report from Your Government: A Survey of Saskatchewan Government Activity* (Regina: Bureau of Publications, 1948), 28; *Progress: A Survey of Saskatchewan Government Activity* (Regina: Bureau of Publications, 1955), 39; McLeod, "Public Enterprise in Saskatchewan," 105; *SAB*, R-907.3, f. 1, "Airways, Sask. Government," J.H. Brockelbank, "The Case for the Expansion and Development of Saskatchewan Government Airways," April 1959.

42 La Ronge Heritage Comm., *Our Roots*, 56; "Government Airways 'Not High' on Northern Development in 1955: Much Optimism in Other Quarters," *Saskatoon Star-Phoenix*, 6 January 1955; *SAB*, R-907.3, f. 1, "Airways, Sask. Government," Govt. of Sask., J.H. Brockelbank submission to Air Transport Board, Re: CPA Ltd. application, 9 October 1958; R-907.3, f. 3a, "Crown Corporations (J.H. Brockelbank: Natural Resources)," D.H.F. Black to Brockelbank, 19 January 1955; R-907.3, f. 6, "Dominion Government (General) (J.H. Brockelbank: Natural Resources)," Brockelbank to L. Chevrier; Chevrier to Brockelbank, 14 June 1949; S-NR 1/4, f. 551 C, "Northern Region," v. 1, 1950-57, C.S. Brown to A.T. Davidson, 12 November 1957.

43 *SAB*, S-M15, Box 23, "Parks,1945-1946," W.A.S. Tegart to J.L. Phelps, 2 April 1946; S-NR 1/4, f. 230, "Northern District – General," v. 2, 1954-56, C.S. Brown to A.T. Davidson, Att. E.E. Chorneyko, 18 March 1955; DNR, *Annual Report*, 1948, 121; DNR, *Annual Report*, 1959, N.A. 27; La Ronge Heritage Comm., *Our Roots*, 53.

44 Bicentennial Committee of Cumberland House, *A History of Cumberland House ... As Told By Its Own Citizens 1774 to 1974* (Cumberland House, SK: Bicentennial Committee, 1974), 6; DNR, *Annual Report*, 1948, 131-132; DNR, *Annual Report*, 1958, 88; *Progress: A Survey*, 16; *SAB*, R-517, v. XIII, f. 9, "Organization," 1951-71, R.F. Badgley to Dr. M.S. Acker, 3 May 1960; R-517, v. XIII, f. 14, "Nursing and Child Health," 1950-70, L. Cowan to Dr. L. Kawula, 15 April 1963; Dr. R.H. MacPherson to Kawula, 24 May 1963; S-M 16, A.M. Nicholson Papers, v. VII, f. 4, "Tour of North Saskatchewan, 1959," "The Present, the Potential, and the Planned for Northern Saskatchewan," background data for the National Northern Development Conference, Edmonton, September 1958, no author given; S-NR 1/4, f. 167 B3, "Northern Region," Min.of N. Dist. Conf., October 7-14, 1955; S-NR 1/4, f. 230, "Northern Region," J.W. Churchman to R.G. Robertson, 23 November 1954.

45 John Richards and Larry Pratt, *Prairie Capitalism: Power and Influence in the New West* (Toronto: McClelland and Stewart, 1979), 113; Richard Wuorinen, *A History of Buffalo Narrows* (Buffalo Narrows, SK: Buffalo Narrows Celebrate Saskatchewan Committee, 1981), 28; *SAB*, R-517, v. XIII, f. 64, "Sandy Bay – Outpost Hospital, 1961-1973," Sister Frances Cecilia to Min. of Northern Affairs, 30 July 1963; Dr. A.C. Irwin to D.L. Hackney, 5 February 1962; S-NR 1/4, f. 235, "La Ronge (1)," C.S. Brown to A.T. Davidson, 27 October 1953; S-NR 1/4, f. 235, "Denare Beach" (2 files), J.W. Churchman to Davidson, Att: Brown, 8 August 1955; S-NR 1/5, v. I, f. 76, (411), "Buffalo Narrows, 1957-1961," J.S. Sinclair to A.H. MacDonald, 18 October 1960; MacDonald to Sinclair, 25 October 1960.

46 Bureau of Publications, *Government in Industry: A Brief Account of Saskatchewan Crown Corporations* (Regina: Bureau of Publications, 1947); *SAB*, R646, Sask. Dept. of Soc. Serv., Info. Services, "Saskatchewan: The Province and its People," 1965.

47 *SAB*, S-NR 1/4, f. 235, "Buffalo Narrows," C.S. Brown to A.T. Davidson, 13 July 1954.

48 *SAB*, R-517, v. XIII, f. 1, *Annual Reports*, 1949-67.

49 *SAB*, R-907.2, v. II, f. 12, "J.J. Wheaton, Northern Administrator," J.L. Phelps to Wheaton, 9 January 1948; S-NR 1/4, f. 235, "Denare Beach" (2 files), C.S. Brown to A.T. Davidson, Att: J.W. Churchman, 23 April 1953; J.W. Churchman to Brown, 28 April 1953.

50 La Ronge Heritage Comm., *Our Roots*, 54-56; *SAB*, S-NR 1/4, f. 137 K3B, "La Ronge" (3

files), R. Hook to A.T. Davidson, 23 June 1955; S-NR 1/4, f. 235, "La Ronge" (1), J.H. Brock-elbank to J.W. Tomlinson, 20 August 1951; J.R. Sarsfield to C.A.L. Hogg, 10 August 1951; J.R. Sarsfield to DNR, 2 December 1954; Sarsfield to Brockelbank, 16 October 1951; Sarsfield to J.W. Churchman, 5 November 1951; Churchman to C.E. Smith, 10 January 1955; A.T. Davidson to Churchman, 22 December 1954; Brockelbank to Churchman, 30 December 1954; Churchman to Davidson, 6 December 1954; Premier's Office to Brockelbank and J.A. Darling, 19 May 1951; Report of J.D. MacLean on Lac la Ronge, 6 November 1950; S-NR 1/5, v. I, f. 41, (235) "La Ronge – 2, 1955-56," Brockelbank to Darling, 11 July 1956; L.E. Gibson to DNR, 22 August 1956.

51　"Historic Motorcade up to Buffalo Narrows," *Saskatoon Star-Phoenix*, 17 November 1956; DNR, *Annual Report*, 1957, 70-71; Wuorinen, *A History of Buffalo Narrows*, 28; *SAB*, S-NR 1/4, f. 235, "Buffalo Narrows," J.W. Churchman to D. Cass-Beggs, 21 October 1955.

52　*SAB*, R-517, v. XIII, f. 66, "Stony Rapids – Outpost Hospital, 1958-1972," Dr. A.C. Irwin to Dr. M.S. Acker, 24 October 1961; S-NR 1/4, f. 235, "Stony Rapids," J.W. Churchman to A.T. Davidson, 23 August 1957.

53　*SAB*, R-517, v. XIII, f. 6, "Newspaper Clippings, 1961-1968," Clipping "Electric power to Cumberland."

54　*SAB*, R-517, v. XIII, f. 64, "Sandy Bay – Outpost Hospital, 1961-1973," Dr. A.C. Irwin to C.E. Smith, 19 June 1961; Smith to Irwin, 30 June 1961.

55　D. Cass-Beggs, "Industrial Development Panel," Northern Saskatchewan Development Conference, Saskatoon, 20-21 November 1957; *SAB*, S-M 16, A.M. Nicholson Papers, v. VII, f. 4, "Tour of North Saskatchewan, 1959," "The Present, the Potential, and the Planned for Northern Saskatchewan," background data for the National Northern Development Conference, Edmonton, September 1958, no author given; Saskpower Facilities, "Power to You – Athabasca Power System," <http://www.saskpower.com/facilities/html/athabasca.html>, 18 February 2001.

56　*SAB*, S-NR 1/3, DNR, Dep. Min., f. G-1-7, "Community Planning, General 1948-50," A.I. Bereskin to C.A.L. Hogg, 9 November 1948.

57　Cass-Beggs, "Industrial Development Panel"; *SAB*, S-M16, v. VII, f. 4, "Tour of North Saskatchewan."

58　Richard H. Bartlett, "Hydroelectric Power and Indian Water Rights on the Prairies," *Prairie Forum* 14, 2 (Fall 1989): 177-193; James B. Waldram, *As Long As the Rivers Run: Hydroelectric Development and Native Communities in Western Canada* (Winnipeg, MB: University of Manitoba Press, 1988).

59　Keith Goulet, "Oral History as an Authentic and Credible Research Base for Curriculum: The Cree of Sandy Bay and Hydroelectric Power Development 1927-67, an Example" (master's thesis, University of Regina, 1986), 85-95, 128.

60　Philip Merasty, interview by author, Island Falls, SK, July 2000; conversations with various residents and former residents of Sandy Bay.

61　Churchill River Board of Inquiry, *Northern Briefs Submitted to the Churchill River Board of Inquiry from the Directly Affected Communities*, 1977; Goulet, "Oral History," 117-144.

62　Churchill River Board of Inquiry, *Churchill River Board of Inquiry Report* (Regina: Saskatchewan Department of Environment, 1978), 170-172; Churchill River Board of Inquiry, *Northern Briefs*, Pelican Narrows Brief, 12; Bartlett, "Hydroelectric Power," 187.

63　Philip Ballantyne, *The Land Alone/Aski-puko* (Saskatchewan: n.p., 1976), 132-134.

64　DNR, *Annual Report*, 1961, 102; Waldram, *As Long As the Rivers Run*, 55-80; *SAB*, S-NR 1/5, v. III, f. 20, "Cumberland House – General, 1962-67," D. Goulet to J. Cuelenaere, 13 July 1964; Cuelenaere to Goulet, 15 September 1964.

65　*SAB*, R-517, v. XIII, f.60, "Hospitals – General, 1953-1968," Dr. G. Kinneard to Dr. A.C. Irwin, 26 September 1955.

66　*SAB*, R-517, v. XIII, f. 22, "Policy – Sanitation," 1951-65, K.A. Mellish, San. Survey of Co-Op Fish. Plant Wollaston Lake, July 1960; Mellish, San. Survey Co-Op Fish. Plant Deschambault Lake, July 1960; Mellish, San. Survey Co-Op Fish. Plant Pinehouse, September 1960; S-NR 1/4, f. 235, "Wollaston Lake," J.F. Gray to C.L. MacLean, 28 July 1950; S-NR 1/4, f. 430, "Game and Fur Branch," A.J. Thompson to J.W. Churchman, 15 April 1953.

67　*SAB*, R-517, v. XIII, f. 22, "Policy – Sanitation," 1951-65, Dist. Sanitary Officer to Schaeffer, 14 April 1953.

68 *SAB*, S-NR 1/4, f. 235, "Cumberland House – General," v. 2, September 1950-57, A.K. Quandt, "Report on the Cumberland House Area to the Hon. J.L. Phelps," 1946.

69 *SAB*, S-NR 1/4, f. 235, "Cumberland House – General," v. 2, September 1950-57, E. Dodds to C.L. MacLean, Att.: J.W. Churchman, 5 September 1951; Dodds to MacLean, 25 October 1951.

70 *SAB*, R-517, v. XIII, f. 10, "Various Services," 1950-73, Dr. G. Kinneard to Dr. F.B. Roth, 31 January 1952; S-NR 1/4, f. 230, "Northern Region," A.I. Bereskin to C.A.L. Hogg, 15 October 1951; Bereskin to Hogg, 15 October 1951; Bereskin to Hogg, 24 October 1951; S-NR 1/4, f. 235, "La Ronge," M.A. Welsh, "Lac La Ronge," 17-20 July 1951; S-NR 1/4, f. 235, "La Ronge (1)," C.L. MacLean to J.W. Churchman, 30 April 1952.

71 *SAB*, R-517, v. XIII, f. 9, "Organization," 1951-71, R.F. Badgley to Dr. M.S. Acker, 3 May 1960.

72 *SAB*, R-517, v. XIII, f. 22, "Policy – Sanitation," 1951-65, K.A. Mellish, San. Survey of Co-Op Fish. Plant Wollaston Lake, July 1960; Mellish, San. Survey Co-Op Fish. Plant Deschambault Lake, July 1960; Mellish, San. Survey Co-Op Fish. Plant Pinehouse, September 1960.

73 *SAB*, R-517, v. XIII, f. 1, "Annual Reports," 1949-67, Dr. A.C. Irwin to Dr. M.S. Acker, 20 June 1962; R-517, v. XIII, f. 22, "Policy – Sanitation," 1951-65, Dr. G. Kinneard to Dr. G.C. Darby, 22 May 1953.

74 DNR, *Annual Report*, 1962, 109-110; T.J. Plunkett, Municipal Government in Northern Saskatchewan (1975), excerpt in David E. Smith, ed., *Building a Province: A History of Saskatchewan in Documents*, Document 37 (Saskatoon: Fifth House Publishers, 1992), 170-173; *SAB*, S-NR 1/4, f. 167 B3, "Northern Region, April 1st, 1956," N. Dist. Field Officers' Conf., Prince Albert, SK, 31 January-1 February 1949; S-NR2, (A), Subject Files – August 1944-April 1949, f. 38, "Northern District (A.K. Quandt)," N. Dist. Field Officers' Conf., 31 January 1949, Discussion summary after J.W. Churchman speech.

75 *SAB*, R-907.2, v. I, f. 2, "Cumberland House Settlement," M.F. Norris to J.J. Wheaton, 22 October 1947, Report attached "Office of the Northern Administrator Report of an Economic and Social Survey of the Cumberland House District," October 1947, Attached: Minutes of Meeting at Community Hall at Cumberland House, 11 October 1947; S-NR2, (A) Subject Files – August 1944-April 1949, f. 38, "Northern District (A.K. Quandt)," Quandt to J.W. Churchman, 13 August 1948; Minutes and proceedings of meeting at Cumberland House, 21 June 1948; Minutes of meeting of Local Council of Cumberland House, 21 June 1948.

76 DNR, *Annual Report*, 1952, 168; *SAB*, S-NR 1/4, f. 230, "Northern Region," J.W. Churchman to C.A.L. Hogg, 26 July 1951; S-NR 1/4, 235, "Denare Beach" (2 files), clipping from Flin Flon newspaper, "C.C. Sparling Heads Denare Beach Ratepayers Assoc.," 30 July 1953; S-NR 1/4, 235, "Ile a la Crosse," W.J. Bague to C.S. Brown, 6 April 1954; S-NR 1/4, f. 235, "La Ronge," C.L. MacLean to J.W. Churchman, 10 December 1951; MacLean to Churchman, 28 December 1951.

77 *SAB*, S-NR 1/5, v. I, f. 88, (426), "Cumberland House – General, 1961," A.H. MacDonald to J.W. Churchman, 20 March 1961; W.J. Bague to MacDonald, 16 March 1961; Walter M. Hlady, "The Cumberland House Fur Project: The First Two Years," in "Cree Studies," special issue of *Western Canadian Journal of Anthropology* 1, 1 (1969): 133-136.

78 Helen L. Buckley, J.E.M. Kew, and John B. Hawley, *The Indians and Metis of Northern Saskatchewan: A Report on Economic and Social Development* (Saskatoon: Center for Community Studies, University of Saskatchewan, 1963), 97-98; *SAB*, S-NR 1/5, v. III, f. 4, "Northern Administration District, 1962-67," E. Kramer to W.S. Lloyd and Cab. Members, 27 January 1964; Office of the Dir. of N. Affairs to J.W. Churchman, 23 December 1963; The Act to Amend The Northern Administration Act, 1964.

79 *SAB*, R-A1113, Joe Phelps, interview by Murray Dobbin, audio tape, 1976; S-NR 1/4, f. 230, "Northern Region," RCMP, "F" Div., to Dep. Min. of DNR, 11 October 1951.

80 *SAB*, S-NR 1/4, f. 235, "Ile a la Crosse," C.S. Brown to A.T. Davidson, Att.: J.W. Churchman, 18 July 1956; Brown to Davidson, 23 August 1956; A.S. Boyd to Churchman, 11 January 1957; S-NR 1/4, f. 230, "Northern Region," A.G. Kuziak to R.A. Walker, 1 October 1957.

81 Kew, *Cumberland House*, 107.

82 *SAB*, S-NR 1/4, f. 230, "Northern Region – General," v. 1, 1948-31 December 1954, E. Dodds to C.L. MacLean, 17 January 1952.

83 *SAB*, S-NR 1/4, f. 235, "Buffalo Narrows," C.S. Brown to A.T. Davidson, 2 April 1954.
84 Wuorinen, *A History of Buffalo Narrows*, 34-35; *SAB*, S-M16, v. VII, f. 3, "Parks and Lands Branch, 1961-63," C.S. Brown to A.T. Davidson, 29 October 1957; A.G. Kuziak to R.A. Walker, 1 November 1947; J.B. McLellan to Brown, 16 October 1957; S-NR 1/5, v. I, f. 39, (230), "Northern Region, 1957-1959," E.N. Shannon to Brown, 27 April 1958; Brown to Davidson, 7 May 1958; S-NR 1/5, v. I, f. 76 (411), "Buffalo Narrows, 1957-1961," Ratepayers Assoc. of Buffalo Narrows, "Buffalo Narrows Brief," 22 October 1957.
85 *SAB*, S-NR 1/4, f. 235, "Sandy Bay," Petition from The Council of Good Order, Sandy Bay, SK, 13 September 1955; D.M. Hunter to Ches, 26 September 1955, J.W. Churchman to J.L. Salterio, 24 October 1955; Salterio to Churchman, 26 October 1955.
86 *SAB*, S-NR 1/4, f. 235, "Denare Beach" (2 files), C.S. Brown to C.N.K. Kirk, 3 September 1957; Brown to A.T. Davidson, 31 August 1953; J.L. Salterio to J.W. Churchman, 16 October 1953.
87 Murray Dobbin, *The One-And-A-Half Men: The Story of Jim Brady and Malcolm Norris, Metis Patriots of the Twentieth Century* (Vancouver: New Star Books, 1981), 199-200.
88 *SAB*, S-M16, v. VII, f. 3, "Parks and Lands Branch, 1961-63," J.B. McLellan to C.S. Brown, 16 October 1957; Brown to A.T. Davidson, 24 October 1957; Brown to Davidson, 29 October 1957; L.M. Reznechenko to Brown, 26 October 1957; Ratepayers Assoc., "Buffalo Narrows Brief," 22 October 1957, A.G. Kuziak to R.A. Walker, 1 November 1947: J.R. Mather to J.S. White, 5 December 1957; White to T.J. Bentley, 18 December 1957.
89 Dept. of Social Welfare and Rehab., *Annual Report*, 1963, 6; *SAB*, S-M16, v. VII, f. 3, "Parks and Lands Branch, 1961-63," Brief by N. Adv. Comm. on Metis of N. Sask., 1955; C.S. Brown to A.T. Davidson, 24 October 1957; "Welfare and Development Policy for Northern Saskatchewan," December 1957; App. A, "On Welfare and Development Policy for Northern Saskatchewan."
90 *SAB*, S-M16, v. VII, f. 3, "Parks and Lands Branch, 1961-63," J.R. Mather to J.S. White, 5 December 1957; White to T.J. Bentley, 18 December 1957.
91 Wuorinen, *A History of Buffalo Narrows*, 34-35.
92 Kew, *Cumberland House*, 107.
93 *SAB*, S-NR 1/4, f. 235, "La Ronge" (1), C.L. MacLean to J.W. Churchman, 2 May 1952.
94 *SAB*, R782, v. I, f. 13, "La Ronge, 1966-1967," J.S. Sinclair to W.R. Parks, 29 March 1967; S-NR 1/4, f. 235, "La Ronge" (1), C.L. MacLean to J.W. Churchman, 30 April 1952.
95 Wuorinen, *A History of Buffalo Narrows*, 35.
96 *SAB*, S-M16, v. VII, f. 3, "Parks and Lands Branch, 1961-63," Brief by N. Adv. Comm. on Metis of N. Sask., 1955.
97 Anne Acco, interview by author, Cumberland House, SK, July 1999.
98 DNR, *Annual Report*, 1964, 45; La Ronge Heritage Comm., *Our Roots*, 64-65; *SAB*, R-907.3, f. 3a, "Crown Corporations (J.H. Brockelbank: Natural Resources)," W.A. Houseman to G.H. Craik, 15 February 1955; Houseman to Craik, 15 March 1955; S-NR2, (A) Subject Files – August 1944-April 1949, f. 37 "Northern Administration (J.J. Wheaton)," Wheaton to Brockelbank, 7 October 1948.
99 Wuorinen, *A History of Buffalo Narrows*, 35.
100 *SAB*, S-NR 1/5, v. I, f. 69, "General – Northern Affairs, 1958-1961," A.H. MacDonald to J.S. Sinclair, February 14, 1961.
101 *SAB*, S-NR 1/5, v. I, f. 88, (426), "Cumberland House – General, 1961," A.H. MacDonald to M. McCutcheon, 17 May 1961; Order in Council 951/61, 26 May 1961.

Chapter 5: Never Before Have We Been So Poor
1 *Saskatchewan Archives Board* [*SAB*], S-NR 1/4, DNR, Dep. Min. and ADM Files, f. 235, "Cumberland House – General," v. 2, September 1950-57, A.K. Quandt, "Report on the Cumberland House Area to the Hon. J.L. Phelps," 1946.
2 DNR, *Annual Report*, 1955, xi.
3 *SAB*, S-M15, Box 16, Joseph Lee Phelps Ministerial Papers, "Game Commissioner, 1944."
4 Helen L. Buckley, J.E.M. Kew, and John B. Hawley, *The Indians and Metis of Northern Saskatchewan: A Report on Economic and Social Development* (Saskatoon: Center for Community Studies, University of Saskatchewan, 1963), 5; G.W. Cadbury, "Planning in Saskatchewan," in *Essays on the Left: Essays in Honour of T.C. Douglas*, ed. Laurier LaPierre et al. (Toronto: McClelland and Stewart, 1971), 62; Lewis H. Thomas, ed., *The Making of a*

Socialist: The Recollections of T.C. Douglas (Edmonton: University of Alberta Press, 1982), 287.

5 F. Laurie Barron, *Walking in Indian Moccasins: The Native Policies of Tommy Douglas and the CCF* (Vancouver: UBC Press, 1997); *SAB*, S-M15, Box 17, "General Correspondence, 1944-1946, (2)," J.L. Phelps to G. Connon, 26 March 1945; S-M15, Box 18, "Hudson's Bay Company, 1945-1946," A. VanderKracht to Phelps, 11 March 1945; Cpl. C.E. Wenzel to Phelps, 27 February 1945; Phelps to Wenzel, 21 February 1945; S.A. Keighley to Phelps, 7 March 1945; Phelps's Secretary to VanderKracht, 2 March 1945; Newspaper clipping, source not given, "Saskatchewan to Probe Hudson's Bay Charter – Regina, March 19."

6 *SAB*, S-M15, Box 15, "Fur Marketing, 1947-1951, (1)," G.W. Burst to J.L. Phelps, 1 November 1944.

7 *SAB*, S-M15, Box 18, "Hudson's Bay Company, 1945-1946," H.F. Kerr to T.C. Douglas, 29 March 1945.

8 Murray Dobbin, "Prairie Colonialism: The CCF in Northern Saskatchewan, 1944-1964," *Studies in Political Economy: A Socialist Review* 16 (1985): 17; Barron, *Walking in Indian Moccasins*.

9 *Glenbow Archives*, M125, James Brady Collection, s. VI, f. 56, "CCF, 1954-1961," Organizational Report – Lac La Ronge C.C.F. Club, January 1960.

10 *SAB*, R-907.2, v. II, f. 12, "J.J. Wheaton, Northern Administrator," J.L. Phelps to Wheaton, 9 January 1948.

11 *SAB*, S-NR 1/4, f. 137 K, "Filleting Plants – General (Ile a la Crosse only)," Proposal to Build a Govt. Filleting Plant at Ile a la Crosse; App. D, V. Valentine, "The Social and Economic Situation of the Ile a la Crosse Metis," 2 May 1956.

12 Virginia McKay, Jean Carriere, Pierre Dorion, and Marie Deschambault, "History and Culture Report: Cumberland House," no date, 71-77.

13 Hugh Mackay Ross, *The Manager's Tale: Saskatchewan District* (Winnipeg, MB: J. Gordon Shillingford Publishing, 1989), Chapter 5.

14 DNR, *Annual Report*, 1958, 37; DNR, *Annual Report*, 1959, W 11-12; *SAB*, R-907.2, J.H. Brockelbank Papers, v. II, f. 10b, "E.L. Paynter, Game Commissioner, September 1953-April 1955," E.L. Paynter, "Fur Conservation," 30 March 1954; R-907.3, J.H. Brockelbank Papers, f. 4, "Dominion Government Departments: Citizenship and Immigration (J.H. Brockelbank: Natural Resources)," Brockelbank to W.E. Harris, 9 August 1950; Harris to Brockelbank, 25 November 1950 and 30 November 1950; S-M16, A.M. Nicholson Papers, v. XIII, f. 264, "Public Assistance, Indians and Metis, 1952-64," A.H. MacDonald, "Treaty Indians and Northern Administration," 18 November 1963; S-M16, v. XV, f. 14, "Indians, 1955-64," Acting Dep. Min., Dept. of Citizenship and Immig., 7 February 1963; S-NR 1/4, f. 430, "Game and Fur Branch, General, 1948-1951," Paynter to J.W. Churchman, 13 October 1948; S-NR 1/4, f. 430; "Game and Fur Branch, General," January 1958-, T.A. Harper, "Northern Fur Conservation Agreement – Federal Provincial," Branch Heads Conf., 3-7 February 1958; S-NR 1/5, v. III, f. 24a, "Fur Advisory Committee, 1960-64," Report of Programme Co-Ord. Comm. to Fur Adv. Comm., 29 January 1965; W.A. Arrowsmith, "Northern Saskatchewan and the Fur Trade" (master's thesis, University of Saskatchewan, 1964), 84.

15 DNR, *Annual Report*, 1947, 66; *SAB*, S-M15, Box 16, "Saskatchewan Fur Marketing Association – Minutes, 1945-1946," Minutes of First Meeting of SFMA, 29 October 1945; S-M15, Box 17, "Game Advisory Committee, 1945-1946"; Thomas Hector Macdonald McLeod, "Public Enterprise in Saskatchewan: The Development of Public Policy and Administrative Controls" (PhD diss., Harvard University, 1959), 87-89.

16 *SAB*, S-NR 1/4, f. 430, "Game and Fur Branch," J.R. Baseheart to "Sirs," 9 September 1953; E.L. Paynter to Baseheart, 24 September 1953. This applied to J.R. Baseheart of Illinois.

17 *SAB*, S-NR 1/4, f. 432, "Complaints," E.L. Paynter to C.A.L. Hogg, 26 March 1951.

18 *SAB*, R-907.3, f. 2, "Churchill River Power (J.H. Brockelbank – NAT. RESOURCES)," R.W. Davis to Brockelbank, 14 September 1949; E.L. Paynter to Brockelbank, 23 December 1949.

19 *SAB*, S-NR 1/4, f. 432, "Complaints," A.L. Akre to W.J. Berezowsky, 7 March 1951; B.A. Matheson to J.W. Churchman, 30 August 1951; C.A.L. Hogg to J.H. Brockelbank, 16 August 1951; Brockelbank to Hogg, 20 August 1951; Churchman to Hogg, 5 September 1951; Berezowsky to Churchman, Att. Hogg and E.L. Paynter, 23 April 1951; Berezowsky to Churchman, 12 April 1951.

20 *SAB*, S-NR 1/4, f. 432, "Complaints," W.J. Berezowsky to Rev. Father Landry, 27 March 1950.
21 V.F. Valentine and R.G. Young, "The Situation of the Metis of Northern Saskatchewan in Relation to His Physical and Social Environment," *The Canadian Geographer* 4 (1954): 55.
22 *SAB*, S-NR 1/4, f. 167 B3, "Northern Region," Minutes of N. Region Cons. Officers' Conf., 15-19 October 1956; S-NR 1/4, f. 430, "Game and Fur Branch, General, 1951-1955," A.T. Davidson to J.W. Churchman, 4 October 1956.
23 DNR, *Annual Report,* 1959, Wi 12.
24 *SAB*, S-NR 1/5, v. III, f. 8, "Buffalo Narrows, 1963-66," Minutes of Buffalo Narrows Reg. Conf., 28 November 1961.
25 *SAB*, S-NR 1/5, v. III, f. 24b, "Fur Advisory Committee, 1964-67," 1965 Annual Meeting Sask. Fur Adv. Comm., 29 January 1965.
26 DNR, *Annual Report,* 1945, Intro. letter from H. Lewis to J.L. Phelps, 1 September 1945; DNR, *Annual Report,* 1950, 90; DNR, *Annual Report,* 1959, Wi 9-10; J.E.M. Kew, *Cumberland House in 1960* (Saskatoon: Center for Community Studies, University of Saskatchewan, 1962), 42-45; *SAB*, R-907.2, v. II, f. 10a, "E.L. Paynter, Game Commissioner, July 1949- June 1953," Minutes of Fur Adv. Conf., 19-20 January 1950; S-M15, Box 2, "Cumberland House, 1944-1945," Cpl. M. Chappuis to The Officer Commanding, RCMP, 27 February 1944; S-M15, Box 5, "Economic Advisory Board Recommendations, 1945-1946," DNR, Summary of 1945 activities and plans for 1946, 3; S-M15, Box 29, "Orders-in-Council, 1944- 1946 (3)," Minister of Nat. Res. to Exec. Council, 3 April 1945; S-M15, Box 36, "Doidge, J. (Publicity)," DNR, Activities summary for 1945 to June 1946, 14 June 1946; S-NR 1/4, f. 430, "Game and Fur Branch," E.L. Paynter, 1951 Game Br. Report to Field Officers' Conf.; James G.E. Smith, "The Ecological Basis of Chipewyan Socio-Territorial Organization," in *Proceedings: Northern Athapaskan Conference, 1971,* vol. 2, ed. A. McFayden Clark, National Museum of Man Mercury Series, Canadian Ethnology Service Paper No. 27 (Ottawa: National Museums of Canada, 1975), 389-461.
27 *SAB*, S-M15, Box 7, "Fish Products, 1944-1946 (2)," A. Vanderkracht to J.L. Phelps, 19 June 1945.
28 *SAB*, S-NR2, DNR-ADM, (A) Subject Files – August 1944-April 1949, f. 21, "Game Branch (E.L. Paynter)," Meeting to discuss Sask. River Delta area, 22 December 1948; Paynter to J.W. Churchman, 3 January 1949; S-NR2, f. 21, "Game Branch (E.L. Paynter)," Paynter to A.K. Quandt, 9 October 1948; Paynter to Churchman, 3 January 1948.
29 *SAB*, S-NR 1/4, f. 430, "Game and Fur Branch, General, 1948-1951," Petition from about sixty Stony Rapids people, Rev. Father R. Gerin interpreter and translator of letter, 15 April 1949; C.L. MacLean to Gerin, 29 April 1949.
30 DNR, *Annual Report,* 1958, 37-38; DNR, *Annual Report,* 1961, 43; Kew, *Cumberland House,* 37-38; Jim Wright, "Saskatchewan's North," *Canadian Geographical Journal* 45, 1 (July 1952): 24; *SAB*, S-NR 1/4, f. 235, "Cumberland House – 1953-1956," E.L. Paynter to J.W. Churchman, 14 January 1955; S-NR2, f. 21, "Game Branch (E.L. Paynter)," Paynter, "Building Our Fur Resources," 11 December 1947.
31 *SAB*, S-M15, Box 5, f. "Dominion-Provincial Conference, 1945-1946 (1)," Document has no title, 14; S-M15, Box 17, "General Correspondence, 1944-1946, (1)," Rev. C.E. Gamache to DNR, 4 December 1945; J.L. Phelps to Gamache, 27 December 1945.
32 *SAB*, R-907.3, f. 7a, "Dominion Government Departments: Resources and Development," Minister of Mines and Resources to J.H. Brockelbank, 22 November 1949; Acting Minister, Dept. of Resources and Development to Brockelbank, 4 August 1950.
33 *SAB*, R-907.3, f. 4, "Dominion Government Departments: Citizenship and Immigration," Report of Sask. Fur Adv. Comm. Mtg, Prince Albert, SK, 18-20 January 1951; S-M15, Box 16, "Game Branch, 1944-1946, (4)," J.L. Phelps to R.D. and K.R. Brooks, 15 January 1945; R.D. and K.R. Brooks to Phelps, 9 January 1945.
34 DNR, *Annual Report,* 1946, Intro. letter from C.A.L. Hogg to J.L. Phelps; DNR, *Annual Report,* 1950, 91-92; *SAB*, S-M15, Box 18, "General Correspondence, 1944-1946," F.X. Gagnon to J.L. Phelps, 9 August 1945.
35 *SAB*, S-M15, Box 18, "General Correspondence, 1944-1946," J. Barnett to J.L. Phelps, 17 August 1945; Phelps to F.X. Gagnon, 14 August 1945.
36 DNR, *Annual Report,* 1948, 70, 75; *Progress: A Survey of Saskatchewan Government Activity* (Regina: Bureau of Publications, 1955), 13; *SAB*, R-907.2, v. II, f. 10a, "E.L. Paynter, Game

Commissioner, July 1949-June 1953," Speech by E.L. Paynter to S.A.R.M. Convention, 13 March 1953; R-907.3, f. 4, "Dominion Government Departments: Citizenship and Immigration," Report on interim meeting Sask. Fur Adv. Comm., Prince Albert, SK, 11-12 July 1952; J.H. Brockelbank to W.E. Harris, 2 October 1952.

37 *SAB*, S-NR 1/5, v. I, f. 93, (462), "Cumberland House – HBC Lease, 1957-1961," H.W. Sutherland to J.W. Churchman, 12 July 1960; E.L. Paynter to Churchman, 7 October 1960; Wayne Runge, *A Century of Fur Harvesting in Saskatchewan*, Wildlife Report Number Five (Prince Albert, SK: Wildlife Branch, Dept. of Environment and Resource Management, 1995), 25.

38 *Glenbow Archives*, M125, s. VI, f. 39, "Historical Notes, 1932-1959," J.P. Brady, "Memorandum Draft Discussion C.C.F. Clubs The Pas and Flin Flon," 1952; M125, s. VI, f. 56, "CCF 1954-1961," J.P. Brady to M. Eninew, 27 May 1960; *SAB*, S-M15, Box 2, "Cumberland House, 1944-1945," M. Chappuis to J.L. Phelps, 20 August 1944; R.C. Corbett to Premier Douglas, 26 March 1945; Phelps to Corbett, 26 March 1945; S-M15, Box 16, "Game Branch, 1944-1946, (4)," J. Angelski to Phelps, 21 January 1945; Phelps to Angelski, 24 January 1945; Petition from residents of Cumberland House, Pine Bluff, and Birch River, received by DNR Minister's Office 31 January 1945; Phelps to R.J. Cheshire, 14 March 1945.

39 *SAB*, S-NR 1/4, f. 235, "Cumberland House, 1953-1956," E.L. Paynter to A.T. Davidson, 15 July 1954.

40 *SAB*, R-907.2, v. II, f 10a, "E.L. Paynter, Game Commissioner, July 1949-June 1953," Paynter to J.H. Brockelbank and C.A.L. Hogg, 21 October 1950; S-NR 1/5, v. I, f. 93, (462), "Cumberland House – HBC Lease, 1957-1961," A.G. Kuziak to H.W. Sutherland, 26 October 1960; Sutherland to J.W. Churchman, 12 July 1960; Kuziak to W.S. Lloyd, 10 November 1960; Paynter to Churchman, 7 October 1960; Runge, *A Century of Fur Harvesting*, 53.

41 *SAB*, S-NR 1/5, v. I, f. 93, (462), "Cumberland House – HBC Lease, 1957-1961," H. Read, "Draft Outline of Cumberland Project," 26 August 1960; A.G. Kuziak to A.J. Cooke, 16 October 1961; E.L. Paynter to J.W. Churchman, 7 October 1960; Walter M. Hlady, "The Cumberland House Fur Project: The First Two Years," in "Cree Studies," special issue of *Western Canadian Journal of Anthropology*, 1, 1 (1969): 124-139.

42 Mary Helen Richards, "Cumberland House: Two Hundred Years of History," *Saskatchewan History* 27, 3 (Autumn, 1974): 112; *SAB*, R-907.3, f. 4, "Dominion Government Departments: Citizenship and Immigration," C.A.L. Hogg to L. Fortier, 28 September 1950; Report on the Interim Meeting Sask. Fur Adv. Comm., Prince Albert, SK, 11-12 July 1952.

43 *SAB*, R-907.2, v. I, f. 2, "Cumberland House Settlement," M.F. Norris to J.J. Wheaton; S-M16, v. VIII, f. 1, "Planning Board, 1953-63" (1 of 2), "Cabinet Conference on Program Planning, May 21-22, 1963"; S-NR 1/5, v. I, f. 93, (462), "Cumberland House – HBC Lease, 1957-1961," H.S. Lee to Premier Douglas and four Ministers, 17 October 1960.

44 *SAB*, R-907.2, v. II, f 10a, "E.L. Paynter, Game Commissioner, July 1949-June 1953," Minutes of Fur Adv. Conf., 19-20 January 1950; R-907.3, f. 4, "Dominion Government Departments: Citizenship and Immigration," Report of Sask. Fur Adv. Comm. Mtg, Prince Albert, SK, 22-24 January 1953; S-NR 1/4, f. 430, "Game and Fur Branch, General, 1951-1955," E.L. Paynter to J.W. Churchman, 11 May 1956.

45 DNR, *Annual Report*, 1963, 40; DNR, *Annual Report*, 1964, 118.

46 DNR, *Annual Report*, 1949, 81, 83, 86; DNR, *Annual Report*, 1959, Wi 11; *Progress: A Survey*, 13; *SAB*, R-907.2, v. II, f. 10a, "E.L. Paynter, Game Commissioner, July 1949-June 1953," "Northern Conservation Area Beaver and Muskrat Harvest 1952-53"; R-907.3, f. 4, "Dominion Government Departments: Citizenship and Immigration," Report of Sask. Fur Adv. Comm. Mtg., Prince Albert, SK, 22-24 January 1953; J.H. Brockelbank to J.W. Pickersgill, 30 September 1954; Report of Sask. Fur Adv. Comm. Mtg., Prince Albert, SK, 24-26 January 1955; Report on Interim Meeting Sask. Fur Adv. Comm., 26 August 1954; S-M15, Box 17, "General Correspondence, 1944-1946, (1)," W.A. Hartwell to J.L. Phelps, 25 February 1946; S-NR2, f. 21, "Game Branch (E.L. Paynter)," Paynter, "Building Our Fur Resources," 11 December 1947.

47 DNR, *Annual Report*, 1948, 71; *SAB*, R-907.2, v. I, f. 2, "Cumberland House Settlement," M.F. Norris to J.J. Wheaton, 22 October 1947, Report attached "Office of the Northern Administrator Report of an Economic and Social Survey of the Cumberland House District," October 1947; R-907.2, v. II, f. 10a, "E.L. Paynter, Game Commissioner, July

1949-June 1953," Paynter to J.H. Brockelbank, 6 December 1951; R-907.3, f. 4, "Dominion Government Departments: Citizenship and Immigration," Report of Sask. Fur Adv. Comm. Mtg., Prince Albert, SK, 18-20 January 1951; Report on Interim Meeting Sask. Fur Adv. Comm., Prince Albert, SK, 11-12 July 1952; S-NR 1/4, f. 430, "Game and Fur Branch," E.L. Paynter, 1951 Game Br. Rpt. to Field Officers' Conf.

48 *SAB*, S-NR 1/4, f. 167 B3, "Northern Region, April 1st, 1956," N. Dist. Field Officers' Conf, 9-13 January 1951.

49 *SAB*, S-NR 1/4, f. 430, "Game and Fur Branch," A. Hansen to J.W. Churchman, 23 June 1952; H. Read to Dear Sirs, 14 July 1952; S-NR 1/4, f. 430, "Game and Fur Branch, General, 1948-1951," E.L. Paynter to J.S. Boardman and C. Forrest, 14 February 1951.

50 *SAB*, S-M15, Box 6, "Fisheries, 1944-1946 (2)," A. Bear to J.L. Phelps, 8 January 1946; S-M15, Box 6, "Fisheries, 1944-1946 (4)," O. Bright to Phelps, 2 February 1945.

51 *SAB*, R-907.3, f. 2, "Churchill River Power," R.W. Davis to Miss B. Green, 22 May 1946; H. Morin to Unknown, 24 March 1946; Secretary of J.L. Phelps to Davis, 12 April 1946.

52 *SAB*, S-NR2, f. 21, "Game Branch (E.L. Paynter)," Petition with names of fifty-six Cumberland House district trappers to A.K. Quandt, 17 April 1948; Quandt to E.L. Paynter, 27 April 1948.

53 *Glenbow Archives*, M125, s. VII, f. 63, Report of meeting of residents at Cumberland House, 6 January 1950.

54 John Hanson, interview by author, Buffalo Narrows, SK, July 1999.

55 *SAB*, R-907.2, v. II, f. 9b, "J.H. Janzen, Legal Branch May 1947-February 1952," Minister of Nat. Res. and Ind. Dev. to Lt. Gov. in Council, 23 February 1949; S-M15, Box 17, "General Correspondence, 1944-1946, (1)," W.A. Hartwell to J.L. Phelps, 25 February 1946; S-NR 1/4, f. 430, "Game and Fur Branch, General," January 1958-, E.L. Paynter to All Fur Dealers, 26 March 1958; Arrowsmith, "Northern Saskatchewan and the Fur Trade," 120.

56 *SAB*, S-M15, Box 4, "Public Health Department, 1944-1946," J.L. Phelps, Report, 9 February 1945; S-M15, Box 16, Minutes, Sask. Fur Marketing Assoc., 1945-46; S-M15, Box 17, "General Correspondence, 1944-1946, (2)," Phelps to T.C. Douglas, 5 September 1944.

57 Helen L. Buckley, *Trapping and Fishing in the Economy of Northern Saskatchewan*, Report No. 3, Economic and Social Survey of Northern Saskatchewan (Saskatoon: Research Division, Center for Community Studies, University of Saskatchewan, 1962), 18.

58 *SAB*, S-M15, Box 15, "Fur Marketing, 1947-1951, (1)," J.L. Phelps to C.G. MacNeil, 10 January 1945.

59 Arrowsmith, "Northern Saskatchewan and the Fur Trade," 120; *SAB*, S-M15, Box 8, "Dickson, K.E., Manager, Fish Filleting Plants, 1946-1948," Minister's Office to K.E. Dickson, 8 October 1947; S-M15, Box 16, "Fur Marketing – A.J. Cooke, 1946-1951," Cooke to "Dear Shipper," 15 November 1946.

60 *SAB*, S-M15, Box 5, "Economic Advisory Board Recommendations, 1945-1946," DNR, Summary of 1945 activities and plans for 1946, 3; S-M15, Box 8, "Fishing – Reindeer Lake, 1945-1946," J.L. Phelps to T. Clarke and J. Clarke, 15 September 1945; S-M15, Box 15, "Fur Marketing, 1947-1951, (1)," Phelps to C.G. MacNeil, 10 January 1945; Phelps to W.H. Lefurgey, 22 November 1945; Lefurgey to Phelps, 19 November 1945; S-M15, Box 16, "Saskatchewan Fur Marketing Association – Minutes, 1945-1946," Minutes of first meeting of SFMA, 29 October 1945; S-M15, Box 36, "Doidge, J. (Publicity)," DNR, Activities summary for 1945 and to June 1946.

61 *SAB*, S-M15, Box 16, "Fur Marketing, 1944-1946, (2)," Nazaire Pelletier, "C.C.F. Fur Exchange Pays $8.25 for Furs Valued At $25.00," *Yorkton Enterprise*, no date given; A. McEwen to J.L. Phelps, 16 May 1945; S-M15, Box 15, "Fur Marketing, 1947-1951, (1)."

62 *SAB*, S-M15, Box 16, "Fur Marketing – A.J. Cooke, 1946-1951," J.S. Bevan to J.H. Brockelbank, 1 December 1949.

63 *SAB*, R-907.2, v. II, f. 12, "J.J. Wheaton, Northern Administrator," G.J. Waite to J.J. Wheaton, 15 December 1948.

64 *SAB*, S-NR 1/4, f. 432, "Complaints – General," L.E. Blanchard to J.H. Brockelbank, 27 July 1949; Brockelbank to Blanchard, 10 August 1949.

65 *SAB*, S-NR 1/4, f. 432, "Complaints – General," Letter, author uncertain, Deschambeault Lake.

66 *SAB*, R-907.2, v. II, f.10b, "E.L. Paynter, Game Commissioner, September 1953-April 1955," R. McKay to J.H. Brockelbank, received 2 August 1954; Brockelbank to McKay, 10 August 1954.

67 John Hanson, interview by author, Buffalo Narrows, SK, July 1999.
68 Vernon C. Serl, "Action and Reaction: An Overview of Provincial Policies and Programs in Northern Saskatchewan," in *A Northern Dilemma: Reference Papers*, vol. 1, ed. Arthur K. Davis et al. (Bellingham, WA: Western Washington State College, 1967), 24; V.F. Valentine, *The Metis of Northern Saskatchewan* (Regina: DNR, 1955), 35.
69 Barron, *Walking in Indian Moccasins*, 177.
70 V.F. Valentine, "Some Problems of the Metis of Northern Saskatchewan," *The Canadian Journal of Economics and Political Science* 20, 1 (1954): 95; Valentine, *The Metis of Northern Saskatchewan*, 23-24.
71 *SAB*, R-907.2, v. I, f. 2, "Cumberland House Settlement," M.F. Norris to J.J. Wheaton, 22 October 1947, Report attached "Office of the Northern Administrator Report of an Economic and Social Survey of the Cumberland House District," October 1947; Minutes, Meeting at C. House, 11 October 1947.
72 *SAB*, S-NR 1/4, f. 235, "Cumberland House – General," v. 1, June 1948 to 31 August 1950, A.K. Quandt to J.W. Churchman, 13 December 1948.
73 Geoffrey R. Weller, "Resource Development in Northern Ontario: A Case Study in Hinterland Politics," in *Resources and the Environment: Policy Perspectives for Canada*, ed. O.P. Dwivedi (Toronto: McClelland and Stewart, 1980), 251-253; *SAB*, S-NR 1/4, f. 235, "La Ronge" (1), J.H. Brockelbank to C.A.L. Hogg, J.W. Churchman, A.H. MacDonald, and O. Linton, 24 August 1949; Valentine, *The Metis of Northern Saskatchewan*, 35.
74 Anne Acco, interview by author, Cumberland House, SK, July 1999; Dobbin, "Prairie Colonialism," 17; Howard Adams (Survey Director), *The Outsiders: An Educational Survey of Metis and Non-Treaty Indians of Saskatchewan* (Saskatoon: Metis Society of Sask., 1972), 6; James C. Scott, *Domination and the Arts of Resistance: Hidden Transcripts* (New Haven, CT/London: Yale University Press, 1990). For a discussion of similar situations in other parts of the world, see James C. Scott, *Weapons of the Weak: Everyday Forms of Peasant Resistance* (New Haven, CT/London: Yale University Press, 1985), xvi.
75 DNR, *Annual Report*, 1953, 119; *Glenbow Archives*, M125, s. II, f. 8, "Personal," 1952-62, M. Kew to Jim, 15 February 1960; Janet Fietz, interview by author, La Ronge, SK, July 1999; Kew, *Cumberland House*, 36-37; *SAB*, R-907.3, f. 4, "Dominion Government Departments: Citizenship and Immigration," Report of the Sask. Fur Adv. Comm. Mtg., Prince Albert, SK, 22-24 January 1953; S-NR 1/5, v. III, f. 24a, "Fur Advisory Committee, 1960-64," Report of the Fur Adv. Comm., 1961.
76 *SAB*, R-907.3, f. 13, "Sask. Raw Fur Dealers' Association," Sask. Raw Fur Dealers Assoc. Brief to J.H. Brockelbank, September 1948; Brockelbank to E.J. Hemming, 5 October 1948; S-M15, Box 15, "Fur Marketing, 1947-1951, (1)," R.H. Chesshire to J.L. Phelps, 17 October 1945; Phelps to Chesshire, 18 October 1945; Schneider and Einarson to Phelps, 13 March 1946; A. Bear to Phelps, 16 March 1946; S-M15, Box 16, "Fur Marketing, 1944-1946, (2)," Carlyle King to Phelps, 29 August 1944; Phelps to L.B. Burroughs, 18 August 1944; Burroughs to T.C. Douglas, 11 August 1944; L.C. Paterson to Phelps, 22 September 1944; Lestock Silver Fox and Fur Assoc. to Phelps, 16 August 1944; Mick Fyck to Phelps, 9 September 1944; Pres., Sask. Prov. Fur Breeders Assoc. to Phelps, 11 August 1944; *Saskatchewan News Letter*, printed by Bureau of Publications, no date given.
77 *SAB*, S-M15, Box 15, "Fur Marketing, 1947-1951, (1)," J.L. Phelps to R.H. Chesshire, 29 December 1945; Chesshire to Phelps, 4 January 1946; S-M15, Box 16, "Fur Marketing, 1944-1946, (2)," Phelps to Chesshire, 16 April 1945; HBC to Phelps, 10 May 1945.
78 DNR, *Annual Report*, 1946, 72; *SAB*, R-907.3, f. 3a, "Crown Corporations," "Statement of Accumulated Surpluses and Deficits of Crown Corporations as at 31 December 1953 or at time of Winding Up Affairs," S-M15, Box 16, "Fur Marketing – A.J. Cooke, 1946-1951," A.J. Cooke to "Dear Shipper," 15 November 1946; Cooke, Mgr's Report for February, 1948; Cooke, Mgr's Report from 1 May-1 September 1947; Cooke to J.H. Brockelbank, 29 June 1949; S-NR 1/4, 167 B3, "Northern Region, April 1st, 1956," N. Dist. Field Officers' Conf, 9-13 January 1951.
79 *SAB*, R-907.2, v. I, f. 2, "Cumberland House Settlement," M.F. Norris to J.J. Wheaton, 22 October 1947, Report attached "Office of the Northern Administrator Report of an Economic and Social Survey of the Cumberland House District," October 1947; Attached Minutes of Meeting at Cumberland House, 11 October 1947; S-NR2, (A) Subject Files – August 1944-April 1949, f. 21, "Game Branch (E.L. Paynter)," M. Norris, excerpt from

"Social and Economic Survey Lac La Ronge"; Norris to J.W. Churchman, 9 November 1948.

80 *SAB*, R-907.2, v. II, f. 10a, "E.L. Paynter, Game Commissioner, July 1949-June 1953," C.A.L. Hogg to various recipients, 17 June 1952; R-907.2, v. II, f. 10b, "E.L. Paynter, Game Commissioner, September 1953-April 1955," Paynter to J.W. Churchman, Report of Northern Trip, 22 September 1953; R-907.3, f. 4, "Dominion Government Departments: Citizenship and Immigration," J.H. Brockelbank to W.E. Harris, 15 February 1954; Brockelbank to J.W. Pickersgill, 30 September 1954; Report of Sask. Fur Adv. Comm. Mtg., Prince Albert, SK, 24-26 January 1955; R-907.3, f. 7a, "Dominion Government Departments: Resources and Development," Brockelbank to C. Gibson, 23 November 1949; S-NR 1/4, f. 430, "Game and Fur Branch," A.T. Davidson to B.A. Matheson, C.S. Brown, W.A. Hartwell, A. Hansen, and C. Schell, 7 June 1955; Brockelbank to Churchman, 16 August 1954; Brockelbank to Churchman and W.A. Houseman, 2 May 1955; Brockelbank to Churchman, 3 June 1955.

81 D. Bruce Sealey and Antoine S. Lussier, *The Métis: Canada's Forgotten People* (Winnipeg, MB: Pemmican Publications, 1981),153.

82 Arrowsmith, "Northern Saskatchewan and the Fur Trade," 121.

83 Buckley, *Trapping and Fishing*, 56; Government Finance Office, *Public Enterprise in Saskatchewan* (Saskatchewan: Government Finance Office, 1964); Arrowsmith, "Northern Saskatchewan and the Fur Trade," 108-109.

84 Buckley, *Trapping and Fishing*, 151; Kew, *Cumberland House*, 42-45; *SAB*, S-NR 1/4, 167 B3, "Northern Region," Minutes of N. District Cons. Officers' Conf., Prince Albert, SK, 4-8 October 1954; S-NR 1/5, v. III, f. 24a, "Fur Advisory Committee, 1960-64," Minutes of Sask. Fur Adv. Comm., Prince Albert, SK, 31 January 1964.

85 Gary Ronald Seymour, "A Geographical Study of the Commercial Fishing Industry in Northern Saskatchewan: An Example of Resource Development" (master's thesis, University of Saskatchewan, 1971), 56-60.

86 J.E. Steen, "Survey of Saskatchewan Fisheries," *Trade News* (publication of the federal Department of Fisheries), November 1959, 5.

87 Buckley, Kew, and Hawley, *The Indians and Metis of Northern Saskatchewan*, 47-48; *SAB*, S-NR 1/5, v. I, f. 39, (230), "Northern Region, 1957-1959," J.W. Churchman, "Our Goals in the North and How We Hope to Achieve Them," 19 April 1959; S-NR 1/5, v. III, f. 8, "Buffalo Narrows, 1963-66," E.L. Paynter to Churchman, 29 December 1961; S-NR 1/5, v. III, f. 24a, "Fur Advisory Committee, 1960-64," Minutes of Sask. Fur Adv. Comm., Prince Albert, SK, 31 January 1964; Runge, *A Century of Fur Harvesting*, 54.

88 DNR, *Annual Report*, 1964, 44; Buckley, *Trapping and Fishing*, 167; Stanford Research Institute, *A Study of Resources and Industrial Opportunities for the Province of Saskatchewan* (Menlo Park, CA: Stanford Research Institute, 1959), Tables 7 and 8; Arrowsmith, "Northern Saskatchewan and the Fur Trade," 142-144.

89 *SAB*, R-907.2, v. II, f. 12, "J.J. Wheaton, Northern Administrator," G.J. Waite to Wheaton, 15 December 1948.

90 *SAB*, R-907.2, v. II, f 10a, "E.L. Paynter, Game Commissioner, July 1949-June 1953," C.A.L. Hogg to J.H. Brockelbank, 2 November 1950; E.L. Paynter to Brockelbank and Hogg, 21 October 1950; S-M15, Box 36, "Elder, Keith (Prince Albert Office)," Elder to J.L. Phelps, 10 June 1946; S-NR 1/4, f. 430, "Game and Fur Branch, General, 1948-1951," B.A. Matheson to Paynter, 21 April 1949; S-NR2, f. 21, "Game Branch (E.L. Paynter)," Paynter to J.W. Churchman, 3 August 1948; S-NR2, (A) Subject Files – August 1944-April 1949, f. 19, "Fisheries Branch (A.H. MacDonald)," Churchman, Summary of meeting at Minister's Office, 16 September likely 1948; S-NR2, (A) Subject Files – August 1944-April 1949, f. 21, "Game Branch (E.L. Paynter)," Mtg. to discuss delta area, 22 December 1948; Paynter to Churchman, Trip report, 3 January 1949.

91 Ross, *The Manager's Tale*, Chapter 6; Kew, *Cumberland House*, 80-82.

92 Arrowsmith, "Northern Saskatchewan and the Fur Trade," 116.

93 Morris C. Shumiatcher, *Welfare: Hidden Backlash* (Toronto: McClelland and Stewart, 1971), 97-105.

94 Ross, *The Manager's Tale*, Chapter 5; *SAB*, R-907.2, v. I, f. 2, "Cumberland House Settlement," M.F. Norris to J.J. Wheaton, 22 October 1947, Report attached "Office of the Northern Administrator Report of an Economic and Social Survey of the Cumberland

House District," October 1947; R-907.2, v. II, f. 12, "J.J. Wheaton, Northern Administrator," M.F. Norris and Wheaton, no recipient shown, 30 December 1947; Minutes of N. Co-Ord. Comm. Mtg., 23 April 1948; S-M15, Box 5, "Economic Advisory Board Recommendations, 1945-1946," G.W. Cadbury to J.L. Phelps, 27 February 1946; S-M15, Box 7, "Fish Products (3)," M. Bodner to Mr. H. Lewis, 8 March 1946; S-M15, Box 7, "Sask. Fish Products – Minutes, 1945-1946," Minutes of Joint Mtg. of SFP and SFMB, 27 January 1946; S-M15, Box 16, "Game Branch, 1944-1946, (4)," HBC, N. posts fur shipments, 1943-44; S-M15, Box 36, "Elder, Keith (Prince Albert Office)," Elder to J.L. Phelps, 10 June 1946.
95 *Progress: A Survey,* 43.
96 *SAB,* R-907.2, v. II, f. 12, "J.J. Wheaton, Northern Administrator," M.F. Norris and Wheaton to J.L. Phelps, 1 October 1947; Wheaton to Phelps, 7 August 1947; S-M15, Box 8, "Dickson, K.E., Manager, Fish Filleting Plants, 1946-1948," Dickson to Phelps, J.H. Brockelbank, G.W. Cadbury, J. Gray, M. Kalmakoff; R.C. Ross to Dickson, 24 July 1947; S-M15, Box 10, "Sask. Lake and Forest Products Corporation – J.F. Gray, 1946-1951, (5)," Gray to Phelps, 8 August 1947; Gray to Dickson, 15 May 1947; S-M15, Box 10, "Sask. Lake and Forest Products Corporation – W. Bague, 1947-1948," Bague to Gray, 2 July 1947.
97 *SAB,* R-907.2, v. II, f. 4a, "J.W. Churchman, Deputy Minister March 1948-March 1949," Churchman to C.A.L. Hogg, 17 September 1948; A.K. Quandt to Churchman, 15 December 1948; S-M15, Box 8, "Dickson, K.E., Manager, Fish Filleting Plants,1946-1948," Dickson to J.F. Gray, 4 September 1947; Dickson to J.L. Phelps, J.H. Brockelbank, G.W. Cadbury, J. Gray, M. Kalmakoff; S-M15, Box 8, "Dickson, K.E., 1946-1951, (1)," Dickson to Gray, 19 November 1947; S-M15, Box 10, "Sask. Lake and Forest Products Corporation – J.F. Gray, 1946-1951, (7)," Gray to Brockelbank, 4 March 1949.
98 *Glenbow Archives,* M125, s. III, "Correspondence, 1933-67," f. 22, "Norris, 1945-1967 (Mining and Native Rights)," M.F. Norris to J. Brady, 5 December 1947; *SAB,* S-M15, Box 10, "Sask. Lake and Forest Products Corporation – J.F. Gray, 1946-1951, (6)," Gray to J.H. Brockelbank, 13 June 1950; S-M15, Box 9, "Sask. Lake and Forest Products Corporation – J.F. Gray, 1946-1951, (3)," Gray, Report to the Bd. of Dirs of SL&FPC; S-M15, Box 10, "Sask. Lake and Forest Products Corporation – J.F. Gray, 1946-1951, (6)," Gray, Report to Chairman and Bd. of Dirs., SL&FPC, 9 June 1949; S-M16, v. VIII, f. 1, "Planning Board, 1953-63" (2 of 2), Minutes of Ann. Cabinet-Planning Bd. Conf., 16-20 November 1953.
99 *SAB,* R-907.2, v. II, f. 10b, "E.L. Paynter, Game Commissioner, September 1953-April 1955," Paynter to J.W. Churchman, Report of Northern Trip, 22 September 1953; R-907.2, v. II, f. 12, "J.J. Wheaton, Northern Administrator," M.F. Norris and J.J. Wheaton (recipient not shown), 30 December 1947; S-M15, Box 9, "Sask. Lake and Forest Products Corporation – J.F. Gray, 1946-1950, (3)," Report of Mtg. 1 December 1947; S-M15, Box 9, "Sask. Lake and Forest Products Corporation – J.F. Gray, 1946-1951, (3)," Gray, Report to the Bd. of Dirs. of SL&FPC.
100 Buckley, *Trapping and Fishing,* 99; *Progress: A Survey,* 43; *Glenbow Archives,* M125, s. VII, f. 60, "Co-Ops 1950-1962," Report of Co-Op School, Prince Albert, 13-21 June 1950; *SAB,* R-907.3, f. 3a, "Crown Corporations (J.H. Brockelbank: Natural Resources)," Brockelbank to "Dear Friend," 16 August 1954; S-M15, Box 10, "Sask. Lake and Forest Products Corporation – J.F. Gray, 1946-1951, (6)," "Field and Supervisory Personnel of Saskatchewan Government Trading"; S-NR 1/5, v. I, f. 20, (162R), "Consultative Committee on Northern Affairs, 1958," Dr. B.N. Arnason, "Report of Advisory Committee on Northern Affairs," Tables 1 and 2 (Draft) (Attachment from Arnason to T.K. Shoyama, 17 July 1958).
101 Barron, *Walking in Indian Moccasins,* 195-198; *SAB,* S-NR 1/4, 167 B3, "Northern Region," Minutes of N. Region Cons. Officers' Conf., 15-19 October 1956; S-NR 1/5, v. 1, f. 16, (137K), "Filleting Plants, 1955-59"; A. Davidson, "Proposal to Build a Government Filleting Plant at Ile a la Crosse," 1956; S-M16, v. VII, f. 3, "Parks and Lands Branch, 1961-63," Minutes of N. Adv. Comm. Mtg., 9 February 1956; "Proposal to Organize a Co-Operative Fish Processing Organization at Ile a la Crosse," 1958; Philip T. Spaulding, "The Metis of Ile-a-la-Crosse" (PhD diss., University of Washington, 1970), 35-37, 124-126.
102 Institute for Northern Studies, *Beauval Community Planning Study* (Saskatoon: University of Saskatchewan, 1979), 13.
103 Ed and Pemrose Whelan, *Touched by Tommy: Stories of Hope and Humour in the Words of Men and Women Whose Lives Tommy Douglas Touched* (Regina: Whelan Publications, 1990), 74; *SAB,* S-M16, v. XIII, f. 293, "Rehabilitation, Metis, La Loche, 1958-62," J.S.

White to T.J. Bentley, 20 June 1958; M. Crawley to W.A. Bourke, 6 June 1958; P. Spaulding to J.T. Phalen, 20 January 1958; Bentley to T.C. Douglas, 25 June 1958; P. Godt, "Co-Operative Store Project for La Loche"; Spaulding to Phalen, 20 January 1958; S-NR 1/5, v. I, f. 20, (162R), "Consultative Committee on Northern Affairs, 1958," Crawley to Bourke, 6 June 1958.

104 DNR, *Annual Report,* 1959, N.A. 6, 9; DNR, *Annual Report,* 1961, 106; *Glenbow Archives,* M125, s. VI, f. 56, "CCF 1954-1961," Organizational Report, Lac La Ronge C.C.F. Club, January 1960: Kew, *Cumberland House,* 104; *SAB,* S-M16, v. VII, f. 3, "Parks and Lands Branch, 1961-63," Brief by N. Adv. Comm. on Metis of N. Sask., 1955; Minutes of N. Adv. Comm. Mtg., 9 February 1956; S-NR 1/5, v. I, f. 20, (162R), "Consultative Committee on Northern Affairs, 1958," Add. Info. re proposed possible Directors; J.W. Churchman to A.G. Kuziak, 31 March 1958; Arrowsmith, "Northern Saskatchewan and the Fur Trade," 110.

105 *Glenbow Archives,* M125, s. VI, f. 41, "Metis, 1952-63," "Co-Ops Are Changing the Northland!"

106 Buckley, *Trapping and Fishing,* 55-56; Buckley, Kew, and Hawley, *The Indians and Metis of Northern Saskatchewan,* Chapter 3.

107 J.T. Phalen, "The Search for an Appropriate Development Program for the People of Northern Saskatchewan," unpublished paper (April 1996); Phalen, "The Co-Operative Development Program for Northern Saskatchewan," unpublished paper (1 June 1997); Phalen, "The Northern Co-Operative Development Program," unpublished paper (1 September 1997); Letter, "Terry" (T. Phalen) to Harold (Harold Chapman), 9 September 1997; Phalen, "An Autobiography of the Life and Times of J.T. (Terry) Phalen," unpublished, undated.

Chapter 6: At the Point of a Gun

1 *Saskatchewan Archives Board* [*SAB*], S-M15, Joseph Lee Phelps Ministerial Papers, Box 5, "Dominion-Provincial Conference, 1945-1946, (1)," Prov. Nat. Res. policy in relation to Dom. proposals, 6; S-M15, Box 9, "Sask. Lake and Forest Products Corporation – J.F. Gray, 1946-1950, (3)," Gray to J.L. Phelps, 17 November 1947.

2 DNR, *Annual Report,* 1945, 58; *SAB,* R-907.2, J.H. Brockelbank Papers, v. II, f. 12, "J.J. Wheaton, Northern Administrator," M.F. Norris and Wheaton, no recipient, 30 December 1947.

3 DNR, *Annual Report,* 1947, 76; *SAB,* S-M15, Box 9, "Sask Lake and Forest Products Corporation, 1946-1949," A.H. MacDonald and K.E. Dickson, "Present Situation and Proposals in Regard to Conditions in Northern Saskatchewan," 1 October 1947; S-M15, Box 36, "Doidge, J. (Publicity)," James Hayes item, 8 June 1946; T.C. Douglas Speech, "Progress Report on Co-Operation Among Fishermen," 1959.

4 Helen L. Buckley, *Trapping and Fishing in the Economy of Northern Saskatchewan,* Report No. 3, Economic and Social Survey of Northern Saskatchewan (Saskatoon: Research Division, Center for Community Studies, University of Saskatchewan, 1962), 64; *SAB,* A 1109, John H. Brockelbank, interview by Murray Dobbin, audio tape, Regina, 19 August 1976; R-A1113, Joe Phelps, interview by Murray Dobbin, audio tape, 1976; S-M15, Box 5, "Economic Advisory Board Recommendations, 1945-1946," G.W. Cadbury to M. Ezekiel, 8 April 1946; S-M15, Box 8, "Lucas, A.A., Office Manager, Fish Board, 1946-1948," Lucas to Phelps, 12 January 1947; S-M15, Box 9, "Sask Lake and Forest Products Corporation, 1946-1949," K.E. Dickson to J.F. Gray, J.H. Brockelbank, Phelps, M. Kalmakoff, Cadbury, 24 September 1947.

5 *SAB,* R-907.2, v. II, f. 12, "J.J. Wheaton, Northern Administrator," Report of third meeting of committee to "Devise Ways and Means of Administering Aid to Isolated Areas," 13 November 1947; S-M15, Box 6, "Fisheries, 1944-1946 (4)," "Fish"; S-NR 1/4, Deputy Minister and Assistant Deputy Minister Files, 167 B3, "Northern Region," G. Beck, "Lake Athabasca Fisheries Summer Season-1953," N. Dist. Conf., 8 October 1953; S-NR2, Department of Natural Resources – Assistant Deputy Minister, (A) Subject Files – August 1944-April 1949, f. 19, "Fisheries Branch (A.H. MacDonald)," J.W. Churchman, Summary of Meeting in Minister's Office, 16 September likely 1948. There were some exceptions to the northern Saskatchewan residents' fishing monopoly. Because people from Saskatchewan showed little interest in fishing Lake Athabasca, Albertans often fished the big lake,

which straddled the Saskatchewan-Alberta border. A 1943 regulation allowed any British subject to obtain a commercial fishing licence for Lake Athabasca. McInnis Products Corporation of Edmonton employed many Scandinavian fishermen in the largest operation there. A government committee in 1947 wanted Saskatchewan fishermen to fish the lake, a move probably aimed at McInnis. About the same time, McInnis moved its operations to Great Slave Lake in the NWT, reportedly over a disagreement with DNR about net mesh size. The company returned in 1951 and again dominated the fishery there, employing about sixty-five people to take the lake limit of about 2.5 million pounds. McInnis also fished some smaller northern lakes with CCF consent.

6 F. Laurie Barron, *Walking in Indian Moccasins: The Native Policies of Tommy Douglas and the CCF* (Vancouver: UBC Press, 1997); *SAB*, S-M15, Box 6, "Fisheries, 1944-1946 (2)," K.E. Dickson to F. Glass, 1 April 1946; S-M15, Box 8, "Lucas, A.A., Office Manager, Fish Board, 1946-1948," Lucas to J.J. Elliott, 24 October 1946; S-M15, Box 9, "Sask Lake and Forest Products Corporation, 1946-1949," Fishermen's Meeting, Beaver Lake, 29 May 1946; A.H. MacDonald and K.E. Dickson, "Present Situation and Proposals in Regard to Conditions in Northern Saskatchewan," 1 October 1947; S-M15, Box 9, "Sask. Lake and Forest Products Corporation – J.F. Gray, 1946-1950, (4)," "A Submission to the Board."

7 *SAB*, S-M15, Box 6, "Fisheries, 1944-1946, (3)," "Report on fishermen's meeting," Meota, SK, 3 November 1945; S-M15, Box 7, "Fish Marketing, 1945-1946," J.L. Phelps to Rev. Father Coady, 17 August 1945; S-M15, Box 10, "Sask. Lake and Forest Products Corporation – J.F. Gray, 1946-1951, (7)," Gray to E.W. Brunsden, 26 November 1948; S-M15, Box 36, "Doidge, J. (Publicity)," DNR, Activities summary, 1945 to June 1946, 14 June 1946.

8 *Glenbow Archives*, M125, James Brady Collection, v. III, "Correspondence, 1933-67," f. 22, "Norris, 1945-1967 (Mining and Native Rights)," M.F. Norris to J. Brady, December 5; *SAB*, S-M15, Box 5, "Economic Advisory Board Recommendations, 1945-1946," DNR, Activities Summary for 1945 and plans for 1946, 3; G.W. Cadbury to J.L. Phelps, 27 February 1946; S-M15, Box 6, "Fisheries, 1944-1946 (3)," Phelps to L.H. Ausman, 19 September 1945; S-M15, Box 7, "Fish Marketing, 1945-1946," April and May 1948 Fish Board Operating Statement; S-M15, Box 8, "Dickson, K.E., 1946-1951," Field and Office Staff, SFMS, 9 March 1950; S-M15, Box 8, "Lucas, A.A., Office Manager, Fish Board, 1946-1948," Lucas to Phelps, 24 January 1947; S-M15, Box 9, "Sask. Lake and Forest Products Corporation, 1946-1949," H.H. Lucas, Address on mechanics of STB, 16 January 1948; J.F. Gray to Phelps, 5 May 1947; Thomas Hector Macdonald McLeod, "Public Enterprise in Saskatchewan: The Development of Public Policy and Administrative Controls" (PhD diss., Harvard University, 1959), 95.

9 *SAB*, S-M15, Box 2, "Bryce, M. Crown Corps.," Minutes, SFP Bd. of Dirs. Mtg., 7 May 1946; S-M15, Box 7, "Bodnar, M. – Fish Board, 1946," Bodner to H. Lewis, 18 July 1946; S-M15, Box 7, "Fish Marketing, 1945-1946," E. Welsh to J.L. Phelps, 20 October 1945; H. Lewis to Phelps, 2 November 1945; Phelps to Mrs. E. Welsh, 3 October 1945; K.F. Harding to "Harry," 22 November 1945; R.H. Carruthers to Phelps, 15 February 1946; Phelps to Carruthers; S-M15, Box 9, "Sask. Lake and Forest Products Corporation – J.F. Gray, 1946-1950, (4)," Gray to K.E. Dickson, 11 October 1947. Although somewhat unclear, the reference from the Trades and Labor Council appears to refer to Welsh. While she worked there, Welsh received a salary of $160 per month, or about $1,920 per year, in contrast to Chairman M. Bodner's $3,600 annual salary. The difference in compensation may have been fair, given the different responsibilities held by the two persons.

10 *SAB*, S-M15, Box 6, "Fisheries, 1944-1946, (2)"; S-M15, Box 6, "Fisheries, 1944-1946, (4)," "Fish"; S-M15, Box 7, "Fish Products, 1944-1946, (2)," J.L. Phelps to T.J. Searle, 13 July 1945.

11 *SAB*, R-907.3, J.H. Brockelbank Papers, f. 5a, "Dominion Government Departments: Fisheries (J.H. Brockelbank Papers: Minister of Natural Resources)," H.V. Dempsey to J.L. Phelps, 7 March 1946; S-M15, Box 6, "Fisheries, 1944-1946, (1)," Phelps to H.P. Evans, 20 December 1944; Phelps to P.C. Hogan, 20 December 1944; Phelps to N.E. Tanner, 28 December 1944; C. Olsen to Phelps, 18 December 1944; Hjalmerson and Einarson, Schneider and Einarson, I. Norman, R. Streittle, W. Russick, A. Custer, M. Dubinak, Derbyshire Bros., R.G. Thomas to T.C. Douglas, 18 December 1944; Phelps, to Hjalmerson and Einarson, Schneider and Einarson, 19 December 1944; S-M15, Box 6, "Fisheries, 1944-1946, (2)," H.W. Pope speech, CKCK, 26 March 1946; S-M15, Box 6, "Fisheries,

1944-1946, (4)," Phelps to J. Pankoski, 7 October 1944; O. Bright to Phelps, 18 September 1944; S-M15, Box 6, "Fish Products, 1944-1946, (5)," A.J. Whitmore to Phelps, 9 October 1945; S-M15, Box 7, "Fish Products, 1944-1946, (1)," D.B. Finn to Phelps, 26 September 1944; S-M15, Box 8, "Dickson, K.E., 1946-1951," Dickson to J.F. Gray, 1 June 1948; The Trimension Group, Spruce River Research, and Office of Northern Affairs, *Examination of the Commercial Fishing Industry in Saskatchewan* (The Trimension Group, 1999), 9.

12 *SAB*, S-M15, Box 7, "Fish Products, 1944-1946, (1)," Letter and Petition, 1 February 1945; J.L. Phelps to A. VanderKracht, 21 February 1945; K.E. Dickson to Phelps, 29 October 1944; J. Jantzen to Phelps, 18 November 1944; L.C. Paterson to Phelps, 14 December 1944; S-M15, Box 7, "Fish Products, 1944-1946, (2)," VanderKracht to Phelps, 13 August 1945; S-M15, Box 7, "Fish Products, 1944-1946, (3)," VanderKracht to Phelps, 19 June 1945; Dr. G.C. Darby to Phelps, 16 April 1946; R. Campbell to Phelps, 22 February 1946; M. Bodner to H. Lewis, 8 March; Gen. Rpt., Lac la Ronge Fish Plant, 1946; M.D. Bryce to Min. of Nat. Res., 22 March 1946; S-M15, Box 8, "McCabe, M.A., Lac La Ronge Plant, 1946-1947," McCabe to Phelps, 13 March 1947; S-M15, Box 10, "Sask. Lake and Forest Products Corporation – J.F. Gray, 1946-1951, (5)," Gray to Phelps, 28 August 1947; S-M15, Box 17, "Game Branch, 1944-1946, (5)," B.L. Keighley to Phelps, 10 August 1944; S-M15, Box 7, "Saskatchewan Fish Products – Minutes, 1945-1946," SFMB meeting minutes, Prince Albert, SK, 29 January 1946.

13 *SAB*, S-M15, Box 2, "Bryce, M. Crown Corps.," W.D. Bryce to J.L. Phelps and G.W. Cadbury, 7 June 1946; S-M15, Box 7, "Fish Products, 1944-1946, (3)," K.E. Dickson to Phelps, 3 November 1945; H.F. Hanreider to Phelps, 19 December 1945; Hanreider to Phelps, 5 January 1946; S-M15, Box 9, "Sask. Lake and Forest Products Corporation – J.F. Gray, 1946-1950, (4)," "A Submission to the Board."

14 *SAB*, S-M15, Box 7, "Fish Marketing, 1945-1946," D. Phelps to J.L. Phelps, 10 February 1946; D. Phelps to J.L. Phelps, 21 February 1946; J.L. Phelps to Frank Needham, 7 December 1945; J.L. Phelps to W.D. Phelps, 4 March 1946; S-M15, Box 7, "Sask. Fish Products – Minutes, 1945-1946," Minutes of SFMB meeting, Prince Albert, SK., 10 January 1946; S-M15, Box 8, "Phelps, W.D., Manager of Fish Warehouse, 1946-1947," W.D. Phelps to J.F. Gray, 21 April 1947.

15 *SAB*, S-M15, Box 7, "Fish Products, 1944-1946, (1)," K.E. Dickson to J.L. Phelps, 29 October 1944; S-M15, Box 7, "Saskatchewan Fish Products – Minutes, 1945-1946," Minutes of SFP directors meeting, Prince Albert, SK, 26 January 1946, 3.

16 *SAB*, R-907.2, v. II, f. 12, "J.J. Wheaton, Northern Administrator," A.H. MacDonald and K.E. Dickson, 7 October 1947; S-M15, Box 8, "Dickson, K.E., 1946-1951, (1)," Dickson to J.F. Gray, 19 November 1947; "Proposed Production Policy for Future Operations," 13 October 1947; S-M15, Box 29, "Questions, 1945-1946, (2)," Question by Mr. Proctor, 7 March 1946.

17 *SAB*, S-M15, Box 7, "Fish Marketing, 1945-1946," D. Phelps to J.L. Phelps, 21 February 1946; S-M15, Box 7, "Fish Products, 1944-1946, (3)," K.E. Dickson to J.L. Phelps, 30 January 1946; Dickson to J.L. Phelps, 8 February 1946; S-M15, Box 8, "Dickson, K.E., Manager, Fish Filleting Plants, 1946-1948," Dickson to J.L. Phelps, "Report on trip to Reindeer and Wollaston Lakes – March 7-8-9/1946."

18 *SAB*, S-M15, Box 8, "Dickson, K.E., 1946-1951," Dickson to SL&FPC Board of Directors, 29 April 1948; S-M15, Box 8, "Lucas, A.A., Office Manager, Fish Board, 1946-1948," Lucas, "Summary Report to the Saskatchewan Fish Board Directors on Findings on the Canadian and Export American Lakefish Markets"; S-M15, Box 8, "Mansfield, A, Fish Board, 1946-1949 (2)," A. Mansfield, "Stocks On Hand," 30 September 1947, S-M15, Box 9, "Sask. Lake and Forest Products Corporation – J.F. Gray, 1946-1950, (4)," "A Submission to the Board."

19 *SAB*, R-907.3, f. 5a, "Dominion Government Departments: Fisheries (J.H. Brockelbank Papers: Minister of Natural Resources)," H.V. Dempsey to J.L. Phelps, 7 February 1947; S. Bates to J.W. Churchman, 11 October 1949; R-907.3, f. 5b, "Dominion Government Departments: Fisheries (J.H. Brockelbank Papers: Minister of Natural Resources)," H.V. Dempsey to Brockelbank, 16 November 1950; S-M15, Box 6, "Fisheries, 1944-1946, (2)," O. Bright to H. Lewis, 28 March 1946; S-M15, Box 8, "Mansfield, A, Fish Board, 1946-1949, (2)," Mansfield to Manager and Chairman of Sask. Fish Board, 4 October 1947; S-NR2, (A) Subject Files – August 1944-April 1949, f. 19, "Fisheries Branch (A.H. MacDonald)," MacDonald to Churchman, 24 July 1948.

20 DNR, *Annual Report*, 1952, 82; Buckley, *Trapping and Fishing*, 65-67; *SAB*, S-M15, Box 8, "Dickson, K.E., Manager, Fish Filleting Plants, 1946-1948," Dickson to J.F. Gray, 9 August 1947; S-M15, Box 9, "Sask Lake and Forest Products Corporation, 1946-1949," Dickson to Gray, J.H. Brockelbank, J.L. Phelps, M. Kalmakoff, G.W. Cadbury, 24 September 1947; S-M15, Box 9, "Sask. Lake and Forest Products Corporation – J.F. Gray, 1946-1951, (3)," Gray to Phelps, 13 January 1948; S-NR 1/4, f. 235, "Cumberland House – General," v. 1, June 1948 to 31 August 1950; A.H. MacDonald to J.W. Churchman, 28 September 1948; S-NR 1/4, 822, "Waite Fisheries – General," L.J. Waite to Brockelbank, 27 March 1951.

21 *SAB*, R-907.3, f. 11, "Fisheries Research Board of Canada (J.H. Brockelbank Papers: Natural Resources)," Brockelbank to A.W. Lantz, 14 April 1949; S-M15, Box 8, "Mansfield, A, Fish Board, 1946-1949, (2)," A. Mansfield, Report to Board of Dirs. of Sask. Fish Bd. for June 1948; S-M15, Box 9, "Sask. Lake and Forest Products Corporation – J.F. Gray, 1946-1951, (2)," J.L. Phelps to Gray, 17 December 1947; S-M15, Box 9, "Sask. Lake and Forest Products Corporation – J.F. Gray, 1946-1950, (4)," Smoking and canning expenses and revenue, 1 April 1947 to 30 September 1947.

22 DNR, *Annual Report*, 1963, 67; Buckley, *Trapping and Fishing*, 62, 71; Buckley, *Working Paper on the Commercial Fishing Industry*, 3; The Trimension Group, *Examination of the Commercial Fishing Industry*, 8.

23 DNR, *Annual Report*, 1947, 78; *SAB*, S-M15, Box 7, "Fish Products, 1944-1946, (2)," K.E. Dickson to J.L. Phelps, 6 August 1945; Phelps to Dickson, 14 August 1945; S-M15, Box 7, "Fish Marketing, 1945-1946," Asst. Sec. to R.H. Woof, 24 December 1945; S-M15, Box 8, "Dickson, K.E., Manager, Fish Filleting Plants, 1946-1948," Dickson to Phelps, 6 May 1946; G.W. Cadbury to Phelps, 10 May 1946; S-M15, Box 8, "McCabe, M.A., Lac La Ronge Plant, 1946-1947," J.L. Phelps, Radio Address, January 1947.

24 *SAB*, S-M15, Box 7, "Fish Marketing, 1945-1946," Mansfield to SFMB, 10 December 1945; S-M15, Box 7, "Fish Products 1945-1946, (3)," A.G. MacAskill to F.R. Glass; S-M15, Box 7, "Sask. Fish Products – Minutes, 1945-1946," SFMB minutes, Prince Albert, SK, 20 January 1946.

25 *SAB*, S-M15, Box 8, "Dickson, K.E., Manager, Fish Filleting Plants, 1946-1948," Dickson to J.L. Phelps, 6 January 1947; S-M15, Box 8, "Lucas, A.A., Office Manager, Fish Board, 1946-1948," Phelps to Lucas, 27 January 1947; S-M15, Box 9, "Sask. Lake and Forest Products Corporation, 1946-1949," J.F. Gray to S. Wopnford, 26 January 1949.

26 Richard Wuorinen, *A History of Buffalo Narrows* (Buffalo Narrows, SK: Buffalo Narrows Celebrate Saskatchewan Committee, 1981), 18-19; *SAB*, S-M15, Box 9, "Federal Department of Fisheries, 1946," R. Campbell to J.L. Phelps, 10 April 1946.

27 *SAB*, R-907.2, v. II, f. 4a, "J.W. Churchman, Deputy Minister March 1948-March 1949," A.H. MacDonald to J.W. Churchman, 25 March 1949; R-A1113, Phelps, interview by Dobbin, 1976; S-M15, Box 6, "Fisheries, 1944-1946, (2)," L.J. Waite to J.L. Phelps, 26 February 1946; S-M15, Box 6, "Fisheries, 1944-1946, (3)," W.G. Tunstead to O. Bright, Supervisor of Fisheries, 11 April 1945; S-M15, Box 7, "Fish Products, 1944-1946, (1)," Phelps to E.H. Tucker, 17 April 1945; Waite Fisheries to Phelps, 14 March 1945; S-M15, Box 8, "Lucas, A.A., Office Manager, Fish Board, 1946-1948," Phelps to Lucas, 27 January 1947; S-M15, Box 9, "Sask. Lake and Forest Products Corporation – J.F. Gray, 1946-1951, (1)," SL&FPC Board and Plant Managers meeting, Regina, 17 January 1947; S-M15, Box 9, "Sask. Lake and Forest Products Corporation – J.F. Gray, 1946-1951, (2)," Phelps to J. Gray, 20 July 1946; S-M15, Box 10, "Sask. Lake and Forest Products Corporation – J.F. Gray, 1946-1951, (5)," Phelps to J. Gray, 2 June 1947; Gray to Phelps, 6 June 1947; S-M15, Box 29, "Questions, 1945-1946, (2)," Question by Mr. Patterson, 5 March (1946).

28 *SAB*, R-907.2, v. II, f. 4a, "J.W. Churchman, Deputy Minister March 1948-March 1949," A.H. MacDonald to Churchman, 25 March 1949; S-M15, Box 6, "Fisheries, 1944-1946, (1)," M.B. Olson to T.C. Douglas, 19 September 1944; S-M15, Box 8, "Dickson, K.E., Manager, Fish Filleting Plants, 1946-1948," "Confidential Report," Dickson to J.L. Phelps, 23 November 1946; S-NR2, (A) Subject Files – August 1944-April 1949, File 19, "Fisheries Branch (A.H. MacDonald)," MacDonald to Churchman, Dore Lake fishermen meeting report, 7 April 1948.

29 *SAB*, S-M15, Box 7, "Fish Products, 1944-1946, (3)," M. Bodner to H. Lewis, 8 March 1946; S-M15, Box 9, "Sask Lake and Forest Products Corporation, 1946-1949," Minutes, Fisherman's Meeting, Pelican Narrows, 19 May 1949; S-M15, Box 10, "Sask. Lake and Forest

Products Corporation – J.F. Gray, 1946-1951, (7)," Gray to T.C. Douglas, 27 May 1948; S-NR2, (A) Subject Files – August 1944-April 1949, f. 34, "Minister of Natural Resources (Hon. J.H. Brockelbank)," J. Johnson, Report on fisheries complaint, R.F. Bradfield, 21 January 1949.

30 *SAB*, S-M15, Box 9, "Sask Lake and Forest Products Corporation, 1946-1949," K.E. Dickson to J.F. Gray, 6 October 1947; S-M15, Box 9, "Sask. Lake and Forest Products Corporation – J.F. Gray, 1946-1950, (4)," Dickson to Gray, 26 September 1947; S-M15, Box 10, "Sask. Lake and Forest Products Corporation – W. Bague, 1947-1948," W.J. Bague to Gray, 2 December 1946.

31 *SAB*, S-M15, Box 9, "Sask Lake and Forest Products Corporation, 1946-1949," A.H. MacDonald and K.E. Dickson, "Present Situation and Proposals in Regard to Conditions in Northern Saskatchewan," 1 October 1947; S-M15, Box 9, "Sask. Lake and Forest Products Corporation – J.F. Gray, 1946-1950, (3)," Gray to MacDonald, W. Tunstead, and J.J. Wheaton; S-M15, Box 9, "Sask. Lake and Forest Products Corporation – J.F. Gray, 1946-1950, (4)," D.F. Corney and M.A. McCabe to J. Gray, 6 October 1947; S-M15, Box 10, "Sask. Lake and Forest Products Corporation – W. Bague, 1947-1948," SL&FPC, Fish Board Div., Profit and Loss statement, 31 March 1947; S-NR2, (A) Subject Files – August 1944-April 1949, f. 19, "Fisheries Branch (A.H. MacDonald)," J.W. Churchman, Summary of Meeting in Minister's Office, 16 September likely 1948.

32 *Progress: A Survey of Saskatchewan Government Activity* (Regina: Bureau of Publications, 1955), 41-42; *SAB*, R-907.3, f. 3a, "Crown Corporations (J.H. Brockelbank: Natural Resources)," Statement of Accumulated Surpluses and Deficits of Crown Corps.," R-907.3, f. 11, "Fisheries Research Board of Canada (J.H. Brockelbank Papers: Natural Resources)," Brockelbank to A.W. Lantz, 14 April 1949; S-NR 1/4, f. 137 K, (3 files), C.A.L. Hogg to J.S. Bevan, 22 April 1949.

33 *SAB*, A 1109, Brockelbank, interview by M. Dobbin, 1976; S-M15, Box 9, "Sask. Lake and Forest Products Corporation, 1946-1949," Minutes, Fisherman's Meeting, Pelican Narrows, 19 May 1949; Fishermen's Meeting, Snake Lake, 21 May 1949; Minutes, Fishermen's Meeting, Deschambeault, 19 May 1949; J.W. Churchman to J.H. Brockelbank, 23 May 1949.

34 Gary Ronald Seymour, "A Geographical Study of the Commercial Fishing Industry in Northern Saskatchewan: An Example of Resource Development" (master's thesis, University of Saskatchewan, 1971), 66-67; Helen L. Buckley, *Working Paper on the Commercial Fishing Industry in Northern Saskatchewan* (Saskatoon: Center for Community Studies, University of Saskatchewan, 1963), 14-19; *SAB*, R-907.3, f. 3b, "Crown Corporations (J.H. Brockelbank: Natural Resources)," J.H. Brockelbank to C.M. Peterson, Clinton, BC, 19 September 1955; S-NR 1/4, 137 K, (3 files), Information about DNR lease to SFMS, including signed copy of lease agreement.

35 DNR, *Annual Report*, 1953, 81; DNR, *Annual Report*, 1958, 54; *SAB*, R-907.3, f. 3b, "Crown Corporations (J.H. Brockelbank: Natural Resources)," A.T. Davidson to J.W. Churchman, 21 February 1956; D.F. Corney to Chairman and Board of Sask. Mktg. Services, 29 February 1956.

36 *SAB*, S-M15, Box 10, "Sask. Lake and Forest Products Corporation – J.F. Gray, 1946-1951, (7)," Gray to Office of the Minister of Nat. Res. and Ind. Dev., 30 September 1948; S-NR 1/4, 137 K, (3 files), F.S. Mitchell to A.H. MacDonald, 23 August 1951; S-NR 1/4, 167 B3, "Northern Region," F. Clinton, "Commercial Fishing – Reindeer Lake," N. Dist. Conf., 7 October 1953; Minutes of N. District Cons. Officers' Conf., Prince Albert, SK, 4-8 October 1954.

37 Miles Goldstick, *Wollaston: People Resisting Genocide* (Montreal: Black Rose Books, 1987), 25-27; *SAB*, R-907.3, f. 3b, "Crown Corporations (J.H. Brockelbank: Natural Resources)," Brief for submission to GFO about plant at Wollaston Lake, 15 March 1956; S-M16, v. XIII, f. 250, "Public Assistance, Social Aid" (a), 1955, H.S. Lee to J.S. White, 15 August 1955; S-NR 1/4, 137 K, (3 files), W.A. Houseman to Brockelbank, 29 June 1955; A.T. Davidson to J.W. Churchman, 18 July 1955; Houseman to Davidson, 18 July 1955; Houseman to C.S. Brown, 11 October 1955; Davidson to D. Corney, 22 May 1956; S-NR 1/5, v. I, f. 16, (137K), "Filleting Plants, 1955-59," Davidson to Houseman, Att. Corney, 28 September 1956; Houseman to Brockelbank, 10 March 1956; Brockelbank to T.C. Douglas, C.M. Fines, Houseman, C.S. Edy, Churchman, 5 March 1956; R.N. Gooding to Davidson, 14

June 1956; Gooding to A.G. Kuziak, 10 September 1956; W.M. Simenson to Gooding, 7 September 1956.

38 DNR, *Annual Report,* 1956, 52, 82; *SAB,* S-NR 1/4, 137 K3B, "La Ronge" (3 files), W.A. Houseman to J.H. Brockelbank, 25 March 1955; A.T. Davidson to J.W. Churchman, 9 December 1954; W.M. Simenson to R.N. Gooding, 30 December 1954.

39 *SAB,* S-NR 1/4, 137 K, (3 files), A.G. Kuziak to E.S. Jones, 25 February 1957; S-NR 1/4, 137 K3, "Northern Region – General" (3 files), J.W. Churchman to Col. L. Fortier, 17 March 1958; A.H. MacDonald to A.T. Davidson, 28 March 1958; Churchman to MacDonald, 17 March 1958; R.N. Gooding to Davidson, 19 March 1958.

40 Buckley, *Trapping and Fishing,* 112-113; *SAB,* S-M15, Box 36, "Doidge, J. (Publicity)," DNR, Activity summary for 1945 to June 1946, 14 June 1946.

41 *SAB,* S-NR 1/4, f. 137 K, (3 files), F.M. Mitchell to A.H. MacDonald, 23 August 1951; G.R. Bowerman to MacDonald, 26 September 1956; S-NR 1/4, 137 K3, "Northern Region – General" (3 files), Office of the N. Admin., E. Dodds to J.W. Churchman, 12 June 1951; S-NR 1/4, f. 444, "Prosecutions," A.H. MacDonald to Churchman, 20 June 1951; S-NR 1/4, f. 822, "Waite Fisheries – General," MacLean to Churchman, 4 September 1951; S-NR 1/5, 144.

42 *SAB,* S-NR 1/4, f. 822, "Waite Fisheries – General," L.J. Waite to J.H. Brockelbank, 27 March 1951.

43 *SAB,* S-NR 1/4, f. 137 K3, "Northern Region – General" (3 files), E. Dodds to C.S. Brown, 30 March 1954; A.H. MacDonald to A.T. Davidson, 6 April 1954; J.H. Brockelbank to H.C. Dunfield, 15 April 1954; S-NR 1/4, f. 235, "Buffalo Narrows," G.E. Couldwell to Davidson, Att.: C.S. Brown, 6 May 1954; S-NR 1/4, f. 822, "Waite Fisheries – General," Waite Fisheries Ltd. to MacDonald, 13 March 1951; MacDonald to J.W. Churchman, 13 March 1951; Churchman to Brockelbank, 14 March 1951; L.J. Waite to Brockelbank, 27 March 1951.

44 *SAB,* S-NR 1/4, f. 137 K, "Filleting Plants – General (Ile a la Crosse only)," Cabinet Minute No. 8369, H.S. Lee to A.G. Kuziak, T.C. Douglas, C.M. Fines, W.S. Lloyd, 4 April 1958; L.J. Waite to G. Couldwell, 1 June 1956; C.S. Brown to A.T. Davidson, 19 February 1957, Proposal to Build a Govt. Filleting Plant at Ile a la Crosse; App. D, Vic Valentine, Social and Economic Situation of Ile a la Crosse Metis, 2 May 1956; S-NR 1/5, v. I, f. 16, (137K), "Filleting Plants, 1955-59," Petition from Île-à-la-Crosse to T.C. Douglas, 1 February 1957; Couldwell, "Meeting Re Assistance to the Fishing Industry – Ile a la Crosse Area," 23 April 1956; W.A. Houseman to J.W. Churchman, 18 April 1956; Churchman to Dr. B.N. Arnason, 7 April 1958; Churchman to J.H. Brockelbank, 20 April 1956; Brockelbank to Churchman, 26 April 1956; S-NR 1/5, f. 144, "Waite Fisheries," Waite Fisheries Ltd. to Kuziak, 22 February 1957; Waite Fisheries Ltd. to Kuziak, 23 July 1957.

45 *SAB,* S-NR 1/4, f. 137 K, (3 files), C.S. Brown to A.T. Davidson, 12 April 1957; S-NR 1/4, f. 137 K3, "Northern Region – General" (3 files), J.W. Churchman to C.L. MacLean, 29 August 1951; S-NR 1/4, f. 444, "Prosecutions," A.H. MacDonald to Churchman, 20 June 1951; S-NR 1/4, f. 822, "Waite Fisheries – General," MacLean to Churchman, 4 September 1951; S-NR 1/5, 144, "Waite Fisheries," Minutes, Processing Plant Board meeting, 3 May 1957; Churchman to MacDonald, 16 May 1957.

46 *SAB,* S-NR 1/5, 144, "Waite Fisheries," Cab. Sec., H.S. Lee to T.C. Douglas, J.H. Brockelbank, C.M. Fines, 9 September 1955; Fisheries Meeting report, 17 April 1957.

47 C.S. Brown, "The Application of Regional Surveys in Provincial Administration, with an Example from the Buffalo Region of Northwestern Saskatchewan," *The Canadian Geographer* 4 (1954): 46; DNR, *Annual Report,* 1951, 72-73; DNR, *Annual Report,* 1958, 54; *Glenbow Archives,* M125, s. VII, f. 65, "Fisheries, 1957-1965," M.M., "Fisheries Policy – as of October 1958," 26 September 1958; Seymour, "A Geographical Study," 68; Buckley, *Trapping and Fishing,* 100-102.

48 *SAB,* R-907.3, f. 10, "Fishermen's Co-Operative Federation," D.G. Macdonald, Summary of W.W. Wood Report on Sask. Fisheries to the Bd. of Dirs. of the Fishermen's Co-Op. Fed., 10-14 March 1949, 12 April 1949; S-M15, Box 7, "Fish Products, 1944-1946, (2)," J.L. Phelps to T.J. Searle, 13 July 1945; S-M15, Box 7, "Sask. Fish Products – Minutes, 1945-1946," Minutes of SFP Bd. of Dirs. Mtg., Regina, 25 February 1946; S-M15, Box 9, "Sask. Lake and Forest Products Corporation, 1946-1949," K.E. Dickson to Phelps, 16 June 1947; S-NR2, (A) Subject Files – August 1944-April 1949, f. 19, "Fisheries Branch (A.H. MacDonald)," MacDonald, "Report on Fisheries Program/February 1946"; T.C. Douglas Speech, "Progress Report on Co-Operation Among Fishermen," 1959.

49 DNR, *Annual Report,* 1952, 87; DNR, *Annual Report,* 1953, Intro. letter from J.W. Churchman to J.H. Brockelbank; J.E.M. Kew, *Cumberland House in 1960* (Saskatoon: Center for Community Studies, University of Saskatchewan, 1962), 47-51; *SAB,* S-M16, A.M. Nicholson Papers, v. VII, f. 3, "Parks and Lands Branch, 1961-63," J.A. Collier to R. Brown, 27 November 1957.

50 *Glenbow Archives,* M125, s. VII, f. 65, "Fisheries, 1957-1965," M.M., Fisheries Policy Committee proposals for est. of Co-Op. Fish Mktg. Service, 14 May 1957; A.G. Kuziak to Premier and all Cabinet Ministers, 23 May 1957.

51 *Glenbow Archives,* M125, s. VII, f. 65, "Fisheries, 1957-1965," M.M., "Fisheries Policy – as of October 1958," 26 September 1958; Seymour, "A Geographical Study," 69; Buckley, *Working Paper on the Commercial Fishing Industry,* 3-19; Barron, *Walking in Indian Moccasins,* 154-155.

52 *Glenbow Archives,* M125, s. VII, f. 60, "Co-Ops 1950-1962," Premier Douglas, News Release, 26 November 1958; Report of meeting in Prince Albert, 26 November 1958; J.W. Churchman to DNR staff, 10 December 1958.

53 *Glenbow Archives,* M125, s. VI, f. 56, "CCF 1954-1961," Organizational Report – Lac La Ronge C.C.F. Club, January 1960.

54 DNR, *Annual Report,* 1959, N.A. 14; DNR, *Annual Report,* 1961, 106; DNR, *Annual Report,* 1963, 67-68; Seymour, "A Geographical Study," 70; Buckley, *Trapping and Fishing,* 103-108; *Glenbow Archives,* M125, s. VII, f. 66, "La Ronge Co-Op Fisheries, 1959-1962," CFL Bd. of Dirs. report for fiscal year ended 31 October 1960 to Second Ann. CFL Mtg., 20 February 1961.

55 In 1962, La Ronge Fishermen's Co-Op. Association and some fishermen asked to have CFL handle all fish from over fifty lakes. Alleged irregularities in supporting signatures and a shortage of signatures repeatedly prevented this from proceeding.

56 Buckley, *Trapping and Fishing,* 184; *SAB,* S-NR 1/5, v. III, f. 8, "Buffalo Narrows, 1963-66," E.L. Paynter to J.W. Churchman, 29 December 1961.

57 Buckley, *Trapping and Fishing,* 31-33, 75-88, 95; DNR, *Annual Report,* 1958, 54; DNR, *Annual Report,* 1962, 67, 108; Edward B. Reed, *Limnology and Fisheries of the Saskatchewan River in Saskatchewan* (Regina: DNR, Fisheries Branch, 1962); *SAB,* R-907.2, v. I, f. 2, "Cumberland House Settlement," M.F. Norris to J.J. Wheaton, 22 October 1947 and attached report on Economic and Social Survey of Cumberland House Dist., October 1947; S-M15, Box 8, "Dickson, K.E., 1946-1951, (1)," Operations summary, Lac la Ronge, Summer, 1947; S-M15, Box 8, "Dickson, K.E., Manager, Fish Filleting Plants,1946-1948," Dickson to J.L. Phelps, 3 December 1946; S-NR 1/4, 167 B3, "Northern Region," J.W. Clouthier, "Commercial Fishing Buffalo Region," N. Dist. Conf., 8 October 1953; S-NR 1/4, f. 235, "Cumberland House – General," v. 1, June 1948 to 31 August 1950; Jack Wilkie, "Report of Trip to Cumberland House," August 1948; S-NR 1/5, v. III, f. 24a, "Fur Advisory Committee, 1960-64," Minutes of Sask. Fur Adv. Comm., Prince Albert, SK, 31 January 1964.

58 Buckley, *Working Paper on the Commercial Fishing Industry,* 8-9.

59 *SAB,* S-M16, v. VII, f. 3, "Parks and Lands Branch, 1961-63," J.A. Collier to R. Brown, 27 November 1957; S-NR 1/4, f. 137 K, "Filleting Plants – General (Ile a la Crosse only)," C.S. Brown to A.T. Davidson, 19 February 1957.

60 DNR, *Annual Report,* 1964, 70; DNR, *Annual Report,* 1965, 13; DNR, *Annual Report,* 1966, 12; Buckley, *Working Paper on the Commercial Fishing Industry,* 18; *SAB,* R-907.3, f. 3a, "Crown Corporations," W.A. Houseman to A.E. Blakeney, Re: "Saskatchewan Fish Marketing Service and Federal Price Support Programme"; R-907.3, f. 4, "Dominion Government Departments: Citizenship and Immigration," J.H. Brockelbank to W.E. Harris, 13 May 1953; Brockelbank to Harris, 17 August 1953; L. Fortier to C.A.L. Hogg, 8 February 1950; Harris to Brockelbank, 27 May 1953; Harris to Brockelbank, 5 October 1953; J.F. Gray to F.W. Woloshyn, 16 March 1950; R-907.3, f. 5a, "Dominion Government Departments: Fisheries," J.L. Phelps to H.F.G. Bridges; Bridges to Phelps, 18 February 1947; S-M15, Box 9, "Sask. Lake and Forest Products Corporation – J.F. Gray, 1946-1950, (4)," "A Submission to the Board," anon., undated; S-M15, Box 10, "Sask. Lake and Forest Products Corporation – J.F. Gray, 1946-1951, (5)," Gray to M. Kalmakoff, G.W. Cadbury, Phelps, Brockelbank, 16 July 1947; Gray, Report to the Bd. of Dirs. of the SL&FPC on SFB Board of Management meeting, 17 May 1948; S-M16, v. XIII, f. 264, "Public Assistance, Indians and Metis, 1952-64," A.H. MacDonald, "Treaty Indians and Northern Administration," 18 November 1963.

61 Stanford Research Institute, *A Study of Resources and Industrial Opportunities for the Province of Saskatchewan* (Menlo Park, CA: Stanford Research Institute, 1959), Tables 7, 8, 81.
62 DNR, *Annual Report*, 1962, 67; DNR, *Annual Report*, 1966, 12; Seymour, "A Geographical Study," 55; Buckley, *Trapping and Fishing*, 64; *SAB*, S-NR 1/4, 167 B3, "Northern Region, April 1st, 1956," N. Dist. Field Officers' Conf., 9-13 January 1951.
63 *SAB*, S-NR 1/4, f. 444, "Prosecutions," C.L. MacLean to R.F. Albus, 4 July 1951; C.F. Oatway to N. Admin., 24 July 1951; Statement of Robert Albus, 31 July 1951; Statement of John Ivanchuk, 4 August 1951; Statement of Joseph Thomas, 4 August 1951; Statement of Duncan Lawson, 5 August 1951; Statement of Larry Roluf, 6 August 1951; Oatway to MacLean, 8 August 1951; J.H. Brockelbank, Press Release, 8 August 1951; MacLean to Brockelbank, 20 September 1951.
64 *SAB*, S-NR 1/4, f. 444, "Prosecutions," A.T. Davidson to C.S. Brown, 18 July 1955; G.J. Fladager to A.H. MacDonald, 27 June 1951; "Prosecutions," anon, undated; S.C. Read to C.L. MacLean, 17 December 1951; E.L. Paynter to MacDonald, 1 December 1951; MacDonald to J.W. Churchman, 2 January 1952.
65 *SAB*, S-NR 1/4, f. 230, "Northern Region," C.S. Brown to A.T. Davidson, 6 August 1953; S-NR 1/4, f. 235, "Cumberland House – General," v. 2, September 1950-57, W. Carriere to T.C. Douglas, 29 July 1953; F. Mitchell to A.H. MacDonald, 4 August 1953.
66 *SAB*, S-M15, Box 7, "Fish Products, 1944-1946, (2)," P.C. Hogan to H.P. Evans, 15 August 1945; "Minutes of a Meeting of the Fishermen Tributary to Big River," 23 August 1944; S-M15, Box 7, "Fish Products (3)," K.E. Dickson to J.L. Phelps, 30 January 1946; S-M15, Box 8, "Dickson, K.E., Manager, Fish Filleting Plants, 1946-1948," Dickson to Phelps, 18 February 1945; S-M15, Box 9, "Sask Lake and Forest Products Corporation, 1946-1949," Dickson to J.F. Gray, J.H. Brockelbank, Phelps, M. Kalmakoff, G.W. Cadbury, 24 September 1947.
67 DNR, *Annual Report*, 1945, 58; DNR, *Annual Report*, 1959, Fi 4-5; DNR, *Annual Report*, 1962, 68-69; Seymour, "A Geographical Study," 56-60; *SAB*, R782, Department of Natural Resources (GR-24-3), v. I, f. 5, "Deputy Minister Correspondence, 1970-1971"; S-M15, Box 16, "Game Branch, 1944-1946, (2)," W.A. Hartwell to J.L. Phelps, 27 July 1945.
68 DNR, *Annual Report*, 1949, 100; Reed, *Limnology and Fisheries of the Saskatchewan River*; Robert Jarvenpa, *The Trappers of Patuanak: Toward a Spatial Ecology of Modern Hunters*, National Museum of Man Mercury Series, Canadian Ethnology Service Paper No. 67 (Ottawa: National Museums of Canada, 1980), 24; *SAB*, S-M15, Box 6, "Fisheries, 1944-1946, (2)," Minutes, Fishermen's Meeting, Flin Flon, 28 February 1946; S-NR 1/4, f. 235, "Cumberland House – General," v. 1, June 1948 to 31 August 1950; Jack Wilkie, "Report of Trip to Cumberland House," August 1948.

Chapter 7: Just One Jump Out of the Stone Age

1 Green Lake, the site of a relocation project for southern Metis since the 1930s, fell outside both the NAD and Northern District. For this reason, although the project limped on through many trials and tribulations during the CCF era, this study does not include it.
2 *Saskatchewan Archives Board* [*SAB*], R-907.2, J.H. Brockelbank Papers, v. I, f. 6, "Land Administration," Report on Div. of Resp. for Land Admin., 1951.
3 Bruce Peel, "Cumberland House," *Saskatchewan History* 3, 2 (Spring 1950): 72-73; Committee on Saskatchewan River Delta Problems, *Resources, Development and Problems of the Saskatchewan River Delta* (Regina: Water Resources Commission, April 1972), 138-139; *Glenbow Archives*, M125, James Brady Collection, s. VI, f. 39, "Historical Notes, 1932-1959," Brady, Draft, C.C.F. Clubs, The Pas and Flin Flon, 1952; *SAB*, S-NR 1/4, Deputy Minister and Assistant Deputy Minister Files, f. 230, "Northern Region," A.G. Kuziak to L.F. McIntosh, 14 November 1956; Virginia McKay, Jean Carriere, Pierre Dorion, and Marie Deschambault, "History and Culture Report: Cumberland House," no date, 27.
4 *SAB*, R-A1113, Joe Phelps, interview by Murray Dobbin, audio tape, 1976; S-NR 1/4, f. 236 E., "Cumberland House Farm," v. 1, July 1948-31 March 1951, A.T. Davidson to C.A.L. Hogg, 28 September 1951; E. Dodds, "Proposed Agricultural Programme for Cumberland House," 1/5/50.
5 *SAB*, S-NR 1/4, f. 235, "Cumberland House – General," v. 2, September 1950-57, A.K. Quandt to J.L. Phelps, Report on Cumberland House area, 1946.
6 *SAB*, R-907.2, v. II, f. 4a, "J.W. Churchman, Deputy Minister," March 1948-March 1949,

Churchman to C.A.L. Hogg, 17 September 1948; S-NR2, DNR-ADM, (A) Subject Files – August 1944-April 1949, f. 38, "Northern District (A.K. Quandt)," Quandt to Churchman, 10 August 1948; Quandt to T. Leia, 10 August 1948; S-NR2, (A) Subject Files – August 1944-April 1949, f. 11, "Co-Operatives, Department of," Churchman to B.N. Arnason, 20 August 1948; S-NR 1/4, f. 236 E, "Cumberland House Farm," v. 1, July 1948-31 March 1951, J.J. Wheaton to E.J. Marshall, 7 July 1948; Office of the Northern Administrator to A.T. Davidson, Att.: E.E. Chorneyko, 9 April 1953; E. Dodds, "Proposed Agricultural Programme for Cumberland House," 1/5/50

7 *SAB*, S-NR 1/4, f. 236 E, "Cumberland House Farm," v. 1. July 1948-31 March 1951, J.H. Brockelbank to J.W. Churchman, 31 December 1949; C.A.L. Hogg to Brockelbank, 29 March 1950; E. Dodds to C.L. MacLean, 25 July 1950; Brockelbank to Hogg, 20 April 1949; Churchman to MacLean, 17 July 1950.

8 DNR, *Annual Report,* 1950, 148; *SAB*, S-M15, Box 36, Phelps Papers, "Christie, C, R.," J.D. Neilson to C.L. McLean, 8 November 1950; C.A.L. Hogg to J.H. Brockelbank, 7 February 1951; S-NR 1/4, f. 236 E, "Cumberland House Farm," v.1, July 1948-31 March 1951, E. Dodds to MacLean, 25 July 1950; R.N. Gooding to J.W. Churchman, 28 June 1950.

9 *SAB*, S-NR 1/4, f. 236 E., "Cumberland House Farm," v. 1, July 1948-31 March 1951, Office of N. Admin. to A.T. Davidson, Att.: E.E. Chorneyko, 9 April 1953; S-NR 1/4, f. 236 E., "Cumberland House Farm," v. 2, April 1951-, J.W. Churchman to J.H. Brockelbank and C.A.L. Hogg, 17 April 1951; Churchman to Brockelbank, 13 June 1951; C.L. MacLean to Churchman, 24 July 1951; MacLean to Churchman, 10 August 1951; E. Dodds to Churchman, 17 April 1951; Dodds to Churchman, 7 June 1951; Brockelbank to Churchman, 5 July 1951; W.J. Bague to MacLean, 23 January 1952; S-NR 1/4, f. 235, "Cumberland House – General," v. 2, September 1950-57, Dodds to MacLean, 25 October 1951; S-NR2, (A) Subject Files – August 1944-April 1949, f. 38, "Northern District (A.K. Quandt)," Quandt to Churchman, 10 August 1948.

10 *SAB*, S-NR 1/4, f. 236 E, "Cumberland House Farm," v. 1, July 1948-31 March 1951, J.W. Churchman to W.M. Miner, 4 December 1952; E. Dodds to Churchman, 10 June 1952; J.H. Brockelbank to C.A.L. Hogg, 8 July 1952; S-NR 1/4, f. 236 E, "Cumberland House Farm," v. 2, April 1951-, Churchman to G. Craik, 5 August 1952; Premier's Office to Brockelbank, J.H. Sturdy, 22 July 1952; Item from J.W. Churchman, 5 August 1952; S-NR 1/4, f. 236 E., "Cumberland House Farm," v. 2, July 1948-31 March 1951, W.M. Miner to Co-Op. Mgmt. Adv., DNR, 10 September 1952; C.S. Brown to Churchman, 14 November 1952; Miner to Brown, 22 November 1952.

11 *Glenbow Archives*, M125, s. VI, f. 39, "Historical Notes, 1932-1959," J.P. Brady, Draft, C.C.F. Clubs The Pas and Flin Flon, 1952; *SAB*, S-NR 1/4, f. 236 E, "Cumberland House Farm," v. 1, July 1948-31 March 1951, J.W. Churchman to Dr. L.B. Thomson, 18 March 1953.

12 DNR, *Annual Report,* 1953, 152; *SAB*, S-NR 1/4, f. 236 E, "Cumberland House Farm," v. 1, July 1948-31 March 1951, E. Dodds to C.S. Brown, 27 November 1953; J.D. Neilson to Brown, 21 October 1953; J.W. Churchman to Dr. L.B. Thomson, 18 March 1953; Churchman to A.T. Davidson, Att.: C.S. Brown, 5 May 1953; Churchman to Davidson, 8 May 1953.

13 *SAB*, S-NR 1/4, f. 236 E, "Cumberland House Farm," v. 1, July 1948-31 March 1951, H.S. Lee to Premier Douglas, C.M. Fines, W.S. Lloyd, J.H. Brockelbank, Re: Cab. Mtg. of 26 January 1954; A.T. Davidson to J.W. Churchman, 16 February 1954; C.S. Brown to Davidson, 5 February 1954; S-NR 1/4, f. 236 E, "Cumberland House Farm," v. 2, Brockelbank to Douglas, 18 February 1954.

14 DNR, *Annual Report,* 1955, 64.

15 *SAB*, S-M16, A.M. Nicholson Papers, v. VII, f. 3, "Parks and Lands Branch, 1961-63," "Welfare and Development Policy for Northern Saskatchewan," December 1957; App. B, V.F. Valentine, Comm. Dev. Res. Project, 10 June 1957; S-NR 1/4, f. 236 E, "Cumberland House Farm," v. 2, 1956-, C.S. Brown to J.D. Neilson, 12 April 1957; J.W. Churchman to A.T. Davidson, 7 May 1957; Minutes, Meeting in office of A.T. Davidson, 4 May 1956.

16 DNR, *Annual Report,* 1961, 108; *Glenbow Archives*, M125, v. II, f. 8, "Personal," 1952-62, M. Kew to Jim, 15 February 1960; *SAB*, R-517, Dept. of Health, Comm. Health Services Br. (GR-278), (Records of Central Office, the 13 Health Regions and the Northern Health District), Northern Health District, v. XIII, f. 50, Relations with Saskatchewan Government Departments, 1961-62; J.E.M. Kew, Talk at the Third Annual Short Course, 10-14 April

1961; S-NR 1/5, v. III, f. 6, "Cumberland House Farm, 1961-65," J.E.M. Kew, "The Cumberland House Farm," undated; "A Review of Recommendations Concerning the Cumberland House Farm," undated.

17 *SAB*, S-NR 1/5, v. I, f. 74, (408), "Cumberland House Farm, 1957-1961," Minutes, Cumberland Community Council, 12 July 1961; A.H. MacDonald, "Proposals for the Cumberland House Farm," 21 April 1961; C.C. Hanson to MacDonald, undated; MacDonald to J.W. Churchman, 14 July 1961; R.I.I. McKay to H.D. McRorie, 8 September 1961; "Summary of Cumberland House Farm Report," 3 January 1962; S-NR 1/5, v. III, f. 6, "Cumberland House Farm, 1961-65," "A Review of Recommendations Concerning the Cumberland House Farm," undated.

18 *SAB*, S-M 16, v. VII, f. 1, J.W. Churchman to A.G. Kuziak, 10 September 1962; S-NR 1/5, v. I, f. 74, (408), "Cumberland House Farm, 1957-1961," Churchman to A.H. MacDonald, 25 July 1962; Kuziak to Treasury Board, 19 February 1962; Kuziak to Treasury Board, 25 July 1962; S-NR 1/5, v. III, f. 6, "Cumberland House Farm, 1961-65," "A Review of Recommendations Concerning the Cumberland House Farm," undated; A.H. MacDonald, "Interim Report of Inter-Departmental Committee on Cumberland House," 11/9/62; E. Dodds to A.H. MacDonald, 20 March 1962; Minutes, Cumberland House Farm Meeting, 15 November 1962; "Report of the Inter-Departmental Committee on Cumberland House," 1963; E.I. Wood to E. Kramer, 15 January 1964; Kramer to W.J. Berezowsky, 27 January 1964; Kramer to Berezowsky, 16 March 1964; Churchman to R. Thommes, 17 April 1964; Treasury Board Minute No. 1943, 24 April 1952.

19 *Glenbow Archives*, M125, s. VI, f. 39, "Historical Notes, 1932-1959," J.P. Brady, Draft, C.C.F. Clubs The Pas and Flin Flon, 1952; *SAB*, S-NR 1/4, f. 235, "Cumberland House – General," v. 1, June 1948-31 August 1950, E. Dodds to C.L. MacLean, 17 April 1950; Office of N. Admin. to J.W. Churchman, Att.: A.I. Bereskin, 21 April 1950; S-NR 1/4, f. 235, "Cumberland House – General," v. 2, September 1950-57, Dodds to MacLean, 25 October 1951; S-NR 1/4, f. 236 E, "Cumberland House Farm," v. 1, July 1948-31 March 1951, A.T. Davidson to C.A.L. Hogg, 22 March 1951; W.J. Bague to MacLean, 23 January 1952; Dodds, "Proposed Agricultural Programme for Cumberland House," 1/5/50; S-NR 1/4, f. 236 E, "Cumberland House Farm," v. 2, April 1951-, Churchman to J.H. Brockelbank and Hogg, 17 April 1951.

20 A.T. Davidson, "Role of Geographers in Northern Saskatchewan," *Canadian Geographer* 4 (1954): 36; Committee on Saskatchewan River Delta Problems, *Resources, Development and Problems*, 9-11; DNR, *Annual Report*, 1953, 152; Helen L. Buckley, J.E.M. Kew, and John B. Hawley, *The Indians and Metis of Northern Saskatchewan: A Report on Economic and Social Development* (Saskatoon: Center for Community Studies, University of Saskatchewan, 1963), 48-49; J.D. Neilson and A.M. Thomson, Presentation for Northern Saskatchewan Development Conference, Saskatoon, 20-21 November 1957; Royal Commission on Agriculture and Rural Life, *Crown Land Settlement in North-Eastern Saskatchewan*, Interim Report (January 1954); *SAB*, S-M 16, v. VIII, f. 1, "Planning Board, 1953-63," (1 of 2), Cabinet Conf. on Program Planning, 21-22 May 1963; S-NR 1/4, f. 235, "Cumberland House – General," v. 2, September 1950-57, R.G. Young to J.W. Churchman, 27 August 1951; S-NR 1/4, f. 236 E, "Cumberland House Farm," v. 1, July 1948-31 March 1951, J.S. Clayton, J.G. Ellis, and A.P. Edwards, "Soil Survey of the Cumberland House Area," 1951; S-NR 1/5, v. I, f. 19, (162G), "Saskatchewan River Reclamation Area, 1953-1960," Minutes, Meeting of PFRA, Man., and Sask. Reps. re: Sask. River Reclamation Project, 6 March 1953; C.A.L. Hogg to J.W. Churchman, 7 March 1953; Hogg to J.H. Brockelbank, 10 March 1953; Brockelbank to J.S. McDiarmid, 13 April 1953; Man. Minister of Mines and Natural Resources to I.C. Nollet, 27 October 1953; Other correspondence; S-NR 1/5, v. I, f. 74, (408), "Cumberland House Farm, 1957-1961," Churchman to A.H. MacDonald, 25 July 1962; A.G. Kuziak to Treasury Board, 25 July 1962; S-NR 1/5, v. III, f. 6, "Cumberland House Farm, 1961-65," MacDonald, "Interim Report of Inter-Dept. Comm. on C. House," 11/9/62.

21 *SAB*, S-NR 1/4, f. 236 E, "Cumberland House Farm," v. 1, July 1948-31 March 1951, R.N. Gooding to J.W. Churchman, 29 June 1950.

22 *SAB*, S-NR 1/4, f. 231 B, "Cumberland House," (2 files), D.E. Denmark to C.A.L. Hogg, 18 March 1953.

23 *SAB*, S-NR 1/4, f. 236 E, "Cumberland House Farm," v. 1, July 1948-31 March 1951, H.C.

Moss, "A Preliminary Study of the Soils of the Churchill River Basin of Northern Saskatchewan," 1950; "Notes on Trip From Meadow Lake to Buffalo River Settlement on Peter Pond Lake," 1943.

24 Neilson and Thomson, Northern Saskatchewan Development Conference; *Proceedings "Resources for People" Saskatchewan Resources Conference*, Saskatoon, SK, 20-21 January 1964, 409; *SAB*, S-NR 1/4, f. 235, "La Ronge," C.S. Brown to C.A.L. Hogg, "An Investigation of Problems Related to the Development of Recreational Resources of Lac la Ronge"; S-NR 1/4, f. 236 E, "Cumberland House Farm," v. 1, July 1948-31 March 1951, H.C. Moss, "A Preliminary Study of the Soils of the Churchill River Basin of Northern Saskatchewan," 1950; A.R. Brown, "Horticultural and Agricultural Possibilities of the Southern Portion of the Churchill River Basin," 31 December 1949.

25 DNR, *Annual Report*, 1948, 130; DNR, *Annual Report*, 1952, 165-167; DNR, *Annual Report*, 1956, 77-78; *SAB*, S-NR 1/4, f. 167 B3, "Northern Region," Minutes of N. District Cons. Officers' Conf., Prince Albert, SK, 4-8 October 1954; S-NR 1/5, v. III, f. 7, "Northern Agriculture, 1961-65," Communication from W.S. Lloyd, 6 October 1961; A.G. Kuziak to Treasury Board, 3 May 1961; J.D. Nielson to A.H. MacDonald, 27 April 1961.

26 DNR, *Annual Report*, 1953, 152; DNR, *Annual Report*, 1954, 63; *SAB*, S-NR 1/4, 167 B3, "Northern Region," Minutes of N. District Cons. Officers' Conf., Prince Albert, SK, 4-8 October 1954.

27 DNR, *Annual Report*, 1961, 108; DNR, *Annual Report*, 1962, 110; *SAB*, S-NR 1/5, v. III, f. 7, "Northern Agriculture, 1961-65," J.D. Neilson, "The Northern Agricultural Program 1963"; "Saskatchewan Co-Operative Extension Program – Planned Program Narrative," Ag. Rep. Dist. 37, 1961-62.

28 *Glenbow Archives*, M125, s. VII, f. 62, "Co-Op agriculture, 1948-1958," From paper for Seminar on Comm. Dev. in the Far North, Activities of Dept. of Agric., 1950-58; *SAB*, S-NR 1/4, f. 231 B, "Buffalo Narrows, 1949-1957," Office of N. Admin. to J.W. Churchman, 15 September 1952; S-NR 1/4, f. 235, "Snake Lake," (2 files), C.L. MacLean to Churchman, 5 April 1950; Churchman to A.T. Davidson, 22 February 1954; S-M16, v. VII, f. 3, "Parks and Lands Branch, 1961-63," Minutes, N. Adv. Comm., 29 March 1954; S-NR 1/4, f. 236 E, "Cumberland House Farm," v. 2, 1956-, Minutes, Meeting in Office of A.T. Davidson, 4 May 1956.

29 *SAB*, S-NR 1/4, f. 167 B3, "Northern Region," Minutes of N. District Cons. Officers' Conf., Prince Albert, SK, 4-8 October 1954; S-NR 1/4, 236 E, "Cumberland House Farm, v. 2, 1956-" Minutes, Meeting in Office of A.T. Davidson, 4 May 1956.

30 DNR, *Annual Report*, 1953, 152; DNR, *Annual Report*, 1954, 63.

31 DNR, *Annual Report*, 1965, 51; *SAB*, S-NR 1/5, v. III, f. 7, "Northern Agriculture, 1961-65," J.D. Neilson, "The Northern Agricultural Program 1963"; S-NR 1/5, v. III, f. 24a, "Fur Advisory Committee, 1960-64," Minutes, Sask. Fur Adv. Comm., Prince Albert, 31 January 1964.

32 DNR, *Annual Report*, 1961, 108; DNR, *Annual Report*, 1962, 110; *Glenbow Archives*, M125, s. VII, f. 62, "Co-Op agriculture, 1948-1958," From paper for Seminar on Comm. Dev. in the Far North, Activities of Dept. of Agric., 1950-58; *SAB*, S-NR 1/4, f. 236 E, "Cumberland House Farm," v. 2, 1956-, Minutes, Meeting in Office of A.T. Davidson, 4 May 1956; S-NR 1/5, v. III, f. 7, "Northern Agriculture, 1961-65," J.D. Neilson, "The Northern Agricultural Program 1963"; "Saskatchewan Co-Operative Extension Program – Planned Program Narrative," Ag. Rep. Dist. 37, 1961-62.

33 *SAB*, S-NR 1/4, DNR, Dep. Min. and ADM Files, f. 235, "Cumberland House – General," v. 1, June 1948-31 August 1950, A.O. Aschim, "Cumberland House Reconnaissance Survey," 2 September 1948.

34 *Glenbow Archives*, M125, s. III, "Correspondence," 1933-67, f. 22, "Norris," 1945-67, M. Norris to Brady, 5 December 1947.

35 *SAB*, S-NR 1/4, f. 235, "Cumberland House – General," v. 1, June 1948-31 August 1950, J.W. Churchman to J.J. Wheaton and A.K. Quandt, 7 July 1948; S-NR2, DNR-ADM, (A) Subject Files, August 1944-April 1949, f. 37, "Northern Administration (J.J. Wheaton)," J.W. Churchman to Wheaton, 11 June 1948.

36 *SAB*, S-NR 1/4, f. 235, "Cumberland House – General," v. 1, June 1948-31 August 1950, A.O. Aschim, "Cumberland House Reconnaissance Survey," 2 September 1948.

37 *SAB*, S-NR 1/4, f. 167 B3, "Northern Region, April 1st, 1956," N. Dist. Field Officers' Conf.,

Prince Albert, SK, 31 January-1 February 1949. Brady cited a need to follow democratic procedures.

38 DNR, *Annual Report,* 1952, 168; DNR, *Annual Report,* 1953, 152; DNR, *Annual Report,* 1954, 63; C.S. Brown, "The Application of Regional Surveys in Provincial Administration, With an Example from the Buffalo Region of Northwestern Saskatchewan," *The Canadian Geographer* 4 (1954): 43; *Progress: A Survey of Saskatchewan Government Activity* (Regina: Bureau of Publications, 1955), 15-16; *SAB,* S-NR 1/4, f. 236, "Rehabilitation and Welfare – General," v. 2, A.T. Davidson to J.W. Churchman, 17 June 1953.

39 *SAB,* S-M16, A.M. Nicholson Papers, v. VII, f. 3, "Parks and Lands Branch, 1961-63," A.G. Kuziak to J.H. Brockelbank, J.W. Erb, T.J. Bentley, and W.S. Lloyd, 9 January 1958; J.A. Collier to R. Brown, 27 November 1957; Brockelbank to Premier Douglas and All Cabinet Members, 10 October 1955; S-NR 1/4, f. 167 B3, "Northern Region," Minutes of N. District Cons. Officers' Conf., Prince Albert, SK, 4-8 October 1954; V.F. Valentine and R.G. Young, "The Situation of the Metis of Northern Saskatchewan in Relation to His Physical and Social Environment," *The Canadian Geographer* 4 (1954): 56.

40 *Glenbow Archives,* M125, s. III, "Correspondence," 1933-67, f. 22, "Norris, 1945-1967," (Mining and Native Rights), M.F. Norris to J.P. Brady, 11 December 1956; *SAB,* S-M16, v. VII, f. 3, "Parks and Lands Branch, 1961-63," "Welfare and Development Policy for Northern Saskatchewan," December 1957; App. B, V.F. Valentine, "Community Development Research Project: A General Proposal for Cumberland House," 10 June 1957.

41 *SAB,* S-NR 1/4, f. 236, "Rehabilitation and Welfare – General," v. 2, A.T. Davidson to J.W. Churchman, 3 October 1957; M. Miller to Churchman, 29 May 1957.

42 DNR, *Annual Report,* 1957, 115; DNR, *Annual Report,* 1958, 107-108; *SAB,* S-M16, v. VII, f. 3, "Parks and Lands Branch, 1961-63," "Welfare and Development Policy for Northern Saskatchewan," December 1957; App. B, V.F. Valentine, "Community Development Research Project: A General Proposal for Cumberland House," 10 June 1957; S-NR 1/4, f. 236, "Rehabilitation and Welfare – General," v. 2, Valentine, "Community Development Research Project: A General Proposal for Cumberland House," 29 May 1957.

43 *SAB,* S-NR 1/4, f. 236, "Rehabilitation and Welfare – General," v. 2, E.N. Shannon to C.S. Brown, 1 November 1957.

44 *SAB,* S-M16, v. VII, f. 3, "Parks and Lands Branch, 1961-63," C.C. Taylor to M. Miller, 10 September 1957.

45 *SAB,* S-M16, v. VII, f. 3, "Parks and Lands Branch, 1961-63," "Welfare and Development Policy for Northern Saskatchewan," December 1957.

46 DNR, *Annual Report,* 1959, xiii, N.A. 8-9; *SAB,* S-M 16, v. VII, f. 4, "Tour of Northern Saskatchewan, 1959," M. Miller, Center for Community Studies, "Some Problems and Premises of Policy for the Development of Northern Saskatchewan," Center for Community Studies Seminar, Saskatoon, 6 October 1958; S-NR 1/5, v. I, f. 39, (230), "Northern Region, 1957-1959," J.W. Churchman, "Our Goals in the North and How We Hope to Achieve Them," 19 April 1959.

47 *SAB,* S-NR 1/4, f. 162, "Center for Community Studies," (4 files), Center for Community Studies, "Community Notebook," v. 1, 2, May 1959; A.K. Davis to W. Churchman, 6 May 1959; W.B. Baker, Address, "The Purpose and Program of the Center for Community Studies," 10 March 1959; Center for Community Studies, *Developing Saskatchewan's Community Resources: Saskatchewan Approaches Community Development, Prerequisites for a Social Technology* (Saskatoon: Center for Community Studies, University of Saskatchewan, 1961); Center for Community Studies, "Program – Far Northern Research" (Saskatoon: Center for Community Studies, University of Saskatchewan, 1959).

48 DNR, *Annual Report,* 1962, 108; *SAB,* NR 1/5, DNR, Dep. Min., v. I, f. 85, "Centre for Community Studies," 1960, Center for Community Studies, "A General Outline of the Approach to be Taken to Contract Obligations with the Department of Natural Resources," 2 February 1960; Copy of unsigned agreement between the Center and DNR.

49 DNR, *Annual Report,* 1961, 102, 108; Center for Community Studies, *Economic and Social Survey of Northern Saskatchewan,* Interim Report No. 1 (March 1961), Preface, 3; W.B. Baker, *Some Observations on the Application of Community Development to the Settlements of Northern Saskatchewan* (Saskatoon: University of Saskatchewan, Center for Community Studies, n.d.), 8.

50 DNR, *Annual Report,* 1962, 110; *Glenbow Archives,* M125, s. II, f. 8, "Personal," 1952-62,

M. Kew to Jim, 9 January 1964; *SAB*, S-NR 1/5, v. III, f. 4, "Northern Administration District, 1962-67," AHM, "Brief on Community Development in the North," 7/9/62; S-NR 1/5, v. III, f. 20, "Cumberland House – General," 1962-67," W.R. Parks to J.W. Churchman, 16 October 1963.

51 DNR, *Annual Report*, 1964, 43; *SAB*, S-NR 1/5, v. III, f. 24a, "Fur Advisory Committee, 1960-64," Minutes, Sask. Fur Adv. Comm., Prince Albert, SK, 31 January 1964.

52 James M. Pitsula, "'Educational Paternalism' Versus Autonomy: Contradictions in the Relationship Between the Saskatchewan Government and the Federation of Saskatchewan Indians, 1958-1964," *Prairie Forum* 22, 1 (Spring 1997): 48, 54, 63.

53 *SAB*, S-NR 1/5, v. I, f. 39, (230), "Northern Region, 1957-1959," A. Darche to G. MacDonald, 18 June 1959; A.H. MacDonald to J.W. Churchman, 13 May 1959; A.H. MacDonald to Churchman, 22 June 1959; M. Miller to Churchman, 3 June 1959; S-NR 1/5, v. III, f. 8, "Buffalo Narrows, 1963-66," Darche to A.M. Nicholson, 25 November 1963; E.I. Wood to E. Kramer, 29 January 1964; Kramer to Treasury Board, 3 February 1964; Churchman to A.H. MacDonald, 15 January 1964; Churchman to A.H. MacDonald, 3 August 1964; Churchman to J.M. Cuelenaere, 10 June 1964; O.D. Reiman to Kramer, 15 April 1964; W.B. Hyshka to A.H. MacDonald, 27 January 1964.

54 Buckley, Kew, and Hawley, *The Indians and Metis of Northern Saskatchewan*, 34-35; J.T. Phalen, "The Search for an Appropriate Development Program for the People of Northern Saskatchewan," unpublished paper (April 1996); Phalen, "The Co-Operative Development Program for Northern Saskatchewan," unpublished paper (1 June 1997); Phalen, "The Northern Co-Operative Development Program," unpublished paper (1 September 1997); Letter, "Terry" (T. Phalen) to Harold (Harold Chapman), 9 September 1997; Phalen, "An Autobiography of the Life and Times of J.T. (Terry) Phalen," unpublished paper, undated. Some northerners later sat on cooperative boards, and Pierre Carriere of Cumberland House became chairman. Phalen says Dr. Arnason, the deputy minister of the Department of Co-operation, "never understood the situation well enough to participate fully in planning sessions with the Planning Board or Treasury Board or Douglas himself."

55 DNR, *Annual Report*, 1963, 40; *Glenbow Archives*, M125, s. VI, f. 39, "Historical Notes, 1932-1959," J.P. Brady, "Memorandum Draft Discussion C.C.F. Clubs The Pas and Flin Flon," 1952; M125, s. II, f. 8, "Personal," 1952-62, Bill, (W.J. Berezowsky,) to Jim, 22 September 1954; *SAB*, R-907.2, v. II, f. 10b, "E.L. Paynter, Game Commissioner, September 1953-April 1955," Paynter to J.W. Churchman, 22 September 1953; S-NR 1/4, f. 235, "Cumberland House – General," v. 2, September 1950-57, H.E. Chapman to Dr. B.N. Arnason, 30 October 1950; S-NR 1/4, f. 236 E, "Cumberland House Farm," v. 1, "July 1948 to 31 March 1951," Churchman to C.A.L. Hogg, 6 June 1952.

56 Ian MacPherson, "The CCF and the Co-Operative Movement in the Douglas Years: An Uneasy Alliance," in *"Building the Co-Operative Commonwealth": Essays on the Democratic Socialist Tradition in Canada*, Canadian Plains Proceedings 13, ed. J. William Brennan (Regina: Canadian Plains Research Center, University of Regina, 1985), 192; Phalen, "The Search for an Appropriate Development Program"; Phalen, "The Co-Operative Development Program"; Phalen, "The Northern Co-Operative Development Program"; "Terry" to Harold, 9 September 1997; Phalen, "An Autobiography"; *SAB*, R-A1113, Phelps, interview by Dobbin, 1976; S-M16, v. VII, f. 3. "Parks and Lands Branch, 1961-63," Minutes of N. Adv. Comm. Mtg., 9 February 1956; S-NR 1/4, f. 230, "Northern Region," "Co-Operation and Northern Problems," undated, no author; S-NR 1/5, v. I, f. 39, (230), "Northern Region, 1957-1959," D.D. Tansley to A.W. Johnson, 10 February 1959.

57 Adelaide Leitch, "Pattern of Progress at Lac La Ronge," *Canadian Geographical Journal* 62, 3 (March 1961): 89; *SAB*, S-NR 1/5, v. I, f. 80, (415), "La Ronge, 1955-1961," A.H. MacDonald to J.W. Churchman, 21 August 1961; J.A. Langford to Churchman, 23 November 1960; Churchman to MacDonald, 13 September 1961; Churchman to Langford, 8 March 1960; S-NR 1/5, v. III, f. 4, "Northern Administration District, 1962-67," AHM "Brief on Community Development in the North," 7/9/64.

58 MacPherson, "The CCF and the Co-Operative Movement," 192, 199; Phalen, "The Search for an Appropriate Development Program"; Phalen, "The Co-Operative Development Program"; Phalen, "The Northern Co-Operative Development Program"; "Terry" to Harold, Phalen, "An Autobiography"; Vernon C. Serl, "Action and Reaction: An Overview of Provincial Policies and Programs in Northern Saskatchewan," in *A Northern Dilemma: Reference*

Papers, vol. 1, ed. Arthur K. Davis et al. (Bellingham, WA: Western Washington State College, 1967), 40; *SAB,* S-NR 1/4, DNR, 167 B3 Northern Region, Minutes of N. Reg. Cons. Officers' Conf., 15-19 October 1956.

Chapter 8: A Pre-Industrial Way of Life

1 DNR, *Annual Report,* 1945, Intro. letter from H. Lewis to J.L. Phelps, September 1945; *Saskatchewan Archives Board* [*SAB*], S-M15, Box 36, "Christie, C, R.," Christie address at Field Officers' Conf., 25 November 1948.

2 Lewis H. Thomas, ed., *The Making of a Socialist: The Recollections of T.C. Douglas* (Edmonton: University of Alberta Press, 1982), 286; *SAB,* R-8453, J.L. Phelps, interview by J. Larmour, audio tape, 1 June 1982; S-M15, Box 4, "Public Health Department, 1944-1946," Report by J.L. Phelps, 9 February 1945; S-M15, Box 9, "Sask. Lake and Forest Products Corporation, 1946-1949," H.H. Lucas, Address on STB at DNR Field Conf., 16 January 1948; J.F. Gray to R. Kenyon, 26 January 1949; S-M15, Box 10, "Forestry – Supervision (Reports, Conferences, Meetings), 1944-1945, (1)," E.H. Roberts to H. Lewis, undated.

3 *SAB,* S-M15, Box 2, "Contract Logging, 1945"; S-M15, Box 5, "District Superintendent Progress Reports, 1945-1946," J. Barnett, September Progress Report, 9 October 1945; S-M15, Box 9, "Sask Lake and Forest Products Corporation, 1946-1949," "Questionnaire re Timber Industry"; S-M15, Box 10, "Forestry – Supervision (Reports, Conferences, Meetings), 1944-1945, (1)," J.L. Phelps to 12 MLAs, 2 August 1945; Phelps to L.M. Marion, 3 August 1945; Thomas Hector Macdonald McLeod, "Public Enterprise in Saskatchewan: The Development of Public Policy and Administrative Controls" (PhD diss., Harvard University, 1959), 98.

4 *SAB,* R-8453, Phelps, interview by Larmour, 1982; S-M15, Box 9, "Sask. Lake and Forest Products Corporation, 1946-1949," H.H. Lucas to J.L. Phelps, 9 March 1948; H.H. Lucas to I. Stewart Ross, 22 August 1947; J.F. Gray to R. Kenyon, 26 January 1949; S-M15, Box 10, "Forestry – Supervision (Reports, Conferences, Meetings), 1944-1945. (1)," A.A. Wenger to Phelps, 19 October 1944; Phelps to Wenger, 25 October 1944; Man. Sask. For. Prods. Assoc. to Phelps, 27 September 1945; S-M15, Box 10, "Sask. Lake and Forest Products Corporation – J.F. Gray, 1946-1951, (5)," Gray to Directors of SL&FPC; Gray, Report to SL&FPC Board; S-M15, Box 10, "Sask. Lake and Forest Products Corporation – J.F. Gray, 1946-1951, (7)," Gray to D.T. Galbraith, 13 September 1948; Gray to T.C. Douglas, 27 May 1948; S-M15, Box 36, "Christie, C, R.," Christie, Address at Field Officers' Conf., 25 November 1948.

5 *SAB,* S-M15, Box 36, "Reed, C. Philip (Field Officer)," Reed to J.L. Phelps, 6 April 1947; Report of Sask. Royal Comm. on Forestry, v. 5, 4; Phelps to Reed, 23 May 1946; Reed to Phelps, 5 June 1946.

6 *SAB,* R-907.2, v. II, f. 5b, "R.T. Cook, Northern Executive Assistant, June 1948-March 1949," F. Beaudoin to H.H. Lucas, Manager, 1 June 1948; F. Beaudoin to Lucas, 12 June 1948.

7 DNR, *Annual Report,* 1946, 5; DNR, *Annual Report,* 1951, Intro. letter from C.A.L. Hogg to J.H. Brockelbank; DNR, *Annual Report,* 1961, 11; Bureau of Statistics, *Saskatchewan Economic Review* (February 1952), 8-9; *Progress Report from Your Government: A Survey of Saskatchewan Government Activity* (Regina: Bureau of Publications, 1948), 32; *SAB,* R-8453, Phelps, interview by Larmour, 1982; S-M15, Box 5, "Dominion-Provincial Conference, 1945-1946, (1)," "Provincial Natural Resources Policy in Their Relation to the Dominion Proposals," 3-4; S-M15, Box 5, "Economic Advisory Board Recommendations, 1945-1946," DNR, Activities summary for 1945 and plans for 1946, 1; S-M15, Box 5, J. Barnett, Report, 14 November 1945; S-M15, Box 18, "O.G. Horncastle, Field Officer, Prince Albert, 1945," Horncastle to All Field Officers and Timber Cruisers, 1 November 1945; S-M15, Box 36, "Christie, C.R.," Christie Address at Field Officers' Conf., 25 November 1948; S-M15, Box 36, "Eisler, H. (Supervisor Forestry Branch at Regina)," Eisler to E.J. Marshall, 28 August 1946; S-M15, Box 36, J.L. Phelps to various DNR officials, "Comments on Forestry Commission," 12 May 1947; S-M15, Box 36, "Doidge, J. (Publicity)," DNR News Release, undated.

8 DNR, *Annual Report,* 1948, 16; DNR, *Annual Report,* 1961, 105; *Progress: A Survey of Saskatchewan Government Activity* (Regina: Bureau of Publications, 1955), 12; *SAB,* S-NR 1/5, v. I, f. 39, (230), "Northern Region, 1957-1959," W.R. Parks to J.W. Churchman, 6 April 1959.

9 Big River History Book Committee, *Timber Trails: History of Big River and District* (North Battleford, SK: Turner-Warwick Printers, 1979), 23, 46-47; La Ronge Heritage Committee, *Our Roots: A History of La Ronge* (La Ronge, SK: Lakeland Press Ltd., 1981), 33; Government Finance Office, *Public Enterprise in Saskatchewan, 1964*; *SAB*, S-M15, Box 9, "Sask. Lake and Forest Products Corporation, 1946-1949," H.H. Lucas to J.L. Phelps, 9 March 1948; S-M15, Box 9, "Sask. Lake and Forest Products Corporation – J.F. Gray, 1946-1950, (4)," List of personnel, STB, October 1947.

10 DNR, *Annual Report*, 1958, 17; DNR, *Annual Report*, 1959, N.A. 11; *SAB*, S-M15, Box 9, "Sask. Lake and Forest Products Corporation, 1946-1949," J.F. Gray to R. Kenyon, 26 January 1949; S-NR2, (A) Subject Files – August 1944-April 1949, f. 38, "Northern District (A.K. Quandt)," A.K. Quandt to J.W. Churchman, 9 December 1948.

11 DNR, *Annual Report*, 1947, 124; DNR, *Annual Report*, 1949, 154; DNR, *Annual Report*, 1950, 148; DNR, *Annual Report*, 1963, 121; DNR, *Annual Report*, 1964, 119; *SAB*, S-NR 1/4, f. 230, "Northern Region – General," v. 1, 1948-31 December 1954, E. Dodds to C.L. MacLean, 31 March 1951; S-NR 1/4, f. 235, "Snake Lake," (2 files), MacLean to W.K. Riese, 29 July 1952; S-NR 1/5, v. III, f. 17 (b), "Municipal Winter Works Program, 1964-67," DNR Dep. Min. to Treasury, Att.: A.T. Wayabayashi, 29 January 1965.

12 *SAB*, R-971, J.L. Phelps, interview by B. Richards, audio tape, 1976.

13 DNR, *Annual Report*, 1951, 149; *SAB*, S-NR 1/4, f. 167 B3, "Northern Region," O. Shaw, "Cumberland House Wood Co-Op," N. Dist. Conf., September 1953; S-NR 1/5, v. I, f. 39, (230), "Northern Region, 1957-1959," W.R. Parks to J.W. Churchman, 6 April 1959.

14 *SAB*, S-M 16, v. XIII, f. 264, "Public Assistance, Indians and Metis, 1952-64," F. Meakes to W.S. Lloyd and All Cabinet Ministers, 9 September 1963: G.F. Porteous, Report on Cumberland House Wood Products Co-Op Ltd., 1963(?); S-NR 1/5, v. III, f. 20, "Cumberland House – General, 1962-67," Dr. B.N. Arnason to J.W. Churchman, 9 November 1964; Churchman to Arnason, 26 November 1964; H.S. Lee, "Cumberland House Wood Products Co-Operative," 24 September 1963.

15 *SAB*, S-NR 1/5, v. III, f. 8, "Buffalo Narrows, 1963-66," D. Mackinnon, P.R. Golla, G.F. Porteous, Report on Buffalo Narrows Sawmill Co-Op. Ltd., undated; J.W. Churchman to E. Kramer, 24 December 1963; Kramer to W.S. Lloyd and Cabinet Members, 3 January 1964; Minister's Office to Churchman, 31 January 1964; A.H. MacDonald to Churchman, 17 February 1964.

16 *SAB*, S-NR2, (A) Subject Files – August 1944-April 1949, f. 25 "Instructions to Branch Heads," On Forest Operations, 1947; *Progress Report from Your Government*, 32.

17 *SAB*, S-NR 1/4, 235, "Stony Rapids," C.A.L. Hogg to J.W. Churchman, 5 April 1949; Other documents in file.

18 *SAB*, R-907.3, J.H. Brockelbank Papers, f. 3a, "Crown Corporations (J.H. Brockelbank: Natural Resources)," W.A. Houseman to Brockelbank, 15 December 1953; W. Roy Bell to L.F. McIntosh, 23 November 1953; R-907.3, f. 14, "Miscellaneous," "H.C. Dunfield, M.L.A. Participated in Budget Debate Recently," *The Progress* (Meadow Lake, SK), 13 May 1954; A. Hansen to Brockelbank, 31 May 1954; S-NR 1/4, f. 167 B3, "Northern Region," I. Berezowsky, "Beaver Lake Lumber Operations," N. Dist. Conf., 5 October 1953.

19 *SAB*, S-M15, Box 9, "Sask. Lake and Forest Products Corporation, 1946-1949," J.F. Gray to R. Kenyon, 26 January 1949.

20 DNR, *Annual Report*, 1952, 165; DNR, *Annual Report*, 1956, 5; DNR, *Annual Report*, 1957, 14, 17; DNR, *Annual Report*, 1958, 17; DNR, *Annual Report*, 1961, 104; "Forest Resources Panel," Northern Saskatchewan Development Conference, Saskatoon, SK, 20-21 November 1957, 6; *Proceedings "Resources for People" Saskatchewan Resources Conference*, Saskatoon, SK, 20-21 January 1964, 256; *SAB*, S-M 16, A.M. Nicholson Papers, v. VII, f. 4, "Tour of North Saskatchewan, 1959," "The Present, the Potential, and the Planned for Northern Saskatchewan," background data for the National Northern Development Conference, Edmonton, August 1958, no author given.

21 *SAB*, S-NR 1/5, v. I, f. 39, (230), "Northern Region, 1957-1959," W.R. Parks to J.W. Churchman, 6 April 1959.

22 DNR, *Annual Report*, 1963, 119; H.B. Hawthorne, ed., *A Survey of the Contemporary Indians of Canada: A Report on Economic, Political, Educational Needs and Policies* (Ottawa: Indian Affairs Branch, vol. 1 – 1966), 152-153.

23 Stanford Research Institute, *A Study of Resources and Industrial Opportunities for the Province of Saskatchewan* (Menlo Park, CA: Stanford Research Institute, 1959), Tables 7 and 8.

24 Dale Eisler, *Rumours of Glory: Saskatchewan and the Thatcher Years* (Edmonton: Hurtig Publishers, 1987), 164-165; Gary William David Abrams, *Prince Albert: The First Century 1866-1966* (Saskatoon: Modern Press, 1966), 361-362; John H. Archer, *Saskatchewan: A History* (Saskatoon: Western Producer Prairie Books, 1980), 272; SAB, S-M15, Box 18, "Sask. Industrial Development Branch, 1944-1946," H.W. Monahan to J.L. Phelps, 26 February 1946; R-907.2, v. II, f. 8, "W.A. Houseman, Saskatchewan Timber Board, Prince Albert," J.W. Churchman to Houseman, 19 July 1956; S-M 16, v. IX, f. 5, "Industrial Development, 1960-63," D.H.F. Black, to R. Brown, 5 November 1962; S-NR 1/3, DNR, C.A.L. Hogg, Deputy Minister Files, f. G-2-4, "Government Policy, 1948-49," Hogg to Churchman, 2 March 1949; S-NR 1/4, f. 167 B3, "Northern Region, April 1st, 1956," N. Dist. Conf., 5-10 October 1953; S-NR 1/4, f. 167 B3, "Northern Region," Minutes, N. Region Cons. Officers' Conf., 15-19 October 1956; Industrial Development Office, *Proceedings of "Building from Within" Industrial Development Conference*, Regina, SK, 29-30 November 1956, 9; S-NR2, (A) Subject Files – August 1944-April 1949, f. 13, "Deputy Minister (C.A.L. Hogg)," Deputy Minister's Office to W.D. Smith, G.N. Munro, and A.J. Williams.
25 *Proceedings "Resources for People" Saskatchewan Resources Conference*, 253-258.
26 DNR, *Annual Report*, 1954, 61; SAB, R-971, J. Phelps, interview by B. Richards, 1976; R-8453, Phelps, interview by Larmour, 1982; S-M15, Box 8, "McCabe, M.A., Lac La Ronge Plant, 1946-1947," Phelps radio address, January 1947.
27 John Richards and Larry Pratt, *Prairie Capitalism: Power and Influence in the New West* (Toronto: McClelland and Stewart, 1979), 111; SAB, S-M15, Box 5, "Disallowance of Legislation," 1945, T.C. Douglas radio address, "The Case Against Disallowance"; Other documents; S-M15, Box 5, "Economic Advisory Board Recommendations, 1945-1946," DNR 1945 activities summary and plans for 1946, 2.
28 DNR, *Annual Report*, 1950, 21; Department of Natural Resources, *The New North: Saskatchewan's Northern Development Program, 1945-1948* (Regina: DNR, 1948), 28; Jean Larmour, "The Douglas Government's Changing Emphasis on Public, Private, and Co-Operative Development in Saskatchewan, 1944-1961," in *"Building the Co-Operative Commonwealth": Essays on the Democratic Socialist Tradition in Canada*, Canadian Plains Proceedings 13, ed. J. William Brennan (Regina: Canadian Plains Research Center, University of Regina, 1985), 166-172; SAB, S-NR2, (A) Subject Files – August 1944-April 1949, f. 2, "Administration Branch (W.H. Roney)," DNR, "Essay Contest Air Trip Itinerary," about 1948.
29 DNR, *The New North*, 28; Larmour, "The Douglas Government's Changing Emphasis," 172; "What Price Encouragement?" *Regina Leader Post*, 27 January 1945.
30 DNR, *Annual Report*, 1950, 18; Kathleen A. Morton, "Northern Saskatchewan," *Western Miner and Oil Review* 34, 10 (October 1961): 68-72; SAB, S-M 16, A.M. Nicholson Papers, v. VII, f. 4, "Tour of North Saskatchewan, 1959."
31 DNR, *Annual Report*, 1949, 50-55; DNR, *Annual Report*, 1951, 30; *Progress: A Survey*, 8; SAB, S-M15, Box 5, "Dominion-Provincial Conference, 1945-1946, (1)," Untitled, 17; S-M15, Box 23, "Prospector's Course, 1944-1946," C.A.L. Hogg to R. McKenzie, 18 February 1946; J.B. Mawdsley to Hogg, 13 January 1945; Hogg to J.L. Phelps, 24 January 1945; "Prospecting Encouraged," *Regina Leader Post*, 25 January 1945; "What Price Encouragement?" *Regina Leader Post*, 27 January 1945.
32 DNR, *Annual Report*, 1949, 55; *Glenbow Archives*, M125, James Brady Collection, s. III, "Correspondence," 1933-67, f. 22, "Norris," 1945-67, M.F. Norris to Dr. R.L. Cheesman, 26 July 1960; SAB, S-NR2, (A) Subject Files – August 1944-April 1949, f. 35, "Municipal Affairs, Department of," J.W. Churchman to J.J. Wheaton, 13 January 1949; Philip Ballantyne, *The Land Alone/Aski-puko* (Saskatchewan: n.p., 1976), 156.
33 W.O. Kupsch and S.D. Hanson, eds., *Gold and Other Stories As Told to Berry Richards* (Regina: Saskatchewan Mining Association, 1986), 160-162.
34 DNR, *Annual Report*, 1959, N.A. 16-17; DNR, *Annual Report*, 1961, 102.
35 DNR, *Annual Report*, 1950, 13; Economic and Planning Board, *Saskatchewan Economic Review* (November 1951), 2-3.
36 Archer, *Saskatchewan*, 327.
37 Department of Mineral Resources, *Saskatchewan's Metallic and Industrial Minerals* (Regina: Department of Mineral Resources, 1961), 40-43; Industrial Development Office, *Proceedings of "Building from Within" Industrial Development Conference*, Regina, SK, 29-30 November 1956, 60; Archer, *Saskatchewan*, 364; SAB, S-M15, Box 18, "C.A.L. Hogg – Assistant

Deputy Minister, DNR," Order in Council 186-44 amended Quartz Mining Regulations; Economic and Planning Board, *Saskatchewan Economic Review,* 15; "Saskatchewan May Soon Be Canada's Largest Uranium Producer," *Musk-Ox* 19 (1976): 77.

38 Dennis Gruending, *Promises to Keep: A Political Biography of Allan Blakeney* (Saskatoon: Western Producer Prairie Books, 1990), 151-152; Murray Dobbin, *The One-And-A-Half Men: The Story of Jim Brady and Malcolm Norris, Metis Patriots of the Twentieth Century* (Vancouver: New Star Books, 1981), 213.

39 E.F. Partridge, presentation on "Mining Resource Panel," Northern Saskatchewan Development Conference, Saskatoon, SK, 20-21 November 1957, 1-3; "Mining Resource Panel," Northern Saskatchewan Development Conference, Saskatoon, SK, 20-21 November 1957. The CCF reinvested only $1 million annually into mining from provincial revenues of $22 million. In contrast, from revenues of about $233,167 in 1944, government spent $34,585, almost 15 percent, on mining.

40 DNR, *Annual Report,* 1959, N.A. 16; *SAB,* R-A1113, Joe Phelps, interview by Murray Dobbin, audio tape, 1976.

41 *SAB,* R-A1113, Phelps, interview by Dobbin, 1976; S-NR 1/4, f. 235, "La Ronge (1)," P.S. Pettit to A.H. MacDonald, 13 June 1949; N. Admin. to G.R. Kennedy, 8 February 1950; S-NR 1/4, f. 231 B, "La Ronge – General," (5 files), A.I. Bereskin to C.A.L. Hogg, 23 August 1949; C.L. MacLean to R.J. Sweet, 18 October 1951; S-NR 1/4, f. 235, "La Ronge," C.S. Brown to Hogg, "An Investigation of Problems Related to the Development of Recreational Resources of Lac la Ronge," 1952; D.S. Rawson and F.M. Atton, *Biological Investigation and Fisheries Management at Lac La Ronge, Saskatchewan* (Regina: DNR, Fisheries Branch, 1953).

42 DNR, *Annual Report,* 1952, 84; DNR, *Annual Report,* 1950, 146; *SAB,* R782, Department of Natural Resources (GR-24-3), v. I, f. 4, "Branch Heads Meetings, 1963-1968," Minutes, Meeting No. 51, Regina, 7 January 1964; S-NR 1/4, f. 235, "La Ronge,"(1), J.P.B. Ostrander to A.H. MacDonald, 6 September 1949; E. Dodds to C.S. Brown, 1 March 1954; A.T. Davidson to D.F. Corney, 15 March 1954.

43 *SAB,* S-NR 1/4, f. 235, "La Ronge, Publicity," A.H. MacDonald to J.W. Churchman, 1 April 1950; C.S. Brown to W.J. Bague, 23 January 1953; S-NR2, (A) Subject Files – August 1944-April 1949, f. 34, "Minister of Natural Resources," A.I. Bereskin to C.A.L. Hogg, D.A. Cunningham, and J.J. Wheaton, 30 March 1948; Churchman to J.L. Phelps, 27 April 1948.

44 *SAB,* S-NR 1/4, f. 235, "La Ronge, Publicity," A. Maxwell to Can. Govt. Travel Bureau, 23 March 1952; G.E. Davis to Tourist Br., undated; D. Snowden to C.M. Fines, 9 April 1952.

45 *SAB,* S-NR 1/4, f. 167 B3, "Northern Region," W.K. Riese, "Tourist Development at Lac La Ronge," N. Dist. Conf., 8 October 1953; S-NR 1/4, f. 235, "La Ronge," (1), J.W. Churchman to D. Snowden, 31 October 1952; S-NR 1/5, v. III, f. 11, "La Ronge, 1962-67," J.M. Cuelenaere to Churchman, 15 October 1964.

46 *SAB,* S-M16, v. VII, f. 2, "Parks and Lands Branch, 1961-64," A.G. Kuziak to Premier and All Cabinet Ministers, 24 July 1962; Minutes, Meeting about sale of islands, 1 August 1962.

47 DNR, *Annual Report,* 1959, Co 5; *SAB,* S-NR 1/4, f. 235, "Denare Beach," (2 files), J.W. Churchman to C.A.L. Hogg, 23 October 1950; S-NR2, (A) Subject Files – August 1944-April 1949, f. 37, "Northern Administration (J.J. Wheaton)," Wheaton to Churchman, 10 June 1948.

48 *SAB,* DNS-1, Dept. of N. Sask., (GS-201), v. VII, f. 10, "Sandy Bay Housing, 1970-1973," G.G. Rathwell to M.A. Laird, 2 November 1970.

49 DNR, *Annual Report,* 1959, N.A. 19; *SAB,* S-NR 1/4, f. 235, "La Ronge, Publicity," C.S. Brown to W.J. Bague, 23 January 1953.

50 DNR, *Annual Report,* 1954, 61; *SAB,* R-517, v. XIII, f. 1, "Annual Reports," 1949-67, Dr. A.C. Irwin to Dr. M.S. Acker, 20 June 1962; S-NR 1/4, f. 167 B3, "Northern Region," Minutes of N. District Cons. Officers' Conf., Prince Albert, SK, 4-8 October 1954.

51 Bicentennial Committee of Cumberland House, *A History of Cumberland House ... As Told By Its Own Citizens 1774 to 1974* (Cumberland House, SK: Bicentennial Committee, 1974), 18, 23; *SAB,* S-NR 1/4, f. 230, "Northern Region," A.T. Davidson to C.A.L. Hogg, 18 June 1951; S-NR 1/5, v. I, f. 39, (230), "Northern Region, 1957-1959," J.W. Churchman, "Our Goals in the North and How We Hope to Achieve Them," 19 April 1959.

52 DNR, *Annual Report,* 1959, N.A. 21.

53 *SAB*, R-907.3, f. 2, "Churchill River Power," J.L. Phelps to R.W. Davis, 10 December 1946; Phelps to Davis, 19 December 1946.
54 *SAB*, S-NR 1/4, f. 430, "Game and Fur Branch, General, 1948-1951," H. Read to E.L. Paynter, 9 February 1951.
55 DNR, *Annual Report*, 1959, N.A. 10, 11, 16, xiii; H. Dryden, "Tourist Development Panel," Northern Saskatchewan Development Conference, Saskatoon, SK, 20-21 November 1957; *SAB*, R782, DNR, (GR-24-3), v. I, f. 4, "Branch Heads Meetings, 1963-1968," Minutes, Branch Heads' Planning and Policy Committee Meeting, 28 October 1963.
56 Stanford Research Institute, *A Study of Resources and Industrial Opportunities*, 287-293.
57 *SAB*, R-907.2, v. II, f. 12, "J.J. Wheaton, Northern Administrator," Wheaton to C.A.L. Hogg, "Re: Progress Report – Northern Administration District – Spring and Summer 1948"; Wheaton to DNR Minister, 25 July 1947; R-907.2, v. II, f. 4a, "J.W. Churchman, Deputy Minister, March 1948-March 1949," Churchman to J.H. Brockelbank, 5 March 1949; S-NR 1/3, f. G-1-7, "Community Planning, General, 1948-50," F.R. Glass to Hogg, 20 December 1948; Hogg to Glass, 12 January 1949; S-NR 1/3, f. G-1-7, "Community Planning, Northern and Parks, 1945-48," A.I. Bereskin, "La Ronge Development"; Other documents in file; S-NR 1/4, f. 235, "Wollaston Lake," J.F. Gray to C.L. MacLean, 28 July 1950.

Chapter 9: Scarcely More Than Palliative

1 Mildred E. Battel, *Children Shall Be First: Child Welfare Saskatchewan 1944-64* (Regina: Saskatchewan Department of Culture and Youth, 1979), 16.
2 James G.E. Smith, "Western Woods Cree," in *Subarctic*, ed. June Helm, vol. 6 of *Handbook of North American Indians*, ed. William C. Sturtevant (Washington: Smithsonian Institution, 1981), 267.
3 James M. Pitsula, "The CCF Government in Saskatchewan and Social Aid, 1944-1964," in *"Building the Co-Operative Commonwealth": Essays on the Democratic Socialist Tradition in Canada*, Canadian Plains Proceedings 13, ed. J. William Brennan (Regina: Canadian Plains Research Center, University of Regina, 1985), 205-225; Lewis H. Thomas, ed., *The Making of a Socialist: The Recollections of T.C. Douglas* (Edmonton: University of Alberta Press, 1982), 174, 249; Battel, *Children Shall Be First*, 16; *Progress Report from Your Government: A Survey of Saskatchewan Government Activity* (Regina: Bureau of Publications, 1948), 42; Economic and Planning Board, *Saskatchewan Economic Review* (September 1953), 4-5.
4 Battel, *Children Shall Be First*, 40; Saskatchewan Archives Board [*SAB*], R-646, "Saskatchewan Department of Social Services," "Fifteen Year History, Department of Social Welfare and Rehabilitation," "For *The Commonwealth*," "Highlights From The Department of Social Welfare and Rehabilitation" November 1957; S-M 16, A.M. Nicholson Papers, v. XVI, f. 1, "Personal Correspondence, 1960-63," (2 of 3), Various items.
5 Dept. of Social Welfare, *Annual Report*, 1945, 10; Dept. of Social Welfare, *Annual Report*, 1948, 11, 14; Dept. of Social Welfare and Rehab., *Annual Report*, 1949, 9, 13; Dept. of Social Welfare and Rehab., *Annual Report*, 1956, 9; Dept. of Social Welfare and Rehab., *Annual Report*, 1963, 7; Battel, *Children Shall Be First*, 8, 14, 16, 19; *SAB*, R646, "Fifteen Year History," "For *The Commonwealth*," "Highlights," November 1957.
6 Dept. of Social Welfare, *Annual Report*, 1947, 12; Dept. of Social Welfare and Rehab., *Annual Report*, 1951, 14-15; *SAB*, R-646, "Fifteen Year History," "Department of Social Welfare and Rehabilitation History," "Disabled Persons' Allowance," "Mothers Allowance"; S-M15, Box 5, Phelps Papers, "Dominion-Provincial Conference, 1945-1946," (2), Dom.-Prov. Conf. on Reconst., 1945-46, Sask.'s reply to Dominion proposals, 45; S-M 16, v. XIII, f. 249, "Public Assistance, Mothers' Allowances, 1952-61," Mothers' All., est. dates. Saskatchewan passed a Blind Persons' Act in 1951, and Disabled Persons' Allowances began in 1954. A means test looked at the assets and income of the applicant, while a needs test added an evaluation of the client's detailed financial needs. Many social welfare professionals wanted to end categorical programs and means tests, preferring one program for all, with eligibility determined by a needs test.
7 *SAB*, R646, Budget Bureau, "Report on a Survey of the Organization of the Department of Social Welfare and Rehabilitation," 30 June 1952.
8 Dept. of Social Welfare, *Annual Report*, 1945, 33; Dept. of Social Welfare, *Annual Report*, 1948, 39, 122; Dept. of Social Welfare and Rehab., *Annual Report*, 1949, 50-52; DNR,

Annual Report, 1950, 149; *SAB,* S-NR 1/3, DNR, Dep. Min., f. NR-8-3, "Child Welfare Wards, 1951-52," C.A.L. Hogg to J.S. White, 13 December 1950; W.A. Houseman to Hogg, 26 March 1951; C.H. Smith to Hogg, 21 April 1951; W.H. Roney to Hogg, 17 December 1951; J.H. Brockelbank to Hogg, 28 February 1952.

9 Department of Social Welfare and Rehabilitation, *Social Welfare in Saskatchewan* (Regina: Department of Social Welfare and Rehabilitation, 1960), 19; Dept. of Social Welfare, *Annual Report,* 1945, 30; Dept. of Social Welfare and Rehab., *Annual Report,* 1958, 11.

10 *SAB,* S-M15, Box 9, "Sask. Lake and Forest Products Corporation, 1946-1949," A.H. Mac-Donald and K.E. Dickson, "Present Situation and Proposals in Regard to Conditions in Northern Saskatchewan," 1 October 1947; S-NR2, DNR-ADM, (A) Subject Files – August 1944-April 1949, f. 37, "Northern Administration (J.J. Wheaton)," A.K. Quandt to Wheaton, 20 May 1948.

11 *SAB,* R-907.2, J.H. Brockelbank Papers, v. II, f. 12, "J.J. Wheaton, Northern Administrator," Report, meeting of prov. and fed. reps. of Dept. of Indian Affairs, 7 October 1947; S-M 16, v. XV, f. 14, "Indians, 1955-64," Dept. of Social Welfare proposals for extending prov. services to Registered Indians, App. 1, November 1963; Department of Citizenship and Immigration, Indian Affairs Branch, *The Indian Today: The Indian in Transition* (Ottawa: Dept. of Citizenship and Immigration, IAB, 1964), 21, 22; Philip Ballantyne, *The Land Alone/Aski-Puko* (Saskatchewan: n.p., 1976), 186-193.

12 Dept. of Social Welfare, *Annual Report,* 1945, 32-33; *SAB,* R-A1113, Joe Phelps, interview by Murray Dobbin, audio tape, 1976; R-907.2, v. II, f. 4a, "J.W. Churchman, Deputy Minister, March 1948-March 1949," Churchman to C.A.L. Hogg, 17 September 1948; R-907.2, v. II, f. 12, "J.J. Wheaton, Northern Administrator," Wheaton to J.L. Phelps, 15 July 1947; Wheaton to Phelps, 7 August 1947; S-NR2, (A) Subject Files – August 1944-April 1949, f. 37, "Northern Administration (J.J. Wheaton)," J.H. Brockelbank to Hogg, 13 September 1948; Wheaton to Churchman, 21 September 1948; S-NR2, f. 38, "Northern District (A.K. Quandt)," N. Dist. Field Officers' Conf., Prince Albert, 31 January 1949; Burgess, Speech; Discussion after Burgess speech.

13 DNR, *Annual Report,* 1949, 155; Dept. of Social Welfare, *Annual Report,* 1948, 41; Dept. of Social Welfare and Rehab., *Annual Report,* 1949, 52-53; Dept. of Social Welfare and Rehab., *Annual Report,* 1950, 47; *SAB,* S-NR2, f. 37, "Northern Administration (J.J. Wheaton)," Wheaton and G. Burgess to K.F. Forster, Social Aid lists, 21 September 1948, 20 October 1948, 23 November 1948, 20 January 1949; S-NR2, f. 38, "Northern District (A.K. Quandt)," N. Dist. Field Officers' Conf., Prince Albert, 31 January 1949, Burgess, Speech; Discussion after Burgess speech.

14 Dept. of Social Welfare and Rehab., *Annual Report,* 1952, 44; Dept. of Social Welfare and Rehab., *Annual Report,* 1955, 29.

15 DNR, *Annual Report,* 1953, 149; V.F. Valentine, "Some Problems of the Metis of Northern Saskatchewan," *The Canadian Journal of Economics and Political Science* 20, 1 (1954): 92-93; V.F. Valentine, *The Metis of Northern Saskatchewan* (Regina: DNR, 1955), 35.

16 DNR, *Annual Report,* 1958, 78; DNR, *Annual Report,* 1959, N.A. 25; Helen L. Buckley, J.E.M. Kew, and John B. Hawley, *The Indians and Metis of Northern Saskatchewan: A Report on Economic and Social Development* (Saskatoon: Center for Community Studies, University of Saskatchewan, 1963), 35-36; J.E.M. Kew, *Cumberland House in 1960* (Saskatoon: Center for Community Studies, University of Saskatchewan, 1962), 70-79; *SAB,* S-NR 1/3, f. NR-8-3, "Child Welfare Wards, 1951-52," W.A. Houseman to C.A.L. Hogg, 26 March 1951; C.H. Smith to Hogg, 21 April 1951; W.H. Roney to Hogg, 17 December 1951; J.H. Brockelbank to Hogg, 28 February 1952; S-NR 1/4, Dep. Min. and Asst. Dep. Min. Files, f. 167 B3, "Northern Region," Minutes, N. Reg. Cons. Officers' Conf., 15-19 October 1956; Minutes, N. Dist. Conf., 7-14 October 1955; N. Dist. Report to Field Officers' Conf., 1951; S-NR 1/4, f. 230, "Northern District – General," v. 2, 1954-56, C.S. Brown to V. Valentine, 2 April 1956; A.T. Davidson to J.W. Churchman, 23 December 1955; Brown to Davidson, 1 December 1955; S-NR 1/5, v. I, f. 39, (230), "Northern Region, 1957-1959," Davidson to Churchman, 12 May 1958; S-NR 1/5, v. I, f. 45, (236), "Rehabilitation and Welfare, 1956-1958," A.H. MacDonald to Churchman, 22 September 1958.

17 Philip T. Spaulding, "The Metis of Ile-a-la-Crosse" (PhD diss., University of Washington, 1970), 122-127; *SAB,* S-NR 1/4, f. 235, "Cumberland House – General," v. 1, June 1948-31 August 1950, Anonymous to Dear Sir, 27 July 1950.

18 Pitsula, "The CCF Government," 220; *SAB*, S-M16, v. VII, f. 3, "Parks and Lands Branch, 1961-63," A.W. Sihvon to Reg. Admin., Prince Albert Region, 4 February 1958; Ballantyne, *The Land Alone/Aski-puko,* 188.

19 Center for Community Studies, *Economic and Social Survey of Northern Saskatchewan,* Interim Report No. 1 (March 1961), 34-35; Dept. of Social Welfare and Rehab., *Annual Report,* 1963, 43; DNR, *Annual Report,* 1962, 109-110; Helen L. Buckley, *Trapping and Fishing in the Economy of Northern Saskatchewan,* Report No. 3, Economic and Social Survey of Northern Saskatchewan (Saskatoon: Research Division, Center for Community Studies, University of Saskatchewan, 1962), 1, 9-12; Kew, *Cumberland House,* 70-79; *SAB*, R-517, Dept. of Health, Comm. Health Serv. Br., (GR-278), (Records of Central Office, the 13 Health Regions and the Northern Health District), Northern Health District, v. XIII, f. 9, "Organization," 1951-71, R.F. Badgley to Dr. M.S. Acker, 3 May 1960.

20 DNR, *Annual Report,* 1963, 120; DNR, *Annual Report,* 1964, 122; Dept. of Social Welfare and Rehab., *Annual Report,* 1962, 15; Dept. of Social Welfare and Rehab., *Annual Report,* 1963, 52; Dept. of Social Welfare and Rehab., *Annual Report,* 1964, 51-52; Spaulding, "The Metis of Ile-a-la-Crosse," 73; *SAB*, S-M 16, v. VIII, f. 1, "Planning Board, 1953-63," (1 of 2), Dept. of Social Welfare, "Mid-Term Review of Progress in Implementation of the 1960 Electoral Platform"; S-NR 1/5, v. I, f. 69, "General – Northern Affairs, 1958-1961," A.H. MacDonald to J.W. Churchman, 25 August 1961.

21 Dept. of Social Welfare and Rehab., *Annual Report,* 1960, 8, 17; Dept. of Social Welfare and Rehab., *Annual Report,* 1961, 6, 16; Dept. of Social Welfare and Rehab., *Annual Report,* 1962, 3-6; Dept. of Social Welfare and Rehab., *Annual Report,* 1963, 10; *SAB*, R-646, "Fifteen Year History," "The Development of Financial Assistance Services in Saskatchewan," 1962, 1; R646, File with various pamphlets, Budget Bureau, "An Examination of Public Assistance Programs in the Department of Social Welfare and Rehabilitation," 10 September 1951.

22 Kew, *Cumberland House,* 78-79; Leon Lavasseur, "Cultural Encounter: Some Differences Between Canada's Indians and Her More Recent Settlers" (Toronto: Indian Eskimo Association of Canada, undated); Various personal interviews.

23 Morris C. Shumiatcher, *Welfare: Hidden Backlash* (Toronto: McClelland and Stewart, 1971), 102; *SAB*, S-M 16, v. XIII, f. 264, "Public Assistance, Indians and Metis, 1952-64," Mrs. E. Montgrand to Dear Sir, 7 November 1963; A.M. Nicholson to Montgrand, 5 December 1963; S-M 16, v. XIII, f. 293, "Rehabilitation, Metis, La Loche, 1958-62," G. McCaw to Mrs. D. Zarski, 12 March 1962.

24 John L. Tobias, "Canada's Subjugation of the Plains Cree, 1879-1885," in *Sweet Promises: A Reader on Indian-White Relations in Canada,* ed. J.R. Miller (Toronto: University of Toronto Press, 1991), 216.

25 DNR, *Annual Report,* 1950, 148; DNR, *Annual Report,* 1948, 126; *SAB*, R-907.2, v. I, f. 2, "Cumberland House Settlement," M.F. Norris to J.J. Wheaton, 22 October 1947; Attached report by Office of N. Admin. on "Economic and Social Survey of the Cumberland House District," October 1947; R-907.2, v. II, f. 12, "J.J. Wheaton, Northern Administrator," J.L. Phelps to Wheaton, 2 September 1947; S-NR 1/4, f. 235, "Cumberland House – General," v. 1, June 1948-31 August 1950, Wheaton to J.W. Churchman, 21 September 1948; S-NR2, f. 1, "Accounts Branch (J.S. Bevan)," Wheaton to Bevan, 21 May 1948; S-NR2, f. 37, "Northern Administration (J.J. Wheaton)," Wheaton to C.A.L. Hogg, 22 October 1948; Wheaton to J. Johnson, 5 June 1948.

26 *SAB*, S-NR 1/4, f. 230, "Northern District – General," v. 2, 1954-56, Letter from B. McKenzie, 27 September 1954; Letter from McKenzie, 29 September 1954; W.J. Berezowsky to A.T. Davidson, 4 October 1954; C.S. Brown to Davidson, Att. R.G. Young, 26 October 1954; Davidson to Berezowsky, 1 November 1954; S-NR 1/4, f. 235, "Cumberland House – General," v. 2, September 1950-57, Davidson to Brown, 26 January 1955.

27 *SAB*, S-M16, v. VII, f. 3, "Parks and Lands Branch, 1961-63," A.W. Sihvon to Reg. Admin., Prince Albert Region, 4 February 1958; M. Crawley to G. McGaw, 24 January 1958; Crawley to McGaw, 14 January 1958; S-NR 1/4, f. 167 B3, Northern Region, Minutes, N. Dist. Conf., 7-14 October 1955; S-NR 1/5, v. III, f. 17 (a), "Municipal Winter Works Program," 1962-64, A.G. Kuziak to Treasury Board, 30 January 1962; W.J. Bague to J.W. Churchman, 11 December 1961.

28 *SAB*, S-M 16, v. XIII, f. 264, "Public Assistance, Indians and Metis, 1952-64," F. Meakes to

W.S. Lloyd and All Cabinet Ministers, 9 September 1963; Attached report by G.F. Porteous, Report on Cumberland House Wood Prods. Co-Op. Ltd; S-NR 1/5, v. III, f. 20, "Cumberland House – General, 1962-67," A.H. MacDonald to J.W. Churchman, 14 May 1963; DNR to Treasury Board, 3 September 1963; Minister's Office to Churchman, 2 October 1963; M.K. McCutcheon to MacDonald, 2 October 1963.

29 DNR, *Annual Report*, 1963, 121; DNR, *Annual Report*, 1964, 119; *SAB*, S-NR 1/5, v. I., "General," f. 131, "Roads – General," 1956-61, A.H. Macdonald to R.N. Gooding, 13 January 1960; S-NR 1/5, v. I, f. 69, "General – Northern Affairs, 1958-1961," Anonymous, "The People and the Problem"; S-NR 1/5, v. I, f. 80, (415), Office of Dir. of N. Affairs to J.W. Churchman, 24 November 1959; A.G. Kuziak to Treasury Board, 28 December 1959; Office of Dir. of N. Affairs to Churchman, 2 October 1961; Ballantyne, *The Land Alone/ Aski-puko*, 146.

30 *SAB*, S-NR 1/5, v. III, f. 17 (a), "Municipal Winter Works Program," 1962-64, E. Kramer to M. Sauve, 9 March 1964; Kramer to Sauve, 26 March 1964; M. McLeod to Kramer, 21 February 1964; "Proposed Municipal Winter Work's Incentive Program, 1963-1964"; A.H. MacDonald to J.W. Churchman, 20 May 1964; Dir. of Const. to R.G. Young, 21 January 1964; Kramer to Treasury Board, 24 October 1963; Churchman to MacDonald, 20 January 1964.

31 *SAB*, S-M 16, v. XIII, f. 264, "Public Assistance, Indians and Metis, 1952-64," E. Kramer to M. Sauve, 26 March 1964; S-NR 1/5, v. III, f. 17 (a), "Municipal Winter Works Program," 1962-64, J. LaMarsh to Kramer, 14 April 1964.

32 Dept. of Social Welfare and Rehab., *Annual Report*, 1963, 11-12.

33 Buckley, Kew, and Hawley, *The Indians and Metis of Northern Saskatchewan*, 36-37; *Glenbow Archives*, M125, James Brady Collection, s. VI, f. 58, 1933-64, CCF, Sask. Sec. of NDP, "BILLION DOLLAR PROVINCE: Keep Saskatchewan Ahead," March 1964; *SAB*, S-NR 1/5, v. III, f. 4, "Northern Administration District, 1962-67," A.C. Towill, "The People and the Problem Northern Saskatchewan," 20 June 1962.

34 Herbert C. Taylor, Jr., "The Parameters of a Northern Dilemma" (Prologue), in *A Northern Dilemma: Reference Papers*, vol. 1, ed. Arthur K. Davis et al. (Bellingham, WA: Western Washington State College, 1967), 4; *SAB*, R-907.2, v. II, f. 12, "J.J. Wheaton, Northern Administrator," Mrs. J.A. Bell to T.C. Douglas, 30 October 1948.

35 DNR, *Annual Report*, 1959, N.A. 21-22; DNR, *Annual Report*, 1961, 103; DNR, *Annual Report*, 1962, 108; *SAB*, S-NR 1/4, 167 B3, "Northern Region," Minutes, N. Dist. Conf., 7-14 October 1955; O.B. McNeil, "Utilization of Caribou in Stony Rapids District," N. Dist. Conf., 8 October 1953; S-NR 1/4, f. 430, "Game and Fur Branch," Dept. of N. Affairs and Nat. Res., Nat. Parks Br., CWS, Ottawa, "Wildlife Management Bulletin," s. 1, nos. 10A and 10B, November 1954, A.W.F. Banfield, "Preliminary Investigation of the Barren Ground Caribou," 1954; H. Read to E.L. Paynter, 20 March 1956.

36 Canada, Dominion Bureau of Statistics, 1946 Census of the Prairie Provinces, Volume II, "Occupations, Industries, Earnings, Employment, and Unemployment," 1949; *SAB*, S-NR 1/3, f. G-8-1, "Residents of Northern Sask. (Annual Income)," C.A.L. Hogg to W.J. Bague, 10 April 1947; Money paid by SFMS, 13 June 1945-13 June 1946; Sask. Fish Board, Beaver Lake Plant payments list, 1 April 1946-31 March 1947; Lac la Ronge Div. list of fishermen and earnings, 1946-47.

37 *SAB*, R-907.2, v. I, f. 2, "Cumberland House Settlement," M.F. Norris to J.J. Wheaton, 22 October 1947; Attached report by Office of the N. Admin. on "Economic and Social Survey of the Cumberland House District," October 1947; S-NR 1/3, f. G-8-1, "Residents of Northern Sask. (Annual Income)," M.S. Deutscher to J.S. Bevan, 6 August 1947; S-NR 1/5, v. I, f. 74, (408), "Cumberland House Farm, 1957-1961," Hist. Chron. of Cumberland House Farm, undated.

38 V.F. Valentine and R.G. Young, "The Situation of the Metis of Northern Saskatchewan in Relation to His Physical and Social Environment," *The Canadian Geographer* 4 (1954): 54-55.

39 *SAB*, S-M16, v. VII, f. 3, "Parks and Lands Branch, 1961-63," M. Crawley to G. McGaw, 14 January 1958.

40 Buckley, Kew, and Hawley, *The Indians and Metis of Northern Saskatchewan*, 16-26; Census of Canada, series 3.3.1, Labour Force, 21-105; Center for Community Studies, *Economic and Social Survey of Northern Saskatchewan*, Interim Report No. 1 (March 1961), 34-35; *SAB*, S-M 16, v. XIII, f. 264, "Public Assistance, Indians and Metis, 1952-64," A.H. MacDonald,

"Treaty Indians and Northern Administration," 18 November 1963; S-NR 1/5, v. III, f. 11, "La Ronge, 1962-67," R. Dafoe, Report, "La Ronge Hospital Background Information," 1966.

41 Center for Community Studies, "Economic and Social Survey," 34-35; Hugh Mackay Ross, *The Manager's Tale: Saskatchewan District* (Winnipeg, MB: J. Gordon Shillingford Publishing, 1989), Chapter 3.

42 DNR, *Annual Report,* 1961, 104; Buckley, *Trapping and Fishing,* 133-134; *SAB,* R-517, v. XIII, f. 65, "Sandy Bay," 1960-72, J.I. Habens to Dr. A.C. Irwin, 9 November 1958; Irwin to Dr. G. Kinneard, 12 November 1958.

43 Buckley, Kew, and Hawley, *The Indians and Metis of Northern Saskatchewan,* 16-19, 29; Ballantyne, *The Land Alone/Aski-puko,* 159, 160, 166, 167.

44 Center for Community Studies, "Economic and Social Survey," Chapter 4; Buckley, Kew, and Hawley, *The Indians and Metis of Northern Saskatchewan,* 16-19, 29; *SAB,* S-NR 1/4, f. 230, "Northern Region," R.G. Young to J.W. Churchman, 26 June 1953; S-NR 1/4, f. 235, "Stony Rapids," J.J. Wheaton to Churchman, 7 July 1949; S-NR 1/4, f. 236A, "Employment Projects," E.N. Shannon to C.L. MacLean, 13 April 1951; C.A.L. Hogg to Churchman, 27 April 1951; MacLean to Churchman, 21 April 1951; Churchman to MacLean, 1 May 1951; Valentine, *The Metis of Northern Saskatchewan,* 30-31; Valentine and Young, "The Situation of the Metis," 55.

45 DNR, *Annual Report,* 1962, 110; A.H. MacDonald, "Co-Operatives and People of Indian Ancestry," *Canadian Co-Operative Digest* 3, 1 (Spring 1960): 31-38; Murray Dobbin, "Prairie Colonialism: The CCF in Northern Saskatchewan, 1944-1964," *Studies in Political Economy: A Socialist Review* 16 (1985): 18-19.

46 *SAB,* S-M 16, v. XIII, f. 264, "Public Assistance, Indians and Metis, 1952-64," J.S. White to A.M. Nicholson, 28 November 1963; W.S. Lloyd to All Cabinet Ministers, 22 October 1963.

47 Buckley, Kew, and Hawley, *The Indians and Metis of Northern Saskatchewan,* 16-19, 29; Buckley, *Trapping and Fishing,* 121-124; Kew, *Cumberland House,* 60-65; *SAB,* R-517, v. XIII, f. 9, "Organization," 1951-71, R.F. Badgley to Dr. M.S. Acker, 3 May 1960; S-NR 1/4, f. 137 K, "Filleting Plants – General," Proposal, Govt. Filleting Plant, Ile a la Crosse; App. D, V. Valentine, "The Social and Economic Situation of the Ile a la Crosse Metis," 2 May 1956; S-NR 1/5, v. 1, f. 20, (162R), "Consultative Committee on Northern Affairs, 1958," M. Crawley to W.A. Bourke, 6 June 1958.

48 DNR, *Annual Report,* 1963, 122; DNR, *Annual Report,* 1965, 51; *SAB,* R-907.2, v. II, f. 12, "J.J. Wheaton, Northern Administrator," Wheaton to C.A.L. Hogg, Re: NAD Progress Report, 1948; Wheaton to J.S. White, 26 May 1948; S-NR 1/4, f. 236A, "Employment Projects," Office of J.W. Churchman to Hogg, 21 September 1951; S-NR2, (A) Subject Files – August 1944-April 1949, f. 37, "Northern Administration (J.J. Wheaton)," Wheaton to Churchman, 10 May 1948; Valentine, "Some Problems of the Metis," 94-95.

49 Helen L. Buckley, "Raising Incomes in Northern Saskatchewan," in *Research Review 1,* ed. Jean Foulds, (Saskatoon: Center for Community Studies, University of Saskatchewan, 1962 or 1963), 12; Buckley, Kew, and Hawley, *The Indians and Metis of Northern Saskatchewan,* 53, 105, Chapter 5; Valentine, "The Situation of the Metis," 53-55.

50 Arthur K. Davis, "Edging into Mainstream: Urban Indians in Saskatchewan," 338-510; and Vernon C. Serl, "Action and Reaction: An Overview of Provincial Policies and Programs in Northern Saskatchewan," in *A Northern Dilemma: Reference Papers,* vol. 1, ed. Arthur K. Davis et al. (Bellingham, WA: Western Washington State College, 1967), 64.

51 *SAB,* R-517, v. XIII, f. 3, "Population, 1954-1966," Population and housing census, Uranium City, SK, undated; S-NR 1/4, f. 235, "Cumberland House – General," v. 1, June 1948-31 August 1950, G. Burgess to J.S. White, 7 October 1948.

52 *SAB,* S-NR 1/4, f. 137 C, "Northern Region," (3 files), C.L. MacLean to J.W. Churchman, 12 June 1950; S-NR 1/4, f. 235, "Ile a la Crosse," A.K. Quandt to J.L. Phelps, 2 June 1948; Father G.E.A. Remy to J.H. Brockelbank, 3 March 1949; Quandt to Churchman, 25 March 1949; E.J. Marshall to Churchman, 26 July 1949; Brockelbank to Remy, 16 November 1949; S-NR 1/5, v. I, f. 39, (230), "Northern Region, 1957-1959," W.R. Parks to Churchman, 6 April 1959.

53 Buckley, Kew, and Hawley, *The Indians and Metis of Northern Saskatchewan,* 25; Kew, *Cumberland House,* 15; Richard W. Bailey, "Housing for Indians and Metis in Northern Saskatchewan," *Habitat* 2, 4 (1968): 19.

54 DNR, *Annual Report,* 1961, 108; *SAB,* NR 1/5, v. I, f. 84, (420), "Northern Housing Project," 1959-61, Cabinet Secretary to Premier Douglas, O.A. Turnbull, A.G. Kuziak, A.M. Nicholson, W.S. Lloyd, 11 July 1961; Cabinet Secretary to Douglas, Kuziak, C.M. Fines, Lloyd, T.J. Bentley, 8 September 1959; A.H. MacDonald to J.W. Churchman, 12 January 1961; H.S. Lee to Lloyd, L.F. McIntosh, J.H. Brockelbank, A.E. Blakeney, Kuziak, Turnbull, 13 December 1961; Churchman to MacDonald, 28 December 1961.

55 DNR, *Annual Report,* 1961, 107; *SAB,* NR 1/5, v. I, f. 84, (420), "Northern Housing Project, 1959-1961," M. Kalmakoff to W.A. Houseman, 9 March 1960.

56 *SAB,* NR 1/5, v. I, f. 84, (420), "Northern Housing Project, 1959-1961," A.H. MacDonald to J.W. Churchman, 4 April 1961; A.G. Kuziak to Treasury Board, 24 April 1961.

57 DNR, *Annual Report,* 1962, 110; *SAB,* S-NR 1/5, v. I, f. 69, "General – Northern Affairs, 1958-1961," L.J. Hutchison to A. Doyle, 24 April 1962; S-NR 1/5, v. III, f. 4, "Northern Administration District, 1962-67," AHM, N. Comm. Dev. Brief, 7/9/64.

58 *SAB,* R-517, v. XIII, f. 25, "Construction and Housing, 1961-1965," M.A. Welsh to Regional Health Services Branch, Att.: Dr. M.S. Acker, 3 January 1963; R-517, v. XIII, f. 21, "Policy – Medical Care," 1955-73, Dr. A.C. Irwin to Acker, 8 April 1963.

59 DNR, *Annual Report,* 1963, 121; DNR, *Annual Report,* 1964, 119; *SAB,* S-NR 1/5, v. III, f. 16a, "Housing – Low Income," 1964-65, A.H. MacDonald to J.W. Churchman, 4 March 1964; Minister's Office to Churchman, 4 February 1964; W.J. Bague to MacDonald, 25 March 1964; S-NR 1/5, v. III, f. 24a, "Fur Advisory Committee, 1960-64," Minutes, Sask. Fur Adv. Comm., Prince Albert, 31 January 1964.

60 *SAB,* S-NR 1/4, 122 D, "Northern Region," (5 files), DNR Auth. No. C-247, 15 April 1958; S-NR 1/4, f. 137 C, "Northern Region," (3 files), A.T. Davidson to J.W. Churchman, 24 July 1953; W.M. Simenson to R.N. Gooding, 13 February 1956; T.H. Preston to Davidson, 16 May 1956.

61 J.E.M. Kew, "Metis-Indian Housing in Northern Saskatchewan," in *Research Review I,* ed. Jean Foulds (Saskatoon: Center for Community Studies, University of Saskatchewan, 1963), 13-16; *SAB,* S-NR 1/5, v. III, f. 8, "Buffalo Narrows, 1963-66," E. Kramer to M. Semchuk, 5 December 1963.

62 *SAB,* R-517, v. XIII, f. 22, "Policy – Sanitation," 1951-65, M.A. Welsh to Dr. S.L. Skoll, 18 May 1965.

63 Dept. of Social Welfare, *Annual Report,* 1946, 18, 20; Dept. of Social Welfare and Rehab., *Annual Report,* 1959, 22; Dept. of Social Welfare and Rehab., *Annual Report,* 1960, 22; Battel, *Children Shall Be First,* 28-30, 43; *SAB,* R-646, "Saskatchewan Department of Social Services," "Fifteen Year History," "The History of Saskatchewan's Department of Social Welfare and Rehabilitation 1944-1949."

64 Dept. of Social Welfare, *Annual Report,* 1945, 14, Dept. of Social Welfare, *Annual Report,* 1946, 9; Dept. of Social Welfare and Rehab., *Annual Report,* 1958, 11; Dept. of Social Welfare and Rehab., *Annual Report,* 1960, 14; Battel, *Children Shall Be First,* 43-44.

65 Dept. of Social Welfare, *Annual Report,* 1947, 64; Dept. of Social Welfare and Rehab., *Annual Report,* 1961, 53; Dept. of Social Welfare and Rehab, *Annual Report,* 1963, 43; Battel, *Children Shall Be First,* 25; *SAB,* S-M16, v. VII, f. 3, "Parks and Lands Branch, 1961-63," Minutes, N. Adv. Comm., 29 March 1954; Minutes, N. Adv. Comm., 29 November 1954; S-M 16, v. XV, f. 14, "Indians, 1955-64," Dept. of Social Welfare, Proposals for extending prov. welfare services to Registered Indians, App. 1, November 1963.

66 *SAB,* S-NR 1/3, f. NR-8-3, "Child Welfare Wards, 1951-52," C.A.L. Hogg to J.S. White, 13 December 1950; C.H. Smith to Hogg, 21 April 1951; J.H. Brockelbank to Hogg, 28 February 1952; W.A. Houseman to Hogg, 26 March 1951; W.H. Roney to Hogg, 17 December 1951.

67 Dept. of Social Welfare and Rehab., *Annual Report,* 1951, 14; Battel, *Children Shall Be First,* 50-51, 83, 87, 103-104, 107, 109; *SAB,* R-646, "Fifteen Year History," "Hist. of Dept. of Soc. Welfare and Rehab., 1944-1949."

68 Dept. of Social Welfare and Rehab., *Annual Report,* 1954, 18; Battel, *Children Shall Be First,* 108-111.

69 Dept. of Social Welfare, *Annual Report,* 1948, 136; Dept. of Social Welfare and Rehab., *Annual Report,* 1949, 27; Dept. of Social Welfare and Rehab., *Annual Report,* 1951, 26; Dept. of Social Welfare and Rehab., *Annual Report,* 1952, 15; Dept. of Social Welfare and Rehab., *Annual Report,* 1962, 44; Battel, *Children Shall Be First,* 127-128; *SAB,* R-646, "Fifteen Year History," "Hist. of Dept. of Soc. Welfare and Rehab., 1944-1949."

70 Battel, *Children Shall Be First*, 116; Dept. of Welfare, *Annual Report*, 1965, 19; *SAB*, S-M 16, v. XIII, f. 49, "Social Welfare, Religion and Child Care, 1962-64," A.M. Nicholson to G. Willis, 5 September 1963.

71 Dept. of Social Welfare and Rehab., *Annual Report*, 1960, 44; Dept. of Social Welfare and Rehab., *Annual Report*, 1961, 24; *SAB*, S-M 16, v. XIII, f. 49, "Social Welfare, Religion and Child Care, 1962-64," A.M. Nicholson to E.A. Johnson, 29 January 1964.

72 Battel, *Children Shall Be First*, 58, 128; *SAB*, R-646, "Fifteen Year History," "Hist. of Dept. of Soc. Welfare and Rehab., 1944-1949," 11, 15.

Chapter 10: Dollars Are Worth More Than Lives

1 C.H. Piercy, *Survey of Educational Facilities in Northern Saskatchewan, Part 1: The Areas in the Remote Northern Part of the Province of Saskatchewan*, unpublished paper (18 December 1944), 4-5.

2 Dean E. McHenry, *The Third Force in Canada: The Co-Operative Commonwealth Federation, 1932-1948* (Westport, CT: Greenwood Press, 1950), 249; Public Health, "Saskatchewan Plans for Health," in *Building a Province: A History of Saskatchewan in Documents*, ed. David E. Smith, Document 92 (Saskatoon: Fifth House Publishers, 1992), 329.

3 Aleck Ostry, "Prelude to Medicare: Institutional Change and Continuity in Saskatchewan, 1944-1962," *Prairie Forum* 20, 1 (Spring 1995): 95; Duane Mombourquette, "'An Inalienable Right:' The CCF and Rapid Health Care Reform, 1944-1948,'" *Saskatchewan History* 43, 3 (Autumn, 1991), 113; Sigerist Health Services Survey Commission, *Report of the Commissioner* (Regina: Public Health, Health Services Survey Commission, 1944); David E. Smith, ed., *Building a Province: A History of Saskatchewan in Documents*, Document 91 (Saskatoon: Fifth House Publishers, 1992), 325; Jack McLeod, "Health, Welfare, and Politics," in *Essays on the Left: Essays in Honour of T.C. Douglas*, ed. Laurier LaPierre et al. (Toronto/Montreal: McClelland and Stewart, 1971), 86; *Progress Report from Your Government: A Survey of Saskatchewan Government Activity* (Regina: Bureau of Publications, 1948), 5; Thomas Hector Macdonald McLeod and Ian McLeod, *Tommy Douglas: The Road to Jerusalem* (Edmonton: Hurtig Publishers, 1987), 128-129.

4 Ostry, "Prelude to Medicare," 101; Lewis H. Thomas, ed., *The Making of a Socialist: The Recollections of T.C. Douglas* (Edmonton: University of Alberta Press, 1982), 169; *Progress Report from Your Government*, 8; Economic and Planning Board, *Saskatchewan Economic Review*, (September 1953), 4-5; Health Survey Committee, *Saskatchewan Health Survey Report*, vol. 1 (Regina: n.p., 1951), xxvii.

5 Betty L. Dyck, *Running to Beat Hell: A Biography of A.M. (Sandy) Nicholson* (Regina: Canadian Plains Research Center, University of Regina, 1988), 187; McLeod and McLeod, *Tommy Douglas*, 145-152; Ostry, "Prelude to Medicare," 89, 101; Health Survey Committee, *Saskatchewan Health Survey Report*, vol. 1, 225-226.

6 Dept. of Social Welfare and Rehab., *Annual Report*, 1949, 10; Mildred E. Battel, *Children Shall Be First: Child Welfare Saskatchewan 1944-64* (Regina: Saskatchewan Department of Culture and Youth, 1979), 59; *Saskatchewan Archives Board [SAB]*, R-517, Dept. of Health, Comm. Health Services Br., (GR-278), (Records of Central Office, the 13 Health Regions and the Northern Health District), Northern Health District, v. XIII, f. 7, "Budget Estimates," 1956-73 (3 folders), "1969-70 Work Program Northern Health District," undated; R-646, "Saskatchewan Department of Social Services," "Fifteen Year History, Department of Social Welfare and Rehabilitation," Chronology.

7 DNR, *Annual Report*, 1948, 126; DNR, *Annual Report*, 1949, 154; *SAB*, R-517, v. XIII, f. 10, "Various Services," 1950-73, Dr. F.D. Mott to Dr. C.R. Totton, 12 January 1950; R-517, v. XIII, f. 60, "Hospitals – General," 1953-68, G.W. Myers to Dr. G. Kinneard, 15 October 1953; S-NR 1/4, Deputy Minister and Assistant Deputy Minister Files, f. 236, "Rehabilitation and Welfare – General," v. 2, Rev. G.J. Waite to N. Admin., 27 November 1950; J.H. Brockelbank to Waite, 18 December 1950; Waite to N. Admin., 30 November 1951; C.L. MacLean to Waite, 15 January 1952.

8 DNR, *Annual Report*, 1958, 78; DNR, *Annual Report*, 1959, N.A. 25; DNR, *Annual Report*, 1964, 119; DNR, *Annual Report*, 1965, 64; *SAB*, S-M 16, A.M. Nicholson Papers, v. VII, f. 4, "Tour of North Saskatchewan, 1959," "The Present, the Potential, and the Planned for Northern Saskatchewan," background data for the National Northern Development Conference, Edmonton, August 1958, no author given; S-M 16, v. VIII, f. 3, "Proposed Legislation,

1959-64," (2 of 2), J.W. Churchman to A.G. Kuziak, 7 March 1961; S-M 16, v. XV, f. 14, "Indians, 1955-64," "Review of Progress in Programs to Promote Integration and Economic Development"; R782, DNR, (GR-24-3), v. I, f. 5, "Deputy Minister Correspondence," 1970-71, J.E. Weymark to D. Dombowsky, 18 November 1970; S-NR 1/5, v. I, f. 39, (230), "Northern Region, 1957-1959," Dr. F.B. Roth to Churchman, 18 July 1958; S-NR 1/5, v. I, f. 69, "General – Northern Affairs, 1958-1961," A.H. MacDonald to Churchman, 15 December 1958; Dept. of Pub. Health, *Outline of Services* (Regina: Saskatchewan Department of Public Health, Division of Health Education, 1958), 33.

9   *SAB*, R-517, v. XIII, f. 9, "Organization," 1951-71, R.G. Ellis to Dr. G. Kinneard, 5 May 1954.

10 *SAB*, R-907.2, J.H. Brockelbank Papers, v. II, f. 12, "J.J. Wheaton, Northern Administrator," Wheaton to J.L. Phelps, 15 April 1948; Wheaton to C.A.L. Hogg, Re: Progress Report, NAD, 1948.

11 *SAB*, R-517, v. XIII, f. 9, "Organization," 1951-71, Dr. F.B. Roth to Dr. G. Kinneard, 9 September 1954; Roth to various recipients, 20 September 1954; Kinneard to Dr. G.C. Darby, 2 July 1954; J.M. Hershey to Dr. F.D. Mott, 10 July 1951; S-NR 1/4, f. 167 B3, "Northern Region," Minutes of N. District Cons. Officers' Conf., Prince Albert, SK, 4-8 October 1954; R-517, v. XIII, f. 7, "Budget Estimates," 1956-73, (3 folders), Northern Health Services, Stats., undated; R-517, v. XIII, f. 10, "Various Services," 1950-73, Dr. G. Kinneard to Dr. F.B. Roth, 31 January 1952; S-NR2, DNR-ADM, (A) Subject Files, August 1944-April 1949, f. 38, "Northern District (A.K. Quandt)," N. Dist. Field Officers' Conf., beginning 31 January 1949, Discussion after G. Burgess speech; Department of Public Health, *Outline of Services*.

12 Mombourquette, "'An Inalienable Right,'" 110; *SAB*, S-NR 1/5, v. I, f. 39, (230), "Northern Region, 1957-1959," Dept. of Public Health, NHD, "Review and Trends of Government Programs Affecting the North," 9 April 1959.

13 Mary Helen Richards, "Cumberland House: Two Hundred Years of History," *Saskatchewan History* 27, 3 (Autumn 1974): 112; Richard Wuorinen, *A History of Buffalo Narrows* (Buffalo Narrows, SK: Buffalo Narrows Celebrate Saskatchewan Committee, 1981), 31-32; *SAB*, R-517, v. XIII, f. 7, "Budget Estimates," 1956-73, (3 folders), Dr. A.C. Irwin to Dr. M.S. Acker, 27 February 1961; Attached, N. Health Dist. Budget Summary; Irwin to Acker, 1 June 1960; S-NR 1/4, f. 235, "Cumberland House – General," v. 1, June 1948-31 August 1950, G. Burgess to J.S. White, 7 October 1948; S-NR 1/4, f. 235, "Cumberland House," 1953-56, Dr. G. Kinneard to A.T. Davidson, 8 December 1955; S-NR 1/4, f. 235, "Ile a la Crosse," Kinneard to Irwin, 24 January 1956; J.W. Churchman to Davidson, 25 January 1956.

14 *SAB*, R-517, v. XIII, f. 1, "Annual Reports," 1949-67, Dr. A.C. Irwin to Dr. S.L. Skoll, 20 January 1965; V.F. Valentine, *The Metis of Northern Saskatchewan* (Regina: DNR, 1955), 26.

15 *Religious History of St. John the Baptist Parish, Ile a la Crosse, 150 Years: The Church, The People of God* (1996), 9-11; *SAB*, R-517, v. XIII, f. 58, "Relations with National Health and Welfare," 1951-73, P.E. Moore to Dr. J.P. Harvey, 8 June 1954; S-NR 1/5, v. I, f. 39, (230), "Northern Region, 1957-1959," Dept. of Public Health, NHD, "Review and Trends of Government Programs Affecting the North," 9 April 1959.

16 *SAB*, R-517, v. XIII, f. 7, "Budget Estimates," 1956-73 (3 folders), Dr. A.C. Irwin to Dr. F.B. Roth, 7 September 1956; Dept. of Public Health, NHS, "Work Programme For Fiscal Year 1964-65"; R-517, v. XIII, f. 58, "Relations with National Health and Welfare," 1951-73, Dr. J.G. Clarkson to Dr. G.D.W. Cameron, 28 December 1964; Irwin to Dr. F.J. Porth, 8 January 1965; R-517, v. XIII, f. 9, "Organization," 1951-71, R.F. Badgley to Dr. M.S. Acker, 3 May 1960; R-517, v. XIII, f. 10, "Various Services," 1950-73, Dr. S.L. Skoll to Irwin, 29 September 1965; Attached "Draft Copy" "Proposed Reorganization of the Northern Health District"; R-517, v. XIII, f. 60, "Hospitals – General," 1953-68, Dr. G. Kinneard to Irwin, 26 September 1955; S-NR 1/4, f. 235, "Cumberland House," 1953-56, Kinneard to A.T. Davidson, 8 December 1955; S-NR 1/4, f. 235, "Ile a la Crosse," Kinneard to Irwin, 24 January 1956; J.W. Churchman to Davidson, 25 January 1956.

17 *SAB*, R-517, v. XIII, f. 63, "Hospitals – St. Martins and La Loche," 1955-72, Dr. C.R. Totton to Rev. J. Bourbonnais, 15 March 1954; Dr. A.C. Irwin to Dr. G. Kinneard, 28 February 1955; Irwin to Dr. H.D. McDonald, 15 November 1961; Kinneard to Irwin, 25 February 1955; S-NR 1/5, v. I, f. 39, (230), "Northern Region, 1957-1959," Dept. of Public Health, NHD, "Review and Trends of Government Programs Affecting the North," 9 April 1959.

18 *SAB*, R-907.2, v. II, f. 12, "J.J. Wheaton, Northern Administrator," Minutes, N. Co-Ord. Comm. Mtg., 23 April 1948.

19 *SAB*, R-517, v. XIII, f. 60, "Hospitals – General," 1953-68, N. Admin. Health Dist., 19 July 1954; Health Survey Committee, *Saskatchewan Health Survey Report*, vol. 2, 22, 36, 66, 146, 160.

20 *SAB*, R-517, v. XIII, f. 7, "Budget Estimates," 1956-73, (3 folders), Dept. of Public Health, NHS, "Work Programme For Fiscal Year 1964-65."

21 J.E.M. Kew, *Cumberland House in 1960* (Saskatoon: Center for Community Studies, University of Saskatchewan, 1962); *SAB*, R-517, v. XIII, f. 7, "Budget Estimates," 1956-73 (3 folders), "Northern Health Services" Summary Sheets; R-517, v. XIII, f. 10, "Various Services," 1950-73, Dr. M.S. Acker to A.K. Davis, 12 February 1963.

22 *SAB*, R-517, v. XIII, f. 21, "Policy – Medical Care," 1955-73, O.J. Rath to Dr. A.C. Irwin, 17 October 1956; R-517, v. XIII, f. 58, "Relations with National Health and Welfare," 1951-73, Rath to Dr. G. Kinneard, 8 December 1958; Kinneard to Rath, 10 December 1958; Irwin to Kinneard, 16 December 1958; Irwin to Rath, 16 December 1958; Rath to Kinneard, 12 January 1959; Rath to Irwin, 16 February 1959; Irwin to Kinneard, 21 April 1959.

23 DNR, *Annual Report*, 1955, 63; *SAB*, S-NR 1/4, f. 230, "Northern District – General," v. 2, 1954-56, C.S. Brown to A.T. Davidson, 18 March 1955; R-517, v. XIII, f. 1, "Annual Reports," 1949-67, *Annual Report*, 1963; Dr. A.C. Irwin to Dr. G. Kinneard, 20 June 1957; Attached "Fiscal Year 1956-57," S-NR 1/5, v. I, f. 39, (230), "Northern Region, 1957-1959," Dept. of Public Health, NHD, "Review and Trends of Government Programs Affecting the North," 9 April 1959; R-517, v. XIII, f. 9, "Organization," 1951-71, R.F. Badgley to Dr. M.S. Acker, 3 May 1960.

24 La Ronge Heritage Committee, *Our Roots: A History of La Ronge* (La Ronge: Lakeland Press Ltd., 1981), 46-48; *SAB*, R-517, v. XIII, f. 1, "Annual Reports," 1949-67, Dr. A.C. Irwin to Dr. G. Kinneard, 20 June 1957; Attached "Fiscal Year 1956-57"; R-517, v. XIII, f. 7, "Budget Estimates," 1956-73 (3 folders), Dept. of Public Health, NHS, "Work Programme For Fiscal Year 1964-65"; R-517, v. XIII, f. 14, "Nursing and Child Health," 1950-70, L. Cowan to Dr. L. Kawula, 15 April 1963; E.M. Broome to Irwin, 3 August 1957; Irwin to Kinneard, 15 August 1957; R-517, v. XIII, f. 60, "Hospitals – General," 1953-68, Kinneard to Irwin, 26 September 1955; Dr. R.H. MacPherson to Kawula, 24 May 1963; S-NR 1/5, v. I, f. 39, (230), "Northern Region, 1957-1959," Dept. of Public Health, NHD, "Review and Trends of Government Programs Affecting the North," 9 April 1959.

25 *SAB*, R-517, v. XIII, f. 7, "Budget Estimates," 1956-73, (3 folders), Dr. A.C. Irwin to Dr. M.S. Acker, 27 February 1961; Attached, NHD Budget Summary; R-517, v. XIII, f. 14, "Nursing and Child Health," 1950-70, Irwin to Dr. V.L. Matthews, 17 April 1964; Dr. S.L. Skoll to Matthews, 7 May 1964; Irwin to Skoll, 25 May 1965; Matthews to Irwin, 15 June 1964; R-517, v. XIII, f. 2, "Visits," 1963-72, Skoll to Acker, 21 July 1964.

26 *SAB*, R-517, v. XIII, f. 9, "Organization," 1951-71, R.F. Badgley to Dr. M.S. Acker, 3 May 1960.

27 *SAB*, R-517, v. XIII, f. 10, "Various Services," 1950-73, Dr. M.S. Acker to A.K. Davis, 12 February 1963; R-517, v. XIII, f. 14, "Nursing and Child Health," 1950-70, Dr. A.C. Irwin to Acker, 19 March 1962; Miss J. Cummine to Irwin, 31 May 1962; E.L. Miner to Acker, 11 July 1962; Irwin to Dr. J.G. Clarkson, 18 March 1964; R. Woollam to Acker, 21 November 1961; Irwin to Acker, 27 December 1961; Dr. S.L. Skoll to File, 24 March 1964.

28 *SAB*, R-517, v. XIII, f. 4, "Infant Mortality," 1955-65, Dr. A.C. Irwin to Dr. G. Kinneard, 1 October 1958; Irwin to Dr. S.C. Best, 9 June 1964; Kinneard to Irwin, 3 October 1958.

29 *SAB*, R-517, v. XIII, f. 1, "Annual Reports," 1949-67, Dr. A.C. Irwin to Dr. S.L. Skoll, 20 January 1965; R-517, v. XIII, f. 7, "Budget Estimates," 1956-73 (3 folders), "Northern Health Services" Summary Sheets; R-517, v. XIII, f. 9, "Organization," 1951-71, R.F. Badgley to Dr. M.S. Acker, 3 May 1960; Irwin to Dr. J.G. Clarkson, 23 October 1964; R-517, v. XIII, f. 10, "Various Services," 1950-73, Acker to R.S. Reid, 2 October 1963; B. McCulloch, Report.

30 G. Graham-Cumming, "Health of the Original Canadians, 1867-1967," *Medical Services Journal of Canada* 23 (February 1967): 127; *SAB*, S-M15, Box 9, Phelps Papers, "Sask. Lake and Forest Products Corporation – J.F. Gray, 1946-1950, (4)," "A Submission to the Board"; R.C. Ross to K.E. Dickson, 23 September 1947; S-NR 1/4, f. 236, "Rehabilitation and Welfare – General," v. 2, "Relief to Destitutes and Administration of Northern Outpost Hospitals," undated; S-NR 1/5, v. I, f. 39, (230), "Northern Region, 1957-1959," Dept. of Public Health, NHD, "Review and Trends of Government Programs Affecting the North," 9 April 1959; R-517, v. XIII, f. 7, "Budget Estimates," 1956-73 (3 folders), "Northern

Health Services" Summary Sheets; R-517, v. XIII, f. 9, "Organization," 1951-71, R.F. Badgley to Dr. M.S. Acker, 3 May 1960; R-517, v. XIII, f. 58, "Relations with National Health and Welfare," 1951-73, Dr. A.C. Irwin to Dr. F.B. Roth, 29 September 1954; Irwin to Roth, 30 September 1954; J.A. Hughes to The Regional Supt., 19 October 1959; Irwin to O.J. Rath, 23 April 1956; Rath to Dr. G. Kinneard, 6 November 1959; Irwin to Rath, 25 November 1959.

31 SAB, R-517, v. XIII, f. 58, "Relations with National Health and Welfare," 1951-73, Dr. A.C. Irwin to Dr. F.B. Roth, 29 September 1954; Irwin to Roth, 30 September 1954.

32 Graham-Cumming, "Health of the Original Canadians," 142-159.

33 SAB, R-517, v. XIII, f. 1, "Annual Reports," 1949-67, Dr. A.C. Irwin to Dr. J.D. Ramsay, 22 February 1960; R-517, v. XIII, f. 9, "Organization," 1951-71, R.F. Badgley to Dr. M.S. Acker, 3 May 1960; R-517, v. XIII, f. 11, "Health Services (Care)," 1964-65, Dr. V.L. Matthews, "Preliminary Report on Health Services Programs in the Northern Health District," September 1964; R-907.2, v. II, f. 12, "J.J. Wheaton, Northern Administrator," Wheaton to Dr. H.S. Doyle, 20 March 1948; S-NR 1/4, 167 B3, "Northern Region, April 1st, 1956," N. Dist. Field Officers' Conf., Prince Albert, SK, 31 January-1 February 1949; S-NR2, (A) Subject Files, August 1944-April 1949, f. 37, "Northern Administration (J.J. Wheaton)," M.F. Norris to C.A.L. Hogg, 25 August 1948.

34 Graham-Cumming, "Health of the Original Canadians," 129-142; P.E. Moore, "Medical Care of Canada's Indians and Eskimos," Canadian Journal of Public Health 47, 6 (June 1956): 227-233; Health Survey Committee, Saskatchewan Health Survey Report, vol. 1, 108-120, 229-230.

35 SAB, R-517, v. XIII, "Communicable Diseases," 1952, Dept. of Public Health, TB death statement for NAD for 1950; R-517, v. XIII, f. 11, "Health Services (Care)," 1964-65, Dr. A.C. Irwin to Dr. J.G. Clarkson, 19 October 1964; Dr. V.L. Matthews, "Preliminary Report on Health Services Programs in the Northern Health District," September 1964; S-NR 1/4, 167 B3, "Northern Region," Minutes of N. District Cons. Officers' Conf., Prince Albert, SK, 4-8 October 1954.

36 SAB, R-517, v. XIII, f. 9, "Organization," 1951-71, R.F. Badgley to Dr. M.S. Acker, 3 May 1960; R-517, v. XIII, f. 10, "Various Services," 1950-73, Dr. A.C. Irwin to Dr. G. Kinneard, 20 October 1954; J. Orr to Kinneard, 4 November 1954; R-517, v. XIII, f. 29, "Policy – Tuberculosis," 1950-69, Irwin to Kinneard, 28 April 1955; S-NR 1/4, f. 230, "Northern Region – General," v. III, 1957-, F. Froh to The Minister, DNR, 12 March 1957; S-NR 1/5, v. I, f. 39, (230), "Northern Region, 1957-1959," Dept. of Public Health, NHD, "Review and Trends of Government Programs Affecting the North," 9 April 1959. S-NR 1/5, v. III, f. 4, "Northern Administration District, 1962-67," Froh to E. Kramer, 27 February 1964; Froh to D.G. Stewart, 28 February 1967.

37 SAB, R-517, v. XIII, f. 3, "Population," 1954-66, Dr. M.S. Acker to Dr. A.C. Irwin, 16 March 1961; R-517, v. XIII, f. 9, "Organization," 1951-71, R.F. Badgley to Acker, 3 May 1960; R-517, v. XIII, f. 29, "Policy – Tuberculosis," 1950-69, Dr. G. Kinneard to Dr. G.D. Barnett, 18 September 1959; Irwin to Kinneard, 21 July 1959; Irwin to Kinneard, 28 April 1955; June Cutt Thompson, "Cree Indians in North-Eastern Saskatchewan," Saskatchewan History 11, 2 (Spring 1958): 52.

38 Dept. of Social Welfare and Rehab., Annual Report, 1962, 65; SAB, R-517, v. XIII, f. 9, "Organization," 1951-71, R.F. Badgley to Dr. M.S. Acker, 3 May 1960; S-M 16, v. XV, f. 14, "Indians, 1955-64," Dept. of Social Welfare, "Proposals to extend prov. welfare services to Registered Indians," App. 1, November 1963; S-NR 1/4, f. 433, "Prosecutions," E. McLean to Attorney General, 19 May 1951; C.L. MacLean to J.W. Churchman, 29 June 1951; E.L. Paynter to C.L. MacLean, 11 June 1951.

39 Progress Report from Your Government, 8; SAB, S-M15, Box 36, "Doidge, J. (Publicity)," DNR, News Release, January 1947; Department of Health, Outline of Services (1958), 22-23; Health Survey Committee, Saskatchewan Health Survey Report, vol. 1, 75-76.

40 SAB, R-907.2, v. II, f. 12, "J.J. Wheaton, Northern Administrator," Wheaton to F. Clavelle, 10 March 1948.

41 SAB, R-907.2, v. II, f. 12, "J.J. Wheaton, Northern Administrator," Wheaton to J.L. Phelps, 3 May 1948; Dr. C.R. Totton, "Suggested Programme For The Far North"; S-NR2, (A) Subject Files – August 1944-April 1949, f. 38, "Northern District (A.K. Quandt)," Quandt to Wheaton, 17 December 1948.

42 *SAB*, R-907.2, v. II, f. 12, "J.J. Wheaton, Northern Administrator," C.A.L. Hogg to T.C. Douglas, 16 November 1948; G.J. Waite to J.J. Wheaton, 15 December 1948; Rev. G.J. Waite to NAD Rep., 24 November 1948; H.S. Udey to Douglas, 26 October 1948; J.J. Wheaton to J.H. Brockelbank, 8 February 1949; Wheaton to J.W. Churchman, 8 November 1948; Wheaton to Waite, 30 November 1948; A. Fremont to Wheaton, 8 December 1948; S-NR2, (A) Subject Files – August 1944-April 1949, f. 37, "Northern Administration (J.J. Wheaton)," Udey to Douglas, undated.

43 *SAB*, S-M15, Box 9, "Sask. Lake and Forest Products Corporation – J.F. Gray, 1946-1951, (3)," Gray, report to SL&FPC Bd. of Dirs. on trip, 20 February 1948.

44 *SAB*, R-517, v. XIII, f. 7, "Budget Estimates," 1956-73, (3 folders), "Northern Health Services" Summary Sheets; R-517, v. XIII, f. 10, "Various Services," 1950-73, Dr. M.S. Acker to R.S. Reid, 2 October 1963; Attached report by Bruce McCulloch; R-517, v. XIII, f. 21, "Policy – Medical Care," 1955-73, Dr. A.C. Irwin to R.G. Ellis, 12 September 1961; S-NR 1/4, f. 167 B3, "Northern Region," Minutes of N. District Cons. Officers' Conf., Prince Albert, SK, 4-8 October 1954; S-NR 1/4, f. 230, "Northern District – General," v. 2, 1954-56, C.S. Brown to A.T. Davidson, Att.: J.W. Churchman, 27 September 1954; S.C. Best et al., "The Pinehouse (Saskatchewan) Nutrition Project II," *Canadian Medical Association Journal* 85 (19 August 1961): 413.

45 *SAB*, R-517, v. XIII, f. 1, "Annual Reports," 1949-67, Dr. C.R. Totton to Dr. F.D. Mott, 25 January 1950; R-517, v. XIII, f. 7, "Budget Estimates," 1956-73 (3 folders), Dept. of Pub. Health, NHS, "Work Programme For Fiscal Year 1964-65"; R-517, v. XIII, f. 14, "Nursing and Child Health," 1950-70, Mrs. W.H. Wilson to "Dear Sirs," 21 February 1962; Dr. S.C. Best to Dr. R.G. Murray, 1 May 1962; R-517, v. XIII, f. 21, "Policy – Medical Care," 1955-73, Dr. A.C. Irwin to Dr. V.L. Matthews, 2 January 1958.

46 *SAB*, R-517, v. XIII, f. 16, "Policy – Dental," 1954-73, C.S. Brown to Dr. A.E. Chegwin, 30 March 1954; Dr. G. Kinneard to Brown, 9 April 1954; Chegwin to Dr. A.C. Irwin, 28 February 1955; Chegwin to Kinneard, 3 April 1954.

47 *SAB*, R-517, v. XIII, f. 7, "Budget Estimates," 1956-73 (3 folders), Dr. A.E. Chegwin to Dr. M.S. Acker, Att.: J. Yerhoff, 28 August 1963; Dr. S.L. Skoll to C.P. Feader, 5 March 1964, (Memo not sent); "Narrative in Support of Inclusion of an Item in the 'A' Budget for Northern Health District Dental Services for Children"; Dept. of Public Health, NHS, "Work Programme For Fiscal Year 1964-65"; R-517, v. XIII, f. 14, "Nursing and Child Health," 1950-70, Chegwin to Dr. A.C. Irwin, 26 March 1956; R-517, v. XIII, f. 16, "Policy – Dental," 1954-73, Canadian Red Cross Society, Brief to Minister of Public Health re: dental care of children in north, undated; Miss H. Lawrence to Chegwin, 12 October 1962; Irwin to Chegwin, 28 February 1962; Chegwin to Acker, 22 January 1963; Chegwin to G. Townshend, 18 December 1962; Dr. G. Kinneard to Dr. F.B. Roth, 25 October 1955; Acker to Townshend, 14 May 1962; Skoll to Dr. V.L. Matthews, 11 September 1963; "Summary of Northern Dental Clinics," undated.

48 *SAB*, R-517, v. XIII, f. 16, "Policy – Dental," 1954-73, Dr. S.L. Skoll to Dr. V.L. Matthews, 11 September 1963; Matthews to Skoll, 18 September 1963; Skoll to Matthews, 7 October 1963; Skoll to Matthews, 22 November 1963.

49 Department of Natural Resources, *The New North: Saskatchewan's Northern Development Program, 1945-1948* (Regina: DNR, 1948), 32; *SAB*, R-517, v. XIII, f. 12, "Policy – General," 1965-73, Excerpt from letter from Dr. L.B. Pett, 28 November 1957; R-907.2, v. II, f. 12, "J.J. Wheaton, Northern Administrator," J.A. Bell to Sask. Div. Can. Red Cross Society, Regina, 24 October 1948; Mrs. J.A. Bell to T.C. Douglas, 30 October 1948; S-NR 1/4, f. 167 B3, "Northern Region, April 1st, 1956," N. Dist. Field Officers' Conf, 9-13 January 1951.

50 *SAB*, S-M 16, v. XIII, f. 293, "Rehabilitation, Metis, La Loche, 1958-62," R. Woollam to W.S. Lloyd, 8 January 1962; G. McCaw to Mrs. D. Zarski, 12 March 1962.

51 *SAB*, R-517, v. XIII, f. 58, "Relations with National Health and Welfare," 1951-73, Dr. A.C. Irwin to Dr. G. Kinneard, 24 May 1957; S-NR 1/5, v. I, f. 39, (230), "Northern Region, 1957-1959," Irwin, "The Nutrition Survey in Northern Saskatchewan," undated, Survey by Dr. L.B. Pett; S-M 16, v. XIII, f. 293, "Rehabilitation, Metis, La Loche, 1958-62," P. Godt, "Co-Operative Store Project for La Loche"; P. Spaulding to J.T. Phalen, 20 January 1958.

52 *SAB*, S-NR 1/5, v. I, f. 39, (230), "Northern Region, 1957-1959," Dept. of Public Health, NHD, "Review and Trends of Government Programs Affecting the North," 9 April 1959; S.C. Best and J.W. Gerrard, "Pine House (Saskatchewan) Nutrition Project," *Canadian*

Medical Association Journal 81 (1 December 1959): 915-917; S.C. Best et al., "The Pine-house (Saskatchewan) Nutrition Project II," 412-414.

53 *SAB*, S-NR2, (A) Subject Files – August 1944-April 1949, f. 19, "Fisheries Branch (A.H. Mac-Donald)," J.W. Churchman, "Summary of a Meeting Held in the Minister's Office," 16 September (1948?); S-NR2, (A) Subject Files – August 1944-April 1949, f. 57, "Surveys Branch (A.I. Bereskin)," Bereskin to J.L. Phelps, C.A.L. Hogg, J.J. Wheaton, 21 July 1948.

54 Helen L. Buckley, J.E.M. Kew, and John B. Hawley, *The Indians and Metis of Northern Saskatchewan: A Report on Economic and Social Development* (Saskatoon: Center for Community Studies, University of Saskatchewan, 1963), 30; Philip T. Spaulding, "The Metis of Ile-a-la-Crosse" (PhD diss., University of Washington, 1970), 103; Valentine, *The Metis of Northern Saskatchewan*, 26.

55 Doris French Shackleton, *Tommy Douglas* (Toronto: McClelland and Stewart, 1975), 207; *SAB*, R-A1113, Joe Phelps, interview by Murray Dobbin, audio tape, 1976. Beginning in 1951, provinces determined whether Status Indians could drink off the reserve. Saskatchewan allowed Indians to do so beginning in 1960.

56 La Ronge Heritage Committee, *Our Roots*, 56; Murray Dobbin, *The One-And-A-Half Men: The Story of Jim Brady and Malcolm Norris, Metis Patriots of the Twentieth Century* (Vancouver: New Star Books, 1981), 186, 200; *SAB*, S-NR 1/4, f. 231 B, "Buffalo Narrows," 1949-57, C.L. MacLean to J.W. Churchman, 27 July 1950; S-NR 1/4, f. 231 B, "La Ronge – General," (5 files), C.A.L. Hogg to C.M. Fines, 22 April 1949; S-NR 1/4, f. 235, "Buffalo Narrows," MacLean to Churchman, 6 September 1951; S-NR 1/4, f. 235, "La Ronge," J.J. Wheaton to Churchman, 19 April 1949.

57 *SAB*, S-NR 1/4, f. 235, "Buffalo Narrows," J.W. Churchman to J.H. Brockelbank, 24 January 1951; D. LeChasseur to Churchman, 23 May 1951; D. LeChasseur and M. LeChasseur to Brockelbank, 1 August 1951; Brockelbank to Mr. and Mrs. LeChasseur, 16 August 1951; Brockelbank to Mr. and Mrs. LeChasseur, 15 January 1952; J.F. Gray to D. LaChasseur, 11 February 1952; Churchman to G.B. Stewart, 7 May 1954; C.S. Brown to A.T. Davidson, 6 December 1954; Churchman to Brown, 3 January 1955; S-NR 1/4, f. 230, "Northern District – General," v. 2, 1954-56, Brown to Davidson, 2 April 1954; S-NR 1/4, f. 822, "Waite Fisheries – General," Churchman to C.L. MacLean, 7 April 1951; S-NR 1/5, v. I, f. 76, (411), "Buffalo Narrows, 1957-1961," A.G. Kuziak to Stewart, 16 August 1961; S-NR 1/5, v. I, f. 88, (426), "Cumberland House – General, 1961," Kuziak to Stewart, 22 August 1961.

58 Alfred Montgrand, interview by author, Prince Albert, SK, August 1999; Churchill River Board of Inquiry, *Churchill River Board of Inquiry Report* (Regina: Sask. Dept. of Environment, 1978), 176-177; *SAB*, S-NR 1/4, f. 230, "Northern Region – General," v. III, 1957-, C.S. Brown to A.T. Davidson, 11 March 1957.

59 Dept. of Social Welfare and Rehab., *Annual Report*, 1954, 11; Dept. of Social Welfare and Rehab., *Annual Report*, 1956, 75; *SAB*, S-M 16, v. XIII, f. 22, "Alcoholism, General, 1962-64," "Alcoholism and the Indian," Conf. proceedings, Fort Qu'Appelle, SK, 8 November 1963; Sask. Bureau on Alcoholism, "Recommendations on a Provincial Alcoholism Program," 1959.

60 *SAB*, A 1109, John H. Brockelbank, interview by Murray Dobbin, audio tape, Regina, 19 August 1976.

61 Piercy, *Survey of Educational Facilities in Northern Saskatchewan*, 12-13; William D. Knill and Arthur K. Davis, "Provincial Education in Northern Saskatchewan: Progress and Bog Down, 1944-1962," in *A Northern Dilemma: Reference Papers*, vol. 1, ed. Arthur K. Davis et al. (Bellingham, WA: Western Washington State College, 1967), 199.

62 Lionel George Marshall, "The Development of Education in Northern Saskatchewan" (master's thesis, University of Saskatchewan, 1966), 157; M.P. Toombs, "The Control and Support of Public Education in Rupert's Land and the Northwest Territories to 1905 and Saskatchewan to 1960" (PhD diss., University of Minnesota, 1962); William D. Knill, "Education and Northern Canada," *The Canadian Administrator* 3, 3 (December 1963): 10.

63 Marshall, "The Development of Education," 159; *SAB*, S-NR 1/4, f. 167 B3, "Northern Region," 1 April 1956, N. Dist. Field Officers' Conf., 9-13 January 1951.

64 *SAB*, R-907.2, v. II, f. 12, "J.J. Wheaton, Northern Administrator," C.H. Piercy and Wheaton to J.L. Phelps, 23 March 1948; Report on meeting between prov. and fed. reps. of Dept. of Indian Affairs, 7 October 1947.

65 Evangeline LeMaigre, "La Loche: Its History and Development," unpublished essay (April

1978); Institute for Northern Studies, *Beauval Community Planning Study* (Saskatoon: University of Saskatchewan, 1979), 12-13; Paul Hurly, "Beauval, Saskatchewan: An Historical Sketch," *Saskatchewan History* 33, 3 (Autumn 1980): 102-110; Marshall, "The Development of Education," 182-188; Spaulding, "The Metis of Ile-a-la-Crosse," 32-33; *SAB*, DNS-1, Dept. of Northern Saskatchewan, (GS-201), v. VIII, f. 11, "History and Culture Report," D. McLeod, "History and Culture Report – Stanley Mission – La Ronge," undated; R-517, v. XIII, f. 62, "Ile a la Crosse," 1963-68, Memo for file, 16 March 1965; S-M16, v. VII, f. 3, "Parks and Lands Branch, 1961-63," Minutes, N. Adv. Comm., 7 January 1954 and 29 March 1954; Wuorinen, *A History of Buffalo Narrows*, 30-31.

66 Kew, *Cumberland House*, 109.

67 La Ronge Heritage Committee, *Our Roots*.

68 Department of Citizenship and Immigration, *Indian Education: The Indian in Transition* (Ottawa: Department of Citizenship and Immigration, IAB, 1964), 4-5; Toombs, "The Control and Support of Public Education"; *SAB*, R-907.2, v. II, f. 12, "J.J. Wheaton, Northern Administrator," Minutes, N. Co-Ord. Comm. Mtg., 23 April 1948; S-M 16, v. XV, f. 14, "Indians, 1955-64," "Review of Progress in Programs to Promote Integration and Economic Development," undated; S-NR 1/4, f. 230, "Northern District – General," v. 2, 1954-56; "Tribal Chief Criticizes North School System," *Hudson Bay Post-Review*, 14 December 1955; William D. Knill, "North of the 53rd, Part 2: The Piercy Era," *The Saskatchewan Bulletin* 30, 3 (March 1964): 46-52; Knill and Davis, "Provincial Education in Northern Saskatchewan," 225.

69 DNR, *The New North*, 30; Knill, "Education and Northern Canada," 10; Knill, "North of the 53rd, Part 2," 46-52; Knill and Davis, "Provincial Education in Northern Saskatchewan," 190; *Progress: A Survey of Saskatchewan Government Activity* (Regina: Bureau of Publications, 1955), 66; Toombs, "The Control and Support of Public Education."

70 Knill and Davis, "Provincial Education in Northern Saskatchewan," 205, 213, 225.

71 *SAB*, S-NR 1/3, Department of Natural Resources Deputy Minister, f. G-1-7, "Community Planning, General, 1948-50," C.A.L. Hogg to A. McCallum, 17 November 1948; McCallum to Hogg, 3 December 1948.

72 *SAB*, S-NR 1/4, f. 235, "Cree Lake," (2 files), J.W. Churchman to C.L. MacLean, 8 July 1952. By the following year, DNR no longer had an officer at Cree Lake.

73 *SAB*, DNS-1, v. VIII, f. 7, "History and Culture Report – Kinoosao," L. Olson, "History and Culture Report – Kinoosao (Co-Op Point)," undated.

74 Kenneth Dalton Collier, "Underdevelopment and Social Spending in the Advanced Periphery: Mid-Wales and Northern Saskatchewan" (PhD diss., University of Wales, 1991), 202; Laurie Barron, *Walking in Indian Moccasins: The Native Policies of Tommy Douglas and the CCF* (Vancouver: UBC Press, 1997); Marshall, "The Development of Education," 163, 167; *SAB*, S-NR 1/5, v. I, f. 69, "General – Northern Affairs, 1958-1961," Treasury Department, Comptroller's Office, Arrangements for vocational training in Saskatoon for Metis children from the NAD, 30 August 1960; Knill and Davis, "Provincial Education in Northern Saskatchewan," 205.

75 Buckley, Kew, and Hawley, *The Indians and Metis of Northern Saskatchewan*, 27, 32; Kew, *Cumberland House*, 20; Marshall, "The Development of Education," 171; Wuorinen, *A History of Buffalo Narrows*, 31; *SAB*, R-517, v. XIII, f. 62, "Ile a la Crosse," 1963-68, Memo for file, 16 March 1965; S-NR 1/5, v. III, f. 20, "Cumberland House – General," 1962-67, J.D. Neilson, "Program Planning Guide for Community of Cumberland House Saskatchewan," 1962.

76 Knill, "North of the 53rd, Part 3," *The Saskatchewan Bulletin* 30, 4 (April 1964): 34-37; Knill and Davis, "Provincial Education in Northern Saskatchewan," 246.

77 K. Izumi and G.R. Arnott, *A Guide for Development: Uranium City and District* (Regina: Community Planning Branch, Department of Municipal Affairs, 1956), 41; *Progress: A Survey*, 66; *SAB*, DNS-1, v. VIII, f. 12, "History and Culture Report – Uranium City," D. Belanger, F. Halkett, C. Dusseault, "History and Culture – Uranium City," undated; R-907.2, v. II, f. 4a, "J.W. Churchman, Deputy Minister, March 1948-March 1949," Churchman to C.A.L. Hogg, 17 September 1948.

78 DNR, *The New North*, 30; Toombs, "The Control and Support of Public Education"; Knill, "North of the 53rd, Part 2," 46-52.

79 *SAB*, S-M16, v. VII, f. 3, "Parks and Lands Branch, 1961-63," Brief by N. Adv. Comm. on

Metis of N. Sask., 1955; S-NR 1/5, v. I, f. 39, (230), "Northern Region, 1957-1959," A. Darche to G. MacDonald, 18 June 1959; A.H. MacDonald to J.W. Churchman, 13 May 1959; A.H. MacDonald to Churchman, 22 June 1959; M. Miller to Churchman, 3 June 1959.

80 DNR, *Annual Report*, 1963, 122; Knill and Davis, "Provincial Education in Northern Saskatchewan, 190.

Epilogue: We Will Measure Our Success

1 DNR, *Annual Report*, 1963, 118; Helen L. Buckley, J.E.M. Kew, and John B. Hawley, *The Indians and Metis of Northern Saskatchewan: A Report on Economic and Social Development* (Saskatoon: Center for Community Studies, University of Saskatchewan, 1963), Foreword, 37, 38, 41, 50, 57, 102.

2 Arthur K. Davis et al., *A Northern Dilemma: Reference Papers*, vols. 1 and 2 (Bellingham, WA: Western Washington State College, 1967); *Glenbow Archives*, M125, James Brady Collection, s. III, "Correspondence," 1933-67, f. 19, "Davis, Arthur K.," 1959-66, Davis to Dear Friend, 22 September 1963.

3 Dale Eisler, *Rumours of Glory: Saskatchewan and the Thatcher Years* (Edmonton: Hurtig Publishers, 1987), 153; *Glenbow Archives*, M125, s. II, v. 8, "Personal," 1952-62, Unrecognized Signature to J. Brady, 28 January 1963.

4 Mildred E. Battel, *Children Shall Be First: Child Welfare Saskatchewan 1944-64* (1979), 16.

5 Ivan Avakumovic, *Socialism in Canada: A Study of the CCF-NDP in Federal and Provincial Politics* (Toronto: McClelland and Stewart, 1978), 173-180; F. Laurie Barron, *Walking in Indian Moccasins: The Native Policies of Tommy Douglas and the CCF* (Vancouver: UBC Press, 1997), 202; Evelyn L. Eager, "The Government of Saskatchewan" (PhD diss., University of Toronto, 1957), 339-383; Norman Penner, *From Protest to Power: Social Democracy in Canada 1900-Present* (Toronto: Lorimer, 1992), 114-116; John Richards and Larry Pratt, *Prairie Capitalism: Power and Influence in the New West* (Toronto: McClelland and Stewart, 1979), 97-210; Leo Zakuta, *A Protest Movement Becalmed: A Study of Change in the CCF* (Toronto: University of Toronto Press, 1964), 86-103.

6 Examples of other governments taking an interest in managing, controlling, and owning northern resources include Alberta's Pacific Western Airlines, Ottawa's Eldorado Mining and Refining, and various provinces' hydroelectric utilities. In each of these cases, governments did not claim a general ideological opposition to the participation of private enterprise in the northern region. Instead, those governments encouraged the continued involvement of private capital in most aspects of northern development.

Bibliography

Primary Sources

Archives

Glenbow Archives
M125. James Brady Collection. Series I, Series II, Series III, Series VI, Series VII. Various files.

Saskatchewan Archives Board – Ministerial Papers
S-M15. Joseph Lee Phelps Ministerial Papers, 1944-48. Box 2, Box 4, Box 5, Box 6, Box 7, Box 8, Box 9, Box 10, Box 11, Box 12, Box 13, Box 14, Box 15, Box 16, Box 18, Box 36.
S-M16. A.M. Nicholson Papers. Files VI.10, VI.11, VII, VIII, IX, XIII.1, XIII.6, XIII.9, XIII.15, XIII.22, XIII.24, XIII.25, XIII.34, XIII.49, XIII.246, XIII.247, XIII.248, XIII.249, XIII.250a, XIII.250b, XIII.251, XIII.264, XIII.293, XV.14, XVI.1, XX.7.
S-M16.1. A.M. Nicholson Papers. Files I.1, I.2, I.3, I.4, I.5a, I.6, III.40.

Records of the Department of Health
R-517. Community Health Services Branch (GR-278). Files XIII.1, XIII.2, XIII.3, XIII.4, XIII.5, XIII.6, XIII.7, XIII.8, XIII.9, XIII.10, XIII.11, XIII.12, XIII.13, XIII.14, XIII.15, XIII.16, XIII.21, XIII.22, XIII.23, XIII.24, XIII.25, XIII.28, XIII.29, XIII.34, XIII.50, XIII.53, XIII.55, XIII.56, XIII.57, XIII,58, XIII.60, XIII.61, XIII.62, XIII.63, XIII.64, XIII.65, XIII.66.
R-1489. Regional Health Services Branch. Files I.1a, I.1b, I.2, I.3, I.4, I.5, I.6, I.7a, I.7b, I.7c, I.8, I.9, I.10, I.11, I.12, I.13a, I.13b, I.13c, I.13d, I.13e, I.13f, I.13g, I.13h, I.13i.

Records of the Department of Natural Resources
S-NR 1/2. Deputy Minister Files, 1936-47. File 135.
R-782. Files I.1, I.2, I.3, I.4, I.5, I.6, I.7, I.8, I.10, I.11, I.12, I.13, I.14, I.15, I.16, I.17, I.18, I.19, I.20, I.21, II.1, II.2, II.3, II.4, II.4, II.5, II.6, II.7, II.8, II.9, III.1, IV.1, IV.2, IV.3, IV.4a, IV.4b, IV.4c, IV.5, IV.5, IV.6.
R-A971. Audiotape. Interview with Phelps re north.
R-A1108. Audiotape. Interview with John H. Brockelbank re north.
R-A1109. Audiotape. Interview with Brockelbank re north.
R-A1113. Audiotape. Interview with Phelps re north.
R-38. Audiotape. Interview with Phelps re CCF history.
R-8452 to 8453. Audiotape. Interview with Phelps re Crown corporations, etc.
S-NR 1/3. C.A.L. Hogg, Deputy Minister Files. Files G-1-7, G-2-4, G-8-1, NR-8-3.
S-NR 1/4. Deputy Minister and Assistant Deputy Minister Files. Files 113C, 112 D, 122 D, 132 A3, 137C, 137C1, 137C2, 137C4, 137C6, 137C7, 137C8, 137C9, 137C10, 137C11, 137C12, 137K, 137K3, 137K3B, 141C, 162, 167B3, 213, 214, 230, 231B, 235, 235A, 236, 236A, 236E, 255, 313C, 412C, 430, 432, 433, 444, 551C, 822.

S-NR 1/5. I. General. Files 16, 19, 20, 39, 41, 45, 69, 74, 76, 80, 84, 85, 88, 93, 131, 132, 134, 144.
   II. Regions. Files 4, 6.
   III. Files 7, 8, 11, 16a, 16b, 17a, 17b, 20, 24a, 24b, 34.
S-NR 2. Assistant Deputy Minister, 1942-55. Files 1 to 63.
S-NR2. C. Personnel Files. Files 14, 77.

Records of the Department of Northern Saskatchewan
DNR-1. Files III.A.120, III.A.122, III.A.123, III.A.170, III.A.172, VII.10, VII.11, VII.18, VII.19, VII.34, VII.35, VII.36, VII.37, VII.38, VII.39, VIII.7, VIII.8, VIII.9, VIII.10, VIII.11, VIII.12.

Records of the Department of Social Services
R-646. Historical information on Department of Social Welfare, 1944-67 and Books and Pamphlets, 1944-65.
R-927. Agricultural Rehabilitation Development Act (ARDA) (GR305). Files 1.4, 1.5, 1.13, 1.50.

Interviews by Author
Acco, Anne. Cumberland House, Saskatchewan. 21 July 1999.
Carriere, Angus. Cumberland House, Saskatchewan. 23 July 1999.
Carriere, John. Cumberland House, Saskatchewan. 22 July 1999.
Charles, Elizabeth. Stanley Mission, Saskatchewan. 14 July 1999.
Chartier, Pierre. Buffalo Narrows, Saskatchewan. 5 July 1999.
Cheechum, Ernestine. La Loche, Saskatchewan. 8 July 1999.
Clarke, Bruce. Buffalo Narrows, Saskatchewan. 9 July 1999.
Fietz, Janet. La Ronge, Saskatchewan. 15 July 1999.
Fosseneuve, Charles. Cumberland House, Saskatchewan. 21 July 1999.
Fosseneuve, Marcel. Cumberland House, Saskatchewan. 22 July 1999.
Gooding, Robert. Prince Albert, Saskatchewan. 4 August 1999.
Goulet, Solomon. Cumberland House, Saskatchewan. 23 July 1999.
Hanson, John and Mary. Buffalo Narrows, Saskatchewan. 5 July 1999.
Lemaigre, Evangeline. Clearwater River Dene Nation, La Loche, Saskatchewan. 6 July 1999.
Lemaigre, Tobie. La Loche, Saskatchewan. 8 July 1999.
L'Heureux, Marcel. La Ronge, Saskatchewan. 15 July 1999.
Merasty, Philip. Island Falls, Saskatchewan. 12 July 2000.
Montgrand, Alfred. Prince Albert, Saskatchewan. 10 August 1999.
Montgrand, Gertrude. Prince Albert, Saskatchewan. 10 August 1999.
Quandt, Allan. La Ronge, Saskatchewan. 16 July 1999.
Sanderson, Henry. La Ronge, Saskatchewan. 14 July 1999.

Other Primary Sources
Amisk Planning Consultants. *A Community Planning Study for Buffalo Narrows.* Prepared for the Buffalo Narrows Local Community Authority and the Department of Northern Saskatchewan. N.p., 1978.
Baker, W.B. *Some Observations on the Application of Community Development to the Settlements of Northern Saskatchewan.* Saskatoon: University of Saskatchewan, Center for Community Studies, n.d.
Ballantyne, Philip. *The Land Alone/Aski-Puko.* A report on the expected effects of the proposed hydro-electric installation at Wintego Rapids upon the Cree of the Peter Ballantyne and Lac La Ronge Bands. Federation of Saskatchewan Indians, Lac La Ronge and Peter Ballantyne Band. Saskatchewan: n.p., 1976.
Bélanger, D., F. Halkett, and C. Dusseault. "History and Culture – Uranium City." n.d.
Brown, C.S. "An Investigation of Problems Related to the Development of Recreational Resources of Lac La Ronge." Planning Division, Department of Natural Resources, Province of Saskatchewan, 1951 or 1952.
Canada. Dominion Bureau of Statistics. Census of Canada. 1941, 1946, 1951, 1956, 1961.

Cass-Beggs, D. "Industrial Development Panel." Northern Saskatchewan Development Conference, Saskatoon, SK, 20-21 November 1957.
–. *Energy and Resource Development*. Report to Saskatchewan Resources Conference, Saskatoon, SK, 20-21 January 1964.
Center for Community Studies. "Program – Far Northern Research." Saskatoon: Center for Community Studies, University of Saskatchewan, 1959.
–. *Developing Saskatchewan's Community Resources. Saskatchewan Approaches Community Development, Prerequisites for a Social Technology*. Report to Council in Social Work Education, Montreal, 4 February 1961.
Churchill River Basin Task Force. *Churchill River Basin Task Force Report*. Report to the Members of the Canada-Saskatchewan-Manitoba Joint Consultative Committee, 1972.
Churchill River Board of Inquiry. *Northern Briefs Submitted to the Churchill River Board of Inquiry from the Directly Affected Communities*. 1977.
–. *Churchill River Board of Inquiry Report*. Regina: Saskatchewan Department of Environment, 1978.
Committee on Saskatchewan River Delta Problems. *Resources, Development and Problems of the Saskatchewan River Delta*. Regina: Water Resources Commission, April 1972.
Co-operative Commonwealth Federation. "Regina Manifesto: Programme of the Co-operative Commonwealth Federation, adopted at First National Convention, held at Regina, Sask., July 1933." Regina: n.p., 1933.
Damas and Smith Ltd. *(Pelican Narrows); Community Planning Study; Summary Report and Recommendations*. Winnipeg, MB: Damas and Smith Ltd., 1977.
Davis, Arthur K., ed. With the assistance of Vernon C. Serl and Philip Spaulding. *A Northern Dilemma: Reference Papers*. Vol. 1 and 2. Bellingham, WA: Western Washington State College, 1967.
Directory of Education, Health, Welfare, Recreation, Rehabilitation Services in Saskatchewan. Regina: Co-Ordinating Council on Rehabilitation (Saskatchewan), 1961.
Douglas, T.C. "Progress Report on Co-Operation Among Fishermen." Speech. 1959.
Dryden, H. "Tourist Development Panel." Presented at the Northern Saskatchewan Development Conference, Saskatoon, SK, 20-21 November 1957.
General Information re: Department of Northern Saskatchewan. Saskatchewan: Department of Northern Saskatchewan, 15 October 1973.
Hamilton, F. Alvin G. Address to Northern Saskatchewan Development Conference, Saskatoon, SK, 20-21 November 1957.
Health Survey Committee. "Index of Hospital Descriptions." *Report to Government of Saskatchewan - Federal Health Survey Grant*. Regina, SK, 1951.
Hlady, Walter M. "Summary, A Social and Economic Study of Sandy Bay." Survey, June-September, 1959. Regina: Saskatchewan Department of Natural Resources and/or Department of the Environment, 1959.
Hylton, John H. *The La Loche Report*. Prepared for the Saskatchewan Municipal Government. Regina: Saskatchewan Municipal Government, 1993.
Institute for Northern Studies. *Beauval Community Planning Study*. Saskatoon: University of Saskatchewan, 1979.
Izumi, K., and G.R. Arnott. *A Guide for Development: Uranium City and District*. Regina: Community Planning Branch, Department of Municipal Affairs, 1956.
Karras, A.L. *North to Cree Lake*. New York: Trident Press, 1970.
–. *Face the North Wind*. Don Mills, ON: Burns and MacEachern, 1975.
Kemp, H.S.M. *Northern Trader*. Toronto: The Ryerson Press, 1956.
Kew, J.E.M. *Cumberland House in 1960*. Saskatoon: Center for Community Studies, University of Saskatchewan, March 1962.
King, Carlyle. "The CCF Sweeps Saskatchewan." *Canadian Forum* 24 (July 1944): 79.
Olson, Laverne. "History and Culture Report – Kinoosao (Co-Op Point)." N.d.
Parres, J.C. "Transportation Panel." Presented at the Northern Saskatchewan Development Conference, Saskatoon, SK, 20-21 November 1957.
Partridge, E.F. Presentation for "Mining Resource Panel," Northern Saskatchewan Development Conference, Saskatoon, SK, 20-21 November 1957.
Phalen, J.T. Letter to Harold (Chapman). 9 September 1997.
Piercy, C.H. *Survey of Educational Facilities in Northern Saskatchewan, Part 1: The Areas in the*

Remote Northern Part of the Province of Saskatchewan. Unpublished paper, 18 December 1944.

Proceedings of the Northern Saskatchewan Development Conference. Sponsored by the Saskatchewan Chamber of Commerce, Saskatoon, SK, 20-21 November 1957.

Proceedings "Resources for People" Saskatchewan Resources Conference. Saskatoon, SK, 20-21 January 1964.

Progress: A Survey of Saskatchewan Government Activity. 4th Edition. Regina: Bureau of Publications, 1955.

Progress Report from Your Government: A Survey of Saskatchewan Government Activity. Regina: Bureau of Publications, 1948.

Richards, J. Howard. *Recreation Potential of the Saskatchewan River Delta Area.* Ottawa, ON: Canada. Department of Forestry and Rural Development, ARDA, 1966.

Roberts, Vicky. "History and Culture – La Ronge." Undated.

Ross, Hugh Mackay. *The Manager's Tale: Saskatchewan District.* Winnipeg, MB: J. Gordon Shillingford Publishing, 1989.

Saskatchewan. Bureau of Publications. *Government in Industry: A Brief Account of Saskatchewan Crown Corporations.* Regina: Bureau of Publications, 1947.

Saskatchewan. Bureau of Statistics. *Saskatchewan Economic Review,* No. 1 to 27. Regina: Bureau of Statistics, 1951 to 1973.

Saskatchewan. Department of Highways. *Travel on Saskatchewan Highways.* Regina: Department of Highways, Planning Branch, 1958-64.

Saskatchewan. Department of Mineral Resources. *Saskatchewan's Metallic and Industrial Minerals.* Regina: Department of Mineral Resources, 1961.

Saskatchewan. Department of Natural Resources. Annual Reports. Regina: Department of Natural Resources, 1944 to 1971.

–. *Saskatchewan's Forests.* Regina: Queen's Printer, 1955.

–. *The New North: Saskatchewan's Northern Development Program, 1945-1948.* Regina: Department of Natural Resources, 1948.

Saskatchewan. Department of Natural Resources and Industrial Development. *The Natural Resources of Saskatchewan.* Regina: Department of Natural Resources and Industrial Development, 1945 and 1947.

–. *"According to Plan": Prospectors' Assistance Plan – Saskatchewan.* Prepared by W. James Bichan (Mineral Resources Branch, director). Regina: Department of Natural Resources and Industrial Development, 1949.

Saskatchewan. Department of Public Health. *Outline of Services.* Regina: Department of Public Health, Division of Health Education, 1958.

Saskatchewan. Department of Social Welfare. Annual Reports. Regina: Department of Social Welfare, 1944-49.

Saskatchewan. Department of Social Welfare and Rehabilitation. Annual Reports. Regina: Department of Social Welfare and Rehabilitation, 1950-64.

–. *Social Welfare in Saskatchewan.* Regina: Department of Social Welfare and Rehabilitation, 1960.

Saskatchewan. Government Finance Office. *Public Enterprise in Saskatchewan.* 1964.

Saskatchewan. Health Survey Committee. *Saskatchewan Health Survey Report.* Vol. 1 and 2. Regina: n.p., 1951.

Saskatchewan. Industrial Development Office. *Proceedings of "Building from Within" Industrial Development Conference.* Sponsored by Industrial Development Office. Regina, SK, 29-30 November 1956.

Saskatchewan. Royal Commission on Agriculture and Rural Life. *Crown Land Settlement in Northeastern Saskatchewan.* Interim Report to the Government of Saskatchewan. Regina: 1954.

Saskatchewan. Urban Affairs (Community Planning Branch). *Buffalo Narrows Planning Study Review: Background Study.* Prepared by Pineridge Consultants, and Village of Buffalo Narrows. 1985.

Saskatchewan Chamber of Commerce. *Report of Northern Saskatchewan Development Conference.* Saskatoon, SK, 20-21 November 1957.

Saskatchewan Plans for Progress: A Summary of Legislation Passed at the Special Session of the Saskatchewan Legislature, October 19-November 10, 1944. Regina: Bureau of Publications, 1945.

Scott, Frank R. *A New Endeavour: Selected Political Essays, Letters, and Addresses.* Edited and introduced by Michiel Horn. Toronto: University of Toronto Press, 1986.

Semchuk, Martin. "Transportation Panel." Northern Saskatchewan Development Conference. Saskatoon, SK, 20-21 November 1957.

Sigerist Health Services Survey Commission. *Report of the Commissioner.* Regina: Public Health, Health Services Survey Commission, 4 October 1944.

Smith, David E. *Building a Province: A History of Saskatchewan in Documents.* Saskatoon: Fifth House Publishers, 1992.

Stanford Research Institute. *A Study of Resources and Industrial Opportunities for the Province of Saskatchewan.* Report prepared for Saskatchewan Industrial Development Office, Economic Advisory and Planning Board. Menlo Park, CA: Stanford Research Institute, 1959.

Thomas, Lewis H., ed. *The Making of a Socialist: The Recollections of T.C. Douglas.* Edmonton: University of Alberta Press, 1982.

Underwood McLellan Ltd. *Pinehouse Planning Study.* Saskatoon: The UMA Group, 1981.

Valentine, V.F. "Some Problems of the Metis of Northern Saskatchewan." *The Canadian Journal of Economics and Political Science* 20, 1 (1954): 89-95.

–. *The Metis of Northern Saskatchewan.* Regina: Department of Natural Resources, 1955.

Valentine, V.F., and R.G. Young. "The Situation of the Metis of Northern Saskatchewan in Relation to His Physical and Social Environment." *The Canadian Geographer* 4 (1954): 49-56.

Worsley, P.M., Helen L. Buckley, Arthur K. Davis. *Economic and Social Survey of Northern Saskatchewan.* Interim Report No. 1. Saskatoon: Center for Community Studies, University of Saskatchewan, March 1961.

Secondary Sources (Reports, Periodicals, and Books)

Abrams, Gary William David. *Prince Albert: The First Century, 1866-1966.* Saskatoon: Modern Press, 1966.

Abramson, Jane A. *Women and Work in Northern Saskatchewan.* Draft. 1975.

Adams, Howard (Survey Director). *The Outsiders: An Educational Survey of Metis and Non-Treaty Indians of Saskatchewan.* Saskatoon: Metis Society of Saskatchewan, June 1972.

Allen, Richard, ed. *A Region of the Mind: Interpreting the Western Canadian Plains.* Regina: Canadian Plains Studies Centre, University of Saskatchewan, Regina, 1973.

Archer, John H. *Saskatchewan: A History.* Saskatoon: Western Producer Prairie Books, 1980.

Arrowsmith, W.A. "Northern Saskatchewan and the Fur Trade." Master's thesis, University of Saskatchewan, 1964.

Avakumovic, Ivan. *Socialism in Canada: A Study of the CCF-NDP in Federal and Provincial Politics.* Toronto: McClelland and Stewart, 1978.

Badgley, Robin F., and Samuel Wolfe. *Doctors' Strike: Medical Care and Conflict in Saskatchewan.* Toronto: Macmillan of Canada, 1967.

Bailey, Richard W. "Housing for Indians and Metis in Northern Saskatchewan." *Habitat* 2, 4 (1968): 18-23.

Barron, F. Laurie. *Walking in Indian Moccasins: The Native Policies of Tommy Douglas and the CCF.* Vancouver: UBC Press, 1997.

Bartlett, Richard H. "Indian and Native Rights in Uranium Development in Northern Saskatchewan." Special edition, "Uranium Development in Saskatchewan," of *Saskatchewan Law Review* 45, 1 (1980-81): 13-51.

–. "Hydroelectric Power and Indian Water Rights on the Prairies." *Prairie Forum* 14, 2 (Fall 1989): 177-193.

Battel, Mildred. *Children Shall Be First: Child Welfare Saskatchewan 1944-64.* Regina: Saskatchewan Department of Culture and Youth, 1979.

The Beaver. 1960 to present.

Beeching, W.C., and Morden Lazarus. "Le Socialisme en Saskatchewan: Trop ou Trop Peu?" *Socialisme 64, Revue du socialisme international et québécois* 2 (Autumn 1964): 16-32.

Best, S.C., and J.W. Gerrard. "Pine House (Saskatchewan) Nutrition Project." *Canadian Medical Association Journal* 81 (December 1959): 915-917.

Best, S.C., J.W. Gerrard, A.C. Irwin, Dorren Kerr, Mildred Flanagan, and Marjorie Black. "The Pine House (Saskatchewan) Nutrition Project. II." *Canadian Medical Association Journal* 85 (August 1961): 412-414.

Bicentennial Committee of Cumberland House. *A History of Cumberland House ... As Told By Its Own Citizens, 1774 to 1974.* Cumberland House, SK: Bicentennial Committee, 1974.

Big River History Book Committee. *Timber Trails: History of Big River and District.* North Battleford, SK: Turner-Warwick Printers, 1979.

Blakeney, A.E. "Saskatchewan's Crown Corporations: A Case Study." In *The Proceedings of the Fifth Annual Conference of the Institute of Public Administration of Canada, Saskatoon, September 9-12, 1953,* edited by Philip T. Clark, 413-420. Toronto: Institute of Public Administration of Canada.

Bone, Robert M. *Canadian Western Northland: Some Observations and Examples from Northern Communities.* Saskatoon: Institute for Northern Studies, University of Saskatchewan, 1974.

–. *The Geography of the Canadian North: Issues and Challenges.* Toronto: Oxford University Press, 1992.

Bone, Robert M. With the assistance of R. Larsen, P.G. Osrunn, and T.W. Foster. *Regional Socio-Economic Development.* Saskatoon: Institute for Northern Studies, University of Saskatchewan, 1973.

Bone, Robert M., ed. *The Chipewyan of the Stony Rapids Region.* Mawdsley Memoir No. 1. Saskatoon: Institute for Northern Studies, University of Saskatchewan, 1973.

Bone, Robert M., and Milford B. Green. "Jobs and Access: A Northern Dilemma." *Journal of Canadian Studies* 18, 3 (Fall 1983): 90-101.

Bourgeault, Ronald Graham. "The Development of Capitalism and the Subjugation of Native Women in Northern Canada." *Alternate Routes* 6 (1983): 109-140.

–. "Class Race and Gender: Political Economy and the Canadian Fur Trade 1670s to 1820s." Master's thesis, University of Regina, 1986.

–. "The Struggle for Class and Nation: The Origin of the Métis in Canada and the National Question." In *1492-1992: Five Centuries of Imperialism and Resistance.* Vol. 8 of *Socialist Studies/Études Socialistes,* edited by Ronald Bourgeault et al., 153-187. Winnipeg, MB/Halifax, NS: Society for Socialist Studies/Fernwood Publishing, 1992.

"Brief History of Social Assistance." In *Issues in Welfare.* Saskatchewan Social Services Planning and Evaluation, 1982.

Brown, C.S. "The Application of Regional Surveys in Provincial Administration, with an Example from the Buffalo Region of Northwestern Saskatchewan." *The Canadian Geographer* 4 (1954): 39-48.

Brownstone, M. "The Douglas-Lloyd Governments: Innovation and Bureaucratic Adaptation." In *Essays on the Left: Essays in Honour of T.C. Douglas,* edited by Laurier LaPierre, Jack McLeod, Charles Taylor, and Walter Young, 65-80. Toronto: McClelland and Stewart, 1971.

Buckley, Helen L. *Trapping and Fishing in the Economy of Northern Saskatchewan.* Report Number 3, Economic and Social Survey of Northern Saskatchewan. Saskatoon: Research Division, Center for Community Studies, University of Saskatchewan, 1962.

–. "Raising Incomes in Northern Saskatchewan." In *Research Review 1,* edited by Jean Foulds, 10-12. Saskatoon: Center for Community Studies, University of Saskatchewan, 1963.

–. *Working Paper on the Commercial Fishing Industry in Northern Saskatchewan.* Saskatoon: Center for Community Studies, University of Saskatchewan, 1963.

Buckley, Helen L., J.E.M. Kew, and John B. Hawley. *The Indians and Metis of Northern Saskatchewan: A Report on Economic and Social Development.* Saskatoon: Center for Community Studies, University of Saskatchewan, 1963.

Cadbury, G.W. "Planning in Saskatchewan." In *Essays on the Left: Essays in Honour of T.C. Douglas,* edited by Laurier LaPierre, Jack McLeod, Charles Taylor, and Walter Young, 51-64. Toronto: McClelland and Stewart, 1971.

Canada. Department of Citizenship and Immigration. Indian Affairs Branch. *Indian Education: The Indian in Transition.* Ottawa: Department of Citizenship and Immigration, IAB, 1964.

–. *The Indian Today: The Indian in Transition.* Ottawa: Department of Citizenship and Immigration, IAB, 1964.

Cheesman, R.L. "A History of Mineral Exploration in Saskatchewan." Paper presented to

Mining Convention of the Prospectors' and Developers' Association, Toronto, 7 March 1967.

Clifton, Archie Wayne. *Highway Engineering in Northern Saskatchewan*. Master's thesis, University of Saskatchewan, 1966.

Coates, Kenneth, and William Morrison. *The Forgotten North: A History of Canada's Provincial Norths*. Toronto: Lorimer, 1992.

–, eds. *For Purposes of Dominion*. North York, ON: Captus Press, 1989.

Collier, Kenneth Dalton. "Underdevelopment and Social Spending in the Advanced Periphery: Mid-Wales and Northern Saskatchewan." PhD diss., University of Wales, 1991.

Crown Investments Corporation of Saskatchewan and Gordon W. MacLean. *Public Enterprise in Saskatchewan*. Regina: Crown Investments Corporation of Saskatchewan, 1981.

Cruikshank, Julie. "Oral Tradition and Oral History: Reviewing Some Issues." *Canadian Historical Review* 75, 3 (1994): 403-418.

–. *The Social Life of Stories: Narrative and Knowledge in the Yukon Territory*. Vancouver/Lincoln: UBC Press/University of Nebraska Press, 1998.

Daniel, Richard C. *A History of Native Claims Processes in Canada, 1867-1979*. Ottawa: Department of Indian Affairs and Northern Development, 1980.

Davidson, A.T. "Role of Geographers in Northern Saskatchewan." *Canadian Geographer* 4 (1954): 33-38.

Davies, W.A. "A Brief History of the Churchill River." *The Musk-Ox* 15 (1975): 30-38.

Davis, Arthur K. "The Saskatchewan CCF." *Our Generation* 6, 4 (1969).

–. "Edging into Mainstream: Urban Indians in Saskatchewan." In *A Northern Dilemma: Reference Papers*. Vol. 1. Edited by Arthur K. Davis et al., 338-530. Bellingham, WA: Western Washington State College, 1967.

Davis, Robert, and Mark Zannis. *The Genocide Machine in Canada: The Pacification of the North*. Montreal: Black Rose Books, 1973.

Dibb, Sandra, ed. *Northern Saskatchewan Bibliography*. Mawdsley Memoir 2. Saskatoon: Institute for Northern Studies, University of Saskatchewan, 1975.

Dobbin, Murray. *The One-And-A-Half Men: The Story of Jim Brady and Malcolm Norris, Metis Patriots of the Twentieth Century*. Vancouver: New Star Books, 1981.

–. "Prairie Colonialism: The CCF in Northern Saskatchewan, 1944-1964." *Studies in Political Economy: A Socialist Review* 16 (1985): 7-40.

Dyck, Betty L. *Running to Beat Hell: A Biography of A.M. (Sandy) Nicholson*. Regina: Canadian Plains Research Center, University of Regina, 1988.

Dyer, Aldrich J. *Indian, Metis and Inuit of Canada in Theses and Dissertations, 1892-1987*. Saskatoon: University of Saskatchewan, 1989.

Eager, Evelyn L. "The Government of Saskatchewan." PhD diss., University of Toronto, 1957.

–. "The Paradox of Power in the Saskatchewan CCF, 1944-1961." In *The Political Process in Canada: Essays in Honour of R. MacGregor Dawson*, edited by J.H. Aitchison, 118-135. Toronto: University of Toronto Press, 1963.

–. "The Conservatism of the Saskatchewan Electorate." In *Politics in Saskatchewan*, edited by Norman Ward and Duff Spafford, 1-19. Don Mills, ON: Longmans Canada, 1968.

–. *Saskatchewan Government: Politics and Pragmatism*. Saskatoon: Western Producer Prairie Books, 1980.

Eisler, Dale. *Rumours of Glory: Saskatchewan and the Thatcher Years*. Edmonton: Hurtig Publishers, 1987.

Fitzgerald, Denis Patrick. "Pioneer Settlement in Northern Saskatchewan." Parts 1 and 2. PhD diss., University of Minnesota, 1966.

Forestry Branch 1945-82. N.d.

Friesen, David W. *The Cree Indians of Northern Saskatchewan: An Overview of the Past and Present*. Saskatoon: Department of Anthropology/Archaeology, University of Saskatchewan, 1973.

Friesen, Gerald. *The Canadian Prairies: A History*. Toronto: University of Toronto Press, 1987.

Glover, R. "Cumberland House." *The Beaver* (December 1951): 4-7.

Goldstick, Miles. *Wollaston: People Resisting Genocide*. Montreal: Black Rose Books, 1987.

Goode, Peter, Joan Champ, and Leslie Amundson. *The Montreal Lake Region: Its History and Geography.* Saskatoon: Sentar Consultants, 1996.

Goulet, Keith. "Oral History as an Authentic and Credible Research Base for Curriculum: The Cree of Sandy Bay and Hydroelectric Power Development 1927-67, an Example." Master's thesis, University of Regina, 1986.

Graham-Cumming, G. "Health of the Original Canadians, 1867-1967." *Medical Services Journal of Canada* 23 (February 1967): 115-166.

Gruending, Dennis. *Promises to Keep: A Political Biography of Allan Blakeney.* Saskatoon: Western Producer Books, 1990.

Gulig, Anthony G. "Sizing up the Catch: Native-Newcomer Resource Competition and the Early Years of Saskatchewan's Northern Commercial Fishery." *Saskatchewan History* 47, 3 (Fall 1995): 3-11.

–. "In Whose Interest? Government-Indian Relations in Northern Saskatchewan and Wisconsin, 1900-1940." PhD diss., University of Saskatchewan, 1997.

Gzowski, Peter. "This Is Our Alabama." *Maclean's,* 6 July 1963, 20-24.

Harding, Bill. "The Two Faces of Public Ownership: From the Regina Manifesto to Uranium Mining." In *Social Policy and Social Justice: The NDP Government in Saskatchewan during the Blakeney Years,* edited by Jim Harding, 281-313. Waterloo, ON: Wilfrid Laurier University Press, 1995.

Hawthorne, H.B., ed. *A Survey of the Contemporary Indians of Canada: A Report on Economic, Political, Educational Needs and Policies.* Vol. 1 and 2. Ottawa: Indian Affairs Branch, 1966 (Vol. 1) and 1967 (Vol. 2).

Helm, June, Edward S. Rogers, and James G.E. Smith. "Intercultural Relations and Cultural Change in the Shield and Mackenzie Borderlands." In *Subarctic,* edited by June Helm, 146-157. Vol. 6 of *Handbook of North American Indians,* edited by William C. Sturtevant. Washington: Smithsonian Institution, 1981.

Higginbotham, C.H. *Off the Record: The CCF in Saskatchewan.* Toronto: McClelland and Stewart, 1968.

Hill, Heather. *Women in Northern Saskatchewan.* Prepared for the Department of Regional Economic Expansion. 1973.

Historical Atlas of Canada. Vol. 3. Toronto: University of Toronto Press, 1993.

Hlady, Walter M. "The Cumberland House Fur Project: The First Two Years." Special issue, "Cree Studies," of *Western Canadian Journal of Anthropology* 1, 1 (1969): 124-139.

Hurly, Paul. "Beauval, Saskatchewan: An Historical Sketch." *Saskatchewan History* 33, 3 (Autumn 1980): 102-110.

Iglauer, Edith. *Inuit Journey: The Co-Operative Adventure in Canada's North.* Madeira Park, BC: Harbour Publishing, 2000.

Institute for Northern Studies. *Directory of Northern Research at the University of Saskatchewan.* Saskatoon: University of Saskatchewan, 1973, 1974. 1973 edition compiled by Linda Hayward. 1974 edition compiled by Sandra Dibb.

Jarvenpa, Robert. "The People of Patuanak: The Ecology and Spatial Organization of a Southern Chipewyan Band." PhD diss., University of Minnesota, 1975.

–. "The Ubiquitous Bushman: Chipewyan-White Trapper Relations of the 1930s." In *Problems in the Prehistory of the North American Subarctic: The Athapaskan Question,* edited by J.W. Helmer, S. Van Dyke, and F.J. Kense, 165-183. Calgary, AB: Archaeological Association, Department of Archaeology, University of Calgary, 1977.

–. "Subarctic Indian Trappers and Band Society: The Economics of Male Mobility." *Human Ecology* 5, 3: (1977) 223-259.

–. *The Trappers of Patuanak: Toward a Spatial Ecology of Modern Hunters.* National Museum of Man Mercury Series, Canadian Ethnology Service Paper No. 67, Ottawa: National Museums of Canada, 1980.

Kew, J.E.M. "Metis-Indian Housing in Northern Saskatchewan." *Research Review 1* (1963): 13-16.

Knill, William D. "Education and Northern Canada." *The Canadian Administrator* 3, 3 (December 1963): 9-12.

–. "North of the 53rd." Parts 1, 2, and 3. *The Saskatchewan Bulletin* 30, 2 (February 1964): 26-31; 30, 3 (March 1964): 46-52; 30, 4 (April 1964): 34-37.

–. "Occupational Aspirations of Northern Saskatchewan Students." *The Alberta Journal of Educational Research* 10, 1 (March 1964): 3-16.

Knill, William D., and Arthur K. Davis. "Provincial Education in Northern Saskatchewan: Progress and Bog Down, 1944-1962." In *A Northern Dilemma: Reference Papers*. Vol. 1. Edited by Arthur K. Davis et al., 170-337. Bellingham, WA: Western Washington State College, 1967.

Koester, C.B., ed. *The Measure of the Man: Selected Speeches of Woodrow Stanley Lloyd*. Saskatoon: Western Producer Prairie Books, 1976.

Kupsch, W.O. *Pioneer Geologists in Saskatchewan*. Regina: Department of Mineral Resources, 1955.

Kupsch, W.O., and S.D. Hanson, eds. *Gold and Other Stories As Told to Barry Richards*. Regina: Saskatchewan Mining Association, 1986.

Kyba, Patrick. "Third Party Leadership in a Competitive Two Party Province: Alvin Hamilton and the Progressive Conservative Party in Saskatchewan, 1949-1957." *Saskatchewan History* 36, 1 (Winter 1983): 1-19.

Larmour, Jean. "The Douglas Government's Changing Emphasis on Public, Private, and Co-Operative Development in Saskatchewan, 1944-1961." In *"Building the Co-Operative Commonwealth": Essays on the Democratic Socialist Tradition in Canada*, Canadian Plains Proceedings 13, edited by J. William Brennan, 161-180. Regina: Canadian Plains Research Center, University of Regina, 1985.

–. "Jack Douglas and Saskatchewan's Highways." *Saskatchewan History* 38, 3 (Autumn 1985): 97-107.

La Ronge Heritage Committee. *Our Roots: A History of La Ronge*. La Ronge, SK: Lakeland Press, 1981.

Lautt, M.L. "Sociology and the Canadian Plains." In *A Region of the Mind: Interpreting the Western Canadian Plains*, edited by Richard Allen, 125-151. Regina: Canadian Plains Studies Centre, 1973.

Lavasseur, Léon. "Cultural Encounter: Some Differences Between Canada's Indians and Her More Recent Settlers." Toronto: Indian Eskimo Association of Canada, n.d.

Lee, H.S., and Laurier LaPierre, eds. "Tommy Douglas." (Audio recording.) The New Democratic Party of Canada, 1971.

"The Legacy of the Fur Trade." *Saskatchewan History* 1, 3 (October 1948): 21-22.

Leitch, Adelaide. "Pattern of Progress at Lac La Ronge." *Canadian Geographical Journal* 62, 3 (March 1961): 88-93.

Lemaigre, Evangeline. "La Loche: Its History and Development." Unpublished essay. April 1978.

Lewis, David. "North America's First Socialist Government." *The Progressive* (March 1949): 15-19.

Lewis, David, and Frank R. Scott. *Make This Your Canada*. Toronto: Central Canada Publishing Co., 1943.

Lewis, Sinclair. *Mantrap*. New York: Harcourt, Brace, 1926.

Lipset, Seymour Martin. "The CCF in Saskatchewan." In *Party Politics in Canada*, edited by H.G. Thorburn, 159-167. Scarborough, ON: Prentice-Hall, 1967.

–. *Agrarian Socialism*. Berkeley: University of California Press, 1968.

Lipset, Seymour Martin, Norman Ward, and John C. Courtney. "CCF Support in Saskatchewan." In *Voting in Canada*, edited by John C. Courtney, 186-190. Toronto: Prentice-Hall, 1967.

Lloyd, Dianne. *Woodrow: A Biography of W.S. Lloyd*. The Woodrow Lloyd Memorial Fund, 1979.

Longpré, Robert. *Ile-a-la-Crosse 1776-1976: Sakitawak Bi-Centennial*. Île-à-la-Crosse, SK: Ile-a-la-Crosse Bi-Centennial Committee and Ile-a-la-Crosse Local Community Authority, 1977.

Lovick, L.D., ed. *Tommy Douglas Speaks*. Lantzville, BC: Oolichan Books, 1979.

MacDonald, A.H. "Co-Operatives and People of Indian Ancestry." *Canadian Co-Operative Digest* 3, 1 (Spring 1960): 31-38.

MacDonald, Christine. *Publications of the Governments of the Northwest Territories 1876-1905 and of the Province of Saskatchewan 1905-1952*. Regina: Legislative Library, 1952.

MacNeish, June Helm. "Leadership Among the Northeastern Athabascans." *Anthropologica* 2 (1956): 131-163.

MacPherson, Ian. "The CCF and the Co-Operative Movement in the Douglas Years: An

Uneasy Alliance." In *"Building the Co-Operative Commonwealth": Essays on the Democratic Socialist Tradition in Canada,* Canadian Plains Proceedings 13, edited by J. William Brennan, 181-203. Regina: Canadian Plains Research Center, University of Regina, 1985.

Marsh, James H., ed. *The Canadian Encyclopedia.* 2nd ed. Edmonton: Hurtig Publishers, 1988.

Marshall, Lionel George. "The Development of Education in Northern Saskatchewan." Master's thesis, University of Saskatchewan, 1966.

–. "The Development of Education in Northern Saskatchewan." *The Musk-Ox* 1 (1967): 19-25.

McCutcheon, M.K., and R.G. Young. "The Development of Uranium City." *The Canadian Geographer* 4 (1954): 57-62.

McHenry, Dean E. *The Third Force in Canada: The Co-Operative Commonwealth Federation, 1932-1948.* Westport, CT: Greenwood Press, 1950.

McKague, Ormond. "The Saskatchewan CCF: Education Policy and the Rejection of Socialism, 1942-1948." *The Journal of Educational Thought* 14, 2 (August 1980): 138-159.

McKay, Virginia, Jean Carriere, Pierre Dorion, and Marie Deschambault. *History and Culture Report: Cumberland House.* Undated.

McLeod, D. "History and Culture Report – Stanley Mission – La Ronge." Undated.

McLeod, Jack. "Health, Wealth, and Politics." In *Essays on the Left: Essays in Honour of T.C. Douglas,* edited by Laurier LaPierre, Jack McLeod, Charles Taylor, and Walter Young, 81-99. Toronto: McClelland and Stewart, 1971.

McLeod, Thomas Hector Macdonald. "Public Enterprise in Saskatchewan: The Development of Public Policy and Administrative Controls." PhD diss., Harvard University, 1959.

McLeod, Thomas Hector Macdonald, and Ian McLeod. *Tommy Douglas: The Road to Jerusalem.* Edmonton: Hurtig Publishers, 1987.

McNab, Miriam. "From the Bush to the Village to the City: Pinehouse Lake Aboriginal Women Adapt to Change." In *"Other Voices": Historical Essays on Saskatchewan Women,* edited by David BeBrou and Aileen Moffatt, 131-143. Regina: Canadian Plains Research Center, University of Regina, 1995.

Mid-Canada Development Corridor ... A Concept. Thunder Bay, ON: Lakehead University, 1972.

Miller, J.R. *Skyscrapers Hide the Heavens: A History of Indian-White Relations in Canada.* Toronto: University of Toronto Press, 1989.

–. *Shingwauk's Vision: A History of Native Residential Schools.* Toronto: University of Toronto Press, 1996.

Miller, J.R., ed. *Sweet Promises: A Reader in Indian-White Relations in Canada.* Toronto: University of Toronto Press, 1991.

Mombourquette, Duane. "'An Inalienable Right': The CCF and Rapid Health Care Reform, 1944-1948." *Saskatchewan History* 43, 3 (Autumn 1991): 101-116.

Moore, P.E. "Medical Care of Canada's Indians and Eskimos." *Canadian Journal of Public Health* 47, 6 (June 1956): 227-233.

Morin, Max. "History and Culture: Ile a la Crosse, Saskatchewan." N.d.

Morton, Kathleen A. "Northern Saskatchewan." *Western Miner and Oil Review* 34, 10 (October 1961): 68-72.

The Musk-Ox. Saskatoon: University of Saskatchewan, Department of Geological Sciences, 1967-94.

Naylor, R.T. "Appendix. The ideological foundations of Social Democracy and Social Credit." In *Capitalism and the National Question in Canada,* edited by Gary Teeple, 251-256. Toronto: University of Toronto Press, 1972.

Ostry, Aleck. "Prelude to Medicare: Institutional Change and Continuity in Saskatchewan, 1944-1962." *Prairie Forum* 20, 1 (Spring 1995): 87-105.

Peel, B. "Cumberland House." *Saskatchewan History* 3, 2 (Spring 1950): 68-73.

Peel, Bruce Braden. *A Bibliography of the Prairie Provinces to 1953.* Toronto: University of Toronto Press, 1973.

Penner, Norman. *The Canadian Left: A Critical Analysis.* Scarborough, ON: Prentice-Hall of Canada, 1977.

–. *From Protest to Power: Social Democracy in Canada 1900-Present.* Toronto: Lorimer, 1992.
Phalen, J.T. "An Autobiography of the Life and Times of J.T. (Terry) Phalen." And Harold Chapman. "Supplement to Autobiography of J.T. (Terry) Phalen." Unpublished, n.d.
–. "The Search for an Appropriate Development Program for the People of Northern Saskatchewan." Unpublished paper. April 1966.
–. "The Co-Operative Development Program for Northern Saskatchewan," "The Reorganization of Provincial Government Services to Meet the Special Needs of the North," "The Production Credit Problem," "Board Policies and Programs," "The Need for Introducing Competition into the Closed Northern Economy," "An Interim Step in the Co-Operative Development Program." Unpublished Paper. 1 June 1997.
–. "The Northern Co-Operative Development Program." Unpublished paper. 1 September 1997.
Pitsula, James M. "The CCF Government in Saskatchewan and Social Aid, 1944-1964." In *"Building the Co-Operative Commonwealth": Essays on the Democratic Socialist Tradition in Canada,* Canadian Plains Proceedings 13, edited by J. William Brennan, 205-225. Regina: Canadian Plains Research Center, University of Regina, 1985.
–. "The Saskatchewan CCF Government and Treaty Indians, 1944-64." *The Canadian Historical Review* 75, 1 (March 1994): 21-54.
–. "The CCF Government and the Formation of the Union of Saskatchewan Indians." *Prairie Forum* 19, 2 (Fall 1994): 131-151.
–. "The Thatcher Government in Saskatchewan and Treaty Indians, 1964-1971: The Quiet Revolution." *Saskatchewan History* 48, 1 (Spring 1996): 3-17.
–. "'Educational Paternalism' Versus Autonomy: Contradictions in the Relationship Between the Saskatchewan Government and the Federation of Saskatchewan Indians, 1958-1964." *Prairie Forum* 22, 1 (Spring 1997): 47-71.
Poelzer, D., and I. Poelzer. *Resident Metis Women's Perceptions of their Local Social Reality in Seven Northern Saskatchewan Communities.* Preliminary descriptive report for submission to the Saskatchewan Native Women's Association and to the women interviewed in the original field research. 1982.
Prairie Forum. 1976-present.
Queen's University, Institute of Local Government. "Municipal Government for Northern Saskatchewan." (T.J. Plunkett, study director.) Kingston, ON: The Institute of Local Government, Queen's University, May 1975.
Rankin, Seth. *An Assessment of Population Data for Saskatchewan C.D. 18, 1941-1976.* Northern Population Series, Report 2. Saskatoon: Institute for Northern Studies, University of Saskatchewan, 1976.
Rawson, D.S. *Limnology and Fisheries of Cree and Wollaston Lakes in Northern Saskatchewan.* Regina: Department of Natural Resources, Fisheries Branch, 1959.
–. *Five Lakes on the Churchill River near Stanley, Saskatchewan.* Regina: Department of Natural Resources, Fisheries Branch, 1960.
Rawson, D.S., and F.M. Atton. *Biological Investigation and Fisheries Management at Lac La Ronge, Saskatchewan.* Regina: Department of Natural Resources, Fisheries Branch, 1953.
Ray, Arthur J. *Indians in the Fur Trade: Their Role As Trappers, Hunters, and Middlemen in the Lands Southwest of Hudson Bay 1660-1870.* Toronto: University of Toronto Press, 1974.
–. "Periodic Shortages, Native Welfare, and the Hudson's Bay Company 1670-1930." In *The Subarctic Fur Trade: Native Social and Economic Adaptations,* edited by Shepard Krech, 1-20. Vancouver: UBC Press, 1984.
–. *The Canadian Fur Trade in the Industrial Age.* Toronto: University of Toronto Press, 1990.
Reed, E.B. *Limnology and Fisheries of the Saskatchewan River in Saskatchewan.* Fisheries Report No. 6. Regina: Saskatchewan Department of Natural Resources, Fisheries Branch, 1962.
Religious History of St. John the Baptist Parish Ile a la Crosse. 150 Years. The Church. The People of God. 1996.
Richards, J. Howard. *Saskatchewan Geography: Physical Environment and Its Relationship with Population and the Economic Base.* Saskatoon: Extension Division, University of Saskatchewan, 1975.
Richards, J. Howard, and K.L. Fung. *Atlas of Saskatchewan.* Saskatoon: University of Saskatchewan and Modern Press, 1969.

Richards, John, and Larry Pratt. *Prairie Capitalism: Power and Influence in the New West.* Toronto: McClelland and Stewart, 1979.

Richards, Mary Helen. "Cumberland House: Two Hundred Years of History." *Saskatchewan History* 27, 3 (Autumn 1974): 108-114.

Ridington, Robin. *Trail to Heaven: Knowledge and Narrative in a Northern Native Community.* Vancouver/Toronto: Douglas and McIntyre, 1988.

–. *Little Bit Know Something: Stories in a Language of Anthropology.* Iowa City: University of Iowa Press, 1990.

Robinson, Ira M. *New Industrial Towns on Canada's Resource Frontier.* Chicago: University of Chicago Press, 1962.

Rogers, Edward S. "History of Ethnological Research in the Subarctic Shield and MacKenzie Borderlands." In *Subarctic,* edited by June Helm, 19-29. Vol. 6 of *Handbook of North American Indians,* edited by William C. Sturtevant. Washington: Smithsonian Institution, 1981.

Rounthwaite, H. Ian. "Uranium Development in Saskatchewan: An Introduction." Special edition, "Uranium Development in Saskatchewan," of *Saskatchewan Law Review* 45, 1 (1980-81): 1-2.

Runge, Wayne. *A Century of Fur Harvesting in Saskatchewan.* Wildlife Report Number Five. Prince Albert, SK: Wildlife Branch, Department of Environment and Resource Management, 1995.

Rusch, T.A. "The Political Thought of the Co-Operative Commonwealth Federation." *The Journal of Politics* 12 (August 1950).

Saskatchewan. Department of Industry and Commerce. "Highways Push Frontier North." *Outdoor Saskatchewan* 19, 1 (Spring 1970): 2.

Saskatchewan. Government Finance Office. *Summary of Results of Operations for Crown Corporations 1945 to 1959.* Regina: Government Finance Office, March 1960.

–. *Public Enterprise in Saskatchewan.* Regina: Government Finance Office, 1964.

Saskatchewan Executive and Legislative Directory, 1905-1970. Saskatoon and Regina: Saskatchewan Archives Board, 1971.

Saskatchewan History. 1948-97.

"Saskatchewan Indians Organize." *Saskatchewan Community* 10, 3 (February Supplement, 1960): 1-4.

"Saskatchewan May Soon Be Canada's Largest Uranium Producer." *The Musk-Ox* 19 (1976): 77.

Scott, James C. *Weapons of the Weak: Everyday Forms of Peasant Resistance.* New Haven, CT: Yale University Press, 1985.

–. *Domination and the Arts of Resistance: Hidden Transcripts.* New Haven, CT/London: Yale University Press, 1990.

–. *Seeing Like a State: How Certain Schemes to Improve the Human Condition Have Failed.* New Haven, CT: Yale University Press, 1998.

Scotton, Anne, ed. *Bibliography of All Sources Relating to the Co-Operative Commonwealth Federation and the New Democratic Party in Canada.* Woodsworth Archives Project, 1977.

Seaborne, Adrian A. "A Population Geography of Northern Saskatchewan." *The Musk-Ox* 12 (1973): 49-58.

Sealey, Bruce D., and Antoine S. Lussier. *The Métis: Canada's Forgotten People.* Winnipeg, MB: Pemmican Publications, 1981.

Serl, Vernon C. "Action and Reaction: An Overview of Provincial Policies and Programs in Northern Saskatchewan." In *A Northern Dilemma: Reference Papers.* Vol. 1. Edited by Arthur K. Davis et al. Bellingham, WA: Western Washington State College, 1967.

Seymour, Gary Ronald. "A Geographical Study of the Commercial Fishing Industry in Northern Saskatchewan: An Example of Resource Development." Master's thesis, University of Saskatchewan, 1971.

Shackleton, Doris French. *Tommy Douglas.* Toronto: McClelland and Stewart, 1975.

Sharp, Henry S. "The Kinship System of the Black Lake Chipewyan." PhD diss., Duke University, 1973.

–. "Trapping and Welfare: The Economics of Trapping in a Northern Saskatchewan Chipewyan Village." *Anthropologica* 17, 1 (1975): 30-44.

Sherdahl, Raymond Merle. "The Saskatchewan General Election of 1944." Master's thesis, University of Saskatchewan, 1966.

Shumiatcher, Morris C. "Saskatchewan Socialism Works." *Canadian Forum* 26, 305 (June 1946): 54-56.
–. *Welfare: Hidden Backlash*. Toronto: McClelland and Stewart, 1971.
Sinclair, Peter R. "The Saskatchewan CCF: Ascent to Power and the Decline of Socialism." *Canadian Historical Review* 54, 4 (December 1973): 419-433.
Smith, David E. "Liberalism in Saskatchewan: The Evolution of a Provincial Party." In *Western Perspectives I*, edited by David J. Bercuson, 101-109. Papers of the Western Canadian Studies Conference, 1973. Toronto: Holt, Rinehart and Winston of Canada, 1974.
–. *Prairie Liberalism: The Liberal Party in Saskatchewan, 1905-1971*. Toronto: University of Toronto Press, 1975.
Smith, James G.E. "The Chipewyan Hunting Group in a Village Context." *Western Canadian Journal of Anthropology* 2, 1 (1970): 60-66.
–. "The Ecological Basis of Chipewyan Socio-Territorial Organization." In *Proceedings: Northern Athapaskan Conference, 1971*. Vol. 2. Edited by A. McFayden Clark, 389-461. National Museum of Man Mercury Series, Canadian Ethnology Service Paper No. 27. Ottawa: National Museums of Canada, 1975.
– "The Emergence of the Micro-Urban Village Among the Caribou-Eater Chipewyan." *Human Organization* 37, 1 (Spring 1978): 38-49.
–. "Western Woods Cree." In *Subarctic*, edited by June Helm, 256-270. Vol. 6 of *Handbook of North American Indians*, edited by William C. Sturtevant. Washington: Smithsonian Institution, 1981.
Spafford, Duff, and Norman Ward, eds. *Politics in Saskatchewan*. Don Mills, ON: Longmans Canada, 1968.
Spaulding, Philip T. "The Metis of Ile-a-la-Crosse." PhD diss., University of Washington, 1970.
Sproat, B., and J. Feather. *Northern Saskatchewan Health Research Bibliography*. Saskatoon: Northern Medical Services, University of Saskatchewan, 1990.
Steen, J.E. "Survey of Saskatchewan Fisheries." *Trade News* (publication of the federal Department of Fisheries), November 1959, 3-5.
Steer, Donald N. "The History and Archaeology of a North West Company Trading Post and a Hudson's Bay Company Transport Depot, Lac La Loche, Saskatchewan." Manuscript Report Number 280. Ottawa: National Historic Parks and Sites Branch, Parks Canada, Department of Indian and Northern Affairs, 1977.
Swerhone, Elise, producer. *Tommy Douglas: Keeper of the Flame*. (Video). National Film Board of Canada, 1980.
Taylor, Herbert C. Jr. "The Parameters of a Northern Dilemma." Prologue in *A Northern Dilemma: Reference Papers*. Vol. 1. Edited by Arthur K. Davis et al., 1-7. Bellingham, WA: Western Washington State College, 1967.
Teeple, Gary. "'Liberals in a Hurry': Socialism and the CCF-NDP." In *Capitalism and the National Question in Canada*, edited by Gary Teeple, 230-250. Toronto: University of Toronto Press, 1972.
Tester, Frank J., and Peter Kulchyski. *Tammarniit (Mistakes): Inuit Relocation in the Eastern Arctic, 1939-63*. Vancouver: UBC Press, 1994.
Thompson, John Herd. "The West and the North." In *Confederation to the Present*. Vol. 2 of *Canadian History: A Reader's Guide*, edited by Doug Owram, 341-373. Toronto: University of Toronto Press, 1994.
Thompson, June Cutt. "Cree Indians in North-Eastern Saskatchewan." *Saskatchewan History* 11, 2 (Spring 1958): 41-58.
Tobias, John L. "Canada's Subjugation of the Plains Cree, 1879-1885." In *Sweet Promises: A Reader in Indian-White Relations in Canada*, edited by J.R. Miller, 212-240. Toronto: University of Toronto Press, 1991.
Toombs, M.P. "The Control and Support of Public Education in Rupert's Land and the Northwest Territories to 1905 and Saskatchewan to 1960." Vol. 1 and 2. PhD diss., University of Minnesota, 1962.
Trimension Training and Consulting Group Inc., Spruce River Research, and Office of Northern Affairs. *Examination of the Commercial Fishing Industry in Saskatchewan*. Saskatoon: Trimension Group, 1999.

Tymchak, Michael. *Our Heritage: The People of Northern Saskatchewan.* Academic Education, Department of Northern Saskatchewan, 1975.

Tyre, Robert. *Douglas in Saskatchewan: The Story of a Socialist Experiment.* Vancouver: Mitchell Press, 1962.

Vanstone, James W. "Changing Patterns of Indian Trapping in the Canadian Subarctic." *Arctic* 16 (September 1963): 158-174.

Waiser, W.A. *Saskatchewan's Playground: A History of Prince Albert National Park.* Saskatoon: Fifth House Publishers, 1989.

–. *The New Northwest: The Photographs of the Frank Crean Expeditions, 1908-1909.* Saskatoon: Fifth House Publishers, 1993.

–. "Writing About Northern Saskatchewan." In *The Historiography of the Provincial North,* edited by Kenneth Coates and William Morrison, 232-247. Thunder Bay, ON: Centre for Northern Studies, Lakehead University, 1996.

Waldram, James B. "The 'Other Side': Ethnostatus Distinctions in Western Subarctic Native Communities." In *1885 and After: Native Society in Transition,* edited by F. Laurie Barron and James B. Waldram, 279-295. Regina: Canadian Plains Research Center, University of Regina, 1986.

–. "Relocation, Consolidation, and Settlement Patterns in the Canadian Subarctic." *Human Ecology* 15, 2 (1987): 117-131.

–. *As Long As the Rivers Run: Hydroelectric Development and Native Communities in Western Canada.* Winnipeg, MB: University of Manitoba Press, 1988.

Weir, Thomas R. *Atlas of the Prairie Provinces.* Toronto: Oxford University Press, 1971.

Weller, Geoffrey R. "Resource Development in Northern Ontario: A Case Study in Hinterland Politics." In *Resources and the Environment: Policy Perspectives for Canada,* edited by O.P. Dwivedi, 243-269. Toronto: McClelland and Stewart, 1980.

–. "Political Disaffection in the Canadian Provincial North." *Bulletin of Canadian Studies* 9, 1 (Spring 1985): 58-86.

–. "Managing Canada's North: The Case of the Provincial North." *Canadian Public Administration* 27, 2 (Summer 1984): 197-209.

Whelan, Ed, and Pemrose Whelan. *Touched by Tommy: Stories of Hope and Humour About Canada's Most Loved Political Leader, T.C. Douglas.* Regina: Whelan Publications, 1990.

Whitehorn, Alan. *Canadian Socialism.* Don Mills, ON: Oxford University Press, 1992.

Worsley, P.M. "Bureaucracy and Decolonization: Democracy from the Top." In *The New Sociology: Essays in Social Science and Social Theory in Honor of C. Wright Mills,* edited by Irving Louis Horowitz, 370-390. New York: Oxford University Press, 1971.

Wright, Jim. "Saskatchewan's North." *Canadian Geographical Journal* 45, 1 (July 1952): 14-33.

Wright, J.F.C. *Saskatchewan: The History of a Province.* Toronto: McClelland and Stewart, 1955.

Wuorinen, Richard. *A History of Buffalo Narrows.* Buffalo Narrows, Saskatchewan: Buffalo Narrows Celebrate Saskatchewan Committee, 1981.

Young, Walter D. "The CCF: The Radical Background." In *The Prairie West: Historical Readings,* edited by R.D. Francis and Howard Palmer, 538-558. Edmonton: University of Alberta Press, 1985.

Zakuta, Leo. *A Protest Movement Becalmed: A Study of Change in the CCF.* Toronto: University of Toronto Press, 1964.

Zaslow, Morris. *The Northward Expansion of Canada 1914-1967.* Toronto: McClelland and Stewart, 1988.

Internet Sources

"Buffalo Narrows Residents." Photographs one, two, and three. <http://www.jkcc.com/evje/photo1.html> (and photo2.html, photo3.html) (10 July 1999).

"Deep River Fur Farm." <http://www.jkcc.com/evje/mink.html> (10 July 1999).

"Fishing on Deep River." <http://www.jkcc.com/evje/mink.html> (10 July 1999).

Saskpower Facilities. "Power to You – Athabasca Power System." <http://www.saskpower.com/facilities/html/athabasca.html> (18 February 2001).

Index